# SIGNALS, SYSTEMS, AND THE COMPUTER

PAUL M. CHIRLIAN
*Stevens Institute of Technology*

INTEXT EDUCATIONAL PUBLISHERS

New York and London

*To Barbara, Lisa, and Peter*

The Intext Series in

**Circuits, Systems, Communications, and Computers**

Consulting Editor

**S. C. Gupta**

Chirlian—SIGNALS, SYSTEMS, AND THE COMPUTER

Gupta, Bayless, and Peikari—CIRCUIT ANALYSIS: With Computer
  Application to Problem Solving

Ingels—INFORMATION AND CODING THEORY

Lathi—SIGNALS, SYSTEMS, AND CONTROLS

Matsch—ELECTROMAGNETIC AND ELECTROMECHANICAL
  MACHINES

Mickle and Sze—OPTIMIZATION IN SYSTEMS ENGINEERING

Sheng—INTRODUCTION TO SWITCHING LOGIC

**Library of Congress Cataloging in Publication Data**

Chirlian, Paul M

  Signals, systems, and the computer.
  (Intext series in circuits, systems, communication, and computers)
  Includes bibliographies.
  1. Electronic data processing—Electric networks. *621.3819535*
  2. Electronic data processing—System analysis. *C541s*

I. Title. *c.2*

TK454.2.C46      621.3819'535      72–84133

ISBN 0–7002–2427–0

Intext Educational Publishers
257 Park Avenue South
New York, New York 10010

# Contents

# Preface

This textbook on signals and systems is intended for use in senior or first-year graduate electrical engineering courses. It is designed to follow a basic network theory course and to provide the student with the mathematical tools needed to analyze a wide variety of systems and the signals processed by them. It may be used for a one or two semester course since material may be considered or omitted according to the instructor's requirements.

Much of the difficulty of such analyses has been greatly reduced by the application of the digital computer to the solution of the mathematical problems. However, the digital computer does not eliminate the need for a thorough understanding of the principles of analysis which are the primary concern of the book. Nevertheless, the student should feel confident that he will be able to write a computer program using FORTRAN IV that can implement the solution of a mathematical problem.

This is not intended to be a handbook of computer programs, hence a computer program is not given for every analysis encountered. Moreover, since this is not a study of numerical analysis, not every common type of numerical analysis is included. Methods for minimizing storage space are discussed and flow charts of many of the programs are included. Programs written for batch processing and timeshared operation are also covered because of the rapidly increasing use of these techniques. Thus we shall at times write programs which are suitable for these operations.

In Chapter 1 the general concepts of systems, and the signals transmitted by them are discussed. The basic idea of digital computation is briefly presented. A direct-current loop-analysis program is written and explained to illustrate how a FORTRAN IV program can simplify one of the most tedious problems that the student has encountered.

In Chapter 2 the Fourier transform is presented using distribution theory. An elementary discussion of distribution theory is covered, which can be easily understood by a student who is unfamiliar with the subject. The theory greatly simplifies the Fourier transform of certain common functions and allows generalized functions, such as the unit impulse and its derivatives, to be treated rigorously but simply. The Fourier transform is derived and its fundamental properties are discussed, and the Fourier series is treated as a special case of the Fourier transform. In addition, the fast Fourier transform and a computer program for implementing it are discussed in great detail.

The convolution theorem, Gibbs phenomenon, and Shannon's sampling theorem are also included.

In Chapter 3 the Laplace transform is derived from the Fourier transform and the ideas of distribution theory are applied. The $0-$, rather than the $0+$, Laplace transform is used and the advantages of this transform in computing the response to an impulse applied at $t = 0$ are thoroughly discussed. The basic theorems and concepts of the Laplace transform used in the solution of differential equations are considered. The inverse Laplace transform is developed, but this may be omitted. It is assumed that the reader is familiar with the basic notions of functions of a complex variable. (Appendix B presents this material.) The convolution theorem and the two-sided Laplace transform are also discussed.

In Chapter 4 the basic principles of state space are considered and the procedures for writing state variable equations are given. Linear, time-invariant, time-varying, and nonlinear systems are discussed and techniques for the solution of state-variable equations are given. Numerical techniques are also discussed in detail and FORTRAN IV programs, which implement these solutions, are presented.

In Chapter 5 the analysis techniques of Chapters 2, 3, and 4 are applied to linear continuous time systems. The relation among transfer functions, impulse response, and sinusoidal steady-state response is given. The response to arbitrary signals in terms of unit step and unit impulse response is discussed and causal sytems are considered. The Hilbert transforms and Bode relations are derived as a consequence of causal systems. Low pass and band pass systems are also discussed. In addition, bounds on system response and the meaning of the effective bandwidth of a signal are considered.

In Chapter 6 discrete time systems are considered. Difference equations are discussed and state variable procedures are presented. Linear, time-invariant, time-varying, and nonlinear systems are considered. The solution of these equations, including computer implementation, is presented. The use of the $z$-transform for the solution of linear, time-invariant systems is discussed.

In Chapter 7 system stability is covered. Linear, time-invariant systems are considered first. The Routh-Hurwitz algorithms and Nyquist criterion are derived. Then, general (nonlinear) systems are considered. State variable procedures are discussed. Liapunov stability is presented in detail. Observability and controllability are discussed. Stability in sampled systems is also considered.

In Chapter 8 basic ideas of probability are presented. Random signals and processes are discussed. A simplified derivation of the central limit theorem is given. The basic ideas of spectral density are discussed. The effects of band pass filtering upon noise probability are covered. Correlation functions and the Weiner-Kinchine relation are discussed. A computer program for the implementation of correlation and the use of correlation to extract signals from noise are discussed.

In Chapter 9 transmission of information is covered and the basic ideas of information theory are used to develop the concepts of channel capacity.

Some basic ideas of encoding are also discussed. The transmission of signals over noisy channels and the extraction of the signals from the noise is considered. Noise-reducing codes are discussed. Next the use of continuous filtering to extract signals from noise is presented, and predicting and causal filters are discussed.

In Chapter 10 distributed systems are presented, and partial differential equations of distributed systems are derived and solved using Laplace transforms. The transient response of special and general transmission lines is discussed. Sinusoidal, steady-state response and standing waves are then considered. A discussion of impedance calculations using the Smith chart is presented. Stub matching is discussed and a computer program to implement this is obtained.

There are three appendixes for review or instruction of material which may be unfamiliar to the reader. Othogonal functions are covered in Appendix A, basic complex variable theory is discussed in Appendix B, and matrices are considered in Appendix C, which includes the Cayley-Hamilton theorem.

My loving and heartfelt thanks, and great appreciation, are given to my wife, Barbara, for typing and correcting the numerous drafts of the manuscript for this book. The author also wishes to thank his colleagues Professors A. C. Gilmore, Jr., G. J. Herskowitz, E. Peskin, H. W. Phair, and S. Smith, and Professors S. C. Gupta and L. Gerhardt for their invaluable suggestions.

# CHAPTER 1

# Introduction to Signals and Systems— The Digital Computer in Signal and System Analysis

In this book we shall study the analysis of *systems* and *signals*. We shall define a system as *a collection of devices which perform some specified objective*. Systems can be very simple or extremely complex. A flashlight consisting of a battery, switch, light, reflector, and case can be considered to be a system. A satellite communications link, which includes transmitters, receivers, satellite, computers, and antennas, is also a system. An electric network can also be considered a system. Thus, the complexity of systems may vary greatly.

Systems of the type that we shall consider respond to certain inputs. These inputs and the system's response, or outputs, will be called *signals*. In the communication system discussed, the input signal could be a signal from a microphone and the output signal the sound from a loud-speaker. A complex system can be assumed to be made up of components each of which is often treated as a system. There are many definitions of signals and systems. For this reason, mathematical procedures are usually used in classifying them.

The digital computer is often used in systems analyses to avoid tedious calculations. Accordingly, we shall often discuss computer programs which can implement analysis procedures. While certain analysis techniques lend themselves to computer solutions and others do not, all of these techniques are important since they usually provide additional insight into the operation of a system.

## 1-1. SOME FUNDAMENTAL ASPECTS OF SYSTEMS

Many systems can be represented by a set of equations which relate the input and output signals. Often, these will be differential equations. For instance, consider the system characterized by the "black box" of Fig. 1–1. There are $k$ inputs $y_1, y_2, y_3, ...,$ $y_k$ and $n$ outputs $x_1, x_2, x_3, ..., x_n$. All of these are functions of time. For example, in an electrical network the $y(k)$ could be voltage generators and the $x(k)$ loop currents. If the system is linear, a set of differential equations which characterize the system could be

$$a_{1m}\frac{d^m x_1(t)}{dt^m} + \cdots + a_{11}\frac{dx_1(t)}{dt} + a_{10}x_1(t) = F_1[y_1(t), y_2(t), ..., y_k(t)]$$

*1*

$$a_{2m}\frac{d^m x_2(t)}{dt^m} + \cdots + a_{21}\frac{dx_2(t)}{dt} + a_{20}x_2(t) = F_2[y_1(t), y_2(t), \ldots, y_k(t)] \qquad (1\text{--}1)$$

$$a_{nm}\frac{d^m x_n(t)}{dt^m} + \cdots + a_{n1}\frac{dx_n(t)}{dt} + a_{n0}x_n(t) = F_n[y_1(t), y_2(t), \ldots, y_k(t)]$$

FIG. 1–1

A "black box" representation of a system with $k$ inputs and $n$ outputs

The $a_{ij}$ are coefficients which may or may not be functions of time.

Let us now consider some terminology:

The *order of a system* is the highest order of the derivative necessary to characterize the system.

The *degree of a system* is the number of simultaneous equations needed to characterize the system.

**Linear and Nonlinear Systems.** Let us discuss a system with $k$ inputs $y_1(t)$, $y_2(t)$, ..., $y_k(t)$ and $n$ outputs $x_1(t)$, $x_2(t)$, ..., $x_n(t)$. Suppose a particular set of inputs $y_{1a}(t), y_{2a}(t), \ldots, y_{ka}(t)$ is applied and that the response to them is $x_{1a}(t), x_{2a}(t), \ldots, x_{na}(t)$. If another set of inputs $y_{1b}(t), y_{2b}(t), \ldots, y_{kb}(t)$ is applied, then the response to them is $x_{1b}(t), x_{2b}(t), \ldots, x_{nb}(t)$. Now suppose that the input signal becomes $y_{1a}(t) + by_{1b}(t), y_{2a}(t) + by_{2b}(t), \ldots, y_{ka}(t) + by_{kb}(t)$, where $b$ is an arbitrary constant; i.e., each input signal becomes the sum of the original input plus $b$ times the second one. The system is a *linear* one if the output is

$$
\begin{aligned}
x_1(t) &= x_{1a}(t) + bx_{1b}(t) \\
x_2(t) &= x_{2a}(t) + bx_{2b}(t) \\
&\quad\text{------------------} \\
x_n(t) &= x_{na}(t) + bx_{nb}(t)
\end{aligned}
\qquad (1\text{--}2)
$$

for all $y$'s and $b$'s. One consequence of Eqs. 1–2 is that a linear system is one whose output, due to a sum of (sets of) inputs, is the sum of the outputs which result when each (set of) input(s) acts separately. Such a system is said to satisfy the principle of *superposition*. For instance, in a linear electrical resistance if $i_1(t)$ results from the application of $v_1(t)$, and $i_2(t)$ results from the application of $v_2(t)$, then $i_1(t) + i_2(t)$ will result from the application of $v_1(t) + v_2(t)$.

Another consequence of Eqs. 1–2 is that if all inputs are multiplied by a constant, then all the outputs will be multiplied by the same constant. Such a system is said to be *homogenous*. In the case of the linear resistance, if $i_1(t)$ results from the application of $v_1(t)$, then $5i_1(t)$ will result from the application of $5v_1(t)$. If a system is linear, then it is characterized by linear simultaneous differential equations.

If a system is not linear, it is said to be *nonlinear*. A nonlinear system is character- ized by a set of nonlinear differential equations. That is, there are products of variables, etc. A resistance whose voltage is given by $5i^3(t)$ is nonlinear. Also transistors are nonlinear devices.

**Time-Invariant and Time-Varying Systems.** A time-invariant system is one whose parameters do not change with time. As an example, consider Fig. 1–2. If the switch remains open (or closed) for all values of time, then this network is time invariant. However, if the switch is open for one value of time and then closed for another (e.g., open for $0 \leq t \leq 1$, closed for $1 < t \leq 2$, open for $2 < t \leq 5$, etc.), then the network is said to be time varying.

Note that the signals in this case $v_1(t)$ and $v_2(t)$, will be functions of time even if the switch remains fixed. However, this does not influence whether or not the system is time varying or time invariant.

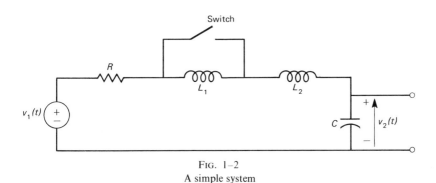

FIG. 1–2
A simple system

**Continuous Time and Discrete Time Systems.** Systems characterized by a set of differential equations, such as those of Eqs. 1–1 are called *continuous time systems*. That is, the inputs and outputs consist of functions of time which can vary at all times. The outputs consist of similar functions of time. In general, all systems are of this type. However, there are systems whose inputs and outputs are *satisfactorily approximated* if they are measured (or determined) only at discrete times, i.e., every second or every 10 seconds, etc. These are called *discrete time systems*. There are special techniques which simplify the analysis of these systems. We shall discuss them in Chapters 6 and 7, where these systems will be represented by *difference equations*.

**Instantaneous Systems and Dynamic Systems.** The response of most systems depends upon all its past history. Consider the network of Fig. 1–2. The value of $v_2(t)$ at $t = t_0$ is a function of $v_1(t)$ for all $t \leq t_0$. This is called a *dynamic system.* Now consider an electric network made up only of linear resistors and voltage generators. At any instant of time $t_0$, the voltage and currents only depend upon the generator voltage at $t_0$; e.g., $i(t_0) = v(t_0)/R$. This is called an *instantaneous system.* In general, most practical systems are dynamic, and we shall mostly study this type of system.

There are other classifications of systems. For instance, the network of Fig. 1–2 is made up of lumped elements (resistors, inductors, and capacitors). This can be called a *lumped-parameter system.* If the elements of a system are distributed continuous, as in a transmission line, then we speak of it as a *distributed-parameter system.*

## 1-2. SOME FUNDAMENTAL ASPECTS OF SIGNALS

The inputs to a system and its responses to them are called *signals.* Many of the signals that we shall consider will be electrical. The input to a high-fidelity amplifier system can be considered to be the electrical output of a phonograph pickup. Similarly, if the system is the suspension of an automobile, the input is all the mechanical forces applied to the wheels, while the output is the motion of the car seat.

Signals can be classified in many ways, some of which we shall discuss here. If a signal $f(t)$ is such that

$$f(t) = f(t + T), \quad \text{for all} \quad t \tag{1-3}$$

where $T$ is a constant, then $f(t)$ is said to be *periodic.* That is, a periodic function repeats itself for each $T$ seconds. We call $T$ the *period* of the signal and $1/T$ its *frequency.* Functions which are not periodic are said to be *nonperiodic.* We shall consider nonperiodic functions in much of this book.

Some signals are known or can be predicted for all time. For instance, suppose the input to a system is

$$\begin{aligned} f(t) &= e^{-t}, & t &> 0 \\ f(t) &= 0, & t &< 0 \\ &= \tfrac{1}{2}, & t &= 0 \end{aligned} \tag{1-4}$$

Then $f(t)$ is known for all times, future, and past.

At times we deal with signals whose future values are unknown and cannot be exactly predicted. For instance, a noise signal which results from the random motion of charge carriers in a semiconductor is such a signal. Signals of this type are called *random.* If $f(t)$ is known for all future times, then it is said to be *nonrandom, deterministic,* or *predictable.* Of course, all real signals are random to some extent. For instance, we cannot predict for all future time what any real signal will be. However, it often is convenient to hypothesize mathematically that a predictable signal is applied to a system and then to compute its response. This often provides much information about the general system response.

Sometimes we must work with random signals whose values as functions of time are not known. However, the total energy contained in the signals can often be specified and probabilistic information is known about the signals. (This is discussed in Chapters 8 and 9.)

## 1-3. COMPUTER SOLUTION OF SIGNAL AND SYSTEM PROBLEMS

The mathematical analysis of system problems is often tedious and time consuming. A digital computer can be utilized to reduce greatly the calculation time and work. Hence, we shall, where practical, discuss computer programs that can be used to implement the analysis procedures considered in this book. These programs will be written in FORTRAN IV. Programs written for batch processing and timeshared operation are very similar. The only differences are minor differences in the input and output statements. Because of its rapidly increasing use, we shall at times write programs which are suitable for timeshared operation.

## 1-4. COMPUTER SOLUTION OF SIMULTANEOUS EQUATIONS

In this and the next section we shall discuss the procedure for performing dc loop analysis using a digital computer. Here we shall consider a program for the solution of a set of simultaneous equations, and in the next section we shall discuss computer procedures for obtaining the simultaneous equations from the network.

The mathematical basis of any computer program must be understood before the program is considered. We shall first discuss a mathematical procedure for the solution of a set of simultaneous equations. The computer program will be considered subsequently. We shall use the *Gauss-Jordan* method for the solution of a set of simultaneous equations. Consider the following equations:

$$a_{11}x_1 + a_{12}x_2 + \cdots + a_{1n}x_n = y_1$$
$$a_{21}x_1 + a_{22}x_2 + \cdots + a_{2n}x_n = y_2$$
$$\text{-----------------------}$$
$$a_{n1}x_1 + a_{n2}x_2 + \cdots + a_{nn}x_n = y_n \qquad (1\text{-}5a)$$

This can be written in matrix form as

$$\hat{a}\hat{x} = \hat{y} \qquad (1\text{-}5b)$$

Note that the "hat" indicates a matrix. In some texts boldface letters are used to indicate a matrix. This is not done here since boldface letters are used to denote complex quantities. (A brief discussion of matrices is given in Appendix C.) The $a_{ij}$ and the $y_j$ are knowns and we must determine the $x_j$. Multiply the first equation by $-a_{21}/a_{11}$ and add the result to the second equation. Then repeat this for each equation in turn; e.g., multiply the first equation by $-a_{31}/a_{11}$ and add the result to the third one. The resulting set of equations becomes

$$a_{11}x_1 + a_{12}x_2 + \cdots + a_{1n}x_n = y_1$$

$$0 + \left( a_{22} - \frac{a_{12}a_{21}}{a_{11}} \right)x_2 + \cdots + \left( a_{2n} - \frac{a_{1n}a_{21}}{a_{11}} \right)x_n = y_2 - \left( \frac{a_{21}}{a_{11}} \right)y_1$$

- - - - - - - - - - - - - - - - - - - - - - - -

$$0 + \left( a_{n2} - \frac{a_{12}a_{n1}}{a_{11}} \right)x_2 + \cdots + \left( a_{nn} - \frac{a_{1n}a_{n1}}{a_{11}} \right)x_n = y_n - \left( \frac{a_{n1}}{a_{11}} \right)y_1 \qquad (1\text{-}6)$$

Once this has been done we shall have no need for the original values of the $a_{ij}$'s or the $y$'s. Let us rename the variables in the following way:

$$a_{ij} \quad \text{remains} \quad a_{ij} \quad \text{if} \quad i = 1.$$

$$a_{ij} \quad \text{becomes} \quad 0 \quad \text{if} \quad j = 1, \quad i \neq 1.$$

$$a_{ij} \quad \text{replaces} \quad a_{ij} - \frac{a_{i1}a_{1j}}{a_{11}} \quad \text{if} \quad i \neq 1, \quad j \neq 1.$$

$$y_1 \quad \text{remains} \quad y_1.$$

$$y_j \quad \text{replaces} \quad y_j - \left( \frac{a_{i1}}{a_{11}} \right)y_1 \qquad j \neq 1.$$

Then Eqs. 1–6 become

$$a_{11}x_1 + a_{12}x_2 + \cdots + a_{1n}x_n = y_1$$

$$0 + a_{22}x_2 + \cdots + a_{2n}x_n = y_2$$

- - - - - - - - - - - - - - - - - - - -

$$0 + a_{n2}x_2 + \cdots + a_{nn}x_n = y_n \qquad (1\text{-}7)$$

where new parameters are used. We rename the variables using old variable names to reduce the number of variables stored during the computer solution.

Now we proceed in the same way but operate on the second to $n$th equations. Before doing this, let us introduce some time-saving notation. Instead of writing the $x_j$'s each time, let us use matrix notation. In addition, we shall include the $y$'s in the matrix by adding an $(n + 1)$th column to the matrix. The array shall be called the *augmented matrix* and will be indicated by $\hat{A}'$. Then

$$a_{j,n+1} = y_j, \qquad j = 1, 2, ..., n \qquad (1\text{-}8)$$

Then the $\hat{A}'$ array is (prior to performing any computation)

$$\hat{A}' = \begin{bmatrix} a_{11} & a_{12} & \cdots & a_{1n} & a_{1,n+1} \\ a_{21} & a_{22} & \cdots & a_{2n} & a_{2,n+1} \\ \hline a_{n1} & a_{n2} & \cdots & a_{nn} & a_{n,n+1} \end{bmatrix} \tag{1-9}$$

Note that this supplies all the information which is given in Eqs. 1–5.

After the operations which lead to Eqs. 1–6 and using the substitutions which lead to Eqs. 1–7, we have

$$\hat{A}' = \begin{bmatrix} a_{11} & a_{12} & \cdots & a_{1n} & a_{1,n+1} \\ 0 & a_{22} & \cdots & a_{2n} & a_{2,n+1} \\ 0 & a_{32} & \cdots & a_{3n} & a_{3,n+1} \\ \hline 0 & a_{n2} & \cdots & a_{nn} & a_{n,n+1} \end{bmatrix} \tag{1-10}$$

Now we multiply the second row by $-a_{32}/a_{22}$ and add the result to the third row, etc. This yields, after replacing the variables (i.e., renaming them as before),

$$\hat{A}' = \begin{bmatrix} a_{11} & a_{12} & a_{13} & \cdots & a_{1n} & a_{1,n+1} \\ 0 & a_{22} & a_{23} & \cdots & a_{2n} & a_{2,n+1} \\ 0 & 0 & a_{33} & \cdots & a_{3n} & a_{3,n+1} \\ \hline 0 & 0 & a_{3n} & \cdots & a_{nn} & a_{n,n+1} \end{bmatrix} \tag{1-11}$$

where the following substitution is made: $a_{ij}$ replaces the "old" $a_{ij} - a_{i2}a_{2j}/a_{22}$ in row 3 and beyond. Repeating this procedure, we eventually obtain

$$\hat{A} = \begin{bmatrix} a_{11} & a_{12} & a_{13} & & \cdots & a_{1n} & a_{1,n+1} \\ 0 & a_{22} & a_{23} & & \cdots & a_{2n} & a_{2,n+1} \\ 0 & 0 & a_{31} & & \cdots & a_{3n} & a_{3,n+1} \\ \hline 0 & 0 & & \cdots & a_{n-1,n-1} & a_{n-1,n} & a_{n-1,n+1} \\ 0 & 0 & & \cdots & 0 & a_{nn} & a_{n,n+1} \end{bmatrix} \tag{1-12}$$

Now divide the first row by $a_{11}$, the second by $a_{22}$, etc. This yields, after replacing the variables by new ones (i.e., $a_{ij}$ replaces $a_{ij}/a_{ii}$)

$$\hat{A}' = \begin{bmatrix} 1 & a_{12} & a_{13} & \cdots & a_{1n-1} & a_{1n} & a_{1,n+1} \\ 0 & 1 & a_{23} & \cdots & a_{2,n-1} & a_{2n} & a_{2,n+1} \\ 0 & 0 & 1 & \cdots & a_{3,n-1} & a_{3n} & a_{3,n+1} \\ \cdots\cdots\cdots\cdots\cdots\cdots\cdots\cdots\cdots\cdots\cdots\cdots\cdots \\ 0 & 0 & 0 & \cdots & 1 & a_{n-1,n} & a_{n-1,n+1} \\ 0 & 0 & 0 & \cdots & 0 & 1 & a_{n,n+1} \end{bmatrix} \tag{1-13}$$

Now multiply the last row by $-a_{n-1,n}$ and add it to the next to last. Then, multiply the last row by $a_{n-2,n}$ and add it to the second from last, etc. This yields

$$
\hat{A}' =
\begin{bmatrix}
1 & a_{12} & a_{13} & \cdots & a_{1n-1} & 0 & a_{1,n+1} - a_{n,n+1}a_{1n} \\
0 & 1 & a_{23} & \cdots & a_{2n-1} & 0 & a_{2,n+1} - a_{n,n+1}a_{2n} \\
0 & 0 & 1 & \cdots & a_{3n-1} & 0 & a_{3,n+1} - a_{n,n+1}a_{3n} \\
\multicolumn{7}{c}{\dotfill} \\
0 & 0 & 0 & \cdots & 1 & 0 & a_{n-1,n+1} - a_{n,n+1}a_{n-1,n} \\
0 & 0 & 0 & \cdots & 0 & 1 & a_{n,n+1}
\end{bmatrix}
\tag{1-14}
$$

Making a replacement of variables in the last column (i.e., $a_{i,n+1}$ replaces $a_{i,n+1} - a_{n,n+1}a_{in}$ for $i \neq n$), we have

$$
\hat{A}' =
\begin{bmatrix}
1 & a_{12} & a_{13} & \cdots & a_{1,n-1} & 0 & a_{1,n+1} \\
0 & 1 & a_{23} & \cdots & a_{2,n-1} & 0 & a_{2,n+1} \\
0 & 0 & 1 & \cdots & a_{3,n-1} & 0 & a_{3,n+1} \\
\multicolumn{7}{c}{\dotfill} \\
0 & 0 & 0 & \cdots & 1 & 0 & a_{n-1,n+1} \\
0 & 0 & 0 & \cdots & 0 & 1 & a_{n,n+1}
\end{bmatrix}
\tag{1-15}
$$

Now, repeat the procedure with the $(n-1)$th row to make all the $a_{i,n-1}$ terms zero (except $a_{n-1,n-1}$). Then repeat this for each of the remaining rows in turn. Thus, we eventually obtain

$$
\hat{A}' =
\begin{bmatrix}
1 & 0 & 0 & \cdots & 0 & a_{1,n+1} \\
0 & 1 & 0 & \cdots & 0 & a_{2,n+1} \\
0 & 0 & 1 & \cdots & 0 & a_{3,n+1} \\
\multicolumn{6}{c}{\dotfill} \\
0 & 0 & 0 & \cdots & 1 & a_{n,n+1}
\end{bmatrix}
\tag{1-16}
$$

Hence, each equation has only one unknown and we have

$$
x_i = a_{i,n+1}, \qquad i = 1, 2, \ldots, n
\tag{1-17}
$$

where $a_{i,n+1}$ represents the final "replaced" value, i.e., after each step the last column is renamed $a_{i,n+1}, i = 1, 2, \ldots, n$.

**Computer Program for the Implementation of the Gauss-Jordan Method.** Now let us discuss a computer program which implements this procedure. The program is called SIMUL and is listed in Fig. 1–3a. The line numbers 00010–00500 (at the left) are *not* part of the FORTRAN program and should *not* be included when the program is typed on the teletype or when cards are punched. However, they can be obtained with almost all computer printouts. Including the line numbers in the listing makes it easy to discuss the program. Note that in some timeshared systems, line numbers can be typed in. The particular computer manual should be checked to see if this can be done.

```
00010          CØMMØN A(10,11),N,NA
00020          TYPE 1
00030     1    FØRMAT(' ENTER NUMBER ØF UNKNØWNS'/)
00040          ACCEPT 2,N
00050     2    FØRMAT(I)
00060          TYPE 3
00070     3    FØRMAT(' ENTER ARRAY ØF CØEF'/)
00080          DØ 10 I=1,N
00090          ACCEPT 5,(A(I,J),J=1,N)
00100    10    CØNTINUE
00110     5    FØRMAT(10F)
00120          NA=N+1
00130          TYPE 4
00140     4    FØRMAT(' ENTER KNØWNS'/)
00150          ACCEPT 5,(A(I,NA),I=1,N)
00160          CALL SIMUL
00170          TYPE 6,(A(I,NA),I=1,N)
00180     6    FØRMAT(' UNKNØWNS ARE'/(' 'E))
00190          STØP
00200          END
00210          SUBRØTINE SIMUL
00220          CØMMØN A(10,11),N,NA
00230          NB=N-1
00240          DØ 20 L=1,NB
00250          IF(A(L,L))16,1000,16
00260    16    CØNTINUE
00270          LA=L+1
00280          DØ 20 I=LA,N
00290          DØ 20 JQ=L,NA
00300          J=NA+L-JQ
00310          A(I,J)=A(I,J)-A(I,L)*A(L,J)/A(L,L)
00320    20    CØNTINUE
00330          IF(A(N,N))17,1000,17
00340    17    CØNTINUE
00350          DØ 60 I=1,N
00360          DØ 60 JQ=1,NA
00370          J=NA+1-JQ
00380          A(I,J)=A(I,J)/A(I,I)
00390    60    CØNTINUE
00400          DØ 100 LQ=1,N-1
00410          L=N-LQ
00420          K=L+1
00430          DØ 100 I=1,L
00440          A(I,NA)=A(I,NA)-A(K,NA)*A(I,K)
00450   100    CØNTINUE
00460          RETURN
00470  1000    TYPE 15
00480    15    FØRMAT(' PRINC DIAG TERM ZERØ')
00490          RETURN
00500          END
```

(a)

Fig. 1-3 (a)

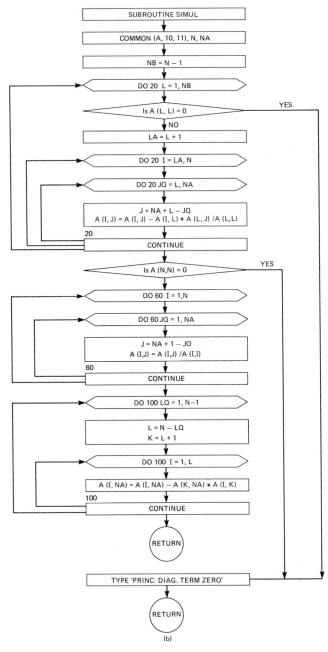

FIG. 1–3 (b)

A program for solving simultaneous equations: (a) SUBROUTINE
SIMUL (lines 210–500) for solving simultaneous equations; (b) Flow
chart for SUBROUTINE SiMUL

Most of the programs which we shall discuss will be given as subroutines since we shall not have to list very similar input and output statements with each program. Thus the program will not be obscured with unnecessary details. This program is written in subroutine form. However, for this case, the input and output statements are included as an example.

Lines 10–200 represent the input-output statements. Line 10 is a common statement which dimensions the matrix A and places A and the integers N and NA in common storage along with some variables of the subroutine. Note that a quantity in common storage should not be included in the calling statement.

Lines 20–50 provide for entering the number of simultaneous equations. The array of coefficients (of the unknowns) is entered using lines 70–110. The DO loop of lines 80–100 is such that the coefficients of the unknown equation are entered in the same relative position that they appear in the equations.

Line 90 accepts the terms of one row of the coefficient array. Each time that the DO loop is cycled, a row of the array is entered. Note that as we have written the program, there can be up to ten unknowns.

The FORMAT statement (statement 110) provides for entering up to ten variables. (This is a *free* type of FORMAT statement and is similar to those found in most time shared computers. No information about columns or decimal points is given. Data are entered without blanks in successive columns. Commas are usually used to separate numbers.) However, the *implied* DO loop of line 90 only cycles $N$ times, where $N$ is the number of unknowns. The main DO loop is then cycled again. Each time that the DO loop is cycled, the ACCEPT statement is executed again. Thus, in effect, it becomes a "new" ACCEPT statement and data are entered on a new line. Thus the entered data appears "natural" to the user.

Lines 80–100 could be replaced by the single line

$$\text{ACCEPT } 5, ((A(I, J), J = 1, N), I = 1, N)$$

However, this has one disadvantage. The ACCEPT statement is only executed once. The coefficients would be entered in the order $A(1, 1), A(1, 2) \ldots A(1, N), A(2, 1)$, $A(2, 2), \ldots$, etc. Ten unknowns would be entered on each line, see statement 110. Thus, unless the array were $10 \times 10$, the imput data would not be in the same form as they are in the equations. (Note that data cannot be entered into a FORMAT statement.) For this reason, we used the three statements 80–110 rather than the single statement given above.

Lines 120–150 provide for entering the knowns and appending them as an $(n + 1)$th column to the A array, see Eq. 1–12. Then, line 160 calls the subroutine SIMUL which obtains the values of the unknowns. Finally, lines 170 and 180 provide for printing the answer.

Now consider the SUBROUTINE SIMUL. A flow chart for this subroutine is given in Fig. 1–3b. The data are entered using the COMMON statements of lines 10 and 220. Let us discuss the DO loop of lines 240–320. If a principal diagonal term is zero, this procedure will not work; lines 250 and 260 terminate calculations in this case. If a principal diagonal term is not zero then the DO loop effectively consists of lines 240 and 270–320.

$$\text{DO } 20 \text{ L} = 1, \text{NB}$$
$$\text{LA} = \text{L} + 1$$
$$\text{DO } 20 \text{ I} = \text{LA}, \text{N}$$
$$\text{DO } 20 \text{ JQ} = \text{L}, \text{NA}$$
$$\text{J} = \text{NA} + \text{L} - \text{JQ}$$
$$A(I, J) = A(I, J) - A(I, L) * A(L, J)/A(L, L)$$
$$20 \qquad \text{CONTINUE}$$

The DO loop carries out the operations indicated in Eqs. 1–6 through 1–12. The $L$th row is multiplied by the constant $A(I, L)/A(L, L)$ and subtracted term by term for the $I$th row. That is, $A(L, J) * A(I, L)/A(L, L)$ is subtracted from $A(I, J)$ for each value of J. Note that the order of performance of this subtraction is "backwards." That is, as the innermost DO loop is cycled, J takes on the values $n + 1, n, n - 1, ..., L$. This is done because the multiplier $A(I, L)$ should be the original one. The new value of $A(I, L)$ is zero. If $A(I, L)$ were set equal to zero first, then zero would replace it in each subsequent calculation and $A(I, J)$ would not be changed as it should. In the program $A(I, L)$ is changed last and this problem does not occur. This backwards cycling is performed in lines 290 and 300. JQ can be considered to be a dummy variable which is cycled from L to NA. Then, line 300 defines J which is cycled in the proper way.

Some compilers (a relatively small number) allow negative increments in their DO loops. If such compilers are used, lines 290 and 300 can be replaced by

$$\text{DO } 20 \text{ J} = \text{NA}, \text{L}, -1$$

Line 250 checks if $A(L, L) = 0$ for all values of L except $A(N, N)$. $A(N, N)$ is checked in line 330.

The DO loops of lines 350–390 divide the $I$th row by $A(I, I)$ as indicated in Eq. 1–13. Again, it is necessary to run one DO loop backwards. This is done using lines 370 and 380. If negative increments are allowed in the DO loop these two statements can be replaced by a single one.

The operations of Eqs. 1–14 through 1–16 are carried out in the DO loop of lines 400–450. Note that in going from Eqs. 1–13 through 1–15 only the $n$th and $(n + 1)$th columns are affected. In addition, the values in the $n$ column do not affect any of the subsequent calculations using other columns. Then, since we only need the values of the $(n + 1)$th column (see Eq. 1–17), we need only compute this column. Each step of this calculation is done in line 410 and repeated by the DO loops. (Note that, as before, one of these is run "backwards.") Control is then returned to the main program and the answers are printed.

If only the subroutine were listed, then only lines 210–500 would be shown. This type of listing will be used for most of the programs of this book. An alternate form of the subroutine is shown in Fig. 1–4. Here lines 210 and 220 have been changed. Common storage is not used and the subroutines' variables are given in its name, i.e.,

```
00210          SUBRØUTINE SIMUL(N,NA,A)
00200          DIMENSIØN A(N,NA)
00230          NB=N-1
00240          DØ 20 L=1,NB
00250          IF(A(L,L))16,1000,16
00260    16    CØNTINUE
00270          LA=L+1
00280          DØ 20 I=LA,N
00290          DØ 20 JQ=L,NA
00300          J=NA+L-JQ
00310          A(I,J)=A(I,J)-A(I,L)*A(L,J)/A(L,L)
00320    20    CØNTINUE
00330          IF(A(N,N))17,1000,17
00340    17    CØNTINUE
00350          DØ 60 I=1,N
00360          DØ 60 JQ=1,NA
00370          J=NA+1-JQ
00380          A(I,J)=A(I,J)/A(I,I)
00390    60    CØNTINUE
00400          DØ 100 LQ=1,N-1
00410          L=N-LQ
00420          K=L+1
00430          DØ 100 I=1,L
00440          A(I,NA)=A(I,NA)-A(K,NA)*A(I,K)
00450    100   CØNTINUE
00460          RETURN
00470    1000  TYPE 15
00480    15    FØRMAT(' PRINC DIAG TERM ZERØ')
00490          RETURN
00500          END
```

FIG. 1-4

An alternate form of the SUBROUTINE SIMUL

SIMUL (N, NA, A). Of course, line 10 in the main program would have to be changed to a DIMENSION statement and line 160 would be changed to CALL SIMUL (N, NA, A).

A sample run of SIMUL is given in Fig. 1–5. In this case the equations

$$5x_1 + x_2 + x_3 + x_4 + x_5 = 15$$
$$x_1 + 2x_2 + x_3 + x_4 - x_5 = 5$$
$$x_1 + x_2 + 6x_3 - x_4 - x_5 = 2$$
$$x_1 - x_2 - x_3 + 9x_4 + x_5 = 29$$
$$x_1 - x_2 - x_3 - x_4 + 8x_5 = 27$$

are solved. The values of the unknowns are

$$x_1 = 1$$
$$x_2 = 2$$
$$x_3 = 1$$
$$x_4 = 3$$
$$x_5 = 4$$

```
ENTER NUMBER ØF UNKNØWNS
5

ENTER ARRAY ØF CØEF
5.,1.,1.,1.,1.,
1.,2.,1.,1.,-1.,
1.,1.,6.,-1.,-1.,
1.,-1.,-1.,9.,1.,
1.,-1.,-1.,-1.,8.,

ENTER KNØWNS
15.,5.,2.,29.,27.,

UNKNØWNS ARE
   0.1000000E+01
   0.2000000E+01
   0.1000000E+01
   0.3000000E+01
   0.4000000E+01
```

FIG. 1–5
A teletype printout of a run of the program
SIMUL

If a principal diagonal term becomes zero, operation terminates (see lines 250 and 330 of Fig. 1–3). If the $n \times n$ matrix of coefficients is singular, then a unique solution cannot be found. In this case, a principal diagonal term will always become zero. However, a principal diagonal term can become zero even if the matrix is nonsingular. In this case, all that need be done is to rearrange the equations and/or the order in which the unknowns are written so that the zero term does not fall on the principal diagonal.

If the principal diagonal terms are smaller, in magnitude, than the other terms in the same column, then large multipliers $A(I, L)/A(L, L)$ can result. After several steps very large terms in the array can result. This can produce several undesirable effects. The large numbers can be beyond the range of the computer, in which case, they are often set at the largest value permitted by the computer and a warning is printed. Hence, the results are in error. In addition, division by one of these large numbers can result in numbers whose magnitudes are so small that they are set equal to zero by the computer. Either of these leads to improper results. The latter may cause a PRINC DIAG TERM ZERO to print even though this is actually not the case. An additional error can result since the subtraction of large nearly equal numbers can result in errors.

A procedure called *pivotal condensation* can eliminate these problems. Here, the equations and order of the variables are arranged so that the (1,1) position of the array has the largest magnitude coefficient. Then, after $n - 1$ terms of the first column are set equal to zero, etc., the order of equations and unknowns is rearranged so that the (2, 2) position has the largest coefficient. (The first column must be unchanged by this operation.) When the principal diagonal magnitude is the largest one, the multipliers will be kept small and the previously discussed problems will not occur. This pivoting procedure is repeated throughout the operation. For an example of a program that used pivoting, see the numerical analysis texts cited in the bibliography at the end of this chapter.

In our case, we do not have to use pivotal condensation. SIMUL will be used to solve DC loop analysis problems. There, the principal diagonal terms will have a magnitude which is always equal to or greater than the sums of the magnitudes of all terms on their row or column. In this case, pivoting is usually not necessary.

## 1-5. DC CIRCUIT ANALYSIS PROGRAM

In this section we shall discuss a simple program which can be used to analyze a dc circuit. We wish to enter the elements, generator values, and some simple information about the topology of the network and then have the computer print the loop currents or the branch currents.

As a review consider the set of loop equations which result from a loop analysis of a dc circuit.

$$R_{11}I_1 + R_{12}I_2 + \cdots + R_{1n}I_n = V_1$$
$$R_{21}I_1 + R_{22}I_2 + \cdots + R_{2n}I_n = V_2$$
$$\cdots\cdots\cdots\cdots\cdots\cdots\cdots\cdots\cdots\cdots\cdots\cdots$$
$$R_{n1}I_1 + R_{n2}I_2 + \cdots + R_{nn}I_n = V_n$$

$$(1-18)$$

where $R_{ii}$ represents the sum of all the resistances in loop i. Loops $i$ and $j$ have resistance $R_{ij} = R_{ji}$ in common. Resistance $R_{ij}$ is positive if $I_i$ and $I_j$ are in the same direction through it, and negative otherwise. $V_1$ is the algebraic sum of the voltage generators in mesh $I$.

To simplify the program we shall slightly restrict the network in the following way.

1. The network must be such that no more than two mesh currents can be in any branch.
2. Each branch contains exactly one resistance and one voltage generator. (Either or both may be zero, the resistance cannot be negative.)
3. No pair of mesh currents have more than one branch in common.
4. Each mesh has no more than one branch which is not in common with any other mesh.

For any network which can be drawn in a plane (i.e., a planar network) loop currents can always be chosen so that condition 1 is satisfied. Condition 2 is just a definition which assumes that all the resistors are positive. Condition 3 can be satisfied in any planar network by choosing mesh currents properly and combining branches, if necessary. Condition 4 can always be satisfied for any network by combining branches, if necessary.

The program which we shall discuss easily enables the user to obtain an augmented matrix (see Section 1–4) which characterizes the network. The subroutine SIMUL (see Section 1–4) is used to solve for the unknown currents. We call the program DCLA (dc loop analysis). It is given in Fig. 1–6. (Again note that the line numbers 00010–00830 are not part of the FORTRAN program; see Section 1–4).

We have written this program so that it can be used by someone who is unfamiliar with FORTRAN. Only the procedure for entering data must be known. Consequently, much of the program consists of input and output statements. For this reason, we shall not use the subroutine form.

Lines 10–90 are comments which do not affect the operation of the program. However, they are printed whenever the program is listed. These comments indicate to the reader the procedure for entering data. (Note that these comments are not listed when the program is run, but only appear when a listing is called for.)

This program will be run in conjunction with the SUBROUTINE SIMUL. Line 100 is a COMMON statement which dimensions the array R and enters the data in the subroutine. Line 110 is a dimension statement for an array which is not used in the SUBROUTINE. Lines 130–160 provide for entering the number of meshes and branches.

The data concerned with the resistances and voltage generators will initially be stored in two arrays $R(I, J)$ and $V(I, J)$. Lines 180–220 set their initial values to zero. These statements are not necessary with all FORTRAN compilers. Some compilers automatically set variables whose values are not entered equal to zero.

Data are entered using the DO loop of lines 260–330. The DO loop cycles NB (the number of branches) times. Each cycle through the DO loop enters a value of I, J, $R(I, J)$, $V(I, J)$, and a SIGN term for a particular branch, where $V(I, J)$ is the generator voltage in the branch in question. If $I \neq J$, then $R(I, J)$ is the coupling between the I and the J loops. SIGN is entered as $+1$ or $-1$. The $+1$ indicates that the loop currents $I(I)$ and $I(J)$ are in the same direction in $R(I, J)$, while $-1$ indicates the opposite. The generator voltage $V(I, J)$ is positive if it "aids" $I(I)$ and negative otherwise. The value of $R(I, J)$ is set equal to SIGN $* R(I, J)$. Thus, the coupling term has the correct sign. $R(J, I)$ is then set equal to $R(I, J)$ in line 300. The sign of $V(I, J)$ is entered with it. Then $V(J, I)$ is calculated using line 310. Note that if a branch lies only in loop I, then SIGN must be entered as $+1$.

The coefficient matrix of the loop analysis now is calculated. If $I \neq J$, then $R(I, J)$ has already been calculated. The value of $R(I, I)$ must be modified. To obtain $R(I, I)$ the *magnitudes* of all coupling resistances between mesh $I$ and all the other meshes plus any resistance that lies only in mesh I are added. This is done in the DO loop of lines 340–400. Note that (see line 350) a dummy variable RR is used here. Each complete cycle of the inner DO loop (lines 360–380) sets $RR$ equal to the sum of all $|R(I, 1)| + |R(I, 2)| + \cdots + |R(I, M)|$. Note that ABS (see line 370) is a function that takes the magnitude of the argument. Then $R(I, I)$ is set equal to $RR$ (see line 390). After this, $RR$ is set equal to zero by the first DO loop and the cycle is repeated with a new value of $I$.

```
00010  C     DC LOOP ANALYSIS PROGRAM
00020  C     PROCEDURE FOR ENTERING DATA:
00030  C     FOR EACH BRANCH ENTER ITS LOOPS(I,J).
00040  C     IF THE MESH CURRENTS ARE IN THE SAME
00050  C     DIRECTION TYPE 1. OTHERWIZE TYPE -1.
00060  C     THEN TYPE BRANCH RESISTANCE EVEN IF 0
00070  C     THEN ENTER BRANCH VOLTAGE. IT IS POSITIVE
00080  C     IF IT AIDS THE FIRST LOOP CURRENT. EXAMPLE
00090  C     2,3,-1,2,3,4.5 OR 1,1,1,2.1,4.,
00100        COMMON R(10,11),M,MA
00110        DIMENSION V(10,10)
00120  2     FORMAT(I)
00130        TYPE 5
00140  5     FORMAT (' ENTER NUMBER OF LOOPS AND BRANCHES'/)
00150        ACCEPT 6,M,NB
00160  6     FORMAT (2I)
00170        MA=M+1
00180        DO 25 I=1,M
00190        DO 25 J=1,M
00200        R(I,J)=0.
00210        V(I,J)=0.
00220  25    CONTINUE
00230        TYPE 7
00240  7     FORMAT (' ENTER DATA'/)
00250        SIGN=0.
00260        DO 35 K=1,NB
00270        ACCEPT 66,I,J,SIGN,R(I,J),V(I,J)
00280  66    FORMAT(2I,3F)
00290        R(I,J)=SIGN*R(I,J)
00300        R(J,I)=R(I,J)
00310        V(J,I)=SIGN*V(I,J)
00320        SIGN=0.
00330  35    CONTINUE
00340        DO 50 I=1,M
00350        RR=0.
00360        DO 51 J=1,M
00370        RR=RR+ABS(R(I,J))
00380  51    CONTINUE
00390        R(I,I)=RR
00400  50    CONTINUE
00410        DO 60 I=1,M
00420        R(I,MA)=0.
00430        DO 60 J=1,M
00440        R(I,MA)=R(I,MA)+V(I,J)
00450  60    CONTINUE
00460        TYPE 11
00470  11    FORMAT(' IF AUGMENTED MATRIX IS DESIRED
00480       +  TYPE 1 AND RETURN.'/' IF NOT DESIRED
00490       +  TYPE 0 AND RETURN'/)
00500        ACCEPT 2,JJJ
00510        IF(JJJ)62,62,61
00520  61    CONTINUE
00530        DO 177 I=1,M
00540        TYPE 13,(R(I,J),J=1,MA)
00550  13    FORMAT(10F7.2)
```

FIG. 1-6(a)

```
00560  177      CØNTINUE
00570  62       CØNTINUE
00580           CALL SIMUL
00590           TYPE 101
00600  101      FØRMAT(' TYPE 0 FØR LISTING ØF ALL
00610      +    CURRENTS, 1 FØR SINGLE'/' LØØP CURRENT
00620      +    -1 FØR BRANCH CURRENT'/)
00630           ACCEPT 2,JJ
00640           IF(JJ)64,621,63
00650  621      TYPE 102,(R(I,MA),I=1,M)
00660  102      FØRMAT(' LØØP CURRENTS'/(E))
00670           STØP
00680  63       TYPE 106
00690  106      FØRMAT(' ENTER DESIRED LØØP CURRENT'/)
00700           ACCEPT 2,IA
00710           TYPE 107,R(IA,MA)
00720  107      FØRMAT(' THE LØØP CURRENT IS',E)
00730           STØP
00740  64       TYPE 103
00750  103      FØRMAT(' TØ ØBTAIN I(J)+OR-I(K) TYPE'/'
00760      +    J,K,1 ØR J,K,-1'/)
00770           ACCEPT 104,JA,KA,A
00780  104      FØRMAT(2I,F)
00790           B=R(JA,MA)+A*R(KA,MA)
00800           TYPE 105,B
00810  105      FØRMAT(' THE BRANCH CURRENT IS',E)
00820           STØP
00830           END
```

FIG. 1–6 (b)

The program DCLA used for solving dc loop analysis problems. The SUBROUTINE SIMUL (lines 210–500) or Fig 1–3a should be appended to this program. Note that the line numbers (e.g., 00010–00830) are not part of this program

The mesh voltages (i.e., the sum of the generator voltages around any particular mesh) are calculated in the DO loops of lines 410–450. These values are included as the last column in the array R.

The augmented array has now been formed. Lines 460–570 provide the user with the option of having it printed. If JJJ is entered as zero, control shifts to line 570 and the array is not printed. If JJJ is entered as 1, the array is typed. Note (see line 550) that a free format is not used. This is because the spacing on the free format is too large to allow all the numbers of the array to be typed on one line. An F field specifier is used here rather than the more desirable E field specifier to save space. Note that this can cause the loss of important significant figures. Note the + sign preceding lines 480 and 490. Any symbol placed in the sixth column indicates that the line is a continuation of the previous one, e.g., lines 470–490 actually represent one FORTRAN statement.

The subroutine SIMUL is then called, the simultaneous equations are solved, and the loop currents are obtained. The user is now provided with three options

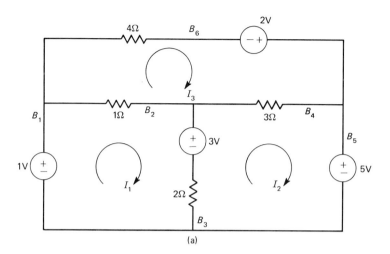

(a)

```
ENTER NUMBER ØF LØØPS AND BRANCHES
3,6

ENTER DATA
1,1,1.,0.,1.,
1,3,-1.,1.,0.,
1,2,-1.,1.,-3.,
2,3,-1.,3.,0.,
2,2,1.,0.,-5.,
3,3,1.,4.,2.,

IF AUGMENTED MATRIX IS DESIRED   TYPE 1 AND RETURN.
IF NØT DESIRED   TYPE 0 AND RETURN
1

   3.00   -2.00   -1.00   -2.00
  -2.00    5.00   -3.00   -2.00
  -1.00   -3.00    8.00    2.00
TYPE 0 FØR LISTING ØF ALL CURRENTS, 1 FØR SINGLE
LØØP CURRENT   -1 FØR BRANCH CURRENT
0

LØØP CURRENTS
-0.1772727E+01
-0.1409091E+01
-0.5000000E+00
```

(b)

FIG. 1–7

(a) Three-loop network ; (b) sample run of the program DCLA

since he may not want all the currents typed (unwanted data can be annoying). These options are indicated in lines 600–620. Either all the loop currents, a single loop current, or the sum or difference between two loop currents (i.e., a branch current) can be typed on the user's teletype. These options are picked by entering 0, 1, or − 1, respectively, for the value of JJ. The IF statement of line 640 then transfers control to the desired option. If a single loop current or a branch current is desired, the number of the loop current or the numbers of the loop currents making up the branch currents are then entered (see lines 700 and 770).

To run this program, the subroutine SIMUL (see Section 1–4) is appended to this one. A network and a sample run of DCLA are included in Fig. 1–7. Note that this greatly reduces the work required to solve for the network currents.

We have illustrated a simple dc loop analysis, but there are many programs which are far more general. For instance, these can perform ac and transient analysis. Many of these are packaged programs supplied by computer centers or companies. The user need not understand the program, but just enters the data in the appropriate way and obtains the results. The best known program of this type is ECAP (electronic circuit analysis program). It was developed by the International Business Machines Corporation. These packaged programs can be very helpful. However, the electrical engineer must often be able to write a program which solves his particular problem; thus, it is also very important to understand how to write programs.

## PROBLEMS

**1-1.** Define signals and systems consistent with the discussions of this chapter.

**1-2.** Consider a complex system which transmits a television signal from one point to another *via* a satellite. Describe the system in terms of its subsystems.

**1-3.** What are the signals for the system of Problem 1-2?

**1-4.** Using a simple electrical network, give examples of a linear system, a nonlinear system, a time-varying system, and a time-invariant system.

**1-5.** Write a set of differential equations that characterize the simple system of Fig. 1–8. What are the order and the degree of this system?

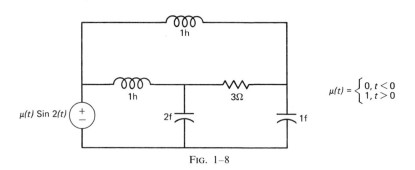

FIG. 1–8

**1-6.** Write a FORTRAN program that accepts the values of the three variables $a$, $b$, and $c$, and then prints out the values of

$$d = a^2 + 2ab + c^2$$
$$e = a + 3ac + b^2$$

**1-7.** Write a FORTRAN program to obtain the results of Problem 1-6 using a FUNCTION to calculate $d$ and $e$.

**1-8.** Repeat Problem 1-7 using a SUBROUTINE.

**1-9.** Repeat Problem 1-8 using a COMMON statement to enter and extract all data.

**1-10.** Write a FORTRAN program that accepts the value of $a_i$, $i = 1, 2, 3, ..., 10$, and $b_i$, $i = 1, 2, ..., 10$, and computes and prints out

$$c_i = (a_i + b_i)^2$$

**1-11.** Rewrite the program of Fig. 1-3a replacing all numerical IF statements by logical IF statements.

**1-12.** Solve the set of simultaneous equations

$$\begin{aligned}
5x_1 + 3x_2 - x_3 - x_4 &= 15 \\
x_1 + 17x_2 - x_3 - x_4 &= 12 \\
x_1 + x_2 + 19x_3 + x_4 &= 15 \\
x_1 + x_2 + x_3 + 17x_4 &= 18
\end{aligned}$$

**1-13.** Why is SIMUL suited to dc network analysis (and the solution of the equations of Problem 1-12), but not to the general solution of simultaneous equations?

**1-14.** Write an original FORTRAN program that can be used to solve simultaneous equations. (This should be different from SIMUL.)

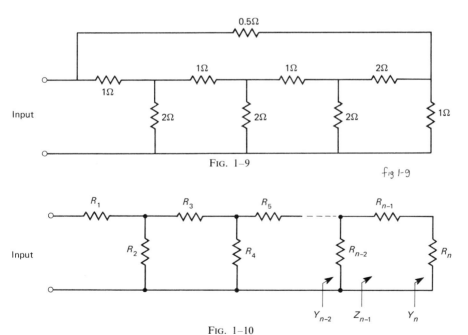

FIG. 1-9

FIG. 1-10

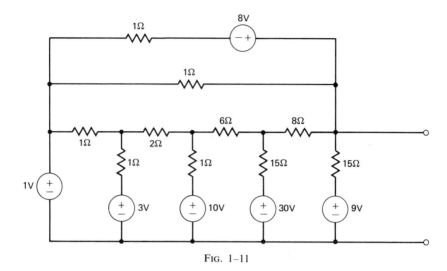

FIG. 1–11

**1-15.** Repeat Problem 1-12 using the program of Problem 1-14. Check your answer with that of Problem 1-12.

**1-16.** Obtain the input resistance of the network of Fig. 1–9. (Use a network analysis program.)

**1-17.** Write a program using features of the program DCLA as a subroutine which determines the input resistance of a network made up of resistors.

**1-18.** Write a program that does not use loop analysis, but that determines the input resistance of the network of Fig. 1–10 for values of $n \leq 10$. *Hint:* $Y_n = 1/R_n$, $Z_{n-1} = R_{n-1} + 1/Y_n$, $Y_{n-2} = 1/R_{n-1} + 1/Z_{n-1}$.

**1-19.** Obtain the Thevenin's equivalent circuit for the network of Fig. 1–11. (Use DCLA to solve for the required values.)

**1-20.** Write a program that determines the Thevenin's equivalent circuit for a general oneport made up of direct voltage generators and resistors.

**1-21.** Write a program that performs nodal analysis in circuits containing only direct current generators and resistors.

## BIBLIOGRAPHY

Carnahan, B., Luther, H.A., and Wilkes, J.O. *Applied Numerical Methods.* Chap. 5. New York: Wiley, 1969.

Hamming, R.W. *Numerical Methods for Scientists and Engineers.* Chaps. 29 and 30. New York: McGraw-Hill, 1962.

Huelsman, L.P. *Digital Computations in Basic Circuit Theory.* Chap. 7. New York: McGraw-Hill, 1968.

McCracken, D.D., and Dorn, W.S. *Numerical Methods and FORTRAN Programming.* Chap. 8. New York: Wiley, 1964.

Pennington, R.H. *Introductory Computer Methods and Numerical Analysis.* Chap. 12. New York: Macmillan, 1965.

Ralston, A. *A First Course in Numerical Analysis.* Chap. 9. New York: McGraw-Hill, 1965.

# CHAPTER 2

# Distribution Theory, Fourier Transform, Fast Fourier Transform

The Fourier transform provides us with an important procedure for analyzing signals and the responses of systems to them. This transform shall be developed using *distribution theory*, which will enable us to discuss such topics as impulse response on a rigorous basis. In addition, the use of distribution theory often simplifies analysis procedures. We shall start with a discussion of distribution theory and then apply it to the Fourier transform.

## 2-1. INTRODUCTION TO DISTRIBUTION THEORY

In this section we shall introduce *distribution theory*. The use of distribution theory not only provides rigor for many of the procedures used by engineers but also it makes some of these procedures simpler. For instance, the response to many commonly used signals, such as the unit step function or a sinusoid turned on a $t = 0$, can be studied far more easily using distribution theory.

Let us begin our discussion by considering a particular function which is often used by the electrical engineer; the *unit impulse*, or *Dirac delta*, function. Then, we can generalize to other functions. We shall start by taking an heuristic approach and then consider distribution theory in general.

Consider the function $\delta_n(t)$ illustrated in Fig. 2–1.

$$\delta_n(t) = \begin{cases} \dfrac{1}{n}, & 0 \leqq t \leqq n \\ 0, & 0 < t, t > n \end{cases} \qquad (2\text{–}1)$$

where $\delta_n(t)$ is a rectangular pulse of height $1/n$ and area unity. In a heuristic, or nonrigorous sense, we can state that the limit as $n$ approaches 0 of $\delta_n(t)$ is the *unit impulse function* $\delta(t)$. That is,

$$\delta(t) = \lim_{n \to 0} \delta_n(t) \qquad (2\text{–}2)$$

Thus the unit impulse is a "pulse of infinite height and unit area." The reader may ask why we are concerned with such pulses since they cannot actually be generated. The response of a system to $\delta(t)$ often very closely approximates its response to a very short pulse of unit area. Usually the response to $\delta(t)$ is more easily calculated

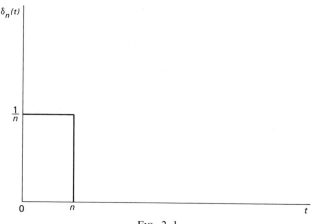

Fig. 2–1

The function $\delta_n(t)$

than the response to the short pulse. In addition, impulse functions facilitate the study of the Fourier transform.

Now consider a function $f(t)$ which is continuous at $t = 0$. Let us determine

$$\lim_{n \to 0} \int_{-\infty}^{\infty} \delta_n(t) f(t)\, dt$$

where $\delta_n(t)$ is zero except at $0 \leq t \leq n$. If $0 \leq t \leq n$, then $\delta_n(t) = 1/n$; thus the integral can be written as

$$\lim_{n \to 0} \int_{-\infty}^{\infty} \delta_n(t) f(t)\, dt \qquad \lim_{n \to 0} \int_0^n \frac{1}{n} f(t)\, dt = \lim_{n \to 0} \frac{1}{n} \int_0^n f(t)\, dt$$

Note that $n$ is a constant for the integration. Also, $f(t)$ is continuous about $t = 0$; thus as $n$ becomes small, $f(t)$ approaches the constant $f(0)$ for $0 \leq t \leq n$. Hence, we can write

$$\lim_{n \to 0} \int_{-\infty}^{\infty} \delta_n(t) f(t)\, dt = \lim_{n \to 0} \frac{1}{n} f(0) \int_0^n dt = f(0) \qquad (2\text{–}3a)$$

Thus, in a nonrigorous sense, we have

$$\int_{-\infty}^{\infty} \delta(t) f(t)\, dt = f(0) \qquad (2\text{–}3b)$$

We cannot, in general, state that the value which a function assumes as it approaches a limit is the same value it actually has at the limit. For example, consider the discontinuous function

$$u(t) = \begin{cases} 1, & t > 0 \\ \frac{1}{2}, & t = 0 \\ 0, & t < 0 \end{cases} \tag{2-4}$$

If we take the limit for positive values of $t$, we obtain

$$\lim_{\substack{t \to 0 \\ t > 0}} u(t) = 1 \tag{2-5a}$$

Similarly, for negative values of $t$ we have

$$\lim_{\substack{t \to 0 \\ t < 0}} u(t) = 0 \tag{2-5b}$$

These limits are different and neither of them is equal to the value of $1/2$ which is *defined* as the value of $u(t)$ at $t = 0$. Thus in the above example the value at the origin is not the value obtained as the origin is approached. However, if we define the function so that its value at $t = 0$ is $+ 1$, then its value at the limit would be its value as approached through positive values.

In the "real world" we encounter functions which may approach some limit, as does the unit impulse. However, we never encounter functions which actually reach the limit. On the other hand, it is often convenient, for mathematical computations, to work with functions "at the limit." Hence, it is often desirable to define functions which are equal to the limit approached by actual ones. Analyses using these functions are often less tedious than ones using the actual ones. The calculated results often very closely approximate the actual ones.

Consider a definition for $\delta_n(t)$ such that its value, when $n = 0$, is equal to the value approached by $\lim_{n \to 0} \delta_n(t)$. The limit of $\delta_n(t)$ is not an ordinary function, thus we must use another procedure for defining $\delta(t)$. Suppose we say that $\delta(t)$ is defined by the relation (see Eq. 2–3b)

$$\int_{-\infty}^{\infty} \delta(t) f(t)\, dt = f(0) \tag{2-6}$$

where $f(t)$ is *any* ordinary function which is continuous at $t = 0$. It may appear strange to define a function in terms of an integral. However, note that Eq. 2–6 must hold for *all* $f(t)$ continuous at $t = 0$. Thus in an heuristic sense $\delta(t)$ must have the properties (i.e., unit area and zero width) that we have attributed to it.

The only time that we shall really use $\delta(t)$ is when it is part of a function which is to be integrated. For instance, to compute the response of a system to an impulse, we work with an integral containing $\delta(t)$. Thus, any definition of $\delta(t)$ is proper as long as the evaluation of the integrals yields the proper results. Let us look at this in a slightly different way. Suppose

$$\int_{-\infty}^{\infty} f_1(t) f_2(t)\, dt = 0 \qquad (2\text{–}7)$$

for all $f_2(t)$. The only time that $f_1(t)$ can be used (or studied) is in this integral; we could then define

$$f_1(t) = 0$$

since this would always give us the proper value of the integral. (Of course, this presupposes that we only work with $f_1(t)$ in the integral.) At times, $f_1(t)$ is manipulated with no use of integration. For instance, we could write

$$f_1(t) f_2(t) = 0$$

However, the integration is implied. (This equation is obtained by application of Eq. 2–7.)

We often encounter functions which can never be actually measured, however, integrals containing them can be. For instance, the Fourier transform is used to relate the time response of a network to its frequency spectrum and the time response can be measured by using an oscilloscope, but the frequency response can *never* actually be measured. Of course, we can infer the frequency response by measuring the time response to a series of sinusoidal input signals. However, the time response to these signals is *actually* measured and the frequency response is determined from these time responses.

The time response can be *calculated* from the frequency response using the Fourier transform. If the frequency response yields the correct time response (integral) then we can state that the frequency response is correct. Thus, we need only concern ourselves with obtaining functions whose integrals give correct values if we cannot check the functions themselves but only their integrals. Then, the definition of $\delta(t)$ given by Eq. 2–6 is allowable.

**Generalized Functions–Distributions.**    Let us now generalize the previous discussion to functions other than impulse functions. We now consider *functionals: A functional is a process which produces a number for each member of a set of functions.* For example, consider

$$\int_{-\infty}^{\infty} f(t)\, dt$$

where $f(t)$ is continuous, bounded, and $\lim_{t \to \pm\infty} |f(t)| < K/t^2$. Then, we can define the above integral as a functional because it produces a single *number* for each $f(t)$. We can use the following notation.

$$N[f(t)] = \int_{-\infty}^{\infty} f(t)\, dt \qquad (2\text{–}8)$$

Here, $N[f(t)]$ is a number which depends upon $f(t)$, thus, Eq. 2–8 is a functional. As an example, we could also write

$$N[f_1(t), f(t)] = \int_{-\infty}^{\infty} f_1(t) f(t) \, dt$$

Assuming that $f(t)$ is fixed, the functional assigns a value for each $f(t)$. We include $f_1(t)$ in the parameters of $N$ since it serves to indicate something of the functional. Consider another functional, the *delta functional*, which is defined as

$$N[\delta(t), f(t)] = f(0)$$

Here, we consider $\delta(t)$ as a functional which yields $f(0)$ when it operates on $f(t)$. We can symbolically write this functional relation as

$$\int_{-\infty}^{\infty} \delta(t) f(t) \, dt$$

Note that this is not an integral in the ordinary sense, but only a convenient notation.

There are other functionals which, like $\delta(t)$, cannot be expressed as ordinary functions. However, they are approached in the limit by ordinary functions. Thus, it is desirable to generalize the previous discussion and consider this type of function rather than just $\delta(t)$. We shall call such functions *generalized functions* or *distributions*. Note that $\delta(t)$ is one example of a distribution. These distributions will be written as $g(t)$; the functional relation which defines them is

$$N[g(t), \phi(t)] = \int_{-\infty}^{\infty} g(t) \, \phi(t) \, dt \qquad (2\text{–}9)$$

where $\phi(t)$ is an ordinary function and $N[g(t), \phi(t)]$ is a number which is assigned by the functional. Equation 2–9 actually represents many different functionals, depending upon $g(t)$ and we shall call these *distribution functionals*. As in the case of $\delta(t)$, the integral of Eq. 2–9 is only a convenient notation; however, it may not represent an integral in the usual sense. Thus, the $\int$ in these equations is actually not an integral sign. Why do we use it then? In all practical cases, the generalized function will be obtained from the limit of an actual one, just as the impulse is obtained from $\delta_n(t)$. The integral of the actual function will exist. Then, $g(t)$ is defined so as to make the value of the "integral" equal to the limit of the integral of the actual function. In the real world, we never reach the limit. We just approach it. Thus, defining the limit to be what we approach is compatible with physical measurements; that is, the use of Eq. 2–9 implies that $g(t)$ is defined by some limit process (e.g., $g(t) = \lim g_n(t)$) and $N[g(t), \phi(t)]$ results from taking $\lim \int_{-\infty}^{\infty} g_n(t) \, \phi(t) \, dt$. In summary, as an example,

$$\lim_{n \to 0} \int_{-\infty}^{\infty} \delta_n(t) f(t) \, dt = f(0)$$

is an actual integral for all nonzero $n$ and

$$\int_{-\infty}^{\infty} \delta(t) f(t)\, dt = f(0)$$

is a definition compatible with it.

In general, when we define operations including generalized functions, we shall make them compatible with operations involving ordinary functions. That is, if the generalized functions are replaced by ordinary functions, the definition should still be valid. This is consistant with our previous discussions and will be illustrated in the next section.

Now consider the definition of generalized functions given by Eq. 2–9. We shall restrict $\phi(t)$ in the following way: $\phi(t)$ will be continuous, possess all its derivatives, and be of compact support; i.e., $f(t) = 0$ for $|t|$ sufficiently large or, equivalently, $f(t) = 0$ for $t > |T_1|$ and $t < -|T_2|$. Note that a function of compact support is nonzero only for a finite length of time. Thus any function that can be physically generated is of compact support. Functions which satisfy these conditions will be called *testing functions* or *test functions*. The set of *all* testing functions which satisfy the above conditions will be said to exist in a space (or set) $D$. We can define our test functions in a slightly different way. The condition of compact support can be replaced by the condition that $\phi(t)$ falls off sufficiently fast (e.g., $e^{-|t|}$ or $1/t^n$, $n$ any integer) as $|t|$ approaches infinity.

## 2.2. PROPERTIES OF DISTRIBUTIONS

In this section we shall define some properties of distributions. Any set of self-consistent rules can be used to define a branch of mathematics. However, if the mathematics is to be used for solving practical problems, the rules must be compatible with physical phenomena.

Since distributions are usually obtained by limit processes, the operations defined should be compatible with those for ordinary functions; that is, if the generalized functions are replaced by ordinary functions, (before the limit is taken), the defined operations should still be valid. Now let us consider some operations.

*Linearity*: Operations with generalized functions are *linear*. Suppose we have two generalized functions

$$N[g_1(t), \phi(t)] = \int_{-\infty}^{\infty} g_1(t)\, \phi(t)\, dt \qquad (2\text{–}10a)$$

and

$$N[g_2(t), \phi(t)] = \int_{-\infty}^{\infty} g_2(t)\, \phi(t)\, dt \qquad (2\text{–}10b)$$

Equivalently, we may state that we have two distribution functionals $N[g_1(t), \phi(t)]$

and $N[g_2(t), \phi(t)]$. Then,

$$N[g_1(t) + g_2(t), \phi(t)] = N[g_1(t), \phi(t)] + N[g_2(t), \phi(t)] \qquad (2-11a)$$

for all $\phi(t)$ in set $D$. Note that this would be true if $g_1(t)$ and $g_2(t)$ were ordinary functions. For example,

$$\int_{-\infty}^{\infty} [g_1(t) + g_2(t)] \phi(t) \, dt = \int_{-\infty}^{\infty} g_1(t) \phi(t) \, dt + \int_{-\infty}^{\infty} g_2(t) \phi(t) \, dt \qquad (2-11b)$$

Linearity can be considered in another way. Suppose we have any two test functions $\phi_1(t)$ and $\phi_2(t)$ in $D$ such that

$$N[g(t), \phi_1(t)]$$

and

$$N[g(t), \phi_2(t)]$$

Then,

$$N[g(t), a_1\phi_1(t) + a_2\phi_2(t)] = a_1 N[g(t), \phi_1(t)] + a_2 N[g(t), \phi_2(t)] \qquad (2-12)$$

where $a_1$ and $a_2$ are constants. Note that $N[g(t), \phi(t)]$ and $N[g(t), \phi_2(t)]$ are just numbers and that Eq. 2–12 would be true if $g(t)$ were an ordinary function; that is,

$$\int_{-\infty}^{\infty} g(t) [a_1\phi(t) + a_2\phi_2(t)] \, dt = a_1 \int_{-\infty}^{\infty} g(t) \phi_1(t) \, dt + a_2 \int_{-\infty}^{\infty} g(t) \phi_2(t) \, dt$$

*Continuity*: We define continuity in the following way. Suppose $\phi_n(t)$ represents a set of test functions in $D$ such that

$$\phi(t) = \lim_{n \to n_0} \phi(t)$$

Then,

$$N[g(t), \phi(t)] = \lim_{n \to 0} N[g(t), \phi_n(t)] \qquad (2-13)$$

Linearity and continuity are fundamental properties of distributions. We shall consider another aspect of continuity in Section 2-3.

*Equality.* Consider a criterion wherein two generalized functions can be set equal to each other. If

$$N[g_1(t) \phi(t)] = N[g_2(t), \phi(t)] \qquad (2-14a)$$

for *all* test functions $\phi(t)$ in $D$, then we state that

$$g_1(t) = g_2(t) \qquad (2-14b)$$

Now consider that $g_1(t)$ and $g_2(t)$ are ordinary functions. It now becomes convenient to use the integral notation; thus Eq. 2–14a is written as

$$\int_{-\infty}^{\infty} g_1(t)\,\phi(t)\,dt = \int_{-\infty}^{\infty} g_2(t)\,\phi(t)\,dt \tag{2-15}$$

Note that Eqs. 2–14a and 2–15 must be satisfied for *all* $\phi(t)$ and not just a single one. In general, if we are dealing with ordinary functions, Eq. 2–14b would be valid except that $g_1(t)$ and $g_2(t)$ could differ by a finite amount at a finite number of isolated points (see Fig. 2–2). In all practical cases, functions which have such differences will not be of consequence, since signals with point discontinuities cannot be physically generated. In addition, a finite number of these finite discontinuities will not affect the value of any integral; accordingly, they will not affect the result of an analysis.

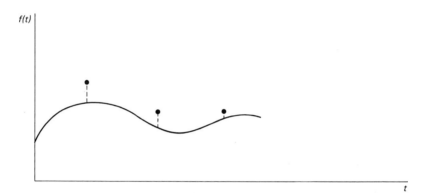

FIG. 2–2
Two functions that differ at three isolated points (one function is the curve and the other is the curve except for the three points)

**Transpose of a Distribution.**  If $g(t)$ represents a distribution, then its *transpose* is defined as $g(-t)$. Let us discuss the effect of replacing $t$ by $-t$. For any $\phi(t)$ in $D$, we define

$$N[g(-t), \phi(t)] = N[g(t), \phi(-t)] \tag{2-16}$$

Note that this is compatible with ordinary functions. Suppose that $f(t)$ is an ordinary function, then,

$$\int_{-\infty}^{\infty} f(-t)\,\phi(t)\,dt = -\int_{\infty}^{-\infty} f(x)\,\phi(-x)\,dx = \int_{-\infty}^{\infty} f(t)\,\phi(-t)\,dt$$

where we substitute $x = -t$ in the second integral and $t = x$ in the third.

We can use the definition of the transpose of a distribution to define the evenness or oddness of distributions. Note that an ordinary function $f(t)$ is said to be *even* if

$$f(t) = f(-t)$$

and *odd* if

$$f(t) = -f(-t)$$

We use a similar definition for distributions. A distribution $g(t)$ is even if it equals its transpose. That is if

$$g(t) = g(-t) \tag{2-17a}$$

A distribution is odd if it equals the negative of its transpose. That is if

$$g(t) = -g(-t) \tag{2-17b}$$

Consider some implications of this. Assume that $g_e(t)$ is an even distribution; then,

$$N[g_e(t), \phi(t)] = N[g_e(-t), \phi(t)] = N[g_e(t), \phi(-t)]$$

Suppose that $\phi_o(t)$ is an odd function. Then, by linearity and Eq. 2–16, we have

$$N[g_e(t), \phi_o(t)] = -N[g_e(t), \phi_o(t)] = 0$$

This expression is equal to zero, since the only number which is equal to its negative is zero. Hence, when an even distribution operates on *any* odd test function in $D$, the result is zero. Similarly, if we have an odd distribution $g_o(t)$, with $\phi_e(t)$ any even test function in $D$, then

$$N[g_o(t), \phi_e(t)] = -N[g_o(t), \phi_e(t)] = 0$$

Thus when an odd distribution operates on any even test function in $D$, the result is zero.

These definitions are compatible with those obtained using ordinary functions. The product of an even function and an odd function will be an odd function. Thus, if $g_e(t)$ and $g_o(t)$ are ordinary functions, then $g_e(t)\phi_o(t)$ and $g_o(t)\phi_e(t)$ will be an odd function $f_0(t)$. Let us consider $\int_{-\infty}^{\infty} f_0(t)\,dt$. Before doing this we must consider a fundamental definition of infinite definite integrals. In general, we shall define infinite definite integrals in the following way:

$$\int_{-\infty}^{\infty} f(t)\,dt = \lim_{b \to \infty} \int_{-b}^{b} f(t)\,dt \tag{2-18}$$

Thus, if $f(t)$ is odd, we have

$$\int_{-\infty}^{\infty} f_o(t)\,dt = 0 \tag{2-19}$$

The integral is zero since the contribution for $t > 0$ is exactly cancelled by the contribution for $t < 0$. Hence,

$$\int_{-\infty}^{\infty} g_e(t)\,\phi_o(t)\,dt = \int_{-\infty}^{\infty} g_o(t)\,\phi_e(t)\,dt = 0$$

Thus, the results for ordinary functions are compatible with the definitions for distributions.

**Product of a Distribution and Ordinary Function.** It is often disirable to determine the product of two distributions. Unfortunately, this usually cannot be done. However, we can often define the product of a distribution and an ordinary function. Suppose an ordinary function $f(t)$ is such that $f(t)\phi(t)$ represents a function in $D$ for *all* $\phi(t)$ in $D$; then we define

$$N[f(t)g(t), \phi(t)] = N[g(t), f(t)\phi(t)] \qquad (2\text{–}20)$$

If we write this using the integral notation, we have

$$\int_{-\infty}^{\infty} f(t)g(t)\phi(t)\,dt = \int_{-\infty}^{\infty} g(t)f(t)\phi(t)\,dt$$

This is certainly true for ordinary functions.

**Differentiation of a Distribution.** We shall now define a value for $dg(t)/dt$; that is, we want to define a value for

$$N\left[\frac{dg(t)}{dt}, \phi(t)\right]$$

in terms of previously developed expressions. The definition that we use is

$$N\left[\frac{dg(t)}{dt}, \phi(t)\right] = -N\left[g(t), \frac{d\phi(t)}{dt}\right] \qquad (2\text{–}21)$$

Here the test function is replaced by the negative of its derivative and the derivative of the distribution is replaced by the distribution. Equivalently, we can use integral notation (see Eq. 2–9), and write

$$\int_{-\infty}^{\infty} \frac{dg(t)}{dt}\phi(t)\,dt = -\int_{-\infty}^{\infty} g(t)\frac{d\phi(t)}{dt}\,dt \qquad (2\text{–}22)$$

We now show that Eqs. 2–21 and 2–22 are compatible with ordinary functions. Consider

$$\int_{-\infty}^{\infty} \frac{df(t)}{dt}\phi(t)\,dt$$

and integrate it by parts. This yields

$$\int_{-\infty}^{\infty} \frac{df(t)}{dt}\phi(t)\,dt = \phi(t)f(t)\bigg|_{-\infty}^{\infty} - \int_{-\infty}^{\infty} f(t)\frac{d\phi(t)}{dt}\,dt \qquad (2\text{–}23)$$

However, $\phi(t)$ is in $D$. Thus, it is of compact support (see Section 2–1). Hence, as $t$ approaches infinity, the first term is zero. Then, Eq. 2–23 is compatible with Eq. 2–21. Note that if Eq. 2–21 is to have meaning, $d\phi(t)/dt$ must be in $D$. This will be the case, since $\phi(t)$ possesses all its derivatives and is of compact support.

We have used the functional notation $N[g(t), \phi(t)]$ and the integral notation

$$\int_{-\infty}^{\infty} g(t)\,\phi(t)\,dt$$

to represent distribution functionals. In much of the remainder of this discussion, we shall use the integral notation.

As an example of the derivative of a distribution, consider the following: let $g(t) = u(t)$, the unit step, where

$$u(t) = \begin{cases} 1, & t > 0 \\ 0, & t < 0 \end{cases} \tag{2-24}$$

Then,

$$\int_{-\infty}^{\infty} \frac{dg(t)}{dt}\,\phi(t)\,dt = -\int_{-\infty}^{\infty} \frac{du(t)}{dt}\,\phi(t)\,dt \tag{2-25}$$

In an ordinary sense, $du(t)/dt$ is zero at all points except $t = 0$, where it does not exist. Suppose $u(t)$ is obtained from Fig. 2–3a by letting $n$ approach zero. The derivative of Fig. 2–3a is given in Fig. 2–3b. Note that this is $\delta_n(t)$ (see Fig. 2–1). Thus, $du(t)/dt$ can be considered a distribution. Now, applying Eq. 2–22 we have

$$\int_{-\infty}^{\infty} \frac{du(t)}{dt}\,\phi(t)\,dt = -\int_{-\infty}^{\infty} u(t)\frac{d\phi(t)}{dt}\,dt$$

Then, substituting Eq. 2–24. we obtain

$$\int_{-\infty}^{\infty} \frac{du(t)}{dt}\,\phi(t)\,dt = -\int_{0}^{\infty} \frac{d\phi(t)}{dt}\,dt = \phi(0) - \phi(\infty)$$

However, $\phi(\infty)$ is assumed to be zero for functions in $D$; hence,

$$\int_{-\infty}^{\infty} \frac{du(t)}{dt}\,\phi(t)\,dt = \phi(0) \tag{2-26}$$

This is true for all $\phi(t)$ in $D$. Hence, if we compare Eq. 2–26 with Eq. 2–6 and then use the definition of equality given in Eqs. 2–14 and 2–15, we have

$$\frac{du(t)}{dt} = \delta(t) \tag{2-27}$$

On a *distribution basis*, the derivative of the unit step is the unit impulse. This result could be expected since the derivative of $u_u(t)$ is $\delta_n(t)$. It is far easier to use distributions instead of using cumbersome limit processes. This is especially true when the equations became more complex. On an ordinary basis the derivative of $u(t)$ does not exist, but distribution theory makes it much easier to work with these functions when integrals are considered.

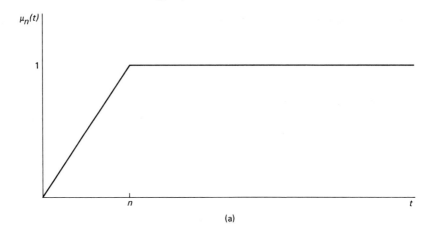

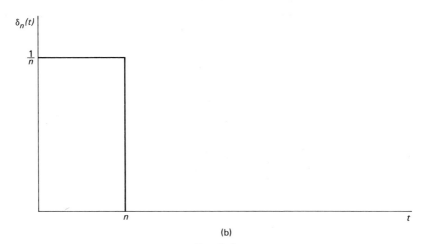

FIG. 2–3

(a) Function $u_n(t)$ which approaches the unit step function as $n$ approaches zero; (b) derivative of $u_n(t)$

Now suppose that we have a function $f(t)$ which consists of the sum of a continuous part $f_c(t)$ plus a jump discontinuity at the origin. That is,

$$f(t) = f_c(t) + au(t) \tag{2–28}$$

where $a$ is a constant and $u(t)$ is the unit step function. Let us evaluate

$$\int_{-\infty}^{\infty} \frac{df(t)}{dt} \phi(t)\, dt = \int_{-\infty}^{\infty} \left[ \frac{df_c(t)}{dt} + a\frac{du(t)}{dt} \right] \phi(t)\, dt$$

Applying linearity and Eq. 2–21, we obtain

$$\int_{-\infty}^{\infty} \frac{df(t)}{dt} \phi(t)\, dt = -\int_{-\infty}^{\infty} \frac{df_c(t)}{dt} \phi(t)\, dt - a \int_{-\infty}^{\infty} u(t) \frac{d\phi(t)}{dt}\, dt \qquad (2\text{–}29)$$

Comparing this equation with Eq. 2–26, we have

$$\int_{-\infty}^{\infty} \frac{df(t)}{dt} \phi(t)\, dt = -\int_{-\infty}^{\infty} \frac{df_c(t)}{dt} \phi(t)\, dt + a\phi(0) \qquad (2\text{–}30)$$

This is true for all $\phi(t)$ in $D$. Thus (see Eq. 2–6), we have

$$\frac{df(t)}{dt} = \frac{df_c(t)}{dt} + a\delta(t) \qquad (2\text{–}31)$$

That is, on a distribution basis, the derivative of a function which is continuous except for a jump discontinuity at $t = 0$ is the sum of the derivative of the continuous part of the function plus an impulse whose area is equal to the height $a$ of the discontinuity.

This result can be extended to a function which has many discontinuities. For example, consider

$$f(t) = f_c(t) + a_1 u(t - t_1) + a_2 u(t - t_2) + \cdots + a_N u(t - t_N) \qquad (2\text{–}32)$$

That is, $f(t)$ consists of a continuous function $f_c(t)$ plus discontinuities of $a_1$ at $t = t_1$, $a_2$ at $t = t_2 \ldots$ (see Fig. 2–4). Proceeding as before, it can be demonstrated that, on a distribution basis,

$$\frac{df(t)}{dt} = \frac{df_c(t)}{dt} + a_1 \delta(t - t_1) + a_2 \delta(t - t_2) + \cdots + a_N \delta(t - t_N) \qquad (2\text{–}33)$$

where $\delta(t - t_1)$ is a unit impulse that occurs at $t = t_1$ instead of at $t = 0$.

If we have a derivative of order $n$, we define

$$\int_{-\infty}^{\infty} \frac{d^n g(t)}{dt^n} \phi(t)\, dt = (-1)^n \int_{-\infty}^{\infty} g(t) \frac{d^n \phi(t)}{dt^n}\, dt \qquad (2\text{–}34)$$

The compatibility of this with ordinary function can be demonstrated by integrating by parts $n$ times.

**Time Shift of a Distribution.** Let us now define the effect of replacing $g(t)$ by $g(t - t_0)$. Then, if

$$\int_{-\infty}^{\infty} g(t) \phi(t)\, dt = N[g(t), \phi(t)]$$

then we define

$$\int_{-\infty}^{\infty} g(t - t_0) \phi(t)\, dt = \int_{-\infty}^{\infty} g(t) \phi(t + t_0)\, dt = N[g(t), \phi(t + t_0)] \qquad (2\text{–}35)$$

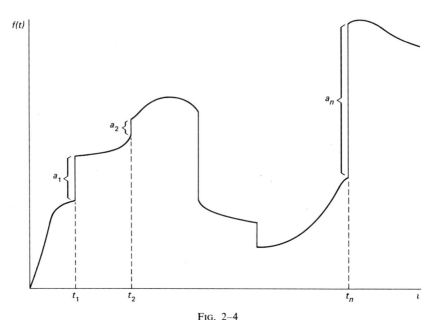

FIG. 2–4

Function which is continuous except for a finite number of jump discontinuities

It can be seen that this is compatible with the results for ordinary functions by considering that $g(t)$ is an ordinary function and replacing $t - t_0$ by $x$. As an example, consider the impulse function

$$\int_{-\infty}^{\infty} \delta(t - t_0)\,\phi(t)\,dt = \phi(t_0) \tag{2-36}$$

**Multiplying the Independent Variable of a Distribution by a Constant.** Let us now define the effect of replacing $g(t)$ by $g(at)$, where $a$ is a constant.

$$\int_{-\infty}^{\infty} g(at)\,\phi(t)\,dt = \frac{1}{|a|}\int_{-\infty}^{\infty} g(t)\,\phi\left(\frac{t}{a}\right) dt \tag{2-37}$$

It can be seen that this is compatible with ordinary functions by replacing $at$ by $x$ in Eq. 2–37. If $a$ is negative, the lower limit of integration becomes $+\infty$, while the upper limit is $-\infty$. Reversing these limits requires that the integral be multiplied by $-1$. Thus, the negative $1/a$ is replaced by its magnitude. This is why the magnitude is included in Eq. 2–37.

## 2-3. SOME SPECIFIC DISTRIBUTIONS

In Section 2-1 and 2-2, we discussed that distributions could be obtained from a limit of ordinary functions. This is not the only way to define distributions. However, for our purposes, it is a very practical procedure. As an example, suppose $g_n(t)$ represents ordinary functions such that the following functional relation is valid.

$$\int_{-\infty}^{\infty} g_n(t)\,\phi(t)\,dt = N[g_n(t), \phi(t)] \qquad (2\text{–}38a)$$

Let us also assume that this approaches a limit (which exists); that is,

$$\lim_{n \to n_0} \int_{-\infty}^{\infty} g_n(t)\,\phi(t)\,dt = \lim_{n \to n_0} N[g_n(t), \phi(t)] \qquad (2\text{–}38b)$$

We shall then define the generalized function $g(t)$ by the relation,

$$\int_{-\infty}^{\infty} g(t)\,\phi(t)\,dt = \lim_{n \to n_0} N[g_n(t), \phi(t)] = N[g(t), \phi(t)] \qquad (2\text{–}39a)$$

We then state that, on a distribution basis

$$\lim_{n \to n_0} g_n(t) = g(t) \qquad (2\text{–}39b)$$

As an example let us find, on a distribution basis,

$$\lim_{\omega \to \infty} e^{j\omega t}$$

In order to determine this limit, we first evaluate

$$\lim_{\omega \to \infty} \int_{-\infty}^{\infty} e^{j\omega t}\,\phi(t)\,dt$$

where $\phi(t)$ is in $D$. Integrating by parts, we obtain

$$\lim_{\omega \to \infty} \int_{-\infty}^{\infty} e^{j\omega t}\,\phi(t)\,dt = \lim_{\omega \to \infty} \frac{1}{j\omega}\,e^{j\omega t}\,\phi(t)\Big|_{-\infty}^{\infty} - \frac{1}{j\omega}\int_{-\infty}^{\infty} \frac{d\phi(t)}{dt}\,e^{j\omega t}\,dt \qquad (2\text{–}40)$$

Since $\phi(t)$ and all its derivatives exist and are of compact support, $e^{j\omega t}\,\phi(t)\big|_{-\infty}^{\infty}$ will be zero and

$$\int_{-\infty}^{\infty} \frac{d\phi(t)}{dt}\,e^{j\omega t}\,dt$$

will be bounded. This integral is divided by $\omega$ (see Eq. 2–40). Hence, in the limit, as $\omega$ approaches infinity, we have

$$\lim_{\omega \to \infty} \int_{-\infty}^{\infty} e^{j\omega t}\,\phi(t)\,dt = 0 \qquad (2\text{–}41)$$

This is true for all $\phi(t)$ in $D$. Equation 2–41 is called the *Riemann-Lebesgue lemma*.

Note that $\phi(t)$ need not have compact support to prove this lemma. Actually, $\phi(t)$ and $d\phi(t)/dt$ need only fall off sufficiently fast (faster than $1/t^2$) as $|t|$ approaches infinity.

Now we shall obtain some distributions. We can write

$$\lim_{\omega \to \infty} \int_{-\infty}^{\infty} e^{j\omega t} \phi(t)\, dt = 0 \qquad (2\text{--}42)$$

for all $\phi(t)$ in $D$. We can also write, for all $\phi(t)$ in $D$,

$$\int_{-\infty}^{\infty} 0\phi(t)\, dt = 0 \qquad (2\text{--}43)$$

Then, using the definition of equality of distributions, we have

$$\lim_{\omega \to \infty} e^{j\omega t} = 0 \qquad (2\text{--}44)$$

This does not mean that $\lim_{\omega \to \infty} e^{j\omega t}$ is zero for all values of time. Indeed, *on an ordinary basis, this limit does not exist.* It is only valid to use Eq. 2–44 when $e^{j\omega t}$ appears in an integral and a limit ($\omega \to \infty$) is taken. Equation 2–44 can be a great convenience, since integrals containing $\lim_{\omega \to \infty} e^{j\omega t}$ can now be readily evaluated.

We can obtain other useful results from Eq. 2–44. Using Euler's equation

$$e^{\pm j\omega t} = \cos \omega t \pm j\sin \omega t \qquad (2\text{--}45)$$

we obtain

$$\lim_{\omega \to \infty} (\cos \omega t + j\sin \omega t) = 0$$

Equating reals and imaginaries, we have

$$\lim_{\omega \to \infty} \cos \omega t = 0 \qquad (2\text{--}46a)$$

$$\lim_{\omega \to \infty} \sin \omega t = 0 \qquad (2\text{--}46b)$$

Note that when we work with a function of two variables, we can proceed on a dual basis. For instance, interchanging $\omega$ and $t$ in Eqs. 2–46a and 2–46b, we have

$$\lim_{t \to \infty} \cos \omega t = 0 \qquad (2\text{--}46c)$$

$$\lim_{t \to \infty} \sin \omega t = 0 \qquad (2\text{--}46d)$$

Note that these results are true on a distribution basis. On an ordinary basis, these limits do not exist. Here, however, they can be very convenient. We can now state, without resorting to cumbersome details, that

$$\lim_{\omega \to \infty} \int_{-\infty}^{\infty} \cos \omega t\, \phi(t)\, dt = 0$$

Let us show how these results can be helpful. Suppose we wish to evaluate

$$F(\omega) = \int_0^\infty \omega \sin \omega t \, dt$$

This yields

$$F(\omega) = \lim_{T \to \infty} \int_0^T \omega \sin \omega t \, dt = \lim_{T \to \infty} (-\cos \omega t)\Big|_0^T$$

Applying Eq. 2–46a, we obtain

$$F(\omega) = 1 - \lim_{T \to \infty} \cos \omega T = 1 \qquad (2\text{–}47)$$

Integrals involving $F(\omega)$ can be evaluated by replacing it by 1. If distribution theory were not used, cumbersome limit processes would have to be used. Note that if $F(\omega)$ is not to be studied in an integral, Eq. 2–47 would *not be valid*.

As an additional example of limit processes, on a distribution basis, consider

$$\lim_{\omega \to \infty} \int_{-\infty}^\infty \frac{\sin \omega t}{\pi t} \phi(t) \, dt$$

It may appear as though we could use the Riemann-Lebesgue lemma to set this integral equal to zero. However, $\phi(t)/t$ is infinite at $t = 0$. Hence, the lemma cannot be used. We shall split the integral into three parts. For any region that does not contain $t = 0$, $\phi(t)/t$ will be bounded and in $D$ and the Riemann-Lebesgue lemma can be used. Hence, we write

$$\lim_{\omega \to \infty} \int_{-\infty}^\infty \frac{\sin \omega t}{\pi t} \phi(t) \, dt = \lim_{\omega \to \infty} \left[ \int_{-\infty}^{-\varepsilon} \frac{\sin \omega t}{\pi t} \phi(t) \, dt + \int_{-\varepsilon}^{\varepsilon} \frac{\sin \omega t}{\pi t} \phi(t) \, dt \right.$$

$$\left. + \int_{\varepsilon}^\infty \frac{\sin \omega t}{\pi t} \phi(t) \, dt \right] \qquad (2\text{–}48)$$

where $\varepsilon$ is an arbitrary positive constant. The Riemann-Lebesgue lemma now can be used to set the first and third integrals equal to zero. Note that we use $e^{j\omega t} = \cos \omega t + j\sin \omega t$ in Eq. 2–41; hence,

$$\lim_{\omega \to \infty} \int_{-\infty}^\infty \frac{\sin \omega t}{\pi t} \phi(t) \, dt = \lim_{\omega \to \infty} \int_{-\varepsilon}^{\varepsilon} \frac{\sin \omega t}{\pi t} \phi(t) \, dt \qquad (2\text{–}49)$$

We can make $\varepsilon$ as small as desired. Thus since $\phi(t)$ is in $D$, we make $\varepsilon$ small enough so that we can replace $\phi(t)$ by $\phi(0)$ in the right-hand integral of Eq. 2–49; hence,

$$\lim_{\omega \to \infty} \int_{-\infty}^\infty \frac{\sin \omega t}{\pi t} \phi(t) \, dt = \phi(0) \lim_{\omega \to \infty} \int_{-\varepsilon}^{\varepsilon} \frac{\sin \omega t}{\pi t} \, dt$$

$$= \phi(0) \lim_{\omega \to \infty} \int_{-\varepsilon\omega}^{\varepsilon\omega} \frac{\sin x}{\pi x} \, dx \qquad (2\text{–}50)$$

where we have substituted $x = \omega t$ in the last integral of Eq. 2–50. Since $\varepsilon$ is very small but not zero, we have

$$\lim_{\omega \to \infty} \int_{-\infty}^{\infty} \frac{\sin \omega t}{\pi t} \phi(t) \, dt = \frac{\phi(0)}{\pi} \int_{-\infty}^{\infty} \frac{\sin x}{x} \, dx$$

but

$$\int_{-\infty}^{\infty} \frac{\sin x}{x} \, dx = \pi$$

Hence,

$$\lim_{\omega \to \infty} \int_{-\infty}^{\infty} \frac{\sin \omega t}{\pi t} \phi(t) \, dt = \phi(0) \qquad (2\text{–}51)$$

From Eq. 2–6, we have

$$\int_{-\infty}^{\infty} \delta(t) \phi(t) \, dt = \phi(0) \qquad (2\text{–}52)$$

Since both of the relations are true for all $\phi(t)$ in $D$, we can, on a distribution basis, state that

$$\delta(t) = \lim_{\omega \to \infty} \frac{\sin \omega t}{\pi t} \qquad (2\text{–}53)$$

Let us now use Eq. 2–53 to evaluate for $t \neq 0$

$$\int_{-\infty}^{\infty} \cos \omega t \, d\omega = \lim_{\Omega \to \infty} \int_{-\Omega}^{\Omega} \cos \omega t \, d\omega = \lim_{\Omega \to \infty} \frac{2 \sin \Omega t}{t}$$

Comparing this with Eq. 2–53, we obtain

$$\int_{-\infty}^{\infty} \cos \omega t \, d\omega = 2\pi\delta(t)$$

Or, equivalently, we can write

$$\delta(t) = \frac{1}{2\pi} \int_{-\infty}^{\infty} \cos \omega t \, d\omega \qquad (2\text{–}54)$$

Thus, we have obtained an alternate expression for $\delta(t)$ on a distribution basis.

Still another expression for $\delta(t)$ will be useful when we work with the Fourier integral. Consider the following:

$$\lim_{\Omega \to \infty} \int_{-\Omega}^{\Omega} \sin \omega t \, d\omega = 0 \qquad (2\text{–}55)$$

This is zero since $\sin \omega t$ is an odd function of $\omega$. Then, adding or subtracting Eq. 2–55 from Eq. 2–54, we have

$$\delta(t) = \frac{1}{2\pi} \int_{-\infty}^{\infty} (\cos \omega t \pm j \sin \omega t) \, d\omega$$

Application of Euler's relation yields

$$\delta(t) = \frac{1}{2\pi} \int_{-\infty}^{\infty} e^{\pm j\omega t}\, d\omega \tag{2-56}$$

As a final example of a distribution consider the function shown in Fig. 2–5. Now let us determine

$$\lim_{n\to 0} \int_{-\infty}^{\infty} f_n(t)\,\phi(t)\,dt = \lim_{n\to 0}\left[ \int_0^n \frac{1}{n^2}\phi(t)\,dt - \int_n^{2n} \frac{1}{n^2}\phi(t)\,dt \right]$$

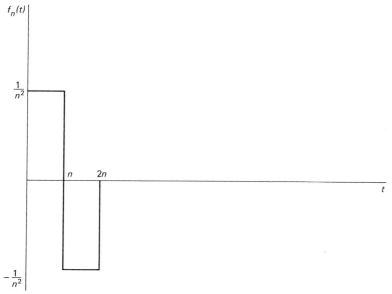

FIG. 2–5
Function $f_n(t)$, which becomes the unit doublet in the limit

Let $x = t$ in the first integral and let $x = t - n$ in the second. This yields

$$\lim_{n\to 0} \int_{-\infty}^{\infty} f_n(t)\,\phi(t)\,dt = \lim_{n\to 0}\frac{1}{n} \int_0^n \frac{\phi(x) - \phi(x+n)}{n}\,dx$$

but, in an ordinary sense,

$$\lim_{n\to 0}\frac{\phi(x) - \phi(x+n)}{n} = -\frac{d\phi(x)}{dx} \tag{2-57}$$

(This is just the definition of the derivative.) Then, interchanging the order of the limit process and the integral which is valid, since $\phi(t)$ is in $D$, we have

$$\lim_{n\to 0} \int_{-\infty}^{\infty} f_n(t)\,\phi(t) = -\lim_{n\to 0}\frac{1}{n} \int_0^n \frac{d\phi(x)}{dx}\,dx$$

As $n$ becomes arbitrarily small, $d\phi(x)/dx$ approaches $d\phi(x)/dx|_{x=0}$ in the range of the integral. Then, removing $d\phi(x)/dx|_{x=0}$ from the integral, we obtain

$$\lim_{n \to 0} \int_{-\infty}^{\infty} f_n(t)\,\phi(t)\,dt = -\frac{d\phi(t)}{dt}\bigg|_{t=0} \tag{2-58}$$

Now consider the following (see Eqs. 2–6 and 2–21):

$$\int_{-\infty}^{\infty} \frac{d\delta(t)}{dt}\,\phi(t)\,dt = -\int_{-\infty}^{\infty} \delta(t)\frac{d\phi(t)}{dt}\,dt = -\frac{d\phi(t)}{dt}\bigg|_{t=0} \tag{2-59}$$

Since Eqs. 2–58 and 2–59 are true for all $\phi(t)$ in $D$, we have

$$\lim_{n \to 0} f_n(t) = \frac{d\delta(t)}{dt} = \delta'(t) \tag{2-60}$$

That is, in the limit, Fig. 2–5 represents the derivative of the unit impulse, on a distribution basis. The derivative of the unit impulse is called the unit *doublet*.

In this section we have derived several distributions using limits. Some of these may seem strange when compared with limits derived on the basis of ordinary functions and the reader may question their validity. Recall that when a limit process is applied to an ordinary integral, the value that this integral approaches as some parameter $n$ approaches a limit $n_0$ is determined. Then, *at the limit*, a distribution is defined so that the value of the integral when $n$ *equals* $n_0$ (i.e., using the distribution) is equal to the value that the actual integral approaches as $n$ approaches $n_0$. Thus, when the distributions are used, the integrals will have the proper values.

## 2-4. FOURIER TRANSFORM

This section shall be concerned with the fundamental relations of the Fourier transform. We shall start by stating the relations of the Fourier transform and then proving that they are valid. Often, the Fourier series, for periodic functions, is presented first and then the Fourier transform, or Fourier integral, is derived by "extending" this to nonperiodic functions. However, we feel that it is more logical to start with the Fourier transform since this is valid for both periodic and nonperiodic functions. Thus, the Fourier series actually is a special case of the Fourier transform. We shall derive this in Section 2-15.

Consider a pair of relations called the *Fourier transform pair*.

$$F(j\omega) = \int_{-\infty}^{\infty} f(t)\,e^{-j\omega t}\,dt \tag{2-61}$$

$$f(t) = \frac{1}{2\pi} \int_{-\infty}^{\infty} F(j\omega)\,e^{j\omega t}\,d\omega \tag{2-62}$$

The first of these obtains a *frequency spectrum* $F(j\omega)$ from a given function of time $f(t)$. (We shall show in Section 2–6 that $F(\omega)$ is the "frequency content" of the signal.) Note that the integrand of Eq. 2–62 is $F(j\omega)(\cos \omega t - j\sin \omega t)$. Hence, Eq. 2–62 represents $f(t)$ as an "infinite sum" of frequency components. In general, $F(j\omega)$ will be a complex function of $\omega$. (Complex time-invariant quantities will be represented by boldface capital letters.) Equation 2–62 reconstitutes the function of time from the frequency spectrum. We have discussed (see Section 2-1 and 2-2) that the function of time can be measured directly, while the frequency spectrum cannot be measured, but can only be inferred from time domain measurements (we shall discuss this further in Chapter 5).

We must now prove that Eqs. 2–61 and 2–62 are valid. That is, we must show that if $F(j\omega)$ is obtained from a given $f(t)$ using Eq. 2–61 and if that $F(j\omega)$ is substituted into Eq. 2–62, then the resulting $f(t)$ must be the same as the original $f(t)$. Assume that $f(t)$ is such that $F(j\omega)$ exists for all $\omega$. (In Section 2-8 conditions on $f(t)$ will be derived such that this is so.) In addition we shall restrict ourselves to functions of time which are continuous or have a finite number of jump discontinuities. (The impulse, etc. will be treated using limit processes on a distribution basis (see Sections 2-1 through 2-3). To aid in the proof of the Fourier transform, we shall use a standard procedure and apply a limit process to Eq. 2–62; that is, we rewrite Eq. 2–62 as

$$f(t) = \lim_{\Omega \to \infty} \frac{1}{2\pi} \int_{-\Omega}^{\Omega} F(j\omega) e^{j\omega t}\, d\omega \tag{2–63}$$

At the start we assume that $f(t)$ is a continuous function of time. Then, substituting Eq. 2–61 into Eq. 2–63, we obtain

$$f(t) = \lim_{\Omega \to \infty} \frac{1}{2\pi} \int_{-\Omega}^{\Omega} \left[ \int_{-\infty}^{\infty} f(\tau) e^{-j\omega \tau}\, d\tau \right] e^{j\omega t}\, d\omega \tag{2–64}$$

where $\tau$ is substituted for $t$ in the second integral to avoid confusion. Assume that $f(t)$ is well behaved so that the integral converges uniformly. Then, the order of integration can be interchanged. Thus, we have

$$f(t) = \lim_{\Omega \to \infty} \frac{1}{2\pi} \int_{-\infty}^{\infty} f(\tau) \left[ \int_{-\Omega}^{\Omega} e^{j\omega(t - \tau)}\, d\omega \right] d\tau \tag{2–65}$$

Evaluating the inner integral, we obtain [see Eq. 2–45]

$$\int_{-\Omega}^{\Omega} e^{j\omega(t - \tau)}\, d\omega = \int_{-\Omega}^{\Omega} \left[ \cos \omega(t - \tau) + j\sin \omega(t - \tau) \right] d\omega = \frac{2 \sin \Omega(t - \tau)}{t - \tau}$$

Remember that we are taking the limit of this as $\Omega$ approaches infinity. From Eq. 2–53, we have

$$\delta(t - \tau) = \lim_{\Omega \to \infty} \frac{\sin \Omega(t - \tau)}{\pi(t - \tau)}$$

Substituting this into Eq. 2–65 and assuming that the order of the limit and the integration can be interchanged, we have

$$f(t) = \int_{-\infty}^{\infty} f(\tau)\,\delta(t - \tau)\,d\tau \tag{2-66}$$

Applying Eq. 2–36, we obtain ($\delta(t - \tau)$ is equivalent to $\delta(\tau - t)$)

$$f(t) = f(t)$$

Thus, the theorem is proved for continuous $f(t)$.

Now let us extend this theorem to discontinuous functions. First, assume that $f(t)$ consists of a continuous part $f_c(t)$ and a single step discontinuity of height $a_1$ occuring at $t = t_0$.

$$f(t) = f_c(t) + a_1 u(t - t_0) \tag{2-67}$$

where $u(t)$ is the unit step function defined in Eq. 2–24. Then, proceeding as before,

$$f(t) = \frac{1}{2\pi} \lim_{\Omega \to \infty} \int_{-\Omega}^{\Omega} \int_{-\infty}^{\infty} [f_c(\tau) + a_1 u(\tau - t_0)]\, e^{-j\omega\tau} e^{j\omega t}\, d\tau\, d\omega$$

Interchanging the order of integration and splitting the function into two parts, we obtain

$$f(t) = \frac{1}{2\pi} \lim_{\Omega \to \infty} \int_{-\infty}^{\infty} f_c(\tau) \int_{-\Omega}^{\Omega} e^{j\omega(t - \tau)}\, d\omega\, d\tau$$

$$+ \frac{1}{2\pi} \lim_{\omega \to \infty} \int_{-\infty}^{\infty} a_1 u(\tau - t_0) \int_{-\Omega}^{\Omega} e^{j\omega(t - \tau)}\, d\omega\, d\tau \tag{2-68}$$

The first integral is the same as Eq. 2–65. Thus, it yields $f_c(t)$. Now consider the second integral. For brevity we shall call that integral $\alpha(t)$. Then,

$$f(t) = f_c(t) + \alpha(t) \tag{2-69}$$

$$\alpha(t) = \frac{1}{2\pi} \lim_{\Omega \to \infty} \frac{1}{2\pi} \int_{-\infty}^{\infty} a_1 u(\tau - t_0) \int_{-\Omega}^{\Omega} e^{j\omega(t - \tau)}\, d\omega\, d\tau \tag{2-70}$$

Evaluating the inner integral as in the case of Eq. 2–65, we have

$$\alpha(t) = \lim_{\Omega \to \infty} a_1 \int_{-\infty}^{\infty} u(\tau - t_0)\, \frac{\sin \Omega(t - \tau)}{\pi(t - \tau)}\, d\tau$$

However,

$$u(t) = \begin{cases} 1, & t > 0 \\ 0, & t < 0 \end{cases}$$

Hence,

$$\alpha(t) = \lim_{\Omega \to \infty} a_1 \int_{t_0}^{\infty} \frac{\sin \Omega(t - \tau)}{\pi(t - \tau)}\, d\tau \tag{2-71}$$

Let $x = \Omega(t - \tau)$; then

$$\alpha(t) = - \lim_{\Omega \to \infty} \frac{a_1}{\pi} \int_{\Omega(t-t_0)}^{-\infty} \frac{\sin x}{x} \, dx$$

or, equivalently,

$$\alpha(t) = \frac{a_1}{\pi} \int_{-\infty}^{0} \frac{\sin x}{x} \, dx + \lim_{\Omega \to \infty} \int_{0}^{\Omega(t-t_0)} \frac{\sin x}{x} \, dx \qquad (2\text{–}72)$$

Consider the upper limit of integration in the second integral. If

$$t > t_0 \qquad \lim_{\Omega \to \infty} (t - t_0) = \infty$$

$$t < t_0 \qquad \lim_{\Omega \to \infty} (t - t_0) = - \infty$$

$$t = t_0 \qquad \lim_{\Omega \to \infty} (t - t_0) = 0$$

Hence,

$$\alpha(t) = \begin{cases} \dfrac{2a_1}{\pi} \displaystyle\int_{0}^{\infty} \dfrac{\sin x}{x} \, dx, & t > t_0 \\[2ex] \dfrac{a_1}{\pi} \displaystyle\int_{0}^{\infty} \dfrac{\sin x}{x} \, dx, & t = t_0 \\[2ex] 0, & t < t_0 \end{cases} \qquad (2\text{–}73)$$

Note that

$$\int_{0}^{\infty} \frac{\sin x}{x} \, dx = \int_{-\infty}^{0} \frac{\sin x}{x} \, dx$$

The value of

$$\int \frac{\sin x}{x} \, dx$$

cannot be obtained exactly for finite limits. However, it can be obtained exactly for infinite limits as [1]

$$\int_{0}^{\infty} \frac{\sin x}{x} \, dx = \frac{\pi}{2} \qquad (2\text{–}74)$$

Substituting in Eq. 2–73, we obtain

$$\alpha(t) = \begin{cases} a_1, & t > t_0 \\[2ex] \dfrac{a_1}{2}, & t = t_0 \\[2ex] 0, & t < t_0 \end{cases} \qquad (2\text{–}75)$$

Thus, we can write

$$\alpha(t) = a_1 u(t - t_0) \qquad (2\text{–}76)$$

where, as before, the unit step function is defined as

$$u(t) = \begin{cases} 0, & t < 0 \\ 1, & t > 0 \end{cases} \qquad \begin{matrix} (2\text{–}77a) \\ (2\text{–}77b) \end{matrix}$$

However, we now add the condition that

$$u(t) = 1/2, \qquad t = 0 \tag{2–77c}$$

Substituting Eq. 2–76 into Eq. 2–69, we have

$$f(t) = f_c(t) + a_1 u(t - t_0) \tag{2–78}$$

Comparing Eq. 2–78 with Eq. 2–67 we see that they are the same. Thus, we have verified that Eqs. 2–61 and 2–62 form a consistant set. Hence, the validity of the Fourier transform has been demonstrated for a continuous function with a single jump discontinuity.

One fact should now be considered: Eq. 2–75 indicates that at a jump discontinuity the Fourier transform converges to a point which is the average of the values on each side of the discontinuity; i.e., it lies midway between the values just on either side of the discontinuity. If the given $f(t)$ is not defined to have this value at the point of discontinuity, then the $f(t)$ obtained from the Fourier transform will not be equal to the given $f(t)$ at the single point of discontinuity. If $f(t)$ is used to compute $F(j\omega)$ and then $F(j\omega)$ is used to compute $f_1(t)$ and there is a finite jump discontinuity in $f(t)$ at $t = t_0$, then

$$f_1(t_0) = \tfrac{1}{2}\Big[\lim_{\substack{t \to t_0 \\ t < t_0}} f(t) + \lim_{\substack{t \to t_0 \\ t > t_0}} f(t)\Big] \tag{2–79}$$

independent of the defined value of $f(t_0)$. Of course, at all values of $t$ where there is no discontinuity $f(t) = f_1(t)$. Note that if $f(t)$ is changed by a finite amount at a finite number of isolated points (see Fig. 2–2), these changes will not affect

$$\int_{-\infty}^{\infty} f(t)\, e^{-j\omega t}\, dt$$

Hence, $f(t_0)$ can be defined as any finite value, and not change $f_1(t)$ for any time. Actually, such single point discontinuities can not be generated in practice and could not be measured even if they were generated. In addition, these isolated, finite point discontinuities do not affect the values of any calculations. Hence, we can say that Eqs. 2–67 and 2–78 show the validity of the Fourier transform for functions with a single jump discontinuity.

Actually, it can be shown that the Fourier transform is unique in the following sense. If both $f_1(t)$ and $f_2(t)$, when substituted into Eq. 2–61 yield the same $F(j\omega)$, then $f_1(t) = f_2(t)$ except possibily at a finite number of isolated points where they differ only by a finite value.

To complete the verification of the Fourier transform, we must consider a function which has a finite number of finite jump discontinuities; that is,

$$f(t) = f_c(t) + a_1 u(t - t_1) + a_2(t - t_2) + \cdots + a_N u(t - t_N) \tag{2–80}$$

where $f_c(t)$ is continuous. We must show that Eqs. 2–61 and 2–62 are valid for such

$f(t)$. Proceeding as before, we have

$$f(t) = \lim_{\Omega \to \infty} \int_{-\Omega}^{\Omega} \int_{\omega}^{\infty} f_c(\tau) e^{-j\omega\tau} e^{j\omega t} \, d\tau \, d\omega$$

$$+ \lim_{\Omega \to \infty} \int_{-\Omega}^{\Omega} \int_{-\infty}^{\infty} \sum_{k=1}^{N} a_k u(\tau - t_k) e^{-j\omega\tau} e^{j\omega t} \, d\tau \, d\omega$$

Proceeding as we did in the case of Eq. 2–68, we obtain

$$f(t) = f_c(t) + \sum_{k=1}^{N} a_k u(t - t_k) \tag{2-81}$$

where $u(t)$ is defined as in Eqs. 2–77a through 2–77c. Hence, we have shown the validity of the Fourier transform for all $f(t)$ which are continuous or are continuous except for a finite number of jump discontinuities. Of course, other functions can be used if they can be represented by a limit of such functions.

Now consider some notation. The function $F(j\omega)$ is called the *Fourier transform* of $f(t)$ and is written as

$$F(j\omega) = \mathscr{F} f(t) \tag{2-82}$$

Similarly, $f(t)$ can be called the inverse Fourier transform of $F(j\omega)$. This is written as

$$f(t) = \mathscr{F}^{-1} F(j\omega) \tag{2-83}$$

Finally, $f(t)$ and $F(j\omega)$ constitute a *Fourier transform pair*; this is written as

$$f(t) \leftrightarrow F(j\omega) \tag{2-84}$$

## 2-5. BASIC GIBBS' PHENOMENON

Let us now study the convergence of the Fourier transform in the region of a discontinuity of $f(t)$, in more detail. If

$$f(t) = a_1 u(t - t_1) \tag{2-85}$$

then, see Eqs. 2–72 and 2–74, taking the Fourier transform of $f(t)$ and then the inverse Fourier transform, we obtain

$$f_1(t) = \lim_{\Omega \to \infty} a_1 \left[ \frac{1}{2} + \frac{1}{\pi} \int_0^{\Omega(t-t_1)} \frac{\sin x}{x} \, dx \right] \tag{2-86}$$

Consider this limit process in detail. Although the integral of $(\sin x)/x$ cannot be evaluated in closed form, it can be evaluated by numerical means and the results are tabulated [2]. This integral is written as

$$Si(y) = \int_0^y \frac{\sin x}{x} \, dx \tag{2-87}$$

A plot of $Si(y)$ is given in Fig. 2–6. Note that as $y$ approaches infinity, $Si(y)$ ap-

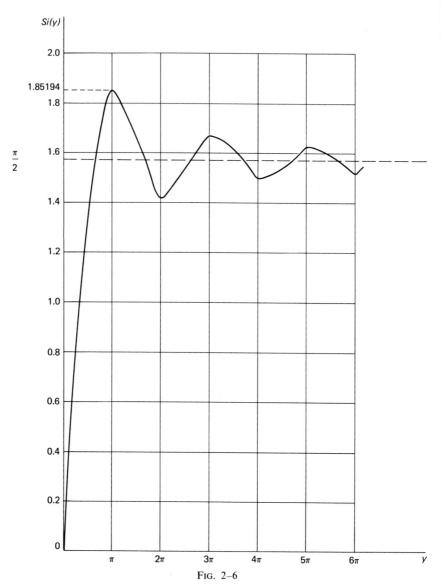

FIG. 2–6

Plot of $Si(y) = \displaystyle\int_0^y \frac{\sin x}{x}\,dx$

proaches $\pi/2$, and that $Si(y)$ *oscillates* around this value. The maximum value of $Si(y)$ occurs at $y = \pi$ and is given by

$$Si(\pi) = 1.85194 \tag{2-88}$$

Another useful fact is that $Si(y)$ is an odd function; i.e., $Si(-y) = -Si(y)$.

Now consider Eq. 2–86. We have

$$f_1(t) = \lim_{\Omega \to \infty} a_1 \left\{ \frac{1}{2} + \frac{1}{\pi} Si[\Omega(t - t_1)] \right\} \tag{2-89}$$

Let us normalize this by dividing by $a_1$. Thus,

$$f_n(t) = \frac{f_1(t)}{a_1} = \lim_{\Omega \to \infty} \frac{1}{2} + \frac{1}{\pi} Si[\Omega(t - t_1)] \tag{2-90}$$

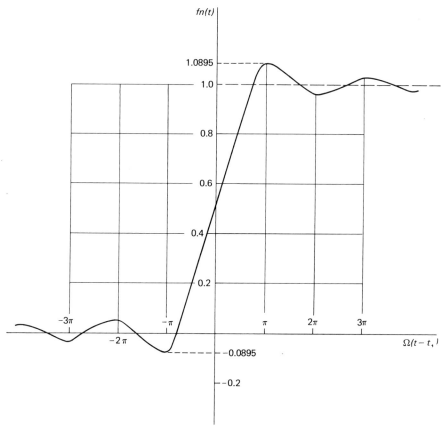

FIG. 2–7
Plot of $f_n(t)$ about a step discontinuity

A plot of this function is shown in Fig. 2–7. The time axis is in units of $\Omega(t - t_1)$; thus, $t = t_1$ corresponds to the origin.

There are several important facts that should be mentioned. At $t = t_1$, $f_n(t)$ is $1/2$, independent of the value of $\Omega$. In addition, for any fixed $\Omega$, $f_n(t)$ oscillates above its final value 1. Note that (for $t > t_1$) $f_n(t)$ "overshoots" and "undershoots" its final value of 1. The maximum value of $f_n(t)$ is

$$f_n(t)|_{max} = 1.0895 \qquad (2\text{–}91)$$

This occurs at $\Omega(t - t_1) = \pi$ or, equivalently, at

$$t - t_1 = \frac{\pi}{\Omega} \qquad (2\text{–}92)$$

In addition, for $t < t_1$, $f_n(t)$ oscillates about zero. The minimum value of $f_n(t)$ is

$$f_n(t)|_{min} = -0.0895 \qquad (2\text{–}93)$$

This occurs at

$$t - t_1 = -\frac{\pi}{\Omega} \qquad (2\text{–}94)$$

Thus, we can say that $f_n(t)$ has a maximum overshoot of 0.0895, or 8.95 % of the height of the discontinuity. (Note that we have been working with the normalized $f_n(t)$.) Similarly, we state that it has an "underswing" of 8.95 %; i.e., at $\Omega(t - t_1) = -\pi$, $f_n(t) = -0.0895$. Also note that the magnitude of the overshoot and underswing are *not* functions of $\Omega$; that is, as $\Omega$ is increased, the sizes of these "ripples" do not decrease. However, as $\Omega$ is increased, *all* the maxima and minima move closer to the discontinuity so that as $\Omega$ approaches $\infty$ (see Eqs. 2–92 and 2–94),

$$f_n(t) \rightarrow \begin{cases} 1, & t > t_0 & (2\text{–}95a) \\ 0, & t < t_0 & (2\text{–}95b) \end{cases}$$

Also,

$$f_n(0) = \tfrac{1}{2} \qquad (2\text{–}95c)$$

Thus, $f_n(t)$ converges as it should.

Since Eq. 2–86 indicates that $\Omega \rightarrow \infty$, why consider smaller values of $\Omega$. This is because all transmission systems attenuate high frequencies (see Section 2-13). This is often equivalent to limiting the value of $\Omega$ in Eq. 2–86. Thus, the response of many systems to the discontinuous portion of a signal is similar to Fig. 2–7. For instance, in such systems there is an overshoot approximately equal to 8.95 % of the discontinuity. This type of output, where the overshoots and underswings do not decrease as $\Omega$ is increased, is called *Gibbs' phenomenon*. (In Section 2-3 we shall see how these overshoots and underswings can be eliminated.)

## 2-6. REAL AND IMAGINARY PARTS OF FOURIER TRANSFORM—SOME EXAMPLES OF FOURIER TRANSFORMS

In general, $F(j\omega)$ will be a complex function of $j\omega$. Let us write it as a sum of real and imaginary terms:

$$F(j\omega) = R(\omega) + jX(\omega) \qquad (2\text{–}96)$$

where $R(\omega)$ and $X(\omega)$ are *both* real functions of $\omega$. Now replace $e^{-j\omega t}$ by Euler's relation (i.e. Eq. 2-45) in Eq. 2-61. This yields

$$F(j\omega) = \int_{-\infty}^{\infty} f(t)(\cos \omega t - j\sin \omega t)\, d\omega$$

In general, $f(t)$ will be a real function of time; thus,

$$R(\omega) = \int_{-\infty}^{\infty} f(t) \cos \omega t\, dt \qquad (2\text{-}97)$$

$$X(\omega) = -\int_{-\infty}^{\infty} f(t) \sin \omega t\, dt \qquad (2\text{-}98)$$

If $f(t)$ is real then $R(\omega)$ is an *even* function of $\omega$ and $X(\omega)$ is an *odd* function of $\omega$. Note that when $\omega$ is replaced by $-\omega$ in Eq. 2-97, $R(\omega)$ remains unchanged and when $\omega$ is replaced by $-\omega$ in Eq. 2-98, $X(\omega)$ must be replaced by $-X(\omega)$.

Now let us substitute Eqs. 2-96 and 2-45 into Eq. 2-62. This yields

$$f(t) = \frac{1}{2\pi} \int_{-\infty}^{\infty} [R(\omega) + jX(\omega)](\cos \omega t + j\sin \omega t)\, d\omega \qquad (2\text{-}99)$$

The integral of an odd function of $\omega$ over symmetric limits is zero. Eliminating the odd portion of the integrand, we have

$$f(t) = \frac{1}{2\pi} \int_{-\infty}^{\infty} R(\omega) \cos \omega t\, d\omega - \frac{1}{2\pi} \int_{-\infty}^{\infty} X(\omega) \sin \omega t\, d\omega \qquad (2\text{-}100)$$

Equations 2-97, 2-98, and 2-100 constitute another form of the Fourier transform pair which is valid for real functions of time. Note that Eqs. 2-61 and 2-62 are valid for complex as well as real $f(t)$.

Equation 2-100 provides us with a physical interpretation of the Fourier transform and $f(t)$ can be considered to be made up of an infinite sum of terms of the form

$$R(\omega) \cos \omega t\, df - X(\omega) \sin \omega t\, df \qquad (2\text{-}101)$$

where

$$\omega = 2\pi f \qquad (2\text{-}102)$$

(Note the $1/2\pi$ in Eq. 2-100.) Relation 2-101 represents a sinusoid of frequency $f$. From discussions of complex numbers, phasors, and sinusoids, we have that the magnitude of the sinusoid is $\sqrt{R^2(\omega) + X^2(\omega)}\, d\omega$. The phase angle, using $\cos \omega t$ as reference, is $\tan^{-1}[X(\omega)/R(\omega)]$. Note that $-\sin x = \cos(x + \pi/2)$. Thus, we can represent each frequency component of $f(t)$ by a phasor:

$$df \sqrt{R^2(\omega) + X^2(\omega)}\; e^{j\tan^{-1}[X(\omega)/R(\omega)]}$$

Thus, from Eq. 2–96, we have this phasor as

$$df\, F(j\omega) = df\, \sqrt{R^2(\omega) + X^2(\omega)}\; e^{j\tan^{-1}[X(\omega)/R(\omega)]} \qquad (2\text{–}103)$$

That is, the Fourier integral of Eq. 2–62 indicates that $f(t)$ is composed of an infinite sum of sinusoidal components. The magnitude of each component is the magnitude of $F(j\omega)$ times $df$, while its phase angle is the phase angle of $F(j\omega)$. Note that, as long as $F(j\omega)$ is finite, the magnitude of each frequency component is differentially small; i.e., $F(j\omega)\,df$. Since there are an infinite number of components to be "summed", the energy contained in any one frequency is differentially small. However, the energy contained in a finite *band* of frequencies can be nonzero. The function $F(j\omega)$ is called the *Fourier spectrum*. It gives the *relative* amplitude and phase angles of all the frequency components of $f(t)$.

As an example, we obtain the Fourier transform of some common time functions. Let us start with

$$f(t) = \begin{cases} 0, & t < 0 \\ e^{-\beta t}, & t > 0 \end{cases} \qquad (2\text{–}104)$$

where $\beta$ is real and positive. Thus, $f(t)$ is 0 for $t < 0$, becomes 1 for $t = 0+$ (i.e., just greater than 0), and then decays exponentially. Substituting in Eqs. 2–61, we obtain

$$F(j\omega) = \int_0^\infty e^{-\beta t} e^{-j\omega t}\, dt = \frac{-1}{\beta + j\omega}\, e^{-(\beta + j\omega)t}\Big|_0^\infty$$

Hence,

$$F(j\omega) = \frac{1}{\beta + j\omega} \qquad (2\text{–}105)$$

We can write this as

$$F(j\omega) = \frac{1}{\sqrt{\beta^2 + \omega^2}}\, e^{-j\tan^{-1}(\omega/\beta)} \qquad (2\text{–}106)$$

Thus, we can state that the Fourier spectrum of $F(j\omega)$ falls off as $1/\sqrt{\beta^2 + \omega^2}$ in magnitude. A plot of $f(t)$ and the magnitude of $F(j\omega)$ are given in Fig. 2–8.

Now let us reconstruct $f(t)$ from $F(j\omega)$. Substituting Eq. 2–105 into Eq. 2–62, we have

$$f(t) = \frac{1}{2\pi}\int_{-\infty}^\infty \frac{1}{\beta + j\omega}\, e^{j\omega t}\, d\omega = \frac{1}{2\pi}\int_{-\infty}^\infty \frac{\beta - j\omega}{\beta^2 + \omega^2}\, e^{j\omega t}\, d\omega$$

Using Eq. 2–45, manipulating and eliminating the odd integrand, we obtain

$$f(t) = \frac{1}{2\pi}\int_{-\infty}^\infty \frac{\beta}{\beta^2 + \omega^2}\cos \omega t\, d\omega + \frac{1}{2\pi}\int_{-\infty}^\infty \frac{\omega}{\beta^2 + \omega^2}\sin \omega t\, d\omega \qquad (2\text{–}107)$$

Since each integrand is even, we have

$$f(t) = \frac{1}{\pi}\int_0^\infty \frac{\beta}{\beta^2 + \omega^2}\cos \omega t\, d\omega + \frac{1}{\pi}\int_0^\infty \frac{\omega}{\beta^2 + \omega^2}\sin \omega t\, d\omega \qquad (2\text{–}108)$$

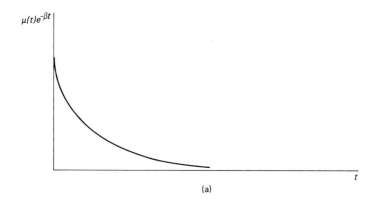

(a)

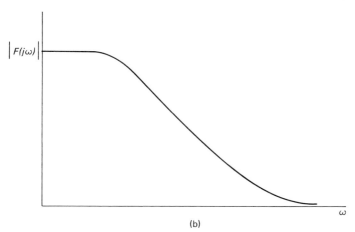

(b)

Fig. 2–8
(a) Plot of $f(t) = u(t) e^{-\beta t}$; (b) magnitude of its Fourier spectrum

It can be shown that

$$\frac{1}{\pi} \int_0^\infty \frac{\beta}{\beta^2 + \omega^2} \cos \omega t \, d\omega = \frac{1}{2} e^{-|\beta t|} \qquad (2\text{–}109a)$$

and

$$\frac{1}{\pi} \int_0^\infty \frac{\omega}{\beta^2 + \omega^2} \sin \omega t \, d\omega = \begin{cases} -\frac{1}{2} e^{\beta t}, & t < 0 \\ \frac{1}{2} e^{-\beta t}, & t > 0 \end{cases} \qquad (2\text{–}109b)$$

Thus adding Eqs. 2–109b, we obtain

$$f(t) = \begin{cases} 0, & t < 0 \\ e^{-\beta t}, & t > 0 \end{cases}$$

as required.

As another example, let us obtain $F(j\omega)$ for the unit impulse. We could use limits; however, since we work with distributions (see Sections 2-1 through 2-3), we need not repeat cumbersome details of the limit process. Thus,

$$F(j\omega) = \int_{-\infty}^{\infty} \delta(t)\, e^{-j\omega t}\, d\omega \qquad (2\text{--}110)$$

Then, using Eq. 2–6, we obtain

$$F(j\omega) = 1 \qquad (2\text{--}111)$$

Thus, the impulse function has a flat or constant Fourier spectrum.

Let us reconstruct $f(t)$ from Eq. 2–111. Substituting in Eq. 2–62, we have

$$f(t) = \frac{1}{2\pi} \int_{-\infty}^{\infty} e^{j\omega t}\, d\omega \qquad (2\text{--}112)$$

Comparing this with Eq. 2–56, we have $f(t) = \delta(t)$, as required.

Now let us obtain the Fourier transform of the unit step response.

$$F(j\omega) = \int_{-\infty}^{\infty} u(t)\, e^{-j\omega t}\, dt = \int_{0}^{\infty} e^{-j\omega t}\, dt \qquad (2\text{--}113)$$

Thus, we can write

$$F(j\omega) = \int_{0}^{\infty} \cos \omega t \, dt - j \int_{0}^{\infty} \sin \omega t \, dt \qquad (2\text{--}114)$$

We use Eq. 2–54 to evaluate the first integral; from this equation we have

$$\delta(\omega) = \frac{1}{2\pi} \int_{-\infty}^{\infty} \cos \omega t \, dt = \frac{1}{\pi} \int_{0}^{\infty} \cos \omega t \, dt \qquad (2\text{--}115)$$

To evaluate the second integral, we use Eq. 2–47; hence,

$$\int_{0}^{\infty} \sin \omega t \, dt = \frac{1}{\omega} \qquad (2\text{--}116)$$

Substituting Eqs. 2–115 and 2–116 into Eq. 2–114, we have

$$F(j\omega) = \pi\delta(\omega) + \frac{1}{j\omega} \qquad (2\text{--}117)$$

(Note that $1/j = -j$.)

Let us interpret this physically. If a function of time consists of just one frequency (e.g., $f(t) = 1$ or $f(t) = \cos \omega_0 t$ for *all* $-\infty < t < \infty$), then *the Fourier spectrum will be zero except at the one frequency in question*. Note that if $f(t) = 1$, then the frequency is zero ($\cos 0t$). If $f(t) = \cos \omega_0 t$ then the frequency in question is $\omega_0$. Thus, a nonzero amount of energy must be contained at a *single, isolated* frequency. Hence, $F(j\omega)\, d\omega$ must be finite (not differentially small) there. Therefore $F(j\omega)$ must be infinite at this single frequency. If $F(j\omega)$ contains an impulse, it is of the proper form; i.e., zero everywhere except at $\omega = \omega_0$, where it is infinite. The case is similar for the unit step (there are some differences), which is constant for all $t > 0$. Thus, its spectrum has an infinite zero frequency component; i.e., $\delta(\omega)$. However, the unit step is not constant for all time; i.e., it is zero for $t < 0$. Thus, its spectrum contains an additional term $1/j\omega$.

As a further example, consider $f(t) = \cos \omega_0 t$; then,

$$F(j\omega) = \int_{-\infty}^{\infty} \cos \omega_0 t \; e^{-j\omega t} \, dt$$

Using the relation

$$\cos \omega_0 t = \frac{e^{j\omega_0 t} + e^{-j\omega_0 t}}{2} \tag{2-118}$$

yields

$$F(j\omega) = \tfrac{1}{2} \int_{-\infty}^{\infty} (e^{-j(\omega - \omega_0)t} + e^{-(\omega + \omega_0)t}) \, dt \tag{2-119}$$

Using Eq. 2-56, we have

$$F(j\omega) = \pi\delta(\omega_0 - \omega) + \pi\delta(\omega_0 + \omega) \tag{2-120}$$

This bears out our previous discussion of impulse functions.

Now let us consider

$$f(t) = u(t) \cos \omega_0 t$$

Then

$$F(j\omega) = \int_{0}^{\infty} \cos \omega_0 t \; e^{-j\omega t} \, dt = \tfrac{1}{2} \int_{0}^{\infty} (e^{-j(\omega - \omega_0)t} + e^{-j(\omega + \omega_0)t}) \, dt$$

This yields

$$F(j\omega) = \tfrac{1}{2} \left[ \frac{e^{-j(\omega - \omega_0)t}}{-j(\omega - \omega_0)} + \frac{e^{-j(\omega + \omega_0)t}}{-j(\omega + \omega_0)} \right]_{0}^{\infty} \tag{2-121}$$

Substitution of the lower limit gives us

$$\frac{1}{2} \left[ \frac{1}{j(\omega - \omega_0)} + \frac{1}{j(\omega + \omega_0)} \right] = \frac{j\omega}{\omega_0^2 - \omega^2} \tag{2-122}$$

To determine the value corresponding to the upper limit, we make use of Eq. 2-53. Rearranging this, we obtain

$$\delta(\omega) = \lim_{t \to \infty} \frac{\sin \omega t}{\pi \omega} \tag{2-123}$$

In addition, we must also determine

$$\lim_{t \to \infty} \frac{\cos \omega t}{\pi \omega}$$

on a distribution basis. To do this, we evaluate

$$\lim_{t \to \infty} \int_{-\infty}^{\infty} \frac{\cos \omega t}{\pi \omega} \phi(\omega) \, d\omega$$

Proceeding as in Eqs. 2–48 through 2–50, we have

$$\lim_{t \to \infty} \int_{-\infty}^{\infty} \frac{\cos \omega t}{\pi \omega} \phi(\omega) \, d\omega = \phi(0) \lim_{t \to \infty} \int_{-\varepsilon t}^{\varepsilon t} \frac{\cos x}{x} \, dx \qquad (2\text{–}124)$$

but $(\cos x)/x$ is an odd function. Thus, this integral is zero; hence,

$$\lim_{t \to \infty} \int_{-\infty}^{\infty} \frac{\cos \omega t}{\pi \omega} \phi(\omega) \, d\omega = 0 \qquad (2\text{–}125)$$

for all $\phi(\omega)$ in $D$. Thus, on a distribution basis

$$\lim_{t \to \infty} \frac{\cos \omega t}{\pi \omega} = 0 \qquad (2\text{–}126)$$

Multiplying Eq. 2–123 by $\pm j$ and adding it to Eq. 2–126, we have

$$\lim_{t \to \infty} \frac{e^{\pm j\omega t}}{\pi \omega} = \pm j\delta(\omega) \qquad (2\text{–}127)$$

Thus, the upper limit of Eq. 2–121 yields

$$\frac{\pi}{2} \left[ \delta(\omega - \omega_0) + \delta(\omega + \omega_0) \right] \qquad (2\text{–}128)$$

Adding Eqs. 2–122 and 2–128, we obtain for $F(j\omega)$

$$F(j\omega) = \frac{\pi}{2} \left[ \delta(\omega - \omega_0) + \delta(\omega + \omega_0) \right] + \frac{j\omega}{\omega_0^2 - \omega^2} \qquad (2\text{–}129)$$

TABLE 2-1

*Fourier Transforms*

| $f(t) \longleftrightarrow$ | $F(j\omega)$ |
|---|---|
| $1$ | $2\pi\delta(\omega)$ |
| $\delta(t)$ | $1$ |
| $u(t)\,e^{-\beta t}$ | $1/(\beta + j\omega)$ |
| $u(t)$ | $\pi\delta(\omega) + 1/j\omega$ |
| $\sin \omega_0 t$ | $j\pi\left[\delta(\omega + \omega_0) - \delta(\omega - \omega_0)\right]$ |
| $\cos \omega_0 t$ | $\pi\left[\delta(\omega + \omega_0) + \delta(\omega - \omega_0)\right]$ |
| $u(t) \sin \omega_0 t$ | $\dfrac{\pi}{2j}\left[\delta(\omega - \omega_0) - \delta(\omega + \omega_0)\right] + \dfrac{\omega_0}{\omega_0^2 - \omega^2}$ |
| $u(t) \cos \omega_0 t$ | $\dfrac{\pi}{2}\left[\delta(\omega - \omega_0) + \delta(\omega + \omega_0)\right] + \dfrac{j\omega}{\omega_0^2 - \omega^2}$ |
| $e^{j\omega_0 t}$ | $2\pi\delta(\omega - \omega_0)$ |

Again we see that if a function contains finite energy at one frequency, then an impulse appears in its transform.

Table 2-1 lists the transforms discussed in this section and some others, which are similarly derived.

## 2-7.  A BRIEF DISCUSSION OF THE COMPUTATION OF TRANSIENT RESPONSE USING THE FOURIER TRANSFORM

In this section we shall illustrate the use of the Fourier transform to solve simple network problems. Parts of this discussion will be heuristic. In Chapter 5 we shall consider analysis techniques with much more detail and rigor. This discussion is given here to provide the reader with a feeling for the Fourier transform.

As an example let us determine the unit step response of the network of Fig. 2–9a. We start by taking the Fourier transform of the unit step (see Table 2–1) of $u(t)$. This is

$$F(j\omega) = \pi\delta(\omega) + \frac{1}{j\omega} \qquad (2\text{-}130)$$

Each frequency component of $F(j\omega)\,df$ (see Section 2-6) represents a sinusoid which has been applied at $t = -\infty$. The function $f(t)$ consists of the infinite sum (i.e., integral) of all these sinusoids. Thus, using superposition we can determine the response to each sinusoid and then add all the responses. Each sinusoid can be analyzed on a steady-state basis since it can be considered to have been applied at $t = -\infty$. (Note that, in this case, $f(t)$ evaluated by the Fourier integral for all $t < 0$ is zero.) Thus, all transients will have died away at some negative (infinite) time. Therefore, in computing the response to the sinusoids, we need only compute the sinusoidal steady-state response. Since $F(j\omega)$ is written as a phasor, we can consider sinusoidal steady-state response on a phasor basis.

The procedure we use is the following: Assume that the input generator is replaced by a sinusoidal steady-state phasor generator (see Fig. 2–9b). Then, compute the output in response to this phasor input as a function of $\omega$. For Fig. 2–9b, we have

$$\frac{V_2(j\omega)}{V_1(j\omega)} = \frac{\dfrac{1}{j\omega C}}{R + \dfrac{1}{j\omega C}} = \frac{1}{1 + j\omega RC} \qquad (2\text{-}131)$$

Thus, the output phasor can be obtained from the input phasor by multiplying it by $1/(1 + j\omega RC)$. Hence, we obtain the Fourier transform of $v_2(t)$ as

$$F_2(j\omega) = \frac{F(j\omega)}{1 + j\omega RC} = \frac{\pi\delta(\omega)}{1 + j\omega RC} + \frac{1}{-\omega^2 RC + j\omega} \qquad (2\text{-}132)$$

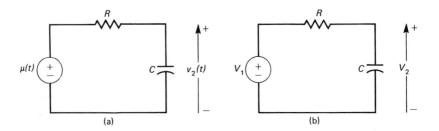

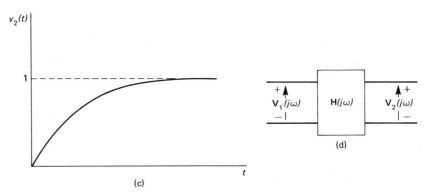

FIG. 2-9

Simple network driven by a unit step of voltage; (b) network for computing its steady-state response; (c) its unit step response; (d) block diagram of this system

Multiply Eq. 2-132 by $\dfrac{1}{2\pi}\,d\omega$ and integrate (see Eq. 2-62). This yields

$$v_2(t) = \frac{1}{2\pi}\int_{-\infty}^{\infty}\frac{\pi\delta(\omega)}{1+j\omega RC}\,e^{j\omega t}\,d\omega + \frac{1}{2\pi}\int_{-\infty}^{\infty}\frac{e^{j\omega t}}{j\omega - \omega^2 RC}\,d\omega \qquad (2\text{-}133)$$

Let us write this as

$$v_2(t) = v_a(t) + v_b(t)$$

Using Eq. 2-6 to evaluate the first integral, we have

$$v_a(t) = \tfrac{1}{2}$$

To evaluate the second integral, we make use of Euler's relation. Substituting Eq. 2-45, and manipulating we have

$$v_b(t) = \frac{-1}{2\pi}\int_{-\infty}^{\infty}\frac{\omega^2 RC + j\omega}{\omega^4 R^2 C^2 + \omega^2}(\cos\omega t + j\sin\omega t)\,d\omega$$

Eliminating the odd integrand yields

$$v_b(t) = -\frac{1}{\pi}\int_{0}^{\infty}\frac{RC}{\omega^2 R^2 C^2 + 1}\cos\omega t\,d\omega + \frac{1}{\pi}\int_{0}^{\infty}\frac{1}{\omega(1+\omega^2 R^2 C^2)}\sin\omega t\,d\omega$$

We make use of the known integrals

$$\int_0^\infty \frac{\cos ax}{B^2 + x^2} \, dx = \frac{\pi}{2B} e^{-|aB|} \tag{2–134a}$$

$$\int_0^\infty \frac{\sin ax}{x(B^2 + x^2)} \, dx = \frac{\pi}{2B^2} (1 - e^{-aB}) \tag{2–134b}$$

Then, the first integral is given by

$$- \tfrac{1}{2} e^{-|t|/RC}$$

and the second is

$$+ \tfrac{1}{2}(1 - e^{-t/RC}), \qquad t > 0$$
$$- \tfrac{1}{2}(1 - e^{+t/RC}), \qquad t < 0$$

Note that the integrand is an odd function of $t$. Thus,

$$v_b(t) = \begin{cases} \tfrac{1}{2} - e^{-t/RC}, & t > 0 \\ -\tfrac{1}{2}, & t < 0 \end{cases}$$

Adding $v_a(t)$ and $v_b(t)$, we have

$$v_2(t) = \begin{cases} 1 - e^{-t/RC}, & t > 0 \\ 0, & t < 0 \end{cases}$$

Alternatively, we can write

$$v_2(t) = (1 - e^{-t/RC}) u(t)$$

This is plotted in Fig. 2–9c. Thus, we have evaluated the transient response, using sinusoidal steady-state analysis and the Fourier transform.

Now consider the application of the Fourier transform to a general class of networks or systems. For instance, the network of Fig. 2–9a is represented by the block diagram of Fig. 2–9d. This box can be used to represent many networks. On a sinusoidal steady-state phasor basis, this box can be characterized by the relation

$$\frac{V_2(j\omega)}{V_1(j\omega)} = H(j\omega) \tag{2–135}$$

on a phasor basis. If the input voltage is $V_1(j\omega)$, the output voltage will be $V_2(j\omega)$. For Fig. 2–9a,

$$H(j\omega) = \frac{1}{1 + j\omega RC}$$

$H(j\omega)$ is called the *transfer function* of the box. In general, the block could contain many elements and $H(j\omega)$ could be far more complex than that given here. In addition, $H(j\omega)$ need not only relate input and output voltages. For instance, it could express the output voltage as a function of the input current. This block diagram could be used for a more general representation. That is, the input and output need not be voltage or current. For example, $H(j\omega)$ could be used to characterize a control system. The output could be the position of the front wheels of an automobile and the input could be the position of the steering wheel.

For example, assume that both the input $v_1(t)$ and output $v_2(t)$ are voltages.

Then, using the notation of relation 2–84,

$$v_1(t) \leftrightarrow V_1(j\omega)$$

Note that $V_1(j\omega)$ is a phasor representation of the spectrum of $v_1(t)$. Then, we can use Eq. 2–135 to obtain $V_2(j\omega)$, the spectrum of $v_2(t)$.

$$V_2(j\omega) = V_1(j\omega) H(j\omega) \qquad (2\text{--}136)$$

Then, to obtain $v_2(t)$, we must take the inverse Fourier transform of the right-hand side of this expression; hence,

$$v_2(t) = \frac{1}{2\pi} \int_{-\infty}^{\infty} V_1(j\omega) H(j\omega) e^{j\omega t} \, d\omega \qquad (2\text{--}137a)$$

Equation 2–137a is a general equation for the response of a system in terms of its transfer function. In general, if the input and output are not voltages, but are arbitrary functions $f_1(t)$ and $f_2(t)$, we can write

$$f_2(t) = \frac{1}{2\pi} \int_{-\infty}^{\infty} F_1(j\omega) H(j\omega) e^{j\omega t} \, d\omega \qquad (2\text{--}137b)$$

where $F_1(j\omega)$ is the Fourier transform of $f_1(t)$.

## 2-8. CONVERGENCE OF FOURIER TRANSFORM

Previously, we had assumed that $f(t)$ was such that $F(j\omega)$ expressed as the integral of Eq. 2–61 exists. Let us now consider the existence of this integral

$$F(j\omega) = \int_{-\infty}^{\infty} f(t) e^{-j\omega t} \, dt \qquad (2\text{--}138)$$

This is an infinite integral. Thus, if the integrand does not fall off rapidly enough, the integral may not exist; i.e., become infinite as $t$ approaches infinity. In addition, $f(t)$ may become infinite at finite values of $t$ in such a way that the integral does not exist. If the integral of Eq. 2–138 does not exist, then $F(j\omega)$ does not exist. In such cases, $f(t)$ does not have a Fourier transform. For example, if

$$f(t) = e^{|t|} \qquad (2\text{--}139)$$

then $F(j\omega)$ will not exist; i.e., $e^{|t|}$ does not have a Fourier transform. Note that if the integral of Eq. 2–138 does not exist in an ordinary sense, but does exist on a distribution basis (e.g., $\int_0^\infty \sin \omega t \, dt$—see Eq. 2–47), then $F(j\omega)$ does exist.

We shall consider some *sufficient conditions* for the existence of $F(j\omega)$. That is, if $f(t)$ satisfies these conditions, then $F(j\omega)$ will exist. However, these conditions are *not* necessary. That is, if $f(t)$ does not satisfy them, then $F(j\omega)$ *may* still exist. To sufficient conditions, let us consider the following inequality

$$\left| \int_{-\infty}^{\infty} f(t) \, dt \right| \leq \int_{-\infty}^{\infty} |f(t)| \, dt \qquad (2\text{--}140)$$

This is true because the positive and negative areas under the curve of $f(t)$ are subtracted when $f(t)$ is integrated. However, when $|f(t)|$ is integrated, all the areas are made positive. Thus, we can state that

$$|F(j\omega)| \leq \int_{-\infty}^{\infty} |f(t)\,e^{j\omega t}|\,dt = \int_{-\infty}^{\infty} |f(t)|\,|e^{j\omega t}|\,dt \qquad (2\text{-}141)$$

but

$$|e^{j\omega t}| = 1 \qquad (2\text{-}142)$$

Thus,

$$|F(j\omega)| \leq \int_{-\infty}^{\infty} |f(t)|\,dt \qquad (2\text{-}143)$$

Hence if $\int_{-\infty}^{\infty} |f(t)|\,dt$ is bounded, then $|F(j\omega)|$ will also be bounded and, therefore, $F(j\omega)$ will exist. Hence, we can state that a *sufficient condition for the existence of the Fourier transform is that*

$$\int_{-\infty}^{\infty} |f(t)|\,dt$$

exist. The reader may ask: since an integral must be evaluated, why not evaluate Eq. 2–138 directly to see if it exists instead of using Eq. 2–143. However, at times, Eq. 2–143 can be more easily evaluated and some simple relations can be obtained from it. Suppose

$$|f(t)| \leq M \qquad (2\text{-}144a)$$

and

$$|f(t)| \leq |K/t^m|\,; \qquad |t| > T_0, \qquad m > 1 \qquad (2\text{-}144b)$$

That is, $f(t)$ is bounded and falls off as fast as $1/t^m$, $m > 1$ for sufficiently large $t$. In this case $F(j\omega)$ will exist. If Eqs. 2–144 are satisfied, then

$$\int_{-\infty}^{\infty} |f(t)|\,dt \leq \int_{T_0}^{T_0} M\,dt + \int_{T_0}^{\infty} \frac{K}{t^m}\,dt - \int_{-T_0}^{-\infty} \left|\frac{K}{t^m}\right|\,dt$$

Evaluating these integrals, we obtain

$$\int_{-\infty}^{\infty} |f(t)|\,dt \leq 2MT_0 + \frac{2K}{(m-1)\,T_0^{m-1}}$$

Since $m > 1$, this will be bounded.

Actually, we can strengthen relations 2–144 somewhat. If $f(t)$ is such that either

$$\int_{-T_0}^{T_0} f(t)\,e^{j\omega t} \quad \text{or} \quad \int_{-T_0}^{T_0} |f(t)|\,dt \qquad (2\text{-}145a)$$

exists and

$$|f(t)| \leq \frac{K}{|t^m|}, \qquad |t| > T_0, \qquad m > 1 \qquad (2\text{-}145b)$$

then $F(j\omega)$ will exist. The development of this follows that of Eqs. 2–144.

Now suppose

$$\int_{-T_0}^{T_0} f(t)\, e^{j\omega t}\, dt$$

exists and that

$$f(t) > 0, \qquad |t| \geq T_0 \tag{2–146a}$$

$$\frac{df(t)}{dt} < 0, \qquad t > T_0 \tag{2–146b}$$

$$\frac{df(t)}{dt} > 0, \qquad t < -T_0 \tag{2–146c}$$

where $f(t)$ is positive and falls off monotonically for $|t| > T_0$. We shall now show that $\int_{T_0}^{\infty} f(t)\, e^{j\omega t}\, dt$ and $\int_{-\infty}^{-T_0} f(t)\, e^{-j\omega t}\, dt$ exist. Consider one of these integrals. The proof for the other is essentially the same

$$\left| \int_{T_0}^{\infty} f(t)\, e^{-j\omega t}\, dt \right| \leq \left| \int_{T_0}^{\infty} f(t) \cos \omega t\, dt \right| + \left| \int_{T_0}^{\infty} f(t) \sin \omega t\, dt \right| \tag{2–147}$$

Consider the integrand of the first integral. It is drawn for values of $t$ somewhat greater than $T_0$ (but within one cycle of $\cos \omega t$) in Fig. 2–10. Note that $f(t)$ is non-negative. Hence, the integrand changes sign whenever $\cos \omega t$ does. The first loop of $f(t) \cos \omega t$ contributes positively to the integral. The next loop produces a negative contribution. However, since $f(t)$ decreases monotonically, the magnitude of the area under the second loop must be equal to or less than that under the first loop. Thus, the algebraic sum of the areas under the first two loops must be positive and

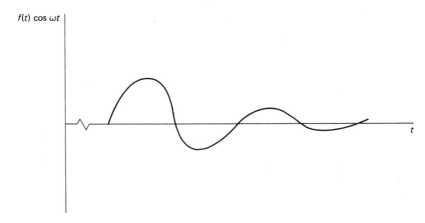

$f(t) \cos \omega t$

$t$

FIG. 2–10

Plot of $f(t) \cos \omega t$, $t > T_0$, and fixed $\omega$

equal to or less than the area under the first loop. Continuing in this way we have that the area under the third loop is positive and less than or equal to the area under the second loop.

The contribution of the second and third loops is thus negative and its magnitude will be equal to or less than the magnitude of the area under the second loop. Thus, we can say that the net contribution of the first three loops will be positive and less than or equal to the area under the first loop. Proceeding in this way, we have that the magnitude of the integral is equal to or less than the area under the first loop. Note that the magnitude of the area under any loop is equal to or greater than the one following it that the signs of these areas alternate. Hence, the magnitude of the integral is bounded.

A similar discussion can be applied to the second integral of Eq. 2–147. Hence, $F(j\omega)$ will exist. Note that Eq. 2–146b can be a weaker condition than Eq. 2–145b. For instance, $f(t)$ need only fall off as fast as $1/t^m$, where $m > 0$ but not $m > 1$.

If $f(t)$ becomes infinite for some finite $t$, then the definition of the integral must be carefully stated. In particular, we shall use the *Cauchy principal value* of the integral. This states that if $f(t)$ is unbounded at $t = t_0$, then we define

$$\int_{-\infty}^{\infty} f(t)\, dt = \lim_{\varepsilon \to 0} \left[ \int_{-\infty}^{t_0 - \varepsilon} f(t)\, dt + \int_{t_0 + \varepsilon}^{\infty} f(t)\, dt \right] \qquad (2\text{–}148)$$

For instance, if $f(t) = 1/t$, then its Fourier transform is

$$F(j\omega) = \lim_{\varepsilon \to 0} \left[ \int_{-\infty}^{-\varepsilon} \frac{e^{-j\omega t}}{t}\, dt + \int_{\varepsilon}^{\infty} \frac{e^{-j\omega t}}{t}\, dt \right]$$

Therefore,

$$F(j\omega) = \lim_{\varepsilon \to 0} \left[ \int_{-\infty}^{-\varepsilon} \frac{\cos \omega t - j \sin \omega t}{t}\, dt + \int_{\varepsilon}^{\infty} \frac{\cos \omega t + j \sin \omega t}{t}\, dt \right]$$

Because of the way the limit process is defined, the odd integrands of the two integrals cancel each other. Thus, $\cos \omega t / t$ (which is unbounded at $t = 0$) can be removed. Hence, we have

$$F(j\omega) = \lim_{\varepsilon \to 0} \left[ \int_{-\infty}^{-\varepsilon} -j\frac{\sin \omega t}{t}\, dt + \int_{\varepsilon}^{\infty} -j\frac{\sin \omega t}{t}\, dt \right]$$

This can be written as

$$F(j\omega) = \lim_{\varepsilon \to 0} \left[ -2j \int_{\varepsilon}^{\infty} \frac{\sin \omega t}{t}\, dt \right]$$

Since $\sin \omega t / t$ is bounded at $t = 0$, we have

$$F(j\omega) = -2j \int_{0}^{\infty} \frac{\sin \omega t}{t}\, dt$$

But

$$\int_0^\infty \frac{\sin ax}{x}\, dx = \begin{cases} \pi/2, & a > 0 \\ 0, & a = 0 \\ -\pi/2, & a < 0 \end{cases} \qquad (2\text{–}149)$$

Hence,

$$F(j\omega) = \begin{cases} -j\pi, & \omega > 0 \\ j\pi, & \omega < 0 \\ 0, & \omega = 0 \end{cases}$$

This can be written as

$$F(j\omega) = -j\pi \operatorname{sgn} \omega$$

where sgn $x$ is defined as

$$\operatorname{sgn} x = \begin{cases} 1, & x > 0 \\ -1, & x < 0 \\ 0, & x = 0 \end{cases} \qquad (2\text{–}150)$$

## 2-9. FOURIER TRANSFORMS OF SOME SPECIAL FUNCTIONS

We shall now restrict $f(t)$ and see how this restricts its Fourier transform $F(j\omega)$. As in Section 2-6, we shall write $F(j\omega)$ in terms of its real and imaginary parts:

$$F(j\omega) = R(\omega) + jX(\omega) \qquad (2\text{–}151)$$

have shown in Section 2-6 that if $f(t)$ is real, then $R(\omega)$ is an even function of $\omega$ and $X(\omega)$ is an odd function of $\omega$. In addition, the converse of this statement is true. That is, if $R(\omega)$ is even and $X(\omega)$ is odd, then $f(t)$ is real. To verify this, consider

$$f(t) = \frac{1}{2\pi} \int_{-\infty}^{\infty} [R(\omega) + jX(\omega)] [\cos \omega t + j\sin \omega t]\, d\omega$$

Eliminating the odd integrand, we have

$$f(t) = \frac{1}{2\pi} \int_{-\infty}^{\infty} [R(\omega) \cos \omega t - X(\omega) \sin \omega t]\, d\omega \qquad (2\text{–}152)$$

Thus, $f(t)$ is real. Unless otherwise indicated, $f(t)$ is always real.

We now consider that $f(t)$ is an even (or odd) function of time. Then its Fourier transform is

$$F(j\omega) = \int_{-\infty}^{\infty} f(t) e^{-j\omega t}\, dt \qquad (2\text{–}153)$$

Using Euler's relation (Eq. 2–45) and Eq. 2–151, we have

$$R(\omega) = \int_{-\infty}^{\infty} f(t) \cos \omega t\, dt \qquad (2\text{–}154a)$$

$$X(\omega) = -\int_{-\infty}^{\infty} f(t) \sin \omega t\, dt \qquad (2\text{–}154b)$$

If $f(t)$ is an even function of time, then

$$R(\omega) = 2 \int_0^\infty f(t) \cos \omega t \, dt \tag{2-155a}$$

$$X(\omega) = 0 \tag{2-155b}$$

Thus, an even function of time has a *real* Fourier transform.
Similarly, if $f(t)$ is an odd function of time, then

$$R(\omega) = 0 \tag{2-156a}$$

$$X(\omega) = -2 \int_0^\infty f(t) \sin \omega t \, dt \tag{2-156b}$$

Thus, an odd function of time has a *purely imaginary* Fourier transform.
The converse of these statements is also true if $f(t)$ is a real function of time. For instance, if $F(j\omega)$ is real, then $f(t)$ will be an even function of time; that is, if

$$F(j\omega) = R(\omega) \tag{2-157}$$

then (see Eq. 2–62)

$$f(t) = \frac{1}{2\pi} \int_{-\infty}^\infty R(\omega)(\cos \omega t + j \sin \omega t) \, d\omega \tag{2-158}$$

Since $f(t)$ is real, $R(\omega)$ will be an even function of $\omega$. Then, eliminating the odd integrand, we have

$$f(t) = \frac{1}{2\pi} \int_{-\infty}^\infty R(\omega) \cos \omega t \, d\omega \tag{2-159}$$

This is an even function of $t$.
Very often, we work with functions of time which are zero for $t < 0$. For instance, we consider that a signal is applied to a network at $t = 0$. Thus, the signal can be assumed to be zero for $t < 0$. In general, the response of the network will also be a signal which is zero for $t < 0$. This will be discussed further in Section 5-4.
Let us now see how the Fourier transform is restricted if $f(t) = 0$ for $t < 0$ (we still assume that $f(t)$ is a real function of time). From Eqs. 2–62, 2–151, and 2–45, we have

$$f(t) = \frac{1}{2\pi} \int_{-\infty}^\infty [R(\omega) + jX(\omega)] [\cos \omega t + j \sin \omega t] \, d\omega \tag{2-160}$$

Since $f(t)$ is real, $R(\omega)$ is an even, while $X(\omega)$ odd (we assume here that $R(\omega)$ and $X(\omega)$ exist). Then, eliminating the odd integrand and manipulating, we obtain

$$f(t) = \frac{1}{\pi} \int_0^\infty R(\omega) \cos \omega t \, d\omega - \frac{1}{\pi} \int_0^\infty X(\omega) \sin \omega t \, d\omega \tag{2-161}$$

where we have assumed that $R(\omega)$ and $X(\omega)$ are bounded at $\omega = 0$ (see Eq. 2–148).

Now replace $t$ by $-t$. This yields

$$f(-t) = \frac{1}{\pi} \int_0^\infty R(\omega) \cos \omega t \, d\omega + \frac{1}{\pi} \int_{-\infty}^\infty X(\omega) \sin \omega t \, d\omega \qquad (2\text{--}162)$$

We are given that

$$f(t) = 0, \qquad t < 0$$

Hence,

$$f(-t) = 0, \qquad t > 0$$

Then substituting Eq. 2–162 into this last equation, we have

$$\frac{1}{\pi} \int_0^\infty R(\omega) \cos \omega t \, d\omega = -\frac{1}{\pi} \int_{-\infty}^\infty X(\omega) \sin \omega t \, d\omega, \qquad t > 0 \qquad (2\text{--}163)$$

Since this equation is valid for all $t > 0$, we can substitute it into Eq. 2–161 so long as we restrict it to values of $t > 0$. Note that $f(t) = 0$, $t < 0$. Thus, we need not evaluate Eq. 2–161 to obtain $f(t)$ for $t < 0$. (The value of $f(0)$ is not defined here. As long as $f(t)$ does not have an impulse, etc. at $t = 0$, this will not be troublesome. Substituting, we have

$$f(t) = \frac{2}{\pi} \int_0^\infty R(\omega) \cos \omega t \, d\omega \qquad (2\text{--}164a)$$

and

$$f(t) = -\frac{2}{\pi} \int_0^\infty X(\omega) \sin \omega t \, d\omega \qquad (2\text{--}164b)$$

Thus, the response for $t > 0$ can be expressed in terms of $R(\omega)$ alone or $X(\omega)$ alone if $f(t)$ is such that $f(t) = 0$ for $t < 0$.

Equation 2–163 indicates that $R(\omega)$ and $X(\omega)$ can not be independently specified if we are restricted to functions of time which are zero for $t < 0$. Actually, we can write $R(\omega)$ in terms of $X(\omega)$ and vice versa. For instance, substitution of Eq. 2–164a into Eq. 2–61 yields

$$F(j\omega) = \frac{2}{\pi} \int_0^\infty \int_0^\infty R(v) \cos vt \, e^{-j\omega t} \, dv \, dt$$

Note that the lower limit of integration of the integral with respect to $t$ is 0 since $f(t) = 0$ for $t < 0$. The lower limit of the second integral is also zero, see Eq. 2–164a. We have substituted $\omega = y$ in Eq. 2–164a to avoid confusion. Solving for the imaginary portion of this relation, we obtain

$$X(\omega) = -\frac{2}{\pi} \int_0^\infty \int_0^\infty R(v) \cos vt \sin \omega t \, dv \, dt \qquad (2\text{--}165)$$

Similarly, substitution of Eq. 2–164b into Eq. 2–61 and solving for the real part yields

$$R(\omega) = -\frac{2}{\pi} \int_0^\infty \int_0^\infty X(v) \sin vt \cos \omega t \, dv \, dt \qquad (2\text{--}166)$$

Thus, for $f(t)$, which is zero for $t < 0$, we have expressed $R(\omega)$ and $X(\omega)$ in terms of each other. (In Chapter 5 we shall study the Hilbert transforms which provide a more convenient way of expressing $R(\omega)$ and $X(\omega)$ in terms of each other.)

## 2-10. BASIC FOURIER TRANSFORM THEOREMS

We shall use the notation of Eq. 2–84 here. If $F(j\omega)$ is the Fourier transform of $f(t)$, we write

$$f(t) \leftrightarrow F(j\omega)$$

This implies that both $f(t)$ and $F(j\omega)$ exist, possibly on a distribution basis.

**Linearity.**   The operations of the Fourier transform are linear; that is, if

$$f_1(t) \leftrightarrow F_1(j\omega) \qquad\qquad (2\text{–}167a)$$

and

$$f_2(t) \leftrightarrow F_2(j\omega) \qquad\qquad (2\text{–}167b)$$

then

$$a_1 f_1(t) + a_2 f_2(t) \leftrightarrow a_1 F_1(j\omega) + a_2 F_2(j\omega) \qquad\qquad (2\text{–}168)$$

where $a_1$ and $a_2$ are constants. This follows directly from the linearity of integration.

**Time Shift.**   Let us determine the changes that occur in $F(j\omega)$ if $f(t)$ is shifted in time; that is, if

$$f(t) \leftrightarrow F(j\omega)$$

we shall determine the Fourier transform of $f(t - \tau)$. Let

$$f(t - \tau) \leftrightarrow F_1(j\omega)$$

Then,

$$F_1(j\omega) = \int_{-\infty}^{\infty} f(t - \tau) e^{-j\omega t}\, dt \qquad\qquad (2\text{–}169)$$

Substituting $x = t - \tau$ and manipulating, we have

$$F_1(j\omega) = \int_{-\infty}^{\infty} f(x) e^{-j\omega(x + \tau)}\, dx = e^{-j\omega\tau} \int_{-\infty}^{\infty} f(x) e^{-j\omega x}\, dx \qquad (2\text{–}170)$$

The second integral of Eq. 2–170 is just $F(j\omega)$, the Fourier transform of $f(t)$; thus,

$$f(t - \tau) \leftrightarrow e^{-j\omega t} F(j\omega) \qquad\qquad (2\text{–}171)$$

If a function of time is delayed by $\tau$ seconds, its Fourier transform is multiplied by $e^{-j\omega t}$.

As an example, let us evaluate the Fourier transform of the pulse $f_T(t)$ shown in Fig. 2–11a. This pulse can be considered the sum of the unit step advanced by $T$ seconds and the negative unit step delayed by $T$ seconds (see Fig. 2–11b). From

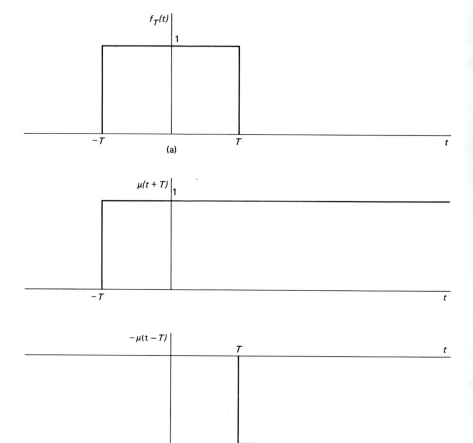

FIG. 2–11

(a) Pulse $f_T(t)$; (b) two functions which, when added, yield $f_T(t)$

Eq. 2–117, we have

$$u(t) \leftrightarrow \pi\delta(\omega) + \frac{1}{j\omega} \qquad (2\text{–}172)$$

Applying Eq. 2–171, we obtain

$$u(t - T) \leftrightarrow e^{-j\omega T} \left[ \pi\delta(\omega) + \frac{1}{j\omega} \right] \qquad (2\text{–}173a)$$

and

$$u(t + T) \leftrightarrow e^{j\omega T} \left[ \pi\delta(\omega) + \frac{1}{j\omega} \right] \qquad (2\text{–}173b)$$

Before proceeding further let us evaluate $f(x)\,\delta(x)$; i.e., the product of the impulse and an ordinary function. From Eq. 2–6, we have

$$\int_{-\infty}^{\infty} \phi(x)\, f(x)\, \delta(x)\, dx = \phi(0)\, f(0)$$

where it is assumed that $f(x)$ is continuous at $x = 0$. Hence, we can write

$$f(x)\,\delta(x) = f(0)\,\delta(x) \qquad (2\text{--}174)$$

Applying this relation to Eq. 2–173 yields

$$u(t - T) \leftrightarrow \pi\delta(\omega) + \frac{e^{-j\omega T}}{j\omega} \qquad (2\text{--}175a)$$

and

$$u(t + T) \leftrightarrow \pi\delta(\omega) + \frac{e^{j\omega T}}{j\omega} \qquad (2\text{--}175b)$$

Now,

$$f_T(t) = u(t + T) - u(t - T)$$

Then, applying linearity, we have

$$f_T(t) \leftrightarrow \frac{e^{j\omega T} - e^{-j\omega T}}{j\omega} = 2\,\frac{\sin \omega T}{\omega} \qquad (2\text{--}176)$$

**Frequency Shift.**   Consider the effect of a shift in frequency; that is, if

$$f(t) \leftrightarrow F(j\omega)$$

what is the inverse Fourier transform of $F[j(\omega - \omega_0)]$? Let $f_a(t) \leftrightarrow F[j(\omega - \omega_0)]$. Then (see Eq. 2–62)

$$f_a(t) = \frac{1}{2\pi} \int_{-\infty}^{\infty} F[j(\omega - \omega_0)]\, e^{j\omega t}\, d\omega$$

Let $x = \omega - \omega_0$. Then, substituting and manipulating, we obtain

$$f_a(t) = \frac{1}{2\pi} \int_{-\infty}^{\infty} F(jx)\, e^{j(x + \omega_0)t}\, dx = \frac{e^{j\omega_0 t}}{2\pi} \int_{-\infty}^{\infty} F(jx)\, e^{jxt}\, dx \qquad (2\text{--}177)$$

The $1/2\pi$ times the second integral of Eq. 2–177 is just the inverse Fourier transform of $F(j\omega)$; hence

$$f(t)\, e^{j\omega_0 t} \leftrightarrow F[j(\omega - \omega_0)] \qquad (2\text{--}178)$$

If $f(t)$ is a real function of time, then $f(t)\, e^{j\omega_0 t}$ will *not* be real. This is to be expected. If $f(t)$ is real, then Re $F(j\omega) = R(\omega)$ will be even while Im $F(j\omega) = X(\omega)$ will be odd. However, if $F(j\omega)$ is translated in $\omega$, then its real part will no longer be even and its imaginary part will no longer be odd.

Let us use Eq. 2–178 to obtain some other Fourier transforms. For example, if $f(t) \leftrightarrow F(j\omega)$, let us determine the Fourier transform of $f(t) \cos \omega_0 t$.

$$f(t) \cos \omega_0 t = \frac{f(t)}{2}\left[e^{j\omega_0 t} + e^{-j\omega_0 t}\right] \tag{2–179}$$

Then, using Eq. 2–178 and linearity, we have

$$f(t) \cos \omega_0 t \leftrightarrow \frac{F[j(\omega - \omega_0)] + F[j(\omega + \omega_0)]}{2} \tag{2–180}$$

In a similar way, we obtain

$$f(t) \sin \omega_0 t \leftrightarrow \frac{F[j(\omega - \omega_0)] - F[j(\omega + \omega_0)]}{2j} \tag{2–181}$$

**Time or Frequency Scaling.**   It sometimes is convenient to be able to adjust the time or frequency scale. For instance, when analog computers are used with pen recorders, the speed of their responses is limited. However, these devices can be used to study rapidly varying signals if the time axis of these signals are scaled; that is, the response of the computer is made to vary such that $t$ is replaced by $bt$, where $b$ is a real constant. Let us determine the effect of such scaling on the Fourier transform of $f(t)$; that is, if

$$f(t) \leftrightarrow F(j\omega)$$

what is the Fourier transform of $f(bt)$? Then,

$$f(bt) \leftrightarrow \int_{-\infty}^{\infty} f(bt) e^{-j\omega t} dt \tag{2–182}$$

Substituting $bt = x$ and manipulating, we obtain (see Eq. 2–37)

$$f(bt) \leftrightarrow \frac{1}{|b|} \int_{-\infty}^{\infty} f(x) e^{-j(\omega/b)x} dx \tag{2–183}$$

Hence,

$$f(bt) \leftrightarrow \frac{1}{|b|} F\left(\frac{\omega}{b}\right) \tag{2–184}$$

That is, $\omega$ is replaced by $\omega/b$ and the transform is divided by $|b|$.

In a similar way, we can scale in the frequency domain. Manipulating Eq. 2–184, we have

$$\frac{1}{|b|} f\left(\frac{t}{b}\right) \leftrightarrow F(b\omega) \tag{2–185}$$

**Symmetry.**   The two integrals in the Fourier transform pair are (see Eqs. 2–61 and 2–62)

$$F(j\omega) = \int_{-\infty}^{\infty} f(t) e^{-j\omega t} dt \tag{2–186a}$$

$$f(t) = \frac{1}{2\pi} \int_{-\infty}^{\infty} F(j\omega) e^{j\omega t} \, d\omega \tag{2-186b}$$

These two integrals of Eqs. 2–186 are almost identical except for a minus sign, interchanging of $t$ and $\omega$, and a factor of $2\pi$. Because of this, there is a symmetry that exists between $f(t)$ and $F(j\omega)$. Note that, in general, $f(t)$ and its Fourier transform $F(j\omega)$ *will have very different forms*. However, a symmetry does exist insofar as general relations are concerned. For instance, Eqs. 2–184 and 2–185 are very similar. The same type of similarities can be seen between Eqs. 2–171 and 2–178.

Let us formalize the symmetry of $f(t)$ and $F(j\omega)$. Replace $t$ by $-t$ in Eq. 2–186b; after rearranging, this yields

$$2\pi f(-t) = \int_{-\infty}^{\infty} F(j\omega) e^{-j\omega t} \, d\omega$$

Now replace $t$ by $\omega$ and $\omega$ by $t$; this yields

$$2\pi f(-\omega) = \int_{-\infty}^{\infty} F(jt) e^{-j\omega t} \, dt \tag{2-187}$$

The integral of Eq. 2–187 represents the Fourier transform of a function $F(jt)$. Note that this is a complex function of time; thus, if

then
$$f(t) \leftrightarrow F(j\omega) \tag{2-188a}$$

$$F(jt) \leftrightarrow 2\pi f(-\omega) \tag{2-188b}$$

This is a formal expression of the symmetry of the Fourier transform.

This symmetry is often convenient. For instance, Eq. 2–176 gave the Fourier transform of the rectangular pulse of Fig. 2–11a. Now suppose we wish the inverse Fourier transform of a pulse in the frequency domain (see Fig. 2–12).

$$F_a(j\omega) = \begin{cases} 1, & -\omega_a \le \omega \le \omega_a \\ 0, & |\omega| > \omega_a \end{cases} \tag{2-189}$$

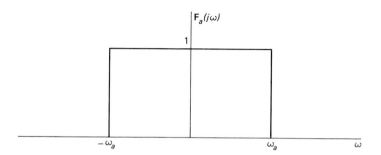

Fig. 2–12
Function $F_a(j\omega)$

Using Eqs. 2-176 and 2-188, we obtain

$$F_a(j\omega) \leftrightarrow \frac{e^{j\omega_a t} - e^{-j\omega_a t}}{2\pi jt} = \frac{\sin \omega_a t}{\pi t} \tag{2-190}$$

**Time Differentiation.**   If $f(t) \leftrightarrow F(j\omega)$, let us determine the Fourier transform of $df(t)/dt$. From Eq. 2-62 we have

$$f(t) = \frac{1}{2\pi} \int_{-\infty}^{\infty} F(j\omega) e^{j\omega t} \, d\omega \tag{2-191}$$

Let us differentiate this and assume that $F(j\omega)$ is such that the order of differentiation and integration can be interchanged. This yields

$$\frac{df(t)}{dt} = \frac{1}{2\pi} \int_{-\infty}^{\infty} j\omega F(j\omega) e^{j\omega t} \, d\omega \tag{2-192}$$

Comparing this with Eq. 2-191, we have

$$\frac{df(t)}{dt} \leftrightarrow j\omega \, F(\omega) \tag{2-193}$$

Differentiating $n$ times and assuming that the order of differentiation and integration can be interchanged at each step, this yields

$$\frac{df^n(t)}{dt^n} = (j\omega)^n \, F(\omega) \tag{2-194}$$

Proceeding in a similar way, we obtain from Eq. 2-61

$$\frac{d^n F(j\omega)}{d\omega^n} \leftrightarrow (-jt)^n \, f(t) \tag{2-195}$$

**Moments.**   Consider a procedure for obtaining a power series expansion for the Fourier transform. This can be of help when the integral of Eq. 2-61 cannot be obtained in closed form. We start by defining the $n$th *moment* $m_n$ of $f(t)$; this is

$$m_n = \int_{-\infty}^{\infty} t^n f(t) \, dt \tag{2-196}$$

The moments may be more easily evaluated than $F(j\omega)$ because no exponential appears in the integral. Let us relate the moments to the Fourier transform. From Eq. 2-195, we have

$$\frac{d^n F(j\omega)}{d\omega^n} = \int_{-\infty}^{\infty} (-jt)^n f(t) e^{-j\omega t} \, dt \tag{2-197}$$

Evaluating this as $\omega = 0$ yields

$$\frac{d^n F(j\omega)}{d\omega^n} \bigg|_{\omega=0} = (-j)^n \int_{-\infty}^{\infty} t^n f(t) \, dt \tag{2-198}$$

Then (see Eq. 2–196)

$$\frac{d^n F(j\omega)}{d\omega^n}\bigg|_{\omega=0} = (-j)^n m_n \tag{2-199}$$

If $F(j\omega)$ is such that it can be expanded in a Taylor's series about the origin, then we have

$$F(j\omega) = \sum_{k=0}^{\infty} \frac{d^k F(j\omega)}{d\omega^k}\bigg|_{\omega=0} \frac{\omega^k}{k!} \tag{2-200}$$

Substituting Eq. 2–199, we obtain

$$F(j\omega) = \sum_{k=0}^{\infty} (-j)^k m_k \frac{\omega^k}{k!} \tag{2-201}$$

Thus, if the Taylor's series exists, we can expand the Fourier spectrum in terms of the moments of $f(t)$.

## 2-11.   CONVOLUTION THEOREMS

We shall now consider a very powerful mathematical tool called *convolution*. In subsequent sections and chapters we shall demonstrate that this procedure can be of great help in the development of important results concerned with the Fourier transform and in the obtaining of the transient response of systems.

We begin by defining convolution and then apply it to the Fourier transform. If we are given two functions $f_1(x)$ and $f_2(x)$, their *convolution* is written as $f_1(x) * f_2(x)$ and is defined by the integral

$$f_1(x) * f_2(x) = \int_{-\infty}^{\infty} f_1(y) f_2(x-y)\, dy \tag{2-202}$$

Note that the integrand consists of the product of the first function multiplied by the second which has been reversed in time (note the $-y$) and time shifted. Note that $x$ is treated as a parameter (constant) in the integration.

If we let $z = x - y$, the convolution becomes

$$f_1(x) * f_2(x) = \int_{-\infty}^{\infty} f_2(z) f_1(x-z)\, dz \tag{2-203}$$

Then,

$$f_1(x) * f_2(x) = f_2(x) * f_1(x) \tag{2-204}$$

Thus, the order of convolution is unimportant, and the convolution of more than two functions can be taken. For example,

$$f_1(x) * f_2(x) * f_3(x)$$

In this case, the convolution $f_1(x) * f_2(x)$ is obtained. The convolution of this function with $f_3(x)$ yields the desired result. Again the order may be changed.

$$f_1(x) * f_2(x) * f_3(x) = [f_1(x) * f_2(x)] * f_3(x) \tag{2-205}$$

$$= f_1(x) * [f_2(x) * f_3(x)]$$

It is often desirable to remove small ripples or rapid variations from a signal. Such a process is called *smoothing*. It is accomplished mathematically by taking the convolution of the function in question and the function $f_T(t)$ which is given in Fig. 2–11a.

$$f(t) * f_T(t) = \int_{-\infty}^{\infty} f(x) f_T(t - x)\, dx \qquad (2\text{–}206)$$

However,

$$f_T(t) = \begin{cases} 1, & -T \leq t \leq T \\ 0, & |t| > T \end{cases} \qquad (2\text{–}207)$$

Thus,

$$f(t) * f_T(t) = \int_{t-T}^{t+T} f(x)\, dx$$

That is, the convolution evaluated at any $t$ represents the average from $t - T$ to $t + T$ of $f(t)$. In this way, any ripples in $f(t)$ whose time duration is short in comparison with $T$ will be "averaged out" or smoothed.

**Time Convolution Theorem.**   Often, in the analysis of networks and system response, we must take the inverse Fourier transform of a function, which is equal to the product of two functions whose inverse transforms are known. The inverse transform of the product can be determined in terms of the inverse transforms of the individual functions by using the *time convolution theorem*. This states that if

$$f_1(t) \leftrightarrow F_1(j\omega) \qquad (2\text{–}208a)$$

$$f_2(t) \leftrightarrow F_2(j\omega) \qquad (2\text{–}208b)$$

then

$$f_1(t) * f_2(t) \leftrightarrow F_1(j\omega)\, F_2(j\omega) \qquad (2\text{–}209)$$

Thus, the Fourier transform of the convolution of two functions of time is the product of their individual Fourier transforms. We assume that the Fourier transform is unique (see Section 2-4). Thus, if $F_a(j\omega)$ is the Fourier transform of $f_a(t)$, then we assume that $f_a(t)$ is the inverse Fourier transform of $F_a(j\omega)$ and vice versa.

To prove this theorem, we apply Eq. 2–61 to the convolution; this yields

$$f_1(t) * f_2(t) \leftrightarrow \int_{-\infty}^{\infty} \left[ \int_{-\infty}^{\infty} f_1(x) f_2(t - x)\, dx \right] e^{-j\omega t}\, dt \qquad (2\text{–}210)$$

Now, assume that $f_1(x)$ and $f_2(x)$ are such that the order of integration can be interchanged; thus,

$$f_1(t) * f_2(t) \leftrightarrow \int_{-\infty}^{\infty} f_1(x) \int_{-\infty}^{\infty} f_2(t - x)\, e^{-j\omega t}\, dt\, dx \qquad (2\text{–}211)$$

The inner integral is just the Fourier transform of $f_2(t)$ delayed by $x$ seconds. Then, applying Eq. 2–171 to evaluate the inner integral, we obtain

$$f_1(t) * f_2(t) \leftrightarrow \int_{-\infty}^{\infty} f_1(x) F_2(j\omega)\, e^{-j\omega x}\, dx \qquad (2\text{–}212)$$

Since $F_2(j\omega)$ is not a function of $x$, it can be removed from the integral; thus,

$$f_1(t) * f_2(t) \leftrightarrow F_2(j\omega) \int_{-\infty}^{\infty} f_1(x) e^{-j\omega x} dx \qquad (2\text{–}213)$$

The integral is the definition of the Fourier transform of $f_1(t)$; hence,

$$f_1(t) * f_2(t) \leftrightarrow F_1(j\omega) F_2(j\omega)$$

Thus, the theorem is proved.

In the proof of the time convolution theorem, we have assumed that the order of integration can be interchanged. The following are two *sufficient* conditions that this can be done: (1) if the integral converges uniformly, then the order of integration can be interchanged; (2) if $\int_{-\infty}^{\infty} |f_1(x)| dx$ *and* $\int_{-\infty}^{\infty} |f_2(x)| dx$ both exist, then the order of integration can be interchanged.

Now let us consider an example of this procedure. Suppose that

$$f_1(t) = u(t) e^{-b_1 t} \leftrightarrow 1/(b_1 + j\omega)$$
$$f_2(t) = u(t) e^{-b_2 t} \leftrightarrow 1/(b_2 + j\omega)$$

where $b_1 > 0$ and $b_2 > 0$. We shall determine the inverse Fourier transform $f(t)$ of

$$F(j\omega) = \frac{1}{(b_1 + j\omega)(b_2 + j\omega)}$$

Applying the time convolution theorem, we have

$$f(t) = f_1(t) * f_2(t)$$

Thus,

$$f(t) = \int_{-\infty}^{\infty} u(x) e^{-b_1 x} u(t - x) e^{-b_2(t-x)} dx$$

Now

$$u(x) = 0, \qquad x < 0$$
$$u(t - x) = 0, \qquad x > t$$

Hence,

$$f(t) = \int_0^t e^{-b_1 x - b_2 t + b_2 x} dx = e^{-b_2 t} \int_0^t e^{-(b_1 - b_2)x} dx, \qquad t > 0$$

Integration yields

$$f(t) = \frac{e^{-b_2 t}}{b_1 - b_2} + \frac{e^{-b_1 t}}{b_2 - b_1}, \qquad t > 0$$

**Frequency Convolution Theorem.** We can proceed in a fashion analogous to that used in obtaining the time convolution theorem to obtain the frequency convolution theorem. This states that if

$$f_1(t) \leftrightarrow F_1(j\omega) \qquad (2\text{–}214a)$$

and

$$f_2(t) \leftrightarrow F_2(j\omega) \qquad (2\text{–}214b)$$

then
$$f_1(t)f_2(t) \leftrightarrow \frac{1}{2\pi} F_1(j\omega) * F_2(j\omega) \qquad (2\text{--}215)$$

The proof is analogous to that for time convolution so the details will be left to the reader. Note that Eq. 2–215 can be written as

$$f_1(t)f_2(t) \leftrightarrow \frac{1}{2\pi} \int_{-\infty}^{\infty} F_1(jx) F_2[j(\omega - x)]\, dx \qquad (2\text{--}216)$$

As an example of the use of frequency convolution, let us obtain the Fourier transform of $u(t)f(t)$ in terms of the transform of $f(t)$. It is assumed that $f(t) \neq 0$ for $t < 0$. Then,

$$f(t) \leftrightarrow F(j\omega)$$

$$u(t) \leftrightarrow \pi\delta(\omega) + \frac{1}{j\omega}$$

(See Eq. 2–117.) From Eq. 2–216, we obtain

$$u(t)f(t) \leftrightarrow \frac{1}{2\pi} \int_{-\infty}^{\infty} F(jx) \left[ \pi\delta(\omega - x) + \frac{1}{j(\omega - x)} \right] dx \qquad (2\text{--}217)$$

Integrating the impulse function, we have

$$u(t)f(t) = \frac{1}{2} F(j\omega) + \frac{1}{2\pi} \int_{-\infty}^{\infty} \frac{F(jx)}{j(\omega - x)}\, dx \qquad (2\text{--}218)$$

Alternatively, we could reverse the order of convolution in Eq. 2–217 and write

$$u(t)f(t) \leftrightarrow \frac{1}{2\pi} \int_{-\infty}^{\infty} \left[ \pi\delta(x) + \frac{1}{jx} \right] F[j(\omega - x)]\, dx$$

Then, proceeding as before, we obtain

$$u(t)f(t) \leftrightarrow \frac{1}{2} F(j\omega) + \frac{1}{2\pi} \int_{-\infty}^{\infty} \frac{F[j(\omega - x)]}{jx}\, dx \qquad (2\text{--}219)$$

(Equations 2–218 and 2–219 are equivalent.)


## 2-12. ENERGY—PARSEVAL'S THEOREM

Very often, we are concerned with the energy supplied by a signal to a load. For instance, if $v(t)$ is the voltage across a resistance, then the total energy supplied to the resistor is

$$W = \int_{-\infty}^{\infty} \frac{v^2(t)}{R}\, dt \qquad (2\text{--}220)$$

If we define

$$f(t) = \frac{v(t)}{\sqrt{R}}$$

we can write

$$W = \int_{-\infty}^{\infty} f^2(t)\, dt \qquad\qquad (2-221)$$

In general, $f(t)$ is real; thus,

$$f^2(t) = |f(t)|^2 \qquad\qquad (2-222)$$

Thus, Eq. 2–221 can be written as

$$W = \int_{-\infty}^{\infty} |f(t)|^2\, dt \qquad\qquad (2-223)$$

The reader may wonder why we write Eq. 2–221 in the form of Eq. 2–223 since they are equivalent for all real $f(t)$. We shall derive results in terms of Eq. 2–223, which are valid for complex as well as for real $f(t)$, while those results derived in terms of Eq. 2–221 are only valid for real $f(t)$. Thus, additional generality is obtained.

Equations 2–221 and 2–223 can be used to express the total energy supplied by a signal. Sometimes, especially if the load is not resistive, the energy is expressed in terms of the product of voltage and current; thus,

$$W = \int_{-\infty}^{\infty} v(t)\, i(t)\, dt \qquad\qquad (2-224)$$

where $v(t)$ is the voltage across the load and $i(t)$ is the current through it. We can write Eq. 2–224 in a more general form as

$$W = \int_{-\infty}^{\infty} f_1(t)\, f_2(t)\, dt \qquad\qquad (2-225)$$

We have expressed the energies in terms of the signals themselves. Let us now see how the Fourier spectrum of a signal is related to its energy content. We shall use the convolution theorem to obtain this relation. Then, using the notation of Eq. 2–84, we have

$$f_1(t) \leftrightarrow F_1(j\omega)$$

$$f_2(t) \leftrightarrow F_2(j\omega)$$

Then (see Eq. 2–115)

$$f_1(t)\, f_2(t) \leftrightarrow \frac{1}{2\pi} F_1(j\omega) * F_2(j\omega) \qquad\qquad (2-226)$$

From the definition of the Fourier transform given in Eq. 2–61, we have

$$f_1(t)\, f_2(t) \leftrightarrow \int_{-\infty}^{\infty} f_1(t)\, f_2(t)\, e^{-j\omega t}\, dt$$

Equating this to the convolution of $(1/2\pi)\, F_1(j\omega)$ and $F_2(j\omega)$, by Eq. 2–216, we obtain

$$\int_{-\infty}^{\infty} f_1(t)\, f_2(t)\, e^{-j\omega t}\, dt = \frac{1}{2\pi} \int_{-\infty}^{\infty} F_1(y)\, F_2(\omega - y)\, dy$$

Letting $\omega = 0$ in this equation yields

$$\int_{-\infty}^{\infty} f_1(t) f_2(t) \, dt = \frac{1}{2\pi} \int_{-\infty}^{\infty} F_1(y) F_2(-y) \, dy$$

or, equivalently

$$\int_{-\infty}^{\infty} f_1(t) f_2(t) \, dt = \frac{1}{2\pi} \int_{-\infty}^{\infty} F_1(\omega) F_2(-\omega) \, d\omega \qquad (2\text{-}227)$$

This is called *Parseval's Theorem*. It states that the *infinite* integral of the product of two time functions is equal to $1/2\pi$ times the *infinite* integral of the product of the frequency spectrums (where in one spectrum, $\omega$ is replaced by $-\omega$). If $f_2(t)$ is real, then $R_2(\omega) = \text{Re} \, F_2(j\omega)$ will be an even function of $\omega$ and $X_2(\omega) = \text{Im} \, F_2(j\omega)$ will be an odd function of $\omega$. Hence, $F_2(-\omega) = F_2^*(\omega)$, where the superscript $*$ indicates the complex conjugate. Thus, Eq. 2–227 can be written as

$$\int_{-\infty}^{\infty} f_1(t) f_2(t) \, dt = \frac{1}{2\pi} \int_{-\infty}^{\infty} F_1(j\omega) F_2^*(j\omega) \, d\omega \qquad (2\text{-}228)$$

Before considering Eq. 2–223, an additional result must be obtained. Consider that

$$f(t) \leftrightarrow F(j\omega)$$

Let us determine the Fourier transform of $f^*(t)$. Here we assume that $f(t)$ may be complex and that $f^*(t)$ is the complex conjugate of $f(t)$; let

$$f^*(t) \leftrightarrow F_1(j\omega) \qquad (2\text{-}229)$$

Then, using Eq. 2–61, we have

$$F(j\omega) = \int_{-\infty}^{\infty} f(t) e^{-j\omega t} \, dt \qquad (2\text{-}230a)$$

$$F_1(j\omega) = \int_{-\infty}^{\infty} f^*(t) e^{-j\omega t} \, dt \qquad (2\text{-}230b)$$

Replace $\omega$ by $-\omega$ in Eq. 2–230b; this yields

$$F_1(-j\omega) = \int_{-\infty}^{\infty} f^*(t) e^{j\omega t} \, dt$$

Now take the conjugate of both sides of the equation

$$F_1^*(-j\omega) = \int_{-\infty}^{\infty} f(t) e^{-j\omega t} \, dt$$

Substituting Eq. 2–230a, we have

$$F_1^*(-j\omega) = F(j\omega) \qquad (2\text{-}231)$$

Replacing $\omega$ by $-\omega$ and taking the conjugate of both sides of the resulting expression yields

$$F_1(j\omega) = F^*(-j\omega)$$

Hence,

$$f^*(t) \leftrightarrow F^*(-j\omega) \tag{2 232}$$

Now let us return to Parseval's theorem. In Eq. 2–228 let

$$f_1(t) = f(t) \leftrightarrow F(j\omega)$$

$$f_2(t) = f^*(t) \leftrightarrow F^*(-j\omega)$$

Then, substituting in Eq. 2–227 (note minus sign), we have

$$\int_{-\infty}^{\infty} |f(t)|^2 \, dt = \frac{1}{2\pi} \int_{-\infty}^{\infty} |F(j\omega)|^2 \, d\omega \tag{2-233}$$

This is an alternate form of Parseval's theorem. It states that the energy contained in a signal can be obtained either by integrating the magnitude in the time domain or by integrating the magnitude in the frequency domain. This is to be expected since the signal can be considered the "sum" of all the sinusoids. The quantity $|F(j\omega)|^2$ is called the *energy spectrum* of $f(t)$. (Note that Parseval's theorem can be applied to arbitrary functions and not only those which are expressible as energies.)

## 2-13. BANDLIMITED SIGNALS—FURTHER DISCUSSION OF GIBBS' PHENOMENON. THE ELIMINATION OF GIBBS' PHENOMENON

When signals are transmitted through systems, the Fourier spectrum of the output signal is given by the product of the Fourier spectrum of the input signal and the transfer function of the system (see Eq. 2–136). In any practical system, the high frequencies will be attenuated; that is, the magnitude of the transfer function $|H(j\omega)|$ will fall off as $|\omega|$ becomes large. If $|H(j\omega)|$ actually becomes 0 for $|\omega| > \omega_a$, then we call this *bandlimiting*. We shall now discuss the effects of bandlimiting by studying some idealized forms of $H(j\omega)$. (In Section 5-4 we shall show that these idealized transfer functions cannot be exactly obtained; however, the results that we obtain using them often closely approximate those obtained in practice.)

Consider that the system response is constant for all frequencies up to

$$|\omega| = \omega_a$$

and then becomes zero. That is, the transfer function is given by $H(j\omega) = F_a(j\omega)$, where (see Eq. 2–189)

$$F_a(j\omega) = \begin{cases} 1, & -\omega_a \leqq \omega \leqq \omega_a \\ 0, & |\omega| > \omega_a \end{cases} \tag{2-234}$$

Suppose a signal $f_i(t)$ is applied to the system, where

$$f_i(t) \leftrightarrow F_1(j\omega) \tag{2-235a}$$

and that the output of the system is $f_o(t)$, where

$$f_o(t) \leftrightarrow F_o(j\omega) \tag{2-235b}$$

Then (see Eq. 2–136)

$$F_0(j\omega) = F_i(j\omega) F_a(j\omega) \tag{2-236}$$

Taking the inverse Fourier transform, we have

$$f_o(t) = \frac{1}{2\pi} \int_{-\infty}^{\infty} F_i(j\omega) F_a(j\omega) e^{j\omega t} \, d\omega \tag{2-237}$$

Substituting Eq. (2–234), we obtain

$$f_o(t) = \frac{1}{2\pi} \int_{-\omega_a}^{\omega_a} F_i(j\omega) e^{j\omega t} \, d\omega \tag{2-238}$$

Consider the response of this bandlimited system to a signal with a discontinuity. In particular, assume that

$$f_i(t) = u(t)$$

Then (see Eq. 2–117),

$$F_i(j\omega) = \pi\delta(\omega) + \frac{1}{j\omega}$$

Hence,

$$f_o(t) = \frac{1}{2\pi} \int_{-\omega_a}^{\omega_a} \left[ \pi\delta(\omega) + \frac{1}{j\omega} \right] e^{j\omega t} \, d\omega$$

Evaluating the integral of the $\delta$-function and substituting Euler's relation (Eq. 2–45)

$$f_o(t) = \frac{1}{2} + \frac{1}{\pi} \int_0^{\omega_a} \frac{\sin \omega t}{\omega} \, d\omega \tag{2-239}$$

Manipulating, we obtain

$$f_o(t) = \frac{1}{2} + \frac{1}{\pi} \int_0^{\omega_a t} \frac{\sin x}{x} \, dx \tag{2-240}$$

This is essentially the same as Eq. 2–86. Thus, $f_o(t)$ will exhibit all of the properties of Gibbs' phenomenon. Hence, this form of bandlimiting leads to all the underswings and overshoots of Gibbs' phenomenon.

Consider this response, now using the convolution theorem. From Eq. 2–190, we have

$$\frac{\sin \omega_a t}{\pi t} \leftrightarrow F_a(j\omega)$$

Thus, using convolution (Eq. 2–209), we obtain

$$f_o(t) = \int_{-\infty}^{\infty} f_i(x) \frac{\sin \omega_a(t - x)}{\pi(t - x)} \, dx \tag{2-241}$$

If $f_i(t) = u(t)$, this relation becomes

$$f_o(t) = \int_{-\infty}^{\infty} u(x) \frac{\sin \omega_a(t - x)}{\pi(t - x)} \, dx \tag{2-242}$$

The function $\sin \omega_a(t - x)/\pi(t - x)$ is called a *scanning function*. As $t$ is varied, it is translated in time; i.e., it scans along $f_i(x)$. Let us discuss why this particular scanning function leads to Gibbs' phenomenon. Consider Fig. 2–13, which illustrates the scanning function for $t = t_0 = \pi/\omega_a$. (Later we shall show that $t_0$ corresponds to the maximum overshoot of $f_o(t)$.) The integrand is the product of the scanning function and $u(x)$. Hence, only that part of the scanning function that lies to the right of the origin is integrated. Thus, for time $t_0$, only the shaded area of Fig. 2–13 is integrated.

Now consider that $t = -\infty$, the scanning function is shifted (infinitely) to the left. Therefore, that part of it to the right of the origin is infinitely small. Thus, $f_o(-\infty) = 0$. As time increases, the scanning function is shifted to the right. Thus, finite areas are integrated. For any fixed $t$, the scanning function is also fixed. The

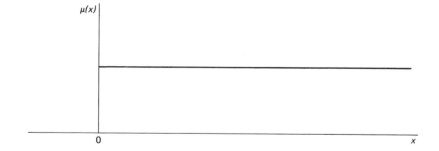

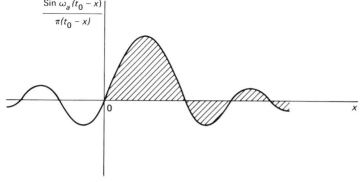

Fig. 2–13

An illustration of the scanning function $\sin \omega_a(t_0 - x)/\pi(t_0 - x)$ where $t_0 = \pi/\omega_a$

positive and negative loops of the scanning function cause the area integrated to increase and decrease as $t$ increases. Note that for each $t$, a specific area is integrated. The area under the positive loop of $(\sin x)/x$ for $-\pi \leqq x \leqq \pi$ is greater than the net area under the remainder of the curve. The discussion following Eq. 2–146 can be used to show this. Similarly, this discussion can be used to show that $t = t_0$ corresponds to the maximum value of $f_o(t)$. Similar arguments show that the net area of the scanning function to the left of the origin in Fig. 2–13 is negative. Thus, as $t$ approaches $\infty$, the response will be less than that at $t_0$. In addition, as $t$ increases from $t_0$, $f_o(t)$ will alternately decrease and increase with the overshoots and underswings of the Gibbs' phenomenon.

The overshoots and undershoots of Gibbs' phenomenon occur because the scanning function has both positive and negative areas. If the scanning function were only positive, then the area integrated would monotonically increase as time increased. Thus, even if $f_i(t)$ had a finite discontinuity, $f_o(t)$ would increase monotonically. The scanning function depends upon the transfer function. Let us now consider another bandlimited transfer function which has a scanning function that is always positive. This transfer function which we call $F_b(j\omega)$ is shown in Fig. 2–14. Note that it is bandlimited in that it is zero for $|\omega| > \omega_a$. However, the response is not constant for $|\omega| < \omega_a$, but falls off linearly; that is

$$F_b(j\omega) = \begin{cases} 1 - \left| \dfrac{\omega}{\omega_a} \right|, & -\omega_a \leqq \omega \leqq \omega_a \\ 0, & |\omega| > \omega_a \end{cases} \qquad (2\text{–}243)$$

Let us obtain the inverse Fourier transform of $F_b(j\omega)$. Since $F_b(j\omega)$ is even, we have

$$f_b(t) = \frac{1}{\pi} \int_0^{\omega_b} F_b(j\omega) \cos \omega t \, d\omega$$

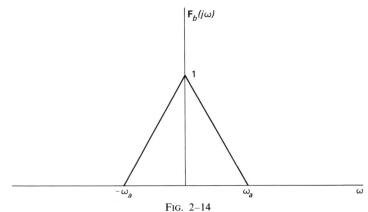

Fig. 2–14
Function $F_b(j\omega)$

Substituting, we obtain

$$f_b(t) = \frac{1}{\pi} \int_0^{\omega_a} \left( 1 - \frac{\omega}{\omega_a} \right) \cos \omega t \, d\omega$$

Integration yields

$$f_b(t) = \frac{1}{\pi \omega_a t^2} (1 - \cos \omega_a t) \qquad (2\text{-}244a)$$

Using the trigonometric identity, $\sin^2 (x/2) = \frac{1}{2}(1 - \cos x)$, we have

$$f_b(t) = \frac{2 \sin^2 (\omega_a t/2)}{\pi \omega_a t^2} \qquad (2\text{-}244b)$$

This is called the *Féjer scanning function*. Note that it is nonnegative. Now assume that the transfer function is $F_b(j\omega)$; thus,

$$F_o(j\omega) = F_i(j\omega) \, F_b(j\omega)$$

Then, using convolution, we have

$$f_o(t) = \int_{-\infty}^{\infty} f_i(x) \, \frac{2\sin^2 \dfrac{\omega_a}{2}(t - x)}{\pi \omega_a (t - x)^2} \, dx \qquad (2\text{-}245)$$

or, if $f_i(t) = u(t)$

$$f_o(t) = \frac{2}{\pi \omega_a} \int_{-\infty}^{\infty} u(x) \, \frac{\sin^2 \dfrac{\omega_a}{2}(t - x)}{(t - x)^2} \, dx \qquad (2\text{-}246)$$

The scanning function is now nonnegative and, thus, the response in the vicinity of a discontinuity will be monotonic. Thus, the ripples of the Gibbs' phenomenon are not present.

In many actual systems where the transfer function falls off very rapidly with frequency, the response to a signal with a discontinuity has overshoots and underswings which are very similar to Gibbs' phenomenon. That is even though the transfer function is not exactly equal to $F_a(j\omega)$, the response to a step discontinuity approximates that of Eq. 2–242 in the neighborhood of discontinuities. Often, the ripples of Gibbs' phenomenon are undesirable. One means of eliminating them is to modify the transfer function so that the very rapid fall off is replaced by a more gradual linear one. Of course these statements are only exactly true if we consider $F_a(j\omega)$ and modify it so that $F_b(j\omega)$ results. However, if the transfer function is reduced over some of the lower frequencies so that a more gradual linear fall off results as $\omega$ increases, the overshoots and underswings in the output caused by a discontinuity of the input can be eliminated. This modification can result in other distortions in $f_o(t)$ which may be more undesirable than the overshoots and underswings.

If a system is bandlimited, then, even if the input has a finite discontinuity, the output will be continuous. This can be demonstrated for the transfer function $F_a(j\omega)$ by considering the scanning function of Fig. 2–13, which is finite for all $t$. Thus, as $t$ increases, the area integrated can only increase or decrease continuously. Therefore, $f_0(t)$ will be continuous. We have demonstrated this for a particular bandlimited transfer function. However, this demonstration was only based on the fact that the scanning function is finite. Hence, it is true for all *finite* bandlimited transfer functions since their inverse Fourier transforms, which are the scanning functions, are finite. Note that a finite *bandlimited* function will always be such that

$$\int_{-\infty}^{\infty} |F(j\omega)| \, d\omega = \int_{-\omega_a}^{\omega_a} |F(j\omega)| \, d\omega$$

will be finite, since the limits of integration are finite. Hence, the inverse Fourier transform of $F(j\omega)$ will be finite (see Section 2-8). In general, the convolution of two finite functions (which we use to obtain the response) will be continuous for the reasons presented in this paragraph.

## 2-14. LEAST SQUARES ERROR PROPERTY OF FOURIER TRANSFORM

When a function $f_1(t)$ is transmitted through a bandlimited system, the output $f_2(t)$ will, in general, differ from the input (see Section 2-13). Often, we do not wish the form of the output to be different from that of the input. Thus, we can state that the system introduces an error. This error is a function of time and is given by

$$\varepsilon(t) = f_1(t) - f_2(t) \tag{2–247}$$

Let $f_1(t) \leftrightarrow F_1(j\omega)$ and assume that $F_1(j\omega)$ is bandlimited by a system whose transfer function is $F_a(j\omega)$ (see Fig. 2–12). Then, if $f_2(t) \leftrightarrow F_2(j\omega)$,

$$F_2(j\omega) = \begin{cases} F_1(j\omega), & -\omega_a \leq \omega \leq \omega_a \\ 0, & |\omega| > \omega_a \end{cases} \tag{2–248}$$

Since $F_2(j\omega)$ differs from $F_1(j\omega)$, then $f_2(t)$ differs from $f_1(t)$, and the error defined in Eq. 2–247 results. If the output of the bandlimited system is passed through another system, the spectrum can be modified further. For instance, consider Fig. 2–15, where $H_c(j\omega)$ is the transfer function of the added system. Let us now determine if the inclusion of such an additional system $H_c(j\omega)$, which changes the Fourier spectrum for $-\omega_a \leq \omega \leq \omega_a$, can correct the frequency response in the sense that it reduces the error. In general, a variation in the Fourier spectrum may reduce the error for one value of time but increase it for another. To determine if an improvement has been made, we must develop an error criterion which gives a *single* figure of merit based on $\varepsilon(t)$. We then must find a corrective $H_c(j\omega)$ which

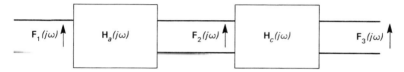

Note: $F_3(j\omega) = H_c(j\omega) F_2(j\omega) = H_a(j\omega) H_c(j\omega) F_1(j\omega)$

FIG. 2–15

Cascading of two systems where $F_3(j\omega) = H_c(j\omega) F_2(j\omega) = H_a(j\omega) H_c(j\omega) F_1(j\omega)$

minimizes this figure of merit. Let us now consider several figures of merit. One would be the *maximum error*; that is,

$$\varepsilon_{max} = |\varepsilon(t)|_{max} = |f_1(t) - f_2(t)|_{max} \qquad (2\text{–}249)$$

In this case, the criterion is defined as a minimization of $\varepsilon_{max}$ which is the largest magnitude of $\varepsilon(t)$. Another figure of merit is the *average error*. This is obtained by averaging the magnitude of the error over all time.

$$\varepsilon_{av} = \int_{-\infty}^{\infty} |\varepsilon(t)| \, dt \qquad (2\text{–}250)$$

Note that a magnitude of the error is chosen such that positive and negative errors do not cancel each other. Taking the magnitude often proves cumbersome and makes integration difficult.

Another figure of merit which eliminates this problem is called the *mean square error*. In this case, the square of the error is averaged; that is,

$$\varepsilon_{MS} = \int_{-\infty}^{\infty} \varepsilon^2(t) \, dt \qquad (2\text{–}251)$$

In general, if we apply a correction to the system which minimizes one figure of merit, it will *not* minimize the others.

There are many error criteria and, in general, they are not equivalent. The one that should be used is the one which best suits the problem. All of these criteria have some practical validity. The maximum error of Eq. 2–249 is useful since the maximum difference between the desired signal and the actual one is limited. For instance, consider that the system under consideration is an oscilloscope amplifier. If $\varepsilon_{max}$ is used as the error criterion and it is much less than the width of the electron beam impinging on the face of the cathode ray tube screen, then, for all practical purposes, the error will not be noticeable. The mean square criterion of Eq. 2–251 is often used when energy is a consideration. It is also often used since, mathematically, it is the most easily applied criterion. However, this should not be an overriding consideration (although it often is). Actually, the mean square error criterion is the only one for which we can simply obtain some general results for the problem of minimizing errors due to bandlimiting.

Now suppose the Fourier spectrum of a signal is bandlimited, as indicated in

Eq. 2–248. What, if any, should be the modification in $F_2(j\omega)$ to reduce the mean square error between $f_1(t)$ and $f_2(t)$? That is (see Fig. 2–15), if $H_a(j\omega)$ is given by

$$H_a(j\omega) = \begin{cases} 1, & -\omega_a \leq \omega \leq \omega_a \\ 0, & |\omega| > \omega_a \end{cases} \tag{2-252}$$

what should be the value of $H_c(j\omega)$ such that the mean square error is reduced? In other words, find $H_c(j\omega)$ such that

$$\varepsilon_{MS} = \int_{-\infty}^{\infty} [f_1(t) - f_3(t)]^2 \, dt \tag{2-253}$$

is minimized. (Note that $f_3(t)$ is used as the output signal.) The Fourier transform of $f_1(t)$ is $F_1(j\omega)$ which we assume is not bandlimited. Rearranging Eq. 2–253, we have

$$\varepsilon_{MS} = \int_{-\infty}^{\infty} |f_1(t)|^2 \, dt - 2 \int_{-\infty}^{\infty} f_1(t) f_3(t) \, dt + \int_{-\infty}^{\infty} |f_3(t)|^2 \, dt \tag{2-254}$$

where we have assumed that $f_1(t)$ and $f_3(t)$ are real. Applying Parseval's theorem (see Eqs. 2–228 and 2–233) yields

$$\varepsilon_{MS} = \frac{1}{2\pi} \int_{-\infty}^{\infty} |F_1(j\omega)|^2 \, d\omega - \frac{1}{\pi} \int_{-\omega_a}^{\omega_a} F_1(j\omega) F_3^*(j\omega) \, d\omega$$
$$+ \frac{1}{2\pi} \int_{-\omega_a}^{\omega_a} |F_3(j\omega)|^2 \, d\omega \tag{2-255}$$

where we have used the notation

$$f_1(t) \leftrightarrow F_1(j\omega)$$
$$f_3(t) \leftrightarrow F_3(j\omega)$$

Note that the limits of integration in the last two integrals of Eq. 2–255 are $-\omega_a$ and $\omega_a$ since $F_3(j\omega) = 0$ for $|\omega| > \omega_a$. This is true since $H_a(j\omega)$ eliminates all frequencies above $\omega_a$ (see Eq. 2–252). We can obtain a somewhat different form of Eq. 2–255 by again applying Eq. 2–228 to the second integral of Eq. 2–254, but now considering that the integrand is $f_3(t) f_1(t)$. This yields

$$\varepsilon_{MS} = \frac{1}{2\pi} \int_{-\infty}^{\infty} |F_1(j\omega)|^2 \, d\omega - \frac{1}{\pi} \int_{-\omega_a}^{\omega_a} F_1^*(j\omega) F_3(j\omega) \, d\omega$$
$$+ \frac{1}{2\pi} \int_{-\omega_a}^{\omega_a} |F_3(j\omega)|^2 \, d\omega \tag{2-256}$$

Adding Eqs. 2–255 and 2–256, and dividing by 2, we have

$$\varepsilon_{MS} = \frac{1}{2\pi} \int_{-\infty}^{\infty} |F_1(j\omega)|^2 \, d\omega + \frac{1}{2\pi} \int_{-\omega_a}^{\omega_a} [-F_1(j\omega) F_3^*(j\omega)$$
$$- F_1^*(j\omega) F_3(j\omega) + |F_3(j\omega)|^2] \, d\omega$$

Breaking the first integral into three parts and combining terms yields

$$\varepsilon_{MS} = \frac{1}{2\pi} \int_{-\infty}^{-\omega_a} |F_1(j\omega)|^2 \, d\omega + \frac{1}{2\pi} \int_{\omega_a}^{\infty} |F_1(j\omega)|^2 \, d\omega + \frac{1}{2\pi} \int_{-\omega_a}^{\omega_a} [\,|F_1(j\omega)|^2$$

$$- F_1(j\omega) F_3^*(j\omega) - F_1^*(j\omega) F_3(j\omega) + |F_3(j\omega)|^2\,]\, d\omega \qquad (2\text{-}257)$$

Noting that $|F(j\omega)|^2 = F(j\omega) F^*(j\omega)$, we obtain

$$\varepsilon_{MS} = \frac{1}{2\pi} \int_{-\infty}^{-\omega_a} |F_1(j\omega)|^2 \, d\omega + \frac{1}{2\pi} \int_{\omega_a}^{\infty} |F_1(j\omega)|^2 \, d\omega$$

$$+ \frac{1}{2\pi} \int_{-\omega_a}^{\omega_a} [F_1(j\omega) - F_3(j\omega)] [F_1^*(j\omega) - F_3^*(j\omega)] \, d\omega \qquad (2\text{-}258)$$

We wish to choose $F_3(j\omega)$ such that this expression is minimized. Since $H_a(j\omega)$ bandlimits $F_1(j\omega)$ (see Eq. 2-252),

$$F_2(j\omega) = \begin{cases} F_1(j\omega), & -\omega_a \leq \omega \leq \omega_a \\ 0, & |\omega| > \omega_a \end{cases} \qquad (2\text{-}259)$$

Then, $H_c(j\omega)$ must be chosen to modify $F_2(j\omega)$ in the range $-\omega_a \leq \omega \leq \omega_a$ such that the resultant $F_3(j\omega)$ minimizes Eq. 2-258. Once the $F_3(j\omega)$ which minimizes Eq. 2-258 is determined, we can then find the $H_3(j\omega)$, which produces the desired $F_3(j\omega)$ by using the relation

$$H_3(j\omega) = \frac{F_3(j\omega)}{F_2(j\omega)} = \frac{F_3(j\omega)}{F_1(j\omega)}, \qquad -\omega_a \leq \omega \leq \omega_a \qquad (2\text{-}260)$$

Since $f_1(t)$ is given, $F_1(j\omega)$ is fixed. Thus, the first two integrals of Eq. 2-258 are fixed. Therefore, to minimize $\varepsilon_{MS}$, we must minimize the last integral. The two bracketed terms of this integrand are complex conjugates. Thus, we can write the last integral as

$$\frac{1}{2\pi} \int_{-\omega_a}^{\omega_a} [F_1(j\omega) - F_3(j\omega)] [F_1^*(j\omega) - F_3^*(j\omega)] \, d\omega$$

$$= \frac{1}{2\pi} \int_{-\omega_a}^{\omega_a} |F_1(j\omega) - F_3(j\omega)|^2 \, d\omega \qquad (2\text{-}261)$$

Since the integrand is a magnitude, *the minimum value that the integral can have is zero.* This value is achieved if we set

$$F_3(j\omega) = F_1(j\omega) \qquad (2\text{-}262)$$

Thus, this $F_3(j\omega)$ minimizes the mean square error.

Let us now consider the physical significance of this. From Eq. 2-260, we have

$$H_3(j\omega) = 1, \qquad -\omega_a \leq \omega \leq \omega_a$$

That is, to minimize the mean square error $\varepsilon_{MS}$, we *leave the bandlimited spectrum unchanged*. This is an important property of the Fourier transform. If a Fourier spectrum is truncated as in Eq. 2–259, then *no modification should be made in the Fourier spectrum, if the minimum mean square error in the time response is desired*. Thus, no corrective network such as $H_c(j\omega)$ in Fig. 2–15 should be used to reduce the mean square error.

If other error criteria are used, this would *not* be true. For instance, if the error criterion was such that there is no overshoot in response to a discontinuity, then the spectrum would be modified as in Section 2-13. In general, error criteria which minimize $|\varepsilon(t)|_{max}$ tend to reduce overshoot. (At a discontinuity, the response is given by Eq. 2–95. Thus, the maximum error cannot be minimized *at* the time of the discontinuity. However, it can be minimized over all time which does not include a neighborhood of the discontinuity.) However, when a mean square error criterion is used, the overshoot may not be reduced even though $\varepsilon_{MS}$ is.

Consider the Gibbs' phenomenon produced by the transfer function of Eq. 2–234. As $\omega_a$ is increased, the width of the overshoots and undershoots are reduced *but their amplitude is unchanged* (see Section 2-5). Then, as $\omega_a$ increases, $\varepsilon_{MS}$ is reduced because the area of the ripples decreases even though the maximum overshoot is unchanged. Thus, the choice of error criterion and the resultant selection of a corrective network can greatly change the form of the output signal.

## 2-15. FOURIER SERIES

We shall obtain the Fourier transform of a *periodic function of time*. That is we shall develop the *Fourier series*. A periodic function is one which satisfies, for all time

$$f(t + T) = f(t) \tag{2–263}$$

where $T$ is a constant called the *period* of the function ($f_0 = 1/T$ is called the *frequency* of the function). Often, in elementary systems of network analysis texts, the Fourier series is discussed first and then the Fourier transform is obtained by generalizing it. However, periodic functions which have a Fourier series are just a subset of all the functions of time that posses Fourier transforms. Hence, the Fourier series is just a special case of the Fourier integral. Thus, it is logical to develop the Fourier series as a special case of the Fourier transform.

Let us assume that $f(t)$ is periodic and obtain its Fourier transform. We shall first consider a special function [3] and obtain its inverse Fourier transform. This will be used to obtain the general Fourier series. This special function is defined as

$$\omega_0 S_{\omega_0}(\omega) = \omega_0 \sum_{n=-\infty}^{\infty} \delta(\omega - n\omega_0) \tag{2–264}$$

Note that $S_{\omega_0}(\omega) = \sum_{n=-\infty}^{\infty} \delta(\omega - n\omega_0)$; that is $S_{\omega_0}(\omega)$ consists of an infinite sequence of impulse functions each displaced by $\omega_0$, where $\omega_0$ is a constant defined in terms of the period of the given periodic function $f(t)$ as

$$\omega_0 = \frac{2\pi}{T} \tag{2-265}$$

Now, let us obtain the inverse Fourier transform of $\omega_0 S_{\omega_0}(\omega)$. From Eq. 2–62, we have

$$\omega_0 S_{\omega_0}(\omega) \leftrightarrow \frac{\omega_0}{2\pi} \int_{-\infty}^{\infty} \sum_{n=-\infty}^{\infty} \delta(\omega - n\omega_0) e^{j\omega t} \, d\omega \tag{2-266}$$

We obtain this integral by a limit process. Define

$$g_N(t) = \frac{\omega_0}{2\pi} \int_{-\infty}^{\infty} \sum_{n=-N}^{N} \delta(\omega - n\omega_0) e^{j\omega t} \, d\omega \tag{2-267}$$

Then,

$$\lim_{N \to \infty} g_N(t) \leftrightarrow \omega_0 S_{\omega_0}(\omega) \tag{2-268}$$

Since the summation of Eq. 2–267 is finite, we can interchange the order of summation and integration; thus,

$$g_N(t) = \frac{\omega_0}{2\pi} \sum_{n=-N}^{N} \int_{-\infty}^{\infty} \delta(\omega - n\omega_0) e^{j\omega t} \, d\omega$$

Integrating and substituting Eq. 2–265, we have

$$g_N(t) = \frac{1}{T} \sum_{n=-N}^{N} e^{jn\omega_0 t} \tag{2-269}$$

We shall express this summation in closed form. Consider the following Taylor's series

$$\frac{1}{1 - e^{j\omega_0 t}} = 1 + e^{j\omega_0 t} + e^{j2\omega_0 t} + e^{j3\omega_0 t} + \cdots \tag{2-270}$$

Then,

$$\frac{e^{-jN\omega_0 t}}{1 - e^{j\omega_0 t}} = e^{-jN\omega_0 t} + e^{-j(N-1)\omega_0 t} + \cdots + 1 + e^{j\omega_0 t} + \cdots$$

$$+ e^{jN\omega_0 t} + e^{j(N+1)\omega_0 t} + \cdots \tag{2-271a}$$

and

$$\frac{e^{j(N+1)\omega_0 t}}{1 - e^{j\omega_0 t}} = e^{j(N+1)\omega_0 t} + e^{j(N+2)\omega_0 t} + \cdots$$

Then subtracting Eq. 2–271b from Eq. 2–271a, we obtain

$$\frac{e^{-jN\omega_0 t} - e^{j(N+1)\omega_0 t}}{1 - e^{-j\omega_0 t}} = \sum_{n=-N}^{N} e^{jN\omega_0 t} \tag{2-272}$$

Substituting in Eq. 2–269, we have

$$g_N(t) = \frac{1}{T} \frac{e^{-jN\omega_0 t} - e^{j(N+1)\omega_0 t}}{1 - e^{j\omega_0 t}}$$

Multiplying numerator and denominator by $e^{-j\omega_0 t/2}$ yields

$$g_N(t) = \frac{1}{T} \frac{e^{-j(N+\frac{1}{2})\omega_0 t} - e^{j(N+\frac{1}{2})\omega_0 t}}{e^{-j\omega_0 t/2} - e^{j\omega_0 t/2}} \qquad (2\text{–}273)$$

Substituting Euler's relation, we obtain

$$g_N(t) = \frac{1}{T} \frac{\sin(N+\frac{1}{2})\omega_0 t}{\sin(\omega_0 t/2)} \qquad (2\text{–}274)$$

This is a periodic function whose period is given by Eq. 2–265. This can be verified by replacing $t$ by $t + T$ in Eq. 2–275 and noting that the new function is equivalent to the original one. The details of this will be left to the reader. Now, to determine the inverse Fourier transform of $\omega_0 S_{\omega_0}(\omega)$, we must take $\lim\limits_{N\to\infty} g_N(t)$, see Eq. 2–268.

Let us rewrite Eq. 2–274 in the following way

$$g_N(t) = \frac{\sin(N+\frac{1}{2})\omega_0 t}{tT} \frac{t}{\sin(\omega_0 t/2)} \qquad (2\text{–}275)$$

We need only study this in the range

$$-\frac{T}{2} \leqq t \leqq \frac{T}{2} \qquad (2\text{–}276)$$

since $g_N(t)$ is periodic with period $T$. Thus, all other periods are replicas of this one. In the range of relation 2–276, $t/\sin(\omega_0 t/2)$ is bounded. Now let us study $\lim\limits_{N\to\infty} \sin(N+\frac{1}{2})\omega_0 t/\pi t$. From Eq. 2–53, we have

$$\lim_{N\to\infty} \frac{\sin Nt}{\pi t} = \delta(t) \qquad (2\text{–}277)$$

Then, considering that as $N$ approaches $\infty$ so does $(N+\frac{1}{2})\omega_0$, we obtain

$$\lim_{N\to\infty} \frac{\sin(N+\frac{1}{2})\omega_0 t}{Tt} = \frac{\pi}{T}\delta(t) \qquad (2\text{–}278)$$

Hence,

$$\lim_{N\to\infty} g_N(t) = \frac{\pi}{T}\delta(t) \frac{t}{\sin(\omega_0 t/2)}, \qquad -\frac{T}{2} \leqq t \leqq \frac{T}{2} \qquad (2\text{–}279)$$

Then, using Eq. 2–174, and the relation

$$\lim_{t\to 0} \frac{t}{\sin(\omega_0 t/2)} = \frac{2}{\omega_0}$$

and also Eq. (2–265), we obtain

$$\lim_{N \to \infty} g_N(t) = \delta(t), \qquad -\frac{T}{2} \leq t \leq \frac{T}{2} \qquad (2\text{–}280)$$

Since $g_N(t)$ is periodic with period $T$, we must repeat this impulse every $T$ seconds; thus,

$$\lim_{N \to \infty} g_N(t) = \sum_{n=-\infty}^{\infty} \delta(t - nT) \qquad (2\text{–}281)$$

Compare this with Eq. 2–264. This has a form which is very similar to $S_{\omega_0}(\omega)$ except that $\omega$ is replaced by $t$ and $\omega_0$ by $T$. Therefore, we can write $\lim_{N \to \infty} g_N(t) = S_T(t)$. Then, substituting in Eq. 2–268, we have

$$S_T(t) \leftrightarrow \omega_0 S_{\omega_0}(\omega) \qquad (2\text{–}282)$$

where

$$S_T(t) = \sum_{n=-\infty}^{\infty} \delta(t - nT) \qquad (2\text{–}283)$$

Now, let us return to a development of the Fourier series. We are working with a periodic function of time $f(t)$ (see Eq. 2–263). Let us define a new function $f_0(t)$ in the following way

$$f_0(t) = \begin{cases} f(t), & -\frac{T}{2} \leq t \leq \frac{T}{2} \\[2mm] 0, & |t| > \frac{T}{2} \end{cases} \qquad (2\text{–}284)$$

That is, $f_0(t) = f(t)$ over one cycle and is zero elsewhere. Let $F_0(j\omega)$ be the Fourier transform of $f_0(t)$

$$f_0(t) \leftrightarrow F_0(j\omega) \qquad (2\text{–}285)$$

Now let us express $f(t)$ in terms of $f_0(t)$. This can be done by means of convolution in the following way:

$$f(t) = f_0(t) * S_T(t) \qquad (2\text{–}286)$$

We can demonstrate this with the following:

$$f_0(t) * S_T(t) = \int_{-\infty}^{\infty} f_0(x) \sum_{n=-\infty}^{\infty} \delta(t - x - nT)\, dx$$

Inverting the order of summation and integration (again a limit process can be used here), we obtain

$$f_0(t) * S_T(t) = \sum_{n=-\infty}^{\infty} \int_{-\infty}^{\infty} f_0(x) \delta(t - x - nT)\, dx$$

Using Eq. 2–6, we have

$$f_0(t) * S_T(t) = \sum_{n=-\infty}^{\infty} f_0(t - nT) \qquad (2\text{--}287)$$

This just consists of an infinite sum of many $f_0(t)$, each displaced in time from the others by $nT$; i.e., an integral multiple of a period. Since $f_0(t)$ only is nonzero for one period, $f(t)$ is reconstructed. Then, applying the convolution theorem to Eq. 2–286, we have

$$f(t) \leftrightarrow \omega_0 F_0(j\omega) S_{\omega_0}(\omega) \qquad (2\text{--}288)$$

Thus, we have obtained the Fourier spectrum of a periodic function in terms of the Fourier spectrum of the nonperiodic $f_0(t)$. Substituting Eq. 2–264 yields

$$f(t) \leftrightarrow \omega_0 F_0(j\omega) \sum_{n=-\infty}^{\infty} \delta(\omega - n\omega_0) = \sum_{n=-\infty}^{\infty} \omega_0 F_0(j\omega) \delta(\omega - n\omega_0)$$

Following a development similar to that of Eq. 2–174 we obtain the following: The product of an ordinary function and an impulse is equal to the value that the ordinary function has when the impulse occurs, times the impulse; hence,

$$f(t) \leftrightarrow \omega_0 \sum_{n=-\infty}^{\infty} F_0(jn\omega_0) \delta(\omega - n\omega_0) \qquad (2\text{--}289)$$

Note that $F_0(j\omega)$ will be continious since $f_0(t) = 0 \; |t| > T$. Thus, the Fourier spectrum of a periodic function of time consists of a sum of impulse functions displaced in frequency by $\omega_0$. Note that the spectrum is discrete since it is zero except at the points where the impulse occurs. This is diagrammatically illustrated in Fig. 2–16. This type of spectrum corresponds to the usual representation of the Fourier series when the function is represented as a sum of sinusoids. Note that the Fourier transform of a sinusoid is a pair of impulse functions (see Table 2–1).

Now let us relate Eq. 2–289 to the conventional representation of the Fourier series. Take the inverse Fourier transform of the right-hand side of Eq. 2–289. This yields

$$f(t) = \frac{\omega_0}{2\pi} \int_{-\infty}^{\infty} \sum_{n=-\infty}^{\infty} F_0(jn\omega_0) \delta(\omega - n\omega_0) e^{j\omega t} \, d\omega$$

Interchanging the order of integration and summation, as before, we have

$$f(t) = \frac{1}{T} \sum_{n=-\infty}^{\infty} F_0(jn\omega_0) e^{jn\omega_0 t} \qquad (2\text{--}290)$$

To be consistant with standard Fourier series notation, let

$$c_n = F_0(jn\omega_0) \qquad (2\text{--}291a)$$

Hence,

$$f(t) = \frac{1}{T} \sum_{n=-\infty}^{\infty} c_n e^{jn\omega_0 t} \qquad (2\text{--}291b)$$

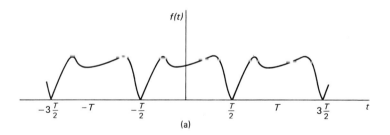

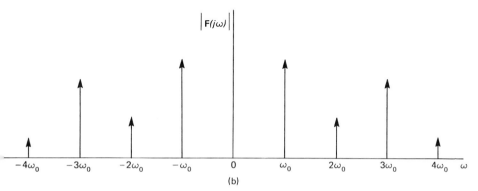

FIG. 2-16

(a) Periodic function of time; (b) typical Fourier spectrum of a periodic function (relative amplitudes of impulses correspond to magnitudes of $F(jn\omega_0)$)

Since $f_0(t)$ is zero for $|t| > T/2$ (see Eq. 2–284), its Fourier transform is

$$F_0(j\omega) = \int_{-T/2}^{T/2} f_0(t)\, e^{-j\omega t}\, d\omega$$

In the range $-T/2 \leqq t \leqq T/2$, $f_0(t) = f(t)$; thus,

$$c_n = F_0(jn\omega_0) = \int_{-T/2}^{T/2} f(t)\, e^{-jn\omega_0 t}\, dt \qquad (2\text{--}292)$$

Equations 2–290 and 2–292 are the conventional ones for the exponential form of the Fourier series. Hence, we have developed the Fourier series as a special case of the Fourier integral.

We can obtain the sine and cosine forms of the Fourier series by writing

$$c_n = a_n - jb_n \qquad (2\text{--}293)$$

From Eq. 2–292, we have

$$c_n^* = c_{-n} = a_n + jb_n$$

Then, substituting in Eq. 2–291b and noting that $\cos x = \cos(-x)$ and that $\sin x = -\sin(-x)$, we obtain

$$f(t) = \frac{1}{T} + \frac{1}{T} \sum_{n=1}^{\infty} a_n \cos n\omega_0 t + b_n \sin n\omega_0 t \qquad (2\text{–}294)$$

Rearranging Eq. 2–292, we have

$$a_n = \int_{-T/2}^{T/2} f(t) \cos n\omega_0 t \, dt \qquad (2\text{–}295a)$$

$$b_n = \int_{-T/2}^{T/2} f(t) \sin n\omega_0 t \, dt \qquad (2\text{–}295b)$$

Equations 2–294 and 2–295 give the sine and cosine form of the Fourier series.

Since the Fourier series is a special case of the Fourier integral, we can apply all the general results obtained for the Fourier integral to the Fourier series. For instance, if the Fourier series is truncated after a finite number of terms, the minimum mean square error results if the coefficients calculated by Eq. 2–292 or 2–295 are *not* changed. In addition, there will be Gibbs' phenomenon in the vicinity of a discontinuity. The Gibbs' phenomenon can be eliminated by reducing the coefficients in accordance with Section 2-13. The discussions of Sections 2-9 and 2-10 are also applicable here (e.g., if $f(t)$ is even, then all $b_n = 0$).

It is assumed that the reader is familiar with basic operations with the Fourier series so they will not be repeated.

## 2-16. POISSON'S SUM FORMULA

A periodic function of time $f(t)$ can be represented using the nonperiodic function $f_0(t)$, which is defined in Eq. 2–284. This representation is given in Eq. 2–287 as

$$f(t) = \sum_{n=-\infty}^{\infty} f_0(t - nT) \qquad (2\text{–}296)$$

where $T$ is the period of $f(t)$. Substituting in Eq. 2–290, we have

$$\sum_{n=-\infty}^{\infty} f_0(t - nT) = \frac{1}{T} \sum_{n=-\infty}^{\infty} F_0(jn\omega_0) e^{jn\omega_0 t} \qquad (2\text{–}297)$$

where

$$f_0(t) \leftrightarrow F_0(j\omega)$$

Equation 2–297 is just a statement of the Fourier series. However, *it is valid even if $f(t)$ is not periodic.* That is, if $f(t)$ is not a periodic function of time and

$$f(t) \leftrightarrow F(j\omega)$$

then

$$\sum_{n=-\infty}^{\infty} f(t - nT) = \frac{1}{T} \sum_{n=-\infty}^{\infty} F(jn\omega_0) e^{jn\omega_0 t} \qquad (2\text{–}298)$$

where $T$ is an *arbitrary* real constant and

$$\omega_0 = \frac{2\pi}{T} \tag{2-299}$$

Note that $T$ can be any finite real constant and it is not the period since $f(t)$ need not be periodic. To derive Eq. 2-298, let us take the convolution of $f(t)$ and $S_T(t)$ (see Eq. 2-283). This yields

$$f(t) * S_T(t) = \int_{-\infty}^{\infty} f(x) \sum_{n=-\infty}^{\infty} \delta(t - nT - x)\, dx \tag{2-300}$$

Interchanging the order of integration and summation, as in Section 2-15, we have

$$f(t) * S_T(t) = \sum_{n=-\infty}^{\infty} f(t - nT) \tag{2-301}$$

Now, using the convolution theorem (see Eqs. 2-209 and 2-282), we obtain

$$\sum_{n=-\infty}^{\infty} f(t - nT) \leftrightarrow \omega_0 F(j\omega) S_{\omega_0}(j\omega) \tag{2-302}$$

Substituting Eq. 2-264 and taking the inverse Fourier transform, we have

$$\sum_{n=-\infty}^{\infty} f(t - nT) = \frac{\omega_0}{2\pi} \int_{-\infty}^{\infty} F(j\omega) \sum_{n=-\infty}^{\infty} \delta(\omega - n\omega_0) e^{j\omega t}\, d\omega$$

Interchanging the order of summation and integration as before; and substitution of Eq. 2-299 yields

$$\sum_{n=-\infty}^{\infty} f(t - nT) = \frac{1}{T} \sum_{n=-\infty}^{\infty} F(jn\omega_0) e^{jn\omega_0 t} \tag{2-303}$$

which is the relation which we set out to prove. Equation 2-303 is called the *Poisson sum relation*.

If $f(t)$ is discontinuous and if any of the $t - nT$ fall at a discontinuity, then the value of $f(t)$ to be used in this summation is the average of the values on either side of the discontinuity (see Eq. 2-79).

An alternative form of Eq. 2-303 can be obtained by noting that, in the summation of Eq. 2-301, $n$ takes on all values both positive and negative; hence,

$$\sum_{n=-\infty}^{\infty} f(t - nT) = \sum_{n=-\infty}^{\infty} f(t + nT)$$

Thus, we can write

$$\sum_{n=-\infty}^{\infty} f(t + nT) = \frac{1}{T} \sum_{n=-\infty}^{\infty} F(jn\omega_0) e^{jn\omega_0 t} \tag{2-304}$$

A special case occurs if we let $t = 0$; thus, substituting in Eq. 2-304, we obtain

$$\sum_{n=-\infty}^{\infty} f(nT) = \frac{1}{T} \sum_{n=-\infty}^{\infty} F(jn\omega_0) \tag{2-305}$$

Relations between various infinite series can be obtained with the Poisson sum formula. For example (see Table 2-1),

$$u(t)\, e^{-\beta t} \leftrightarrow \frac{1}{\beta + j\omega}$$

Substituting in Eq. 2–303, we have

$$\frac{1}{2} + \sum_{n=1}^{\infty} e^{-\beta n T} = \frac{1}{T} \sum_{n=-\infty}^{\infty} \frac{1}{\beta + jn\omega_0} \qquad (2\text{–}306\text{a})$$

Note that $u(0) = 1/2$ (see Eq. 2–77). We can rewrite Eq. 2–306a by making use of the fact that

$$\frac{1}{\beta + jn\omega_0} + \frac{1}{\beta - jn\omega_0} = \frac{2\beta}{\beta^2 + n^2\omega_0^2}$$

Substituting in Eq. 2–306a, we obtain

$$\frac{1}{2} + \sum_{n=1}^{\infty} e^{-\beta n T} = \frac{1}{\beta T} + \frac{2}{T} \sum_{n=1}^{\infty} \frac{\beta}{\beta^2 + n^2\omega_0^2} \qquad (2\text{–}306\text{b})$$

If $\beta = 2$ and $T = 1$, we have

$$\sum_{n=1}^{\infty} e^{-2n} = \sum_{n=1}^{\infty} \frac{1}{1 + n^2\pi^2} \qquad (2\text{–}306\text{c})$$

Similarly, relations between other series can be obtained using Poisson's sum formula.


## 2-17. SHANNON'S SAMPLING THEOREM

Compare two signals $f_1(t)$ and $f_2(t)$ which are of essentially the same magnitude. If $f_1(t)$ varies at a much more rapid rate than $f_2(t)$, then, in general, the Fourier spectrum of $f_1(t)$ will contain larger high-frequency components than will the Fourier spectrum of $f_2(t)$. That is, all other things being equal, rapid variations in the signal are obtained from high-frequency sinusoidal components. Conversely, if a signal is bandlimited, as in Section 2-13, then its variation with time is restricted. These remarks are very unrigorous and are just given to provide the reader with a feel for the situation. In this section we shall rigorously develop a theorem called *Shannon's sampling theorem* [4] which mathematically demonstrates the effect of bandlimiting on a signal. We shall prove that such a signal can be completely determined from a set of discrete samples.

Let us now consider the Shannon's theorem. It states that: *if*

$$f(t) \leftrightarrow F(j\omega)$$

*and*

$$|F(j\omega)| = 0, \qquad |\omega| \geq \omega_a \qquad (2\text{–}307)$$

*then*

$$f(t) = \sum_{n=-\infty}^{\infty} f\left(n\,\frac{\pi}{\omega_a}\right) \frac{\sin(\omega_a t - n\pi)}{\omega_a t - n\pi} \qquad (2\text{–}308)$$

Thus, to completely determine $f(t)$, we need only know the values of $f(n\pi/\omega_a)$; i.e., the values of $f(t)$ at *discrete values of time spaced* $\pi/\omega_a$ *seconds apart*. Note that an infinite set of points is required.

Before we derive this theorem, consider the Fourier spectrum $F(j\omega)$. It is zero for $|\omega| > \omega_a$ (see Eq. 2–307). We form a new function $F_P(j\omega)$ which is defined by

$$F_P(j\omega) = F(j\omega), \qquad -\omega_a \leq \omega \leq \omega_a \qquad (2\text{–}309a)$$

$$F_P[j(\omega + 2\omega_a)] = F_P(j\omega) \qquad (2\text{–}309b)$$

Here, $F_P(j\omega) = F(j\omega)$ in the range $-\omega_a \leq \omega \leq \omega_a$. However, $F_P(j\omega)$ is periodic in $\omega$ with period $2\omega_a$. An illustration of an $F(j\omega)$ and the $F_P(j\omega)$ formed from it is shown in Fig. 2–17. Normally, we consider functions which are periodic in the time domain and express them in terms of a Fourier series. However, because of the symmetry of the Fourier transform (see Eq. 2–188), the periodic $F_P(j\omega)$ can be expanded in a Fourier series also. This development parallels that given in Section 2–15 and will not be repeated. Here, we shall just state the results. If $F_P(j\omega)$ is periodic with period $\Omega$, then we can write

$$F_P(j\omega) = \sum_{n=-\infty}^{\infty} C_n e^{-jn2\pi\omega/\Omega} \qquad (2\text{–}310)$$

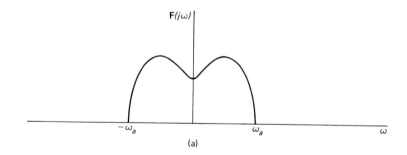

(a)

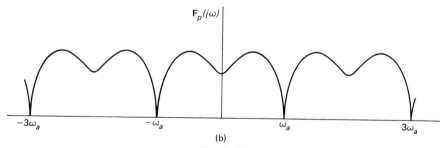

(b)

Fɪɢ. 2–17

(a) Bandlimited Fourier spectrum; (b) periodic spectrum $F_P(j\omega)$ obtained from $F(j\omega)$

where

$$C_n = \frac{1}{\Omega} \int_{-\Omega/2}^{\Omega/2} F_P(j\omega)\, e^{jn2\pi\omega/\Omega}\, d\omega \tag{2-311}$$

For the case, which we are studying, $\Omega = 2\omega_a$; thus,

$$F_P(j\omega) = \sum_{n=-\infty}^{\infty} C_n e^{-jn\pi\omega/\omega_a} \tag{2-312a}$$

and

$$C_n = \frac{1}{2\omega_a} \int_{-\omega_a}^{\omega_a} F(j\omega)\, e^{jn\pi\omega/\omega_a}\, d\omega \tag{2-312b}$$

We can use $F(j\omega)$ instead of $F_P(j\omega)$ in Eq. 2–312b since $F_P(j\omega) = F(j\omega)$ for $-\omega_a \leqq \omega \leqq \omega_a$.

Now we shall develop the sampling theorem. Since $f(t) \leftrightarrow F(j\omega)$ and the Fourier spectrum is bandlimited as in Eq. 2–307, we have for the inverse Fourier transform of $F(j\omega)$

$$f(t) = \frac{1}{2\pi} \int_{-\omega_a}^{\omega_a} F(j\omega)\, e^{j\omega t}\, d\omega \tag{2-313}$$

Since $F(j\omega) = F_P(j\omega)$ for $\omega_a \leqq \omega \leqq \omega_a$ and $F(j\omega) = 0$ for $|\omega| > \omega_a$, we can write

$$F(j\omega) = F_a(j\omega)\, F_P(j\omega) \tag{2-314}$$

where $F_a(j\omega)$ is the bandlimiting spectrum given in Fig. 2–12. Comparing Eqs. 2–312b and 2–313, we have

$$C_n = \frac{\pi}{\omega_a} f\left(\frac{n\pi}{\omega_a}\right) \tag{2-315}$$

Substituting of Eqs. 2–315 and 2–312a into Eq. 2–314 yields

$$F(j\omega) = \frac{\pi}{\omega_a} \sum_{n=-\infty}^{\infty} f\left(\frac{n\pi}{\omega_a}\right) F_a(j\omega)\, e^{-jn\pi\omega/\omega_a} \tag{2-316}$$

Using Eq. 2–62, we obtain the inverse transform of $F(j\omega)$

$$f(t) = \frac{1}{2\pi} \int_{-\infty}^{\infty} \sum_{n=-\infty}^{\infty} \frac{\pi}{\omega_a} f\left(\frac{n\pi}{\omega_a}\right) F_a(j\omega)\, e^{-jn\pi\omega/\omega_a}\, e^{j\omega t}\, d\omega$$

Note that $f(n\pi/\omega_a)$ is not a function of $\omega$. The inverse Fourier transform of $F_a(j\omega)$ is given in Eq. 2–190. Then, interchanging the order of summation and integration, (see Section 2-15) and using Eq. 2–171, we obtain

$$f(t) = \sum_{n=-\infty}^{\infty} f\left(\frac{n\pi}{\omega_a}\right) \frac{\sin(\omega_a t - n\pi)}{\omega_a t - n\pi} \tag{2-317}$$

This is the result we set out to prove.

Thus, we have shown that a bandlimited signal can be completely determined from a set of samples spaced $\pi/\omega_a$ seconds apart. This result is very important and is used in studying the transmission of information in bandlimited systems.

The converse of Shannon's sampling theorem also is true. That is, if $f(t)$ can be expressed as Eq. 2–317, then the Fourier spectrum of $f(t)$ will be bandlimited; i.e., $F(j\omega) = 0$ for $|\omega| > \omega_a$. Note that

$$\frac{\sin(\omega_a t - n\pi)}{\omega_a t - n\pi} \leftrightarrow \frac{\pi}{\omega_a} F_a(j\omega) e^{-jn\pi\omega/\omega_a}$$

where $F_a(j\omega)$ is the bandlimited spectrum given in Fig. 2–12. Thus, the spectrum of $f(t)$ will be bandlimited.

Often, we are given an $f(t)$ which has an infinite spectrum and we wish to approximate it with a function $f_a(t)$. The Fourier spectrum of $f_a(t)$ should be bandlimited. The optimum bandlimited $f_a(t)$ depends upon the criterion used. For instance, if a mean square error criterion is applied, then the Fourier spectrum is simply truncated (see Section 2-14).

Consider another procedure which yields a bandlimited approximation. In this case, we desire that $f_a(t)$ exactly equal $f(t)$ at a discrete set of points:

$$f_a(n\pi/\omega_a) = f(n\pi/\omega_a) \tag{2–318}$$

where $n$ is *any* integer.

To accomplish this, we define $f_a(t)$ using Eq. 2–317:

$$f_a(t) = \sum_{n=-\infty}^{\infty} f\left(\frac{n\pi}{\omega_a}\right) \frac{\sin(\omega_a t - n\pi)}{\omega_a t - n\pi} \tag{2–319}$$

The discussion of the last paragraph indicates that this is bandlimited. Note that if we substitute $t = k\pi/\omega_a$, where $k$ is an integer, we obtain

$$f_a\left(\frac{k\pi}{\omega_a}\right) = f\left(\frac{k\pi}{\omega_a}\right)$$

(The details of this substitution are left to the reader.) Thus, we have achieved the desired approximation. Since $f(t)$ is not bandlimited, it will, in general, not be equal to $f_a(t)$ except at the discrete points given in Eq. 2–318. The procedure whereby a bandlimited signal approximates one which is not bandlimited in the sense of Eq. 2–318 is called *bandlimited interpolation*.

The practical implications of Shannon's sampling theorem are extremely important. Suppose that we want to transmit a telephone conversation. We need only sample it at discrete intervals. Thus, a continuous conversation can be transmitted by a set of discrete pulses spaced $\pi/\omega_a$ seconds apart. A second sampled conversation can be transmitted by transmitting its pulses, spaced $\pi/\omega_a$ seconds apart, in the "spaces between the pulses" of the first conversation. In this way, many conversations can be transmitted over the same pair of telephone wires.

Samples pulses can be encoded in such a way that signals can be transmitted in the presence of noise. Such encoding can also reduce the effects of distortion (see Sections 9-2 through 9-5).

## 2-18. NUMERICAL INTEGRATION

In the remainder of this chapter, we shall consider procedures for the evaluation of the Fourier integral using the digital computer. In this section we shall consider a simple procedure for evaluating definite integrals. In the next section we shall discuss how this can be applied to the evaluation of the Fourier transform. It will be pointed out that this simple procedure presents some difficulties and an alternate procedure will be developed. In Section 2-20, we shall extend this (alternate) procedure to one which is still better suited to the evaluation of the Fourier transform.

Before considering the computer program to evaluate an integral, we present a numerical integration procedure called the *trapezoidal rule*. We choose this method because it is simple and often gives good results. (Other procedures are given in the numerical analysis texts in the bibliography at the end of the chapter.)

In the trapezoidal rule, a curve is approximated by confluent straight line segments whose intersections lie on the curves (see Fig. 2–18). Suppose we wish to evaluate

$$y = \int_{x_a}^{x_b} f(x)\,dx \qquad (2\text{-}320)$$

Then, the interval between $x_a$ and $x_b$ is divided into $N$ areas of equal width. Let the "width" of the area be

$$\Delta x = \frac{x_b - x_a}{N} \qquad (2\text{-}321)$$

Then, we define the following:

$$x_0 = x_a$$

$$x_1 = x_0 + \Delta x$$

$$x_2 = x_0 + 2\Delta x$$

$$\vdots$$

$$x_k = x_0 + k\Delta x \qquad (2\text{-}322)$$

$$\vdots$$

$$x_N = x_0 + N\Delta x = x_b$$

Straight line segments are drawn between each pair of adjacent $f(x_k)$ and $f(x_{k+1})$ as shown in Fig. 2–18. These straight line segments are used to approximate the curve for $f(x)$. Thus, the integral of Eq. 2–320 is approximated by the area under the straight line segments. In general, the accuracy of the approximation increases as $N$ is increased. Let us now compute the area under the straight line segments. The total area in Fig. 2–18 is composed of the sum of many trapezoidal area. The area of a trapezoid (see Fig. 2–19), is $(a + b)\,c/2$. Thus, for Fig. 2–18,

$$\int_{x_a}^{x_b} f(x)\,dx \approx \left[ \frac{f(x_0) + f(x_1)}{2} + \frac{f(x_1) + f(x_2)}{2} + \frac{f(x_2) + f(x_3)}{2} \right.$$

$$\left. + \cdots + \frac{f(x_{n-1}) + f(x_n)}{2} \right] \Delta x$$

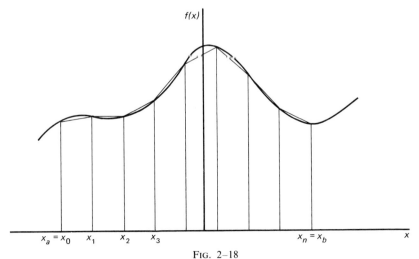

FIG. 2-18

Approximation of a curve by straight line segments

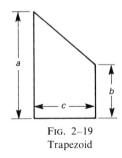

FIG. 2-19

Trapezoid

where $\Delta x$ is given in Eq. 2-321. Combining terms, we have

$$\int_{x_a}^{x_b} f(x)\,dx \approx \left[\frac{f(x_0)}{2} + f(x_1) + f(x_2) + f(x_3)\right.$$

$$\left. + \cdots + f(x_{N-1}) + \frac{f(x_N)}{2}\right]\Delta x \qquad (2\text{-}323)$$

This can be written in compact form as

$$\int_{x_a}^{x_b} f(x)\,dx = -\frac{[f(x_0) + f(x_N)]\Delta x}{2} + \sum_{n=0}^{N} f(x_n)\,\Delta x \qquad (2\text{-}324)$$

The limits of integration must be finite if a numerical integration procedure is to be used. If the limits of integration are infinite then an infinite number of calculations would have to be made. However, there are times when we desire to evaluate integrals which have infinite limits. This is especially true in the case of the Fourier transform. To evaluate such integrals using numerical methods, we must approximate the infinite range of integration by a finite one. Of course, this introduces an error. If the integrand falls off rapidly enough for large $|x|$, the error can easily be bounded. For instance consider

$$y = \int_0^\infty e^{-x} \cos 3x^2 \sin x^3 \, dx$$

We approximate this by

$$y_Y = \int_0^Y e^{-x} \cos 3x^2 \sin x^3 \, dx$$

The error that results from this approximation is

$$\varepsilon(Y) = \int_Y^\infty e^{-x} \cos 3x^2 \sin x^3 \, dx$$

Applying Eq. 2–140 and noting that

$$|\cos 3x^2| \le 1$$

and

$$|\sin x^3| \le 1$$

we obtain

$$|\varepsilon(Y)| \le \int_Y^\infty e^{-x} \, dx = e^{-Y}$$

(Note that $e^{-x} = |e^{-x}|$ for real $x$.) Thus, we have bounded the error caused by assuming that the upper limit is finite. Now, we choose $Y$ sufficiently large so that the bound on the error given by $e^{-Y}$ is acceptably small. Note that we can bound the error without having to evaluate the original integral. In general, if

$$y = \int_0^\infty f(x) \, dx \tag{2–325}$$

and we approximate this by

$$y_Y = \int_0^Y f(x) \, dx \tag{2–326}$$

then the resultant error is

$$\varepsilon(Y) = \int_Y^\infty f(x) \, dx \tag{2–327}$$

If we can find a function $g(x)$ which can be integrated in closed form and is such that

$$|f(x)| \le g(x), \qquad x \ge Y \tag{2–328}$$

then the error can be bounded by

$$|v(Y)| \le \int_Y^\infty g(x)\,dx \qquad (2\text{-}329)$$

Since $g(x)$ can be integrated in closed form, the bound on the error is easily obtained. Thus, a value of $Y$, which insures that the error will be sufficiently small, is used. Then Eq. 2–326 is evaluated using numerical analysis procedures.

The computer program, which we use to implement the trapezoidal integration process, is called TRPINT (see Fig. 2–20). It is given in SUBROUTINE form. The values of $x_0$, $x_N$, and $N$ are entered using the SUBROUTINE name. $\Delta x$ is calculated in line 30. The *integrand* is obtained using a FUNCTION. This is listed in lines 170–200. In this case, we have chosen the integrand as $(\sin x)/x$.

The integration procedure will follow Eq. 2–324. The quantity $[f(x_0) + f(x_N)]\,\Delta x/2$ is calculated in line 40. Lines 50, 60, and the DO loop (lines 70–120) compute the summation of Eq. 2–324. This summation is multiplied by $\Delta x$ in line 130. Finally, the value of the integral is obtained in line 140.

The value of the integrand is given in line 180. To change the integrand (i.e., to integrate a different function) this line must be changed. Most timesharing systems have simple editing procedures that allow this to be done easily. In a batch processed program, a single card must be changed.

```
00010              SUBRØUTINE TRPINT(XO,XN,N,ANS)
00020              AN=N
00030              DELTX=(XN-XO)/AN
00040              B=(FX(XO)+FX(XN))*DELTX/2.
00050              Z=0.
00060              Y=FX(XO)
00070              DØ 100 I=1,N
00080              AI=I
00090              XI=XO+DELTX*AI
00100              Z=FX(XI)
00110              Y=Y+Z
00120        100   CØNTINUE
00130              YB=Y*DELTX
00140              ANS=YB-B
00150              RETURN
00160              END
00170              FUNCTIØN FX(X)
00180              FX=SIN(X)/X
00190              RETURN
00200              END
```

(a)

FIG. 2–20(a)

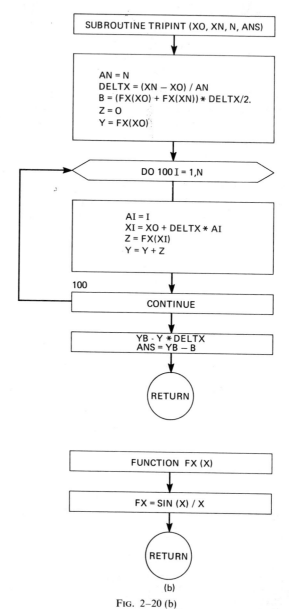

FIG. 2-20 (b)

Fig. 2-20 (b)

(a) SUBROUTINE TRPINT in this case sin $x/x$ is integrated. To change the integrand change line 180; (b) flow chart of TRPINT

After the integral is evaluated, it should be re-evaluated using a larger value of $N$. If the two answers are substantially different, then too small a value of $N$ has been chosen. The value of $N$ should be increased until the point where substantial increases in $N$ do not change the computed value of the integral. The value of $N$ which must be used depends upon $f(x)$. If the slope of $f(x)$ varies rapidly with $x$, then $N$ must be large. In general, $N$ should be large enough so that the straight line segments closely approximate the curve. If the slope of $f(x)$ changes rapidly, then many points will be needed for a close approximation of curve, since it ripples up and down rapidly.

For the particular function that we are integrating, there may be a problem if the range of integration includes $x = 0$ since the denominator of $(\sin x)/x$ becomes zero; i.e., we are dividing by zero. Even though $(\sin x)/x$ is bounded at $x = 0$, many computers do not allow this operation to occur. The user should check his computer manual in such cases. If an integral from 0 to $Y$ is desired, it can be approximated by replacing the lower limit by a small value. For the integrand in question, most computers will perform satisfactorily if the lower limit is $10^{-6}$ or even less. In such cases, E rather than F notation should be used ($10^{-6} = 1.0$ E-6).

## 2-19. NUMERICAL EVALUATION—THE DISCRETE FOURIER TRANSFORM—THE BINARY NUMBER SYSTEM

The numerical integration procedures developed in the last section can be applied to evaluation of the direct and inverse Fourier transform. However, there are better means of evaluating them. Here we shall use the trapezoidal integration procedure as an introduction and then present a better technique. Consider the numerical evaluation of the direct Fourier transform of Eq. 2–61. The evaluation of the inverse Fourier transform (see Eq. 2–62) will follow on a dual basis.

The integrand of Eq. 2–61 is complex. A simple procedure for its evaluation is to break it into the sum of two real integrals (see Eq. 2–154). Thus, we have

$$F(j\omega) = R(\omega) + jX(\omega) \tag{2–330}$$

where

$$R(\omega) = \int_{-\infty}^{\infty} f(t) \cos \omega t \, dt \tag{2–331a}$$

and

$$X(\omega) = -\int_{-\infty}^{\infty} f(t) \sin \omega t \, dt \tag{2–331b}$$

Each of these integrals can be evaluated using TRPINT (see Fig. 2–20). For instance, if $f(t) = e^{-at}$ then, to evaluate Eq. 2–331a, line 180 of TRPINT is replaced by these three lines

AX $= -a * $X

WX $= \omega_0 * $X

FX $=$ EXP (AX) cos (WX)

where $\omega_0$ is a particular value of $\omega$, and $a$ is the given numerical value. Note that $a$ and $\omega_0$ are actual real numbers, not variables (AX $= -2.*$X). Then $R(\omega_0)$ is evaluated. This procedure must be repeated using all the values of $\omega_0$ that are desired so the second line must be changed each time $\omega_0$ is changed. The program can be modified by the inclusion of a DO loop so that $\omega_0$ is automatically varied. (This modification will be left to the reader.) The integral of Eq. 2–331a has an infinite limit. However, the procedure discussed in Section 2-18 can be used to change it to a finite value.

In general, as $\omega_a$ increases, the variation of $f(t) \cos \omega_a t$ or $f(t) \sin \omega_a t$ increases. Thus, if the accuracy of the numerical integration is to remain constant, $\Delta x$ must be made smaller as $\omega_a$ increases (see Section 2-18). Equivalently, $N$ (see Eq. 2–321) must be made larger.

FORTRAN IV has provision for working with complex numbers directly. This allows $F(j\omega)$ to be evaluated in one step. In this case, the complex variables must be declared. For example, to evaluate Eq. 2–61, TRPINT would be modified in the following way. A statement immediately following line 10 would be

COMPLEX ANS, Y, Z, B, YB, FX

Call this line 15. Line 170 would be changed to read

COMPLEX FUNCTION FX (X)

Note that FX is declared complex in line 15 even though it is also declared complex in the function name. (This need not, and should not, be done with all compilers.) Immediately following (the new) line 170 would be the following lines:

COMPLEX XA
XB $= -1.*\omega_0*$X
XA $=$ CMPLX (0.,XB)
AX $= -1.*$X$*a$

Then line 180 is replaced by

FX $=$ EXP (AX)$*$CEXP (XA)

Note that, as before, $\omega_0$ and $a$ are real numbers and not variables. Let us explain these modifications. First, XA is declared to be complex. Then, CEXP is a built-in FORTRAN IV SUBROUTINE which yields the complex value of an exponential. Note that it does not have to be declared complex. However, XA must be declared to be a complex variable. Then we calculate XB $= -\omega_0 t$; i.e., $-\omega_0 x$. Then, in the next line, $x_a$ is set equal to $0 - j\omega t = 0 - j\omega_0 x$. Note that CMPLX indicates that the two values enclosed in the parentheses are the real and imaginary part of the complex variable. If A, B, and C are all complex variables (which have been so declared and defined) a valid FORTRAN statement is C $=$ A$*$B. Finally, FX is calculated as $e^{-ax} e^{-j\omega_0 x} = e^{-at} e^{-j\omega_0 t}$. The integral is then evaluated as before.

Complex numbers actually consist of two parts; e.g., $x = 1 + j2$. Hence, in FORMAT statements, provision must be made for two numbers. For use in TRPINT, if ANS is a complex number, then the following statement could be used to print the data

TYPE 1, ANS

1 FORMAT ('ANS = ', 2E10.3)

The remaining details of the modification of the program will be left to the reader.

**Discrete Fourier Transform.** When numerical methods are applied to the evaluation of the Fourier transform, $F(j\omega)$ is obtained only at a discrete set of points. The numerical integration only uses a discrete set of values of $f(t)$. Thus, a discrete set of points in the time domain transforms into a discrete set of points in the frequency domain and vice versa. This transform is called the *discrete Fourier transform.* Although the numerical integration which we have discussed can be used to obtain the discrete Fourier transform, other procedures, which require less computation, are available. We shall discuss some of these procedures here. To simplify the analysis, we shall modify the numerical integration procedure somewhat as shown in Fig. 2–21. This figure illustrates

$$\int_{x_a}^{x_b} f(x)\, dx$$

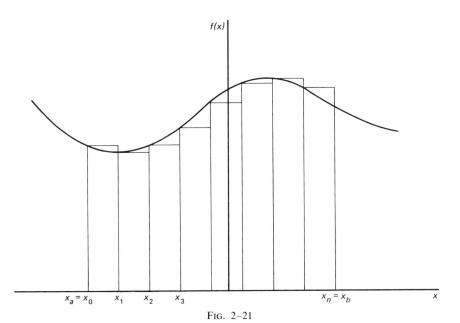

FIG. 2–21

Approximation to a curve using horizontal and vertical line segments

where $x_a = x_0$ and $x_b = x_N$. Instead of using a trapezoidal approach, $f(x)$ is assumed to be constant at $f(x_k)$ for $x_k \leq x \leq x_{k+1}$; that is,

$$f(x) = f(x_k), \qquad x_k \leq x \leq x_{k+1} \tag{2-332}$$

This approximation may not appear to be as good as the trapezoidal one (see Fig. 2–18). However, when very many samples are used, both approximations can be very good. Then, if the curve is divided into $N$ equal areas,

$$\Delta x = \frac{x_b - x_a}{N} = \frac{x_N - x_0}{N} \tag{2-333}$$

The area of the $k$th rectangle is $f(x_{k-1})\,\Delta x$. Hence, the approximate form of the integral is given by

$$\int_{x_a}^{x_b} f(x)\,dx = \Delta x \sum_{n=0}^{N-1} f(x_n) \tag{2-334}$$

Applying this to the Fourier transform of Eq. 2–61, we have

$$F(j\omega) = \Delta t \sum_{n=-N/2}^{N/2-1} f(t_n)\,e^{-j\omega t_n} \tag{2-335}$$

Note that we have chosen $N$ as an even number so that we could integrate symmetrically about $t = 0$. For most practical cases, $f(t) = 0$ for $t < 0$. In such cases, we integrate from $t = 0$ to $t = \infty$. Thus, the approximation is of the form

$$F(j\omega) = \Delta t \sum_{k=0}^{N-1} f(t_k)\,e^{-j\omega t_k} \tag{2-336}$$

(Recall that the approximation of infinite integrals by integrals with finite limits was discussed in Section 2-18.) Proceeding in a similar fashion, we can approximate the inverse Fourier transform of Eq. 2–62 by

$$f(t) = \frac{1}{2\pi} \Delta\omega \sum_{n=-N/2}^{N/2-1} F(j\omega_n)\,e^{j\omega_n t} \tag{2-337}$$

where

$$\Delta\omega = \frac{2\omega_{N/2}}{N} \tag{2-338}$$

We have chosen $N$ to be the same in the frequency and time domains. This will simplify the analysis. To evaluate Eq. 2–336, we only require discrete values of $f(t)$, i.e., $f(t_k)$. Similarly, only a discrete set of $F(j\omega_n)$ are needed in Eq. 2–337. The discrete Fourier transform form usually takes this into account, and Eqs. 2–336 and 2–337 are written as

$$F(j\omega_n) = \Delta t \sum_{k=0}^{N-1} f(t_k)\,e^{-j\omega_n t_k} \tag{2-339a}$$

$$f(t_k) = \frac{1}{2\pi} \Delta\omega \sum_{n=-N/2}^{N/2-1} F(j\omega_n) e^{j\omega_n t_k} \qquad (2\text{--}339\text{b})$$

It may appear as though Eqs. 2–339 are limited, since they only calculate their respective functions at discrete values. However, the summations represent approximations; thus, it would be unreasonable to use them to calculate an infinite number of values. For instance, $F(j\omega)$ calculated using Eq. 2–339a will probably be equal to the actual $F(j\omega)$ only at a discrete set of points.

Now let us consider a procedure for evaluating Eq. 2–339a. However, the application of these results to Eq. 2–339b is essentially the same, hence the details will be left to the reader.

First we shall relate $\Delta\omega$ and $\Delta t$. Let $T$ be the entire time integrated:

$$T = t_N - t_0 \qquad (2\text{--}340)$$

Hence,

$$\Delta t = \frac{T}{N} \qquad (2\text{--}341)$$

We are sampling the signal every $\Delta t$ seconds. Then, from Shannon's sampling theorem (Eq. 2–308), the maximum bandwidth of the signal $\omega_a$ is given by $\pi/\omega_a = \Delta t$ or $\omega_a = \pi/\Delta t$. Since we have chosen $N$ samples in both the time and frequency domains, $\omega_a = N\Delta\omega/2$. (Note that there are both positive and negative values of $\omega$) Equating these two values of $\omega_a$, we obtain

$$\Delta\omega = \frac{2\pi}{N\Delta t}$$

Substituting Eq. 2–341, we have

$$\Delta\omega = \frac{2\pi}{T} \qquad (2\text{--}342)$$

We shall make the substitutions

$$t_k = k\Delta t \qquad (2\text{--}343\text{a})$$

$$\omega_n = n\Delta\omega \qquad (2\text{--}343\text{b})$$

Substituting Eqs. 2–341 through 2–343 in Eqs. 2–339, we have

$$F(j\omega_n) = \Delta t \sum_{k=0}^{N-1} f(k\Delta t) e^{-j2\pi kn/N} \qquad (2\text{--}344\text{a})$$

$$f(t_k) = \frac{\Delta\omega}{2\pi} \sum_{n=-N/2}^{N/2-1} F(jn\Delta\omega) e^{j2\pi kn/N} \qquad (2\text{--}344\text{b})$$

Note that $F(j\omega)$ is only nonzero for $-\omega_a \leq \omega \leq \omega_a$. Thus, this limitation should be included in addition to Eq. 2–344a. We do not write it there for convenience as we shall now discuss.

Now we shall make use of the fact that the *expression* of Eq. 2–344a is periodic in $n$ with period $N$. Note that $n$ only occurs in the exponent. Replace $n$ by $n + N$; this yields

$$\frac{2\pi k(n + N)}{N} = \frac{2\pi kn}{N} + 2\pi k$$

Thus, $F(j\omega)$ has the period $N$. We can write Eq. 2–344b as

$$f(t_k) = \frac{\Delta\omega}{2\pi} \left[ \sum_{n=0}^{N/2-1} F(jn\Delta\omega)\, e^{j2\pi kn/N} + \sum_{-N/2}^{-1} F(jn\Delta\omega)\, e^{2\pi kn/N} \right]$$

Now consider the second summation. Because of the periodicity of Eq. 2–344a, we can write

$$F\left[ j\left(-\frac{N}{2} + a\right)\Delta\omega \right] = F\left[ j\left(\frac{N}{2} + a\right)\Delta\omega \right]$$

In addition.

$$e^{j2\pi k[-(N/2)+a]/N} = (-1)^k e^{j2\pi ka/N} = e^{j2\pi k[(N/2)+a]/N}$$

Thus, the summation from $-N/2$ to $-1$ can be replaced by one from $N/2$ to $N-1$. Hence, Eq. 2–344b can be written as

$$f(t_k) = \frac{\Delta\omega}{2\pi} \sum_{n=0}^{N-1} F(jn\Delta\omega)\, e^{j2\pi kn/N} \tag{2–345}$$

When $F(jn\Delta\omega)$ is considered for $0 \leq n \leq N-1$, it will be symmetric about the frequency corresponding to $n = N/2$. Note that $F(j\omega)$ is actually symmetric about $\omega = 0$. The frequency $(N/2)\Delta\omega$ is called the *aliasing frequency* or the *Nyquist folding frequency*. Remember that the actual $F(j\omega)$ exists for $-\omega_a \leq \omega \leq \omega_a$ and the one for $0 \leq \omega \leq 2\omega_a$ gives the proper results, but actually is just a mathematical convenience.

For purposes of abbreviation, we use the following notation:

$$f_k = \Delta t f(k\Delta t) \tag{2–346a}$$

$$F_n = F(jn\Delta\omega) \tag{2–346b}$$

$$f'_k = f(k\Delta t) \tag{2–346c}$$

$$F'_n = \frac{\Delta\omega}{2\pi} F(jn\Delta\omega) \tag{2–346d}$$

Substituting in Eqs. 2–344a and 2–345, we obtain

$$F_n = \sum_{k=0}^{N-1} f_k e^{-(j2\pi/N)nk} \tag{2–347}$$

$$f'_k = \sum_{n=0}^{N-1} F'_n e^{(j2\pi/N)kn} \tag{2–348}$$

Consider the solution of Eq. 2–347. (The solution of Eq. 2–348 proceeds on a dual basis.) Now let

$$W = e^{-j2\pi/N} \tag{2-349}$$

Then,

$$F_n = \sum_{k=0}^{N-1} f_k W^{nk} \tag{2-350}$$

In general, for all $N$ values of $F_n$, we can write

$$
\begin{aligned}
F_0 &= W^{0(0)} f_0 + W^{0(1)} f_1 + \cdots + W^{0(N-1)} f_{N-1} \\
F_1 &= W^{1(0)} f_0 + W^{1(1)} f_1 + \cdots + W^{1(N-1)} f_{N-1} \\
&\text{- - - - - - - - - - - - - - - - - - - - - - - - - - - - - - - - -} \\
F_{N-1} &= W^{(N-1)(0)} f_0 + W^{(N-1)(1)} f_1 + \cdots + W^{(N-1)(N-1)} f_{N-1}
\end{aligned}
\tag{2-351}
$$

We can write this in matrix form as

$$\hat{F} = \hat{W}\hat{f} \tag{2-352}$$

where

$$
F = \begin{bmatrix} F_0 \\ F_1 \\ \vdots \\ \hat{F}_{N-1} \end{bmatrix}
\tag{2-353a}
$$

$$
f = \begin{bmatrix} f_0 \\ f_1 \\ \vdots \\ f_{N-1} \end{bmatrix}
\tag{2-353b}
$$

and

$$
W = \begin{bmatrix}
W^{0(0)} & W^{0(1)} & \cdots & W^{0(N-1)} \\
W^{1(0)} & W^{1(1)} & \cdots & W^{1(N-1)} \\
\hline
W^{(N-1)(0)} & W^{(N-1)(1)} & \cdots & W^{(N-1)(N-1)}
\end{bmatrix}
\tag{2-353c}
$$

As an example, assume that $N = 4$. Then, carrying out the indicated multiplications in the exponent, we have

$$
\begin{bmatrix} F_0 \\ F_1 \\ F_2 \\ F_3 \end{bmatrix}
=
\begin{bmatrix}
W^0 & W^0 & W^0 & W^0 \\
W^0 & W^1 & W^2 & W^3 \\
W^0 & W^2 & W^4 & W^6 \\
W^0 & W^3 & W^6 & W^9
\end{bmatrix}
\begin{bmatrix} f_0 \\ f_1 \\ f_2 \\ f_3 \end{bmatrix}
\tag{2-354}
$$

We can simplify the previous result by noting the facts that, when $N = 4$, $W = e^{j2\pi/4}$; then,

$$W^0 = e^{-j0} = 0 \tag{2-355a}$$

$$W^1 = e^{-j2\pi/4} = e^{-j\pi/2} = W^1 \tag{2-355b}$$

$$W^2 = e^{-j4\pi/4} = e^{-j\pi} = W^2 \tag{2-355c}$$

$$W^3 = e^{-j6\pi/4} = e^{-j3\pi/2} = W^3 \tag{2-355d}$$

$$W^4 = e^{-j8\pi/4} = e^{-j2\pi} = W^0 \tag{2-355e}$$

$$W^5 = e^{-j10\pi/4} = e^{-j\pi/2} = W^1 \tag{2-355f}$$

$$W^6 = e^{-j12\pi/4} = e^{-j\pi} = W^2 \tag{2-355g}$$

$$W^7 = e^{-j14\pi/4} = e^{-j3\pi/2} = W^3 \tag{2-355h}$$

$$W^8 = e^{-j16\pi/4} = e^{-j2\pi} = W^0 \tag{2-355i}$$

$$W^9 = e^{-j18\pi/4} = e^{-j\pi/2} = W^1 \tag{2-355j}$$

Thus, Eq. 2-354 can be written as

$$\begin{bmatrix} F_0 \\ F_1 \\ F_2 \\ F_3 \end{bmatrix} = \begin{bmatrix} 1 & 1 & 1 & 1 \\ 1 & W^1 & W^2 & W^3 \\ 1 & W^2 & W^0 & W^2 \\ 1 & W^3 & W^2 & W^1 \end{bmatrix} \begin{bmatrix} f_0 \\ f_1 \\ f_2 \\ f_3 \end{bmatrix} \tag{2-356}$$

Hence, we need not compute any power of $W$ higher than the third.

In the previous example we have demonstrated that only $N$ powers of $W$ were required: $W^0$, $W^1$, $W^2$, and $W^3$. Now let us determine a general expression for the high powered $W$'s in terms of the lower powered ones.

$$W^{nk} = e^{-j(2\pi/N)nk}$$

Now consider the fraction $nk/N$. Let us write this as

$$nk/N = Q + \frac{R}{N} \tag{2-357}$$

where $Q$ is the quotient and is an integer. Then, $R$ is the remainder. It is important to note that $R < N$; thus,

$$W^{-nk} = e^{-j[2\pi Q + j2\pi(R/N)]} = e^{-j2\pi R/N} = W^{-R} \tag{2-358}$$

We define $R$ as $nk$ modulo $N$; that is, if $A/B = Q + R/B$, where $Q$ is an integer and $R < B$, then we have

$$R = A \text{ modulo } B$$

Modulo is a built-in SUBROUTINE in FORTRAN IV. The statement used to obtain $R$ is

$$C = NA*K$$
$$R = AMOD(C, N)$$

Note that NA is the FORTRAN designation we have used for $n$ since N is the total number of samples. In FORTRAN IV, AMOD, C, and N are all real numbers. (For integers, use MOD (I, K). It might appear as though a program to implement the calculation of the discrete Fourier transform should be given here. However, in the next section, we shall modify this procedure, which will lend itself more readily to actual calculations.

**Binary and Octal Number Systems.** Before proceeding with modifications of the procedure for obtaining the discrete Fourier transform, let us digress and discuss number systems. These will be used in part of our future discussion. The conventional number system is the decimal system which uses 10 integers (0, 1, 2, 3, 4, 5, 6, 7, 8, 9). Digital computers basically utilize either the presence or absence of signals. Hence, there are only two digits used. This is called the *binary* number system where the digits 0 and 1 are used. Another system used in computers is the *octal number system* with digits 0, 1, 2, 3, 4, 5, 6, 7. Table 2-2 compares the various number systems.

TABLE 2–2

| Decimal | Octal | Binary |
|---------|-------|--------|
| 0 | 0 | 0 |
| 1 | 1 | 1 |
| 2 | 2 | 10 |
| 3 | 3 | 11 |
| 4 | 4 | 100 |
| 5 | 5 | 101 |
| 6 | 6 | 110 |
| 7 | 7 | 111 |
| 8 | 10 | 1000 |
| 9 | 11 | 1001 |
| 10 | 12 | 1010 |
| 11 | 13 | 1011 |
| 12 | 14 | 1100 |
| 13 | 15 | 1101 |
| 14 | 16 | 1110 |
| 15 | 17 | 1111 |
| 16 | 20 | 10000 |
| 17 | 21 | 10001 |

The rules are essentially the same in all number systems; only the number of symbols is limited. Thus, in octal, $6 + 1 = 7$ but $7 + 2 = 11$ since the digits 8 and 9 are not allowed. Similarly, in binary $10 + 1 = 11$ but $11 + 1 = 100$, since only 0 and 1 are allowed.

Now let us consider a general procedure for converting a number in binary form to one in digital form. We shall write the binary number as

$$b_n \ldots b_2 \, b_1 \, b_0 \tag{2–359}$$

For instance, for the binary number 101, we will have

$$b_0 = 1$$
$$b_1 = 0$$
$$b_2 = 1$$

The decimal number that corresponds to 101 is 5 (see Table 2-2). This can be written as

$$5 = 2^2 (1) + 2^1 (0) + 2^0 (1) = 4(1) + 2(0) + 1(1) \tag{2–360}$$

In general, we can write $N_d$, a digital number in terms of a binary number as

$$N_d = 2^n b_n + 2^{n-1} b_{n-1} + \cdots + 2^2 b_2 + 2^1 b_1 + 2^0 b_0 \tag{2–361}$$

Table 2-2 will verify this for $N_d$ up to 17. The first (right most) binary digit represents the number of $2^0$ in the number, the next binary digit represents the number of $2^1$ in the number, etc. This is equivalent to the decimal system, except that powers of ten are involved there.

## 2-20. FAST FOURIER TRANSFORM

We shall now discuss modifications of the procedure for evaluating the discrete Fourier transform which greatly reduce the number of computations involved and, thus, results in a great saving in the computation time. This procedure is called the *Fast Fourier transform* (FFT), which was developed by J.W. Cooley and J.W. Tukey [5]. Hence, the fast Fourier transform is also called the *Cooley-Tukey algorithm*.

To use the FFT, only certain discrete values of $N$, the total number of samples will be allowed. This is done to make the computation simpler. In general, $N$ should be an integral power of 2.

$$N = 2^\gamma \tag{2–362}$$

where $\gamma$ is an integer. The discrete Fourier transform is given by Eq. 2–347

$$F_n = \sum_{k=0}^{N-1} f_k e^{-j(2\pi/N)nk} = \sum_{k=0}^{N-1} f_k W^{nk} \tag{2–363}$$

Now consider discrete Fourier transforms for two other functions. The first is for a set of $N/2$ samples which consist of $f_k$ for all *even* values of $k$. The second transform is a set of $N/2$ samples which consist of $f_k$ for all *odd* values of $k$. Let

$$g_k = f_{2k} \tag{2-364a}$$

and

$$h_k = f_{2k+1}, \qquad k = 0, 1, ..., \frac{N}{2} - 1 \tag{2-364b}$$

Then $g_k$ corresponds to $f_k$ for all even values of $k$ and $h_k$ corresponds to $f_k$ for all odd values of $k$. The discrete Fourier transforms of $g_k$ and $h_k$ are given by

$$G_n = \sum_{k=0}^{(N/2)-1} g_k e^{-j(4\pi/N)nk} \tag{2-365a}$$

$$H_n = \sum_{k=0}^{(N/2)-1} h_k e^{-j(4\pi/N)nk}, \qquad n = 0, 1, ..., \frac{N}{2} - 1 \tag{2-365b}$$

Note that $4\pi/N$ rather than $2\pi/N$ appears in the exponent since $N$ is replaced by $N/2$ in each of these summations. Also note that since $g_k$ has only half of the number of sample points, $G_n$ can only be evaluated for $N/2$ values. A similar statement can be made for $h_k$ and $H_n$. Now let us relate $F_n$ to $G_n$ and $H_n$. First, we substitute the values of $g_k$ and $h_k$ (see Eqs. 2–364) for $f_k$ in the discrete Fourier transform. The indices of summation and the value of the subscripts of the last terms of the summations must be changed since the subscripts of $g_k$ and $h_k$ are different from the corresponding subscripts of $f_k$; thus (see Eq. 2-363),

$$F_n = \sum_{k=0}^{(N/2)-1} g_k e^{-j(2\pi/N)2nk} + \sum_{k=0}^{(N/2)-1} h_k e^{-j(2\pi/N)(2k+1)n} \tag{2-366}$$

Comparing this with Eq. 2–365, we have

$$F_n = G_n + e^{-j(2\pi/N)n} H_n, \qquad n = 0, 1, ..., \frac{N}{2} - 1 \tag{2-367}$$

Since $G_n$ and $H_n$ are only defined by $N/2$ values, they can only be used to define the first $N/2$ values of $F_n$. However, Eq. 2–367 (after the appropriate substitutions are made) yields exactly the same summation as does Eq. 2–363. Thus, if we formally substitute in Eq. 2–367 for values of $n$ between $N/2$ and $N - 1$, the correct results will be obtained. Also, $G_n$ and $H_n$ will themselves be periodic with period $N/2$; hence,

$$G_{(N/2)+n} = G_n \tag{2-368a}$$

$$H_{(N/2)+n} = H_n \tag{2-368b}$$

Then, substituting in Eq. 2–367, we have

$$F_{(N/2)+n} = G_n + e^{-j(2\pi/N)[(N/2)+n]} H_n$$

Rearranging, we have

$$F_{(N/2)+n} = G_n - e^{-j(2\pi/N)n} H_n$$

Substituting Eq. 2–349, we obtain

$$F_n = G_n + W^n H_n, \qquad n = 0, 1, ..., \frac{N}{2} - 1 \qquad (2\text{–}369\text{a})$$

$$F_{(N/2)+n} = G_n - W^n H_n, \qquad \frac{N}{2} + n = \frac{N}{2}, ..., N - 1 \qquad (2\text{–}369\text{b})$$

Note that

$$W^{[r+(N/2)]} = e^{-[j(2\pi/N)][r+(N/2)]} = -e^{-j(2\pi/N)r} = -W^r \qquad (2\text{–}370)$$

Thus, using Eqs. 2–368 and 2–370, Eqs. 2–369 can be written as

$$F_n = G_n + W^n H_n, \qquad n = 0, 1, ..., n - 1 \qquad (2\text{–}371)$$

We have thus expressed the discrete Fourier transform using $N$ samples in terms of two discrete Fourier transforms using $N/2$ samples each. Let us discuss the advantage of doing this. If $N$ samples are used, in general, on the order of $N^2$ arithmetic operations are required to evaluate the discrete Fourier transform. Thus, to evaluate both $G_n$ and $H_n$, we require $2(N/2)^2 = N^2/2$ operations. Therefore, *both* of these transforms can be evaluated using half the operations needed to evaluate $F_n$. In general, $2N$ operations (multiplication and addition) are required to obtain $F_n$ from $G_n$ and $H_n$. However, $(N^2/2) + 2N$ is usually much less than $N^2$ when $N$ is large.

We shall now discuss that the number of operations can still be greatly reduced. Consider $G_n$ and $H_n$. Each of them is the discrete Fourier transform of $g_n$ and $h_n$, respectively. Each of these discrete Fourier transforms can be split into a sum of two transforms corresponding to $N/4$ samples. Similarly each of these transforms can be split into two discrete Fourier transforms, each corresponding to $N/8$ samples each. (This is why $N$ is chosen equal to $2^\gamma$. See Eq. 2–362.) This operation can be repeated until the transform of a one-point function is taken. (The discrete Fourier transform of a one-point function is the function itself, see Eq. 2–363.) This complete operation is the fast Fourier transform (FFT). In general, it can be shown that $\frac{3}{2}N \log_2 N$ arithmetic calculations are required in the FFT while $N^2$ are required in the discrete Fourier transform. This represents a saving of $(1.5 \log_2 N)/N$. For large $N$, this can be substantial. For example, if $N = 1024$, $(1.5 \log_2 N)/N = 0.0146$. Thus, 0.0146 times the computation time of that for the discrete Fourier transform is required to evaluate the FFT if $N = 1024$.

We have considered the general ideas behind the FFT. Now let us discuss the details. To do this, let us assume a specific value of $N$. We shall choose $N = 8$. This is small enough so that the discussion is not cluttered by unnecessary detail and large enough so that the pertinent details can be included. The signal flow graph of Fig. 2–22 [6] will be used to illustrate the first step in the FFT algorithm. The input signals $f_0, f_1$, will be used to illustrate the first step in the FFT algorithm. The input signals $f_0, f_1$, ..., $f_7$ are divided into the odd and even samples and their discrete Fourier transforms

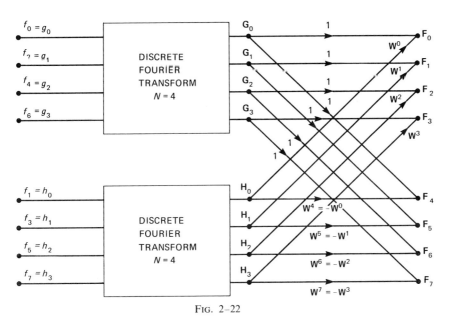

FIG. 2-22

are taken. (Assume that the box in the figure automatically takes the transform.) These are $G_0, G_1, ..., G_4$ and $H_0, H_1, ..., H_4$. Then, $F_0, F_1, ..., F_7$ are calculated according to Eq. 2–371. For example, $F_0 = G_0 + W^0 H_0$, $F_1 = G_1 + W^1 H_1$, etc. Note that, in a signal flow graph, the value of a node is the sum of all the signals (i.e., the input node times the branch transadmittance) of all the branches *incident* on the node. also, the signal flow graph can be simplified (see Eq. 2–370); for example, $W^7 = -W^3$.

In Fig. 2–23, the "FFT Process" is carried one step further. That is each set of inputs $g_0$, $g_1$, $g_2$, and $g_3$ and $h_0$, $h_1$, $h_2$ and $h_3$ of Fig. 2–22 are broken up into odd and even sequences (of two terms each) and their discrete Fourier transforms are taken. This results in $G'_0, G'_1, G''_0, G''_1, H'_0, H'_1, H''_0$, and $H''_1$. Equation 2–371 is then applied to $G'_0, G'_1, G''_0$ and $G''_1$ to obtain $G_0, G_1, G_2$ and $G_3$. Similarly, Eq. 2–371 is applied to the $H'_0, H'_1, H''_0$, and $H''_1$. This is illustrated in the portion of the signal flow graph indicated by Part A. Note that the exponents of $W$ do not seem to agree with those given in Eq. 2–371. If this equation is to be used, $W = e^{-j(2\pi/N)}$, where $N$ is the number of samples. However, at the start, we have 8 samples. The next step results in two sequences of 4 samples each. Hence we should use $W = e^{j2\pi/8}$ for the transform between $F_1 .... F_7$. However, for $G_0 .... G_3$ and $H_0 .... H_3$ in Part A, $W$ should be $e^{j2\pi/4}$ (since there are only four samples in each part). It would be confusing to use two different values for $W$. Hence, we use $W = e^{j2\pi/8}$ throughout the diagram. Therefore, the power of $W$ in part A of Fig. 2–23 appears to be twice the value given by Eq. 2–371.

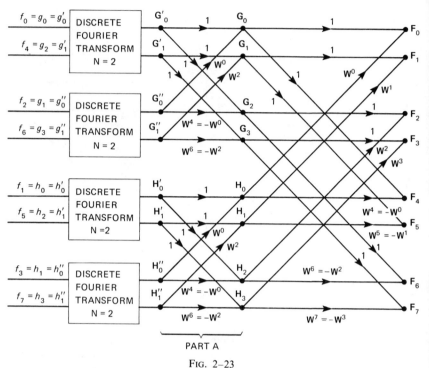

PART A

Fig. 2–23

The representation of Fig. 2–22 carried one step further. Note $W = e^{-j2\pi/8}$

Carrying this procedure to its final step, we break the discrete Fourier transform of two samples into two parts. The transform of a single sample is itself. Hence, applying Eq. 2–371, we obtain Fig. 2–24.

Consider some facts about these signal flow graphs. Pairs of variables are used to calculate other pairs. For instance, $f_0$ and $f_4$ are used to calculate $G'_0$ and $G'_1$ but $f_0$ and $f_4$ *are not used to calculate any other values.* In addition, $f_0$ and $f_4$, but no other variables, are needed to calculate $G'_0$ and $G'_1$. Similarly, $G_2$ and $H_2$ are the only values used to calculate $F_2$ and $F_6$, and $G_2$ and $H_2$ are not used to calculate any other values. This property is very convenient since it reduces the amount of storage required in the computer. For instance, after $G'_0$ and $G'_1$ are calculated, the values of $f_0$ and $f_4$ are *never* needed again. Hence, $G'_0$ and $G'_1$ can be stored in the storage locations used for $f_0$ and $f_4$. Of course, the values of $f_0$ and $f_4$ are then lost. Thus, the storage locations required for the original list of variables can be used to store all the intermediate data and, eventually, the final answers. Clearly, this storage must be for complex numbers.

The value of $f$ (i.e., the data) does not appear in numerical order in the signal flow graph. Let us consider a procedure for obtaining this sequence. First we write the

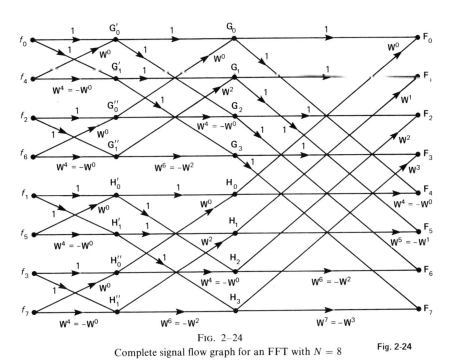

Fig. 2-24

FIG. 2–24

Complete signal flow graph for an FFT with $N = 8$

numbers 0 through 7 in binary form; then we reverse the sequence of the digits and write the decimal number corresponding to the reversed sequence of digits. This is shown in Table 2-3.

TABLE 2–3

| Decimal Number | Binary Number | Reverse Binary Number | Decimal Number Corresponding to Reversed Binary Number |
|---|---|---|---|
| 0 | 000 | 000 | 0 |
| 1 | 001 | 100 | 4 |
| 2 | 010 | 010 | 2 |
| 3 | 011 | 110 | 6 |
| 4 | 100 | 001 | 1 |
| 5 | 101 | 101 | 5 |
| 6 | 110 | 011 | 3 |
| 7 | 111 | 111 | 7 |

(Note that the last column in Table 2-3 is in the order of the input data.) Each binary digit is called a *bit*. The procedure for obtaining the input order is the following:

write the input sequence 0 through 7 in binary numbers, reverse the bits, and use these (reversed) binary numbers to obtain the decimal numbers. (This will be shown subsequently.)

Now let us discuss a mathematical procedure which formally gives us the FFT. From 2–363, we have

$$F_n = \sum_{k=0}^{N-1} f_k W^{nk} \tag{2-372}$$

where

$$W = e^{-j2\pi/N} \tag{2-373}$$

Suppose $N = 8$ and write the subscripts in binary form (see Eq. 2–359); thus,

$$n = 4n_2 + 2n_1 + n_0 \tag{2-374a}$$

$$k = 4k_2 + 2k_1 + k_0 \tag{2-374b}$$

where $n_2, n_1, n_0$ and $k_2, k_1, k_0$ are the binary digits. Let

$$F_n = F(n_2, n_1, n_0) \tag{2-375a}$$

$$f_k = f(k_2, k_1, k_0) \tag{2-375b}$$

Substituting in Eq. 2–372, we obtain

$$F(n_2, n_1, n_0) = \sum_{k_2=0}^{1} \sum_{k_1=0}^{1} \sum_{k_0=0}^{1} f(k_2, k_1, k_0) \, W^{(4k_2 + 2k_1 + k_0)(4n_2 + 2n_1 + n_0)} \tag{2-376}$$

Now let us simplify this:

$$W^{(4k_2 + 2k_1 + k_0)} W^{(4n_2 + 2n_1 + n_0)}$$
$$= W^{(4n_2 + 2n_1 + n_0)4k_2} W^{(4n_2 + 2n_1 + n_0)2k_1} W^{(4n_2 + 2n_1 + n_0)k_0} \tag{2-377}$$

Consider each of the factors on the right-hand side in turn.

$$W^{(4n_2 + 2n_1 + n_0)4k_2} = \left[ W^{8(2n_2 + n_1)k_2} \right] W^{4n_0 k_2} = W^{4n_0 k_2} \tag{2-378a}$$

$$W^{(4n_2 + 2n_1 + n_0)2k_1} = \left[ W^{8n_2 k_1} \right] W^{(2n_1 + n_0)2k_1} = W^{(2n_1 + n_0)2k_1} \tag{2-378b}$$

(Each of the terms enclosed in the brackets equals 1.) For example,

$$W^{8(2n_2 + n_1)k_2} = e^{-j(2\pi/N)(2n_2 + n_1)8k_2}$$

The numbers $n_2$, $n_1$, and $k_2$ can each be either 0 or 1. If $k_2 = 0$, then the exponent is zero. If $n_1$ and $n_2$ are both zero, again the exponent is zero. If *both* $n_1$ and $n_2$ are not zero and $k_2 = 1$, then the exponent is $j2\pi(K)$, where $K$ is an integer. This results in $W = 1$. Substituting in Eq. 2–376, we obtain

$$F(n_2, n_1, n_0)$$
$$= \sum_{k_2=0}^{1} \sum_{k_1=0}^{1} \sum_{k_0=0}^{1} f(k_2, k_1, k_0) \, W^{4n_0 k_2} W^{2k_1(2n_1 + n_0)} W^{k_0(4n_2 + 2n_1 + n_0)} \tag{2-379}$$

Since the sums are finite, we can interchange the order of summation; thus,

$F(n_2, n_1, n_0)$

$$= \sum_{k_0=0}^{1} \sum_{k_1=0}^{1} \sum_{k_2=0}^{1} f(k_2, k_1, k_0) \, W^{4n_0 k_2} \, W^{2k_1(2n_1+n_0)} \, W^{k_0(4n_2+2n_1+n_0)} \qquad (2\text{--}380)$$

Since we now cycle $k_2$ first, then $k_1$, and finally $k_0$, this is equivalent to reversing the order of the bits. Now let us make the following substitutions. Let

$$f_0(k_2, k_1, k_0) = f(k_2, k_1, k_0) \qquad (2\text{--}381\text{a})$$

$$f_1(n_0, k_1, k_0) = \sum_{k_2=0}^{1} f_0(k_2, k_1, k_0) \, W^{4n_0 k_2} \qquad (2\text{--}381\text{b})$$

$$f_2(n_0, n_1, k_0) = \sum_{k_1=0}^{1} f_1(n_0, k_1, k_0) \, W^{2k_1(2n_1+n_0)} \qquad (2\text{--}381\text{c})$$

and

$$f_3(n_0, n_1, n_2) = \sum_{k_0=0}^{1} f_2(n_0, n_1, k_0) \, W^{k_0(4n_2+2n_1+n_0)} \qquad (2\text{--}381\text{d})$$

Thus,

$$F(n_2, n_1, n_0) = f_3(n_0, n_1, n_2)$$

To clarify these substitutions, we reconstruct Fig. 2–24 but now use the notation of Eqs. 2–381. This is done in Fig. 2–25. (This can be verified by substitution in Eqs. 2–381 and comparing with Fig. 2–25.) Higher-ordered signal flow graphs can be obtained by extending this procedure, e.g., for $N = 16$, add a fourth summation, etc.

There is one fact that should be noted about Fig. 2–25. Consider a pair of $f$'s; i.e., $f_0(0)$ and $f_0(4)$, $f_0(3)$ and $f_0(7)$, $f_1(1)$ and $f_1(3)$, or $f_2(4)$ and $f_2(5)$. There are two powers of $W$ associated with each pair. For instance, with $f_2(4)$ and $f_2(5)$ we have $W^1$ and $W^5$. Then, see Eq. 2–370, $W^1 = -W^5$. This will be true for each pair of $W$ (see Eq. 2–370).

Consider a FORTRAN program for the evaluation of the FFT (see Fig. 2–26). At first glance, it might appear as though the program should implement Eqs. 2–381 directly. That is the binary digits $k_0$, $k_1$, $k_2$, $n_0$, $n_1$, and $n_2$ should be manipulated directly. However, it becomes awkward if the values of N can be varied in the program. For example, if $N = 16$ (i.e., $\gamma = 4$), then Eqs. 2–381 would be replaced by equations with four summations. Also, one additional equation would be required. To avoid this difficulty, we shall use Eqs. 2–381 and the signal flow graph of Fig. 2–25, but not the binary digits directly. Since the program is somewhat complex, we shall consider some small segments of it at first to illustrate its basic ideas.

If we are to save storage space (i.e., use only one list of variables) then the sub-

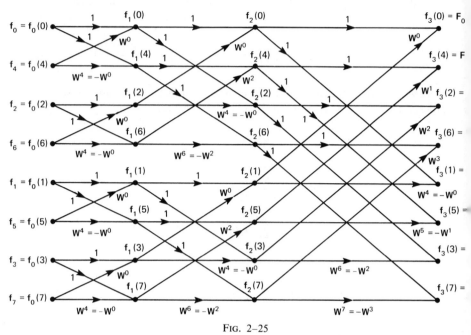

FIG. 2–25

Signal flow graph of Fig. 2–24 reconstructed to conform with Eqs. 2–381

scripts must be computed in pairs and the new variables corresponding to these subscripts are calculated and then stored in the storage space used for the old variables. The new variables are said to be *written over* the old variables. (Of course, the old variables are no longer available.) For instance, $f_0(1)$ and $f_0(4)$ are such a pair. They are used to compute $f_1(0)$ and $f_1(4)$, but are not used again. Hence, $f_0(1)$ and $f_0(4)$ can be written over by $f_1(0)$ and $f_1(4)$, respectively. Pairs such as $f_2(4)$ and $f_2(5)$ exist throughout the program.

We now consider a short program segment which will produce pairs of numbers that correspond to the subscripts of a pair of variables. For instance, for $f_0$, the pairs would be (0, 4), (2, 6), (1, 5), and (3, 7), and for $f_1$ the pairs are (0, 2), (4, 6), (1, 3), and (5, 7). We shall state the program segment [7] and then explain it.

$$
\begin{aligned}
&\text{KM} = \text{IG} - 1 \\
&\text{DO } 100 \text{ LQ} = 1, \text{KM} + 1 \\
&\text{L} = \text{LQ} - 1 \\
&\text{IG1} = 2{**}(\text{IG} - \text{L} - 1) \\
&\text{M} = 0 \\
&\text{KK} = 2{**}\text{L} \\
&\text{DO } 100 \text{ I} = 1, \text{KK}
\end{aligned}
$$

```
          DO 50 J = 1, IG1
          KA = M
          KB = M + IG1
          M = M + 1
50        CONTINUE
          M = M + IG1
100       CONTINUE
```

IG corresponds to the variable $\gamma$; that is, there are $2^\gamma$ samples. KA and KB are the integers that correspond to each pair. For the first pair of $f_0$ given above (i.e., (0, 4)), KA = 0 and KB = 4. For $\gamma = 3$, the program can be verified by substituting and comparing with Fig. 2–25. A similar procedure can be used for larger $\gamma$.

Let us now explain the program. Note that (see Fig. 2–23) at the $f_0$ level the numbers of each pair differ by 4, at the $f_1$ level they differ by 2, and at the $f_2$ level, they differ by 1. This geometric progression is general. The ratio of numbers in each pair is IG1 = 2**(IG − L − 1). Each time L is increased, IG1 is reduced by a factor of 2, as it should be. Suppose IG = 3 ($\gamma = 3$); this corresponds to Fig. 2–25. For the first cycle IG1 = 4. Then the complete set of pairs is obtained in one cycle of the "J" DO loop.

Now suppose the pairs corresponding to $f_1$ are being chosen. Then L = 1. If N = 0, then the (0, 2) pair is obtained first. (Note that IG1 = 2 in this case.) Next the (1, 3) pair is obtained. If N were to be increased by 1, a pair (2, 3) would be found, but this would be incorrect. However, in this case, the "J" DO loop is only traversed twice; i.e., IG1 = 2. After this, M is increased to M + IG1 and the "J" DO loop is again traversed twice. This yields the remaining pairs (4, 6), and (5, 7). Finally this operation is performed four times in obtaining the coefficients corresponding to the $f_2$ pair. Note that most compilers do not allow 0 as one of the DO loop parameters. In the outer DO loop, we desire L to vary from 0 to KM. Thus we define the DO loop index as LQ and have it vary from 1 to KM + 1. We then set L = LQ − 1.

Now let us discuss a program segment which will obtain the power of $W$ that corresponds to KB (see Eq. 2–371) in the above program segment. Note (see Fig. 2–25) that the multiplier of $f$ that corresponds to KA is always 1. We shall first list the segment and then explain it.

```
          K1 = M/IG1
          K2 = 0
          DO 20 K = 1, IG
          K4 = K1/2
          K3 = K1 − 2*K4
          K1 = K1/2
          IF (K3.EQ.0) GO TO 20
          K2 = K2 + 2**(IG − K)
20        CONTINUE
```

If an integer is set equal to a real number, the fractional part of the number is discarded. For instance, if $A = 1.5$, then $K = A$ results in K having the value 1. Thus, if $M = 3$ and $IGI = 2$, then $K1 = M/IGI$ results in $K1 = 1$, and K2 is the desired exponent of W. The first two lines establish the value of K1 and initially set $K2 = 0$.

Now consider the DO loop. For all even K1, we have $K3 = 0$; for all odd K1, we have $K3 \neq 0$. (Note that K3 is not directly used in the computations.) However, because of the IF statement, if $K3 \neq 0$, then K2 is increased by 2 and raised to an integral power. This power is $IG - K$, where $IG = \gamma$ and K represents the number of times that the DO loop has been cycled. By comparing the computed value of K2 with the desired exponents, it can be verified that the correct results are obtained. Now consider the complete FFT program which is illustrated in Fig. 2–26. In line 20, the complex functions are declared and the F array is dimensioned. Up to 1024 samples can be taken ($\gamma = 1, 2, ..., 10$). If larger values of N are desired, the dimension should be increased. In lines 30–160, the data is entered. (A constant A is calculated in line 120.) Note that line 160 is FORMAT(2F). Here 2 is used since the F array consists of complex numbers. Also, since $f(t)$ is usually real, a single number will usually be entered and the carriage returned. This will set the imaginary part of F equal to zero. (Actually, complex numbers could be entered here and the FFT could still be evaluated.) (The field specific is given without column specification. This is convenient when timesharing is used. Note that not all compilers have provision for such specification.) Note that the subscripts of the F array run from 1 to N, not from 0 to $N - 1$. This is because most compilers require that the first subscript in an array be 1 and not 0. Then $A = T/N$ (see Eq. 2–341) is calculated in line 120. Each F is multiplied by A (see Eq. 2–346a) in the DO loop of lines 170–190. In lines 200–220, W is evaluated.

Line 230 and the DO loop of lines 240–500 utilizes the first program segment we discussed. The values KA and KB are obtained as discussed in the segment. However, we have increased both KA and KB by 1. This is because the subscripts of the F array run from 1 to $N$, not from 0 to $N - 1$. The second program segment is enclosed within this one in lines 330–410. This gives K2 which is used as an exponent of W. These exponents are in reduced form so that modulo need not be used. (See the discussion following Eq. 2–358. The values of X and Y computed in lines 430 and 440 correspond to the new values of F. In lines 450 and 460, they are written over the old values. (Note if a fixed number of samples is used, then the values of the powers of W can be computed once and stored in the program as data. This greatly reduces computation time.)

The final value of F is the discrete Fourier transform and it is printed in lines 520–630. The details of the printing are important. This is why we have listed a complete program and not just a subroutine. To avoid using zero as a DO loop parameter, we utilize lines 560 and 570. That is, JQ, the DO loop index, varies from 1 to $NN + 1$. In the next line, we calculate $J = JQ - 1$. Then, J is used as the "actual index" in the DO loop. Note that a relatively small number of compilers do allow

```
00010   C         DIRECT FAST FØURIER TRANSFØRM
00020             CØMPLEX F(1024),W,X,Y,W1
00030             TYPE 1
00040   1         FØRMAT(' ENTER GAMMA'/)
00050             ACCEPT 2,IG
00060   2         FØRMAT(I)
00070             N=2**IG
00080             TYPE 3
00090   3         FØRMAT(' ENTER TØTAL TIME DURATIØN'/)
00100             ACCEPT 4,T
00110   4         FORMAT(F)
00120             A=T/N
00130             TYPE 5
00140   5         FØRMAT(' ENTER N TIME SAMPLES'/)
00150             ACCEPT 6,(F(K),K=1,N)
00160   6         FØRMAT(2F)
00170             DØ 7 I=1,N
00180             F(I) = A*F(I)
00190   7         CØNTINUE
00200             WR=CØS(2.*3.14159/N)
00210             WI=-1.*SIN(2.*4.14159/N)
00220             W=CMPLX(WR,WI)
00230             KM=IG-1
00240             DØ 100 LQ=1,KM+1
00250             L=LQ-1
00260             IGI=2**(IG-L-1)
00270             M=0
00280             KK=2**L
00290             DØ 100 LL=1,KK
00300             DØ 50 J=1,IG1
00310             KA=M+1
00320             KB=M+IG1+1
00330             K1=M/IG1
00340             K2=0
00350             DØ 20 K=1,IG
00360             K4=K1/2
00370             K3=K1-2*K4
00380             K1=K1/2
00390             IF(K3.EQ.0)GØ TØ 20
00400             K2=K2+2**(IG-K)
00410   20        CØNTINUE
00420             W1=W**K2
00430             X=F(KA)+W1*F(KB)
00440             Y=F(KA)-W1*F(KB)
00450             F(KA)=X
00460             F(KB)=Y
00470             M=M+1
00480   50        CØNTINUE
00490             M=M+IG1
00500   100       CØNTINUE
00510             DW=2.*3.14159/T
00520             TYPE 10
00530   10        FØRMAT(' THE DIRECT DISCRETE
00540       +     FØURIER TRANSFØRM IS'/)
00550             NN=N-1
```

Fig. 2–26

```
00560                 DØ 200 JQ=1,NN+1
00570                 J=JQ-1
00580                 AQ=J
00590                 DWN=AQ*DW
00600                 K=IREV(J,IG)+1
00610                 TYPE 12,DWN,F(K)
00620       12        FØRMAT(' F(J',E,')=',E,'+J(',E,')')
00630       200       CØNTINUE
00640                 STØP
00650                 END
00660                 FUNCTIØN IREV(J,IG)
00670                 DIMENSIØN I(10)
00680                 MZ=IG-1
00690                 DØ 300 LQ=1,MZ+1
00700                 L=LQ-1
00710                 I(L+1)=0
00720       300       CØNTINUE
00730                 DØ 500 KJQ=1,MZ+1
00740                 KJ=MZ+1-KJQ
00750                 IF(J-2**KJ.LT.0)GØ TØ 500
00760                 I(KJ+1)=I(KJ+1)+1
00770                 J=J-2**KJ
00780       500       CØNTINUE
00790                 IREV=0
00800                 DØ 1000 LQ=1,MZ=1
00810                 L=MZ+1-LQ
00820                 IREV=IREV+I(MZ-L+1)*2**L
00830       1000      CØNTINUE
00840                 RETURN
00850                 END
```

FIG. 2–26
Program FFT, which takes the direct FFT

zero as a DO loop parameter. In this case, lines 560 and 570 could be combined to a
single line: DO 200 J = 0, NN. In line 510, DW corresponds to the frequency spacing
(see Eq. 2–342). Then, DWN (see line 590) corresponds to W for the value of F
corresponding to J. (Note that line 580 converts J to a real number.) When
the output $F(j)$ is printed we must have a reversal of binary digits of the subscripts
of the $f_\gamma(j)$.

The FUNCTION IREV(J, IG) results in a number which corresponds to the
reversal of the binary digits. Let us discuss this function. In the DO loop of lines
690–720, all the values of I(L) are set equal to zero. Note that the subscripts must
run from 1 to $\gamma$ instead of from 0 to $\gamma - 1$. We have used lines 690 and 700 to avoid
using zero as a DO loop parameter (see discussion of lines 560 and 570).

Now consider the DO loop of lines 730–780. Here we want the DO loop to be
cycled backwards. That is, we want KJ to vary from MZ to 0 in steps of $-1$. Most
compilers do not allow such negative increments. However, the use of lines 730 and

```
00010    C           INVERSE FAST FØURIER TRANSFØRM
00020                CØMPLEX F(1024),W,X,Y,W1
00030                TYPE 1
00040    1           FØRMAT(' ENTER GAMMA'/)
00050                ACCEPT 2,IG
00060    2           FØRMAT (I)
00070                N=2**IG
00080                TYPE 3
00090    3           FØRMAT (' ENTER TØTAL FREQ. DUR*2 PI'/)
00100                ACCEPT 4,T
00110    4           FØRMAT(F)
00120                A=T/(2.*3.14159*N)
00130                TYPE 5
00140    5           FØRMAT(' ENTER N FREQ. SAMPLES'/)
00150                ACCEPT 6,(F(K),K=1,N)
00160    6           FØRMAT(2F)
00170                DØ 7 I=1,N
00180                F(I) = A*F(I)
00190    7           CØNTINUE
00200                WR=CØS(2.*3.14159/N)
00210                WI=SIN(2.*3.14159/N)
00220                W=CMPLX(WR,WI)
00230                KM=IG-1
00240                DØ 100 L=0,KM
00250                IG1=2**(IG-L-1)
00260                M=0
00270                KK=2**L
00280                DØ 100 LL=1,KK
00290                DØ 50 J=1,IG1
00300                KA=M+1
00310                KB=M+IG1+1
00320                K1=M/IG1
00330                K2=0
00340                DØ 20 K=1,IG
00350                K4=K1/2
00360                K3=K1-2*K4
00370                K1=K1/2
00380                IF(K3.EQ.0)GØ TØ 20
00390                K2=K2+2**(IG-K)
00400    20          CØNTINUE
00410                W1=W**K2
00420                X=F(KA)+W1*F(KB)
00430                Y=F(KA)-W1*F(KB)
00440                F(KA)=X
00450                F(KB)=Y
00460                M=M+1
00470    50          CØNTINUE
00480                M=M+IG1
00490    100         CØNTINUE
00500                DW=2.*3.14159/T
00510                TYPE 10
00520    10          FØRMAT(' THE INVERSE DISCRETE
00530    +           FØURIER TRANSFØRM IS'/)
00540                NN=N-1
00550                DØ 200 J=0,NN
```

FIG. 2–27

```
00560              AQ=J
00570              DWN=AQ*DW
00580              K=IREV(J,IG)+1
00590              TYPE 12,DWN,F(K)
00600    12        FØRMAT(' F(',E,')=',E,'J(',E,')')
00610    200       CØNTINUE
00620              STØP
00630              END
00640              FUNCTIØN IREV(J,IG)
00650              DIMENSIØN I(10)
00660              MZ=IG-1
00670              DØ 300 L=0,MZ
00680              I(L+1)=0
00690    300       CØNTINUE
00700              DØ 500 KJQ=1,MZ+1
00710              KJ=MZ+1-KJQ
00720              IF(J-2**KJ.LT.0)GØ TØ 500
00730              I(KJ+1)=I(KJ+1)+1
00740              J=J-2**KJ
00750    500       CØNTINUE
00760              IREV=0
00770              DØ 1000 LQ=1,MZ+1
00780              L=MZ+1-LQ
00790              IREV=IREV+I(MZ-L+1)*2**L
00800    1000      CØNTINUE
00810              RETURN
00820              END
```

FIG. 2–27

Program IFFT, which takes the inverse FFT

740 avoids the use of negative DO loop parameters. Note that KJ varies as desired, while the DO loop parameter KJQ varies in increments of $+1$. If this program is run on a compiler that allows negative DO loop increments and 0 as a DO loop parameter, then lines 730 and 740 can be replaced by the single line DO 500 KJ = MZ, 0, $-1$. The comments of this paragraph also apply to lines 800 and 810.

Consider the operation of this FUNCTION. Suppose that IG = 3. Then, a binary number would be of the form:

$$J = I(3)*2**2 + I(2)*2**1 + I(1)*2**0$$

The DO loop calculates the $I(L + 1)$. (Note that the subscripts are 1 too high.) In the DO loop, the value of $I(3)$ is determined in lines 750–780. Then, J is reduced by $2^2$ and the process repeated. Finally, in the DO loop of lines 800–830, the resulting IREV is calculated using the binary digits in reverse order.

The program we have discussed used the FFT to obtain the direct discrete Fourier transform. However, it need only be slightly modified to obtain the inverse transform. The English text that is printed must be slightly modified. In addition, A of line 120 is changed to

$$A = T/(2*3.14159*N)$$

where T is the total bandwidth (see Eq. 2–342). In addition, $-1$ is deleted from line 210. This changes the exponential from $e^{-j\omega t}$ to $e^{j\omega t}$. Thus, the symmetry in the Fourier transform allows essentially the same program to be used for the direct and the inverse FFT. This inverse FFT program is given in Fig. 2–27.

In these programs we have entered the data as a sequence of numbers. Actually, if $f(t)$ or $F(j\omega)$ consists of a known function whose Fourier transform does not exist in closed form, the data can be entered automatically from a FUNCTION. Such a procedure is illustrated in Fig. 2–20. In this case, the FUNCTION would be used to enter data into the F array. These details will be left to the reader.

## PROBLEMS

**2-1.** Discuss the need for distribution theory.

**2-2.** Determine

$$\int_{-\infty}^{\infty} \delta(t) \frac{\sin 2t}{t} \, dt$$

on a distribution basis.

**2-3.** Discuss why the definitions of operations with generalized functions should be compatible with those of ordinary functions.

**2-4.** Demonstrate that $\delta(t)$ is an even distribution.

**2-5.** Determine

$$\int_{-\infty}^{\infty} \frac{d\delta(t)}{dt} e^{-t} \cos t \, dt$$

**2-6.** Determine

$$\int_{-\infty}^{\infty} \frac{d^2 \delta(t)}{dt^2} e^{-t} \cos t \, dt$$

**2-7.** On a distribution basis, determine $d/dt \left[ u(t) e^{-t} \right]$.

**2-8.** On a distribution basis, determine

$$\frac{d}{dt} \left[ u(t) \cos t + \sum_{k=1}^{10} ku(t-k) \right]$$

**2-9.** On a distribution basis, determine

$$\int_{-\infty}^{\infty} \left[ \frac{d}{dt} u(t-1) \right] \left[ e^{-t} \sin t \right] dt$$

**2-10.** On a distribution basis, determine

$$\lim_{t \to \infty} \frac{t^2 + 2t + 1}{2t^2 + 3} \cos 3t$$

**2-11.** Evaluate

$$\int_{-\infty}^{\infty} e^{-j\omega t} \, dt$$

**2-12.** Evaluate

$$\int_{-\infty}^{\infty} \frac{1}{t} \, dt$$

**2-13.** Given: $f(t)$ has a Fourier transform $F(\omega)$ and $f(t)$ is continuous except at $t = t_0$, where it has a jump discontinuity. If

$$g(t) = \frac{1}{2\pi} \int_{-\Omega}^{\Omega} F(j\omega) e^{j\omega t} \, d\omega$$

then, in the limit, as $\Omega \to \infty$, what is $g(t_0)$ and the maximum value of $|f(t) - g(t)|$?

**2-14.** Determine the Fourier spectrum of

$$f(t) = e^{-\beta |t|}$$

where $\beta > 0$. Verify your result by taking the inverse Fourier transform of the $F(j\omega)$ obtained.

**2-15.** Repeat Problem 2-14 for

$$f(t) = u(t) e^{-\beta t} \sin \omega_0 t$$

where $\beta > 0$.

**2-16.** Repeat Problem 2-14 for

$$f(t) = e^{-t^2}$$

**2-17.** For the Fourier spectrum obtained in Problem 2-14, find $R(\omega)$ and $X(\omega)$.

**2-18.** Repeat Problem 2-17 for the spectrum of Problem 2-15.

**2-19.** Repeat Problem 2-17 for the spectrum of Problem 2-16.

**2-20.** Repeat Problem 2-14 for

$$f(t) = \cos t - \tfrac{1}{3} \cos 3t$$

**2-21.** Repeat Problem 2-14 for

$$f(t) = u(t)(\cos t - \tfrac{1}{3} \cos 3t)$$

**2-22.** Repeat Problem 2-14 for

$$f(t) = u(t)(\cos t - \tfrac{1}{3} \cos 3t + \tfrac{1}{5} \sin 5t)$$

**2-23.** Use the Fourier transform to determine the response $v_2(t)$ for the network of Fig. 2–28 if $v_1(t)$ is a unit step.

**2-24.** Repeat Problem 2-23, but now use

$$v_1(t) = u(t) \sin t$$

**2-25.** Repeat Problem 2-24, but now assume that $R = 0$.

**2-26.** Repeat Problem 2-23 for the network of Fig. 2–29.

**2-27.** Repeat Problem 2-24 for the network of Fig. 2–29.

**2-28.** Prove that the Fourier transform of $f(t)$ will always exist if $f(t)$ is continuous, bounded, and

$$f(t) \leq e^{-|t|}, \qquad t > T$$

**2-29.** Given $g(t)$, where $g(t)$ is a real function of time, such that

$$e^{jg(t)} \leftrightarrow G_1(j\omega)$$

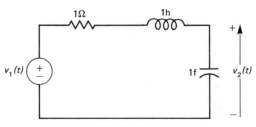

FIG. 2–28

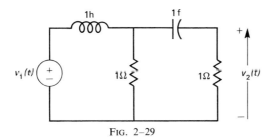

FIG. 2–29

Shows that

$$\cos g(t) \leftrightarrow \tfrac{1}{2}[G_1(j\omega) + G_1^*(-j\omega)]$$

where the asterisk indicates complex conjugate.

**2-30.** Repeat Problem 2-27, but now show that

$$\sin g(t) \leftrightarrow \frac{1}{2j}[G_1(j\omega) - G_1^*(-j\omega)]$$

**2-31.** Find the Fourier transform of

$$f(t) = u(t - 1)\cos \omega_0(t - 1)$$

**2-32.** Find the Fourier transform of

$$f(t) = \cos(t - 2\pi)$$

**2-33.** Use the results of Problem 2-14 to obtain the inverse Fourier transform of

$$F(j\omega) = e^{-\beta|\omega|}$$

**2-34.** Use the time differentiation theorem to relate the Fourier transforms of $\cos \omega_0 t$ and $\sin \omega_0 t$.

**2-35.** Use the convolution theorem to obtain the Fourier transform of

$$u(t)\, e^{-\beta t}\cos \omega_0 t$$

**2-36.** Repeat Problem 2-35 for the function

$$u(t)\, e^{-\beta t}\sin \omega_0 t$$

**2-37.** Use the convolution theorem to obtain the inverse Fourier transform of

$$\frac{1}{(j\omega + a)}\left[\frac{\omega_0}{(\omega_0^2 - \omega^2)} + \frac{\pi}{2j}[\delta(\omega - \omega_0) - \delta(\omega + \omega_0)]\right]$$

**2-38.** Repeat Problem 2-37 for the function

$$\frac{1}{(j\omega + a)}\left[\frac{j\omega}{(\omega_0^2 - \omega^2)} + \frac{\pi}{2}[\delta(\omega - \omega_0) + \delta(\omega + \omega_0)]\right]$$

**2-39.** Use the convolution theorem to prove that if $h(t)$ is the unit impulse response of a network, then the response of the network to a function $f(t) \leftrightarrow F(j\omega)$ is given by

$$\int_{-\infty}^{\infty} h(x)\, f(t - x)\, dx$$

**2-40.** Verify Parseval's theorem for

$$f(t) = u(t)\, e^{-\beta t}$$

**2-41.** Obtain the response of a filter, whose transfer function is given by Eq. 2–234, to an input given by

$$f(t) = u(t) e^{-\beta t}$$

**2-42.** The transfer function of the filter of Problem 2-41 is to be modified by cascading with it another filter, whose response is 0 for $|\omega| > \omega_a$. The second filter is such that the output does not exhibit Gibbs' phenomenon. Determine a transfer function for the added filter. (Note that the overall transfer function is the product of the two transfer functions.)

**2-43.** Repeat Problem 2-41 for the input given by

$$f(t) = u(t) \cos \omega_0 t$$

**2-44.** If $f(t) \leftrightarrow F(j\omega)$ and

$$g(t) = \frac{1}{2\pi} \int_{-\omega_a}^{\omega_a} F_1(j\omega) e^{j\omega t} d\omega$$

and it is desired to minimize $|f(t) - g(t)|_{max}$, does a simple choice for $F_1(j\omega)$ exist? Discuss your answer.

**2-45.** Determine the mean square error (when the input and output are compared) produced by the filter of Problem 2-41.

**2-46.** Discuss various error criteria and why they are, or are not, used.

**2-47.** Given a function

if

$$f_0(t) = e^{-t}, \quad 0 \leq t \leq 1$$

$$f(t) = f_0(t), \quad 0 \leq t \leq 1$$

and

$$f(t) = f(t + 1)$$

for all $t$, find the Fourier transform of $f(t)$. Express $f(t)$ in a Fourier series.

**2-48.** Determine the Fourier transform and Fourier series of the square wave

$$f(t) = \begin{cases} 1, & 0 \leq t \leq \frac{1}{2} \\ -1, & \frac{1}{2} \leq t \leq 1 \end{cases}$$

$$f(t + 1) = f(t)$$

**2-49.** For the square wave of Problem 2-48, let $f_N(t)$ be the function which results from the summation of the first $N$ terms of the Fourier series. Does this exhibit Gibbs phenomenon? Verify your answer.

**2-50.** Modify the coefficients of the Fourier series of Problem 2-49 so that it does not exhibit Gibbs phenomenon.

**2-51.** Obtain an alternate form of the series

$$\sum_{n=-\infty}^{\infty} u(n) e^{-n} \cos n$$

**2-52.** Prove the following theorem: Given two continuous functions of time $f_1(t)$ and $f_2(t)$, which both possess Fourier transforms. If

$$f_1 \left( \frac{n\pi}{1000} \right) = f_2 \left( \frac{n\pi}{1000} \right)$$

for all integers $n$, and if $f_1(t) \neq f_2(t)$ for other values of time, then $f_1(t)$ or $f_2(t)$, or both, must have bandwidths which are greater than $\omega = 1000$ radians/sec.

**2-53.** Write a FORTRAN program which computes the definite integral of a function $f(t)$ and uses the approximation of Fig. 2–21.

**2-54.** Use the program developed in Problem 2-53 to evaluate

$$\int_1^{10} \frac{\sin x}{x}\, dx$$

Compare your answer using subroutine TRPINT (see Fig. 2-20). Use $N = 10$, 100, and 1000. Compare all answers.

**2-55.** Write a FORTRAN program based on subroutine TRPINT that evaluates the discrete Fourier transform. Use complex functions in your program.

**2-56.** Use the program of Problem 2-55 to obtain the discrete Fourier transform of

$$f(t) = u(t)\, e^{-t} \sin t^2$$

Use 128 points spaced 0.1 sec. apart starting at $t = 0$.

**2-57.** Write a FORTRAN program based on Eqs. 2–352 and 2–358 which evaluates the discrete Fourier transform.

**2-58.** Use the program of Problem 2-57 to obtain the Fourier transform for the function of Problem 2-56.

**2-59.** Write the number 123 using the digital number system.

**2-60.** Write the digital number 101001 in the decimal number system.

**2-61.** Write the number 96 in the octal number system.

**2-62.** Write the octal number 123 in the decimal number system.

**2-63.** Without referring to Figs. 2–26 or 2–27, write a FORTRAN program to evaluate the discrete Fourier transform using the FFT.

**2-64.** Use the program of Fig. 2–26 to obtain the discrete Fourier transform of the function given by $f(0) = 0$, $f(1) = 1, f(2) = 2$, $f(3) = 3$, $f(4) = 4$, $f(5) = -4$, $f(6) = -3$, and $f(7) = -2$.

**2-65.** Repeat Problem 2-64 for a function whose values at 1 second intervals (starting at $t = 0$) are given by $0, 1, 2, 3, 4, 3, 2, 1, 0, -1, -2, -3, -4, -3, -2, -1$.

**2-66.** Modify the program FFT of Fig. 2–26 so that the input can be obtained from a FUNCTION.

**2-67.** Use the program of Problem 2-66 to evaluate the discrete Fourier transform of the function given in Problem 2-56.

**2-68.** Compare the number of calculations required and the computer operating time for the computations of Problems 2-56, 2-58, and 2-67. This should illustrate the great saving of the FFT.

# REFERENCES

1. Pierce, B. O. *A Short Table of Integrals.* Boston: Ginn, 1929, Eq. 484.
2. Janke, L., Emde, F., and Lösch, F. *Tables of Higher Functions.* New York: McGraw-Hill, 1960, pp. 17–25.
3. Papoulis, A. *The Fourier Integral and its Applications.* New York: McGraw-Hill, 1962, pp. 42–47.
   Zemanian, A. H. *Distribution Theory and Transform Calculus.* New York: McGraw-Hill, pp. 50–57, 332–333.
4. Shannon, C. E. "Communication in the Presence of Noise." In *Proc. IRE.* Vol. 37, 1949, pp. 10–21.
5. Cooley, J. W., and Tukey, J. W. "An Algorithm for the Machine Calculation of Complex Fourier Series". In *Math of Computation.* Vol. 19. April 1965, pp. 297–301.

6.  Cochran, W. T. et al. "What is the Fast Fourier Transform?". In *Proc. IRE.* Vol. 55, 1967, pp. 1664–1674.
7.  Bice, P. K. "Speed up the Fast Fourier Transform". In *Electronic Design.* Vol. 9, 1970, pp.66–69.

## BIBLIOGRAPHY

Bracewell, R. M. *The Fourier Transform and its Applications.* Chaps. 1–10. New York: McGraw-Hill, 1965.
Chirlian, P. M. *Basic Network Theory.* Chap. 11. New York: McGraw-Hill, 1969.
Cooper, G. R., and McGillem, C. D. *Methods of Signal and System Analysis.* Chap. 5. New York: Holt, 1967.
Hamming, R. W. *Numerical Methods for Scientists and Engineers.* Chap. 12. New York: McGraw-Hill, 1962.
Hovanessian, S. A., and Pipes, L. A. *Digital Computer Methods in Engineering.* Chap. 4. New York: McGraw-Hill, 1969.
Huelsman, L. P. *Digital Computations in Basic Circuit Theory.* Chap. 3. New York: McGraw-Hill, 1968.
Kunz, K. S. *Numerical Analysis.* Chap. 7. New York: McGraw-Hill, 1957.
Lathi, B. P. *Signals, Systems and Communication.* Chaps. 3–4. New York: Wiley, 1965.
Papoulis, A. *The Fourier Integral and its Applications.* Chaps. 1–4. New York: McGraw-Hill, 1962.
Schwarz, M. *Information Transmission, Modulation, and Noise.* Chap. 2. 2d ed. New York: McGraw-Hill, 1970.
Zemanian, A. H. *Distribution Theory and Transform Analysis.* Chap. 1–7. New York: McGraw-Hill, 1965.

# CHAPTER 3

# Laplace Transform

In this chapter we shall use the Fourier transform to develop another procedure for obtaining the response of a system to signals. This procedure is called the *Laplace transform*. Later, we shall show that certain signals which do not possess Fourier transforms have Laplace transforms. When linear integral-differential equations are solved in closed form, the Laplace transform is often more convenient to use than the Fourier transform. However, the Fourier transform is usually preferable if the frequency response of a system is known, the general characteristics of systems are desired, or a computer solution is used. However, we shall later show that a computer solution can be used with the Laplace transform.

## 3-1. DEVELOPMENT OF THE ONE-SIDED LAPLACE TRANSFORM FROM THE FOURIER TRANSFORM

We shall use the Fourier transform pair as the starting point in our development of the Laplace transform and shall mainly concern ourselves with functions of time which are zero for $t < 0$. Thus, we shall consider signals which are applied at $t = 0$. The Laplace transform of such signals is called the *one-sided Laplace transform* and we shall call such signals *one-sided signals*. The Laplace transform which deals with functions of time which, in general, are nonzero for both positive and negative time is called the *two-sided Laplace transform* or the *bilateral Laplace transform* (see Section 3-15). In general, when we refer to the one-sided Laplace transform, we shall just call it the Laplace transform.

The Fourier transform for a one sided function of time is given by (see Eqs. 2-61 and 2-62)

$$F(j\omega) = \int_0^\infty f(t) e^{-j\omega t} dt \qquad (3-1)$$

$$f(t) = \frac{1}{2\pi} \int_{-\infty}^\infty F(j\omega) e^{j\omega t} d\omega \qquad (3-2)$$

Unless we state otherwise, in this chapter, we shall assume that $f(t) = 0$ for $t < 0$. This could be written as $f(t) u(t)$. However, we shall often omit the unit step function, unless it is necessary for clarity.

Now let us obtain the Fourier transform of the function $f(t) e^{-\sigma t}$, where $\sigma$ is real, and assume that $f(t) e^{-\sigma t}$ possesses a Fourier transform. Then (see Eqs. 3-1 and 3-2) its Fourier transform is

$$F'(j\omega) = \int_0^\infty f(t)\, e^{-\sigma t} e^{-j\omega t}\, dt \qquad (3\text{-}3a)$$

and

$$f(t)\, e^{-\sigma t} = \frac{1}{2\pi} \int_{-\infty}^{\infty} F'(j\omega)\, e^{j\omega t}\, d\omega \qquad (3\text{-}3b)$$

Now let us define a new variable $s$, where

$$s = \sigma + j\omega \qquad (3\text{-}4)$$

(Note that $s$ is a complex number.) Then, substituting in Eqs. 3–3 and manipulating, we have

$$F'(j\omega) = \int_0^\infty f(t)\, e^{-st}\, dt \qquad (3\text{-}5a)$$

$$f(t) = \frac{1}{2\pi} \int_{-\infty}^{\infty} F'(j\omega)\, e^{st}\, d\omega \qquad (3\text{-}5b)$$

Equations 3–5 represent a transform pair. That is Eq. 3–5a yields a function $F'(j\omega)$, which is obtained from a given $f(t)$; when this $F'(j\omega)$ is substituted into Eq. 3–5b, the original $f(t)$ results. This transform is unique in the same sense as the Fourier transform (see Section 2-4). For instance, if two $f(t)$ have the same $F'(j\omega)$, then the $f(t)$'s can only differ at isolated points by a finite amount (see Fig. 2–2). Thus, for all practical cases, we can state that the transform given by Eqs. 3–5 is unique.

Since $j\omega$ does not explicitly appear on the right hand-side of Eq. 3–5a, while $s$ does, we can state that this is a function of $s$. Let us then write

$$F(s) = \int_0^\infty f(t)\, e^{-st}\, dt \qquad (3\text{-}6a)$$

Since $\sigma$ is a constant for Eq. 3–5, we have

$$ds = j d\omega$$

Hence, substituting in Eq. 3–5b, we obtain

$$f(t) = \frac{1}{2\pi j} \int_{\sigma - j\infty}^{\sigma + j\infty} F(s)\, e^{st}\, ds \qquad (3\text{-}6b)$$

This notation, which is conventional, may appear confusing since $F(j\omega)$ is the Fourier transform of $f(t)$ while $F(s)$ is the Fourier transform of $f(t)\, e^{-\sigma t}$ and, in general, $F(s)$ cannot be obtained from $F(j\omega)$ simply by replacing $j\omega$ by $s$. The two functions $F(j\omega)$ and $F(s)$ could be distinguished by a subscript; however, this is not conventional. If the $j$ is included with the variable (i.e., $F(j\omega)$), then we refer to the Fourier transform of $f(t)$. If the $j$ is not included, we refer to $F(s)$, the Fourier transform of $f(t)\, e^{-\sigma t}$. (Later, we shall call this the Laplace transform of $f(t)$.)

If Eqs. 3–6 are to have meaning, the value of $\sigma$ cannot be arbitrary. For example, if $f(t) = u(t)$ and $\sigma < 0$ $\left( \text{e.g., } f(t)\, e^{-\sigma t} = u(t)\, e^{+2t} \right)$ the Fourier transform of $f(t)\, e^{-\sigma t}$

does not exist. On the other hand, if $\sigma > 0$, the transform exists since the exponential falls off with time. In Section 2-8 we showed that the Fourier transform of a function exists if $\int_{-\infty}^{\infty} |f(t)| \, dt$ exists. Thus, for Eq. 3–6a, if $\int_{0}^{\infty} |f(t)| e^{-\sigma t} \, dt$ exists, then $F(s)$ exists. In general, if

$$\int_{0}^{M} |f(t)| e^{-\sigma t} \, dt \qquad (3\text{--}7a)$$

exists, where $M$ is arbitrarily large, but bounded (i.e., $f(t)$ is such that its integral for arbitrary finite limits exists) and, in addition, if

$$\lim_{t \to \infty} f(t) e^{-\sigma_0 t} = 0 \qquad (3\text{--}7b)$$

then $F(s)$ exists, for $\sigma > \sigma_0$. Note that if $\sigma > \sigma_0$, then $f(t) e^{-\sigma t} = [f(t) e^{-\sigma_0 t}] e^{-\sigma_1 t}$, where $\sigma_1 = \sigma - \sigma_0 > 0$. Thus, for sufficiently large $t$, $f(t) e^{-\sigma_0 t}$ is bounded and $e^{-\sigma_1 t}$ will fall off exponentially; thus, the integral exists. For example, suppose $f(t) = e^{5t}$. If we write $f(t) e^{-\sigma_0 t}$, we have $e^{(5-\sigma_0)t}$. If $\sigma_0$ is greater than 5, then the exponent will be negative and $f(t) e^{-\sigma_0 t}$ will fall off exponentially. Thus, the integral of $f(t) e^{-\sigma_0 t}$ will converge.

Let us discuss another example. Suppose

$$f(t) = t^5$$

Now consider $f(t) e^{-\sigma_0 t}$. In general if $\sigma_1 > 0$, then

$$\lim_{t \to \infty} t^5 e^{-\sigma_1 t} = 0$$

Suppose $\sigma_0 > \sigma_1$. Then,

$$t^5 e^{-\sigma_0 t} = (t^5 e^{-\sigma_1 t}) e^{-(\sigma_0 - \sigma_1)t}$$

As $t$ becomes large, $(t^5 e^{-\sigma_1 t})$ will be bounded. (Actually, it becomes arbitrarily small.) Also the term $(\sigma_0 - \sigma_1) t$ is positive. Thus, as $t$ approaches infinity, $t^5 e^{-\sigma_0 t}$ will fall off exponentially. Again, the integral of this function will converge. Functions which satisfy Eqs. 3–7 are said to be of *exponential order*.

In view of this discussion Eq. 3–6a is not complete, so we must write

$$F(s) = \int_{0}^{\infty} f(t) e^{-\sigma t} \, dt, \qquad \text{Re } \sigma > \sigma_0 \qquad (3\text{--}8a)$$

That is, $F(s)$ only exists for those values of $s$ whose real part is greater than $\sigma_0$. Of course, there are some functions which are such that there is no value of $\sigma_0$ which will cause $F(s)$ to exist. For example,

$$f(t) = e^{t^2}$$

However, there are many functions which do *not* have Fourier transforms, but for which $F(s)$ does exist; for example,

$$f(t) = e^{at}, \qquad a > 0$$

Equation 3–6b must be evaluated in a region where $F(s)$ exists. Hence, we must introduce such a restriction. Later we shall show that the value of the integral is independent of the value of $\sigma$ as long as $\sigma > \sigma_0$. Thus, Eq. 3–6b is usually written as

$$f(t) = \frac{1}{2\pi j} \int_{c-j\infty}^{c+j\infty} F(s) e^{st} ds, \qquad C > \sigma_0 \tag{3–8b}$$

Equations 3–8a and 3–8b constitute a transform pair. They are called the *Laplace transform pair*, and $F(s)$ is called the *Laplace transform* of $f(t)$ and $f(t)$ is the *inverse Laplace transform* of $F(s)$. The notation we use is

$$f(t) \leftrightarrow F(s) \tag{3–9a}$$

This is the same as the notation used for the Fourier transform; however, usually it is clear which transform is meant. If it is not, then clarifying statements will be made or clarifying notation will be used. The following notation is also used

$$F(s) = \mathscr{L}f(t) \tag{3–9b}$$

$$f(t) = \mathscr{L}^{-1} F(s) \tag{3–9c}$$

In summary, the Laplace transform pair is given by

$$F(s) = \int_0^\infty f(t) e^{-st} dt, \qquad \mathrm{Re}\, s = \sigma > \sigma_0 \tag{3–10}$$

$$f(t) = \frac{1}{2\pi j} \int_{c-j\infty}^{c+j\infty} F(s) e^{st} ds, \qquad C > \sigma_0 \tag{3–11}$$

The Laplace transform was derived from the Fourier transform. Since distribution theory (generalized functions) was used for the Fourier transform, it can also be used for the Laplace transform. Thus, all the advantages of distribution theory can be applied to the Laplace transform. Since generalized functions can be used, particular attention must be paid to the lower limit of Eq. 3–10. For example, suppose

$$f(t) = \delta(t)$$

The lower limit (i.e., 0) can be interpreted in two ways: either

$$F(s) = \lim_{\substack{a \to 0 \\ a > 0}} \int_a^\infty f(t) e^{-st} dt \tag{3–12a}$$

or

$$F(s) = \lim_{\substack{a \to 0 \\ a > 0}} \int_{-a}^\infty f(t) e^{-st} dt \tag{3–12b}$$

That is, the lower limit can approach 0 either through positive or through negative values. In the first case, if $f(t) = \delta(t)$, then $F(s) = 0$ since the origin is not included in the integral. In the second case, using Eq. 2–6, $F(s) = 1$, since the origin is included. (We shall make this more rigorous subsequently.)

Valid results can be obtained using either of these definitions as long as one is consistent. However, we shall show that the second one is often more convenient when there are impulses, or doublets, which occur at $t = 0$. The second definition also conforms easily to the definition for distribution. For example, if

$$f(t) - 0, \qquad t < 0$$

then.

$$\int_{-\infty}^{\infty} f(t) e^{-st} dt = \lim_{\substack{a \to 0 \\ a > 0}} \int_{-a}^{\infty} f(t) e^{-st} dt \qquad (3\text{-}13)$$

The right-hand integral is equivalent to the "integrals" used in distribution theory. For all of these reasons we shall use the definition of Eq. 3–12b.

Consider some notation:

$$\lim_{\substack{a \to 0 \\ a > 0}} a = 0 + \qquad (3\text{-}14\text{a})$$

$$\lim_{\substack{a \to 0 \\ a > 0}} -a = 0 - \qquad (3\text{-}14\text{b})$$

The terms *zero plus* and *zero minus* are used to indicate the limits. Thus, Eq. 3–10 can be written

$$F(s) = \int_{0-}^{\infty} f(t) e^{-st} dt \qquad (3\text{-}15)$$

It is conventional to write the lower limit of integration as 0 rather than as 0 −. Thus, the Laplace transform is written in the form of Eq. 3–10, although Eq. 3–15 is understood.

## 3-2. LAPLACE TRANSFORMS OF SOME COMMONLY USED TIME FUNCTIONS

First, consider the unit step function:

$$f(t) = u(t)$$

Then,

$$F(s) = \int_{0}^{\infty} e^{-st} dt, \qquad \text{Re } s = \sigma > 0 \qquad (3\text{-}16)$$

Note that Re $s = \sigma > 0$. If this is so, then the integrand will fall off exponentially and the integral will exist on an ordinary basis. Integrating, we obtain

$$F(s) = \frac{1}{s}, \qquad \text{Re } s = \sigma > 0$$

or, equivalently,

$$u(t) \leftrightarrow \frac{1}{s}, \qquad \text{Re } s = \sigma > \sigma_0 = 0 \qquad (3\text{-}17)$$

Notice that we have indicated $\sigma_0$ as the value that Re $s$ must be greater than if $F(s)$ is to exist.

Now we obtain the Laplace transform of the unit impulse $\delta(t)$. Then (see Eq. 3–13)

$$F(s) = \int_{0-}^{\infty} \delta(t) e^{-st} dt = \int_{-\infty}^{\infty} \delta(t) e^{-st} dt \qquad (3\text{–}18)$$

Note that no restriction is imposed on Re $s$ (i.e., $s > \sigma_0 = -\infty$), since the behavior of $e^{-st}$ for large $t$ does not affect the integral. Then, integrating Eq. 3–18 (see Eq. 2–6), we have

$$\delta(t) \leftrightarrow 1 \qquad (3\text{–}19)$$

As a third example, consider the Laplace transform of $f(t) = e^{at}$; then,

$$F(s) = \int_{0}^{\infty} e^{at} e^{-st} dt, \qquad \text{Re } s = \sigma > \sigma_0 = a$$

Integrating, we have

$$u(t) e^{at} \leftrightarrow \frac{1}{s - a}, \qquad \text{Re } s > \sigma_0 = a \qquad (3\text{–}20)$$

Table 3-1 lists the Laplace transforms of some other functions. These are obtained in a similar way.

TABLE 3-1

| $f(t) \longleftarrow \quad \longrightarrow F(s)$ | $F(s)$ | $\sigma_0$ |
|---|---|---|
| $u(t)$ | $1/s$ | $0$ |
| $\delta(t)$ | $1$ | $-\infty$ |
| $\dfrac{d^n \delta(t)}{dt^n}$ | $s^n$ | $-\infty$ |
| $u(t) e^{-at}$ | $1/(s + a)$ | $-a$ |
| $u(t) e^{+at}$ | $1/(s - a)$ | $a$ |
| $u(t) e^{j\omega_0 t}$ | $1/(s - j\omega_0)$ | $0$ |
| $u(t) \cos \omega_0 t$ | $s/(s^2 + \omega_0^2)$ | $0$ |
| $u(t) \sin \omega_0 t$ | $\omega_0/(s^2 - \omega_0^2)$ | $0$ |
| $u(t) e^{-at} \cos \omega_0 t$ | $(s + a)/[(s + a)^2 + \omega_0^2]$ | $-a$ |
| $u(t) e^{-at} \sin \omega_0 t$ | $\omega_0/[(s + a)^2 + \omega_0^2]$ | $-a$ |
| $u(t) t^n$ | $n!/s^{n+1}$ | $0$ |
| $u(t) t \cos \omega_0 t$ | $(s^2 - \omega_0^2)/(s^2 + \omega_0^2)^2$ | $0$ |

The Laplace transforms of functions are often characterized by their poles and zeros (see Section B-4). Polar plots of the $s$-plane (see Section B-1) are also often used here. Such $s$-plane plots for some typical functions are shown in Fig. 3–1. These diagrams illustrate some facts that shall be covered later. For example, $F(s)$ is analytic in its region of existence (Re $s > \sigma_0$). Poles in the left half plane lead to functions of time multiplied by $e^{-at}$, $a > 0$, while poles in the right half plane lead to functions of time multiplied by $e^{at}$, $a > 0$. Simple poles on the $j\omega$ axis lead to functions which neither increase nor decrease with time (e.g., $u(t) \sin \omega_0 t$ or $u(t)$). Multiple poles on the $j\omega$ axis lead to functions of time which are multiplied

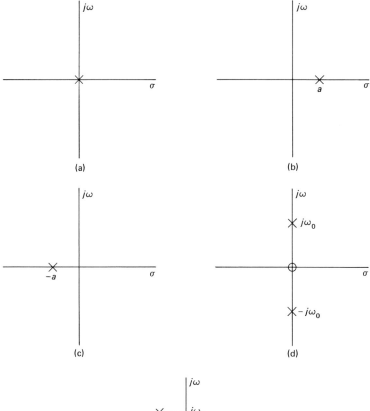

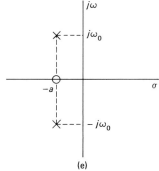

FIG. 3–1

Pole-zero plots of the Laplace transforms of certain $f(t)$; (a) $f(t) = u(t)$; (b) $f(t) = u(t) e^{at}$, $a > 0$; (c) $f(t) = u(t) e^{-at}$, $a > 0$; (d) $f(t) = u(t) \cos \omega_0 t$; (e) $f(t) = u(t) e^{-at} \cdot \cos \omega_0 t$, $a > 0$

by $t^n$. Complex conjugate poles result in functions which contain sinusoids and/or cosinusoids.

## 3-3. ANALYTICITY OF THE LAPLACE TRANSFORM

We shall now develop a result that is of fundamental importance in Laplace transform theory: that *the Laplace transform is analytic in its region of existence.* We must show that $F(s)$ possesses all its derivatives and is single valued for $s$, where $\mathrm{Re}\, s > \sigma_0$.

We shall start by working with the function

$$F_T(s) = \int_0^T f(t)\, e^{-st}\, dt \tag{3-21}$$

and let $T$ approach infinity. Note that this is consistent with the ideas of distribution theory.

Using the basic definition of the derivative, we have

$$\frac{dF_T(s)}{ds} = \lim_{a \to 0} \frac{F_T(s + a) - F_T(s)}{(s + a) - s} \tag{3-22}$$

Substituting Eq. 3–21, we obtain

$$\frac{dF_T(s)}{ds} = \lim_{a \to 0} \int_0^T \frac{f(t)\, e^{-(s+a)t} - f(t)\, e^{-st}}{a}\, dt \tag{3-23}$$

where we have combined both transforms in a single integral. Noting that $e^{-(s+a)t} = e^{-st} e^{-at}$ and manipulating, we obtain

$$\frac{dF_T(s)}{ds} = \lim_{a \to 0} \int_0^T f(t)\, e^{-st} \left( \frac{e^{-at} - 1}{a} \right) dt \tag{3-24}$$

Expand $e^{-at}$ in a Taylor's series. Then, we have

$$e^{-at} = 1 - at + \frac{(at)^2}{2!} + \ldots \ldots \tag{3-25}$$

Substituting into Eq. 3–24, interchanging the order of the integration and limit process, and then taking the limit, we have

$$\frac{dF_T(s)}{ds} = \int_0^T (-t)\, f(t)\, e^{-st}\, dt \tag{3-26}$$

The order of the limit and the integrand can be interchanged since it is assumed that $f(t)$ is such that there is uniform convergence. Now, proceeding similarly, we can differentiate Eq. 3–26 and use the same development with $tf(t)$ instead of $f(t)$. Repeating this $n$ times, we obtain

$$\frac{d^n F_T(s)}{ds^n} = \int_0^T (-t)^n f(t)\, e^{-st}\, dt \tag{3-27}$$

Since the limits of integration are finite and since we assume that $f(t)$ is bounded within the range of integration, the integrand of Eq. 3–27 exists for all integral values of $n$. Hence, all the derivatives of $\mathbf{F}_T(s)$ exist.

Now let us show that these results apply at $T$ approaches infinity. Assume that $t^n f(t)$ is of exponential order. Then, for sufficiently large $T$,

$$\left| t^n f(t) \right| \leq M e^{+\sigma_0 t}, \qquad t \geq T \tag{3-28}$$

Now consider

$$\int_0^T (-t)^n f(t) e^{-st} dt + \int_T^\infty (-t)^n f(t) e^{-st} dt = \frac{d\mathbf{F}_T(s)}{ds^n} + \delta \tag{3-29}$$

where

$$\delta = \int_T^\infty (-t)^n f(t) e^{-st} dt$$

Equation 3–29 can be interpreted in the following way. If the derivative of $\mathbf{F}(s)$ is approximated by the first integral, then the second integral is an *error* term. We must show that for large, but finite, $T$, $\delta$ can be made arbitrarily small. Substituting Eq. 3–28 into the expression for $\delta$ and if $\operatorname{Re} s = \sigma > \sigma_0$, we have

$$|\delta| \leq \int_T^\infty M e^{-\sigma_1 t} dt = \frac{M}{\sigma_1} e^{-\sigma_1 T} \tag{3-30}$$

where $\sigma_1 = \sigma - \sigma_0 > 0$; thus,

$$\lim_{T \to \infty} \delta = 0 \tag{3-31}$$

if $\operatorname{Re} s > \sigma_0$. Thus, we have shown that $\delta$ can be made arbitrarily small; therefore,

$$\frac{d^n \mathbf{F}(s)}{ds^n} = \int_0^\infty (-t)^n f(t) e^{-st} dt, \qquad \operatorname{Re} s > \sigma_0 \tag{3-32}$$

Hence, as long as $\operatorname{Re} s > \sigma_0$, all the derivatives of $\mathbf{F}(s)$ exist. Note that the integral of Eq. 3–32 will exist since the integral of Eq. 3–27 exists and $\delta$ can be made arbitrarily small.

We now must show that $\mathbf{F}(s)$ is single valued. $f(t) e^{-st}$ is a single-valued function of $s$ and $t$. For $\operatorname{Re} s > \sigma_0$, the Laplace transform integral converges uniformly. Hence, $\mathbf{F}(s)$ will be a single-valued function of $s$. Thus, we have shown that the Laplace transform is analytic in its region of existence.

Note that $\sigma_0$ must be such that Eq. 3–28 is valid for all integral $n$. That is, $t^n f(t)$ is considered for all $n$ in obtaining $\sigma_0$. Usually, multiplying a function by $t^n$ will not alter its being of exponential order, nor will it change the value of $\sigma_0$.

We limit the region of existence by the statement $\operatorname{Re} s = \sigma > \sigma_0$. However, we often treat the function in almost the entire $s$-plane. For example, the Laplace transform of $u(t)$ is $F(s) = 1/s$, $\operatorname{Re} s > 0$. However, we often consider $F(s) = 1/s$. As an example we often expand complicated $F(s)$ in partial fractions about its poles. The reader may question how this can be done since $F(s)$ does not exist there. However, if a function is analytic in a region, then it may be extended into other regions, where it is analytic, using the process of analytic continuation (see Section B-7). Thus, in the previously cited example, $F(s)$ can be analytically continued from the right half plane into the left half plane. The origin is a singular point. Hence, analytic continuation cannot be used here, but $F(s)$ can be extended to all other points in the $s$-plane.

## 3-4. THE RELATION BETWEEN THE LAPLACE TRANSFORM AND THE FOURIER TRANSFORM

The Laplace transform is closely related to the Fourier transform. In fact, we developed the Laplace transform from the Fourier transform. Let us now determine the relation between the Laplace and Fourier transforms of specific functions. Since we will be working with both the Laplace and Fourier transforms in this section, we shall use the following notation to avoid confusion. The Fourier transfrom will be written as $F_F(j\omega)$, while the Laplace transform will be written as $F(s)$.

In general, we have, for the Laplace transform

$$f(t) \leftrightarrow F(s), \qquad \operatorname{Re} s = \sigma > \sigma_0 \tag{3-33}$$

There are three cases which we shall consider. These correspond to $\sigma_0 > 0$, $\sigma_0 < 0$, and $\sigma_0 = 0$, which will be discussed in turn:

Case I: $\sigma_0 > 0$

In this case, the Laplace transform is given by

$$F(s) = \int_0^\infty f(t) e^{-st} dt, \qquad \operatorname{Re} s > \sigma_0 > 0 \tag{3-34}$$

The Fourier transform of a one-sided function, if it exists, is given by

$$F_F(j\omega) = \int_0^\infty f(t) e^{-j\omega t} dt \tag{3-35}$$

Thus, the expression for $F_F(j\omega)$ can be obtained by the Laplace transform by setting $\operatorname{Re} s = \sigma = 0$ since $s = \sigma + j\omega$.

However, the assumption that $\sigma_0 > 0$ implies that the integral of Eq. 3–34 *does not exist* if $\operatorname{Re} s = \sigma = 0$. Hence, if $f(t)$ is such that its Laplace transform does not exist for $\operatorname{Re} s = 0$, then $f(t)$ does not have a Fourier transform.

For example, if $f(t) = e^{at}$, $a > 0$, then

$$F(s) = \frac{1}{s - a}, \qquad \operatorname{Re} s > a$$

In this case, $f(t)$ does not possess a Fourier transform even though it has a Laplace transform. Note that $\int_0^\infty e^{at} e^{j\omega t}\, dt$ does not exist because of the exponential buildup of $e^{at}$.

**Case II:** $\sigma_0 < 0$

If $f(t)$ is such that Re $s = 0$ is an allowable value, then an allowable value of the Laplace transform variable $s$ is $s = 0$. Thus, we can write

$$F(s)\Big|_{\sigma=0} = \int_0^\infty f(t) e^{-j\omega t}\, d\omega \tag{3–36}$$

This is identical to the Fourier integral. Hence, if $\sigma_0 < 0$, the Fourier transform of $f(t)$ can be found from its Laplace transform by setting $s = j\omega$. That is,

$$F_F(j\omega) = F(s)\big|_{s=j\omega} = F(j\omega) \tag{3–37}$$

For example, if $f(t) = e^{-at}$, $a > 0$, then its Laplace transform is

$$F(s) = \frac{1}{s+a}, \qquad \text{Re } s > -a$$

and the Fourier transform of $f(t)$ is given by

$$F_F(j\omega) = \frac{1}{j\omega + a}$$

**Case III:** $\sigma_0 = 0$

This is a borderline case. In general, the Fourier transform of these functions will contain impulse functions, or their derivatives. For example (see Table 2-1), $u(t)\cos\omega_0 t$ has a Fourier transform which is given as

$$u(t)\cos\omega_0 t \leftrightarrow \frac{\pi}{2}\left[\delta(\omega-\omega_0) + \delta(\omega+\omega_0)\right] + \frac{j\omega}{\omega_0^2 - \omega^2} \tag{3–38a}$$

The Laplace transform of the same function is

$$u(t)\cos\omega_0 t \leftrightarrow \frac{s}{\omega_0^2 + s^2}, \qquad \text{Re } s > 0 \tag{3–38b}$$

Thus, when $\sigma_0 = 0$, the Fourier transform cannot be obtained from the Laplace transform by this simple substitution of $j\omega$ for $s$.

We now develop a procedure whereby the Fourier transform can be obtained from the Laplace transform for certain cases. We shall do this by considering a class of function and, in a general sense, compare their Fourier and Laplace transforms.

If $F(s)$ is such that $\sigma_0 = 0$, then $F(s)$ must have singularities (see Section B-4) on the $j\omega$ axis. Note that (see Section 3-3) $F(s)$ is analytic to the right of the line defined by Re $s = \sigma_0$. We shall assume, at the start, that the only singularities are simple poles on the $j\omega$ axis. Then we write

$$F(s) = F_a(s) + \sum_{k=1}^{N} \frac{b_k}{s - j\omega_k} \tag{3-39}$$

where $F_a(s)$ is a function that is analytic on the $j\omega$ axis and in the right half $s$-plane and the $b_k$ are constants. (Because of the linearity of integration, if $f(t) = f_1(t) + f_2(t)$ and $f_1(t) \leftrightarrow F_1(s)$ and $f_2(t) \leftrightarrow F_2(s)$, then $f(t) \leftrightarrow F_1(s) + F_2(s)$.) Let $f_a(t) \leftrightarrow F_a(s)$. (Note that the Laplace transform is unique in the same sense as the Fourier transform.) Then (see Table 3-1)

$$f(t) = f_a(t) + \sum_{k=1}^{N} b_k e^{j\omega_k t} u(t) \tag{3-40}$$

Now we obtain the Fourier transform of $f(t)$. Since $F_a(s)$ is such that it is analytic for Re $s = 0$, we have for the Fourier transform of $f_a(t)$

$$F_{F_a}(j\omega) = F_a(j\omega) \tag{3-41}$$

The Fourier transform of $u(t)\, e^{j\omega_0 t}$ can be found from Table 2-1 by noting that

$$u(t)\, e^{j\omega_0 t} = u(t) \cos \omega_0 t + j u(t) \sin \omega_0 t$$

Then,

$$u(t)\, e^{j\omega_0 t} \leftrightarrow \pi \delta(\omega - \omega_0) + \frac{1}{j(\omega - \omega_0)} \tag{3-42}$$

Thus, the Fourier transform of $f(t)$ is given by

$$F_F(j\omega) = F_a(j\omega) + \sum_{k=1}^{N} b_k \left[ \pi \delta(\omega - \omega_k) + \frac{1}{j\omega + j\omega_k} \right] \tag{3-43}$$

Now consider the Laplace transform evaluated at $\sigma = 0$.

$$F(j\omega) = F_a(j\omega) + \sum_{k=1}^{N} \frac{b_k}{j\omega + j\omega_k} \tag{3-44}$$

Substituting in Eq. 3–43, we obtain

$$F_F(j\omega) = F(j\omega) + \pi \sum_{k=1}^{N} b_k \delta(\omega - \omega_0) \tag{3-45}$$

That is if the Laplace transform of an $f(t)$ is analytic in the right-half plane and on the $j\omega$ axis, except for a finite number of simple poles on the $j\omega$ axis, then the Fourier transform of that function is obtained by replacing $s$ by $j\omega$ and adding the appropriate delta functions.

As an example consider Eq. 3–38b. We can write

$$\frac{s}{\omega_0^2 + s^2} = \frac{1/2}{s + j\omega} + \frac{1/2}{s + j\omega}$$

Then, using Eq. 3–45, we obtain Eq. 3–38a.

Now consider the case of multiple poles on the $j\omega$ axis in the Laplace transform.

If

$$F(s) = \frac{1}{(s - j\omega_0)^n} \qquad (3-46)$$

then, it can be shown that

$$f(t) = u(t)\frac{t^{n-1}e^{j\omega_0 t}}{(n-1)!} \qquad (3-47)$$

It can also be shown that the Fourier transform of $f(t)$ is

$$F_F(j\omega) = \frac{\pi j^{n-1}}{(n-1)!}\delta^{(n-1)}(\omega - \omega_0) + \frac{1}{(j\omega - j\omega_0)^n} \qquad (3-48)$$

Then, proceeding as we did in the case of simple $j\omega$ axis poles, we can use Eqs. 3-46 and 3-48 to derive the following. If the Laplace transform of a function of time is given by

$$F(s) = F_a(s) + \sum_{s=1}^{N}\frac{b_k}{(s + j\omega_k)^{n_k}} \qquad (3-49)$$

where $F_a(s)$ is analytic on the $j\omega$ axis and in the right half plane, the Fourier transform of this function of time is given by

$$F_F(j\omega) = F_a(j\omega)$$

$$+ \sum_{k=1}^{N}b_k\left[\frac{\pi j^{n_k-1}}{(n_k-1)!}\delta^{(n_k-1)}(\omega - \omega_k) + \frac{1}{(j\omega + j\omega_k)^{n_k}}\right] \qquad (3-50a)$$

Comparing this with Eq. 3-49, we have

$$F_F(j\omega) = F(j\omega) + \pi\sum_{k=1}^{N}\frac{b_k j^{n_k-1}}{(n_k-1)!}\delta^{(n_k-1)}(\omega - \omega_k) \qquad (3-50b)$$

We have considered obtaining the Fourier transform from the Laplace transform. Of course, if we are given a Fourier transform and it *exactly* follows Eq. 3-50, including the relation between the constants of the impulse, or its derivatives and the residues of the appropriate $j\omega$ axis poles, then these equations can be used in a converse fashion to obtain the Fourier transform from the Laplace transform.

Actually, we have considered some special cases; however, in general, if we have $F(s)$, Re $s > 0$, then we can obtain $f(t)$ by taking the inverse Laplace transform. Then, the Fourier transform of $f(t)$ is obtained if it exists; this is $F_F(j\omega)$.

The results of this section show how the factor of $e^{-\sigma t}$ in the Laplace transform integrand aids in the convergence of the integral. Note that some functions of time (Case II) possess Laplace transforms, but do not have Fourier transforms. For Case III, the Fourier transforms have impulse functions or their derivatives, on a distribution basis, while the Laplace transform does not. Any function which has a Fourier transform will also have a Laplace transform, while the converse is not always true.

## 3-5. LAPLACE TRANSFORM OF DERIVATIVE AND INTEGRAL—SOLUTIONS OF LINEAR DIFFERENTIAL EQUATIONS WITH CONSTANT COEFFICIENTS

The Laplace transform is often the most convenient way of obtaining the solution of linear differential equations with constant coefficients in closed form. In order to use the Laplace transform for this purpose, we shall obtain the Laplace transform of the derivative and the integral.

**Laplace Transform of the Derivative.** Consider a function $f(t)$ whose Laplace transform is $F(s)$ and we wish to determine the Laplace transform of $df(t)/dt$ in terms of $F(s)$. We start by substituting $df(t)/dt$ in Eq. 3–10. This yields

$$\frac{df(t)}{dt} \leftrightarrow \int_{0-}^{\infty} \frac{df(t)}{dt} e^{-st} dt, \qquad \text{Re } s > \sigma_0 \tag{3-51}$$

We have explicitly written the lower limit as $0-$ here, since we must use it subsequently. Of course, $\sigma_0$ depends on $df(t)/dt$ and not upon $f(t)$. Evaluating the integral by parts we have

$$\int_{0-}^{\infty} u \, dv = uv \Big|_{0-}^{\infty} - \int_{0}^{\infty} v \, du \tag{3-52}$$

Then, in Eq. 3–51, let

$$u = e^{-st} \tag{3-53a}$$

$$dv = \frac{df(t)}{dt} dt = df(t) \tag{3-53b}$$

Hence,

$$du = -se^{-st} dt \tag{3-54a}$$

$$v = f(t) \tag{3-54b}$$

Then, integrating by parts, we obtain

$$\frac{df(t)}{dt} \leftrightarrow [f(t) e^{-st}]_{0-}^{\infty} + \int_{0-}^{\infty} sf(t) e^{-st} dt, \qquad \text{Re } s > \sigma_0 \tag{3-55}$$

In general, $\sigma_0$ must be large enough so that $\lim_{t \to \infty} f(t) e^{-st} = 0$; therefore,

$$[f(t) e^{-st}]_{0-}^{\infty} = -f(0-) \tag{3-56}$$

Now consider the integral. Since $s$ is a constant, it can be removed from the integral. The remaining integral is just $F(s)$, the Laplace transform of $f(t)$; hence,

$$\frac{df(t)}{dt} \leftrightarrow -f(0-) + sF(s), \qquad \text{Re } s > \sigma_0 \tag{3-57}$$

Thus, the Laplace transform of the derivative of a function is just $s$ times the transform of the function minus the initial $(0-)$ value of the function.

Remember that $\sigma_0$ is based on $df(t)/dt$ and it may be different from the $\sigma_0$ defined for $f(t)$. For example, if $f(t) = u(t)\sin\omega_0 t$, then $df(t)/dt = u(t)\omega_0\cos\omega_0 t$, and $\sigma_0 = 0$ for both. On the other hand, if $f(t) = u(t)[1 - e^{-t}]$, then $\sigma_0 = 0$. However, $df(t)/dt = u(t)e^{-t}$ and $\sigma_0 = -1$. Thus, $\sigma_0$ for the function is greater than $\sigma_0$ for the derivative. Finally, consider $f(t) = \sin e^t$. Then, $\sigma_0 = 0$. However, $df(t)/dt = e^t\cos e^t$, so $\sigma_0 = 1$. In this case, $\sigma_0$ for the function is less than $\sigma_0$ for the derivative. Often, $f(t)$ is an unknown. However, $\sigma_0$ can also be obtained from its Laplace transform directly by observing its region of analyticity (see Section 3-3).

The initial value is $f(0-)$ and not $f(0+)$. This is often a great convenience. Suppose $f(t)$ represents a current in an inductive circuit and an impulse of voltage is applied. Under these conditions, the current *can* change instantly. Thus, $f(0+)$ and $f(0-)$ differ. The known initial conditions occur prior to the application of the signal. Thus, it is $f(0-)$, while $f(0+)$ is unknown. Hence, the use of $0-$ rather than of $0+$ simplifies the work greatly. There are certain conceptual problems introduced by the use of $0-$. For example, a signal is often applied by closing a switch at $t = 0$. Thus, the system in question is not really in existence at $t = 0-$. (Usually, the initial conditions are set up previous to $0-$; i.e., a current is set up in an inductance and then switches are opened or closed.) This problem can often be eliminated by supposing that the generators in series or parallel with the switches are replaced by generators whose $f(t)$ are multiplied by unit step functions. The use of such unit step function usually resolves the problem of opening or closing switches since the system can be assumed to be in existence at $t = 0-$. (An alternative procedure is (conceptually) to replace the switches by generators whose voltages or currents equal the voltages across the switches or the currents through them.)

Consider some examples. If

$$f(t) = u(t)\sin\omega_0 t$$

then (see Table 3-1)

$$F(s) = \frac{\omega_0}{s^2 + \omega_0^2}$$

Then, using Eq. 3–57, we have

$$\frac{df(t)}{dt} \leftrightarrow \frac{s\omega_0}{s^2 + \omega_0^2}$$

Note that $\dfrac{df(t)}{dt} = \omega_0 u(t)\cos\omega_0 t$. Thus, the result is verified, see Table 3–10.

Let us discuss another example: if

$$f(t) = u(t)\cos\omega_0 t \leftrightarrow \frac{s}{s^2 + \omega_0^2}$$

then, using Eq. 3–57, we have

$$\frac{df(t)}{dt} \leftrightarrow \frac{s^2}{s^2 + \omega_0^2}$$

Note that $f(0-) = 0$ because of the unit step function. We now use distribution theory to obtain the derivative of $f(t)$ (see Section 2-2). This must be done since $f(t)$ is discontinuous at $t = 0$; thus,

$$\frac{df(t)}{dt} = \delta(t) - \omega_0 \sin \omega_0 t$$

Taking the Laplace transform of this, we have

$$\frac{df(t)}{dt} \leftrightarrow 1 - \frac{\omega_0^2}{s^2 + \omega_0^2} = \frac{s^2}{s^2 + \omega_0^2}$$

This checks out as it should.

Equation 3–57 can be extended to higher-ordered derivatives. For example,

$$\frac{d^2f(t)}{dt^2} = \frac{d}{dt}\left[\frac{df(t)}{dt}\right]$$

Now, apply Eq. 3–57, noting that $df(t)/dt$ replaces $f(t)$ there; hence,

$$\frac{d^2f(t)}{dt^2} \leftrightarrow s\mathscr{L}\frac{df(t)}{dt} - \frac{df(t)}{dt}\bigg|_{t=0-} \tag{3–58}$$

Substituting Eq. 3–57 for the Laplace transform of the derivative, we have

$$\frac{d^2f(t)}{dt^2} \leftrightarrow s^2F(s) - sf(0-) - \frac{df(t)}{dt}\bigg|_{t=0-} \tag{3–59}$$

Successively applying this procedure, we obtain

$$\frac{d^nf(t)}{dt^n} = s^nF(s) - s^{n-1}f(0-) - s^{n-2}\frac{df(t)}{dt}\bigg|_{t=0-} - \cdots - \frac{d^{n-1}f(t)}{dt^{n-1}}\bigg|_{t=0-} \tag{3–60}$$

**Laplace Transform of the Integral.** Now we shall obtain the Laplace transform of the integral of a function in terms of the transform of the function itself. The following notation will be used:

$$f^{(-1)}(t) = \int f(t)\,dt \tag{3–61}$$

Actually, in most systems, the indefinite integral represents the integral from $t = -\infty$ to $t = t$, an arbitrary time. Hence, we shall write Eq. 3–61 as

$$f^{(-1)}(t) = \int_{-\infty}^{0-} f(\tau)\,d\tau + \int_{0-}^{t} f(\tau)\,d\tau \tag{3–62}$$

Note that we have used $\tau$ as the variable of integration to avoid confusion between the limit $t$ and $\tau$. As an example, suppose $f(t)$ represents the current into a capacitor. Then, $\int_{-\infty}^{0-} f(\tau) d\tau$ represents the initial stored charge (at $t = 0 -$). Let us write this constant as

$$f^{(-1)}(0 -) = \int_{-\infty}^{0-} f(t) dt \qquad (3-63)$$

Differentiating both sides of Eq. 3–61, we obtain

$$\frac{d}{dt}[f^{(-1)}(t)] = f(t) \qquad (3-64)$$

Now, take the Laplace transform of both sides of Eq. 3–64, using Eq. 3–57; this yields

$$s\mathscr{L}[f^{(-1)}(t)] - f^{(-1)}(0 -) = F(s)$$

Therefore, we have

$$\mathscr{L}[f^{(-1)}(t)] = \mathscr{L}\left[\int f(t) dt\right] = \frac{F(s)}{s} + \frac{f^{(-1)}(0 -)}{s} \qquad (3-65)$$

Thus, the Laplace transform of the indefinite integral of a function is the Laplace transform of the function divided by $s$ plus the *initial value* of the integral divided by $s$.

As an example, let us solve the differential equation

$$\frac{df(t)}{dt} + 3f(t) + 2\int f(t) dt = u(t) \qquad (3-66)$$

where the given initial conditions are

$$f(0 -) = 2 \quad \text{and} \quad f^{(-1)}(0 -) = 0$$

Now take the Laplace transform of both sides of Eq. 3–66; this yields

$$sF(s) - f(0 -) + 3F(s) + 2\frac{F(s)}{s} + \frac{2f^{(-1)}(0 -)}{s} = \frac{1}{s}$$

where $F(s)$ is unknown and is the Laplace transform of the desired $f(t)$. Then, substituting the initial conditions and solving for $F(s)$, we have

$$F(s) = \frac{2s + 1}{s^2 + 3s + 2}$$

This can be expanded in partial fractions to obtain

$$F(s) = \frac{-1}{s + 1} + \frac{1}{s + 2}$$

(It is assumed that the reader is familiar with partial fraction expansion techniques.

The basic network theory texts in the bibliography are references for this.) Then, using Table 3-1, we have

$$f(t) = u(t)\left[-e^{-t} + 3e^{-2t}\right]$$  (3-67)

Clearly, the Laplace transform greatly reduces the work required to solve this equation, since the initial conditions are substituted at the beginning and an additional set of simultaneous equations does not have to be solved to obtain the arbitrary constants.

## 3-6. A BRIEF DISCUSSION OF THE COMPUTATION OF THE TRANSIENT RESPONSE USING THE LAPLACE TRANSFORM. AN ILLUSTRATION OF THE ADVANTAGE OF USING 0 – RATHER THAN 0 +

The transient response of a simple network will be obtained. In a subsequent chapter, we shall discuss analysis techniques with much more detail and rigor. Here we just present a simple example. Let us determine the unit step response of the network of Fig. 3–2a. The differential equation of this network is

$$Ri(t) + L\frac{di(t)}{dt} + \frac{1}{C}\int i(t)\, dt = u(t)$$  (3-68)

Taking the Laplace transform of both sides of this equation, we have

$$RI(s) + LsI(s) - Li(0-) + \frac{I(s)}{C} + v(0-) = \frac{1}{s}$$  (3-69)

Note that $1/C \int_{-\infty}^{0-} i\, dt$ represents the known initial voltage across the capacitor and $i(0-)$ is the known initial current through the inductor. We have assumed that an external circuit, removed just prior to $t = 0-$, has established the initial conditions. This equation is very similar to Eq. 3–66, hence details of its solution will not be repeated. Equation 3–69 is the transformed form of Eq. 3–68.

Suppose we draw a circuit whose equation is given by Eq. 3–69, where the currents and voltages are in transformed form and a generator for each inductor and capacitor is included. These generators supply the terms corresponding to the initial conditions. Such a circuit is shown in Fig. 3–2b. This is called the *transformed form of the circuit* of Fig. 3–2a.

In general, there are several transformed forms of impedance and admittance for inductors and capacitors. These are shown in Fig. 3–3. The details of the development of the transformed form of the impedance are not given since it is assumed that the reader is familiar with the elementary use of the Laplace transform for the solution of simple network problems (see basic network texts in the bibliography at the end of this chapter).

We now consider the solution of the circuit of Fig. 3–2 with the generator now

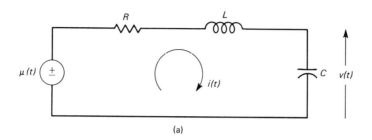

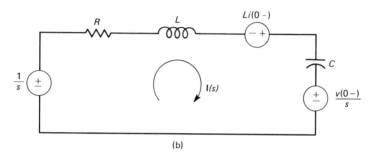

FIG. 3-2
(a) A simple network; (b) transformed form of this network

replaced by one that produces a unit impulse of voltage. The equation for this circuit is

$$Ri(t) + L\frac{di(t)}{dt} + \frac{1}{C}\int i(t)\, dt = \delta(t) \qquad (3\text{–}70)$$

Taking the Laplace transform of both sides of this equation, we obtain

$$RI(s) + LsI(s) - Li(0-) + \frac{I(s)}{Cs} + \frac{v(0-)}{s} = 1 \qquad (3\text{–}71)$$

Again, the equation can be solved using techniques similar to those used to solve Eq. 3–66. Note that the impulse presents no problems and that this circuit is analyzed in essentially the same way as the one in which the generator was a unit step.

When an impulse of voltage and/or current occurs in a network, the current through the inductances and the voltage across the capacitors can change instantaneously. Thus, even though $i_L(0-)$ and $v_C(0-)$ are known initial conditions, $i_L(0+)$ and $v_C(0+)$ are not. (If impulses are not present, $i_L(0-) = i_L(0+)$ and $v_C(0-) = v_C(0+)$. However, generally, this is not true.) Now suppose $0+$ is used instead of $0-$ as the lower limit of the Laplace transform integral. Then 3–71 would be replaced by

$$RI(s) + LsI(s) - Li(0+) + \frac{I(s)}{Cs} + \frac{v(0+)}{s} = 0 \qquad (3\text{–}72)$$

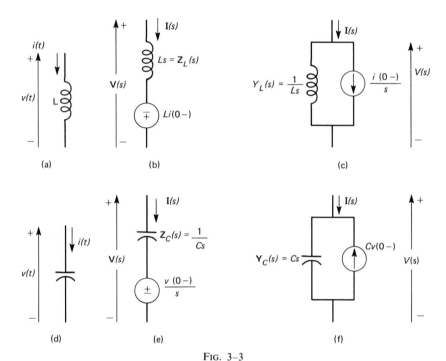

Fig. 3–3

Transformed forms; (a) inductor; (b) transformed form of this inductor suitable for use in loop analysis; (c) transformed form of the inductor suitable for use in nodal analysis; (d) capacitor; (e) transformed form of this capacitor suitable for use in loop analysis; (f) transformed form of this capacitor suitable for use in nodal analysis

Note that when $0 +$ is used $L[\delta(t)] = 0$ (see Section 3-1). The important thing to note here is that $i(0 +)$ and $v(0 +)$ are *unknowns*. Procedures do exist for finding them; however, these require tedious extra steps. The $0 -$ Laplace transform eliminates these steps. Thus, if there is no instant change of the current through the inductor or the voltage across the capacitor, the $0 -$ and $0 +$ transforms become equivalent. However, if such things as the response to an impulse are desired, the $0 -$ form is more desirable.

## 3-7. SOME BASIC LAPLACE TRANSFORM THEOREMS

In this section we shall consider some basic theorems which are often helpful when the Laplace transform is used. Many of the theorems (and their proofs) are similar to those developed for the Fourier transform. Therefore, such proofs will not be repeated. We shall indicate that $F(s)$ is the Laplace transform of $f(t)$ by

$$f(t) \leftrightarrow F(s) \tag{3-73}$$

This implies that both $f(t)$ and $F(s)$ exist, possibly on a distribution basis.

**Linearity.** The operations of the Laplace transform are linear; thus,

$$f_1(t) \leftrightarrow F_1(s) \tag{3-74a}$$

and

$$f_2(t) \leftrightarrow F_2(s) \tag{3-74b}$$

Then,

$$a_1 f_1(t) + a_2 f_2(t) \leftrightarrow a_1 F_1(s) + a_2 F_2(s) \tag{3-75}$$

where $a_1$ and $a_2$ are constants. This follows directly from the linearity of integration.

**Time Shift.** Suppose that $u(t) f(t) \leftrightarrow F(s)$. Let us determine the Laplace transform of $u(t - T) f(t - T)$. (Note that the time function is delayed by $T$ seconds.) Then,

$$u(t - T) f(t - T) \leftrightarrow e^{-sT} F(s) \tag{3-76}$$

Thus, if $f(t)$ is delayed by $T$ seconds, the resulting transform is the transform of $f(t)$ multiplied by $e^{-sT}$. This proof follows that of Eq. 2-171.

**Complex Frequency Shift.** If $f(t) \leftrightarrow F(s)$, then

$$f(t) e^{s_0 t} \leftrightarrow F(s - s_0) \tag{3-77}$$

where $s_0$ is a constant which may be complex. This proof follows that of Eq. 2-178.

**Time or Complex Frequency Scaling.** If $f(t) \leftrightarrow F(s)$, then

$$f(bt) \leftrightarrow \frac{1}{|b|} F\left(\frac{s}{b}\right) \tag{3-78}$$

The proof follows that of Eq. 2-184.

**Frequency Differentiation.** If $f(t) \leftrightarrow F(s)$, then

$$(-t)^n f(t) \leftrightarrow \frac{d^n F(s)}{ds^n}, \qquad \text{Re } s > \sigma_0 \tag{3-79}$$

From Eq. 3-32, we have

$$\frac{d^n F(s)}{ds^n} = \int_0^\infty (-t)^n f(t) e^{-st} dt, \qquad \text{Re } s > \sigma_0$$

However, the integrand is just the Laplace transform of $(-t)^n f(t)$. Thus, Eq. 3-79 is proved.

**Frequency Integration.** If $f(t) \leftrightarrow F(s)$, then

$$\frac{f(t)}{t} \leftrightarrow \int_s^\infty F(s_1) \, ds_1, \qquad \text{Re } s > \sigma_0 \tag{3-80}$$

Note that the variable of integration has been made $s_1$ since one limit of integration is $s$. To prove this theorem, integrate both sides of Eq. 3–10; thus,

$$\int_s^\infty F(s_1)\,ds_1 = \int_s^\infty \int_0^\infty f(t)\,e^{-s_1 t}\,dt\,ds_1, \qquad \text{Re } s_1 > \sigma_0$$

Assume that $f(t)$ and $\sigma_0$ are such that the integral converges uniformly and thus the order of integration can be interchanged; hence,

$$\int_s^\infty F(s_1)\,ds_1 = \int_0^\infty f(t)\int_s^\infty e^{-s_1 t}\,ds_1\,dt \tag{3–81}$$

Evaluating the inner integral, we have

$$\int_s^\infty F(s_1)\,ds_1 = \int_0^\infty \frac{f(t)}{t}\,e^{-st}\,dt \tag{3–82}$$

The integral on the right-hand side is just the Laplace transform of $f(t)/t$; hence, Eq. 3–80 is proved.

This theorem can be extended to multiple integrals in the following way. Integrating both sides of Eq. 3–10, $n$ times, we have

$$\int_s^\infty \int_{s_1}^\infty \cdots \int_{s_{n-1}}^\infty F(s_n)\,ds_n\,ds_{n-1}\cdots ds_1$$

$$= \int_s^\infty \int_{s_1}^\infty \cdots \int_{s_{n-1}}^\infty \int_0^\infty f(t)\,e^{-s_n t}\,dt\,ds_n\,ds_{n-1}\cdots ds_1 \tag{3–83}$$

Then, again assuming that the integrals converge uniformly and interchanging the order of integration, so that the integration with respect to $t$ is performed last, we have after integrating $n$ times with respect to $s$

$$\int_s^\infty \int_{s_1}^\infty \cdots \int_{s_{n-1}}^\infty F(s_n)\,ds_n\,ds_{n-1}\cdots ds_1 = \int_0^\infty \frac{f(t)}{t^n}\,e^{-st}\,dt \tag{3–84}$$

Thus, we have shown that

$$\frac{f(t)}{t^n} \leftrightarrow \int_s^\infty \int_{s_1}^\infty \cdots \int_{s_{n-1}}^\infty F(s_n)\,ds_n\,ds_{n-1}\cdots ds_1 \tag{3–85}$$

## 3-8. ONE-SIDED PERIODIC (SEMIPERIODIC) FUNCTIONS

Very often, we deal with a function which repeats itself (as a periodic function does) for $t > 0$, but is zero for $t < 0$. Such functions are called *one-sided periodic*, or *semiperiodic*, functions. (A typical one is shown in Fig. 3-4.) They are characterized by the relations

$$f(t) = \begin{cases} f(t+T); & t \geqq 0, \qquad t+T \geqq 0 \tag{3–86a} \\ 0, & t < 0 \end{cases} \tag{3–86b}$$

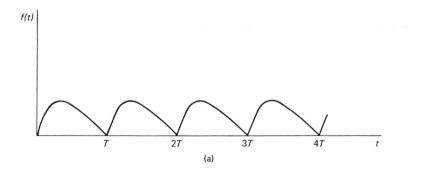

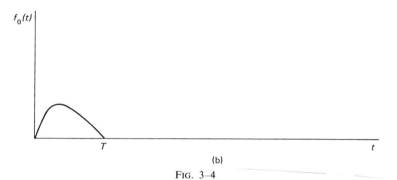

FIG. 3–4

(a) One-sided periodic function $f(t)$; (b) function equal to $f(t)$ for the first cycle and zero elsewhere

Now consider another function $f_0(t)$ which is equal to $f(t)$ for the first "cycle" but is zero elsewhere (see Fig. 3-4b).

$$f_0(t) = \begin{cases} f(t), & 0 \leq t \leq T \\ 0, & t \leq 0, \quad t \leq T \end{cases} \tag{3–87}$$

Let

$$f_0(t) \leftrightarrow F_0(s), \qquad \text{Re } s > \sigma_0 = -\infty \tag{3–88}$$

Note that $\sigma_0 = -\infty$ since $f_0(t) = 0$ for sufficiently large $t$. We now obtain the Laplace transform of $f(t)$ in terms of $F_0(s)$. $f(t)$ can be expressed in terms of $f_0(t)$ in the following way:

$$f(t) = f_0(t) + f_0(t - T) + f_0(t - 2T) + \dots \tag{3–89}$$

Then, applying the time shift theorem (see Eq. 3–76), we obtain

$$f(t) \leftrightarrow F_0(s)(1 + e^{-sT} + e^{-2sT} + \dots) \tag{3–90}$$

This can be written in a more compact form by noting that

$$\frac{1}{1 - e^{sT}} = 1 + e^{-sT} + e^{-2sT} + \ldots, \qquad \text{Re } sT > 0 \qquad (3\text{-}91)$$

Note that $\text{Re } sT > 0$ is necessary if the Taylor's expansion expression is to be valid. Since $T > 0$, this condition reduces to $\text{Re } s > 0$. Then, substituting in Eq. 3–90, we obtain

$$\boldsymbol{F}(s) = \frac{\boldsymbol{F}_0(s)}{1 - e^{sT}}, \qquad \text{Re } s > \sigma_0 = 0 \qquad (3\text{-}92)$$

Let us consider $\sigma_0$ for Eq. 3–92 independent of the condition for Eq. 3–91. In general, for $\boldsymbol{F}_0(s)$, $\text{Re } s$ is unrestricted (i.e., $\sigma_0 = -\infty$). (Note that $f(t)$ does not rise or fall with time.) If $f_0(t)$ is bounded, then any exponential falloff in $e^{-st}$ will cause the Laplace transform integral to converge. Also, any exponential increase in $e^{-st}$ will guarantee divergence. Thus, for Eq. 3–92,

$$\sigma_0 = 0 \qquad (3\text{-}93)$$

This is identical to the condition of Eq. 3–91.

In general, no impulses are present in this transform. In contrast to the case of the Fourier series. Again, the decay of $e^{-\sigma t}$ simplifies the convergence of the transform.

## 3-9. INITIAL VALUE THEOREM

At times, we wish to determine the initial value of a function or its derivative. For example, $df(t)/dt$ evaluated at $t = 0 +$ gives an indication of the initial rate of rise of $f(t)$. We shall develop a procedure whereby the initial value of a function at $t = 0 +$ and its derivatives can be obtained from the Laplace transform of a function without having to evaluate the inverse transform. We can use this procedure to evaluate "initial values" after the application of impulses. Usually, if impulses etc. are not present, then $f(0 +) = f(0 -)$. Assume that

$$f(t) \leftrightarrow \boldsymbol{F}(s)$$

and that $\boldsymbol{F}(s)$ is known, while $f(t)$ is not known.

In order to use this procedure we must have a knowledge of any impulses, doublets, etc, which occur at $t = 0$, in $f(t)$. Let us see how these can be obtained without having to take the inverse Laplace transform. Assume that $\boldsymbol{F}(s)$ is expressed as the ratio of two polynomials in $s$; thus,

$$\boldsymbol{F}(s) = \frac{a_n s^n + a_{n-1} s^{n-1} + \cdots + a_1 s + a_0}{b_m s^m + b_{m-1} s^{m-1} + \cdots + b_1 s + b_0} \qquad (3\text{-}94)$$

If $m \geq n$, then $f(t)$ will not contain any impulses or their derivatives since (see Table 3-1) they all have transforms of the form $s^k$, $k = 0, 1, 2, \ldots$. If $n > m$, there will be an impulse and/or its derivatives. In this case, carry out the long division of Eq.

3–94 until the remainder is a proper fraction:

$$F(s) = K_{n-m}s^{n-m} + K_{n-m-1}s^{n-m-1} + \cdots + K_1 s + K_0$$

$$+ \frac{d_{m-1}s^{m-1} + d_{m-2}s^{m-2} + \cdots + d_1 s + d_0}{b_m s^m + b_{m-1}s^{m-1} + \cdots + b_1 s + b_0} \tag{3-95}$$

Now let us write

$$F(s) = F_1(s) + F_0(s)$$

where

$$F_1(s) = K_{n-m}s^{n-m} + K_{n-m-1}s^{n-m-1} + \cdots + K_1 s + K_0 \tag{3-96}$$

By applying linearity (see Eq. 3–75), if

$$f_1(t) \leftrightarrow F_1(s) \tag{3-97a}$$

$$f_0(t) \leftrightarrow F_0(s) \tag{3-97b}$$

then

$$f(t) = f_1(t) + f_0(t)$$

Therefore, all of the impulses, doublets, etc. contained in $f(t)$ will be in $f_1(t)$. Taking the inverse transform of Eq. 3–96, using Table 3-1, we have

$$f_1(t) = K_0\delta(t) + K_1\delta'(t) + \cdots + K_{n-m}\delta^{(n-m)}(t) \tag{3-98}$$

Thus, for the original $f(t)$, we can write (see Eq. 3–97)

$$f(t) = f_0(t) + K_0\delta(t) + K_1\delta'(t) + K_2\delta''(t) + \cdots \tag{3-99}$$

Hence, by carrying out the long division of $F(s)$, we can determine the coefficients of the impulses, doublets, etc. in $f(t)$ without evaluating the inverse Laplace transform.

We now develop the *initial value theorem*. From Eqs. 3–51 and 3–57, we have

$$\int_{0-}^{\infty} f'(t)\, e^{-st} dt = sF(s) - f(0-) \tag{3-100}$$

where $f'(t) = df(t)/dt$ and $f(t) \leftrightarrow F(s)$. Break up the integral in the following way

$$\int_{0-}^{\infty} f'(t)\, e^{-st} dt = \int_{0-}^{0+} f'(t)\, e^{-st} dt + \int_{0+}^{\infty} f'(t)\, e^{-st} dt \tag{3-101}$$

Consider the first integral on the right. Substituting Eq. 3–99, we obtain

$$\int_{0-}^{0+} f'(t)\, e^{-st} dt = \int_{0-}^{0+} f_0'(t)\, e^{-st} dt + \int_{0-}^{0+} K_0\delta'(t)\, e^{-st} dt$$

$$+ \int_{0-}^{0+} K_1\delta''(t)\, e^{-st} dt + \cdots \tag{3-102}$$

We shall consider this term by term.

For the first integral on the right, $e^{-st} = 1$ over the range of integration; i.e., $e^0 = 1$. Hence,

$$\int_{0-}^{0+} f_0'(t) e^{-st} dt = \int_{0-}^{0+} f_0'(t) dt = f_0(0+) - f_0(0-) \qquad (3\text{--}103)$$

The remaining integrals are of the form

$$K_{m-1} \int_{0-}^{0+} \delta^{(m)}(t) e^{-st} dt$$

Then, proceeding as in Eq. 3–13, we can write

$$K_{m-1} \int_{0-}^{0+} \delta^{(m)}(t) e^{-st} dt = K_{m-1} \int_{-\infty}^{\infty} \delta^{(m)}(t) e^{-st} dt \qquad (3\text{--}104)$$

Then, using Eqs. 2–6 and 2–21, we obtain

$$K_{m-1} \int_{0-}^{0+} \delta^m(t) e^{-st} dt = K_{m-1} s^m \qquad (3\text{--}105)$$

Substituting Eqs. 3–102 and 3–105 into Eq. 3–101 and then substituting into Eq. 3–100, we have

$$f(0+) - f(0-) + K_0 s + K_1 s^2 + K_2 s^3 + \cdots + \int_{0+}^{\infty} f'(t) e^{-st} dt = sF(s) - f(0-)$$

Solving for $f(0+)$ yields

$$f(0+) = s[F(s) - K_0 - K_1 s - K_2 s^2 - \cdots] - \int_{0+}^{\infty} f'(t) e^{-st} dt \qquad (3\text{--}106)$$

This relation is true for all values of $s$. Let us choose the one value of $s$ that makes the evaluation easiest. In particular, we would like to choose a value of $s$ which eliminates the need for evaluating the integral. We assume that $f'(t)$ is of exponential order. Then, $\lim_{s \to \infty} f'(t) e^{-st} = 0$, for all $t > 0$. Note that $0+ \leq t \leq \infty$ in the integral so that $t > 0$ for all values of $t$ in this range. This is why the integral was broken up as indicated in Eq. 3–101. If the lower limit were $0-$, then $t = 0$ would be an allowed value and we could not state that the integrand became zero as $s \to \infty$, since $st$ would be zero. Thus since $0+ \leq t \leq \infty$, letting $s$ approach infinity causes the integrand and, hence the integral, to be zero; therefore,

$$f(0+) = \lim_{s \to \infty} s[F(s) - K_0 - K_1 s - K_2 s^2 - \cdots] \qquad (3\text{--}107)$$

If $f(t)$ contains no impulses or their derivatives at $t = 0$, this Eq. 3–107 becomes

$$f(0+) = \lim_{s \to \infty} sF(s) \qquad (3\text{--}108)$$

**Initial Value of Derivative.** If $F(s)$, the Laplace transform of $f(t)$, is known, and, in addition, if the value of $f(t)$ and its derivatives are known at $t = 0-$, then Eq. 3–107 or 3–108 can be used to evaluate the derivatives of $f(t)$ at $t = 0+$. Equation 3–60 is used to obtain the Laplace transform of the derivatives. The initial value theorem is then applied to each of them in turn.

Let us now discuss some examples. First consider

$$u(t) \cos \omega_0 t \leftrightarrow \frac{s}{s^2 + \omega_0^2}$$

The power of the denominator is greater than that of the numerator. Hence, there are no impulses etc. Using Eq. 3–108, we have

$$\lim_{t \to 0+} u(t) \cos \omega_0 t = \lim_{s \to \infty} \frac{s^2}{s^2 + \omega_0^2} = 1$$

We work with a function which has an impulse at $t = 0$. From Section 3-5, we have

$$\frac{d[u(t) \cos \omega_0 t]}{dt} \leftrightarrow \frac{s^2}{s^2 + \omega_0^2} = 1 - \frac{\omega_0^2}{s^2 + \omega_0^2}$$

Thus (see Eq. 3–107) $K_0 = 1$. Substituting in Eq. 3–107, we have

$$\lim_{t \to 0+} \frac{d}{dt} [u(t) \cos \omega_0 t] = \lim_{s \to \infty} s \left( \frac{s^2}{s^2 + \omega_0^2} - 1 \right) = 0$$

This is true since

$$\frac{d}{dt} [u(t) \cos \omega_0 t] = \delta(t) + u(t) \sin \omega_0 t$$

## 3-10. FINAL VALUE THEOREM

We now develop a theorem which enables us to obtain the *final value* of a function from its Laplace transform without having to take the inverse transform. From Eq. 3–57, we have

$$\int_{0-}^{\infty} f'(t) e^{-st} dt = sF(s) - f(0-)$$

Now let $s$ approach 0. Then $e^{-st}$ becomes unity; hence, we have

$$\int_{0-}^{\infty} f'(t) dt = \lim_{s \to 0} sF(s) - f(0-) \tag{3–109}$$

However,

$$\int_{0-}^{\infty} f'(t) dt = \lim_{t \to \infty} f(t) - f(0-) \tag{3–110}$$

Substituting in Eq. 3–109, we obtain

$$\lim_{t \to \infty} f(t) = \lim_{s \to 0} sF(s) \tag{3-111}$$

This is called the *final value theorem*.

Now let us consider an example. From Table 3-1,

$$u(t)\left[1 - e^{-t}\right] \leftrightarrow \frac{1}{s} - \frac{1}{s+1} - \frac{1}{s(s+1)}$$

Then, applying Eq. 3–111, we have

$$\lim_{t \to \infty} u(t)\left[1 - e^{-t}\right] = \lim_{s \to 0} \frac{1}{s+1} = 1$$

As another example, let us consider

$$u(t) \cos \omega_0 t \leftrightarrow \frac{s}{s^2 + \omega_0^2}$$

$$\lim_{t \to \infty} u(t) \cos \omega_0 t = \lim_{s \to 0} \frac{s^2}{s^2 + \omega_0^2} = 0$$

In an ordinary sense, $\cos \omega_0 t$ has no defined final value. However, on a distribution basis, $\lim_{t \to \infty} \cos \omega_0(t) = 0$ (see Eq. 2–46). *The final value given by* Eq. 3–111 *will be on a distribution basis.* This should be remembered when the theorem is used.

If an $f(t)$ is such that its Laplace transform $F(s)$ has poles in the right half plane, then $f(t)$ will build up exponentially with time. In this case, $F(s)$ does not exist for $s = 0$. Thus we cannot take the limit as $s$ approaches zero. Hence the final value theorem cannot be used.

In general, to apply the final value theorem, $F(s)$ must be analytic in the right-half plane and can have only poles on the $j\omega$ axis. That is, if $f(t)$ is such that it possesses a Fourier transform, then the final value theorem can be applied to the Laplace transform of $f(t)$. If distribution theory is not used, then there can be no poles on the $j\omega$ axis or in the right-half plane.

## 3-11. INVERSE LAPLACE TRANSFORM—JORDAN'S LEMMA

We have thus far utilized the uniqueness of the Laplace transform to obtain the inverse Laplace transform; that is, we used Eq. 3–10 to obtain $F(s)$ from a given $f(t)$. We then stated that the inverse Laplace transform of $F(s)$ was $f(t)$. This procedure is acceptable. However, if an $F(s)$ does not appear in the known list of transforms, its inverse transform cannot be obtained by this procedure. In such cases, we must evaluate Eq. 3–11 to obtain $f(t)$ from $F(s)$.

The integrand of Eq. 3–11 is a function of a complex variable. It is assumed that the reader is familiar with the integration of such functions (see Sections B-5 through B-9). The inverse Laplace transform Eq. 3–11 is evaluated along the straight line path $C + j\omega$, $-\infty \leq \omega \leq \infty$. This line is called the *Bromwich path* and is illustrated in Fig. 3–5. The integral of Eq. 3–11 can be evaluated using formal complex integration. However, in very many circumstances, *residues* can be used to evaluate this integral more easily. Residue theory can be simply applied when the only singularities of $F(s)$ are poles. In this section, we shall assume that this is so. In the next, we shall consider branch point singularities. At the start we shall assume that $F(s)$ only has a finite number of poles. Then, we shall extend the result to an infinite number of poles.

**Finite Number of Poles—Jordan's Lemma.** Assume that $F(s)$ is analytic to the right of the line $s = \sigma_0$ and that the only singularities that $F(s)$ has are poles, which lie to the left of the line $s = \sigma_0$. Finally, we assume that

$$\lim_{s \to \infty} F(s) = 0 \qquad (3-112)$$

(This last equation is necessary if we are to apply residue theory.)

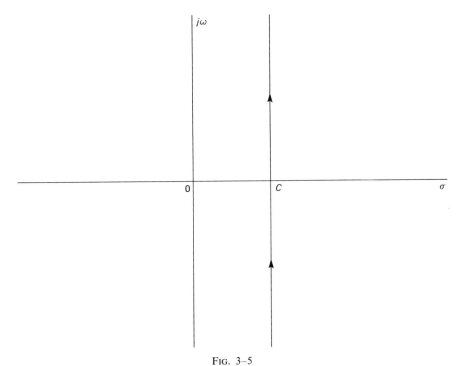

FIG. 3–5

Path of integration of the inverse Laplace transform integral

Consider the integral along the contour in Fig. 3–6 in the limit as $R$ approaches infinity. It could be equal to the integral along the straight line portion of the path; i.e., the Bromwich path (see Eqs. B–70 through B–76). The path would then be closed and residue theory could be applied to evaluate the integral. Using the integral of the inverse Laplace transform, we can write

$$\int_{C-j\infty}^{C+j\infty} F(s)\, e^{st}\, ds + \int_{C_R} F(s)\, e^{st}\, ds = \oint_{C_C} F(s)\, e^{st}\, ds \qquad (3\text{–}113)$$

where $C_R$ represents the circular portion of the path and $C_C$ corresponds to the

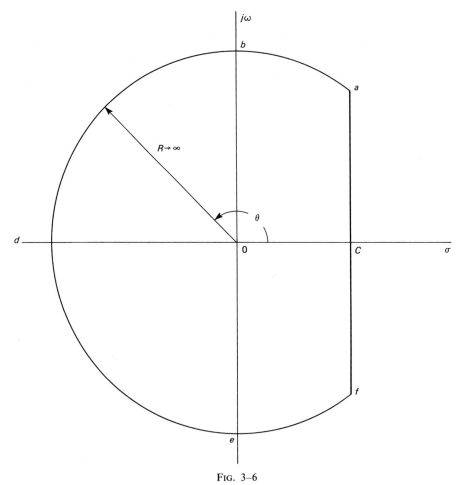

FIG. 3–6

Closed contour of integration for illustrating the inverse Laplace transform integral for $t > 0$ if Jordan's lemma is applicable

*entire* closed path. If we can show that

$$\int_{C_R} F(s) e^{st} ds = 0 \tag{3-114}$$

Then we can write

$$f(t) = \frac{1}{2\pi j} \int_{C-j\infty}^{C+j\infty} F(s) e^{st} ds = \frac{1}{2\pi j} \oint_{C_C} F(s) e^{st} ds \tag{3-115}$$

Note that $C_C$ and $C_R$ are considered in the limit as $R$ approaches $\infty$. If Eq. 3–115 is true, then (see Eq. B–73), we have

$$f(t) = \frac{1}{2\pi j} \int_{C-j\infty}^{C+j\infty} F(s) e^{st} ds$$

$$= \sum [\text{Residues of } F(s) e^{st} \text{ to left of } s = C + j\infty] \tag{3-116}$$

We must now show that if $F(s)$ satisfies the conditions outlined at the beginning of this part of the section, then Eq. 3–114 is satisfied. To do this we shall assume that $R$ is finite and consider the integral over a finite arc $C_{R_1}$; i.e., $C_R = \lim_{R \to \infty} C_{R_1}$. We choose the starting value of $R$ large enough so that it includes *all* the poles of $F(s)$. Now let us break $C_{R_1}$ up into several segments:

$$\int_{C_{R_1}} F(s) e^{st} ds = \int_a^b F(s) e^{st} ds + \int_b^d F(s) e^{st} ds$$

$$+ \int_d^e F(s) e^{st} ds + \int_e^f F(s) e^{st} ds \tag{3-117a}$$

or, equivalently,

$$\int_{C_R} F(s) e^{st} ds = f_1(t) + f_2(t) + f_3(t) + f_4(t) \tag{3-117b}$$

On the circle $C_{R_1}$.

$$s = Re^{j\theta} \tag{3-118}$$

and

$$ds = jRe^{j\theta} d\theta \tag{3-119}$$

Thus, we have

$$f_1(t) = jR \int_{\phi_a}^{\pi/2} F(s) e^{tR\cos\theta} e^{jtR\sin\theta} d\theta \tag{3-120}$$

where

$$\phi_a = \cos^{-1} \frac{C}{R} = \frac{\pi}{2} - \sin^{-1} \frac{C}{R} \tag{3-121}$$

On the arc $ab$, Re $s$ is bound by

$$\text{Re } s = R \cos\theta \leqq C \tag{3-122}$$

On $C_{R_1}$, let $F_R$ be the maximum value of $|F(s)|$; thus,

$$|F(s)| \leq F_R \tag{3-123}$$

Then

$$|f_1(t)| \leq R \int_{\phi_a}^{\pi/2} F_R e^{Ct} d\theta = RF_R e^{Ct} \left( \frac{\pi}{2} - \phi_a \right)$$

Substituting Eq. 3–121, we have

$$|f_1(t)| \leq RF_R e^{Ct} \sin^{-1} \frac{C}{R}. \tag{3-124}$$

For large $R$,

$$\sin^{-1} \frac{C}{R} \approx \frac{C}{R}$$

Substituting in Eq. 3–124, we obtain

$$|f_1(t)| \leq CF_R e^{Ct} \tag{3-125}$$

where $e^{Ct}$ is bound for all finite $t$. Then, from Eq. 3–112, we have

$$\lim_{R \to \infty} F_R = 0 \tag{3-126}$$

Hence,

$$\lim_{R \to \infty} |f_1(t)| = 0 \tag{3-127}$$

Proceeding in essentially the same way, we can show that

$$\lim_{R \to \infty} |f_4(t)| = 0 \tag{3-128}$$

Now consider the integral over the circular arc $bd$:

$$f_2(t) = j \int_{\pi/2}^{\pi} F(s) e^{tR\cos\theta} e^{jt\sin\theta} R \, d\theta \tag{3-129}$$

Thus,

$$|f_2(t)| \leq \int_{\pi/2}^{\pi} |F(s)| e^{tR\cos\theta t} R \, dt \tag{3-130}$$

Now, we make the substitution

$$\phi = \theta - \frac{\pi}{2} \tag{3-131}$$

Thus, Eq. 3–130 becomes

$$|f_2(t)| \leq \int_0^{\pi/2} |F(s)| e^{-tR\sin\theta} R \, d\phi \tag{3-132}$$

in which we have made use of the trigonometric identity

$$\cos\left( \frac{\pi}{2} + \phi \right) = -\sin\phi$$

Now we make use of a well-known inequality

$$\sin \phi \geq \frac{2\phi}{\pi}, \qquad 0 \leq \phi \leq \frac{\pi}{2} \tag{3-133}$$

(This can be verified by plotting $y = \sin \phi$. It intersects the straight line $y = 2\phi/\pi$ at the origin and at $\phi = \pi/2$; $\sin \theta$ is above this straight line at all other points.) Then, substitution in Eq. 3–132 yields

$$|f_2(t)| \leq \int_0^{\pi/2} |F(s)| \, e^{-2tR\phi/\pi} R \, d\phi \tag{3-134}$$

Substituting Eq. 3–123 and integrating, we have

$$|f_2(t)| \leq F_R R \frac{\pi}{2tR} (1 - e^{-tR})$$

or, equivalently,

$$|f_2(t)| \leq \frac{\pi F_R}{2t} (1 - e^{-tR}) \tag{3-135}$$

For all $t > 0$, $e^{-tR} \leq 1$ and $1/t$ is bounded. Hence, for $t > 0$, applying Eq. 3–126, we have

$$\lim_{R \to \infty} |f_2(t)| = 0 \tag{3-136}$$

Proceeding in a similar manner, we can show that

$$\lim_{R \to 0} f_3(t) = 0 \tag{3-137}$$

Note that these results are only valid if $t > 0$. Thus, we have shown that Eq. 3–114 is true. We can now write

$$f(t) = \frac{1}{2\pi j} \int_{C-j\infty}^{C+j\infty} F(s) \, e^{st}, \, ds, \qquad \text{Re } C > \sigma_0$$

$$= \sum [\text{Res } F(s) \, e^{st} \, ds \text{ to left of } s = C], \qquad t > 0 \tag{3-138}$$

Equations 3–10 and 3–11 are derived from the Fourier transform. In deriving Eq. 3–10, we assumed that $f(t) = 0$ for $t < 0$. However, no such assumption was made in deriving Eq. 3–11; thus, it should be valid for both positive and negative time. Equation 3–138 can only be used for $t > 0$. This restriction was imposed because $e^{-tR}$ appears in Eq. 3–135. If $t < 0$, the exponent would be positive and $e^{-tR}$ would increase as $R$ increases. This is equivalent to saying that in the left half plane $e^{st}$ falls off as $|s|$ increases, if $t > 0$. To obtain an equivalent result which is valid for negative time, we shall use the path shown in Fig. 3–7. We must show that the integral over the circular arc vanishes as $R$ approaches $\infty$. Let

$$f_5(t) = \int_a^g F(s) \, e^{-st} \, ds \tag{3-139}$$

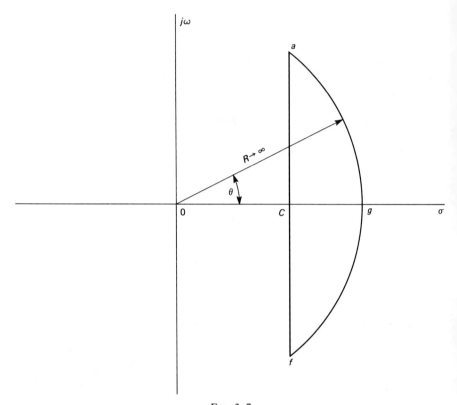

FIG. 3–7
Closed contour of integration for illustrating the inverse Laplace transform for $t < 0$
if Jordan's lemma is applicable

Substituting Eq. 3–118, we have

$$|f_5(t)| \leq \int_{\phi_a}^{0} |F(s)| \, e^{tR\cos\theta} R \, d\theta \qquad (3\text{–}140)$$

where $\phi_a$ is given in Eq. 3–121; but $0 < \phi_a < \pi/2$; hence,

$$|f_5(t)| \leq \int_{\pi/2}^{0} |F(s)| \, e^{tR\cos\theta} R \, d\theta$$

Then, following the development of Eq. 3–134, we have

$$|f_5(t)| \leq \int_{0}^{-\pi/2} |F(s)| \, e^{-2R\phi/\pi} R \, d\phi \qquad (3\text{–}141)$$

Substituting of Eq. 3–123 and integrating yields

$$|f_5(t)| \leq \frac{\pi}{2t} F_R(1 - e^{tR}) \qquad (3\text{--}142)$$

If $t < 0$, then $e^{tR} \leq \phi$ for all values of $R$. Hence, using Eq. 3–126 we have

$$\lim_{R \to \infty} |f_5(t)| = 0 \qquad (3\text{--}143)$$

Similarly, we can show that

$$\lim_{R \to \infty} |f_6(t)| = \lim_{R \to \infty} \left| \int_g^f F(s) e^{st} \, ds \right| = 0 \qquad (3\text{--}144)$$

Hence, we can state that

$$f(t) = -\frac{1}{2\pi j} \int_{C-j\infty}^{C+j\infty} F(s) e^{st} \, ds, \qquad C > \sigma_0$$

$$\qquad (3\text{--}145)$$

$$= -\frac{1}{2\pi j} \sum [\text{Res } F(s) e^{st} \text{ to right of } s = \sigma], \qquad t < 0$$

Note that the minus sign is included since the closed path of integration is clockwise instead of counterclockwise. Combining Eqs. 3–138 and 3–145, we obtain

$$f(t) = \begin{cases} \sum [\text{Res } F(s) e^{st} \text{ to left of } s = \sigma_0], & t > 0 \\ -\sum [\text{Res } F(s) e^{dt} \text{ to right of } s = \sigma_0], & t < 0 \end{cases} \qquad (3\text{--}146)$$

These results are called *Jordan's lemma.*

We have evaluated $f(t)$ for $t > 0$ and $t < 0$. Now let us consider $f(0)$. The Laplace transform is derived from the Fourier transform; thus (see Eq. 2–79),

$$f(0) = \tfrac{1}{2}[f(0+) + f(0-)] \qquad (3\text{--}147)$$

Consider some examples of this procedure. We shall evaluate the inverse Laplace transform of

$$F(s) = \frac{s}{s^2 + \omega_0^2}, \qquad \text{Re } s > \sigma_0 = 0$$

Then,

$$f(t) = \frac{1}{2\pi j} \int_{C-j\infty}^{C\infty j\infty} \frac{s}{s^2 + \omega_0^2} e^{st} \, ds, \qquad C > 0$$

$se^{st}/(s^2 + \omega_0^2)$ has a pair of poles on the $j\omega$ axis. They lie to the left of the path of integration. Then, for $t > 0$,

$$f(t) = [\text{Res } F(s) e^{st} \text{ at } s = j\omega_0] + [\text{Res } F(s) e^{st} \text{ at } s = -j\omega_0]$$

We shall use Eq. B–63b to evaluate the residues

$$[\text{Res } F(s) e^{st} \text{ at } s = j\omega_0] = \dfrac{se^{st}}{\dfrac{d}{ds}(s^2 + \omega_0^2)}\Bigg|_{s=j\omega_0} = \dfrac{j\omega_0 e^{j\omega_0 t}}{2j\omega_0} = \dfrac{e^{j\omega_0 t}}{2}$$

$$[\text{Res } F(s) e^{st} \text{ at } s = -j\omega_0] = \dfrac{-j\omega_0 e^{-j\omega_0 t}}{-2j\omega_0} = \dfrac{e^{-j\omega_0 t}}{2}$$

Thus,

$$f(t) = \dfrac{(e^{j\omega_0 t} + e^{-j\omega_0 t})}{2}$$

Hence,

$$f(t) = \cos \omega_0 t, \qquad t > 0$$

There are no poles to the right of the Bromwich path; therefore,

$$f(t) = 0, \qquad t < 0$$

Then, $f(0+) = 1$ and $f(0-) = 0$; hence,

$$f(0) = \tfrac{1}{2}$$

Thus,

$$f(t) = u(t) \cos \omega_0 t$$

As another example, we evaluate the inverse Laplace transform of

$$F(s) = \dfrac{1 - e^{-s}}{s}, \qquad \text{Re } s > \sigma_0 = -\infty$$

This function does not have a pole at $s = 0$ since the numerator also becomes zero there. Apply L'Hopital's rule: $\lim_{s \to 0} F(s) = \lim_{s \to 0} e^{-s} = 1$. The function $F(s)$ is analytic in the entire plane. Such functions are called *entire functions*.

$\text{Lim}_{s \to \infty} F(s) \neq 0$ because of the exponential. Thus, Jordan's lemma cannot be directly applied. However, we can use linearity to split this up into two transforms.

$$F(s) = F_1(s) + F_2(s)$$

where

$$F_1(s) = \dfrac{1}{s}$$

and

$$F_2(s) = \dfrac{-e^{-s}}{s}$$

We cannot use Jordan's lemma to evaluate $F_2(s)$. However, once the inverse Laplace transform of $F_1(s)$ is obtained, $\mathscr{L}^{-1} F_2(s)$ can be employed using the time shift theorem (see Eq. 3–76).

Let us now evaluate $\mathscr{L}^{-1} F_1(s)$. Since $\sigma_0 = -\infty$, the Bromwich path $s = C + j\omega$ can be put at any value of $C$. Choose the path to the right of the origin; i.e., $C > 0$. Then, using Eq. 3–146

$$f_1(t) = \begin{cases} \left( \text{Res } \dfrac{e^{st}}{s} \text{ at } s = 0 \right), & t > 0 \\ 0, & t < 0 \end{cases}$$

Solving for the residue, we have

$$f_1(t) = \begin{cases} 1, & t > 0 \\ 0, & t < 0 \end{cases}$$

Hence,

$$f_1(t) = \mu(t)$$

Then, using the time shift theorem, we obtain

$$f_2(t) = -u(t-1)$$

Hence,

$$f(t) = u(t) - u(t-1)$$

This represents a pulse of height 1 which persists for 1 second.

Now let us again evaluate this example, but using the Bromwich path to the *left* of the origin; i.e., $C < 0$. Thus, there are no singularities of $F_1(s)$ to the left of the path, while there is one to the right; hence (see Eq. 3–146),

$$f_1(t) = \begin{cases} 0, & t > 0 \\[2mm] \left[ -\operatorname{Res} \dfrac{e^{st}}{s} \text{ at } s = 0 \right], & t < 0 \end{cases}$$

Therefore,

$$f_1(t) = \begin{cases} 0, & t > 0 \\ -1, & t < 0 \end{cases}$$

Thus, $f_1(t) = -u(-t)$. But $f_2(t)$ is obtained by delaying this by 1 second and multiplying by $-1$; hence,

$$f_2(t) = \begin{cases} 0, & t > 1 \\ 1, & t < 1 \end{cases}$$

or

$$f_2(t) = u(1-t)$$

Thus,

$$f(t) = -u(-t) + u(1-t)$$

Of course, this yields the same pulse as before.

**Infinite Number of Poles.**  Now suppose we wish to obtain the inverse transform of an $F(s)$ whose only singularities are an infinite number of poles. If all the poles of $F(s)$ lie to the left of the line $s = \sigma_0$ and within a finite distance of the origin, then Jordan's lemma still applies; that is, the radius $R$ is chosen large enough to include all the poles as before and $\lim_{R \to \infty}$ is taken. If all the poles do not lie in a finite region, then this procedure must be modified somewhat. For instance suppose

$$F(s) = \frac{1}{s \cosh s} \tag{3–148}$$

Thus, poles occur at

$$s = 0 \tag{3-149a}$$

and

$$s_n = \pm j\frac{\pi}{2}(2n - 1), \qquad n = 1, 2, \ldots \tag{3-149b}$$

(Note that $\cosh jx = \cos x$.) It can be shown that these are simple poles by demonstrating that $(s - s_n)/\cosh s|_{s=s_n}$ is bounded and nonzero. (L'Hôpital's rule is used.) The details of this will be left to the reader. We cannot apply Jordan's lemma directly in this case since it is necessary that, on the infinite circular contour of integration $\lim_{s\to\infty} F(s) \to 0$. However, since there are an infinite number of poles, infinitely distributed, at least one point on the contour will periodically become infinite as the contour *passes through the poles*.

It may seem as though Jordan's lemma could not be applied in this case. However, often a sequence of discrete circular arcs of radii $R_1, R_2, \ldots$ can be drawn such that $F(s)$ falls off to zero on the contours of this sequence. Such a set of contours is illustrated in Fig. 3–8; that is, if $C_k$ corresponds to $R_k$,

$$\lim_{n\to\infty} |F(s)|_{\text{on } C_n} = 0 \tag{3-150}$$

For instance, in the previous example, choose $R_k$

$$R_k = \frac{\pi}{2}(2k) = k\pi, \qquad k = 1, 2, \ldots \tag{3-151}$$

Then, on the $j\omega$ axis, $\cosh jk\pi = \pm 1$. Hence, $1/\cosh s$ is bounded on these contours. In these cases, $|F(s)|$ falls off as $|1/s|$ on the $j\omega$ axis on these discrete contours. Using this fact, we can develop an equivalent to Jordan's lemma for an infinite set of poles.

If $F(s)$ is analytic to the right of the line $s = \sigma_0$, and the only singularities of $F(s)$ are poles which lie to the left of the line $s = \sigma_0$ and on an infinite sequence of circular arcs $C_n$ of radius $R_n$ where $\lim_{n\to\infty} R_n \to \infty$, then

$$\lim_{n\to\infty} |F(s)| = 0 \tag{3-152}$$

$$f(t) = \begin{cases} \sum [\text{Res } F(s)\, e^{st} \text{ to left of } s = \sigma_0], & t > 0 \\ -\sum [\text{Res } F(s)\, e^{st} \text{ to right of } s = \sigma_0], & t < 0 \\ \frac{1}{2}[f(0+) + f(0-)], & t = 0 \end{cases} \tag{3-153}$$

Once the infinite set of contours has been established, the proof of this form of Jordan's lemma follows the one previously developed. Thus, the details will not be repeated here.

Now consider an example:

$$F(s) = \frac{1}{s \cosh s}, \qquad \text{Re } s > \sigma_0 = 0 \tag{3-154}$$

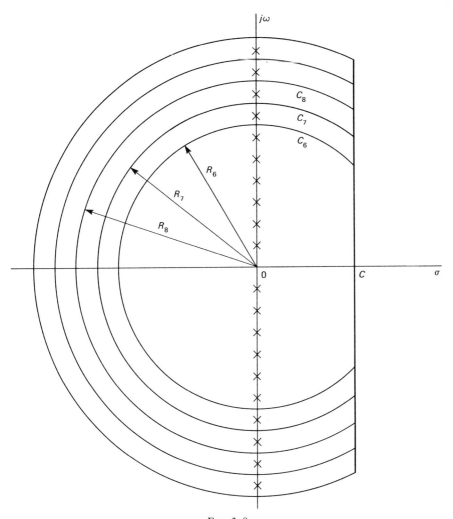

FIG. 3–8

The discrete contours of integration for evaluating the inverse Laplace transform for $t > 0$ if Jordan's lemma is applicable and there are infinitely many poles

For $t > 0$ (see Eq. 3–149),

$$f(t) = \left[\text{Res } \mathbf{F}(s)\, e^{st} \text{ at } s = 0\right] + \sum_{n=1}^{\infty} \left[\text{Res } \mathbf{F}(s)\, e^{st} \text{ at } s = s_n\right]$$

Applying Eq. B–63b, we have

$$\text{Res} = \left.\frac{e^{st}}{\cosh s + s \sinh s}\right|_{s=s_n}, \qquad n = 0, 1, \ldots$$

where $s_0 = 0$. Evaluating, we obtain

$$f(t) = 1 + \sum_{n=1}^{\infty} \frac{e^{j(\pi/2)(2n-1)t}}{j(2n-1)\frac{\pi}{2}\sinh j(2n-1)\frac{\pi}{2}} + \frac{e^{-j(\pi/2)(2n-1)t}}{j(2n-1)\frac{\pi}{2}\sinh j\frac{\pi}{2}(2n-1)}$$

but

$$\sinh j\frac{\pi}{2}(2n-1) = j\sin\frac{\pi}{2}(2n-1) = j(-1)^{n+1}$$

and

$$\cos x = \tfrac{1}{2}e^{jx} + e^{-jx}$$

Substituting and manipulating, we obtain

$$f(t) = \begin{cases} 1 + \dfrac{4}{\pi}\displaystyle\sum_{n=1}^{\infty}\dfrac{(-1)^n\cos\frac{\pi}{2}(2n-1)t}{(2n-1)}, & t > 0 \qquad (3\text{--}155) \\[4mm] 0, & t < 0 \qquad (3\text{--}156) \end{cases}$$

since there are no singularities to the right of the line $s = 0$. Then, combining Eqs. 3–155 and 3–156, we have

$$f(t) = u(t)\left[1 + \frac{4}{\pi}\sum_{n=1}^{\infty}\frac{(-1)^n\cos\frac{\pi}{2}(2n-1)t}{(2n-1)}\right] \qquad (3\text{--}157)$$

## 3-12. EVALUATING INVERSE LAPLACE TRANSFORM WHEN *F* (*s*) HAS BRANCH POINTS

Now let us consider *multiple-valued* functions. Actually, these are not functions, however by making the appropriate branch cuts, we can cause them to become single valued (see Section B-4). For example, consider

$$F(s) = \frac{e^{-\sqrt{s}}}{\sqrt{s}} \qquad (3\text{--}158)$$

This is not single valued. However, if a branch cut is made from the branch point, which is the origin, to $\infty$, so that the angle of $s$ is restricted (i.e., $-\pi \leqq \not{\asymp} s < \pi$) then the function becomes single valued. We shall consider several examples which will illustrate some important ideas in the evaluation of $F(s)$ which have branch point singularities. This will not be an exhaustive study. However, the procedures illustrated here can be used to evaluate many Laplace transforms.

For the first example, consider the $F(s)$ as given by Eq. 3–158. This function has a branch point at $s = 0$. Let us use the negative $\sigma$ axis as the branch cut. Therefore the contour of integration cannot cross this axis. A possible path of integration that can be used is shown in Fig. 3-9. Let us consider the integral over various parts of the contour, in turn. $F(s)$ is analytic on and within the entire contour. Then,

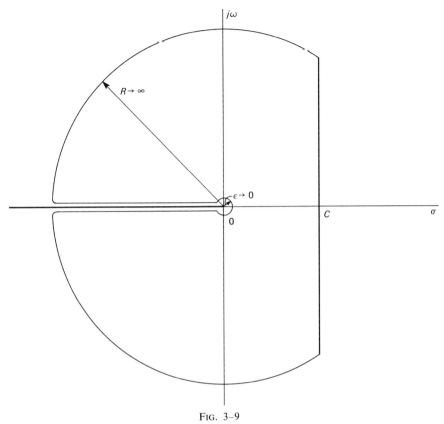

FIG. 3–9

Contour of integration that can be used when $F(s)$ has a branch point at $s = 0$

since on the infinite arc,

$$\lim_{s \to \infty} F(s) = 0$$

the integrals on the infinite arcs are zero for $t > 0$. This follows the development of Jordan's lemma.

Now consider the integral on the small circle of radius $\varepsilon$. We shall let $\varepsilon$ approach 0 and express $s$ in polar form on this circle; then,

$$s = \varepsilon e^{j\theta} \tag{3–159}$$

As $\varepsilon$ approaches zero, $e^{st} \approx 1$ and $e^{\sqrt{s}} \approx 1$.

$$\lim_{\varepsilon \to 0} \oint \frac{e^{\sqrt{s}} e^{st}}{\sqrt{s}} \, ds = \lim_{\varepsilon \to 0} \oint \frac{j\varepsilon e^{j\theta} \, d\theta}{\sqrt{\varepsilon}\, e^{j(\theta/2)}} = \lim_{\varepsilon \to 0} \oint j\sqrt{\varepsilon}\, e^{j(\theta/2)} \, d\theta$$

Note that, in the limit, this path approaches a closed circle.

$$\oint e^{j\theta/2}\, d\theta \leqq \int_0^{2\pi} d\theta = 2\pi$$

Thus, the integral is bounded. It is multiplied by $\sqrt{\varepsilon}$; hence,

$$\lim_{\varepsilon \to 0} \oint_\varepsilon \frac{e^{\sqrt{s}}e^{st}}{\sqrt{s}}\, ds = 0$$

Then, in the limit as $R \to \infty$ and $\varepsilon \to 0$, we have

$$\frac{1}{2\pi j}\left[ \int_{c-j\infty}^{c+j\infty} \frac{e^{-\sqrt{s}}e^{st}}{\sqrt{s}}\, ds + \int_{-\infty}^{0} \frac{e^{-\sqrt{s}}e^{st}}{\sqrt{s}}\, ds + \int_0^{-\infty} \frac{e^{-\sqrt{s}}e^{st}}{\sqrt{s}}\, ds \right] = 0 \quad (3\text{--}160)$$

Note that, since these paths are on opposite sides of the branch cut, the angle of $s$ in $\pi$ in the first integral and $-\pi$ in the second. Thus, these two integrals do not cancel each other. The first integral is $f(t)$; thus,

$$f(t) = -\frac{1}{2\pi j}\left[ \int_{-\infty}^{0} \frac{e^{-\sqrt{s}}e^{st}}{\sqrt{s}}\, ds + \int_0^{-\infty} \frac{e^{-\sqrt{s}}e^{st}}{\sqrt{s}}\, ds \right] \quad (3\text{--}161)$$

Now make the substitution

$$z = \sqrt{s} \quad (3\text{--}162)$$

This halves the angle. Thus, for the first integral of Eq. 3–161, the path of integration becomes from $j\infty$ to $0$, while, for the second (where the original path of integration was at an angle of $-\pi$), the path of integration becomes from $0$ to $-j\infty$. Then, substituting Eq. 3–162 and combining the two integrals yields

$$f(t) = -\frac{1}{j\pi} \int_{j\infty}^{-j\infty} e^{-z+tz^2}\, dz$$

or, equivalently

$$f(t) = \frac{1}{j\pi} \int_{-j\infty}^{j\infty} e^{-z+tz^2}\, dz \quad (3\text{--}163)$$

Now, substitute

$$u = -j\sqrt{t}\, z + j\frac{1}{2\sqrt{t}} \quad (3\text{--}164)$$

Rearranging, we obtain

$$f(t) = \frac{1}{\pi\sqrt{t}}\, e^{-1/4t} \int_{-\infty+j(2\sqrt{t})}^{\infty+j/(2\sqrt{t})} e^{-u^2}\, du \quad (3\text{--}165)$$

where $e^{-u^2}$ is analytic in the finite $u$-plane. Also, $\lim_{|u|\to\infty} e^{-u^2} = 0$ along the contour or a path parallel to it. Hence, the value of the integral will be unchanged if we shift the contour of integration parallel to itself by $1/(2\sqrt{t})$, therefore,

$$f(t) = \frac{1}{\pi\sqrt{t}}e^{-1/(4t)} \int_{-\infty}^{\infty} e^{-u^2}\, du \quad (3\text{--}166)$$

It can be shown that

$$\int_{-\infty}^{\infty} e^{-u_2}\, du = \sqrt{\pi} \qquad (3\text{–}167)$$

Hence,

$$f(t) = \frac{1}{\sqrt{\pi t}}\, e^{-1/4t}, \qquad t > 0 \qquad (3\text{–}168)$$

For $t < 0$, we can choose the path to the right as in Fig. 3–7, since there is no branch cut in the right half plane. In this case, the results follow those of the last section; hence,

$$f(t) = 0, \qquad t < 0$$

It may appear as though all that this procedure accomplishes is to shift the path of integration from the path $s = C + j\omega$ to the path along the negative $\sigma$ axis on each side of the cut. However, more powerful results are available. For instance, suppose $F(s)$ contains poles to the left of the line $s = C + j\omega$. For instance,

$$F(s) = \frac{e^{-\sqrt{s}}}{\sqrt{s}\,[(s+1)^2 + 2]\,[(s+2)^2 + 3]}$$

Then, Eq. 3–160 would become

$$f(t) + \frac{1}{2\pi j}\left[\int_{-\infty}^{0} F(s)\, e^{st}\, ds + \int_{0}^{-\infty} F(s)\, e^{st}\, ds\right]$$

$$= \sum [\text{Res } F(s)\, e^{st} \text{ enclosed in contour}], \qquad t > 0 \qquad (3\text{–}169)$$

In this case, two residues would be evaluated. Thus, certain more complex $F(s)$ can also be considered.

As another second example, suppose

$$F(s) = \frac{1}{\sqrt{s^2 + 1}} \qquad (3\text{–}170)$$

There are two branch points which occur at $s = \pm j$. Let us take the branch cut between them as shown in Fig. 3–10. We now consider the contour $C_R$ of radius $R$ and the Bromwich path $s = C + j\omega$. Since $\lim_{s \to \infty} F(s) = 0$, we can apply the theory of the last section to obtain

$$\lim_{R \to \infty} \int_{C_R} F(s)\, e^{st}\, ds = 0, \qquad t > 0 \qquad (3\text{–}171)$$

Thus,

$$f(t) = \frac{1}{2\pi j}\int_{C-j\infty}^{C+j\infty} \frac{e^{st}}{\sqrt{s^2 + 1}}\, ds = \frac{1}{2\pi j}\oint_{C_1} \frac{e^{st}}{\sqrt{s^2 + 1}}\, ds, \qquad t > 0 \qquad (3\text{–}172)$$

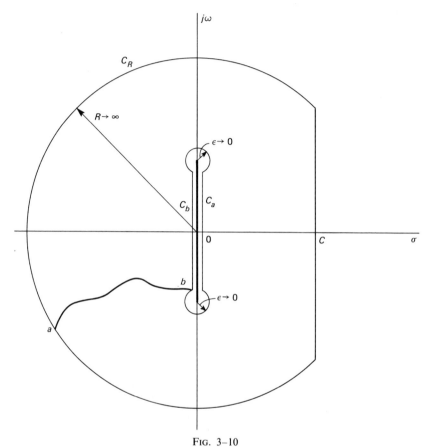

FIG. 3–10
Contour of integration that can be used when $F(s)$ has branch points at $s = \pm j\omega_0$

where the closed contour $C_1$ consists of $C_R$ and the Bromwich path $s = C + j\omega$. In this case, $F(s)$ is not analytic inside the path and the singularities are not just poles. To evaluate the integral, consider the additional contour shown in Fig. 3–10; i.e., the path from $a$ to $b$, the straight lines $C_a$ and $C_b$, and the two circles of radius $\varepsilon$. Now suppose the path of integration is as follows: from $C - j\infty$ to $C + j\infty$, then along $C_R$ to $a$, then from $a$ to $b$, then along $C_b$ to the upper circle of radius $\varepsilon$, around the circle down $C_a$ to the lower circle of radius $\varepsilon$, then back to boint $b$ along this circle, back along the path from $b$ to $a$, and finally along the lower part of $C_R$ to $C - j\infty$. Note that $F(s)$ is analytic within this path.

We have already shown that the integral on $C_R$ is zero. The path from $a$ to $b$ is traversed twice, once from $a$ to $b$ and then from $b$ to $a$. Since $F(s)$ is single valued there, these two integrals cancel. Now let us consider the contribution along the circle of radius $\varepsilon$ centered at $s = j$.

$$f_\varepsilon(t) = \oint_\varepsilon \frac{1}{\sqrt{s^2 + 1}} e^{st} \, ds \tag{3-173}$$

On the circle, let

$$s = j + \varepsilon e^{j\theta} \tag{3-174}$$

Then, $|e^{st}| < e^{\varepsilon t}$. On the circle,

$$\left|\sqrt{s^2 + 1}\right| = \left|\sqrt{(s + j)(s - j)}\right| \geqq \sqrt{\varepsilon(2 - \varepsilon)}$$

Thus,

$$\lim_{\varepsilon \to 0} |f_\varepsilon(t)| \leq \lim_{\varepsilon \to 0} \int_0^{2\pi} \frac{e^{\varepsilon t}}{\sqrt{\varepsilon(2 - \varepsilon)}} \varepsilon d\theta = \lim_{\varepsilon \to 0} \frac{\sqrt{\varepsilon} \, e^{\varepsilon t}}{\sqrt{2 - \varepsilon}} 2\pi = 0 \tag{3-175}$$

The same result is obtained for the integral over the lower circle; therefore,

$$\frac{1}{2\pi j} \int_{C-j\infty}^{C+j\infty} \frac{e^{-st}}{\sqrt{s^2 + 1}} \, ds + \frac{1}{2\pi j} \int_{C_b} \frac{e^{-st}}{\sqrt{s^2 + 1}} \, ds + \frac{1}{2\pi j} \int_{C_a} \frac{e^{-st}}{\sqrt{s^2 + 1}} \, ds = 0 \tag{3-176}$$

On contour $C_b$, $\sqrt{1 + s^2} = \sqrt{1 - \omega^2}$, while on $C_a$, $\sqrt{1 + s^2} = -\sqrt{1 - \omega^2}$. Then, substituting $f(t)$ for the first integral of Eq. 3-176 and $j\omega$ for $s$ on the contour, we have

$$f(t) = \frac{1}{2\pi} \int_{-1}^{1} \frac{e^{j\omega t}}{\sqrt{1 - \omega^2}} \, d\omega - \frac{1}{2\pi} \int_{1}^{-1} \frac{e^{j\omega t}}{\sqrt{1 - \omega^2}} \, d\omega$$

Thus (replacing $\omega$ by $-\omega$ in the second integral), we obtain

$$f(t) = \frac{1}{\pi} \int_{-1}^{1} \frac{\cos \omega t}{\sqrt{1 - \omega^2}} \, d\omega \tag{3-177}$$

If a series solution is used to evaluate the integral, it can be shown to equal Bessel's function of the first kind of order zero; hence,

$$f(t) = J_0(t), \qquad t > 0 \tag{3-178}$$

As before, since $F(s)$ is analytic to the right of the Bromwich path $f(t) = 0$, $t < 0$.

As in the case of the last example, if $F(s)$ is such that it has poles to the left of the Bromwich path, then Eq. 3-176 must be modified by replacing the zero on the right-hand side by the sum of the residues.

## 3-13. COMPUTER PROGRAMS FOR EVALUATING RESIDUES OF THE LAPLACE INVERSION INTEGRAL —SOME POLYNOMIAL MANIPULATIONS

The Laplace transform, with its complex inversion integrals does not easily lend itself to computer evaluation. However, for purposes of illustration we shall demonstrate a compute program which will evaluate residues of the inversion integrand at simple poles. This will also illustrate computer procedures used for polynomials. If we have a function $N(s) e^{st}/D(s)$, where $D(s)$ is a polynomial in $s$ with simple roots and $N(s) e^{st}$ is analytic in the $s$-plane, then the residue is given by (see Eq. B–63b)

$$a_{-1} = \frac{N(s) e^{st}}{\dfrac{d}{ds} D(s)} \Bigg|_{s=s_0} \tag{3–179}$$

where $s_0$ is the root. Assume that the roots of the denominator are known. If not, they can be found by a root location program. Such programs are given in standard numerical analysis texts. Now let us consider the inversion integral

$$f(t) = \frac{1}{2\pi j} \int_{c-j\infty}^{c+j\infty} F(s) e^{st}\, ds \tag{3–180}$$

We shall assume that the only singularities are simple poles and that Jordan's lemma applies. Thus, for $t > 0$ (see Eq. 3–146),

$$f(t) = \sum [\text{Res } F(s) e^{st} \text{ to right of Bromwich path}] \tag{3–181}$$

Assume that $F(s)$ is the ratio of two polynomials in $s$; thus,

$$F(s) = \frac{N(s)}{D(s)} \tag{3–182}$$

Then, for a simple pole at $s = s_0$, we have the contribution to $f(t)$ as (see Eq. 3–179)

$$\text{Res} = \frac{N(s_0) e^{s_0 t}}{D'(s_0)} \tag{3–183}$$

The quantity that we wish to calculate is $R = N(s_0)/D'(s_0)$. The program is written in subroutine form and is listed in Fig. 3–11. It consists of three SUBROUTINES. The first is RES (lines 10–90) which call for $N(s_0) = AN$ and $D'(s_0) = BN$, and takes their ratio (lines 50–70). Note that these may be complex quantities. Thus, a COMPLEX declaration (line 30) is necessary. The coefficients of the numerator polynomial are in the $A$ array while the coefficients of the polynomial in the denominator are in the B array. The C array is one which will contain the coefficients of the derivative of $D(s)$. Note that NN is the highest power of the numerator + 1 and MM is the highest power of the denominator + 1. Since arrays must start with the coefficient 1 and not 0, we write the polynomials in the form

$$N(s) = a_{n+1} s^n + \cdots + a_3 s^2 + a_2 s + a_1$$

Note that these arrays are entered into the SUBROUTINES by a COMMON statement.

There are two SUBROUTINES that are called upon by RES. One is POLVAL, which evaluates a polynomial at a specified value of $s$ and the other is PLDRIV, which evaluates the derivative of a polynomial at a specified value of $s$.

```
00010   C       SUBRØUTINE TØ EVALUATE RESIDUES
00020           SUBRØUTINE RES(S,R)
00030           CØMPLEX S,R,AN,BN
00040           CØMMØN A(20),B(20),C(20),NN,MM
00050           CALL PØLVAL(S,AN)
00060           CALL PLDRIV(S,BN)
00070           R=AN/BN
00080           RETURN
00090           END
00100   C       SUBRØUTINE TØ EVALUATE PØLYNØMIAL
00110           SUBRØUTINE PØLVAL(S,AN)
00120           CØMPLEX AN,S
00130           CØMMØN A(20),B(20),C(20),NN,MM
00140           AN=A(1)
00150           DØ 100 I=2,NN
00160           AN=AN+A(I)*S**(I-1)
00170   100     CØNTINUE
00180           RETURN
00190           END
00200   C       SUBRØUTINE TØ DIFFERENTATE A PØLYNØMIAL
00210   C       AND GIVE ITS VALUE
00220           SUBRØUTINE PLDRIV(S,BN)
00230           CØMPLEX BN,S
00240           CØMMØN A(20),B(20),C(20),NN,MM
00250           J=MM-1
00260           DØ 200 I=1,J
00270           C(I)=B(I+1)*I
00280   200     CØNTINUE
00290           BN=C(1)
00300           DØ 300 I=2,J
00310           BN=BN+C(I)*S**(I-1)
00320   300     CØNTINUE
00330           RETURN
00340           END
```

FIG. 3-11

SUBROUTINES: RES, PLOVAL, and PLDRIV that evaluate the residue of the ratio of two polynomials with simple poles, evaluate a polynomial, and differentiate a polynomial and evaluate it, respectively

The COMMON statements in all three SUBROUTINES (as well as in the main program) enter the required data. Note that POLVAL does not need the B array, while PLDRIV does not need the A array. However, no storage space is lost by entering these all into the COMMON statement.

Now let us consider POLVAL (lines 100–190). Its flow chart is given in Fig. 3–12. Data, except for S, are entered by means of the COMMON statement. The complex quantities are declared and then AN is set equal to A(1) in line 140. In the DO loop of lines 150–170, AN is successively increased by $a_i s^{i-1}$ for $i = 2$, NN until the final value of the polynomial is obtained; i.e., the polynomial is computed term by term.

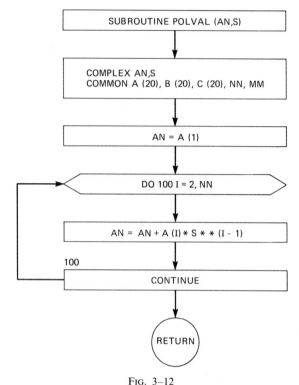

Fig. 3–12
Flow chart for POLVAL

The derivative is computed in PLDRIV (lines 200–340). The flow chart for this SUBROUTINE is given in Fig. 3–13. Again, data, except for $s$, are entered through the COMMON statement. The complex quantities are then declared. Since the array of the derivative will have one term less than the B array, a constant MM-1 is calculated. Now consider the polynomial

$$B = b_{n+1}s^n + b_n s^{n-1} + \cdots + b_3 s^2 + b_2 s + b_1 \qquad (3\text{-}184)$$

It derivative is given by

$$\frac{dB}{ds} = n b_{n+1} s^{n-1} + (n-1) b_n s^{n-2} + \cdots + 2 b_3 s + b_2 \qquad (3\text{-}185)$$

Hence, if

$$\frac{dB}{ds} = c_n s^{n-1} + c_{n-1} s^{n-2} + \cdots + c_2 s + c_1$$

we have

$$c_k = k b_{k+1} \qquad (3\text{-}186)$$

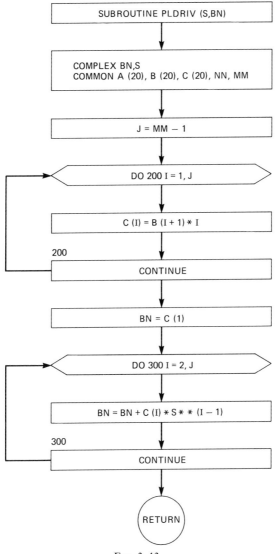

FIG. 3–13
Flow chart for PLDRIV

This is calculated in the DO loop of lines 260–280. In lines 290–320, the C polynomial is evaluated. Thus, the program calculates the desired residues. (The C array is not actually needed since we only want the value of the derivative at a single value of $s$. However if the value of the derivative is to be calculated at many points, then using the C array could reduce the number of calculations. The details of this will be left to the reader.) Note that we have only obtained the residues of $N(s)/D(s)$ and not the complete inverse transform. To do this, each residue should be multiplied by $e^{s_0 t}$. The sum of all the terms (one for each residue) must be evaluated for each value of $t$ desired. These details will be left to the reader. The SUBROUTINE could be extended to multiple poles. However, we shall not do so since general procedures such as the fast Fourier transform (see Chapter 2) or state variable procedures (see Chapter 4) are far better to use when a computer solution is desired.

### 3-14. CONVOLUTION THEOREMS

The convolution theorem developed in Section 2-11 for the Fourier transform can be applied to the Laplace transform. The proofs of the theorem for the Laplace transform are similar to those for the Fourier transform. However, there are differences which make it desirable to include the proofs for the Laplace transform here. The explanatory comments made throughout Section 2-11 are pertinent.

**Time Convolution Theorem.**   If

$$f_1(t) \leftrightarrow F_1(s), \qquad \text{Re } s > \sigma_1 \qquad\qquad (3\text{--}187a)$$

$$f_2(t) \leftrightarrow F_2(s), \qquad \text{Re } s > \sigma_2 \qquad\qquad (3\text{--}187b)$$

then

$$f_1(t) * f_2(t) \leftrightarrow F_1(s) F_2(s); \qquad \text{Re } s > \sigma_1, \qquad \text{Re } s > \sigma_2 \qquad (3\text{--}188)$$

Consider the convolution of two functions of time:

$$f_1(t) * f_2(t) = \int_{-\infty}^{\infty} f_1(x) f_2(t - x)\, dx \qquad\qquad (3\text{--}189)$$

Now let us derive Eq. 3–188. From Eq. 3–11, we have

$$f_1(t) = 0, \qquad t < 0$$

$$f_2(t) = 0, \qquad t < 0$$

Therefore, Eq. 3–189 can be written as

$$f_1(t) * f_2(t) = \int_0^t f_1(x) f_2(t - x)\, dx = \int_0^{\infty} f_1(x) f_2(t - x)\, dx \qquad (3\text{--}190)$$

Now let us derive Eq. 3–188. From Eq. 3–11, we have

$$F_1(s) F_2(s) \leftrightarrow \frac{1}{2\pi j} \int_{C-j\infty}^{C-j\infty} F_1(s) F_2(s) e^{st} dt; \qquad C > \sigma_1, \qquad C > \sigma_2 \qquad (3\text{–}191)$$

The analyticity of $F_1(s) F_2(s)$ depends upon the singularities of $F_1(s)$ and $F_2(s)$ separately. Note that $C$ should be chosen to the right of all these singularities. In general, $C$ must be greater than both $\sigma_1$ and $\sigma_2$. This may not always be true. For instance, a zero of $F(s)$ may cancel a pole of $F(s)$. Now replace $F_1(s)$ by Eq. 3–10

$$F_1(s) F_2(s) \leftrightarrow \frac{1}{2\pi j} \int_{C-j\infty}^{C+j\infty} F_2(s) e^{st} \int_0^\infty f_1(x) e^{-sx} dx \, ds; \qquad (3\text{–}192)$$

$$\operatorname{Re} s > \sigma_1, \qquad C > \sigma_1, \qquad C > \sigma_2, \qquad \operatorname{Re} s > \sigma_2$$

The last condition is equivalent to $C > \sigma_2$ since the Bromwich path is along the line $C + j\omega$. We assume $F_1(s)$, $F_2(s)$, $C$, and $\operatorname{Re} s$ are such that the integral converges uniformly. Thus, we can interchange the order of integration.

$$F_1(s) F_2(s) \leftrightarrow \int_0^\infty f_1(x) \frac{1}{2\pi j} \int_{C-j\infty}^{C+j\infty} F_2(s) e^{s(t-x)} \, ds \, dx \qquad (3\text{–}193)$$

The inner integral is just the inverse Laplace transform integral with $t$ replaced by $t - x$. Hence, its evaluation yields $f_2(t - x)$; therefore,

$$F_1(s) F_2(s) \leftrightarrow \int_0^\infty f_1(x) f_2(t - x) \, dx; \qquad \operatorname{Re} s > \sigma_1, \qquad \operatorname{Re} s > \sigma_2 \qquad (3\text{–}194)$$

Thus, the time convolution theorem is proved.

We now consider some examples of this theorem. Thus, we shall evaluate $f(t)$, the inverse Laplace transform of $1/[s^2(s + a)]$. Using Eq. 3–188 and Table 3-1, we have

$$f(t) = tu(t) * e^{-at} u(t)$$

$$f(t) = \int_0^t (t - x) e^{-ax} dx, \qquad t > 0$$

Note that we have included the condition $t > 0$ to avoid having to write the unit step functions in the integrand. Carrying out the integration, we have

$$f(t) = u(t) \left( \frac{e^{-at}}{a^2} + \frac{t}{a} - \frac{1}{a^2} \right)$$

As a second example, we evaluate the inverse Laplace transform of $1/s^n F(s)$, where $f(t) \leftrightarrow F(s)$. Then, using Eq. 3–188 and Table 3-1, we have

$$\frac{1}{s^n} F(s) \leftrightarrow u(t) \frac{t^{n-1}}{(n-1)!} * f(t)$$

or, equivalently

$$\frac{1}{s^n} F(s) \leftrightarrow \frac{1}{(n-1)!} \int_0^t (t - x)^{n-1} f(x) \, dx \qquad (3\text{–}195)$$

We can use this result to obtain a general result for multiple integrals. From Eq. 3–65, we have

$$\int_{-\infty}^{t} f(x)\,dx \leftrightarrow \frac{F(s)}{s} + \frac{1}{s}\int_{-\infty}^{0^{-}} f(t)\,dt \qquad (3\text{–}196)$$

Now define $f(t) = 0$, $t < 0$. Then, Eq. 3–196 becomes

$$\int_{0}^{t} f(x)\,dx \leftrightarrow \frac{F(s)}{s} \qquad (3\text{–}197)$$

Thus, the Laplace transform of the definite integral of $f(t)$ is $F(s)$ divided by $s$. We now integrate $n$ times. In this case, the transform is given by

$$\int_{0}^{t}\int_{0}^{t_{1}} \cdots \int_{0}^{t_{n-1}} f(t_{n})\,dt_{n}\,dt_{n-1} \cdots dt_{1} \leftrightarrow \frac{F(s)}{s^{n}} \qquad (3\text{–}198)$$

Comparing this with Eq. 3–195, we obtain

$$\int_{0}^{t}\int_{0}^{t_{1}} \cdots \int_{0}^{t_{n-1}} f(t_{n})\,dt_{n}\,dt_{n-1} \cdots dt_{1} = \frac{1}{(n-1)!}\int_{0}^{t} (t-x)^{n-1} f(x)\,dx \qquad (3\text{–}199)$$

**Complex Frequency Convolution Theorem.**   Now let us consider convolution in the $s$ domain; that is, if

$$f_{1}(t) \leftrightarrow F_{1}(s), \qquad \text{Re } s > \sigma_{1} \qquad (3\text{–}200a)$$

$$f_{2}(t) \leftrightarrow F_{2}(s), \qquad \text{Re } s > \sigma_{2} \qquad (3\text{–}200b)$$

then

$$f_{1}(t)f_{2}(t) \leftrightarrow \frac{1}{2\pi j} F_{1}(s) * F_{2}(s) \qquad (3\text{–}201)$$

where the complex convolution of $F_{1}(s)$ and $F_{2}(s)$ is defined as

$$F_{1}(s) * F_{2}(s) = \frac{1}{2\pi j}\int_{C-j\infty}^{C+j\infty} F_{1}(z) F_{2}(s-z)\,dz; \qquad (3\text{–}202)$$

$$\text{Re } s > \sigma_{1} + \sigma_{2}, \qquad \sigma_{1} < C < \text{Re } s - \sigma_{2}$$

Note the restrictions on Re $s$ and $C$. They are important. We shall discuss them subsequently.

We now derive Eq. 3–201. From Eq. 3–10, we have

$$f_{1}(t)f_{2}(t) \leftrightarrow \int_{0}^{\infty} f_{1}(t)f_{2}(t) e^{-st}\,dt, \qquad \text{Re } s > \sigma_{1} + \sigma_{2} \qquad (3\text{–}203)$$

Note that Re $s > \sigma_{1} + \sigma_{2}$ since if, for sufficiently large $t$, $|f_{1}(t)| < K_{1}e^{\sigma_{1}t}$ and $|f_{2}(t)| < K_{2}e^{\sigma_{2}t}$, then $|f_{1}(t)f_{2}(t)| < K_{1}K_{2}e^{(\sigma_{1}+\sigma_{2})t}$. Now, using Eq. 3–11 to substitute for $f_{2}(t)$, we obtain

$$f_1(t)f_2(t) \leftrightarrow \int_0^\infty f_2(t) e^{-st} \frac{1}{2\pi j} \int_{C-j\infty}^{C+j\infty} F_1(z) e^{zt} \, dz \, dt; \qquad (3\text{-}204)$$

$$\mathrm{Re}\, s > \sigma_1 + \sigma_2, \qquad C > \upsilon_1$$

Again assume that the functions are such that there is uniform convergence so that the order of integration can be interchanged; thus,

$$f_1(t)f_2(t) \leftrightarrow \frac{1}{2\pi j} \int_{C-j\infty}^{C+j\infty} F_1(z) \int_0^\infty f_2(t) e^{-(s-z)t} \, dz \, dt; \qquad (3\text{-}205)$$

$$\mathrm{Re}\, s > \sigma_1 + \sigma_2, \qquad C > \sigma_1, \qquad \mathrm{Re}(s - z) > \sigma_2$$

The third condition $\mathrm{Re}(s - z) > \sigma_2$ is added to insure that the inner integral converges. Let us consider the third condition. In general, $\mathrm{Re}\, z = C$, since the integral with respect to $z$ is on the Bromwich path. Thus, the third condition can be written as $\mathrm{Re}\, s - C > \sigma_2$, or equivalently, $C < \mathrm{Re}\, s - \sigma_2$. The inner integral of Eq. 3–205 is just Eq. 3–10 with $s$ replaced by $s - z$. Hence, the evaluation of this integral yields $F_2(s - z)$; then

$$f_1(t)f_2(t) \leftrightarrow \frac{1}{2\pi j} \int_{C-j\infty}^{C+j\infty} F_1(z) F_2(s - z) \, dz; \qquad (3\text{-}206)$$

$$\mathrm{Re}\, s > \sigma_1 + \sigma_2, \qquad \mathrm{Re}\, s - \sigma_2 > C > \sigma_1$$

Alternatively, we can write

$$f_1(t)f_2(t) \leftrightarrow \frac{1}{2\pi j} \int_{C-j\infty}^{C+j\infty} F_1(s - z) F_2(z) \, dz; \qquad (3\text{-}207)$$

$$\mathrm{Re}\, s > \sigma_1 + \sigma_2, \qquad \mathrm{Re}\, s - \sigma_1 > C > \sigma_2$$

The restrictions on $\mathrm{Re}\, s$, and $C$ must be very carefully observed in the case of the complex convolution. We shall illustrate this with an example: Find the Laplace transform of $t^3 u(t)$ using complex convolution.

$$t^3 u(t) = [tu(t)] [t^2 u(t)]$$

Using Table 3-1 and Eq. 3–206, we have

$$t^3 u(t) \leftrightarrow \frac{1}{2\pi j} \int_{C-j\infty}^{C+j\infty} \frac{2}{z^3} \frac{1}{(s - z)^2}; \qquad (3\text{-}208)$$

$$\mathrm{Re}\, s > 0 + 0 = 0, \qquad \mathrm{Re}\, s - 0 > C > 0$$

Now consider the path of integration. It must lie to the right of the origin of the $z$-plane. However, $\mathrm{Re}\, s$ must be greater than $C$. (Note that $s$ is a constant as far as the integration is concerned.) The integrand has poles at $z = 0$ and $z = s$.

This is illustrated in Fig. 3–14. Note that the path of integration must lie between the two singularities. The integrand satisfies Eq. B–74. Hence, the integral on an infinite circular arc will be zero. Thus, we can use residues to evaluate this integral. Note that there is no factor of $e^{st}$ in the integrand. Hence (see Fig. 3–14) we can use either the solid arc to the right or the dashed one to the left to "close the path." We shall consider each of these in turn. If we close to the left, then

$$t^3 u(t) \leftrightarrow \operatorname{Res} \frac{2}{z^3 (s + z)^2} \quad \text{at} \quad z = 0$$

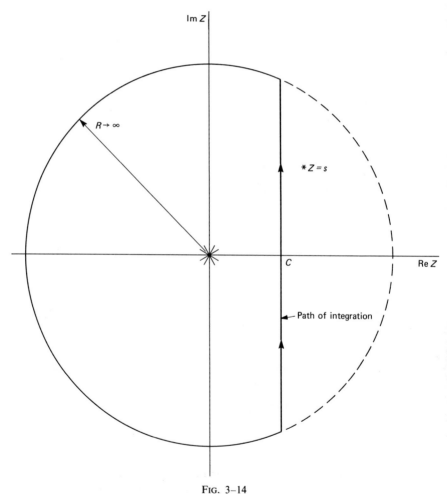

FIG. 3–14
Path of integration and the singularities of the integral in Eq. 3–208

The pole at $z = 0$ is a third-order pole. To evaluate the residue, we use Eq. B–62. This yields

$$t^3 u(t) \longleftrightarrow \frac{1}{2} \frac{d^2}{dz^2} \frac{2}{(s - z)^7} \bigg|_{z=0}$$

Evaluating the derivative, we have

$$t^3 u(t) \longleftrightarrow \frac{6}{s^4}, \qquad \text{Re } s > 0$$

Now suppose we close the path to the right; then

$$t^3 u(t) \longleftrightarrow - \text{Res} \frac{2}{z^3 (s - z)^2} \quad \text{at} \quad z = s \qquad (3\text{--}209\text{a})$$

The minus sign is included since the path of integration is closed to the right. Then (see Eq. B–62), the residue for the second-order pole is

$$t^3 u(t) = - \frac{d}{dz} \frac{2}{z^3} \bigg|_{z=s}$$

$$t^3 u(t) \longleftrightarrow \frac{6}{s^4} \quad \text{at} \quad \text{Re } s > 0 \qquad (3\text{--}209\text{b})$$

Of course, Eqs. 3–209a and 3–209b yield the same result. Note that the contour of integration must be positioned carefully. It *cannot* be arbitrarily placed to the right of all the singularities.

## 3-15. THE TWO-SIDED (BILATERAL) LAPLACE TRANSFORM

In Section 3-1, we developed the one-sided Laplace transform from the Fourier transform. In many applications, the functions of time are one sided; i.e., zero for $t < 0$. However, sometimes they are not. The one-sided restriction need not be imposed and the Laplace transform can be developed for two-sided functions as well as for one-sided ones. That is, the development of Eqs. 3–1 through 3–11 applies, with slight modification, if we replace the lower limit of integration which is 0, by $- \infty$ in the Laplace transform integral. Equations 3–10 and 3–11 then become

$$F(s) = \int_{-\infty}^{\infty} f(t) e^{-st} \, dt, \qquad \sigma_1 > \text{Re } s > \sigma_2 \qquad (3\text{--}210)$$

$$f(t) = \frac{1}{2\pi j} \int_{C-j\infty}^{C+j\infty} F(s) e^{st} \, ds, \qquad \sigma_1 > C > \sigma_2 \qquad (3\text{--}211)$$

When the one-sided Laplace transform is used, only positive values of $t$ are used. Hence, as Re $s$ increases and $e^{-st}$ falls off more rapidly as $t$ approaches

∞. However, now negative time is also considered. In this case, Re $s$ must not be too large, since increasing Re $s$ causes $e^{-st}$ to increase for $t < 0$ as $|t|$ increases. Thus, Re $s$ is restricted to lie in a strip. That is, the Laplace transform exists in that strip. Assume that $\sigma_1 > \sigma_2$. If it does not, then the Laplace transform does not exist. In taking the inverse Laplace transform, the Bromwich path $s = C + j\omega$ must be chosen in the region of existence; here $\sigma_1 > C > \sigma_2$.

The Laplace transform that is valid for two-sided functions is called the *two-sided (bilateral) Laplace transform*. As an example, let us obtain the Laplace transform of

$$f(t) = \begin{cases} e^{+bt}, & t < 0 \\ e^{-at}, & t > 0 \end{cases} \tag{3-212}$$

Then,

$$F(s) = \int_{-\infty}^{0} e^{bt} e^{-st}\, dt + \int_{0}^{\infty} e^{-at} e^{-st}\, dt, \qquad b > \text{Re } s > -a \tag{3-213}$$

If the first integral exists, then $b > \text{Re } s$; similarly, if the second integral exists, Re $s > -a$. It is assumed here that $b > -a$. Then, carrying out the integration, we have

$$F(s) = \frac{1}{s-b} + \frac{1}{s+a} = -\frac{a+b}{(s+a)(s-b)}, \qquad b > \text{Re } s > -a \tag{3-214}$$

Note that $a$ and/or $b$ can be negative as long as $b > -a$. Thus, both poles can lie in the left-half plane or both can lie in the right-half plane, or the pole at $s = -a$ can lie in the left-half plane, while the pole at $s = b$ lies in the right-half plane.

Now consider the integral of Eq. 3–210. Let us split this integral into two integrals; then,

$$F(s) = \int_{-\infty}^{0} f(t)\, e^{-st}\, dt + \int_{0}^{\infty} f(t)\, e^{st}\, dt, \qquad \sigma_1 > \text{Re } s > \sigma_2 \tag{3-215}$$

or, equivalently,

$$F(s) = F_1(s) + F_2(s) \tag{3-216}$$

The second integral is just the one-sided Laplace transform. Hence, $F_2(s)$ is analytic for Re $s > \sigma_2$. Using arguments which are essentially the same as those given in Section 3-3, we can demonstrate that $F_1(s)$ is analytic for $\sigma_1 > \text{Re } s$. Hence, *the two-sided Laplace transform is analytic in its strip of existence*.

Now consider the inverse two-sided Laplace transform. When the inverse Laplace transform of Eq. 3–11 was derived from the Fourier transform, no consideration was given to the fact that $f(t)$ was one sided. Thus, Eq. 3–11 can be directly applied to obtain the inverse Laplace transform of two-sided Laplace transforms. Of course, $C$ must lie in the region of existence. Similarly, all the discussions of Sections 3-11 and 3-12 for the evaluation of the complex integral of the inverse Laplace transform are applicable to the two-sided Laplace transform. In fact, we deliberately considered the response for both positive and negative time. Note that when Jordan's lemma is applied, the path is closed to the left (see Fig. 3–6) to evaluate $f(t)$ for $t > 0$ and the path is closed to the right (see Fig. 3–7) to evaluate $f(t)$ for $t < 0$. Thus, Eq. 3–146 can be used in obtaining the inverse Laplace transform.

As an example, let us obtain the inverse Laplace transform of $F(s)$ given in Eq. 3–214. The $s$-plane, with an allowable Bromwich path is shown in Fig. 3–15. Note that, depending upon the given values of $a$ and $b$, the origin can lie at any point on the $\sigma$ axis; that is, both $a$ and $b$ can be in the left-half plane or right-half plane, or $a$ can lie in the left-half plane and $b$ in the right-half plane. Thus, from Eq. 3–146, we have

$$f(t) \begin{cases} \left[\operatorname{Res} - \dfrac{a+b}{(s+a)(s-b)} e^{st} \text{ at } s = -a\right], & t > 0 \\[4mm] \left[-\operatorname{Res} - \dfrac{a+b}{(s+a)(s-b)} e^{st} \text{ at } s = b\right], & t < 0 \end{cases} \tag{3-217}$$

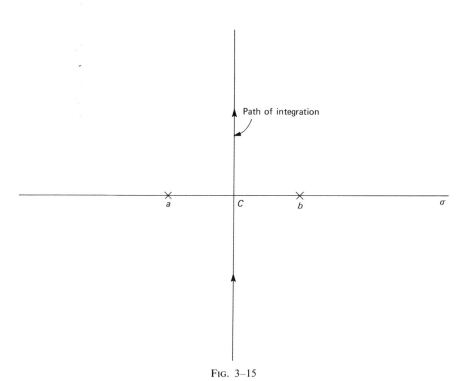

Path of integration

FIG. 3–15

Path of integration for evaluating the inverse Laplace transform of Eq. 3–114. (The $j\omega$ axis is not drawn since the location of the origin, which lies on the $\sigma$ axis, depends upon $a$ and $b$, $b > a$.)

Evaluating the residues, we obtain

$$f(t) = \begin{cases} e^{-at}, & t > 0 \\ e^{bt}, & t < 0 \end{cases} \tag{3-218}$$

Note that shifting the position of the Bromwich path can change the value of $f(t)$. For instance, if $C > b$, then $f(t) = 0$, $t < 0$, etc. Thus, care should be taken to locate the position of the path correctly.

**Relations between the Onesided and Two-Sided Transforms.** Suppose that we write $f(t)$ in the following way

$$f(t) = u(-t)f_1(t) + u(t)f_2(t) \tag{3-219}$$

That is $f_2(t)$ contributes to $f(t)$ for positive time, while $f_1(t)$ contributes to $f(t)$ for negative time. Now consider another function $u(t)f_1(-t)$. This is the mirror image of $f_1(t)$ and it exists only for positive time. A typical example of such functions is shown in Fig. 3–16. Then, the one-sided functions $u(t)f_1(-t)$ and $u(t)f_2(t)$ each have one-sided Laplace transforms:

$$u(t)f_1(-t) \leftrightarrow F_1(s), \qquad \operatorname{Re} s > \sigma_1 \tag{3-220a}$$

$$u(t)f_2(t) \leftrightarrow F_2(s), \qquad \operatorname{Re} s > \sigma_2 \tag{3-220b}$$

Let us relate these to the two-sided Laplace transform of $f(t)$ of Eq. 3–219:

$$F(s) = \int_{-\infty}^{0} f_1(t)\, e^{-st}\, dt + \int_{0}^{\infty} f_2(t)\, e^{-st}\, dt, \qquad -\sigma_1 > \operatorname{Re} s > \sigma_2 \tag{3-221}$$

Note the $-\sigma_1$. Let $x = -t$ in the first integral:

$$F(s) = \int_{0}^{\infty} f_1(-x)\, e^{sx}\, dx + \int_{0}^{\infty} f_2(t)\, e^{-st}\, dt, \qquad -\sigma_1 > \operatorname{Re} s > \sigma_2 \tag{3-222}$$

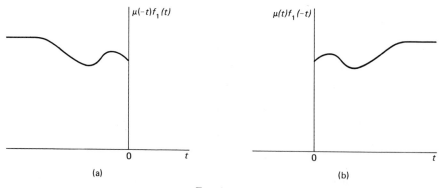

FIG. 3–16

(a) Function $u(-t)\, f_1(t)$; (b) its mirror image $u(t)\, f_1(-t)$

The first integral is just the Laplace transform of $u(t)f_1(-t)$ with $s$ replaced by $-s$. Then (see Eq. 3–221)

$$F(s) = F_1(-s) + F_2(s), \qquad -\sigma_1 > \text{Re } s > \sigma_2 \qquad (3\text{–}223)$$

Thus, we have related the two-sided and one-sided Laplace transforms.

Consider the result if $f(t)$ is even. Then, $f_1(-t) = f_2(t)$ and $F_1(s) = F_2(s)$. Thus, for even $f(t)$, Eq. 3–223 becomes

$$F(s) = F_2(-s) + F_2(s), \qquad -\sigma_2 > \text{Re } s > \sigma_2 \qquad (3\text{–}224)$$

Note that $F(s)$ is an even function of $s$. Note if $F(s)$ is to exist then $\sigma_2$ must be non-positive.

Many of the theorems derived for the one-sided Laplace transform are also applicable to the two-sided transform. However, for the two-sided transform, the initial conditions occur at $t = -\infty$. Usually, we assume that $f(-\infty) = 0$. Consider the two-sided Laplace transform of the derivative of $f(t)$ (see Section 3-5). Thus, if $f(t) \leftrightarrow F(s)$, then (see Eq. 3–57)

$$\frac{df(t)}{dt} \leftrightarrow sF(s), \qquad \sigma_1 > \text{Re } s > \sigma_2 \qquad (3\text{–}225)$$

Note that $\sigma_1$ and $\sigma_2$ are determined from $df(t)/dt$ (see Section 3-5). In addition (see Eq. 3–65),

$$\int f(t)\, dt \leftrightarrow \frac{F(s)}{s} \qquad (3\text{–}226)$$

The basic theorems of Section 3-7 are applicable to the two-sided Laplace transforms. Of course, the region of existence must be modified to a strip; i.e., $\sigma_1 > \text{Re } s > \sigma_2$, not $\text{Re } s > \sigma_0$.

The convolution theorem can be applied to the two-sided Laplace transform. In the case of time convolution, the development parallels that of Section 3-14, except that the region of existence of the Laplace transform must be modified. For example, if

$$f_a(t) \leftrightarrow F_a(s), \qquad \sigma_{1a} > \text{Re } s > \sigma_{2a} \qquad (3\text{–}227a)$$

$$f_b(t) \leftrightarrow F_b(s), \qquad \sigma_{1b} > \text{Re } s > \sigma_{2b} \qquad (3\text{–}227b)$$

Then

$$\int_{-\infty}^{\infty} f_a(x) f_b(t-x)\, dx$$

$$\leftrightarrow F_a(s) F_b(s); \qquad \sigma_{1a} > \text{Re } s > \sigma_{2a}, \qquad \sigma_{1b} > \text{Re } s > \sigma_{2b} \qquad (3\text{–}228)$$

It is assumed that $\sigma_{1a}$, $\sigma_{2a}$, $\sigma_{1b}$, and $\sigma_{2b}$ are such that an allowed range of $\text{Re } s$ exists. If it does not, then the transform in question does not exist. That is, $F_a(s) F_b(s)$ may not be a valid two-sided Laplace transform, even though $F_a(s)$ and $F_b(s)$ are.

For complex convolution, the results are similar to those of Section 3-14, except that the restrictions on Re $s$ and the location of the Bromwich path must be extended. In this case, we have

$$f_a(t)f_b(t) \leftrightarrow \frac{1}{2\pi j} \int_{C-j\infty}^{C+j\infty} F_a(z)\,F_b(s-z)\,dz; \quad \sigma_{1a} + \sigma_{1b} > \operatorname{Re} s > \sigma_{2a} + \sigma_{2b},$$

$$\sigma_{1b} > \operatorname{Re} s - C > \sigma_{2b}, \qquad \sigma_{1a} > C > \sigma_{2a} \qquad\qquad (3\text{–}229)$$

The development of the restrictions on Re $s$ and $C$ essentially parallel those restrictions in Eq. 3–206, except that both positive and negative values of time are allowed, so that Re $s$ and $C$ have both upper and lower bounds.

## PROBLEMS

**3-1.** For the function $f(t) = e^{3t} \cos 2t^2 u(t)$, determine the value $\sigma_0$ (see Eq. 3–10) which defines the region of existence of $F(s)$, where $f(t) \leftrightarrow F(s)$.

**3-2.** Repeat Problem 3-1 for $f(t) = t^2 e^{-3t} u(t)$.

**3-3.** Obtain the Laplace transform of $u(t)\,t^n$. Verify your result using Table 3-1.

**3-4.** Obtain the Laplace transform of $\delta^{(n)}(t)$. Verify your result using Table 3-1.

**3-5.** If $f(t) \leftrightarrow F(s)$, Re $s > \sigma_0$, show that $f(t)\,e^{-at} \leftrightarrow F(s+a)$, Re $s > \sigma_0 - a$. (Note that $a$ is real.)

**3-6.** Determine the region of analyticity for the Laplace transform of Problem 3-5.

**3-7.** Determine the Laplace transform of $u(t)\,e^{-at}$, $a > 0$. Then use the Laplace transform to obtain the Fourier transform of the function.

**3-8.** Repeat Problem 3-7 for the function

$$f(t) = u(t)(1 - e^{-at}), \; + \; a > 0$$

**3-9.** Repeat Problem 3-7 for the function

$$f(t) = u(t)(1 \quad t + e^{-3t} \sin 2t + \cos 3t)$$

**3-10.** Can Problem 3-7 be performed for the function

$$f(t) = u(t)(e^{3t} + e^{-3t})$$

**3-11.** Use Eq. 3–57 to find the Laplace transform of $(d/dt)\,u(t)\,e^{-t} \sin 3t$. Verify your result by differentiating first and then taking the Laplace transform.

**3-12.** Repeat Problem 3-11 for $(d/dt)\,u(t)\,e^{-t}$.

**3-13.** Use Eq. 3–59 to find the Laplace transform of $(d^2/dt^2)\,u(t)\,e^{-t} \sin t$. Verify your result by differentiating first and then taking the Laplace transform.

**3-14.** Repeat Problem 3-13 for $(d^2/dt^2)\,u(t)\,e^{-t}$.

**3-15.** Use Eq. 3–65 to obtain the Laplace transform of $u(t) \int e^{-2t} \sin t\, dt$.

**3-16.** Use the Laplace transform to solve the following differential equation for $x$:

$$\frac{d^2 x}{dt^2} + 3\frac{dx}{dt} + 2x = u(t)$$

where $x(0-) = 1$ and $\left.\dfrac{dx}{dt}\right|_{t=0-} = 2$.

**3-17.** Use the Laplace transform to find all the mesh currents in the network of Fig. 3-17. The initial conditions are $v_c(0-) = 1$ volt, $i_L(0-) = 1$ ampere.

**3-18.** Repeat Problem 3-17, but now assume that the generator voltage is $\delta(t)$. Also find $v_c(0+)$ and $i_L(0+)$.

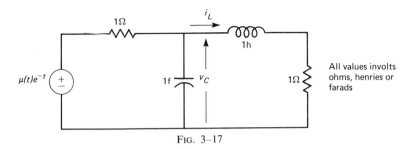

FIG. 3–17

**3-19.** Repeat Problem 3-18, but now assume that the generator voltage is $\delta^{(3)}(t)$.

**3-20.** Discuss why it is desirable to use $0-$ as a lower limit of integration in the Laplace transform integral.

**3-21.** Show that the response of a system to a unit impulse input is the derivative of its response to a unit step input.

**3-22.** Use Eq. 3–76 to obtain the Laplace transform of

$$f(t) = \begin{cases} \sin t, & 0 \leq t \leq 2\pi \\ 0; & t > 2\pi, \quad t < 0 \end{cases}$$

*Note*: express $f(t)$ in terms of $u(t) \sin t$ and a delayed function.

**3-23.** Repeat Problem 3-22 for

$$f(t) = \begin{cases} t, & 0 \leq t \leq 1 \\ 2 - t, & 1 \leq t \leq 2 \\ 0; & t > 2, \quad t < 0 \end{cases}$$

**3-24.** How does the application of Eq. 3–76 change the region of analyticity of the Laplace transform?

**3-25.** Repeat Problem 3-24 for Eq. 3–77.

**3-26.** Use Eq. 3–79 to obtain the Laplace transform of $f(t) = u(t) t \sin 2t$.

**3-27.** Use Eq. 3–80 to obtain the Laplace transform of $f(t) = u(t) (\sin 2t)/t$.

**3-28.** Determine the Laplace transform of

$$f(t) = \mu(t) \left| \sin t \right|$$

**3-29.** Repeat Problem 3-28 for

$$f(t) = \begin{cases} 1, & 0 \leq t \leq 1/2 \\ -1, & 1/2 < t < 1 \end{cases}$$

and

$$f(t + 1) = f(t), \qquad t > 0$$

**3-30.** Find the value of $f(0+)$ for the function whose Laplace transform is given by

$$F(s) = \frac{s^2 + 2s + 1}{(s + 1)(s + 2)(s + 3)}$$

**3-31.** Repeat Problem 3-30 for

$$F(s) = \frac{s^3 + s^2 + 2s + 1}{(s + 1)(s + 2)(s + 3)}$$

**3-32.** Repeat Problem 3-30 for

$$F(s) = \frac{s^3 + s^2 + 2s + 1}{s^2 + 2s + 1}$$

**3-33.** Find the initial value of $f'(t)|_{t=0+}$ of the first derivative of the function given in Problem 3-30; assume that $f(0-) = f(0+)$.

**3-34.** Find the final value of the function whose Laplace transform is given by

$$F(s) = \frac{s^2 + 2s + 1}{(s+1)(s+2)(s+3)}$$

**3-35.** Repeat Problem 3-34 for

$$F(s) = \frac{s^2 + 2s + 3}{(s^2 + \omega_0^2)(s+1)}$$

The answer should be on a distribution basis.

**3-36.** Can the final value theorem be applied to $F(s) = 1/(s-1)$. Explain your answer.

**3-37.** Find the inverse Laplace transform of

$$F(s) = \frac{1}{(s+1)(s+2)}, \qquad \text{Re } s > -1$$

**3-38.** Repeat Problem 3-37 for

$$F(s) = \frac{s^3 + s^2 + 1}{(s+1)(s+2)}, \qquad \text{Re } s > -1$$

Note that $F(s)$ does not satisfy Jordan's lemma. Perform the long division until a proper fraction results and apply Jordan's lemma to this fraction. Use Table 3-1 to obtain the transform of the impulse, etc.

**3-39.** Repeat Problem 3-37 for

$$F(s) = \frac{s^2 + s + 1}{s^3(s+1)(s+2)}, \qquad \text{Re } s > 0$$

**3-40.** Repeat Problem 3-37 for

$$F(s) = \frac{s^2 + s + 3}{s[(s+1)^2 + 4](s+2)}, \qquad \text{Re } s > 0$$

**3-41.** Repeat Problem 3-37 for

$$F(s) = \frac{1}{\sinh s}, \qquad \text{Re } s > 0$$

**3-42.** Repeat Problem 3-37 for

$$F(s) = \frac{1}{s \cosh \sqrt{s}}, \qquad \text{Re } s > 0$$

**3-43.** Repeat Problem 3-37 for

$$F(s) = \frac{1}{\sqrt{s}}, \qquad \text{Re } s > 0$$

**3-44.** Repeat Problem 3-37 for

$$F(s) = \frac{e^{-\sqrt{2}}}{(s^2 + 1)\sqrt{s}}$$

Part of the answer can be left in the form of a real integral.

**3-45.** Repeat Problem 3-37 for

$$F(s) = \frac{s + 2}{\sqrt{s^2 + 1}\,(s + 1)(s + 3)}$$

Part of the answer can be left in the form of a real integral.

**3-46.** Write a computer program that can be used to evaluate the residues of second-degree poles.

**3-47.** Repeat Problem 3-46 for third-degree poles.

**3-48.** Write a main program for the subroutine RES (see Fig. 3-11).

**3-49.** Use the convolution theorem to obtain the inverse Laplace transform of

$$F(s) = \frac{1}{s}\frac{1}{s + 1}, \qquad \mathrm{Re}\,s > 0$$

**3-50.** Repeat Problem 3-49 for

$$F(s) = \frac{1}{[(s + 1)^2 + 1](s + 2)}, \qquad \mathrm{Re}\,s > -1$$

**3-51.** Use the convolution theorem to obtain the Laplace transform of

$$f(t) = u(t)\,e^{-t}e^{-2t}$$

**3-52.** Repeat Problem 3-51 for

$$f(t) = u(t)\sin t\,e^{-t}$$

**3-53.** Repeat Problem 3-51 for

$$f(t) = u(t)\sin t$$

**3-54.** Find the two-sided Laplace transform of

$$f(t) = \begin{cases} 1, & \pm < 0 \\ e^{-3t}, & t > 0 \end{cases}$$

**3-55.** Repeat Problem 3-54 for

$$f(t) = \begin{cases} e^{-t}, & t < 0 \\ e^{-2t}, & t > 0 \end{cases}$$

**3-56.** Repeat Problem 3-54 for

$$f(t) = \begin{cases} \sin t, & t < 0 \\ e^{-t}\sin t, & t > 0 \end{cases}$$

**3-57.** Obtain the inverse Laplace transform of

$$F(s) = \frac{1}{s - 2} + \frac{1}{s + 1}, \qquad 2 > \mathrm{Re}\,s > -1$$

**3-58.** Repeat Problem 3-57 for

$$F(s) = \frac{1}{s - 2} + \frac{1}{s + 1}, \qquad \mathrm{Re}\,s > 2$$

**3-59.** Repeat Problem 3-57 for

$$F(s) = \frac{1}{s - 2} + \frac{1}{s - 1}, \qquad 2 > \mathrm{Re}\,s > 1$$

**3-60.** Repeat Problem 3-57 for

$$F(s) = \frac{1}{(s-2)^2+1} + \frac{1}{(s+3)^2+4}, \qquad 2 > \operatorname{Re} s > -3$$

**3-61.** Use the results of Problem 3-54 to obtain the Laplace transform of $f(t+1)$.

**3-62.** Repeat Problem 3-61 for $f(t+1)$.

**3-63.** Use the convolution theorem to obtain the inverse Laplace transform of the product of these two transforms

$$F_1(s) = \frac{-1}{s-1} + \frac{1}{s+1}, \qquad 1 > \operatorname{Re} s > -1$$

$$F_2(s) = \frac{-1}{s-2} + \frac{1}{s+2}, \qquad 2 > \operatorname{Re} s > -2$$

**3-64.** Use the convolution theorem to obtain the Laplace transform of the product of the two time functions

$$f_1(t) = \begin{cases} e^{+t}, & t < 0 \\ e^{-t}, & t > 0 \end{cases}$$

and

$$f_2(t) = \begin{cases} e^{+2t}, & t < 0 \\ e^{-2t}, & t > 0 \end{cases}$$

## BIBLIOGRAPHY

Chirlian, P. M. *Basic Network Theory*. Chap. 5. New York: McGraw-Hill, 1969.

Cooper, G. R., and McGillem, C. D. *Methods of Signal and System Analysis*. Chaps. 6–7. New York: Holt, 1967.

Gardner, M. F. and Barnes, J. L. *Transients in Linear Systems*. Chaps. 1–8. New York: Wiley, 1942.

Lathi, B. P. *Signals, Systems and Communications*. Chap. 5. New York: Wiley, 1965.

Papoulis, A. *The Fourier Integral and Its Applications*. Chap. 9. New York: McGraw-Hill, 1962.

Peskin, E. *Transient and Steady State Analysis of Electric Networks*. Chaps. 2–3. Princeton, N. J.: Van Nostrand, 1961.

# CHAPTER 4

# State Variables

In this chapter we shall consider another technique for obtaining the response of a system to its inputs. We have previously discussed the Fourier and Laplace transforms as procedures for analyzing linear systems; that is, systems characterized by linear differential equations. We shall now develop a method called the *state variable analysis procedure* or the *state space analysis procedure*. This technique can be applied to *nonlinear* and *time-varying*, as well as to *linear*, systems. Computer solutions can be readily obtained using state variable analysis procedures. This procedure is a very important and powerful one.

State variable equations are actually a set of simultaneous differential equations which characterize a system. However, they are in a different form from conventional differential equations which makes them superior for computer solutions.

## 4-1. AN INTRODUCTION TO STATES, STATE EQUATIONS, STATE SPACE, AND TRAJECTORY

In this section we shall introduce the basic ideas of state space, but we shall restrict the discussion, in the introduction, to simple, linear, time-invariant systems (see Section 1-1). In the next section we shall extend our discussion to general systems including nonlinear and time-varying ones. In general, a linear system can be characterized by a set of linear differential equations with constant coefficients (see Eqs. 1–1). Such a set of equations is

$$a_{1m}\frac{d^m x_1(t)}{dt^m} + \cdots + a_{11}\frac{dx_1(t)}{dt} + a_{10}x_1(t) = F_1\left[y_1(t), y_2(t), \ldots, y_k(t)\right]$$

$$a_{2m}\frac{d^m x_2(t)}{dt^m} + \cdots + a_{21}\frac{dx_2(t)}{dt} a_{20}x_2(t) = F_2\left[y_1(t), y_2(t), \ldots, y_k(t)\right]$$

$$\cdots\cdots\cdots\cdots\cdots\cdots\cdots\cdots\cdots\cdots\cdots\cdots\cdots\cdots\cdots\cdots\cdots\cdots\cdots\cdots\cdots\cdots\cdots\cdots\cdots\cdots \qquad (4\text{–}1)$$

$$a_{nm}\frac{d^m x_n(t)}{dt^m} + \cdots + a_{n1}\frac{dx_n(t)}{dt} + a_{n0}x_n(t) = F_n\left[y_1(t), y_2(t), \ldots, y_k(t)\right]$$

where the $a_{ij}$ are constants, and $F_j[y_1(t), y_2(t), \ldots, y_k(t))]$ is a function of the independent variables $y_1(t), y_2(t), \ldots, y_k(t)$. (It can contain constant terms.) Equations 4–1 characterize a system which has $n$ unknown output signals (i.e., dependent variables) $x_1(t), x_2(t), \ldots, x_n(t)$ and $k$ driving signals (i.e., independent variables) $y_1(t), y_2(t), \ldots, y_k(t)$. (Such a system is represented in Fig. 1–1, and a short general discussion of systems is given in Chapter 1.)

If Eqs. 4–1 characterize an electric network, then $y_1(t), y_2(t), ..., y_k(t)$ could be the voltages and/or currents of the known generators. Then $x_1(t), x_2(t), ..., x_n(t)$ could be the unknown loop currents and/or node voltages of the network.

Alternatively, we could consider the system to be a linear approximation of an airplane. The $y_1(t), y_2(t), ..., y_k(t)$ could represent the wind velocity, thrust of the engines, etc. These are assumed known. Then, the unknowns $x_1(t), x_2(t), ..., x_n(t)$ could represent the airplane's velocity, acceleration, position in three dimensions, altitude, and attitude, etc.

Note that each equation of Eqs. 4–1 has only one unknown. The equations may have been obtained by solving a set of simultaneous differential equations. (It is assumed that the reader is familiar with classical differential equations.)

Equations 4–1 are classical form of representing a linear system. However, they are *not* the form that we shall use here. Another form called the *state variable form*, or *normal form*, shall be used. This form is readily solved using computer techniques that can be applied to linear, nonlinear, and time-varying systems.

In state variable procedures, a new set of unknowns called *state variables* are defined. The old variables $x_1(t), x_2(t), ..., x_n(t)$ will be expressed in terms of the state variables which are characterized by a set of *first-order* differential equations of special form.

Let us discuss a simple example which will illustrate this discussion. We shall generalize the ideas in the next section. Consider the RLC series circuit illustrated in Fig. 4–1. The integral differential equations for the circuit are

$$Ri(t) + L\frac{di(t)}{dt} + \frac{1}{C}\int i(t)\,dt = V \tag{4–2}$$

Now differentiate the equation so that it is in the form of Eqs. 4–1. Thus, we obtain after manipulating

$$\frac{d^2i(t)}{dt^2} + \frac{R}{L}\frac{di(t)}{dt} + \frac{1}{LC}i(t) = 0 \tag{4–3}$$

The system is characterized by a second-order differential equation. We now wish to find a new set of unknowns, such that each is characterized by a first-order dif-

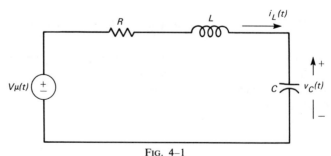

FIG. 4–1
Simple RLC circuit

ferential equation and is such that each equation contains only the derivative of *one* unknown. Choose the unknowns as $i_L(t)$, the current through the inductor, and $v_C(t)$, the voltage across the capacitor. Then, Eq. 4–2 can be written as

$$Ri_L(t) + L\frac{di_L(t)}{dt} + v_C(t) = V \tag{4-4}$$

Also,

$$v_C(t) = \frac{1}{C}\int i_L(t)\,dt \tag{4-5}$$

Differentiating this, we obtain

$$\frac{dv_C(t)}{dt} = \frac{1}{C}i_L(t) \tag{4-6}$$

Equations 4–4 and 4–6 can be written as

$$\frac{di_L(t)}{dt} = -\frac{R}{L}i_L(t) - \frac{1}{L}v_C(t) + \frac{V}{L} \tag{4-7a}$$

$$\frac{dv_C(t)}{dt} = \frac{1}{C}i_L(t) \tag{4-7b}$$

Equations 4–7 are called the *state equations* of the network. In this case, $i_L(t)$ and $v_C(t)$ are the *state variables*.

In the state equations the first derivative of a state variable is set equal to a function of all the state variables and known input signals. This function should not contain any derivatives of either the state variables or the input signals. The numerical values of all the state variables at any instant of time is called the *state* of the system at that time. Thus, the state of a system, at all times, describes its behavior.

The initial conditions are important to the solution of differential equations. In the example, the two initial conditions are $i_L(0-)$ and $v_C(0-)$. These are initial values of the state variables. The state of the system at $t = 0-$ is called the *initial state* of the system. If all the initial conditions are zero, then the system is said to be in the *zero state*.

In Sections 4–6 to 4–9 we shall develop procedures for solving equations in state variable form. However, in this and the next few sections, we shall consider the definition and formulation of these equations. We shall assume that the solutions of Eqs. 4–7 are known and use these solutions to define some additional quantities. (Note that the solution for $i_L(t)$ and $v_C(t)$ can be obtained using standard procedures.) Now consider a specific solution where $R = 2\sqrt{L/C}$. In this case, the solution is

$$i_L(t) = \frac{V}{L}te^{-\omega_0 t} \tag{4-8a}$$

and

$$v_C(t) = V[1 - e^{-\omega_0 t}(\omega_0 t + 1)] \tag{4-8b}$$

where

$$\omega_0 = \frac{1}{\sqrt{LC}} \tag{4-8c}$$

We could represent $i_L(t)$ and $V_C(t)$ by separate plots versus time as shown in Fig. 4–2. However, we can also plot both variables on a *single* graph using the state variables (i.e., $i_L(t)$ and $v_C(t)$) as axes. Such a graph is shown in Fig. 4–3. To obtain this graph, proceed as follows: Choose a time $t_0$, determine $i_L(t_0)$ and $v_C(t_0)$, and plot the point $[i_L(t_0), v_C(t_0)]$ on the $i_L$ versus $v_C$ axes. When this is done for all time, the curve of Fig. 4–3 results. Note that time is not indicated on the axes, but the time corresponding to a point can be labelled on the graph.

The space where the state variables are plotted is called the *state space*. If there are more than three state variables, then the state space has more than three dimensions. Of course, such a space cannot be drawn. However, the general concept of a state space can be applied to $n$ dimensions. A two-dimensional state space, such as that of Fig. 4–3, is called a *phase plane*. The actual curve in the state space is called the *trajectory*. A point on the trajectory at $t = t_0$ gives the state of the system at $t = t_0$. A line drawn from the origin of the state space to a point on the trajectory

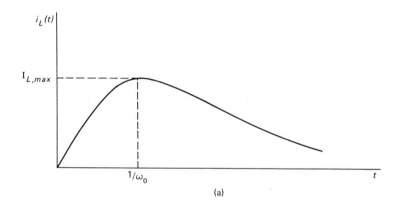

(a)

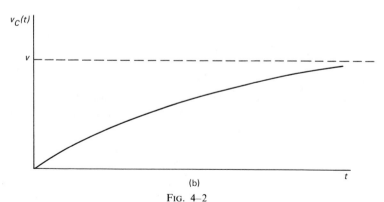

(b)

FIG. 4–2

(a) Plot of $i_L(t)$ given by Eq. 4–8a; (b) plot of $v_C(t)$ given by Eq.4–8b

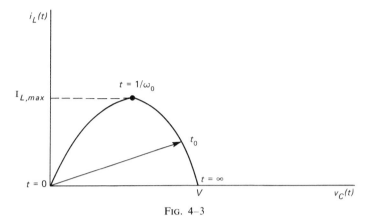

FIG. 4–3
State space and trajectory for the network of Fig. 4–1 for $R = 2\sqrt{L/C}$

can be considered to be a *vector* whose coordinates are the state variables. Vectors can be represented by a one-column matrix (see Appendix C). We shall designate a matrix by a "hat" (^) over the variables or by square brackets. If we call the state vector $\hat{q}(t)$, then, for the state space of Fig. 4–3, we have

$$\hat{q}(t_0) = \begin{bmatrix} i_L(t_0) \\ v_C(t_0) \end{bmatrix} \tag{4–9}$$

The trajectory can have other forms than that illustrated in Fig. 4–3. For example, if $R = 0$ in the network of Fig. 4–1, then

$$i_L(t) = \frac{V}{\omega_0 L} \sin \omega_0 t \tag{4–10a}$$

$$V_C(t) = V(1 - \cos \omega_0 t) \tag{4–10b}$$

These are the parametric equations of an ellipse. In this case, the trajectory has the form shown in Fig. 4–4. Note that it continuously repeats itself.

All of the variables of the network of Fig. 1–1 can be expressed as functions of the state variables and the known input signal, i.e., $V$. (Note that the constants of the network $R$, $L$, and $C$ may be part of the function.) For example,

$$i(t) = i_L(t) \tag{4–11a}$$

$$v_L(t) = -Ri_L(t) - v_C(t) + V \tag{4–11b}$$

$$v_R(t) = Ri_L(t) \tag{4–11c}$$

## 4-2.  BASIC STATE VARIABLE EQUATIONS FOR SYSTEMS

We shall now express the equations of state variables in general terms. Suppose we have a general system which may be nonlinear or time varying. There are $k$ independent variables or signals $y_i(t), i = 1, 2, ..., k$ could represent the known

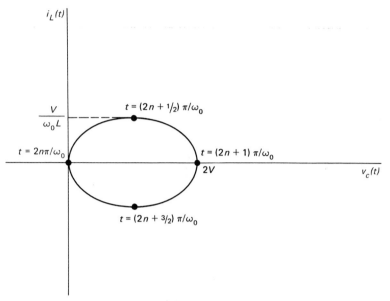

Fig. 4–4

State space and trajectory for Eq. 4–10; $n$ is any integer

generators in an electric network. The unknown signals of the system will be designated by $x_i(t)$, $i = 1, 2, ..., m$. We now choose a new set of variables, the *state variables*,
which shall be designated by $q_i(t)$, $i = 1, 2, ..., n$. The state variables have the following properties: the first derivative of each will be defined as a function of all the
state variables and known driving functions; only one derivative with respect to
time, the derivative of the state variable in question, will appear in each defining
equation; all of the system's unknowns will be expressible in terms of the state
variables, the knowns, and time.

The set of state variable equations will be written in the form

$$\frac{dq_1(t)}{dt} = f_1\left[q_1(t), q_2(t), ..., q_n(t), y_1(t), y_2(t), ..., y_k(t), t\right]$$

$$\frac{dq_2(t)}{dt} = f_2\left[q_1(t), q_2(t), ..., q_n(t), y_1(t), y_2(t), ..., y_k(t), t\right]$$

$$\cdots\cdots\cdots\cdots\cdots\cdots\cdots\cdots\cdots\cdots\cdots\cdots\cdots\cdots\cdots\cdots \qquad (4\text{--}12)$$

$$\frac{dq_n(t)}{dt} = f_n\left[q_1(t), q_2(t), ..., q_n(t), y_1(t), y_2(t), ..., y_k(t), t\right]$$

The first derivative of each state variable is expressed as a function of all the
state variables, the known signal, and time. The functions $f_1, f_2, ..., f_n$ are, in general,

different. These functions do not contain any derivative with respect to time. However, they may be nonlinear or time varying.

Since the equations are cumbersome, it is very convenient to use matrix notation here. We shall define the following matrices

$$\hat{q}(t) = \begin{bmatrix} q_1(t) \\ q_2(t) \\ \cdot \\ \cdot \\ \cdot \\ q_n(t) \end{bmatrix} \tag{4–13}$$

$$\hat{y}(t) = \begin{bmatrix} y_1(t) \\ y_2(t) \\ \cdot \\ \cdot \\ \cdot \\ y_k(t) \end{bmatrix} \tag{4–14}$$

$$\hat{f}[\hat{q}(t), \hat{y}(t), t] =$$

$$\begin{bmatrix} f_1[q_1(t), q_2(t), ..., q_n(t), y_1(t), y_2(t), ..., y_k(t), t] \\ f_2[q_1(t), q_2(t), ..., q_n(t), y_1(t), y_2(t), ..., y_k(t), t] \\ .................................................... \\ f_n[q_1(t), q_2(t), ..., q_n(t), y_1(t), y_2(t), ..., y_k(t), t] \end{bmatrix} \tag{4–15}$$

Then, we can write Eqs. 4–12 in the compact form

$$\frac{d\hat{q}(t)}{dt} = \hat{f}[\hat{q}(t), \hat{y}(t), t] \tag{4–16}$$

Note that: *the derivative of a matrix is defined as the derivative of each element of the matrix.*

The matrix $\hat{q}(t)$ is an $n$-dimensional vector which gives the state of the system at time $t$. The tip of the vector drawn from the origin of the $n$-dimensional state space to $\hat{q}(t)$ traces out the trajectory of the system. Also, the $\hat{y}(t)$ vector is a vector in $k$-dimensional space.

In general, the state variables are chosen so that all the unknowns of the system can be expressed as functions of the state variables, the known signals, and time. That is, we can write

$$x_1(t) = h_1[q_1(t), q_2(t), ..., q_n(t), y_1(t), y_2(t), ..., y_k(t), t]$$
$$x_2(t) = h_2[q_1(t), q_2(t), ..., q_n(t), y_1(t), y_2(t), ..., y_k(t), t]$$
$$.................................................... \tag{4–17}$$
$$x_m(t) = h_m[q_1(t), q_2(t), ..., q_n(t), y_1(t), y_2(t), ..., y_k(t), t]$$

where the $h_1, h_2, \ldots, h_m$ are functions of the state variables, input signals, and time. Let us define a matrix

$$\hat{x}(t) = \begin{bmatrix} x_1(t) \\ x_2(t) \\ \cdot \\ \cdot \\ \cdot \\ x_m(t) \end{bmatrix}$$

(4–18)

Then, in matrix form, Eqs. 4–17 become

$$\hat{x}(t) = \hat{h}[\hat{q}(t)\,\hat{y}(t), t]$$

(4–19)

Equations 4–16 and 4–19 are such that they can apply to linear, nonlinear, time invariant, and/or time-varying systems. We shall consider all such systems in subsequent sections. However, for purposes of example we now restrict ourselves to linear, time-invariant systems. In this case, the functions $f_k$ and $h_k$ (see Eqs. 4–16 and 4–19) become linear combinations of the variables. For example, Eq. 4–16 can be written as

$$\frac{dq_1(t)}{dt} = a_{11}q_1(t) + a_{12}q_2(t) + \cdots + a_{1n}q_n(t)$$
$$+ b_{11}y_1(t) + b_{12}y_2(t) + \cdots + b_{1k}y_k(t)$$

$$\frac{dq_2(t)}{dt} = a_{21}q_1(t) + a_{22}q_2(t) + \cdots + a_{2n}q_n(t)$$
$$+ b_{21}y_1(t) + b_{22}y_2(t) + \cdots + b_{2k}y_k(t)$$

(4–20)

$$\cdots\cdots\cdots\cdots\cdots\cdots\cdots\cdots\cdots\cdots\cdots\cdots\cdots\cdots\cdots$$

$$\frac{dq_n(t)}{dt} = a_{n1}q_1(t) + a_{n2}q_2(t) + \cdots + a_{nn}q_n(t)$$
$$+ b_{n1}y_1(t) + b_{n2}y_2(t) + \cdots + b_{nk}y_k(t)$$

where the $a_{ij}$ and $b_{ij}$ are constants. We can write this in more compact form by using matrix notation.

$$\hat{a} = \begin{bmatrix} a_{11} & a_{12}\ldots a_{1n} \\ a_{21} & a_{22}\ldots a_{2n} \\ \cdots\cdots\cdots\cdots \\ a_{n1} & a_{n2}\ldots a_{nn} \end{bmatrix}$$

(4–21)

$$\hat{b} = \begin{bmatrix} b_{11} & b_{12}\ldots b_{1k} \\ b_{21} & b_{22}\ldots b_{2k} \\ b_{n1} & b_{n2}\ldots b_{nk} \end{bmatrix}$$

(4–22)

Then, Eqs. 4–20 can be written as

$$\frac{d\hat{q}(t)}{dt} = \hat{a}\,\hat{q}(t) + \hat{b}\,\hat{y}(t)$$

(4–23)

As an example, consider Eqs. 4–7. Here

$$\hat{q}(t) = \begin{bmatrix} i_L(t) \\ v_C(t) \end{bmatrix} \tag{4-24a}$$

$$\hat{y}(y) = [V]$$

$$\hat{a} = \begin{bmatrix} -R/L & -1/L \\ 1/C & 0 \end{bmatrix} \tag{4-24b}$$

$$\hat{b} = \begin{bmatrix} 1/L \\ 0 \end{bmatrix}$$

In the linear, time-invariant case, the system unknowns will be linear functions of the state variables and the unknown input signals. Thus, we can write

$$\begin{aligned}
x_1(t) &= c_{11}q_1 + c_{12}q_2(t) + \cdots + c_{1n}q_n(t) \\
&\quad + d_{11}y_1(t) + d_{12}y_2 + \cdots + d_{1k}y_k(t) \\
x_2(t) &= c_{21}q_1(t) + c_{22}q_2(t) + \cdots + c_{2n}q_n(t) \\
&\quad + d_{21}y_1(t) + d_{22}y_2(t) + \cdots + d_{2k}y_k(t) \\
&\cdots\cdots\cdots\cdots\cdots\cdots\cdots\cdots\cdots\cdots\cdots\cdots\cdots\cdots \\
x_m(t) &= c_{m1}q_1(t) + c_{m2}q_2(t) + \cdots + c_{mn}q_n(t) \\
&\quad + d_{m1}y_1(t) + d_{m2}y_2(t) + \cdots + d_{mk}y_k(t)
\end{aligned} \tag{4-25}$$

where the $c_{ij}$ and $d_{ij}$ are constants. Now let us define the matrices

$$\hat{c} = \begin{bmatrix} c_{11} & c_{12} & c_m \\ c_{21} & c_{22} & \cdots & c_{2n} \\ \cdots\cdots\cdots\cdots\cdots \\ c_{m1} & c_{m2} & \cdots & c_{mn} \end{bmatrix} \tag{4-26}$$

and

$$\hat{d} = \begin{bmatrix} d_{11} & d_{12} & \cdots & d_{1k} \\ d_{21} & d_{22} & \cdots & d_{2k} \\ \cdots\cdots\cdots\cdots\cdots \\ d_{m1} & d_{m2} & \cdots & d_{mk} \end{bmatrix} \tag{4-27}$$

Then, Eqs. 4–25 can be written as

$$\hat{x}(t) = \hat{c}\hat{q}(t) + \hat{d}\hat{y}(t) \tag{4-28}$$

For example, suppose that the desired unknowns are given in Eqs. 4–11, then,

$$\hat{x}(t) = \begin{bmatrix} i(t) \\ v_L(t) \\ v_R(t) \end{bmatrix}$$

$$\hat{c} = \begin{bmatrix} 1 & 0 \\ -R & -1 \\ R & 0 \end{bmatrix}$$

$$\hat{d} = \begin{bmatrix} 0 \\ 1 \\ 0 \end{bmatrix}$$

where $\hat{q}(t)$ and $\hat{y}(t)$ are defined in Eqs. 4–24.

Now let us show how the state variable equations for a linear, time-invariant system can be obtained from its differential equations. The procedure will be general. However, there is not one unique set of state variables. Often, for specific systems, a better choice of state variables exists than the one generated by this procedure. In the next section, we shall illustrate a less cumbersome procedure for obtaining the state variable of linear, time-invariant networks. Suppose we have a set of equations such as those given by Eqs. 4–1. However, let us express the right-hand side as a single known function of time $y_j(t)$. We now present a method that will replace each equation by a set of state variable equations. The set of all such sets are the state variable equations for the system. Then let us write a typical equation as

$$\alpha_n \frac{d^n x(t)}{dt^n} + \alpha_{n-1} \frac{d^{n-1} x(t)}{dt^{n-1}} + \cdots + \alpha_1 \frac{dx(t)}{dt} + \alpha_0 x(t) = y(t) \qquad (4\text{–}29)$$

where, for brevity, we have omitted the subscripts from the $x(t)$ and $y(t)$. Choose the state variables in the following way

$$q_1(t) = x(t)$$

$$q_2(t) = \frac{dx(t)}{dt} = \frac{dq_1(t)}{dt}$$

$$q_3(t) = \frac{d^2 x(t)}{dt^2} = \frac{dq_2(t)}{dt} \qquad (4\text{–}30)$$

$$\cdots \cdots \cdots \cdots \cdots \cdots \cdots \cdots \cdots \cdots$$

$$q_n(t) = \frac{d^{n-1} x(t)}{dt^{n-1}} = \frac{dq_{n-1}(t)}{dt}$$

The first $n - 1$ state variables are obtained from Eqs. 4–30.

$$\frac{dq_1(t)}{dt} = q_2(t)$$

$$\frac{dq_2(t)}{dt} = q_3(t)$$

$$\cdot$$
$$\cdot \qquad\qquad (4\text{-}31)$$
$$\cdot$$

$$\frac{dq_{n-1}(t)}{dt} = q_n(t)$$

The $n$th equation is obtained by substituting Eqs. 4–30 into Eq 4–29 and solving for $dq_n(t)$; note that

$$\frac{dx^n(t)}{dt} = \frac{dq_n(t)}{dt}$$

Hence,

$$\frac{dq_n(t)}{dt} = -\frac{\alpha_0}{\alpha_n}q_1(t) - \frac{\alpha_1}{\alpha_n}q_2(t) - \cdots - \frac{\alpha_{n-1}}{\alpha_n}q_n(t) + \frac{1}{\alpha_n}y_n(t) \qquad (4\text{-}32)$$

Equations 4–31 and 4–32 constitute a set of state variable equations. Such a set can be obtained for each equation in Eqs. 4–1. All of these constitute the equations of state of the network.

If the function $y(t)$ represents a single input signal or a linear combination of the input signals, then the method just discussed is satisfactory. However, in order to form equations of the type of Eqs. 4–1, often the system equations have to be differentiated, and simultaneous equations solved. In this case, $y(t)$ could contain derivatives of the input generator functions. Then, Eqs. 4–31 and 4–32 would violate our definition of state variable equations since the right-hand side of the equations would now contain derivatives. This problem can be resolved by redefining our choice of state variables. Because this procedure is more difficult than the one just discussed, we shall work with a specific example before indicating the general procedure.

As an example, consider the differential equation

$$\alpha_2 \frac{d^2x(t)}{dt^2} + \alpha_1 \frac{dx(t)}{dt} + \alpha_0 x(t) = \beta_2 \frac{d^2y(t)}{dt^2} + \beta_1 \frac{dy(t)}{dt} + \beta_0 y(t) \qquad (4\text{-}33)$$

Now let us define the state variable $q_1(t)$ in the following way

$$q_1(t) = x(t) - \frac{\beta_2}{\alpha_2}y(t) \qquad (4\text{-}34)$$

Solving for $x(t)$ and substituting into Eq. 4–33 yields

$$\alpha_2 \frac{d^2q_1(t)}{dt} + \alpha_1 \frac{dq_1(t)}{dt} + \alpha_0 q_1(t) = \left(\beta_1 - \frac{\alpha_1}{\alpha_2}\beta_2\right)\frac{dy(t)}{dt} + \left(\beta_0 - \frac{\alpha_0}{\alpha_2}\beta_2\right)y(t) \qquad (4\text{-}35)$$

The highest order derivative of $y(t)$ has been cancelled from the equation. Note that instead of choosing $q_1(t) = x(t)$ as was done in Eqs. 4–30, we now add a function of $y(t)$ so that its derivative cancels the derivative of $y(t)$ whose order is equal to the order of the highest derivative of $x(t)$. If $y(t)$ does not have a derivative whose order is equal to the highest derivative of $x(t)$, then $q_1(t) = x(t)$.

Now chose $q_2(t)$ in the following way

$$q_2(t) = \frac{dq_1(t)}{dt} - \frac{\beta_1 - \alpha_1\beta_2/\alpha_2}{\alpha_2} y(t) \qquad (4\text{–}36)$$

Substituting in Eq. 4–35, we have

$$\alpha_2 \frac{dq_2(t)}{dt} + \alpha_1 q_2(t) + \alpha_0 q_1(t) = \left[ \beta_0 - \frac{\alpha_0}{\alpha_2}\beta_2 - \frac{\alpha_1}{\alpha_2}\left(\beta_1 - \frac{\alpha_1\beta_2}{\alpha_2}\right) \right] y(t) \qquad (4\text{–}37)$$

Again, the state variable has a constant term or function of $y(t)$ added to it so that the highest-order derivative of $y(t)$ is cancelled. Equations 4–36 and 4–37 can be rearranged to obtain the state variable equations of the network; thus,

$$\frac{dq_1(t)}{dt} = q_2(t) + \frac{\beta_1 - \alpha_1\beta_2/\alpha_2}{\alpha_2} y(t) \qquad (4\text{–}38a)$$

$$\frac{dq_2(t)}{dt} = -\frac{\alpha_0}{\alpha_2}q_1(t) - \frac{\alpha_1}{\alpha_2}q_2(t) + \frac{1}{\alpha_2}\left[ \beta_0 - \frac{\alpha_0}{\alpha_2} - \frac{\alpha_1}{\alpha_2}\left(\beta_1 - \frac{\alpha_1\beta_2}{\alpha_2}\right) \right] y(t) \qquad (4\text{–}38b)$$

Let us consider this procedure in general terms. Suppose the original differential equation is of the form

$$\sum_{i=0}^{n} \alpha_i \frac{d^i x(t)}{dt^i} = \sum_{j=0}^{k} \sum_{i=0}^{n} \beta_{ij} \frac{d^i y_j(t)}{dt^i} \qquad (4\text{–}39)$$

That is we have $k$ different independent variables, all of whose derivatives, up to the $n$th order, can appear on the right-hand side of the equation. Then, we define the first state variable in the following way

$$x(t) = q_1(t) + \sum_{j=1}^{k} \gamma_{j1} y_j(t) \qquad (4\text{–}40)$$

Equation 4–40 is then substituted into Eq. 4–39. Each $\gamma_{j1}$ is then chosen so that the coefficient of the $n$th derivative of $y_j(t)$ becomes zero in the resulting equation. This is illustrated in Eqs. 4–34 and 4–35. The next state variable is defined by the equation

$$\frac{dq_1(t)}{dt} = q_2(t) + \sum_{j=1}^{k} \gamma_{j2} y_j(t) \qquad (4\text{–}41)$$

This equation is then substituted into the equation that resulted when Eq. 4–40 was substituted into Eq. 4–39. (Equation 4–41 is substituted there for all the derivatives of $q_1(t)$.) Then, the values of $\gamma_{j2}$ are chosen so that the coefficients of the $(n-1)$th derivative of $y_j(t)$ becomes zero. This procedure is repeated. In general, we define the state variables by the equation

$$\frac{dq_{i-1}t}{dt} = q_i(t) + \sum_{j=1}^{k} \gamma_{ji} y_j(t), i = 1, 2, ..., n \qquad (4\text{-}42)$$

where the $\gamma_{ji}$ are determined by substitution in successive equations and cancelling the appropriate derivative of $y_j(t)$. Note that we define $dq_0(t)/dt = x(t)$ (see Eq. 4–40).

This procedure can be used as long as the order of the highest derivative of $y_j(t)$ is equal to or less than the order of the highest derivative of $x(t)$. This will usually be the case with linear, time-invariant systems.

The method that we have just discussed is a purely general one for formulating a set of state variables for linear, time-invariant networks. However, it is not the only one. There are others that use different state variables and are often less cumbersome to formulate, or solve. The specific details depend upon the specific system in question.

In general, we can express $n$ other variables in terms of a linear combination of the $n$ state variables; for example,

$$\hat{g}(t) = \hat{M}\hat{q}(t) \qquad (4\text{-}43)$$

where $\hat{M}$ is an $n \times n$ matrix of constants (i.e., Eq. 4–43 represents a set of $n$ linear simultaneous equations). Then, if $\hat{M}$ is nonsingular (i.e., $\hat{M}^{-1}$ exists—see Section C-2, we can write

$$\hat{q}(t) = \hat{M}^{-1}\hat{g}(t) \qquad (4\text{-}44)$$

Substituting into Eq. 4–23, we obtain

$$\hat{M}^{-1}\frac{d\hat{g}(t)}{dt} = \hat{a}\hat{M}^{-1}\hat{g}(t) + \hat{b}\hat{y}(t)$$

Premultiplying by $M$ (see Section C-1) yields

$$\frac{d\hat{g}(t)}{dt} = \hat{M}\hat{a}\hat{M}^{-1}\hat{g}(t) + \hat{M}\hat{b}\hat{y}(t) \qquad (4\text{-}45)$$

Thus, we have a new valid set of state variable equations, where $\hat{g}(t)$ now represents the state variables. This procedure, in general, can only be used with linear systems.

## 4-3. STATE VARIABLE EQUATIONS FOR ELECTRIC NETWORKS

In this section we shall consider a system for choosing the state variables in an electric network. However, before starting we shall discuss some elementary network topology. Although this discussion is self-contained, it will be brief and cover only the necessary material. (The reader is referred to the network analysis texts in the bibliography for a further discussion.)

**Some Basic Ideas and Definitions of Network Topology.** We begin by discussing some basic definitions. A connection of branches is called a *network* or *graph*. The ends of branches are called *nodes*. Branches may only be connected at nodes. If a node is the end of a branch, then that branch is said to be *incident* on the node. A *path* is defined in the following way. Start at one node in the network and move along a branch until we reach another node. Then, leave that node along a different branch. If the procedure is continued, traveling over as many branches as desired, and no node is encountered more than once; then the set of branches and nodes traversed is called a path. In Fig. 4–5a, branches 1, 2, 3, 7, 9, and 10 constitute a path.

A network is said to be *connected* if a path can be drawn between every pair of nodes. For example, the network of Fig. 4–5a is connected while the network of Fig. 4–5b is not connected since, for instance, a path cannot be drawn between nodes 3 and 6. We shall confine our discussion to connected networks. A *subnetwork* is part of the original network. The remainder of the network is called the *complement* of the subnetwork.

Now we shall define a *mesh*, or *loop*. Start at a node, say node *b*, traverse a path but finally choose a branch which has node *b* as its endpoint. The collection of branches forms a "closed path" or mesh or loop. For example, in Fig. 4–5a, branches 1, 2, 3, and 5 constitute a loop. Similarly, branches 1, 2, 6, 7, and 5 constitute a loop.

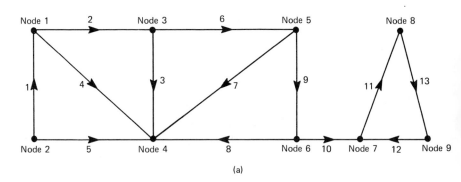

(a)

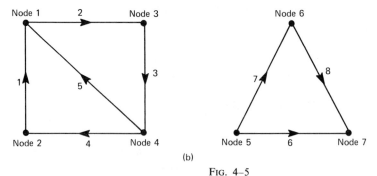

(b)

Fig. 4–5
(a) Connected network; (b) nonconnected network

However, branches 1, 2, 3, and 4 do not constitute a loop since node 1, which is *not* the starting node, is encountered *twice*.

A *tree* is a connected subnetwork of a connected network that contains all the nodes but no loops. That is, a tree is a subnetwork which is such that a path can be drawn between any pair of nodes and the tree contains no loops. For example, Fig. 4–6a is a connected network and several possible trees for this network are shown in Figs. 4–6b and c. In general, several trees exist for a given network. The branches that we have drawn could represent impedances or generators of an electric network. Now assume that the voltage across all the tree branches of a network are known. Since the tree is connected and contains all the nodes of the network, the voltages between any pair of nodes can be determined from the tree's branch voltages. This is done by taking the path in the tree between any two nodes in question and algebraically adding the tree branch voltages along the path. Thus the voltage across any branch can be determined from the tree branch voltages.

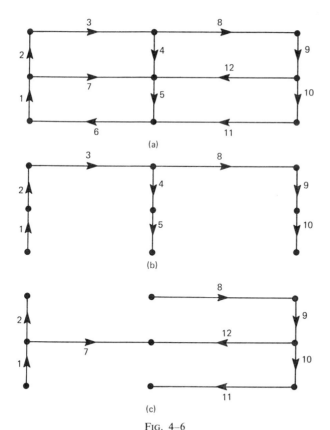

FIG. 4–6
(a) Connected network; (b) and (c) trees of this network

Once a tree has been chosen, the branches of the network fall into two classes; those in the tree and those not in the tree. The branches *not* in the tree are called *chords* or *links*. By applying Kirchhoff's current law, all of the tree branch currents can be expressed in terms of the current in the chords. This can be shown in the following way. Every tree will have at least two nodes with only one incident tree branch. At that node, all other branches are chords. Thus, the chord currents will, by Kirchhoff's law, uniquely determine that tree branch current. Now consider the subtree consisting of all the tree branches except the one whose current has been determined. A subtree will have all the characteristics of a tree, except that one node is missing. Thus, it will have two nodes with only one incident tree branch. All other branches incident to that node are chords or the tree branch whose current has been expressed in terms of the chord currents. Hence, the current in the second tree branch is expressible in terms of the chord currents. Repeat this procedure for all the tree's branches. Then all branch currents will be expressed in terms of the chord currents.

A *cut-set* is a minimal set of branches which, when removed from a network, splits it into *two* and no more than two parts. The word, *minimal*, means that if *any* one of the branches of the cut-set is replaced, then the network becomes a connected network. For example, in Fig. 4–6a, branches 3, 6, and 7 constitute a cut-set. One part of the network consists of branches 1 and 2, while the other consists of branches 4, 5, 8, 9, 10, 11, and 12. Another cut-set consists of branches 2 and 3. Note that one part of the network is, in this case, a single node. Branches 3, 6, 7, and 5 do not constitute a cut-set since branch 5 is superfluous. A cut-set divides a network into two parts, say A and B. The net current from part A to part B must be in the branches of the cut-set.

Now consider a closed surface which completely encloses part A while part B is completely outside of the volume. The branches of the cut-set and only those branches pass through the surface of the volume. For example, in Fig. 4–6a, if the cut-set consists of branches 3, 6, and 7, then part A could consist of branches 1 and 2, while part B could consist of branches 4, 5, 8, 9, 10, 11, and 12. The net current into any closed volume is zero. This is a generalized statement of Kirchhoff's current law. Thus, the algebraic sum of the current through the branches of a cut-set is zero. (The positive direction is into the closed volume.)

**State Variable Equations for Linear, Time-Invariant Electric Networks.** We shall, at the start, restrict ourselves to networks which satisfy the following two conditions: (1) There can be *no* loop which contains *only* voltage generators and capacitors; (2) there can be *no* cut-set which contains only current generators and inductors. A network which satisfies these conditions is called a *proper* network. We shall subsequently discuss the advantages of working with proper networks and the state variable equations for improper networks. However, for now, we shall restrict ourselves to proper networks.

We shall show that, in a proper network, which is linear and time invariant, a valid choice for state variables is *all* the voltages across the capacitors and *all* the currents through the inductors. We must show that if we make such a choice, then a set of equations of the form of Eqs. 4–12 or 4–20 can be obtained. In addition, it must be shown that all of the network currents and voltages can be expressed as functions of the state variables and the known signal generators. Note that the resistors of the network are assumed to be part of the functions (see the simple example of Section 4-1).

To derive a general procedure for obtaining the state variable equations, we make use of the following simple network theorem. *If the voltage $v(t)$ across, or the current $i(t)$ through, a circuit element is known, then the element can be replaced by a voltage generator $v(t)$ or a current generator $i(t)$ without changing conditions in the rest of the network.*

For example, consider Fig. 4–7. If the element of Fig. 4–7a is replaced by either of the generators in Fig. 4–7b or c, then the conditions in the remainder of the circuit will be unchanged. To prove this theorem for $v(t)$, we use loop analysis.

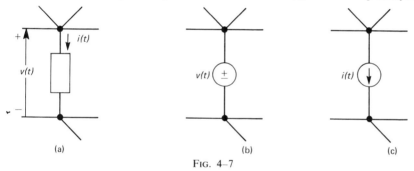

(a)                    (b)               (c)

FIG. 4–7

(a) An arbitrary element in a network; (b) voltage generator equivalent to (a) as far as conditions external to the element are concerned; (c) current generator equivalent to (a) as far as conditions external to the element are concerned

Each term in the equations represents a voltage drop across an element. Thus, replacing an impedance by a voltage generator does not change the loop equations. Hence, the currents in the network are unchanged. (Nodal analysis is used to demonstrate the equivalence of the current generator.)

Now, let us obtain the state variable equations. Define the state variables as all the currents through the inductors and all the voltages across the capacitors, and treat these currents as voltages as though they were known. That is, replace each inductor by a current generator with current $i_{Lj}(t)$ and each capacitor by a voltage generator $v_{Cj}(t)$. (These are just symbols. However in the subsequent network analysis, we shall treat them as though they were known.) The network now consists only of generators and resistors. We call such a network the *equivalent network*. Then an analysis of the equivalent network can be performed to obtain any current or voltage in terms of state variables and independent generators.

We must now show that the state variable equations can be obtained in the correct form. Consider the capacitor voltage terms first. Since we can determine any current or voltage in terms of the state variables and the independent generators, we can determine each capacitor *current* in terms of them, thus,

$$i_{Cm}(t) = f_{Cm}[q_1(t), q_2(t), ..., q_n(t), y_1(t), y_2(t), ..., y_k(t), t] \qquad (4\text{--}46)$$

where the $q_i(i = 1, 2, ..., n)$ are the chosen state variables, the $y_i(i = 1, 2, ..., k)$ are the independent generators, and $f_{Cm}$ represents a linear, time–invariant function of these variables. In general, for a linear, time-invariant capacitor

$$i_{Cm} = C_m \frac{dv_{Cm}(t)}{dt} \qquad (4\text{--}47)$$

Substituting in Eq. 4–46, we obtain

$$\frac{dv_{Cm}(t)}{dt} = \frac{1}{C_m} f_{Cm}[q_1(t), q_2(t), ..., q_n(t), y_1(t), y_2(t), ..., y_k(t), t] \qquad (4\text{--}48)$$

Note that there is a $q_j(t)$ for each $v_{Ck}(t)$. For instance, $q_2(t) = v_{C3}(t)$, etc. Equation 4–48 is the same form as Eq. 4–12. Thus, we have obtained part of the state variable equations.

Now we can analyze the equivalent network to obtain the voltages across the inductors. Thus, we have

$$v_{Lm}(t) = f_{Lm}[q_1(t), q_2(t), ..., q_n(t), y_1(t), y_2(t), ..., y_k(t), t] \qquad (4\text{--}49)$$

where $f_{Lm}$ is a linear, time-invariant function. The voltage across an inductor is

$$v_{Lm}(t) = L_m \frac{di_{Lm}(t)}{dt} \qquad (4\text{--}50)$$

Substituting in Eq. 4–49 and manipulating, we have

$$\frac{di_{Lm}(t)}{dt} = \frac{1}{L_m} f_{Lm}[q_1(t), q_2(t), ..., q_n(t), y_1(t), y_2(t), ..., y_k(t), t] \qquad (4\text{--}51)$$

Thus, we have obtained a set of state variable equations for a linear, time-invariant network.

The initial conditions for electric networks are usually given in terms of the voltages across the capacitors and the currents through the inductors. Then, choosing the state variables as the voltages across the capacitors and the currents through the inductors guarantees that the initial state will be specified, so it will not have to be calculated.

As an example of this procedure, let us obtain a set of state variable equations for the network of Fig. 4–8a. The equivalent network for the circuit is shown in Fig. 4–8b. First, we obtain the loop currents in terms of the state variables. Since $i_1(t)$ is the only loop current through the current generator, we have

$$i_1(t) = i_L(t) \qquad (4\text{--}52a)$$

The equation for the second loop is

$$-v_C = -R_2 i_1(t) + R_2 i_2(t) \qquad (4\text{--}52b)$$

Substituting Eq. 4–52a and manipulating, we have

$$i_{\angle}(t) = i_L(t) - \frac{v_c(t)}{R_2} \tag{4–52c}$$

Equations 4–52b and 4–52c express all the loop currents in terms of the state variables and known generators. Hence, they are in the form of Eqs. 4–25.

We now obtain the state variable equations. Solve Fig. 4–8b for the voltage across the inductor, and substitute Eq. 4–52a. This yields

$$v_L(t) = -R_1 i_L(t) - v_C(t) + v(t) \tag{4–53}$$

Substituting Eq. 4–50· we obtain

$$\frac{d i_L(t)}{dt} = -\frac{R_1}{L} i_L(t) - \frac{1}{L} v_C(t) + \frac{1}{L} v(t) \tag{4–54}$$

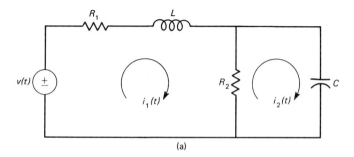

(a)

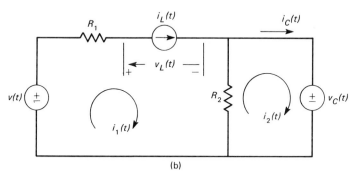

(b)

Fig. 4–8

(a) Simple network; (b) equivalent network used in obtaining state variables

The current through the capacitor is equal to $i_2(t)$. Thus, from Eq. 4–52c, we have

$$i_C(t) = i_L(t) - \frac{v_C(t)}{R_2} \tag{4–55}$$

Substituting Eq. 4–47, we obtain

$$\frac{dv_C(t)}{dt} = \frac{1}{C}i_L(t) - \frac{1}{R_2C}v_C(t) \qquad (4\text{–}56)$$

Equations 4–54 and 4–56 constitute a set of state variable equations for the network, they are

$$\frac{di_L(t)}{dt} = -\frac{R_1}{L}i_L(t) - \frac{1}{L}v_C(t) + \frac{1}{L}v(t) \qquad (4\text{–}57\text{a})$$

$$\frac{dv_C(t)}{dt} = \frac{1}{C}i_L(t) - \frac{1}{R_2C}v_C(t) \qquad (4\text{–}57\text{b})$$

Using the notation of Eqs. 4–20 through 4–23, we have

$$\hat{q}(t) = \begin{bmatrix} i_L(t) \\ v_C(t) \end{bmatrix} \qquad (4\text{–}58\text{a})$$

$$\hat{a} = \begin{bmatrix} -R_1/L & -1/L \\ 1/C & -1/R_2C \end{bmatrix} \qquad (4\text{–}58\text{b})$$

$$\hat{b} = \begin{bmatrix} 1/L \\ 0 \end{bmatrix} \qquad (4\text{–}58\text{c})$$

$$\hat{v}(t) = [v(t)] \qquad (4\text{–}58\text{d})$$

Also, using the notation of Eqs. 4–25 through 4–28, we can represent Eqs. 4–52a and 4–52c by the matrices

$$\hat{x}(t) = \begin{bmatrix} i_1(t) \\ i_2(t) \end{bmatrix} \qquad (4\text{–}58\text{e})$$

$$\hat{c} = \begin{bmatrix} 1 & 0 \\ 1 & -1/R_2 \end{bmatrix} \qquad (4\text{–}58\text{f})$$

$$\hat{d} = \begin{bmatrix} 0 \\ 0 \end{bmatrix} \qquad (4\text{–}58\text{g})$$

We have shown that all the network voltages and currents can be expressed in terms of the state variables and the known generators. Let us now discuss this using network topology. At the beginning of the section we discussed that the tree-branch voltages determined all the branch voltages, while the chord currents determined all the branch currents. Hence, we wish to find a tree which contains *all* the capacitors and voltage generators, but *no* current generators or inductors. There may be resistors in the tree branch or chords. However, their currents and/or voltages can be calculated by the procedure we have discussed. A tree which satisfies the above discussed conditions is called a *proper* tree. *If a network has at least one proper tree, it is a proper network and vice versa.* Let us prove this statement. Condition (1) of a proper network states that *there are no loops containing only voltage generators and capacitors.* Thus, if all of these branches can be chosen as tree branches, then no loop will be formed by these branches. Condition (2) states that *there are no cut-sets composed entirely of inductors or current generators.* If all the inductors and current generators lie in the chords, there must be at least one branch not an inductor or a current generator between each two parts of the network. Note that resistive branches can always be used to complete the tree if necessary.

**Improper Networks.** Now let us consider the problems that arise if the network is not proper. Suppose that there is a loop which consists only of capacitors and voltage generators. Then, when the equivalent network is formed, there will be a loop consisting only of voltage generators. Hence, one of these generators must be expressed in terms of all the others, if Kirchhoff's voltage law is not to be violated. Thus, we do not have the freedom to consider each capacitor voltage as an independent generator. Similarly, if all the elements of a cut-set are current generators or inductors, then, in the equivalent network we would encounter a cut-set which was comprised only of current generators. Again we would have to specify one generator in terms of the others so as not to violate Kirchhoff's current law. We shall illustrate the problems that arise with an example and then see what can be done to obtain the state variable equations of improper networks.

Consider the circuit of Fig. 4–9a. Its equivalent network is given in Fig. 4–9b. The outer loop consists only of three voltage generators. Thus, one must be expressed in terms of the other two. Here we have chosen

$$v_{C2}(t) = v(t) - v_{C1}(t) \tag{4–59}$$

Now, let us try to obtain the loop current in terms of the state variables and the known generator voltage. One of them is

$$i_1(t) = i_L(t) \tag{4–60}$$

However, we cannot obtain an equation for $i_2(t)$ since it only is through the generators. A different choice of loop currents would not eliminate this problem. For example, suppose we use $i_1(t)$ and $i_a(t)$ as the loop currents, then

$$i_1(t) - i_a(t) = i_L(t) \tag{4–61}$$

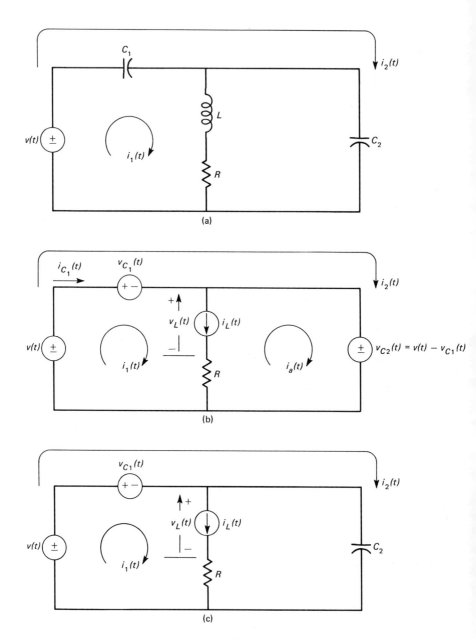

Fig. 4–9
(a) Improper network; (b) equivalent network that cannot be used to obtain state variables; (c) equivalent network used to obtain state variables

However, we cannot obtain a second independent equation in terms of $v(t)$ as the state variable since the voltage drop across the inductor is unknown. Thus, the procedure fails for improper networks.

We can resolve the difficulty by *not* replacing one of the capacitors in the improper loop. The voltage of that capacitor is not a state variable. Note that there is no need for it to be such since it can be expressed in terms of the other generators in the loop. Similarly, if we had a cut-set composed only of current generators and inductors, we would not replace one of the inductors in the equivalent network and its current would not be a state variable. The equivalent network that we use is given in Fig. 4–9c. Now we have

$$i_1(t) = i_L(t) \tag{4-62}$$

$$v(t) = v_{C_1}(t) + \frac{1}{C_2} \int i_2(t)\, dt \tag{4-63a}$$

Solving for $i_2(t)$ yields

$$i_2(t) = -C_2 \frac{dv_{C_1}(t)}{dt} + C_2 \frac{dv(t)}{dt} \tag{4-63b}$$

Thus, we have expressed the loop current in terms of the state variables and known generators.

Now let us obtain the state variable equations. From Fig. 4–9c, we have

$$v_L(t) = -Ri_L(t) - v_{C_1}(t) + v(t)$$

Substitution of Eq. 4–50 and manipulating yields

$$\frac{di_L(t)}{dt} = -\frac{R}{L}i_L(t) - \frac{1}{L}v_{C_1}(t) + \frac{1}{L}v(t) \tag{4-64}$$

Then, $i_{C_1}(t) = i_1(t) + i_2(t)$. Substituting Eqs. 4–62, 4–63b, and 4–47 and manipulating, we obtain

$$\frac{dv_{C_1}(t)}{dt} = \frac{1}{C_1 + C_2}i_L(t) + \frac{C_2}{C_1 + C_2}\frac{dv(t)}{dt} \tag{4-65}$$

Equations 4–64 and 4–65 can be considered to be the state variable equations of the network. Note that this is not strictly true since a derivative of an imput quantity appears on the right-hand side of Eq. 4–65. This difficulty can be resolved in one of two ways. We could assume that $dv(t)/dt$, as well as $v(t)$ are input variables. This would put the equation in the proper form, alternatively, we could replace $v_{C_1}(t)$ by the state variable

$$q_1(t) = v_{C_1}(t) - \frac{C_2}{C_1 + C_2}v(t) \tag{4-66}$$

Substituting in Eq. 4–65, we obtain

$$\frac{dq_1(t)}{dt} = \frac{1}{C_1 + C_2}i_L(t) \tag{4-67}$$

Of course, Eq. 4–66 should be substituted in Eq. 4–64 to replace $v_{C_1}(t)$ by the state variable $q_1(t)$. Then, a set of state variable equations would be obtained in proper form.

In general, the procedure whereby appropriate capacitors and/or inductors are not replaced in the equivalent network of an improper network will always work. Note that the capacitor voltage or inductor current in question can always be expressed in terms of state variables or known quantities. However, there is one drawback to this procedure. The equivalent network no longer only consists of generators and resistors. It will contain capacitors and/or inductors. Thus, in solving the equivalent network, we must solve a differential equation. This is tedious in the case of linear networks. We shall discuss, in the next section, that this is considerably more difficult in the case of nonlinear or time-varying networks.

## 4-4. STATE VARIABLE EQUATIONS FOR TIME-VARYING SYSTEMS

Now let us obtain the state variable equations for systems whose parameters can vary with time. We assume (in this section) that the systems are linear. Before discussing these systems in general, we consider a specific case: a time-varying electric network, i.e., a network whose resistors, inductors, and/or capacitors are functions of time.

If a resistor varies with time, its voltage-current relation is still given by Ohm's law. Hence, we have

$$v_{Rm}(t) = R_m(t) i_{Rm}(t) \tag{4-68}$$

Then, if a resistor in a time-invariant network were replaced by a time-varying one, the constant $R$ would be replaced by $R(t)$ in the network differential equations.

If a capacitor is time varying, we cannot obtain the network equations from those of the time-invariant network simply by replacing the constant $C$ by a time-varying one. It can be shown that the current-voltage relation for a time-varying capacitor is

$$i_{Cm}(t) = C_m(t) \frac{dv_{Cm}(t)}{dt} + v_{Cm}(t) \frac{dC_m(t)}{dt} \tag{4-69}$$

Let us see how this affects the state variable equations.

If the network is a proper one, we can apply the procedure of Section 4–3 and use the equivalent network to express all the capacitor currents in terms of the state variables and the known generator signals. The state variables are all the voltages across the capacitors and all the currents through the inductors. Then Eq. 4–46 could be determined for a time-varying network. Substituting Eq. 4–69 into Eq. 4–46 and manipulating, we have

$$\frac{dv_{Cm}(t)}{dt} = \frac{f_{Cm}}{C_m(t)} \left[ q_1(t), q_2(t), \ldots, q_n(t), y_1(t), y_2(t), \ldots, y_k(t), t \right]$$

$$- \frac{v_{Cm}(t)}{C_m(t)} \frac{dC_m(t)}{dt} \tag{4-70}$$

(Note that one of the $q_i(t) = v_{Cm}(t)$.) Thus, the right-hand side of Eq. 4–70 is a function of the state variables, generator voltages, and/or currents. If the network is linear, then $f_{Cm}$ is a linear function. Observe that there are no time derivatives of the state variables on the right-hand side of this equation. There is a derivative of $C(t)$ on the right-hand side. This is a known function and is usually allowed.

The procedure for obtaining the state variable equations for the currents through the inductors is similar to that just given. The voltage across a time-varying inductor is given by

$$v_{Lm}(t) = L_m(t)\frac{di_{Lm}(t)}{dt} + i_{Lm}(t)\frac{dL_m(t)}{dt} \tag{4–71}$$

Substituting in Eq. 4–49 and manipulating, we obtain

$$\frac{di_{Lm}(t)}{dt} = \frac{f_{Lm}}{L_m(t)}\left[q_1(t), q_2(t), ..., q_n(t), y_1(t), y_2(t), ..., y_k(t), t\right]$$

$$-\frac{i_{Lm}(t)}{L_m(t)}\frac{dL_m(t)}{dt} \tag{4–72}$$

As an example of this procedure, we shall again determine the state variable equations for the network of Fig. 4–8a, but now we assume that the elements are time varying. The equivalent network of Fig. 4–8b is still valid, therefore Eqs. 4–52 are valid, if we replace the constant resistors by time-varying ones. Thus, Eq. 4–53 gives the voltage across the inductor. Since the resistors are time varying, we write the equation as

$$v_L(t) = -R_1(t)i_L(t) - v_C(t) + v(t) \tag{4–73}$$

Then, substituting Eq. 4–71 and manipulating, we obtain

$$\frac{di_L(t)}{dt} = -\frac{1}{L(t)}\left[R_1(t) + \frac{dL(t)}{dt}\right]i(t) - \frac{1}{L(t)}v_C(t) + \frac{1}{L(t)}v(t) \tag{4–74}$$

To obtain the second state variable equation we solve for the current through the capacitor. From Eq. 4–55, we have

$$i_C(t) = i_L(t) - \frac{v_C(t)}{R_2(t)} \tag{4–75}$$

Then, substituting Eq. 4–69 and manipulating, we obtain

$$\frac{dv_C(t)}{dt} = \frac{1}{C(t)}i_L(t) - \frac{1}{C(t)}\left[\frac{1}{R_2(t)} + \frac{dC(t)}{dt}\right]v_C(t) \tag{4–76}$$

Thus, Eqs. 4–74 and 4–76 constitute the state variable equations of the network. The loop currents can be obtained from Eqs. 4–52 with the constant resistors replaced by the time-varying ones.

The fact that the network elements vary with time does not complicate the formulation of state variable equations in the case of proper networks. This is because the equivalent network only contains generators and resistors. Thus, no differential equations need be solved to obtain the state variable equations. In the case of improper networks, there will be inductors and/or capacitors in the equivalent network. Hence, linear differential equations with nonconstant coefficients may have to be solved to obtain the state variable equations. Thus, obtaining the state variable equations becomes more difficult.

Let us now discuss the state variable equations of general time-varying, linear systems. Equations 4–74 and 4–76 have the same form as Eq. 4–23, except that now the $\hat{a}$ and $\hat{b}$ matrices are functions of time. For instance, in Eq. 4–74, $di_L(t)/dt$ is expressed as a linear combination of the state variables, the generator voltages, and the known time-varying parameter values. Thus, in general,

$$\frac{d\hat{q}(t)}{dt} = \hat{a}(t)\hat{q}(t) + \hat{b}(t)\hat{y}(t) \tag{4–77}$$

Similarly, Eq. 4–28 can be used to express all of the system variables in terms of the state variables. However, now the $\hat{c}$ and $\hat{d}$ matrices can contain elements which are functions of time, hence,

$$\hat{x}(t) = \hat{c}(t)\hat{q}(t) + \hat{d}(t)\hat{y}(t) \tag{4–78}$$

Then, the procedure for forming the state variable equations for linear, time-varying systems are similar to those for linear, time-invariant systems.

## 4-5. STATE VARIABLE EQUATIONS FOR NONLINEAR SYSTEMS

We shall now discuss procedures, for obtaining the state variable equations for nonlinear systems. At times, some restrictions must be imposed upon nonlinear systems if we are to obtain equations which have unique solutions. However, in many practical cases, these restrictions do not limit the applicability of the procedure. We shall start by considering a specific example, the nonlinear electric network and then discuss nonlinear systems in general.

Consider a proper electric network. Then we begin by forming the equivalent network. The voltage across the inductors and the current through the capacitors are obtained from a network containing only resistors and generators, as before (see Section 4–3). However, the resistors may be nonlinear. (This complicates the solution.) Note that a nonlinear resistor is one which is a function of the current through it and/or the voltage across it. For instance, we could write

$$v_{Rk}(t) = R_k(i)i_k(t) \tag{4–79a}$$

or

$$i_k(t) = \frac{1}{R_k(v)}v_k(t) \tag{4–79b}$$

In Eq. 4–79a we have assumed that the nonlinear resistance is a function of the current through it, while in Eq. 4–79b the resistance is a function of the voltage across it. It may not always be possible to do this. Consider Fig. 4–10a, which gives the voltage-current characteristic of a nonlinear resistor. For voltages between $V_1$ and $V_2$, the current is not a single-valued function of the voltage. Thus, the current cannot be obtained as a function of the voltage there; i.e., if $v$ lies between $V_1$ and $V_2$, the current can be one of three values. Hence, for Fig. 4–10a, we cannot express $R(v)$. However, we can work with $R(i)$ since the voltage is a (single-valued) function of the current. Such resistors are called *current-controlled* nonlinear resistors. The nonlinear resistor whose voltage-current characteristic is given in Fig. 4–10b is

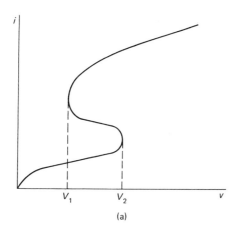

(a)

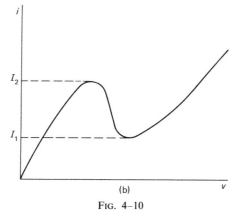

(b)

FIG. 4–10

(a) Current-controlled, nonlinear resistance; (b) voltage-controlled, nonlinear resistance

called a *voltage-controlled* nonlinear resistor. Some nonlinear resistors are both voltage controlled and current controlled. Of course, this concept can be extended to other nonlinear devices, not just resistances or electric elements.

As we have just seen, circuits containing nonlinear resistors and known generators cannot always be solved. In general, if a proper tree can be found such that all the voltage-controlled, nonlinear resistors lie in the chords, then the voltage across them can be expressed in terms of the tree branch voltages. Similarly, if all the current-controlled, nonlinear resistors lie in the tree branches then the currents will be expressable in terms of the chord currents. If a proper tree can be formed such that these conditions are met then a solution for the network currents and voltages probably exists. We shall assume here that the networks are solvable. If the network is proper, then we shall use all the currents through the inductors and all the voltages across the capacitors as the state variables.

Now consider nonlinear inductors. To guarantee a solution, we restrict ourselves to inductors whose flux linkages are functions of the current through them. Fortunately, this is usually the case with nonlinear inductors, thus,

$$\phi = F_L(i) \tag{4-80}$$

The voltage across the inductor is $d\phi/dt$. Substituting Eq. 4-80, we obtain

$$v_L(t) = \frac{dF_L(i)}{di}\bigg|_i \frac{di_L(t)}{dt} \tag{4-81}$$

Note that the derivative of $F_L(t)$ with respect to $i$ is evaluated at the instantaneous current of the inductance. It is assumed that we know $f_L(i)$; it may be in the form of graphic or tabular data. Hence, such data can be used to obtain $dF_L(i)/di$ and incorporated in a computer solution. The state variable equations for the currents through the inductors are found by solving the equivalent network for the voltage across the inductors. Equating this to Eq. 4-81, we obtain

$$\frac{dF_{Lm}(i)}{di}\bigg|_{i_{Lm}} \frac{di_{Lm}(t)}{dt} = f_{Lm}[q_1(t), q_2(t), ..., q_n(t), y_1(t), y_2(t), ..., y_k(t), t] \tag{4-82}$$

From this, we have

$$\frac{di_{Lm}(t)}{dt} = \frac{1}{dF_L(i)/di}\bigg|_{i_{Lm}} f_{Lm}[q_1(t), q_2(t),$$

$$..., q_n(t), y_1(t), y_2(t), ..., y_k(t), t] \tag{4-83}$$

This is in the correct state variable form. Note that there is a derivative of $F_{Lm}$ on the right-hand side of the equation. However, this is a known function and also is not a derivative with respect to time, hence it is usually allowable.

Now consider nonlinear capacitors. Here, we restrict ourselves to capacitors whose charge (transferred from one plate to the other) is a function of the voltage across the capacitor. Most nonlinear capacitors are of this form; then,

$$q_C = F_C(v) \tag{4-84}$$

The current into the capacitor is $dq_C/dt$; hence,

$$i_C(t) = \frac{dF_C(v)}{dv}\bigg|_v \frac{dv_C(t)}{dt} \tag{4-85}$$

Then, we use the equivalent network to solve for the current through the capacitor. Substituting Eq. 4–85 into this equation and manipulating, we obtain

$$\frac{dv_{Cm}(t)}{dt} = \frac{1}{dF_{Cm}(v)/dt}\bigg|_{v_{Cm}} f_{Cm}\big[q_1(t), q_2(t),$$

$$\dots, q_n(t), y_1(t), y_2(t), \dots, y_k(t), t\big] \tag{4-86}$$

This is the correct form for a set of state variable equations.

Consider an example of this procedure. We again obtain the state variable equations for the network of Fig. 4–8a, but now assume that all the elements are nonlinear, $R_1$ is current controlled, and the voltage across $R_1$ is

$$v_{R1} = f_{R1}(i_1) \tag{4-87}$$

Also assume that $R_2$ is voltage controlled and that the current through it (with positive current down) is

$$i_{R2} = f_{R2}(v_C) \tag{4-88}$$

Note that $v_C(t)$ is the voltage across $R_2$. Thus, we have

$$i_1 = i_L(t) \tag{4-89a}$$

$$i_2(t) = i_1(t) - f_{R2}(v_C) \tag{4-89b}$$

The voltage across the inductance is

$$v_L(t) = -f_{R1}(i_L) - v_C(t) + v(t) \tag{4-90}$$

Then, substituting Eq. 4–81 and manipulating, we obtain

$$\frac{di_L(t)}{dt} = -\frac{1}{df_L(i_L)/di_L}\bigg|_{i_L} f_{R1}(i_L) - \frac{1}{df_L(i_L)/di_L}\bigg|_{i_L} v_C(t)$$

$$+ \frac{1}{df_L(i_L)/di_L}\bigg|_{i_L} v(t) \tag{4-91}$$

The current through the capacitor is $i_2(t)$. Substituting Eqs. 4–89a and 4–85 into Eq. 4–89b and manipulating, we have

$$\frac{dv_C(t)}{dt} = \frac{1}{df_C(v_C)/dv_C}\bigg|_{v_C} i_L(t) - \frac{1}{df_C(v_C)/dv_C}\bigg|_{v_C} f_{R2}(v_C)$$

Thus, Eqs. 4–91 and 4–92 are the state variable equations for the network.

As a further example, let us consider specific functions for the nonlinear elements; thus, let

$$f_{R1}(i_L) = i_L + \alpha_2 i_L^2 \tag{4-93a}$$

$$f_{R2}(v_C) = v_C^3 \tag{4-93b}$$

$$f_L(i) = i_L + \beta_3 i_L^3 \tag{4-93c}$$

$$q = v_C + \gamma_4 v_C^4 \tag{4-93d}$$

Substitution in Eqs. 4–91 and 4–92 yields

$$\frac{di_L(t)}{dt} = -\frac{i_L(t) - \alpha_2 i_L^2(t)}{1 + 3\beta_2 i_L^2(t)} - \frac{v_C(t)}{1 + 3\beta_3 i_L^2(t)} + \frac{v(t)}{1 + 3\beta_3 i_L^2(t)} \tag{4-94}$$

$$\frac{dv_C(t)}{dt} = \frac{i_L(t)}{1 + 4\gamma_4 v_C^3(t)} - \frac{v_C^3(t)}{1 + 4\gamma_4 v_C^3(t)} \tag{4-95}$$

If the networks are improper, the procedure discussed in Section 4–3 can be used if a solution exists for the inproper network. However, now nonlinear differential equations must be solved to obtain the state variable equations. This can make the problem extremely difficult.

We have considered the example of a nonlinear electric network. However, the formulation of the state variable equations for general nonlinear systems follows the same ideas. The specific way that the nonlinearity affects the differential equations for each system must be considered. The general form of the state variable equations will be of the form of Eq. 4–16 and 4–19. Often, the formulation of the state variable equations for nonlinear systems is not much more difficult than it is for linear systems. However, the solution of the equations for nonlinear systems usually cannot be obtained in closed form. We shall discuss in Section 4-8 and 4-9 a numerical analysis computer solution that can be used to solve general state variable equations including those of nonlinear or time-varying systems.

## 4-6. THE SOLUTION OF STATE VARIABLE EQUATIONS FOR LINEAR, TIME-INVARIANT SYSTEMS—THE STATE TRANSITION MATRIX

In this section we shall consider the solution of the state variable equations of linear time-invariant systems using classical procedures. In the next we shall apply Laplace transform procedures to the solution of these equations. Finally, (Sections 4-8 and 4-9) we shall develop numerical analysis computer procedures which can be applied to the solution of linear, or nonlinear and/or time-invariant and/or time-varying systems.

The general form of state variable equations of linear, time-invariant systems is given by Eq. 4–23 as

$$\frac{d\hat{q}(t)}{dt} = \hat{a}\,\hat{q}(t) + b\,\hat{y}(t) \tag{4-96}$$

where $a$ and $b$ are matrices of constants.

Before considering the general solution of this matrix differential equation, let us discuss the solution of a simple scalar equation; i.e., one in which the matrices only have single elements. In this case, Eq. 4-96 becomes

$$\frac{dq_1(t)}{dt} = a_{11}q_1(t) + b_{11}y_1(t) \tag{4-97}$$

First assume that $y_1(t) = 0$. Then, we must solve the homogeneous equation

$$\frac{dq_1(t)}{dt} - a_{11}q_1(t) = 0 \tag{4-98}$$

Multiplying both sides of this equation by $e^{-ta_{11}}$ yields

$$e^{-ta_{11}}\frac{dq_1(t)}{dt} - e^{-ta_{11}}a_{11}q_1(t) = 0 \tag{4-99}$$

The left-hand side of this expression can be written as $d[e^{-ta_{11}}q_1(t)]/dt$; hence, we have

$$\frac{d[e^{-ta_{11}}q_1(t)]}{dt} = 0 \tag{4-100}$$

Multiplying by $dt$ and integrating, we obtain

$$\int d[e^{-ta_{11}}q_1(t)]\,dt = 0 \tag{4-101}$$

Carrying out the integration yields

$$e^{-ta_{11}}q_1(t) = K \tag{4-102}$$

Rearranging, we have

$$q_1(t) = Ke^{ta_{11}} \tag{4-103}$$

where $K$ is a constant of integration and at $t = 0-$, $q(t) = q(0-)$, the initial condition. Substituting in Eq. 4-103 yields $K = q(0-)$. Then, substituting this value into Eq. 4-103, we obtain

$$q_1(t) = e^{ta_{11}}q_1(0-) \tag{4-104}$$

Now let us turn our attention to the solution of the matrix differential equation of Eq. 4-96. First consider the homogeneous equation; that is, assume that $\hat{y}(t) = 0$. Thus, we wish to solve

$$\frac{d\hat{q}(t)}{dt} = \hat{a}\,\hat{q}(t) \tag{4-105}$$

We shall guess at a solution to this equation and then verify our guess by substituting in Eq. 4–104. By analogy, with Eq. 4–103, we guess that the solution is

$$\hat{q}(t) = e^{t\hat{a}}\hat{K} \tag{4-106}$$

where $K$ is a column matrix of constant terms. Let us define the matrix $e^{t\hat{a}}$

Consider the power series for the scalar expression

$$e^{ta_{11}} = 1 + ta_{11} + \frac{(ta_{11})^2}{2!} + \frac{(ta_{11})^3}{3!} + \ldots \tag{4-107}$$

Then we define the *matrix function*

$$e^{t\hat{a}} = \hat{U} + t\hat{a} + \frac{t^2}{2!}\hat{a}^2 + \frac{t^3}{3!}\hat{a}^3 + \ldots \tag{4-108}$$

where $\hat{U}$ is the unit matrix of the same order as $\hat{a}$. $t$, $t^2/2!$, $t^3/3!$, ... are scalars which multiply each element of the appropriate matrix and $\hat{a}^k$ means multiply $\hat{a}$ by itself $k$ times. Note that the $\hat{a}$ is a square matrix so that this is allowed (see Section C-1). Now let us verify our choice of $\hat{q}(t)$. Substitute Eq. 4–106 into the left-hand side of Eq. 4–105; hence, we have

$$\frac{d\hat{q}(t)}{dt} = \frac{d}{dt}\left[\hat{U} + t\hat{a} + \frac{t^2}{2!}\hat{a}^2 + \frac{t^3}{3!}\hat{a}^3 + \ldots\right]\hat{K}$$

Differentiating, we obtain (note $\hat{a}$ is a matrix of constants)

$$\frac{d\hat{q}(t)}{dt} = \left[\hat{a} + t\hat{a}^2 + \frac{t^2}{2!}\hat{a}^3 + \frac{t^3}{3!}\hat{a}^4 + \ldots\right]\hat{K}$$

$$\frac{d\check{q}(t)}{dt} = \hat{a}\left[\hat{U} + t\hat{a} + \frac{t^2}{2!}\hat{a}^2 + \frac{t^3}{3!}\hat{a}^3 + \ldots\right]K \tag{4-109}$$

The bracketed series on the right is just $e^{t\hat{a}}$; thus,

$$\frac{d\hat{q}(t)}{dt} = \hat{a}e^{t\hat{a}}\hat{K}$$

Substituting Eq. 4–106, we have

$$\frac{d\hat{q}(t)}{dt} = \hat{a}\hat{q}(t) \tag{4-110}$$

Compare this with Eq. 4–105. They are the same. Thus, we have verified that Eq. 4–106 is a solution to Eq. 4–105.

Now let us evaluate the constant matrix $\hat{K}$. At $t = 0-$, $\hat{q}(t) = \hat{q}(0-)$, the initial state. Substituting into Eq. 4–106, we have

$$K = \hat{q}(0-) \tag{4-111}$$

Note that when $t = 0$ is substituted into Eq. 4–108, we obtain $e^{0\hat{a}} = \hat{U}$. Hence, the solution to the homogeneous state variable equation of Eq. 4–105 is

$$\hat{q}(t) = e^{t\hat{a}}\hat{q}(0-) \qquad (4-112)$$

The matrix $e^{t\hat{a}}$ is called the *state transition matrix* and is often written as

$$\hat{\phi}(t) = e^{t\hat{a}} \qquad (4-113)$$

The state transition matrix can be evaluated using Eq. 4–108.

Now let us obtain the solution for the nonhomogeneous state variable equation

$$\frac{d\hat{q}(t)}{dt} = \hat{a}\hat{q}(t) + \hat{b}\hat{y}(t) \qquad (4-114)$$

We shall proceed in analogous fashion to the previous development. Premultiply both sides of Eq. 4–114 by $e^{-t\hat{a}}$ and rearrange. This yields

$$e^{-t\hat{a}}\frac{dq(t)}{dt} - e^{-t\hat{a}}\hat{a}\hat{q}(t) = e^{-t\hat{a}}\hat{b}\hat{y}(t) \qquad (4-115)$$

Now we will show that

$$\frac{d[e^{-t\hat{a}}\hat{q}(t)]}{dt} = e^{-t\hat{a}}\frac{d\hat{q}(t)}{dt} - e^{-t\hat{a}}\hat{a}\hat{q}(t) \qquad (4-116)$$

Note that this is true for scalars. However, it is not obvious that it is true for vectors. Thus, substituting Eq. 4–108 (with $t$ replaced by $-t$) into the left-hand side of Eq. 4–116, we obtain

$$\frac{d[e^{-t\hat{a}}\hat{q}(t)]}{dt} = \frac{d}{dt}\left[\left(\hat{U} - t\hat{a} + \frac{t^2\hat{a}^2}{2!} - \frac{t^3\hat{a}^3}{3!} + \cdots\right)\hat{q}(t)\right]$$

Differentiating, substituting Eq. 4–108 with $t$ replaced by $-t$ and manipulating, we have

$$\frac{d[e^{-t\hat{a}}\hat{q}(t)]}{dt} = e^{-t\hat{a}}\frac{d\hat{q}(t)}{dt} - \left(\hat{U} - t\hat{a} + \frac{t^2}{2!}\hat{a}^2 - \cdots\right)\hat{a}\hat{q}(t) \qquad (4-117)$$

Substituting Eq. 4–108 into Eq. 4–117, we obtain the right-hand side of Eq. 4–116. Hence, we have shown that Eq. 4–116 is valid. Then, substituting Eq. 4–116 into Eq. 4–115, we obtain

$$\frac{d[e^{-t\hat{a}}\hat{q}(t)]}{dt} = e^{-t\hat{a}}\hat{b}\hat{y}(t) \qquad (4-118)$$

Multiply both sides of Eq. 4–118 by $dt$ and integrate both sides from $-\infty$ to $t$. This yields

$$\int_{-\infty}^{t} d[e^{-t\hat{a}}\hat{q}(\tau)] = \int_{-\infty}^{t} e^{-\tau\hat{a}}\hat{b}\hat{y}(\tau)\,d\tau \qquad (4-119)$$

Note that *the integral of a matrix is just the integral of each term in the matrix.* Assume that $\hat{q}(-\infty) = 0$; hence,

$$e^{-t\hat{a}}\hat{q}(t) = \int_{-\infty}^{t} e^{-\tau\hat{a}}\hat{b}\hat{y}(\tau)\,d\tau \tag{4-120}$$

Let us write

$$\int_{-\infty}^{0-} e^{-\tau\hat{a}}\hat{b}\hat{y}(\tau)\,d\tau = \hat{K} \tag{4-121}$$

Then,

$$e^{-t\hat{a}}\hat{q}(t) = \int_{0}^{t} e^{-\tau\hat{a}}\hat{b}\hat{y}(\tau)\,d\tau + \hat{K} \tag{4-122}$$

Now we wish to find the inverse of $e^{-ta}$ so that we can premultiply both sides of Eq. 4-122 by it (see Section C-2). Let us demonstrate that

$$[e^{-t\hat{a}}]^{-1} = e^{t\hat{a}} \tag{4-123}$$

We must show that $e^{-t\hat{a}}e^{t\hat{a}} = \hat{U}$. Substituting Eq. 4-108, we obtain

$$e^{t\hat{a}}e^{-t\hat{a}} = \left(\hat{U} + t\hat{a} + \frac{t^2}{2!}\hat{a}^2 + \ldots\right)\left(\hat{U} - t\hat{a} + \frac{t\hat{a}^2}{2!} - \ldots\right)$$

Multiplying, we have

$$e^{t\hat{a}}e^{-t\hat{a}} = \hat{U} + t\hat{a} - t\hat{a} + t^2\hat{a}^2 - t^2\hat{a}^2 + \ldots = \hat{U} \tag{4-124}$$

Thus, we have found the desired inverse matrix. Then, multiplying both sides of Eq. 4-122 by $e^{t\hat{a}}$, we obtain

$$\hat{q}(t) = e^{t\hat{a}}\hat{K} + e^{t\hat{a}}\int_{0-}^{t} e^{-\tau\hat{a}}\hat{b}\hat{y}(\tau)\,d\tau \tag{4-125}$$

Now let $t = 0 -$. The integral becomes zero since its upper and lower limits are the same. In addition,

$$e^{t\hat{a}}\big|_{t=0-} = \hat{U} \tag{4-126}$$

This can be seen by substituting in Eq. 4-108; hence,

$$\hat{q}(0-) = \hat{K}$$

Substituting in Eq. 4-125, we obtain

$$\hat{q}(t) = e^{t\hat{a}}\hat{q}(0-) + e^{t\hat{a}}\int_{0-}^{t} e^{-\tau\hat{a}}\hat{b}\hat{y}(\tau)\,d\tau \tag{4-127}$$

　　Thus, we have obtained a general expression for the solution of state variable equations of linear, time-invariant systems.

　　Now consider an example of this procedure. We shall evaluate the response of the network of Fig. 4-1 for the case $R = 0$. The state variable equations are obtained from Eqs. 4-7. With $R = 0$ they are

$$\frac{di_L}{dt} = -\frac{1}{L}v_C(t) + \frac{V}{L} \tag{4-128a}$$

$$\frac{dv_C}{dt} = \frac{1}{C} i_L(t) \tag{4-128b}$$

The various matrices are

$$\hat{q}(t) = \begin{bmatrix} i_L(t) \\ v_C(t) \end{bmatrix} \tag{4-129a}$$

$$\hat{a} = \begin{bmatrix} 0 & -1/L \\ 1/C & 0 \end{bmatrix} \tag{4-129b}$$

$$\hat{b} = \begin{bmatrix} 1/L \\ 0 \end{bmatrix} \tag{4-129c}$$

$$\hat{y}(t) = [V] \tag{4-129d}$$

To simplify the computations, we assume that

$$\hat{q}(0-) = \hat{0}$$

Then, substituting Eq. 4–129 into Eq. 4–127, we obtain

$$\hat{q}(t) = \exp\left(t\begin{bmatrix} 0 & -1/L \\ 1/C & 0 \end{bmatrix}\right)\int_0^t \left(\hat{U} - \tau\begin{bmatrix} 0 & -1/L \\ 1/C & 0 \end{bmatrix}\right.$$

$$\left. + \frac{\tau^2}{2!}\begin{bmatrix} 0 & -1/L \\ 1/C & 0 \end{bmatrix}\begin{bmatrix} 0 & -1/L \\ 1/C & 0 \end{bmatrix} + \cdots\right)\begin{bmatrix} V/L \\ 0 \end{bmatrix} d\tau \tag{4-130}$$

Therefore,

$$\hat{q}(t) = \exp\left(t\begin{bmatrix} 0 & -1/L \\ 1/C & 0 \end{bmatrix}\right)\int_0^t \left(\begin{bmatrix} 1 & 0 \\ 0 & 1 \end{bmatrix}\right.$$

$$\left. - \tau\begin{bmatrix} 0 & -1/L \\ 1/C & 0 \end{bmatrix} - \frac{\tau^2}{2!}\begin{bmatrix} 1/LC & 0 \\ 0 & 1/LC \end{bmatrix} + \cdots\right)\begin{bmatrix} V/L \\ 0 \end{bmatrix} d\tau \tag{4-131}$$

Integrating, we obtain

$$\hat{q}(t) = \exp\left(t\begin{bmatrix} 0 & -1/L \\ 1/C & 0 \end{bmatrix}\right)\left(t\begin{bmatrix} 1 & 0 \\ 0 & 1 \end{bmatrix}\right.$$

$$\left. - \frac{t^2}{2!}\begin{bmatrix} 0 & -1/L \\ 1/C & 0 \end{bmatrix} - \frac{t^3}{3!}\begin{bmatrix} 1/LC & 0 \\ 0 & 1/LC \end{bmatrix} + \cdots\right)\begin{bmatrix} V/L \\ 0 \end{bmatrix} \tag{4-132}$$

Substituting Eq. 4–108 and manipulating, we have

$$\hat{q}(t) = \left\{ \begin{bmatrix} 1 & 0 \\ 0 & 1 \end{bmatrix} + t \begin{bmatrix} 0 & -1/L \\ 1/C & 0 \end{bmatrix} + \frac{t^2}{2!} \begin{bmatrix} 1/LC & 0 \\ 0 & 1/LC \end{bmatrix} \right.$$

$$\left. + \cdots \right\} \left\{ t \begin{bmatrix} V/L \\ 0 \end{bmatrix} - \frac{t^2}{2!} \begin{bmatrix} 0 \\ V/LC \end{bmatrix} - \frac{t3}{3!} \begin{bmatrix} V/L^2C \\ 0 \end{bmatrix} - \cdots \right\} \quad (4\text{–}133)$$

Multiplying and combining terms, we obtain

$$\hat{q}(t) = \begin{bmatrix} Vt/L + 0 - Vt^3/3! \ L^2C + \cdots \\ 0 + Vt^2/2LC + 0 + \cdots \end{bmatrix} \quad (4\text{–}134)$$

Substitution of Eq. 4–129a yields

$$\begin{bmatrix} i_L(t) \\ v_C(t) \end{bmatrix} = V \begin{bmatrix} \dfrac{1}{L}t - \dfrac{t^3}{3!L^2C} + \cdots \\ 0 + \dfrac{t^2}{2!LC} - \cdots \end{bmatrix} \quad (4\text{–}135)$$

Substituting $\omega_0 = 1/\sqrt{LC}$ (see Eq. 4–8c), we obtain

$$i_L(t) = \frac{V}{\omega_0 L}\left(\omega_0 t - \frac{\omega_0^3 t^3}{3!}\right) \quad (4\text{–}136a)$$

$$v_C(t) = V\left(\frac{\omega_0 t^2}{2!} - \cdots\right) \quad (4\text{–}136b)$$

In closed form, the series are

$$i_L(t) = \frac{V}{\omega_0 L}\sin \omega_0 t \quad (4\text{–}137a)$$

$$v_C(t) = V(1 - \cos \omega_0 t) \quad (4\text{–}137b)$$

(This can be shown by taking additional terms in the series.) This checks with Eqs. 4–10.

The state variable procedure seems to be much more tedious than Laplace transform procedures. In the case of simple networks, it may be. However, if the solution actually requires a series, or a computer is used to obtain a solution, then the state variable procedure is a very powerful one. In addition, we shall now discuss a procedure for evaluating the state transition matrix in closed form.

**State Transition Matrix.**   We have shown that the transition matrix

$$\hat{\phi}(t) = e^{t\hat{a}} \qquad (4\text{-}138)$$

is of prime importance in the solution of state variable equations. We now evaluate this matrix. A direct, and often practical, procedure for doing this is simply to substitute in the series of Eq. 4–108. For instance, this was done in the preceding example. However, there is also a procedure which can be used that will evaluate $\phi(t)$, which is a function of a square matrix in closed form. We use the *Cayley-Hamilton* theorem here (see Section C-4). It is shown there that a function $F(\hat{a})$ of a square matrix of degree $n$ can be written in closed form in the following way

$$F(\hat{a}) = \alpha_0 \hat{U} + \alpha_1 \hat{a}_1 + \cdots \alpha_{n-1} \hat{a}^{n-1} \qquad (4\text{-}139)$$

where $\alpha_0, \alpha_1, ..., \alpha_{n-1}$ are scalar constants and $\hat{U}$ is the unit matrix of degree $n$. To obtain the $\alpha_k$ we solve the following scalar equations

$$F(\lambda_1) = \alpha_0 + \alpha_1 \lambda_1 + \cdots + \alpha_{n-1}\lambda_1^{n-1}$$
$$F(\lambda_2) = \alpha_0 + \alpha_1 \lambda_2 + \cdots + a_{n-1}\lambda_2^{n-1}$$
$$\cdots\cdots\cdots\cdots\cdots\cdots\cdots\cdots\cdots\cdots\cdots\cdots\cdots \qquad (4\text{-}140)$$
$$F(\lambda_n) = \alpha_0 + \alpha_1 \lambda_1 + \cdots + \alpha_{n-1}\lambda_n^{n-1}$$

Note that $F(\lambda_k)$ is a scalar quantity which obtained by replacing the matrix $\hat{a}$ by the scalar $\lambda_k$. For example, in Eq. 4–138 we have

$$\phi(\lambda_k) = e^{t\lambda_k}$$

The $\lambda_1, \lambda_2, ..., \lambda_k$ are the *eigenvalues* of $\hat{a}$ (see Section C-3). (Several examples of this procedure are given in Section C-4.) We now specifically apply this procedure to the state transition matrix $\phi(t)$. Suppose

$$F(\hat{a}) = \hat{\phi}(t) = e^{\hat{a}t} \qquad (4\text{-}141)$$

Then, Eq. 4–139 becomes

$$e^{t\hat{a}} = \alpha_0 \hat{U} + \alpha_1 \hat{a} + \cdots + \alpha_{n-1}\hat{a}^{n-1} \qquad (4\text{-}142)$$

and Eqs. 4–140 become the *scalar* equations:

$$e^{t\lambda_1} = \alpha_0 + \alpha_1 \lambda_1 + \cdots + \alpha_{n-1}\lambda_1^{n-1}$$
$$e^{t\lambda_2} = \alpha_0 + \alpha_1 \lambda_2 + \cdots + \alpha_{n-1}\lambda_2^{n-1}$$
$$\cdots\cdots\cdots\cdots\cdots\cdots\cdots\cdots\cdots\cdots\cdots\cdots\cdots \qquad (4\text{-}143)$$
$$e^{t\lambda_n} = \alpha_0 + \alpha_1 \lambda_n + \cdots + \alpha_{n-1}\lambda_n^{n-1}$$

where $\lambda_1, \lambda_2, ..., \lambda_n$ are the eigenvalues of $\hat{a}$. Then, Eqs. 4–143 are solved for $\alpha_0, \alpha_1, ..., \alpha_{n-1}$ and these values are substituted into Eq. 4–142 to obtain $e^{t\hat{a}}$ in closed form.

As an example we now consider the solution of Eqs. 4–128, where we have assumed $q(0-) = 0$. The solution is given by

$$\hat{q}(t) = e^{t\hat{a}} \int_{0-}^{t} e^{-\tau\hat{a}} \hat{b} \hat{y}(\tau)\, d\tau \tag{4-144}$$

Let us evaluate the exponential matrices $e^{t\hat{a}}$ and $e^{-t\hat{a}}$ in closed form. From Eq. 4-129b,

$$\hat{a} = \begin{bmatrix} 0 & -1/L \\ 1/C & 0 \end{bmatrix}$$

To determine the eigenvalue of this matrix, we solve the determinant,

$$\begin{vmatrix} -\lambda & -1/L \\ 1/C & -\lambda \end{vmatrix} = 0 \tag{4-145}$$

Evaluating the determinant, we have

$$\lambda^2 + \frac{1}{LC} = 0$$

Thus, the eigenvalues are

$$\lambda = \pm j \frac{1}{\sqrt{LC}} = \pm j\omega_0 \tag{4-146}$$

Substituting in Eqs. 4-143, we have

$$e^{j\omega_0 t} = \alpha_0 + j\omega_0 \alpha_1$$

$$e^{-j\omega_0 t} = \alpha_0 - j\omega_0 \alpha_1$$

Solving, we obtain

$$\alpha_0 = \frac{e^{j\omega_0 t} + e^{-j\omega_0 t}}{2} = \cos \omega_0 t \tag{4-147a}$$

$$\alpha_1 = \frac{e^{j\omega_0 t} - e^{-j\omega_0 t}}{2j\omega_0} = \frac{\sin \omega_0 t}{\omega_0} \tag{4-147b}$$

Then, substitution in Eq. 4-142 yields

$$e^{t\hat{a}} = \cos \omega_0 t \begin{bmatrix} 1 & 0 \\ 0 & 1 \end{bmatrix} + \frac{\sin \omega_0 t}{\omega_0} \begin{bmatrix} 0 & -1/L \\ 1/C & 0 \end{bmatrix} \tag{4-148}$$

Similarly,

$$e^{-t\hat{a}} = \cos \omega_0 t \begin{bmatrix} 1 & 0 \\ 0 & 1 \end{bmatrix} - \frac{\sin \omega_0 t}{\omega_0} \begin{bmatrix} 0 & -1/L \\ 1/C & 0 \end{bmatrix} \tag{4-149}$$

Then, substituting in Eq. 4–144 yields

$$\hat{q}(t) = \left\{ \cos \omega_0 t \begin{bmatrix} 1 & 0 \\ 0 & 1 \end{bmatrix} + \frac{\sin \omega_0 t}{\omega_0} \begin{bmatrix} 0 & -1/L \\ 1/C & 0 \end{bmatrix} \right\} \left\{ \int_0^t \left( \cos \omega_0 \tau \begin{bmatrix} 1 & 0 \\ 0 & 1 \end{bmatrix} \right. \right.$$

$$\left. \left. - \frac{\sin \omega_0 \tau}{\omega_0} \begin{bmatrix} 0 & -1/L \\ 1/C & 0 \end{bmatrix} \right) \begin{bmatrix} 1/L \\ 0 \end{bmatrix} [V] d\tau \right\} \tag{4–150}$$

Carrying out the matrix multiplication of the integrand, we obtain

$$q(t) = \left\{ \cos \omega_0 t \begin{bmatrix} 1 & 0 \\ 0 & 1 \end{bmatrix} + \frac{\sin \omega_0 t}{\omega_0} \begin{bmatrix} 0 & -1/L \\ 1/C & 0 \end{bmatrix} \right\} \left\{ \int_0^t \left( \cos \omega_0 \tau \begin{bmatrix} V/L \\ 0 \end{bmatrix} \right. \right.$$

$$\left. \left. - \frac{\sin \omega_0 \tau}{\omega_0} \begin{bmatrix} 0 \\ V/LC \end{bmatrix} \right) d\tau \right\} \tag{4–151}$$

Integrating, we have

$$\hat{q}(t) = \left\{ \cos \omega_0 t \begin{bmatrix} 1 & 0 \\ 0 & 1 \end{bmatrix} + \frac{\sin \omega_0 t}{\omega_0} \begin{bmatrix} 0 & -1/L \\ 1/C & 0 \end{bmatrix} \right\} \left\{ \frac{\sin \omega_0 t}{\omega_0} \begin{bmatrix} V/L \\ 0 \end{bmatrix} \right.$$

$$\left. + \left( \frac{\cos \omega_0 t}{\omega_0{}^2} - \frac{1}{\omega_0{}^2} \right) \begin{bmatrix} 0 \\ V/LC \end{bmatrix} \right\} \tag{4–152}$$

Combining terms yields

$$\hat{q}(t) = \begin{bmatrix} \cos \omega_0 t & -\dfrac{\sin \omega_0 t}{\omega_0 L} \\ \dfrac{\sin \omega_0 t}{\omega_0 C} & \cos \omega_0 t \end{bmatrix} \begin{bmatrix} V \dfrac{\sin \omega_0 t}{\omega_0 L} \\ V(\cos \omega_0 t - 1) \end{bmatrix}$$

Note that $\omega_0{}^2 = 1/LC$. Carrying out the multiplication gives us

$$\hat{q}(t) = \begin{bmatrix} V (\sin \omega_0 t)/\omega_0 L \\ V(1 - \cos \omega_0 t) \end{bmatrix} \tag{4–153}$$

These results check with Eqs. 4–137.

## 4-7. LAPLACE TRANSFORM FOR SOLVING STATE VARIABLE EQUATIONS FOR LINEAR, TIME-INVARIANT SYSTEMS

We define the Laplace transform of a matrix as the transform of each element of the matrix; thus,

$$\mathscr{L}\,\hat{q}(t) = \mathscr{L}\begin{bmatrix} q_1(t) \\ q_2(t) \\ \cdot \\ \cdot \\ \cdot \\ q_n(t) \end{bmatrix} = \hat{Q}(s) = \begin{bmatrix} Q_1(s) \\ Q_2(s) \\ \cdot \\ \cdot \\ \cdot \\ Q_n(s) \end{bmatrix} \qquad (4\text{--}154)$$

We now use the Laplace transform to solve the basic state variable equations (see Eq. 4–96). Take the Laplace transform of both sides of this equation. This yields

$$s\hat{Q}(s) - \hat{q}(0-) = \hat{a}\hat{Q}(s) + \hat{b}\hat{Y}(s) \qquad (4\text{--}155)$$

where $\hat{Y}(s)$ is the Laplace transform of $y(t)$. We then obtain

$$(s\hat{U} - \hat{a})\hat{Q}(s) = \hat{b}Y(s) + \hat{q}(0-) \qquad (4\text{--}156)$$

Note that

$$s\hat{U}\,\hat{Q}(s) = s\hat{Q}(s) \qquad (4\text{--}157)$$

Assume that $\hat{a}$ is such that the inverse of $(s\hat{U} - \hat{a})$ exists, (see Section C-2). This will usually be the case with linear, time-invariant systems. Then, premultiplying both sides of Eq. 4–156 by $(s\hat{U} - \hat{a})^{-1}$, we have

$$\hat{Q}(s) = (s\hat{U} - \hat{a})^{-1}[\hat{b}\hat{Y}(s) + \hat{q}(0-)] \qquad (4\text{--}158)$$

Then, taking the inverse Laplace transform of each element of $\hat{Q}(s)$ yields $\hat{q}(t)$. Thus, we have obtained the solution of the state variable equations.

As an example, let us solve Eqs. 4–128 assuming that $q(0-) = 0$. The various various matrices are given in Eq. 4–129. The voltage generator produces a unit step function times $V$, i.e., $u(t)V$; hence,

$$Y(s) = [V/s] \qquad (4\text{--}159)$$

Substituting Eqs. 4–129 and 4–159 into Eq. 4–158, we obtain

$$\hat{Q}(s) = \left( s\begin{bmatrix} 1 & 0 \\ 0 & 1 \end{bmatrix} - \begin{bmatrix} 0 & -1/L \\ 1/C & 0 \end{bmatrix} \right)^{-1} \begin{bmatrix} V/Ls \\ 0 \end{bmatrix} \qquad (4\text{--}160a)$$

Rearranging, we obtain

$$\hat{Q}(s) = \begin{bmatrix} s & 1/L \\ -1/C & s \end{bmatrix}^{-1} \begin{bmatrix} V/Ls \\ 0 \end{bmatrix} \qquad (4\text{--}160b)$$

$$\hat{Q}(s) = \begin{bmatrix} \dfrac{s}{s^2 + \dfrac{1}{LC}} & \dfrac{-1/L}{s^2 + \dfrac{1}{LC}} \\[2em] \dfrac{1/C}{s^2 + \dfrac{1}{LC}} & \dfrac{s^2}{s^2 + \dfrac{1}{LC}} \end{bmatrix} \begin{bmatrix} V/Ls \\[2em] 0 \end{bmatrix} \tag{4-160c}$$

Multiplying, we obtain

$$\hat{Q}(s) = \begin{bmatrix} \dfrac{V/L}{s^2 + \dfrac{1}{LC}} \\[2em] V\left(\dfrac{1}{s} - \dfrac{s}{s^2 + \dfrac{1}{LC}}\right) \end{bmatrix} \tag{4-160d}$$

Then, taking the inverse Laplace transform of each element of the matrix and substituting $\omega_0 = 1/\sqrt{LC}$ yields

$$\hat{q}(t) = \begin{bmatrix} \dfrac{V}{\omega_0 L} \sin \omega_0 t \\[1.5em] V(1 - \cos \omega_0 t) \end{bmatrix} \tag{4-161}$$

This checks with Eq. 4–153.

The Laplace transform procedure is often considerably less difficult than the classical ones for solving the state variable equations for linear, time-invariant networks. However, computer techniques are often developed from classical analysis procedures.

## 4-8. A NUMERICAL PROCEDURE FOR SOLVING STATE VARIABLE EQUATIONS OF LINEAR, NONLINEAR, TIME-INVARIANT, AND TIME-VARYING SYSTEMS

The method that we shall use can be easily implemented using computer procedures (see Section 4-9). This procedure approximates the trajectory by a set of confluent straight line segments. An example of this type of approximation is shown in Fig. 4–11. For convenience, we choose equal increments between successive times where the confluent straight line approximation becomes equal to the curve; that is,

$$\Delta t = t_1 - 0 = t_2 - t_1 = t_3 - t_2 = \cdots \tag{4-162}$$

On any straight line trajectory,

$$\frac{d\hat{q}(t)}{dt} = K \tag{4-163}$$

Equation 4–163 represents the $n$ scalar equations:

$$\frac{dq_1(t)}{dt} = K_1$$

$$\frac{dq_2(t)}{dt} = K_2$$

$$\vdots \tag{4-164}$$

$$\frac{dq_n(t)}{dt} = K_n$$

As $\Delta t$ approaches zero, the approximate trajectory approaches the actual one. Thus, this approximation procedure can be made as accurate as desired.

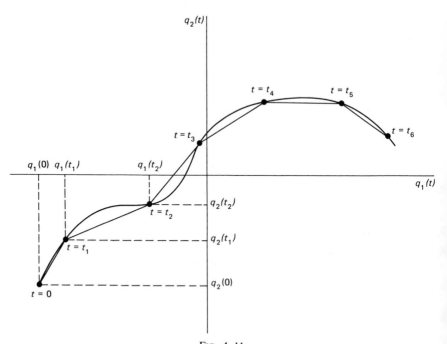

FIG. 4–11

Approximation of a trajectory by straight line segments

Now we wish to solve the general state variable equations (see Eq. 4–16)

$$\frac{d\hat{q}(t)}{dt} = \hat{f}\left[\hat{q}(t), \hat{y}(t), t\right]$$

where the initial state $\hat{q}(0-)$ is specified. The function on the right-hand side of Eq. 4–165 is a known function of $\hat{q}(t)$, $\hat{y}(t)$, and $t$ (where $\hat{y}(t)$ and $t$ are known, but $\hat{q}(t)$ is unknown). However, we do know $\hat{q}(0-)$. Substituting this into the right-hand side of Eq. 4–165 yields

$$\frac{d\hat{q}(t)}{dt}\bigg|_{t=0-} = f\left[\hat{q}(0-), \hat{y}(0-), 0-\right] \tag{4–166}$$

Thus, we have obtained the derivatives at $t = 0-$. The evaluation of the right-hand side of Eq. 4–166 is usually not difficult even in the case of nonlinear or time-varying systems since it involves the substitution of known values into known functions. However, it may be tedious if computer implementation is not used.

We are approximating the trajectory by straight line segments. Then, in the range $0 \leq t \leq t_1$, all the derivatives of the state variables are constant at their initial values, which have been computed in Eq. 4–166. Thus, on the straight line segments for $0 \leq t \leq t_1$,

$$\hat{q}(t) = \hat{q}(0-) + t\frac{d\hat{q}(t)}{dt}\bigg|_{t=0-} \tag{4–167}$$

To simplify the notation, we adopt the following somewhat incorrect notation:

$$\frac{d\hat{q}(t_0)}{dt} = \frac{d\hat{q}(t)}{dt}\bigg|_{t=t_0} \tag{4–168}$$

Then, for $0 \leq t \leq t_1$, we have

$$\hat{q}(t) = \hat{q}(0-) + t\frac{d\hat{q}(0-)}{dt} \tag{4–169}$$

If we substitute $t = t_1$ in Eq. 4–169, we obtain $\hat{q}(t_1)$. This can then be substituted in Eq. 4–165 to evaluate $d\hat{q}(t_1)/dt$; this is

$$\frac{d\hat{q}(t_1)}{dt} = f\left[\hat{q}(t_1), \hat{y}(t_1), t_1\right] \tag{4–170}$$

Thus, on the straight line segment for $t_1 \leq t \leq t_2$,

$$\hat{q}(t) = \hat{q}(t_1) + (t - t_1)\frac{d\hat{q}(t_1)}{dt_1} \tag{4–171}$$

We can use Eq. 4–171 to evaluate $\hat{q}(t_2)$. Substitution in Eq. 4–165 yields $d\hat{q}(t_2)/dt$. Then, for $t_2 \leq t \leq t_3$,

$$\hat{q}(t) = \hat{q}(t_2) + (t - t_2)\frac{d\hat{q}(t_2)}{dt} \tag{4–172}$$

We can proceed in this way. Hence, for $t_j \leq t \leq t_{j+1}$,

$$\hat{q}(t) = \hat{q}(t_j) + (t - t_j) \frac{d\hat{q}(t_j)}{dt} \qquad (4\text{--}173)$$

The approximate trajectory consists of confluent straight line segments. Thus, we need only compute $\hat{q}(0-), \hat{q}(t_1), \hat{q}(t_2), \ldots$ and connect these points by straight lines to obtain the trajectory.

As an example, let us solve the nonlinear state variable equations given by Eqs. 4–94 and 4–95. We shall use the following values for the constants

$$\alpha = 0$$

$$\beta = \tfrac{1}{3}$$

$$\gamma = 0$$

Assume that the input signal is a unit step function

$$v(t) = 1u(t)$$

Also assume that $v(0-) = 1$. We do this since, over the range $-0 \leq t \leq t_1, v(t) = 1$ for almost all the range. Thus, we shall use $v(0-) = 1$ even though it is actually zero. Note that, in the limit, as $\Delta t$ approaches zero, we need not do this. Then, Eqs. 4–94 and 4–95 are

$$\frac{di_L(t)}{dt} = - \frac{i_L(t)}{1 + i_L^2(t)} - \frac{v_C(t)}{1 + i_L^2(t)} + \frac{1}{1 + i_L^2(t)} \qquad (4\text{--}174a)$$

and

$$\frac{dv_C(t)}{dt} = i_L(t) - v_C^3(t) \qquad (4\text{--}174b)$$

Assume that the initial state is

$$i_L(0-) = 0 \qquad (4\text{--}175a)$$

$$v_C(0-) = 0 \qquad (4\text{--}175b)$$

Substituting these values into Eqs. 4–174, we obtain

$$\frac{di_L(0-)}{dt} = 1 \qquad (4\text{--}176a)$$

$$\frac{dv_C(0-)}{dt} = 0 \qquad (4\text{--}176b)$$

We choose $t = 0.1$. The accuracy depends upon the choice of $\Delta t$. In general, the accuracy increases as $\Delta t$ decreases. After the solution is obtained, the calculations should be repeated using a smaller value of $\Delta t$. If this gives substantially different results, then the calculations should be repeated using a still smaller value of $\Delta t$. This process should be repeated until a set of data are obtained that is not substantially changed by decreasing $\Delta t$.

Proceeding with the calculations, we have

$$i_L(0.1) = i_L(0-) + 0.1 \frac{di_L(0-)}{dt} = 0.1 \qquad (4\text{-}177a)$$

$$v_C(0.1) = v_C(0-) + 0.1 \frac{dv_C(0-)}{dt} = 0.0 \qquad (4\text{-}177b)$$

Substituting these values into Eq. 4–174, we obtain

$$\frac{di_L(0.1)}{dt} = 0.891 \qquad (4\text{-}178a)$$

$$\frac{dv_C(0.1)}{dt} = 0.1 \qquad (4\text{-}178b)$$

Use Eqs. 4–178 to calculate $\hat{q}(0.2)$ :

$$i_L(0.2) = 0.1 + 0.1(0.891) = 0.1891 \qquad (4\text{-}179a)$$

$$v_C(0.2) = 0.0 + 0.1(0.1) = 0.01 \qquad (4\text{-}179b)$$

Then, substituting Eqs. 4–179 into Eqs. 4–174, we obtain

$$\frac{di_L(0.2)}{dt} = 0.773 \qquad (4\text{-}180a)$$

$$\frac{dv_C(0.2)}{dt} = 0.1891 \qquad (4\text{-}180b)$$

Hence,

$$i_L(0.3) = 0.1891 + 0.1(0.773) = 0.2664 \qquad (4\text{-}181a)$$

$$v_C(0.3) = 0.01 + 0.1(0.1891) = 0.02891 \qquad (4\text{-}181b)$$

This procedure can be continued for as long as desired.

In general, most systems approach a final equilibrium state. That is, for sufficiency large $t$, the state variables approach constant values. The calculations should be carried out until this occurs. In addition, as discussed earlier, the calculations should be carried out using a smaller $\Delta t$ to check the accuracy. (Actually, in this example, for accuracy, a smaller $\Delta t$ than 0.1 should be used. However, 0.1 was used for purposes of illustration.)

For some systems the trajectory will be similar to Fig. 4–4; that is, it does not approach a final value. In general, even in nonlinear networks, such trajectories will approach a repeating path. The calculations can stop once the trajectory begins to traverse a repeating path.

In some cases, the trajectory is an increasing spiral, or some other curve that increases without limit. In such cases, the trajectory should be calculated for as long as desired or practical.

## 4-9. COMPUTER PROGRAMS FOR SOLVING STATE VARIABLE EQUATIONS OF LINEAR, NONLINEAR, TIME-INVARIANT, AND TIME-VARYING SYSTEMS

In this section we discuss FORTRAN programs, based on the numerical analysis procedure of Section 4-8 that can be used to evaluate the state variable equations for general systems. We shall cover linear, time-invariant time-varying, and nonlinear systems separately, since their programs differ.

**Linear, Time-Invariant Systems.** The state variable equations of linear, time-invariant systems will be of the form (see Eq. 4–23)

$$\frac{d\hat{q}(t)}{dt} = \hat{a}\hat{q}(t) + \hat{b}\hat{y}(t) \qquad (4\text{--}182)$$

where $\hat{a}$ and $\hat{b}$ are known matrices of constants and $\hat{y}$ is a matrix of known functions. The initial state $\hat{q}(0-)$ is assumed to be given. Equation 4–182 represents $n$ scalar equations. There are $n$ state variables $q_1(t), q_2(t), ..., q_n(t)$ and $k$ independent variables $y_1(t), y_2(t), ..., y_k(t)$. Then, $\hat{a}$ will be an $n \times n$ array while $\hat{b}$ will be an $n \times k$ array. The analysis that we shall implement is that given in Section 4-8; thus, we have (see Eqs. 4–168 through 4–173)

$$\frac{dq_i(0-)}{dt} = \sum_{j=1}^{n} a_{ij}q_j(0-) + \sum_{j=1}^{k} b_{ij}y_j(0-), \qquad i = 1, 2, ..., n \qquad (4\text{--}183)$$

Thus, all the $dq/dt$ are calculated at $t = 0-$. Then, using these values, we obtain

$$q_i(t_1) = q_i(0-) + \Delta t \, \frac{dq_i(0-)}{dt}, \qquad i = 1, 2, ..., n \qquad (4\text{--}184)$$

In general, we have

$$\frac{dq_i(t_h)}{dt} = \sum_{j=1}^{n} a_{ij}q_j(t_h) + \sum_{j=1}^{k} b_{ij}y_j(t_h), \qquad i = 1, 2, ..., n \qquad (4\text{--}185)$$

and

$$q_i(t_{h+1}) = q_i(t_h) + \Delta t \, \frac{dq_i(t_h)}{dt}, \qquad i = 1, 2, ..., n \qquad (4\text{--}186)$$

These are the equations that we shall implement in the FORTRAN program. The program is listed in SUBROUTINE STATEL in Fig. 4–12. Its flow chart is given in Fig. 4–13. Data are entered in the main program. These data are transferred to the SUBROUTINE using a COMMON statement. The following data are

```
00010    C       SUBRØUTINE FØR EVALUATIØN ØFLINEAR
00020    C       TIME INVARIENT STATE VARIABLE EQUATIØNS
00030            SUBRØUTINE STATEL
00040            CØMMØN A(20,20),B(20,20),Q(20),DELT,AI,N,K
00050            DIMENSIØN DQ(20),Y(20)
00060            T=AI*DELT
00070            TT=T-DELT
00080            Y(1)=24./(1.+TT)
00090            Y(2)=24.*TT/(1.+TT)
00100            DØ 75 I=3,K
00110            Y(I)=0.
00120    75      CØNTINUE
00130            DØ 200 I=1,N
00140            DQ(I)=0.
00150            DØ 150 J=1,N
00160            DQ(I)=DQ(I)+A(I,J)*Q(J)
00170    150     CØNTINUE
00180    200     CØNTINUE
00190            DØ 300 I=1,N
00200            DØ 250 J=1,K
00210            DQ(I)=DQ(I)+B(I,J)*Y(J)
00220    250     CØNTINUE
00230    300     CØNTINUE
00240            DØ 400 I=1,N
00250            Q(I)=Q(I)+DQ(I)*DELT
00260    400     CØNTINUE
00270            RETURN
00280            END
```

Fig. 4–12

SUBROUTINE STATEL that is used to evaluate the state variable equations of linear time-invariant systems

entered in this way. The $\hat{a}$ and $\hat{b}$ arrays, N and K, the number of state variables and independent variables, respectively, and DELT $= \Delta t$ are entered. In addition, the initial value of $\hat{q}(t)$, i.e., $\hat{q}(0-)$, is entered in the main program and then in the SUBROUTINE using the COMMON statement. The AI is a floating point equivalent of an integer which is generated in the main program. Each time the SUBROUTINE is called, AI is increased by one. Two other arrays that are used only in the SUBROUTINE are dimensioned in line 50. The quantities T and TT are calculated in lines 60 and 70, the T represents the time at which the $\hat{q}(t)$ matrix is evaluated. Then, TT represents $t - \Delta t$. Note (see Eqs. 4–185 and 4–186 that TT is used in the calculations. The SUBROUTINE first computes $d\hat{q}(0-)/dt$ using Eq. 4–183 and then computes $\hat{q}(t_1)$. These values are written over the $\hat{q}(0-)$ array. Thus, $\hat{q}(t_1)$ is now stored in the Q(I) array. Note also that $\hat{q}(t_j)$ is computed from $d\hat{q}(t_{j-1})/dt$. The main program then has the $\hat{q}(t)$ values printed. The value AI is increased by 1 and the procedure is repeated.

Now consider the SUBROUTINE in detail. Lines 40 and 50 are the COMMON and DIMENSION statements. In general, $\hat{y}(t)$ will not be a matrix of constant values but of functions. Thus, we cannot simply enter them as data but must enter

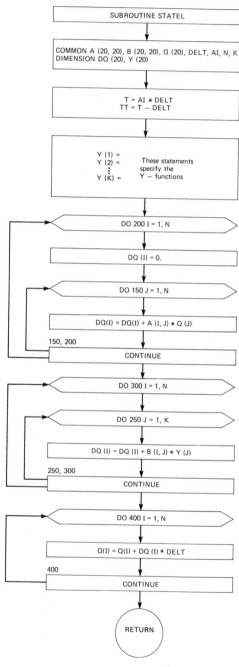

FIG. 4–13
Flow chart for SUBROUTINE STATEL

them as functions. In lines 80 and 90 we define

$$y_1(t) = 24/(1 + t)$$

$$y_2(t) = 24t/(1 + t)$$

Note that $t_{j-1}$ is used here. This is done because, in computing $\hat{q}(t_j)$, we must first compute $d\hat{q}(t_{j-1})/dt$. We have assumed that all other $y_j(t)$ are 0; that is,

$$y_3(t) = y_4(t) = \ldots = y_k(t) = 0$$

This is done in lines 100 through 120.

In the inner DO loop of lines 150–170, we compute the summation

$$\mathrm{DQ(I)} = \sum_{j=1}^{n} a_{ij}q_j$$

The outer DO loop of lines 130–180 computes this for each I.

In the inner DO loop of lines 200–220, DQ(I) is increased by

$$\sum_{j=1}^{k} b_{ij}y_j \qquad \text{.}$$

The outer DO loop of lines 190–230 causes this calculation to be repeated for each I. Thus, DQ(I) is computed as in Eq. 4–185.

In the DO loop of lines 240–260, the value of $q_i$ is computed in accordance with Eq. 4–186. The Q array now contains the new value of $\hat{q}(t)$. The main program, which is not listed, prints the array. Then, the value of AI is increased by one. The SUBROUTINE is called again and the process is repeated. Each time the SUBROUTINE is called, the $\hat{q}(t)$ matrix is evaluated for a new value at $t$.

**Time-Varying Systems.** When time-varying equations are to be solved, the program must be modified. We can still consider that there are $a$ and $b$ arrays, but now they are functions of time; i.e., $\hat{a}(t)$ and $\hat{b}(t)$ (see Eqs. 4–77). We shall enter these functions in the same way as the $\hat{y}(t)$ array was entered in STATEL. For example assume that we have the state variable equations

$$\frac{dq_1(t)}{dt} = tq_1(t) + 2q_2(t) + y_1(t) + 2ty_2(t) \qquad (4\text{–}187a)$$

$$\frac{dq_2(t)}{dt} = \frac{24}{1+t}q_1(t) + 2tq_2(t) + y_1(t) \qquad (4\text{–}187b)$$

where

$$y_1(t) = \frac{48}{(1+t)}$$

$$y_2(t) = 2$$

A SUBROUTINE, called STATET, that can be used to solve these equations is given in Fig. 4–14. Note that the A and B arrays are not put in common storage but

```
00010   C       SUBRØUTINE FØR EVALUATIØN ØFLINEAR
00020   C       TIME VARYING STATE VARIABLE EQUATIØNS
00030           SUBRØUTINE STATET
00040           CØMMØN Q(20),AI,DELT,N,K
00050           DIMENSIØN A(20,20),B(20,20),DQ(20),Y(20)
00060           T=AI*DELT
00070           TT=T-DELT
00080           Y(1)=48./(1.+TT)
00090           Y(2)=2.
00100           A(1,1)=TT
00110           A(1,2)=2.
00120           A(2,1)=24./(1+TT)
00130           A(2,2)=2*TT
00140           B(1,1)=1.
00150           B(1,2)=2.*TT
00160           B(2,1)=1.
00170           B(2,2)=0.
00180           DØ 200 I=1,N
00190           DQ(I)=0.
00200           DØ 150 J=1,N
00210           DQ(I)=DQ(I)+A(I,J)*Q(J)
00220   150     CØNTINUE
00230   200     CØNTINUE
00240           DØ 300 I=1,N
00250           DØ 250 J=1,K
00260           DQ(I)=DQ(I)+B(I,J)*Y(J)
00270   250     CØNTINUE
00280   300     CØNTINUE
00290           DØ 400 I=1,N
00300           Q(I)=Q(I)+DQ(I)*DELT
00310   400     CØNTINUE
00320           RETURN
00330           END
```

FIG. 4-14

SUBROUTINE STATET that is used to evaluate the state variable equations of a linear time-varying system

are computed in the subroutine in lines 100–170. Lines 180–330 correspond to lines 130–280 of SUBROUTINE STATEL (see Fig. 4–12). Thus, most of the description of Fig. 4–12 applies and we shall not repeat it here. Note that for purposes of example, we have dimensioned the arrays for 30 variables. In a specific case, the DIMENSION and COMMON statements should be changed so that excess storage is not required. In this case, the A array would be dimensioned as $A(2, 2)$.

**Nonlinear Systems.** When nonlinear systems are to be solved, we often cannot define $\hat{a}$ and $\hat{b}$ matrices. In this case, it is most convenient to write the expression for each $dq_j(t)/dt$ as a statement of the subroutine. Let us illustrate this by obtaining a program to solve Eqs. 4–147 which we repeat here.

$$\frac{dq_1(t)}{dt} = \left[ -q_1(t) - q_2(t) + y_1(t) \right] / \left[ 1 + q_1^2(t) \right] \qquad (4\text{–}188a)$$

$$\frac{dq_2(t)}{dt} = q_1(t) - q_2{}^3(t) \tag{4-188b}$$

where

$$y_1(t) = 1 \tag{4-188c}$$

The SUBROUTINE STATEN, which is used to solve these equations is listed in Fig. 4–15. Lines 10–70 are similar to the previous state variable programs of Figs. 4–14 and 4–12. Note that lines 60 and 70 which calculate TT are unnecessary in this specific program since $y(t) = 1$, a constant. If $y(t)$ varied with time, then TT would be used to calculate it. Lines 60 and 70 are just included as an example. Equations 4–188a and 4–188b are computed directly in lines 90 and 100. Note that DO loops are not used here. The DO loop of lines 110–130 computes the new Q array as before. As in the other state variable programs, each time that the main program causes the SUBROUTINE to be run, DQ(I), I = 1, N is evaluated using the last calculated value of Q(I), I = 1, N. Then, the new DQ(I) is used to calculate a new value of Q(I), I = 1, N. Note that, as an example, we have dimensioned the arrays for 20 variables. If, as in this case, there are only two state variables, then the DIMENSION statement should be appropriately changed.

This technique could also be used to evaluate nonlinear, time-varying equations. For instance, lines 90 and 100 could be functions of TT as well as of Q(1) and Q(2). Of course, the procedure could also be used for linear, time-invariant state variable equations. For instance, in Fig. 4–12, the DO loops of lines 130–230 could be replaced by a set of statements giving DQ as a function of Q and Y directly. However, in the case of linear, time-invariant networks, the DO loops save much effort.

```
00010   C       SUBRØUTINE FØR EVALUATIØN ØF NØNLINEAR
00020   C       STATE VARIABLE EQUATIØNS
00030           SUBRØUTINE STATEN
00040           CØMMØN Q(20),AI,DELT,N
00050           DIMENSIØN DQ(20),Y(20)
00060           T=AI*DELT
00070           TT=T-DELT
00080           Y(1)=1.
00090           DQ(1)=(-Q(1)-Q(2)+Y(1))/(1.+Q(1)**2)
00100           DQ(2)=Q(1)-Q(2)**3
00110           DØ 400 I=1,N
00120           Q(I)=Q(I)+DQ(I)*DELT
00130   400     CØNTINUE
00140           RETURN
00150           END
```

FIG. 4–15

SUBROUTINE STATEN that is used to evaluate the state variable equations of a nonlinear system

In this section we have discussed programs that can be used to solve all types of state variable equations. The state variable procedure is one of the best to use when digital computers are used to solve the differential equations of systems. This is especially true of nonlinear and time-varying systems.

## 4-10. BLOCK-DIAGRAM REPRESENTATION OF STATE VARIABLE AND OTHER DIFFERENTIAL EQUATIONS

Block diagrams consist of elements some of which have the form shown in Fig. 4–16. The first block represents an integrator. Its output is the integral of its input; that is, if $f(t)$ is its output, then $df(t)/dt$ its input. The block only transmits in one direction. The arrowhead indicates the direction of transmission. For example, applying $df(t)/dt$ at the left-hand side of Fig. 4–16a results in $f(t)$ appearing at the right-hand side. (The converse is not true.) Figure 4–16b is a block which differentiates its input. Thus, $df(t)/dt$ is the output if $f(t)$ is the input. Figure 4–16c represents a block which multiplies the input by a constant. The circle of Fig. 4–16d is a summer. The output is the sum, or difference of its inputs. The inputs are designated by the arrowheads. The $+$ or $-$ signs indicate whether the quantities are to be added or subtracted.

Block diagrams can just be a schematic representation of a set of differential equations. However, each block can actually represent a component of the system. Hence, the block diagram can be a representation of an actual system. The integrator in Fig. 4–16a could represent a network whose transfer function is $1/s$. In fact, at times, block diagrams are drawn on a transformed basis and then the integrator would be designated by a $1/s$ in the block.

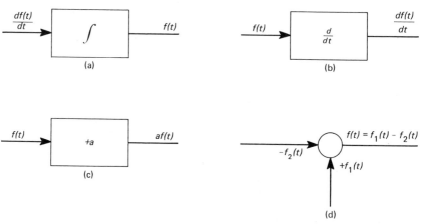

FIG. 4–16

Some typical block-diagram elements: (a) integrator; (b) differentiator; (c) constant multiplier (d) summer

If a block diagram for a set of differential equations can be found and each block represents a subsystem that can actually be built, then a system can be built using the block diagram as a guide which "solves" the differential equations; that is, the outputs of the system are then the solution to the set of differential equations. That is, integrators, summers, and constant multipliers can be built. They then are interconnected in accordance with the block diagram. The output of the system is the solution of the differential equations. This is called *analog simulation*. The circuit is called an *analog computer*.

Now let us obtain a block-diagram representation of the linear differential equation with constant coefficients.

$$\frac{d^2 x(t)}{dt^2} + a_1 \frac{dx(t)}{dt} + a_0 x(t) = y(t) \qquad (4\text{-}189\text{a})$$

Rewrite this as

$$\frac{d^2 x(t)}{dt^2} = -a_1 \frac{dx(t)}{dt} - a_0 x(t) + y(t) \qquad (4\text{-}189\text{b})$$

Now consider the diagram of Fig. 4–17. For the moment assume that the connection from the summer to the leftmost integrator is broken and that a signal $d^2 x(t)/dt^2$ is applied to the input of the leftmost integrator. The signals $dx(t)/dt$ and $x(t)$ will appear as shown. Thus, the output of the summer will be

$$-a_1 \frac{dx(t)}{dt} - a_0 x(t) + y(t)$$

Now assume that the signal $d^2 x(t)/dt^2$ is removed and that the connection between the summer and the integrator is replaced. This physically sets the input to that integrator equal to the output of the summer. Now let us call the input to the

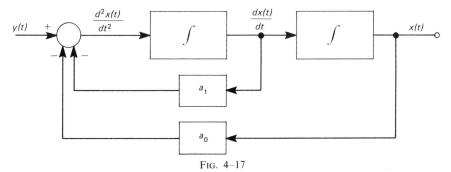

FIG. 4–17
Block diagram for Eq. 4–189

leftmost integrator $d^2x(t)/dt^2$. Thus, Eq. 4–189 will be satisfied. Then, since the proper $y(t)$ is applied at the input and the equilibrium conditions of the system must be satisfied, the proper $x(t)$ is obtained at the output.

Now let us obtain the block diagram for the equation

$$\frac{d^3x(t)}{dt^3} + a_2 \frac{d^2x(t)}{dt^2} + a_1 \frac{dx(t)}{dt} + a_0 x(t)$$

$$= b_2 \frac{d^2y(t)}{dt^2} + b_1 \frac{dy(t)}{dt} + b_0 y(t) \qquad (4\text{–}190)$$

The block diagram for the differential equation is given in Fig. 4–18. Again the block diagram can be formulated by writing

$$\frac{d^3x(t)}{dt^3} = - a_2 \frac{d^2x(t)}{dt^2} - a_1 \frac{dx(t)}{dt} - a_0 x(t) + b_2 \frac{d^2y(t)}{dt^2} + b_1 \frac{dy(t)}{dt} + b_0 y(t)$$

We can also draw block diagrams for simultaneous differential equations or for those with multiple inputs. We shall illustrate these when we discuss the block diagrams for state variable equations.

Let us consider a set of state variable equations. For instance, suppose we represent Eq. 4–189 in the following way:

$$q_1(t) = x(t) \qquad (4\text{–}191a)$$

$$q_2(t) = \frac{dx(t)}{dt} = \frac{dq_1(t)}{dt} \qquad (4\text{–}191b)$$

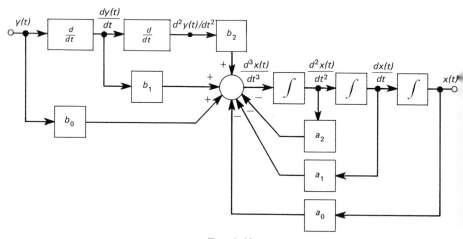

FIG. 4–18
Block diagram for Eq. 4–190

Then, the state variable equations are

$$\frac{dq_1(t)}{dt} = q_2(t) \tag{4-192a}$$

$$\frac{dq_2(t)}{dt} = - a_0 q_1(t) - a_1 q_2(t) + y(t) \tag{4-192b}$$

Figure 4–17 represents Eq. 4–189 and, thus it represents the set of state variable equations. However, the state variables are not explicitly defined in the block diagram. Now consider a block diagram which does this. This is shown in Fig. 4–19. Note that the same ideas are used to draw the block diagram. Now there are two signals $q_1(t)$ and $q_2(t)$. Now let us consider the representation of a set of state variables where there is more than one independent variable.

$$\frac{dq_1(t)}{dt} = a_{11}q_1(t) + a_{12}q_2(t) + b_{11}y_1(t) + b_{12}y_2(t) \tag{4-193a}$$

$$\frac{dq_2(t)}{dt} = a_{21}q_1(t) + a_{22}q_2(t) + b_{21}y_1(t) + b_{22}y_2(t) \tag{4-193b}$$

Assume that we want the variable $x_1(t)$, which is given by

$$x_1(t) = c_{11}q_1(t) + c_{12}q_2(t) + d_{11}y_1(t) \tag{4-193c}$$

The block diagram that represents these equations is given in Fig. 4–20. In general, higher ordered sets of state variables can be represented by extending these ideas.

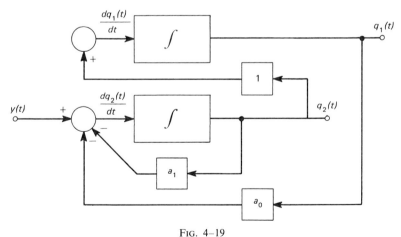

FIG. 4–19
Block diagram of the state variable Eqs. 4–192

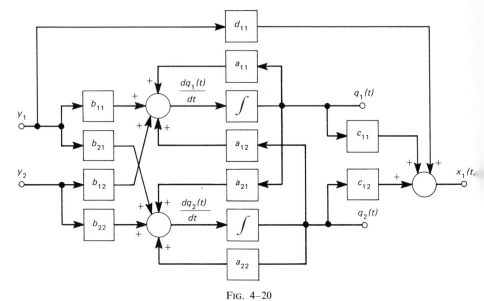

FIG. 4–20
Block diagram representation of the state variable Eqs. 4–193

The block diagram could represent a time-varying system if the $a_{ij}$, $b_{ij}$, $c_{ij}$, and $d_{ij}$ became functions of time. If such a system were built, the elements of the system must be time variable.

If nonlinear equations are to be represented, a block which multiplies or divides is used. In this way, $q_2(t)q_3(t)$, etc. can be generated.

## PROBLEMS

**4-1.** For the network of Fig. 4–1, L = 1 henry, R = 3 ohms, and C = 4 farads. Plot the trajectory in state space.

**4-2.** Repeat Problem 4-1, but now use R = 1 ohm and R = 0.5 ohm.

**4-3.** Write the state variable equations of Eqs. 4–7 in matrix form.

**4-4.** A system is characterized by the linear differential equations

$$\frac{d^2x_1(t)}{dt^2} + 3\frac{dx_1(t)}{dt} + 2x_1(t) = y_1(t) + y_2(t)$$

$$\frac{d^2x_2(t)}{dt^2} + 4\frac{dx_2(t)}{dt} + x_2(t) = y_1(t) - 3y_2(t)$$

where $y_1(t)$ and $y_2(t)$ are known functions of time. Find a set of state variable equations that characterize this system.

**4-5.** A system is characterized by the linear simultaneous integral differential equations

$$\int x_1(t)\,dt + \frac{dx_1(t)}{dt} + 2\,\frac{dx_2(t)}{dt} = y_1(t)$$

$$\frac{dx_1(t)}{dt} - 4\,\frac{dx_2(t)}{dt} = y_2(t)$$

Find a set of state variable equations that characterize the system.

**4-6.** Obtain a set of state variable equations that characterize the network of Fig. 4–21. Then, express the loop currents in terms of the state variables. The answer should be expressed in matrix form.

**4-7.** Repeat Problem 4-6 for the network of Fig. 4–22.

**4-8.** Repeat Problem 4-6 for the network of Fig. 4–23.

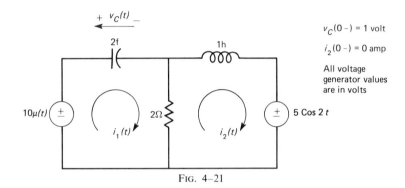

FIG. 4–21

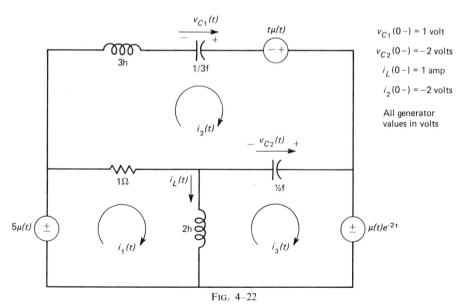

FIG. 4–22

**4-9.** Repeat Problem 4-6 for the network of Fig. 4–24.

**4-10.** Repeat Problem 4-6, but now assume that the 2 farad capacitor is replaced by one whose capacitance is given by $C(t) = 2 + e^{-t}$ farads and the 1 henry inductor is replaced by one whose inductance is $L(t) = 1 + 0.5 \sin 2t$ henries.

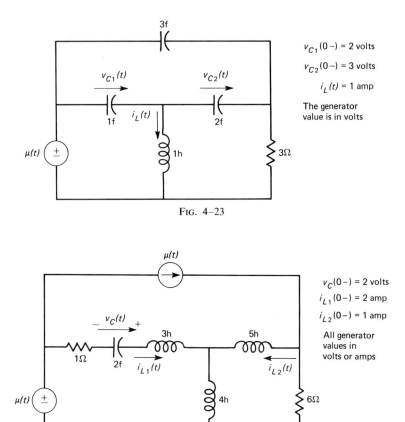

$v_{C_1}(0-) = 2$ volts

$v_{C_2}(0-) = 3$ volts

$i_L(t) = 1$ amp

The generator value is in volts

FIG. 4–23

$v_C(0-) = 2$ volts

$i_{L_1}(0-) = 2$ amp

$i_{L_2}(0-) = 1$ amp

All generator values in volts or amps

FIG. 4–24

**4-11.** Repeat Problem 4-10, but now assume that the 2 ohm resistor is replaced by one whose resistance is $R(t) = 2 + e^{-t} \cos t$.

**4-12.** Repeat Problem 4-7, but now assume that the 3 henry inductor is replaced by one whose inductance is $3 + 2e^{-t}$ henries, the 2 henry inductor is replaced by one whose inductance is $2 + \cos t$ henries and the 1/2 farad capacitor is replaced by one whose capacitance is $0.5 + e^{-t}$ farads.

**4-13.** Repeat Problem 4-12, but now assume that the 1 ohm resistor is replaced by one whose resistance is $1 + e^{-t} \cos t$.

**4-14.** Repeat Problem 4-6, but now assume that the 2 farad capacitor is replaced by one whose charge is given by

$$q = 2v + \tfrac{1}{2} v^3$$

where $v$ is the voltage across the capacitor, and that the 1 henry inductor is replaced by one whose flux linkages are given by $\phi = 2i^3$, where $i$ is the current through the inductance.

**4-15.** Repeat Problem 4-14, but now assume that the 2 ohm resistor has the voltage-current relation

$$i = \tfrac{1}{2} v^3$$

**4-16.** Solve the state variable equations

$$\frac{dq_1(t)}{dt} = -2q_1(t) - q_2(t) + 3$$

$$\frac{dq_2(t)}{dt} = -q_1(t) - 3q_2(t) + 1$$

The initial state is given by

$$q(0-) = \begin{bmatrix} 0 \\ 0 \end{bmatrix}$$

Use the classical procedures to obtain the solution. Express the answer as a power series.

**4-17.** Repeat Problem 4-16, but obtain the answer in closed form.

**4-18.** Repeat Problem 4-16, but now assume that the initial state is given by

$$q(0-) = \begin{bmatrix} 1 \\ -1 \end{bmatrix}$$

**4-19.** Repeat Problem 4-16 for the state variable equations of Problem 4-6.

**4-20.** Obtain the solution to Problem 4-19 in closed form.

**4-21.** Repeat Problem 4-16 for the state variable equations of Problem 4-7.

**4-22.** Obtain the solution to Problem 4-21 in closed form.

**4-23.** Use Laplace transform procedures to obtain the solution of the state variable equations of Problem 4-16.

**4-24.** Repeat Problem 4-23 for the state variable equations of Problem 4-18.

**4-25.** Repeat Problem 4-23 for the state variable equations of Problem 4-6.

**4-26.** Repeat Problem 4-23 for the state variable equations of Problem 4-7.

**4-27.** Repeat Problem 4-23 for the state variable equations of Problem 4-8.

**4-28.** Repeat Problem 4-16 but now use the approximation procedure of Section 4–8. Compare your results with those of Problem 4-16 or 4-17.

**4-29.** Repeat Problem 4-28, but now use the initial state of Problem 4-18.

**4-30.** Repeat Problem 4-28 for the state variable equations of Problem 4-10.

**4-31.** Repeat Problem 4-28 for the state variable equation of Problem 4-11.

**4-32.** Repeat Problem 4-28 for the state variable equations of Problem 4-12.

**4-33.** Repeat Problem 4-28 for the state variable equations of Problem 4-14.

**4-34.** Repeat Problem 4-28 for the state variable equations of Problem 4-15.

**4-35.** Write a main program for the SUBROUTINE STATEL of Fig. 4–12.

**4-36.** Write a computer program and use it to solve the state variable equations of Problem 4-16. Assume that $\Delta t$ and the total number of samples are to be entered by the user in the program.

**4-37.** Repeat Problem 4-36 for the state variable equations of Problem 4-18.
**4-38.** Repeat Problem 4-36 for the state variable equations of Problem 4-11.
**4-39.** Repeat Problem 4-36 for the state variable equations of Problem 4-12.
**4-40.** Repeat Problem 4-36 for the state variable equations of Problem 4-13.
**4-41.** Repeat Problem 4-36 for the state variable equations

$$\frac{dq_1(t)}{dt} = e^{-t}q_1(t) + q_2(t) + \frac{t}{1+t^2}q_3(t) + 2te^{-t}$$

$$\frac{dq_2(t)}{dt} = -q_1(t) - q_2(t) + e^{-t^2}q_3(t) - t/(1+t^2)$$

$$\frac{dq_3(t)}{dt} = -q_1(t) - q_2(t) - tq_3(t)$$

Assume that $\hat{q}(0-) = 0$.
**4-42.** Repeat Problem 4-36 for the state variable equations of Problem 4-14.
**4-43.** Repeat Problem 4-36 for the state variable equations of Problem 4-15.
**4-44.** Repeat Problem 4-36 for the state variable equations

$$\frac{dq_1(t)}{dt} = e^{-t}\left[-q_1(t)q_2(t)\,q_3^2(t) + q_2(t) + te^{-t}q_3(t)\right] + e^{-t}$$

$$\frac{dq_2(t)}{dt} = e^{-t^2}\left[e^t q_1(t) + q_2^2(t) - q_3(t)\right] + te^{-t}$$

$$\frac{dq_3(t)}{dt} = e^{-t}\left[q_1(t) + q_2(t)q_3(t) + q_3^2(t)\right]$$

The initial state is given by

$$\hat{q}(0-) = \begin{bmatrix} 1 \\ -1 \\ 0 \end{bmatrix}$$

# BIBLIOGRAPHY

Chirlian, P. M. *Basic Network Theory.* Chaps. 3 and 7. New York: McGraw-Hill, 1969.
Cooper, G. R., and McGillem, C. D. *Methods of Signals and System Analysis.* Chap. 8. New York: Holt, Rinehart, and Winston, 1967.
Kuo, B. C. *Linear Networks and Systems.* Chaps. 5 and 6. New York: McGraw-Hill, 1967.
Roe, P. H. *Networks and Systems.* Chap. 5. Reading, Mass.: Addison-Wesley, 1966.
Rohrer, R. A. *Circuit Theory: An Introduction to the State Variable Approach.* New York: McGraw-Hill, 1970.
Schwarz, R. J., and Friedland, B. *Linear Systems.* pp. 51–60. New York: McGraw-Hill, 1965.

# CHAPTER 5

# Linear, Continuous Time Systems

In this chapter we shall apply the analysis techniques discussed in Chapters 2, 3, and 4 to linear continuous time systems. A *linear system* is one which is characterized by a linear differential equation (see Section 1-1). A *continuous time system* is one whose output signals can be measured for all values of time. Many systems fall into this category. For instance, the output of a high-fidelity amplifier system produces a continuous output signal. Another such system is the response of an automobile to its engine.

Still another such system is the response of an electric network to applied signal generators. Some systems are such that their signals can be satisfactorily characterized if they are only sampled at discrete times. Also there are systems which can only provide data at discrete times. Such systems are said to be *discrete*. (Discrete time systems will be discussed in the next chapter.) Linear, continuous time systems can either be time invariant or time varying (see Section 1-1).

## 5-1. LINEAR SYSTEM RESPONSE; RELATION TO TRANSFER FUNCTION, IMPULSE RESPONSE AND SINUSOIDAL STEADY-STATE RESPONSE—STATE VARIABLE CHARACTERIZATION IN RELATION TO THE TRANSFER FUNCTION

In this section, we shall discuss the response of a linear, time-invariant network. The concept of a transfer function (see Section 2-7) will be discussed in detail. Let us first consider some definitions. Assume that we are dealing with a system which has a single input $f(t)$ and whose response to it is $g(t)$. Such a system is illustrated, in block diagram form in Fig. 5–1. As an aid in the discussion we shall adopt the following notation [1]. If the input $f(t)$ to a linear system results in an output $g(t)$, we shall write

$$T\{f(t)\} = g(t) \tag{5-1}$$

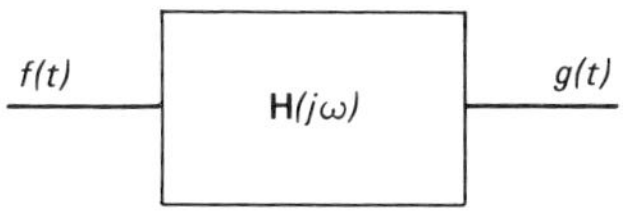

Fig. 5–1
System whose transfer function is $H(j\omega)$

259

**Linearity.** At first we shall assume that a system is linear, but not necessarily time invariant. A linear system is one which is characterized by a set of linear differential equations, see Section 1-1. These equations are such that if $g_1(t)$ is the response to $f_1(t)$, and $g_2(t)$ is the response to $f_2(t)$, then $g_1(t) + g_2(t)$ is the response to $f_1(t) + f_2(t)$. In general, if

$$T\{f_k(t)\} = g_k(t), \qquad k = 1, 2, \ldots \tag{5-2}$$

then

$$T\left\{\sum_{k=1}^{N} a_k f_k(t)\right\} = \sum_{k=1}^{N} a_k g_k(t) \tag{5-3}$$

where the $a_k$ are constants. Then, substituting Eq. 5–2 into the right-hand side of Eq. 5–3, we have

$$T\left\{\sum_{k=1}^{N} a_k f_k(t)\right\} = \sum_{k=1}^{N} a_k T\{f_k(t)\} \tag{5-4}$$

Thus, *the response to a sum of signals is the sum of the responses to individual signals.* We shall extend this definition and consider that $N$ can be infinite. This is consistent with the ideas of limit discussed in distribution theory, see Section 2-3.

Now suppose the input signal is a very specific one, the unit impulse, $\delta(t)$. We shall use the notation that the response of the system to a unit impulse is $h(t)$.

$$T\{\delta(t)\} = h(t) \tag{5-5}$$

Also suppose the impulse function is shifted in time, i.e., the input is $\delta(t - T)$. Then, we write the response as $h(t, T)$. If the system is time varying, its response depends upon when the signal is applied. That is why we write the response as a function of both $t$ and $T$.

$$T\{\delta(t - T)\} = h(t, T) \tag{5-6}$$

We now shall show that the response of a linear system to an arbitrary $f(t)$ can be expressed in terms of its impulse response. First, let us express $f(t)$ in terms of $\delta(t)$. From Eq. 2–36, we have

$$f(t) = \int_{-\infty}^{\infty} f(y)\,\delta(t - y)\,dy \tag{5-7}$$

where we have used $y$ as the variable of integration.

Now, consider a function $f_\Delta(t)$ such that

$$f_\Delta(t) = \sum_{n=-\infty}^{\infty} f(n\Delta y)\,\delta(t - n\Delta y)\,\Delta y \tag{5-8}$$

Note that $\Delta y$ is a constant; thus $f(n\Delta y)$ is also a constant. Then, we have

$$\lim_{\Delta y \to 0} n\Delta y = y \tag{5-9}$$

In the limit as $\Delta y$ approaches zero, $n\Delta y$ becomes the variable $y$. Since $n$ takes on all values from $-\infty$ to $+\infty$ and $\Delta y$ is infinitesimally small, $n\Delta y$ can take on all values. Then, Eq. 5–8 becomes, in the limit, the definition of the Riemann integral.

However, there is a distribution $\delta(t)$ as part of the integrand. Thus, we must use the properties of limits (see Sections 2-1 through 2-3). Hence, we can define

$$\lim_{\Delta y \to 0} f_\Delta(t) = f(t) \qquad (5\text{--}10)$$

Now, substituting Eq. 5-8 into Eq. 5-4, we obtain

$$T\left\{ \sum_{n=-\infty}^{\infty} f(n\Delta y)\, \delta(t - n\Delta y)\, \Delta y \right\} = \sum_{n=-\infty}^{\infty} f(n\Delta y)\, T\{\delta(t) - n\Delta y)\}\, \Delta y \qquad (5\text{--}11)$$

Note that $f(n\Delta y)\, \Delta y$ is constant. Then, substituting Eq. 5-6, we have

$$T\left\{ \sum_{n=-\infty}^{\infty} f(n\Delta y)\, \delta(t - n\Delta y)\, \Delta y \right\} = \sum_{n=-\infty}^{\infty} f(n\Delta y)\, h(t_1 n\Delta y)\, \Delta y \qquad (5\text{--}12)$$

Now take the limit as $\Delta y \to 0$. We assume that the limit and the operation on the left-hand side can be interchanged. The summation on the left-hand side then becomes $f(t)$. The summation on the right-hand side becomes the Riemann integral, thus,

$$T\{f(t)\} = \int_{-\infty}^{\infty} f(y)\, h(t, y)\, dy \qquad (5\text{--}13)$$

Hence, we have expressed the response of a system to an arbitrary $f(t)$ in terms of its response to a unit impulse.

Actually the preceding discussion is not completely rigorous. In Eq. 5-8, a function whose limit is $\delta(t)$ should be used to replace the impulse. The interchanging of the limit process with the $T\{\ \}$ appearing on the right-hand side of Eq. 5-12 should be thoroughly studied. However, the ideas which we have discussed here are consistent with the general ideas discussed in Sections 2-1 to 2-3.

Substituting Eq. 5-1 into Eq. 5-13, we have

$$g(t) = \int_{-\infty}^{\infty} f(y)\, h(t, y)\, dy \qquad (5\text{--}14)$$

**Time-Invariant System.** We have thus far assumed that the system was linear. Now assume that it is also time invariant. If a system does not vary with time and if the input is delayed in time by $T$ seconds, the only effect on the output signal is that it will be delayed by $T$ seconds, hence,

$$T\{f(t - T)\} = g(t - T) \qquad (5\text{--}15)$$

Another way of looking at this is if a system is time invariant, *it does not matter* when the signal is applied. We call the time of application $t = 0$. Then, Eq. 5-6 becomes, for linear time-invariant systems,

$$T\{\delta(t - T)\} = h(t - T) \qquad (5\text{--}16)$$

Substituting in Eq. 5-14, we have

$$g(t) = \int_{-\infty}^{\infty} f(y)\, h(t - y)\, dy \qquad (5\text{--}17)$$

This integral is simply the convolution of $f(t)$ and $h(t)$, (see Eq. 2–202). Thus, the convolution of the input signal $f(t)$ and the impulse response yields the response of a linear, time-invariant network to $f(t)$.

**Transfer Function.** We can now develop the concept of a transfer function in rigorous terms. Let us again write

$$T\{\delta(t)\} = h(t) \tag{5–18}$$

Assume that the Fourier transform of $h(t)$ exists and is given by

$$h(t) \leftrightarrow H(j\omega) \tag{5–19}$$

We shall relate these transforms to the Fourier transform of $g(t)$, the response to $f(t)$. Assume that both of these possess Fourier transforms which are given by

$$f(t) \leftrightarrow F(j\omega) \tag{5–20a}$$
$$g(t) \leftrightarrow G(j\omega) \tag{5–20b}$$

Use the time convolution theorem, (see Eq. 2–209) to take the Fourier transform of both sides of Eq. 5–17. This yields

$$G(j\omega) = H(j\omega)\,F(j\omega) \tag{5–21a}$$

or, equivalently,

$$H(j\omega) = G(j\omega)\,/F(j\omega) \tag{5–21b}$$

Thus, *the Fourier transform of the output of a system is the Fourier transform of the impulse response times the Fourier transform of the input.* We therefore call the Fourier transform of the response to a unit impulse the *transfer function.* In general (see Eq. 5–21b) the transfer function is the ratio of the input and output Fourier transforms. Note that Eqs. 5–21 hold also for the impulse function, since (see Eq. 2–111)

$$\delta(t) \leftrightarrow 1 \tag{5–22}$$

Thus, we have shown that $H(j\omega)$ is not only the Fourier transform of the impulse response, but it is also far more general since it is the transfer function that can be used to obtain the response to arbitrary signals. Note that $H(j\omega)$ can be found not only from the response to an impulse, but also from the response to many signals. For instance, if $f(t)$ is such that $F(j\omega) \neq 0$, then, by measuring the response $g(t)$ and taking its Fourier transform, we can compute $H(j\omega)$ using Eq. 5–21b.

Now we shall extend the generalization of $H(j\omega)$ further by relating it to the sinusoidal steady-state response. Consider the response of a system to the signal $e^{j\omega_0 t}$. Of course, we cannot, in practice, generate a signal which is a complex function. However, almost all the analysis procedures discussed in Chapter 2 are valid if $f(t)$ is complex. Now let

$$f(t) = e^{j\omega_0 t} \tag{5–23}$$

Then, the response to $f(t)$ is $g(t)$

$$T\{e^{j\omega_0 t}\} = g(t)$$

Assume that the system is linear and time invariant, hence (see Eq. 5–15)

$$T\{e^{j\omega_0(t+t_1)}\} = g(t + t_1) \tag{5-24}$$

We can write

$$e^{j\omega_0(t+t_1)} = e^{j\omega_0 t}e^{j\omega_0 t_1} \tag{5\ 25}$$

Then, since $e^{j\omega_0 t_1}$ is a constant, we have, (see Eq. 5–3)

$$T\{e^{j\omega_0(t+t_1)}\} = T\{e^{j\omega_0 t}e^{j\omega_0 t_1}\} = e^{j\omega_0 t_1}g(t) \tag{5-26}$$

Then, comparing Eqs. 5–24 and 5–26, we have

$$g(t + t_1) = e^{j\omega_0 t_1}g(t) \tag{5-27}$$

Since this expression is valid for all $t$, let $t = 0$, then,

$$g(t_1) = e^{j\omega_0 t_1}g(0) \tag{5-28}$$

where $g(0)$ is a constant. However, $t_1$ is an *arbitrary* constant. Thus, we can let it take on any value. Let us write it as $t$

$$g(t) = e^{j\omega_0 t}g(0) \tag{5-29}$$

Thus, the output signal is equal to the input signal times a constant. It may appear as though the constant $t_1$ has been arbitrarily changed into a variable. To show that the previous computations are valid, consider the following. Equation 5–24 is valid for all $t_1$. Hence, we can allow $t_1$ to take on all values and compute $g(t + t_1)$. Thus, $t_1$ has all the attributes of a variable.

The response to $e^{j\omega_0 t}$ is a constant times $e^{j\omega_0 t}$. In general, if

$$T\{f(t)\} = Kf(t) \tag{5-30}$$

then $f(t)$ is called an *eigenfunction*, or *characteristic function*, of the system and $K$ is the *eigenvalue*, or *characteristic value*. Thus, $e^{j\omega_0 t}$ and $g(0)$ are the eigenfunctions and eigenvalues of the system, respectively. (The constant $\omega_0$ can take on different values and $g(0)$ will be a function of these values.)

Now let us relate $g(0)$ to the transfer function of the system. The Fourier transform of $e^{j\omega_0 t}$ is given by

$$e^{j\omega_0 t} \leftrightarrow 2\pi\delta(\omega - \omega_0) \tag{5-31}$$

(See Table 2-1.) Then, if $e^{j\omega_0 t}$ is the input to a system and $e^{j\omega_0 t}g(0)$ is its output, we have

$$g(0)e^{j\omega_0 t} \leftrightarrow 2\pi g(0)\delta(\omega - \omega_0) \tag{5-32}$$

since $g(0)$ is a constant. Then, applying Eqs. 5–21b, 5–31, and 5–32, we obtain

$$H(j\omega_0) = g(0) \tag{5-33}$$

That is, $g(0)$ is equal to the transfer function evaluated at $\omega_0$. Substituting in Eq. 5–29, we have

$$T\{e^{j\omega_0 t}\} = H(j\omega_0)e^{j\omega_0 t} \tag{5-34}$$

Now let us use Euler's relation

$$e^{j\omega_0 t} = \cos\omega_0 t + j\sin\omega_0 t$$

In addition, let us write $H(j\omega)$ in polar form as

$$H(j\omega_0) = |H(j\omega_0)| e^{j\theta(\omega_0)} \qquad (5\text{-}35)$$

Then, substituting Eq. 5-35 and Euler's equation into Eq. 5-34, we have

$$T\{\cos \omega_0 t + j\sin \omega_0 t\} = |H(j\omega_0)| \cos [\omega_0 t + \theta(\omega_0)]$$
$$+ j|H(j\omega_0)| \sin [\omega_0 + \theta(\omega_0)] \qquad (5\text{-}36)$$

We wish now to use Eq. 5-36 to obtain the response of the system to $\cos \omega_0 t$ and $\sin \omega_0 t$. In general, we cannot simply equate reals and imaginaries in Eq. 5-36, since systems can be mathematically formulated so that the response to a real input is complex. However, all systems that can be physically built have transfer functions which are such that the response to a real input is itself real. Thus, in a physical system, if we *compute* the response to $j$ times a real function, we will obtain a purely imaginary response. Assuming we have such a system, if

$$T\{f_1(t) + jf_2(t)\} = g_1(t) + jg_2(t) \qquad (5\text{-}37)$$

where $f_1(t)$, $f_2(t)$, $g_1(t)$, and $g_2(t)$ are real, then

$$T\{f_1(t)\} = g_1(t) \qquad (5\text{-}38a)$$

and

$$T\{f_2(t)\} = g_2(t) \qquad (5\text{-}38b)$$

Thus, for Eq. 5-36, we have

$$T\{\cos \omega_0 t\} = |H(j\omega_0)| \cos [\omega_0 t + \theta(\omega_0)] \qquad (5\text{-}39a)$$
$$T\{\sin \omega_0 t\} = |H(j\omega_0)| \sin [\omega_0 t + \theta(\omega_0)] \qquad (5\text{-}39b)$$

Thus, the response to a sinusoidal signal is itself a sinusoid. (Note that the sinusoid is assumed to be applied at $t = -\infty$.)

In general, to measure the transfer function of a system on a sinusoidal steady-state basis, we apply a sinusoid of frequency $\omega_0$. The ratio of the magnitude of the rms output sinusoid to the magnitude of the rms input signal is defined as the magnitude of the transfer function at $\omega = \omega_0$. The phase shift of the output sinusoid with respect to the input sinusoid is defined as the phase angle of the transfer functions at $\omega = \omega_0$. Thus, $H(j\omega_0)$ is the sinusoidal steady-state transfer function at $\omega = \omega_0$. Hence, in general, $H(j\omega)$ is the sinusoidal steady-state transfer function, the transfer function on a Fourier transform basis, and also the Fourier transform of the unit impulse response. We cannot actually apply the sinusoid at $t = -\infty$. However, if it is applied at $t = t_0$ and the measurements are made after all transients become zero, the results will yield $H(j\omega)$; i.e., applying the signal at $t = -\infty$ implies that all transients have become zero. Now consider the transfer function on a Laplace transform basis. Let us call the Laplace transform of $h(t)$, $H_L(s)$, thus (see Table 3-1),

$$h(t) \leftrightarrow H_L(s) \qquad (5\text{-}40)$$

Let us denote the Laplace transform of the input and output signals, respectively, by

$$f(t) \leftrightarrow F_L(s)$$
$$g(t) \leftrightarrow G_L(s)$$

Then, applying the convolution theorem (see Eq. 3–188) to Eq. 5–17, we have

$$G_L(s) = H_L(s) F_L(s) \tag{5–41}$$

Comparing this with Eq. 5–21, we have the $H_L(s)$ in the Laplace transform domain has the same significance as $H(j\omega)$ in the Fourier transform domain. Often (see Section 3-4) $H_L(s)$ can be obtained from $H(j\omega)$ simply by replacing $j\omega$ by $s$ and vice versa.

If we wish to compute the output of a system in response to an input, we can take the inverse Laplace transform of Eq. 5–41 or the inverse Fourier transform of Eq. 5–21a. Alternatively, we can use Eq. 5–17.

As an example of the use of Eq. 5–41, assume that a system has the transfer function

$$H(s) = \frac{1}{(s + 1)(s + 2)}$$

and we wish to determine its unit step response. Then, $F_L(s) = 1/s$. Hence, the Laplace transform of the output is given by

$$G_L(s) = \frac{1}{s(s + 1)(s + 2)} = \frac{1/2}{s} - \frac{1}{s + 1} + \frac{1/2}{s + 2}$$

Thus, the unit step response of this system is given by

$$g(t) = u(t)(\tfrac{1}{2} - e^{-t} + \tfrac{1}{2}e^{-2t})$$

**State Variable Characterization in Terms of the Transfer Function.** When the system transfer function is simple and the input signal has a simple Laplace transform, the inverse transform can be taken as in the above example. However, this often proves extremely tedious, so computer techniques should be used. In this case, it is desirable to work with state variables.

Let us now consider how a system can be characterized using state variables if its transfer function is known. Assume that the system transfer function is

$$H(s) = \frac{\beta_m s^m + \beta_{m-1} s^{m-1} + \cdots + \beta_1 s + \beta_0}{\alpha_n s^n + \alpha_{n-1} s^{n-1} + \cdots + \alpha_1 s + \alpha_0}$$

The system output, in terms of the system input and the transfer function is given by Eq. 5–41. Substituting into this equation, we obtain

$$(\alpha_n s^n + \alpha_{n-1} s^{n-1} + \cdots + \alpha_1 s + \alpha_0) G_L(s)$$
$$= (\beta_m s^m + \beta_{m-1} s^{m-1} + \cdots + \beta_1 s + \beta_0) F_L(s) \tag{5–42a}$$

Now take the inverse Laplace transform of both sides of this equation, this yields

$$\alpha_n \frac{d^n g(t)}{dt^n} + \alpha_{n-1} \frac{d^{n-1} g(t)}{dt^{n-1}} + \cdots + \alpha_1 \frac{dg(t)}{dt} + \alpha_0 g(t)$$

$$= \beta_m \frac{d^m f(t)}{dt^m} + \beta_{m-1} \frac{d^{m-1} f(t)}{dt^{m-1}} + \cdots + \beta_1 \frac{df(t)}{dt} + \beta_0 f(t) \quad (5\text{–}42b)$$

If we take the Laplace transform of Eq. 5–42b and assume that there are zero initial conditions at $t = 0 -$, then Eq. 5–42a results. At $t = 0 -$, the output (and all its derivatives) of a system with no stored energy in response to a signal applied at $t = 0$ is zero. (Note that the signal is applied *after* $t = 0 -$.) Thus, if we solve Eq. 5–42b for $g(t)$ we shall obtain the system response. However, this is not in "state variable form." Let us see how we can obtain the desired form. Equation 5–41b is essentially the same as Eq. 4–39. Hence, we can use the procedure of Eqs 4–40 through 4–42 to obtain the state variable equations of this system.

Consider the previous example and obtain the state variables of the system whose transfer function is $1/(s + 1)(s + 2)$. Then, we have

$$(s + 1)(s + 2) G(s) = F(s)$$

Taking the inverse Laplace transform, assuming zero initial conditions, we obtain

$$\frac{d^2 g(t)}{dt^2} + 3 \frac{dg(t)}{dt} + 2g(t) = f(t)$$

This is a relatively simple form and we can use the procedure of Eqs. 4–30 through 4–32 to obtain the state variables. In this case, we have

$$q_1(t) = g(t)$$

$$q_2(t) = \frac{dg(t)}{dt} = \frac{dq_1(t)}{dt}$$

Thus, the state variable equations are

$$\frac{dq_1(t)}{dt} = q_2(t)$$

$$\frac{dq_2(t)}{dt} = -2q_1(t) - 3q_2(t) + f(t)$$

These are one set of state variable equations which characterize the system.

## 5-2. UNIT IMPULSE AND UNIT STEP RESPONSES

Very often, we wish the response of a system to have the same form as the input. For instance, in an amplifier, if the input is $f(t)$, it would be ideal if the output $g(t)$

were a constant times the input:

$$g(t) = Kf(t) \qquad (5\text{--}43)$$

Usually, we do not know exactly what signals are to be applied to the system. For instance suppose the system is an oscilloscope in which many different signals may be tested. It is convenient to be able to rate the system response. In general, we showed in Section 5-1 that the transfer function could be found from the response to a large class of signals (see Eq. 5–21). Then, the transfer function can be used to obtain the response to all signals. Thus, it may appear as though any signal could be used to rate the system. However, in practice, we wish, without difficulty, to compare input and output signals. Thus, it has become common to rate systems in terms of their response to signals which are such that the deviation of the output from the input can be readily observed. The two most widely used signals are the unit step and unit impulse responses. Both of these functions are such that differences between the input and output signals can be readily discerned.

The computation of these responses can be obtained using the Fourier transform, Laplace transform, or state variable procedures (see Chapters 2, 3, and 4).

**Unit Impulse Response.** If the transfer function of the system is $H(j\omega)$ on a Fourier transform basis or $H_L(s)$ on a Laplace transform basis, we need only take the inverse Fourier or inverse Laplace transforms to obtain the response.

It is often desirable to use a computer solution. Then, the fast Fourier transform (FFT) is probably the desirable procedure to use (see Section 2-20). A program for the inverse FFT is given in Fig. 2–27. This program can be applied to $H(j\omega)$ to obtain $h(t)$.

State variable procedures can also be used to obtain the impulse response. In this case, the independent variable $y(t)$ is assumed to be $\delta(t)$. Note that the state variable procedure is probably best, if computer solutions are desired for nonlinear or time-varying networks.

When computer solutions are used, it is not possible to enter $\delta(t)$. However, $\delta(t)$ can be approximated by a rectangular pulse of unit area. The time duration $T_0$ of the pulse should be so short that the system response cannot change significantly in $T_0$ seconds. When computer calculations are made, it is often desirable to characterize the network using state variables (see Section 5-1).

**Unit Step Response.** The unit step response can be found using procedures similar to those for the unit impulse response. The Fourier and Laplace transforms of the unit step response are given in Tables 2-1 and 3-1, respectively. These transforms can be multiplied by $H(j\omega)$ or $H_L(s)$ (the system transfer functions on a Fourier or Laplace transform basis, respectively) to obtain the transform of the output. Then, $g(t)$ is obtained by taking the inverse transform. Again, if computer calculations, on a transform basis, are to be performed, the FFT should be used. In this case, the input signal is assumed constant. The number of samples and the spacing between them in time is chosen. Then, the program of Fig. 2–26 is used to obtain the discrete Fourier transform of $u(t)$. This discrete Fourier spectrum is then multiplied (term by term) by $H(j\omega)$. For example, if F(I), I = 1, N is an array which contains the discrete Fourier transform terms of $u(t)$, and

$$H(j\omega) = \frac{1}{1 + j\omega} = \frac{1}{1 + \omega^2} - \frac{j\omega}{1 + \omega^2}$$

the transform of the output can be written over the F(I) array with the following program segment

```
      DO 150 J = 1, N
      AQ = J
      DW = 2 * 3.14159/T
      DWN = DW * AQ                                    (5-44)
      HR = 1./(1. + DWN ** 2)
      HI = - DWN/(1. + DWN ** 2)
      H = CMPLX(HR, HI)
      F(J) = F(J) * H
150   CONTINUE
```

The variables H and F must be declared complex. Note (see lines 90, 100, and 500–570 of Fig. 2–26) that T is the total time duration. Then, DWN represents $\omega$. Thus, HR and HI are the real and imaginary parts of $H(j\omega)$. In the last line, the new value of F(I) is computed and written over the old one. Then, the inverse FFT (see Fig. 2–27) is computed to obtain the unit step response. Of course, the programs should be modified so that the data can be entered directly without having to use the input statements of the inverse FFT program.

State variable procedures can, of course, also be used. Then the calculations directly follow the procedure given in Chapter 4. The known signal is now the unit step.

**Relations between the Unit Step and Unit Impulse Responses.**    First, let us use 5–17 to compute the unit step response. Then, $f(t) = u(t)$. Substituting in Eq. 5–17, we have

$$a(t) = \int_{-\infty}^{\infty} u(y)h(t - y)\,dy \qquad (5\text{--}45)$$

where we have used $a(t)$ to represent the unit step response. Since the convolution of $f_1(t) * f_2(t) = f_2(t) * f_1(t)$ (see Eq. 2–204), Eq. 5–45 can be rewritten as

$$a(t) = \int_{-\infty}^{\infty} h(y)u(t - y)\,dy \qquad (5\text{--}46)$$

However, $u(t - y) = 0$ for $y > t$, hence,

$$a(t) = \int_{-\infty}^{t} h(y)\,dy \qquad (5\text{--}47)$$

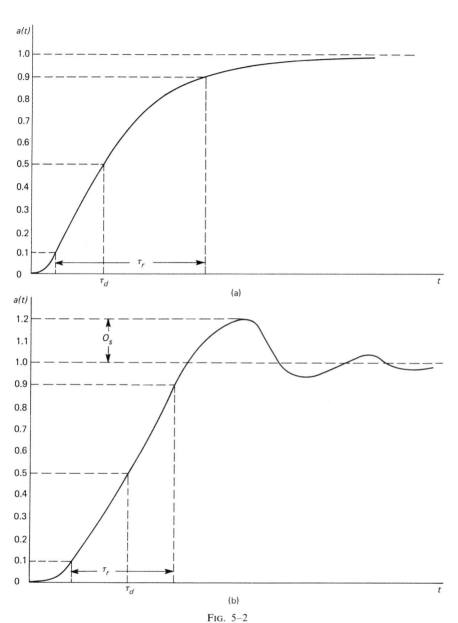

Fig. 5-2

Typical normalized unit step responses; (a) without overshoot; (b) with overshoot

Thus, the unit step response is the integral of the unit impulse response. Differentiating Eq. 5–47, we obtain

$$h(t) = \frac{da(t)}{dt} \qquad (5\text{–}48)$$

Thus, the unit impulse response is the derivative of the unit step response.

**Rise Time, Overshoot, and Delay Time.** Very often, it is desirable to have some figure of merit that can be used to rate the unit step response of a system. There is some danger in working with figures of merit since, in using them, we attempt to describe a curve in terms of one or two values. However, the responses of many systems are often similar in shape. In these cases, it becomes practical to use figures of merit.

Consider the typical unit step response shown in Fig. 5–2. One figure of merit that appears useful is the time it takes for the system response to reach unity. (Note that we have normalized the unit step response so that the final value is unity.) In Fig. 5–2a, $a(t)$ approaches 1 asymptotically. Thus, it takes an infinite time to reach unity. Hence, we must modify the choice of a figure of merit. We could choose the figure of merit as the time it takes $a(t)$ to reach unity for all practical purposes. Usually, 0.9 of the final value is chosen as the practical final value. Note that 0.9 has no special significance and, for instance, 0.95 or 0.85 could be used if the particular case warranted it. Unless otherwise stated, we shall use 0.9 here.

Actually, the rise time is used as an indication of how fast the system can respond. Consider Fig. 5–2b. Notice that the response stays close to zero for a time. The system can be supposed to have introduced delay. Often such delay does not affect the system's response and should not be charged against the rate of response. For instance a high fidelity audio amplifier would be considered perfect if it faithfully reproduced the input signal even if all signals were delayed by 0.1 second. For this reason, the response of the system is often assumed not to start until $a(t)$ has reached one tenth of its final value (again note that the value, one tenth, can be changed in specific instances). Thus, we often use the 10 to 90 percent rise time $\tau_r$ as a figure of merit; $\tau_r$ is illustrated in Fig. 5–2.

There is one circumstance when time delay should be charged against the response of a system. In digital computers, signals in the form of pulses are processed in sequence. The next device cannot process a pulse until it has reached a sufficiently large value. Thus, time delay will slow the speed of response of a system and should be charged against it.

Often, the time it takes for $a(t)$ to reach 0.5 of its final value is arbitrarily called the *delay time* $\tau_d$.

There is another parameter that is commonly used to rate the unit step response of a system. Note in Fig. 5–2b that $a(t)$ overshoots and undershoots the final value. This is characteristic of the Gibbs' phenomenon (see Section 2-5). The *overshoot*, $O_s$ is used to rate this

$$O_s = \frac{a(t)_{max} - a(\infty)}{a(\infty)} \qquad (5\text{–}49)$$

The 10 to 90 percent rise time and the overshoot are two values that are usually used to rate the unit step response of systems. It is difficult to obtain an expression for them in closed form. However, we can obtain their values using simple computer programs. Assume that the unit step response has been calculated using FFT (see Section 2-20) or state variable procedures (see Section 4-8) and that the response is stored in an array $F(I)$, $I = 1$, N. We shall now discuss two subroutines that can be used to obtain the 10 to 90 percent rise time and the overshoot.

Consider the SUBROUTINE RISE (see Fig. 5–3) that computes the 10 to 90 percent rise time of the unit step response. Common statements are used to transfer data into the SUBROUTINE and to transfer the rise time TR back to the main program. That is the array F of the unit step response, the number of terms N in the array, the time between samples DELTA, and the 10 to 90 percent rise time TR are placed in common storage. Consider the DO loop of lines 40–80. In line 50, $F(I)$ is normalized. That is, it is replaced by $F(I)/F(N)$. Assume that a sufficient number of samples is taken, so that $F(N)$ accurately represents the final value of $a(t)$. Now consider lines 60 and 70 of the DO loop. First we set a variable T2 = I. In line 70 $F(I)$ is compared with 0.9. If $F(I) \geq 0.9$, the operation of the DO loop is terminated. Thus, the final value of T2 equals the last used value of I. This corresponds to $F(I) \geq 0.9$. This is not exact since $F(I)$ can be greater than 0.9, but it is assumed that the samples are close enough together in line so that no significant error results if we use I or I–1 in the calculations.

The DO loop of lines 100–130 repeats this procedure, but now $F(I) \leq 0.1$ is the criterion used and T1 is set equal to I. We do not have to normalize here since all of the F array that we need was normalized in the first DO loop. Finally, in line 150, TR = (T2 − T1) * DELTA is computed. Note that TR is returned to the main program through common storage.

Now consider Fig. 5–4 which lists the SUBROUTINE OVER that computes the overshoot of the unit step response. Again, common storage is used to enter the F array and the number of terms N, and to return OS, the overshoot, to the

```
00010    C        SUBRØUTINE TØ CØMPUTE ØVERSHØØT
00020             SUBRØUTINE ØVER
00030             CØMMØN F(64),N,ØS
00040             NN=N-1
00050             ØS=F(N)
00060             DØ 300 I=1,NN
00070             IF(F(I)-ØS.GT.0.)ØS=F(I)
00080    300      CØNTINUE
00090             ØS=(ØS-F(N))/F(N)
00100             RETURN
00110             END
```

(a)

FIG. 5–3(a)

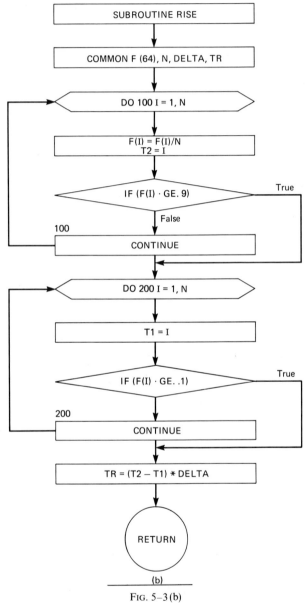

FIG. 5–3 (b)

(a) SUBROUTINE RISE that is used to compute the 10–90 percent rise
time of the unit step response; (b) flow chart for this SUBROUTINE

main program. First OS is set equal to the final value F(N). Now consider the DO
loop of lines 60–80. In line 70 F(I) is compared with OS. Then, in this line, the value
of OS is set equal to F(I) if F(I) > OS. Thus, as the DO loop is cycled, OS is set
equal to the largest member of the F array. In line 90 the value of OS is computed
using Eq. 5–49. This value is then returned to the main program. It may seem that
the programs of Figs. 5–3 and 5–4 are of limited use, since, once the data are in
array form, the rise time and overshoot can easily be determined. However, the data
can be entered into the arrays by means of a FUNCTION. This eliminates the need
for much calculation.

```
00010   C         SUBRØUTINE TØ CØMPUTE 10-90 PERCENT RISE TIME
00020             SUBRØUTINE RISE
00030             CØMMØN F(64),N,DELTA,TR
00040             DØ 100 I=1,N
00050             F(I)=F(I)/F(N)
00060             T2=I
00070             IF(F(I).GE..9)GØ TØ 150
00080   100       CØNTINUE
00090   150       CØNTINUE
00100             DØ 200 I=1,N
00110             T1=I
00120             IF(F(I).GE..1)GØ TØ 250
00130   200       CØNTINUE
00140   250       CØNTINUE
00150             TR=(T2-T1)*DELTA
00160             RETURN
00170             END
```

FIG. 5–4
SUBROUTINE OVER that is used to compute the overshoot of the unit step response

Sometimes it is desirable to have a simple relation which gives the 10 to 90
percent rise time in closed form. Unfortunately, this cannot be obtained. However,
there are some definitions for delay and rise times that have been proposed by
Elmore [2]. These are often fairly accurate for systems whose unit step responses
increase monotonically. The definitions are:

$$\tau_d = \frac{\int_0^\infty t h(t)\, dt}{\int_0^\infty h(t)\, dt} \tag{5-50}$$

$$\tau_r = \left[ \frac{2\pi \int_0^\infty (t - \tau_d)^2 h(t)\, dt}{\int_0^\infty h(t)\, dt} \right]^{1/2} \tag{5-51}$$

where $h(t)$ is the unit impulse response. The relations cannot be derived. They can be very inaccurate if $h(t) \leqq 0$ for any time. If $h(t) \geqq 0$ for all $t$ then, in many typical circumstances, Eqs. 5–50 and 5–51 yield fairly accurate results. However, they are not exact.

Some interesting results can be obtained if we relate the speed of response (i.e., the rise time of the unit step response) to the pole zero diagram. Let us consider a specific example first. Suppose the unit step response is given by

$$a(t) = u(t)(1 - e^{-t/T})$$

As $T$ becomes smaller the speed of response increases. For instance, it takes $T$ seconds for the response to reach 0.632 of its final value. Taking the Laplace transform of this unit step response, yields

$$a(t) \leftrightarrow \frac{1/T}{s[s + (1/T)]} = \frac{T}{sT(sT + 1)}$$

The poles of this function occur at $s = 0$ and $s = 1/T$. As $T$ decreases, the diagram *becomes larger*, i.e., the pole moves out from the origin. In general, if we have a function of time $f(t)$ whose Laplace transform is given by

$$f(t) \leftrightarrow F_1(sT)$$

Similar results will be obtained. As $T$ is decreased, the general shape of $f(t)$ will be unchanged, but its speed of response will be increased. Alternatively, we can state that a plot of $f(t)$ versus $t/T$ will be unchanged. This can be rigorously shown by applying Eq. 3–78. Decreasing $T$ will cause the entire pole-zero diagram to *increase in size*. However, the relative pole-zero locations will be unchanged. Thus, as the poles and zeros are moved further from the origin, the speed of response increases.

## 5-3. RELATION BETWEEN THE UNIT IMPULSE RESPONSE, THE UNIT STEP RESPONSE, AND THE RESPONSE TO ARBITRARY SIGNALS

In general, for a linear, time-invariant system, if we know the unit impulse response, the unit step response, or the response to an arbitrary signal whose Fourier spectrum is not zero for any value of $\omega$, we can find the response to any arbitrary signal. For example, Eq. 5–21b can be used to obtain the transfer function $H(j\omega)$ if the Fourier spectrum of the input and output signals are known.

We have also expressed $g(t)$, the response of a system to an input signal $f(t)$, in terms of the impulse response $h(t)$. This relation is (see Eq. 5–17)

$$g(t) = \int_{-\infty}^{\infty} f(y) h(t - y) \, dy \qquad (5-52a)$$

This is the convolution of $f(t)$ and $h(t)$. Thus, it can also be written as (see Eq. 2–204)

$$g(t) = \int_{-\infty}^{\infty} h(y)f(t-y)\,dy \tag{5-52b}$$

Now let us express the system response in terms of the unit step response. Substituting Eq. 5–48 into Eq. 5–52b, yields

$$g(t) = \int_{-\infty}^{\infty} \frac{da(y)}{dy} f(t-y)\,dy \tag{5-53}$$

Applying Eq. 2–21 yields

$$g(t) = -\int_{-\infty}^{\infty} a(y)\frac{df(t-y)}{dy}\,dy \tag{5-54a}$$

Similarly, we can work with Eq. 5–52a and obtain

$$g(t) = \int_{-\infty}^{\infty} a(t-y)\frac{df(y)}{dy}\,dy \tag{5-54b}$$

In Eqs. 5–53 and 5–54 we have assumed that the derivatives exist, on a distribution basis. If they do not, then these equations do not exist.

As an example, suppose that the system is such that its unit impulse response is given by

$$h(t) = e^{-at}u(t)$$

Then, using Eq. 5–47, the unit step response is given by

$$a(t) = \int_{0}^{t} e^{-at}\,dt = \frac{1-e^{-at}}{a}u(t)$$

Now, let us find the response of the system to a signal:

$$f(t) = u(t)\,t$$

Substituting in Eq. 5–52b, we have

$$g(t) = \int_{0}^{t} e^{-ay}(t-y)\,dy, \qquad t \geq 0$$

Integration yields

$$g(t) = \left[ -\frac{1}{a^2} + \frac{t}{a} + \frac{e^{-at}}{a^2} \right]u(t)$$

Similarly, using Eq. 5–54a, we have

$$g(t) = -\int_{0}^{t} \frac{1-e^{-ay}}{a}\frac{d}{dy}(t-y)\,dy, \qquad t \geq 0$$

$$= \int_{0}^{t} \frac{1-e^{-ay}}{a}\,dy$$

Integrating, we obtain

$$g(t) = \left[ -\frac{1}{a^2} + \frac{t}{a} + \frac{e^{-at}}{a^2} \right] u(t)$$

If $f(t)$ is discontinuous, its derivative must be evaluated on a distribution basis (see Eq. 2–33). Suppose $f(t)$ is 0 for $t < 0$, continuous for $t > 0$, but has a jump discontinuity at $t = 0$, then,

$$\frac{df(t)}{dt} = f(0+)\delta(t) + \frac{df(t)}{dt}, \qquad t > 0 \tag{5–55}$$

Substituting in Eq. 5–54b, yields

$$g(t) = f(0+)a(t) + \int_{0+}^{\infty} a(t-y)\frac{df(y)}{dy}\,dy \tag{5–56}$$

## 5-4. CAUSAL SYSTEMS

Consider a system such as that shown in Fig. 5–1 whose input is $f(t)$ and whose output is $g(t)$. Let us assume that

$$f(t) = 0, \qquad t < t_1 \tag{5–57}$$

If the system is such that, for all $f(t)$ satisfying Eq. 5–57, $g(t)$ is such that

$$g(t) = 0, \qquad t < t_1 \tag{5–58}$$

then the system is said to be *causal*. That is, a causal system is one whose output does not precede the input. Most systems encountered are of this type. Any linear system which is passive; that is, one which has no energy sources within it and does not violate the law of conservation of energy will be causal.

If a system is such that its response to a unit impulse applied at $t = 0$ is 0 for for $t < 0$, then the system is causal. Let us demonstrate this: Assume that

$$h(t) = 0, \qquad t < 0 \tag{5–59}$$

From Eq. 5–71, we have

$$g(t) = \int_{-\infty}^{\infty} f(y)h(t-y)\,dy$$

but

$$f(y) = 0, \qquad y < 0 \tag{5–60a}$$

and

$$h(t-y) = 0 \qquad t < y \tag{5–60b}$$

Thus, we can rewrite the integral as

$$g(t) = \int_{t_1}^{t} f(y)h(t-y)\,dy \tag{5–61}$$

If $t < t_1$, then in the integrand $y < t_1$ over the entire range of integration. Then, substituting Eq. 5–60a, we have

$$g(t) = 0, \qquad t < t_1 \tag{5–62}$$

Thus, we have shown that a system will be causal if its impulse response is 0 for $t < 0$.

Another fact can be ascertained from Eq. 5–61. Consider $g(t_2), t_2 > t_1$. Then, only those values of $f(t)$ for $t_1 \leqq t \leqq t_2$ are used in the integral. Thus, the response of a causal system at time $t$ only depends upon the input signal for times equal to or less than $t$. That is, the response of a causal system at any time $t$ does not depend upon any future value of the input signal.

## 5-5. HILBERT TRANSFORMS

If a system is causal, then certain restrictions are imposed upon its transfer function. For instance, if $f(t) = 0, t < 0$, then the real and imaginary parts of its Fourier transform are related by Eqs. 2–165 and 2–166. If $f(t)$ is replaced by $h(t)$, the impulse response of the system, then its Fourier transform is the transfer function of the network. Thus, the real and imaginary parts of the transfer function are related by Eqs. 2–165 and 2–166. These relations are often difficult to use. In this section we shall derive a different set of relations between the real and imaginary parts of the transfer function of a causal system. These relations are called *Hilbert transforms*.

The reader may ask why study these transforms. Often a circuit designer specifies the real (imaginary) part of an impedance function or a transfer function. Knowledge of the imaginary (real) part of the function would aid in its synthesis. A form of Hilbert transform called the *Bode relation*, discussed in the next section, is widely used in the design of feedback systems.

We shall begin our discussion of the Hilbert transform with

$$h(t) \leftrightarrow H(j\omega) \qquad (5\text{–}63)$$

where $h(t)$ is the impulse response of the system and $H(j\omega)$, its Fourier transform, is the transfer function of the system.

In general, any function can be expressed as a sum of an even function and an odd function. Thus,

$$h(t) = h_e(t) + h_0(t) \qquad (5\text{–}64)$$

where

$$h_e(t) = h_e(-t) \qquad (5\text{–}65a)$$

$$h_0(t) = -h_0(-t) \qquad 5\text{–}65b)$$

First assume that $h(t)$ contains no impulses at $t = 0$. Thus, there is no problem about expressing its value at $t = 0$. Then, using the relation

$$h(-t) = h_e(t) - h_0(t)$$

and Eq. (5–64), we obtain

$$h_e(t) = \frac{h(t) + h(-t)}{2} \tag{5-66a}$$

$$h_o(t) = \frac{h(t) - h(-t)}{2} \tag{5-66b}$$

We assume that the system is causal, hence,

$$h(t) = 0, \qquad t < 0 \tag{5-67}$$

Therefore, we equivalently have

$$h(-t) = 0, \qquad t > 0 \tag{5-68}$$

Then, substituting Eqs. 5–67 and 5–68 into Eqs. 5–66, we obtain

$$h_e(t) = \begin{cases} h_o(t), & t > 0 & (5\text{-}69a) \\ -h_o(t), & t < 0 & (5\text{-}69b) \end{cases}$$

We can write this in a form which is valid for all $t$ using the sgn $t$ function (see Eq. 2–150)

$$h_e(t) = h_0(t)\, \text{sgn}\, t \tag{5-70a}$$

or
$$h_o(t) = h_e(t)\, \text{sgn}\, t \tag{5-70b}$$

where
$$\text{sgn}\, t = \begin{cases} 1, & t > 0 \\ 0, & t = 0 \\ -1, & t < 0 \end{cases} \tag{5-71}$$

We shall need the Fourier transform of sgn $t$ in the derivation. Substituting sgn $t$ in Eq. 2–61, we have

$$\text{sgn}\, t \leftrightarrow \int_{-\infty}^{\infty} (\text{sgn}\, t)\, e^{-j\omega t}\, dt = -2j \int_{0}^{\infty} \sin \omega t \, dt$$

Then, using Eq. 2–46, we obtain

$$\text{sgn}\, t \leftrightarrow 2/j\omega \tag{5-72}$$

Now we proceed with the development of the Hilbert transform. Let us write $H(j\omega)$ in terms of its real and imaginary parts

$$H(j\omega) = R(\omega) + jX(\omega) \tag{5-73}$$

In Eqs. 2–153 through 2–156, we have shown that the Fourier transform of an even function was real, while that of an odd function was a pure imaginary, hence,

$$h_e(t) \leftrightarrow R(\omega) \tag{5-74a}$$

$$h_o(t) \leftrightarrow jX(\omega) \tag{5-74b}$$

Substituting Eqs. 5–70 yields

$$h_o(t) \operatorname{sgn} t \leftrightarrow R(\omega) \tag{5–75a}$$
$$h_e(t) \operatorname{sgn} t \leftrightarrow jX(\omega) \tag{5–75b}$$

Now applying the frequency convolution theorem (see Eq.2–215) to Eq. 5–75, we have

$$R(\omega) = \frac{1}{2\pi} jX(\omega) * \frac{2}{j\omega} \tag{5–76a}$$

$$jX(\omega) = \frac{1}{2\pi} R(\omega) * \frac{2}{j\omega} \tag{5–76b}$$

Applying Eq. 2–216 to Eq. 5–76b, we obtain

$$jX(\omega) = \frac{1}{2\pi} \int_{-\infty}^{\infty} \frac{2R(y)}{j(\omega - y)} dy$$

Rearranging, we have

$$X(\omega) = -\frac{1}{\pi} \int_{-\infty}^{\infty} \frac{R(y)}{\omega - y} dy \tag{5–77}$$

(We have assumed that $h(t)$ contained no impulses at $t = 0$.) Then, $R(\omega)$ will not contain any constant terms and Eq. 5–77 exists. Note that if no impulse or its derivatives are present, then $|H(j\omega)|$, which is the ratio of two polynomials in $j\omega$, will fall off as $\omega$ approaches $\infty$.

Now apply Eq. 2–216 to Eq. 5–76a. This yields

$$R(\omega) = \frac{1}{\pi} \int_{-\infty}^{\infty} \frac{X(y)}{\omega - y} dy \tag{5–78}$$

Now assume that $h(t)$ does contain an impulse at $t = 0$. Let us write this as $\delta(t) K_0 + h_1(t)$. The inclusion of $\delta(t)$ adds a real constant to $H(j\omega)$ (see Table 2-1). The contribution of $h_1(t)$ to $H(j\omega)$ at $\omega = \infty$ is zero; then,

$$K_0 = \lim_{\omega \to \infty} H(j\omega) = R(\infty)$$

Thus, if we allow $h(t)$ to have an impulse at the origin, then $X(\omega)$ will be unaffected, while $R(\omega)$ will have an additional constant. Then, Eq. 5–78 becomes

$$R(\omega) = R(\infty) + \frac{1}{\pi} \int_{-\infty}^{\infty} \frac{X(y)}{\omega - y} dy \tag{5–79}$$

Equations 5–77 and 5–79 constitute the *Hilbert transforms*, we shall repeat them here:

$$X(\omega) = -\frac{1}{\pi} \int_{-\infty}^{\infty} \frac{R(y)}{\omega - y} dy \tag{5–80a}$$

$$R(\omega) = R(\infty) + \frac{1}{\pi}\int_{-\infty}^{\infty}\frac{X(y)}{\omega - y}\,dy \qquad (5\text{--}80b)$$

Note that when $y = \omega$, the integrand becomes infinite. In such cases, we work with the Cauchy principal value of the integral (see Eq. 2–148), then,

$$\int_{-\infty}^{\infty}\frac{F(y)}{\omega - y}\,dy = \lim_{\varepsilon\to 0}\left[\int_{-\infty}^{\omega-\varepsilon}\frac{F(y)}{\omega - y}\,dy + \int_{\omega+\varepsilon}^{\infty}\frac{F(y)}{\omega - y}\,dy\right] \qquad (5\text{--}81)$$

We have based the derivation of the Hilbert transform on the fact that the system is causal. The converse is also true; that is, given a transfer function whose real and imaginary parts satisfy Eqs. 5–80, then the system will be causal. This can be demonstrated in the following way. Remove the impulse at $t = 0$ from $h(t)$. Then, Eqs. 5–80b become Eq. 5–78. Using Eqs. 5–78 and 5–80a, the frequency convolution theorem, the fact that the transform of an even function is a real function and that of an odd function is a pure imaginary function, and Eqs. 5–70, we obtain

$$h_e(t) = -h_o(t), \qquad t < 0$$

Hence,

$$h(t) = 0, \qquad t < 0$$

**Alternative Derivation of Hilbert Transform.** We now discuss an alternative derivation of the Hilbert transforms, which is based upon the Laplace transform. Suppose that $H_L(s)$ is the transfer function of a causal system in transformed form. Assume that $H_L(s)$ is analytic on the $j\omega$ axis and in the right-half plane, then (see Section 3-4)

$$H_L(j\omega) = H(j\omega) \qquad (5\text{--}82)$$

Thus, the Fourier transform can be obtained from the Laplace transform by replacing $s$ by $j\omega$ and vice versa. Thus, we can write

$$H_L(s) = H(s)$$

Now we form the function

$$\frac{H(s)}{s - j\omega_0}$$

and integrate it over the closed contour shown in Fig. 5–5. Since $H(s)$ is analytic in the right-half plane and on the $j\omega$ axis, the only singularity of $H(s)/(s - j\omega_0)$ in the right-half plane or on the $j\omega$ axis is a simple pole at $s = j\omega_0$. Thus, $H(s)/(s - j\omega_0)$ is analytic on and within the contour of the figure, hence,

$$\oint \frac{H(s)}{s - j\omega_0}\,ds = 0 \qquad (5\text{--}83)$$

Now let us consider the integral over various portions of the contour. Consider

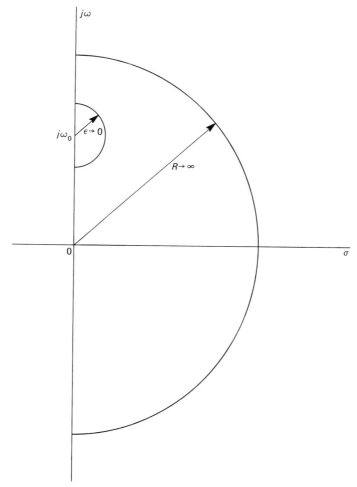

FIG. 5–5
Contour of integration used to derive Hilbert transforms

the infinite semicircle first. Let us assume that, as $s$ approaches infinity, $\boldsymbol{H}(s)$ approaches either zero or a real positive constant.

$$\lim_{s \to \infty} \boldsymbol{H}(s) = R(\infty) \qquad (5\text{--}84)$$

Then, in the infinite semicircle, let

$$s = Re^{j\theta} \qquad (5\text{--}85)$$

Hence,

$$\lim_{R \to \infty} \int_R \frac{H(s)}{s - j\omega_0} \, ds = R(\infty) \lim_{R \to \infty} \int_{\pi/2}^{-\pi/2} \frac{jRe^{j\theta} d\theta}{Re^{j\theta} - j\omega_0} = -j\pi R(\infty) \quad (5\text{–}86)$$

Now let us consider the integral over the semicircle of radius $\varepsilon$, note that

$$\lim_{\varepsilon \to 0} H(s) = H(j\omega_0) = R(\omega_0) + jX(\omega_0) \quad (5\text{–}87)$$

That is, as $\varepsilon$ approaches zero, the entire semicircle approaches the point $s = j\omega_0$. On the semicircle let

$$s - j\omega_0 = \varepsilon e^{j\theta} \quad (5\text{–}88)$$

Then,

$$\lim_{\varepsilon \to 0} \int_\varepsilon \frac{H(s)}{s - j\omega_0} \, ds = [R(\omega_0) + jX(\omega_0)] \lim_{\varepsilon \to 0} \int_{-\pi/2}^{\pi/2} \frac{j\varepsilon e^{j\theta}}{\varepsilon e^{j\theta}} \, d\theta$$

$$= j\pi [R(\omega_0) + jX(\omega_0)] \quad (5\text{–}89)$$

The remaining part of the integral is that on the $j\omega$ axis, this is given by

$$\lim_{\varepsilon \to 0} \left[ j \int_{-\infty}^{\omega_0 - \varepsilon} \frac{H(j\omega)}{j\omega - j\omega_0} \, d\omega + j \int_{\omega_0 + \varepsilon}^{\infty} \frac{H(j\omega)}{j\omega - j\omega_0} \, d\omega \right]$$

Since we use the Cauchy principal value of the integral, we can write this integral as

$$\int_{-\infty}^{\infty} \frac{H(j\omega)}{\omega - \omega_0} \, d\omega = \int_{-\infty}^{\infty} \frac{R(\omega) + jX(\omega)}{\omega - \omega_0} \, d\omega \quad (5\text{–}90)$$

Substituting Eqs. 5–86, 5–89, and 5–90 into Eq. 5–83, we obtain

$$-j\pi R(\infty) + j\pi [R(\omega_0) + jX(\omega_0)] + \int_{-\infty}^{\infty} \frac{R(\omega) + jX(\omega)}{\omega - \omega_0} \, d\omega = 0 \quad (5\text{–}91)$$

Replace $\omega$ by $y$ and then replace $\omega_0$ by $\omega$ in Eq. 5–91. Then, equating reals and imaginaries yields

$$X(\omega) = -\frac{1}{\pi} \int_{-\infty}^{\infty} \frac{R(y)}{\omega - y} \, dy \quad (5\text{–}92)$$

$$R(\omega) = R(\infty) + \int_{-\infty}^{\infty} \frac{X(y)}{\omega - y} \, dy \quad (5\text{–}93)$$

Hence, we have derived the Hilbert transforms in an alternative way.

Now consider an example of the procedure: given

$$R(\omega) = \frac{1}{1 + \omega^2}$$

let us find $X(\omega)$ such that the system is causal. From Eq. 5–92, we have

$$X(\omega) = -\frac{1}{\pi}\lim_{\varepsilon \to 0}\left[\int_{-\infty}^{\omega-\varepsilon}\frac{1}{(1+y^2)(\omega-y)}\,dy + \int_{\omega+\varepsilon}^{\infty}\frac{1}{(1+y^2)(\omega-y)}\,dy\right]$$

Integrating we obtain

$$X(\omega) = -\frac{1}{\pi}\lim_{\varepsilon \to 0}\left\{\left[\frac{1}{2}\ln\frac{(1+y)^2}{(\omega-y)^2} + \omega\tan^{-1}y\right]_{-\infty}^{\omega-\varepsilon}\right.$$

$$\left. + \left[\frac{1}{2}\ln\frac{(1+y)^2}{(\omega-y)^2} + \omega\tan^{-1}y\right]_{\omega+\varepsilon}^{\infty}\right\}\cdot\frac{1}{\omega^2+1}$$

$$= \frac{-1}{\pi(\omega^2+1)}\left\{\pi\omega + \lim_{\varepsilon \to 0}\frac{1}{2}\ln\left[\frac{[1+(\omega-\varepsilon)^2]}{\varepsilon^2}\cdot\frac{\varepsilon^2}{[1+(\omega+\varepsilon)^2]}\right]\right\}$$

Then, since $\ln 1 = 0$, we have

$$X(\omega) = \frac{-\omega}{\omega^2+1}$$

**Analytical Signals.** All practical functions of time are real; however, as a mathematical exercise, we could consider that functions of time were complex. Many of the relations that we have derived would still be valid. For instance, most of the relations of the Fourier transform are valid if $f(t)$ is complex. Let us regard $f(t)$ as the real part of a complex function of time:

$$f(t) = \text{Re}\,f_c(t)$$

We could specify the imaginary part of $f_c(t)$ arbitrarily. However, sometimes $\text{Im}\,f_c(t)$ is specified so that it is the Hilbert transform of $f(t)$. In this case, $f_c(t)$ is called an *analytical signal*. These signals have some use in the discussion of such things as modulated carriers and bandwidth; however, they are so specialized that we shall not consider them further.

## 5-6. BODE RELATIONS—MINIMUM PHASE-SHIFT FUNCTIONS

In the last section, we derived relations between the real and imaginary parts of the transfer function of a causal system. Now we derive similar relations between the magnitude and phase angle of the transfer function of a causal system. However, in order to obtain these relations, we must impose one additional restriction upon $H(s)$: we assume (as for the Hilbert transforms) that $H(s)$ is analytic in the right-half plane and on the $j\omega$ axis. We must also assume that $H(s)$ has no zeros in the right-half plane. Such a function is called a *minimum phase-shift function*. Let us digress for a moment and discuss these functions.

**Minimum Phase-Shift Functions.** Consider a function of the form

$$H_1(s) = \frac{(s - s_0)(s - s_0^*)}{(s + s_0)(s + s_0^*)} \tag{5-94}$$

where the asterisk indicates a complex conjugate. A pole-zero plot of this function is shown in Fig. 5-6a. The poles and zeros are symmetric about the $j\omega$ axis. Now let us evaluate $H_1(j\omega)$.

$$H_1(j\omega) = \frac{(j\omega - s_0)(j\omega - s_0^*)}{(j\omega + s_0)(j\omega + s_0^*)} = 1e^{j\phi(\omega)} \tag{5-95}$$

The magnitude $|H_1(j\omega)|$ is unity. Thus, if a transfer function is multiplied by $H_1(j\omega)$; its amplitude will be unchanged, while its phase angle will be altered. Since the transfer function $H_1(j\omega)$ passes all frequencies with equal amplitude it is called an *all pass function*. Another pole-zero plot of an all pass function is shown in Fig. 5-6b. In general, any transfer function whose pole-zero plot has the type of mirror symmetry about the $j\omega$ axis, illustrated in Fig. 5-6, will be an all pass function.

Consider a general transfer function which has a pair of zeros in the right-half plane

$$H_2(s) = H_a(s)(s - s_0)(s - s_0^*) \tag{5-96}$$

We can write this as

$$H_2(s) = H_a(s)(s + s_0)(s + s_0^*)\frac{(s - s_0)(s - s_0^*)}{(s + s_0)(s + s_0^*)} \tag{5-97}$$

Let

$$H_b(s) = H_a(s)(s + s_0)(s + s_0^*) \tag{5-98}$$

Then, $H_b(s)$ has no zeros in the right-half plane. Note that $(s + s_0)$ and $(s + s_0^*)$ introduce zeros into the left-half plane. Thus, we have expressed $H_2(s)$ as a minimum phase function and an all pass function. In effect, we have removed the *excess phase* from the function $H_b(s)$.

**Bode Relations.** Now let us develop the relations between amplitude and phase. Assume that $H(s)$, the Laplace transform of the transfer function, is analytic in the right-half plane and on the $j\omega$ axis. Also we assume that $H(s)$ has no zeros in the right-half plane or on the $j\omega$ axis. We shall now use logarithms; we write

$$H(j\omega) = e^{-\alpha(\omega) - j\phi(\omega)} \tag{5-99}$$

or, equivalently

$$\ln H(j\omega) = -\alpha(\omega) - j\phi(\omega) \tag{5-100}$$

Now form the function

$$\frac{\ln H(s)}{s^2 + \omega_0^2}$$

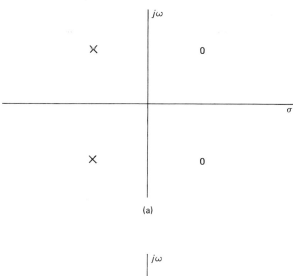

(a)

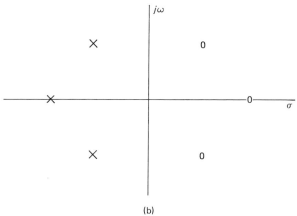

(b)

FIG. 5-6
Pole-zero plots for typical all pass functions

and integrate it over the contour shown in Fig. 5–7. The integrand is analytic on and within the path. Thus, we have

$$\oint \frac{\ln H(s)}{s^2 + \omega_0^2} \, ds = 0 \tag{5–101}$$

Now let us discuss each part of the contour of Fig. 5–7. First, consider the infinite semicircle and assume that $H(s)$ approaches $Ks^n$ as $s$ approaches $\infty$. Then,

$$\lim_{s \to \infty} \ln H(s) = n \ln s + \ln K \tag{5–102}$$

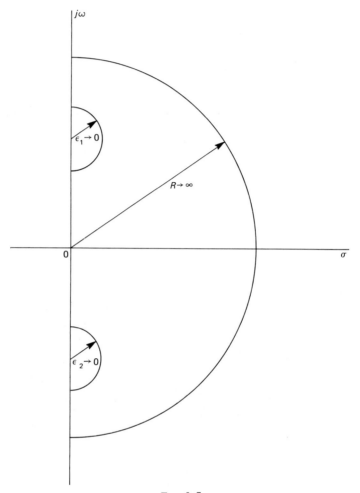

FIG. 5–7
Path of integration for Eq. 5–101

where $K$ is a constant. In the integrand, we let

$$s = Re^{j\theta}$$

so that

$$\lim_{s \to \infty} \ln H(s) = n \ln R + jn\theta + \ln K$$

Then,

$$\lim_{R \to \infty} \left| \int_R \frac{\ln H(s)}{s^2 + \omega_0^2} \, ds \right| \leq \lim_{R \to \infty} \left| (n \ln R + jn\theta + \ln K) \int_{\pi/2}^{-\pi/2} \frac{jRe^{j\theta} d\theta}{R^2 e^{j2\theta}} \right| = 0 \quad (5\text{–}103)$$

Note $\lim\limits_{R \to \infty} (\ln R)/R = 0$. Thus, the factor of $s^2$ in the denominator is necessary to make this integral become zero. This is one reason why the simple denominator of Eq. 5–83 is not used here. Now consider the integral over the path of radius $\varepsilon_1$. We define

$$s - j\omega_0 = \varepsilon_1 e^{j\theta} \qquad (5\text{-}104)$$

Noting that

$$s^2 + \omega_0^2 = (s + j\omega_0)(s - j\omega_0)$$

we obtain

$$\lim_{\varepsilon_1 \to 0} \int_{\varepsilon_1} \frac{\ln H(s)}{s^2 + \omega_0^2} \, ds = \frac{\ln H(j\omega_0)}{2j\omega_0} \int_{-\pi/2}^{\pi/2} \frac{je^{j\theta}}{e^{j\theta}} \, d\theta = \frac{\pi}{2\omega_0} \ln H(j\omega_0) \qquad (5\text{-}105)$$

Similarly, we have

$$\lim_{\varepsilon_2 \to 0} \int_{\varepsilon_2} \frac{\ln H(s)}{s^2 + \omega_0^2} \, ds = -\frac{\pi}{2\omega_0} \ln H(-j\omega_0) \qquad (5\text{-}106)$$

The integral along the $j\omega$ axis is given by

$$\lim_{\substack{\varepsilon_2 \to 0 \\ \varepsilon_1 \to 0}} j \left[ \int_{-\infty}^{-\omega_0 - \varepsilon_2} \frac{\ln H(j\omega)}{\omega_0^2 - \omega^2} \, d\omega + \int_{-\omega_0 + \varepsilon_2}^{\omega_0 - \varepsilon_1} \frac{\ln H(j\omega)}{\omega_0^2 - \omega^2} \, d\omega \right.$$

$$\left. + \int_{\omega_0 + \varepsilon_1}^{\infty} \frac{\ln H(j\omega)}{\omega_0^2 - \omega^2} \, d\omega \right] = j \int_{-\infty}^{\infty} \frac{\ln H(j\omega)}{\omega_0^2 - \omega^2} \, d\omega \qquad (5\text{-}107)$$

where the integral defined in Eq. 5–107 is the Cauchy principal value. Then, substituting Eqs. 5–103, 5–105, 5–106, and 5–107 into Eq. 5–101, we obtain

$$\frac{\pi}{2\omega_0} \ln H(j\omega_0) - \frac{\pi}{2\omega_0} \ln H(-j\omega_0) + j \int_{-\infty}^{\infty} \frac{\ln H(j\omega)}{\omega_0^2 - \omega^2} \, d\omega = 0 \qquad (5\text{-}108)$$

Substituting Eq. 5–100 and noting that

$$\alpha(-\omega) = \alpha(\omega) \qquad (5\text{-}109a)$$

$$\phi(-\omega) = -\phi(\omega) \qquad (5\text{-}109b)$$

we have

$$-j \int_{-\infty}^{\infty} \frac{\alpha(\omega)}{\omega_0^2 - \omega^2} \, d\omega + \int_{-\infty}^{\infty} \frac{\phi(\omega)}{\omega_0^2 - \omega^2} \, d\omega$$

$$+ \frac{\pi}{2\omega_0} [-\alpha(\omega_0) - j\phi(\omega_0) + \alpha(\omega_0) - j\phi(\omega_0)] = 0 \qquad (5\text{-}110)$$

The second integral is zero since $\phi(\omega)$ is an odd function of $\omega$. Thus, we have

$$\phi(\omega_0) = -\frac{\omega_0}{\pi} \int_{-\infty}^{\infty} \frac{\alpha(\omega)}{\omega_0^2 - \omega^2} \, d\omega \tag{5-111}$$

The real part of Eq. 5–110 is zero. Thus, this equation did not supply us with $\alpha(\omega)$ in terms of $\phi(\omega)$. To obtain this, we must form a new function and integrate over a new contour. The function is

$$\frac{\ln H(s)}{s(s^2 + \omega_0)^2}$$

and the contour is shown in Fig. 5–8. Since the integrand is analytic within and on the contour of integration

$$\oint \frac{\ln H(s)}{s(s^2 + \omega_0^2)} \, ds = 0 \tag{5-112}$$

Then, proceeding as before, we have

$$\lim_{R \to \infty} \int_R \frac{\ln H(s)}{s(s^2 + \omega_0^2)} \, ds = 0 \tag{5-113}$$

$$\lim_{\varepsilon_1 \to 0} \int_{\varepsilon_1} \frac{\ln H(s)}{s(s^2 + \omega_0^2)} \, ds = \frac{\pi}{2j\omega_0^2} \ln H(j\omega_0) \tag{5-114a}$$

$$\lim_{\varepsilon_2 \to 0} \int_{\varepsilon_2} \frac{\ln H(s)}{s(s^2 + \omega_0^2)} \, ds = \frac{\pi}{2j\omega_0^2} \ln H(-j\omega_0) \tag{5-114b}$$

$$\lim_{\varepsilon_0 \to 0} \int_{\varepsilon_0} \frac{\ln H(s)}{s(s^2 + \omega_0^2)} \, ds = \frac{j\pi \ln H(j0)}{\omega_0^2} \tag{5-115}$$

Proceeding as before, substituting in Eq. 5–112 and equating reals and imaginaries, we obtain

$$\alpha(\omega_0) = \alpha(0) + \frac{\omega_0^2}{\pi} \int_{-\infty}^{\infty} \frac{\phi(\omega)}{\omega(\omega_0^2 - \omega^2)} \, d\omega \tag{5-116}$$

Equations 5–111 and 5–116 relate the amplitude and phase of all pass transfer functions. These are called the *Bode relations*. We now rewrite them in slightly different form.

$$\phi(\omega) = \frac{\omega}{\pi} \int_{-\infty}^{\infty} \frac{\alpha(y)}{y^2 - \omega^2} \, dy \tag{5-117}$$

$$\alpha(\omega) = \alpha(0) - \frac{\omega^2}{\pi} \int_{-\infty}^{\infty} \frac{\phi(y)}{y(y^2 - \omega^2)} \, dy \tag{5-118}$$

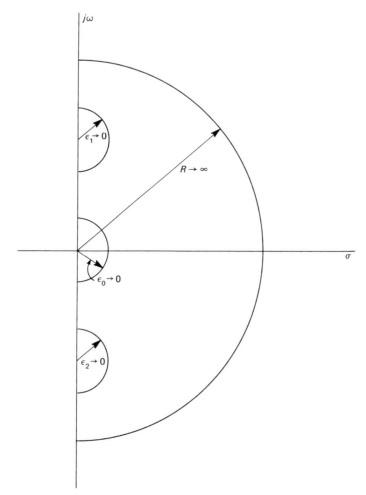

FIG. 5–8
The path of integration for Eq. 5–112

Consider an example of this procedure. Suppose

$$|H(j\omega)| = \begin{cases} 1, & \omega_c \leq \omega \leq 0 \\ d, & |\omega| > \omega_c \end{cases} \qquad (5\text{–}119)$$

Now, let us find the phase shift of the minimum phase network that corresponds to this. Substituting in Eq. 5–117 and noting that $\ln 1 = 0$, we have

$$\phi(\omega) = -\frac{2\omega}{\pi} \int_{\omega_c}^{\infty} \frac{\ln d}{y^2 - \omega^2} \, dy \qquad (5\text{–}120)$$

If $\omega < \omega_c$, the integrand does not become infinite. Then, we obtain

$$\phi(\omega) = -\frac{2\omega}{\pi} \ln d \left[ \frac{1}{2\omega} \ln \left( \frac{y - \omega}{\omega + y} \right) \right]_{\omega_c}^{\infty}$$

Substituting the limits, we have

$$\phi(\omega) = \frac{-\ln d}{\pi} \ln \frac{\omega_c + \omega}{\omega_c - \omega} \tag{5-121a}$$

If $\omega > \omega_c$, the integrand becomes infinite and we must use the Cauchy principal value:

$$\phi(\omega) = -\frac{2\omega \ln d}{\pi} \lim_{\varepsilon \to 0} \left[ \int_{\omega_c}^{\omega - \varepsilon} \frac{dy}{y^2 - \omega^2} + \int_{\omega + \varepsilon}^{\infty} \frac{dy}{y^2 - \omega^2} \right]$$

Integration yields,

$$\phi(\omega) = -\frac{2\omega \ln d}{\pi} \lim_{\varepsilon \to 0} \left[ \frac{-1}{2\omega} \left| \frac{\omega - \omega_c}{\omega + \omega_c} \right| + \ln \left( \frac{\varepsilon}{2\omega - \varepsilon} \cdot \frac{2\omega + \varepsilon}{\varepsilon} \right) \right]$$

Since $\ln 1 = 0$, we have

$$\phi(\omega) = -\frac{\ln d}{\pi} \ln \left| \frac{\omega + \omega_c}{\omega - \omega_c} \right|, \qquad \omega > \omega_c \tag{5-121b}$$

Comparing Eqs. 5-121a and 5-121b, we obtain

$$\phi(\omega) = \frac{\ln d}{\pi} \ln \left| \frac{\omega - \omega_c}{\omega + \omega_c} \right| \tag{5-122}$$

## 5-7. RESISTANCE INTEGRAL THEOREM

Suppose we are working with a causal system whose transfer function is analytic on the $j\omega$ axis and in the right-half plane. Assume, as in the case in some common systems, that $H(s)$, the Laplace transform of the transfer functions, falls off as $1/s$, as $s$ approaches infinity, that is,

$$\lim_{s \to \infty} H(s) = \frac{K}{s} \tag{5-123}$$

Since $H(s)$ is analytic on the $j\omega$ axis and in the right-half plane, the Fourier transform can be obtained from the Laplace transform simply be replacing $s$ by $j\omega$. Then, from Eq. 2-62, we have

$$h(t) = \frac{1}{2\pi} \int_{-\infty}^{\infty} H(j\omega) e^{j\omega t} d\omega$$

Now let t = 0, then,

$$h(0) = \frac{1}{2\pi} \int_{-\infty}^{\infty} H(j\omega) \, d\omega \qquad (5\text{--}124)$$

We now express

$$H(j\omega) = R(\omega) + jX(\omega) \qquad (5\text{--}125)$$

Since $h(t)$ is assumed to be a real function of time, then $R(\omega)$ is even and $X(\omega)$ is odd (see Eqs. 2–155 and 2–156), hence,

$$h(0) = \frac{1}{\pi} \int_{0}^{\infty} R(\omega) \, d\omega \qquad (5\text{--}126)$$

From Eq. (2–79), we have

$$h(0) = \tfrac{1}{2}[h(0-) + h(0+)] \qquad (5\text{--}127)$$

However, $h(0-) = 0$, since we are working with a causal system. Then, substituting Eq. 5–127 into Eq. 5–126, we have

$$h(0+) = \frac{2}{\pi} \int_{0}^{\infty} R(\omega) \, d\omega \qquad (5\text{--}128)$$

Now apply the initial value theorem to $H(s)$. $h(t)$ contains neither an impulse nor its derivatives (see Eq. 5–123 and Section 3–9). Then, we have, (see Eq. 3–108),

$$h(0+) = \lim_{s \to \infty} sH(s)$$

Substitution of Eq. 5–123 yields

$$h(0+) = K \qquad (5\text{--}129)$$

Substituting Eq. 5–129 into Eq. 5–128, we obtain

$$\int_{0}^{\infty} R(\omega) \, d\omega = \frac{K\pi}{2} \qquad (5\text{--}130)$$

Equation 5–121 indicates that if $H(s)$ falls off as $1/s$, for large $s$, then the area under the curve of $R(\omega)$ is fixed. This is called the *resistance integral theorem.*

The terminals of any practical electric network will be shunted by a capacitor C. Thus, the driving point impedance will fall off as $1/sC$. To apply Eq. 5–130 to such networks, we set $K = 1/C$, then Eq. 5–130 becomes

$$\int_{0}^{\infty} R(\omega) \, d\omega = \frac{\pi}{2C} \qquad (5\text{--}131)$$

where now $R(\omega)$ is the resistive component of the driving point impedance. This accounts for the name of the theorem.

## 5-8. LOW PASS SYSTEMS

Many systems have transfer functions that are relatively constant for low values of $\omega$. However, their magnitudes fall off as $\omega$ is increased. Audio and video amplifiers fall into this category. The responses of many mechanical systems also are of this type. Usually, the Fourier spectrums of the outputs of such systems fall off at high frequencies and can, in general, be ignored at sufficiently high frequencies. These systems are called *low pass systems*, since they only effectively pass the low frequency component of signals. Often, for frequencies greater than some value $\omega_c$, the Fourier spectrum of signals applied to these systems has a magnitude which is small and falls off rapidly with frequency. Often, the frequencies above $\omega_c$ can be ignored without introducing a significant error (see Section 5-11).

**Ideal Low Pass Filters.** Consider a system which has the following characteristics. If $f(t)$, the input to the system, has a Fourier spectrum $F(j\omega)$, which is such that

$$F(j\omega) = 0, \qquad |\omega| > \omega_c \tag{5-132}$$

Then, the output $g(t)$ will be equal to $f(t)$ multiplied by a constant or be equal to $f(t)$ multiplied by a constant and delayed in time, that is,

$$g(t) = Kf(t - T) \tag{5-133}$$

In this case, the output waveform will be the same shape as the input waveform and the system is said to be *distortionless*.

Consider the transfer function $H(j\omega)$ of such a distortionless system. If $T = 0$, then $g(t) = Kf(t)$ then (see Eq. 5-21),

$$H(j\omega) = K, \qquad -\omega_c \leqq \omega \leqq \omega_c \tag{5-134}$$

Let us see how $H(j\omega)$ is modified if the system delays the signal. Using the time shift theorem (see Eq. 2-171), we have,

$$H(j\omega) = Ke^{-j\omega T} \tag{5-135}$$

Thus, the magnitude of $H(j\omega)$ is constant and its phase angle varies linearly with time if the system is distortionless.

We often desire a network which will pass, without distortion, signals whose Fourier spectrum is 0 for $|\omega| > \omega_c$. That is the signal is characterized by Eq. 5-132. In addition these systems reject all frequency components for which $|\omega| > \omega_c$. Such a system is a *filter*. It removes unwanted frequency components which might interfere with the desired signal. Thus, the transfer function of such a filter is

$$H(j\omega) = \begin{cases} e^{-j\omega T}, & -\omega_c \leqq \omega \leqq \omega_c \\ 0, & \omega > \omega_c \end{cases} \tag{5-136}$$

where, for convenience, we have set $|H(j\omega)| = 1$ for $-\omega_c \leqq \omega \leqq \omega_c$. This transfer function represents an *ideal low pass filter*. It is illustrated in Fig. 5-9.

Let us determine the impulse response of the ideal low pass filter. Applying Eq. 2-62 and noting that $\delta(t) \rightarrow 1$, we have

$$h(t) = \frac{1}{2\pi} \int_{-\omega_c}^{\omega_c} e^{j\omega(t-T)} \, d\omega$$

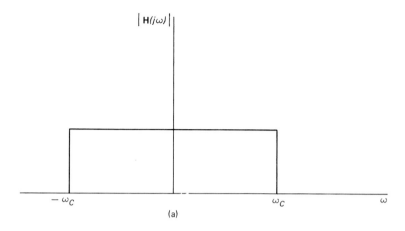

(a)

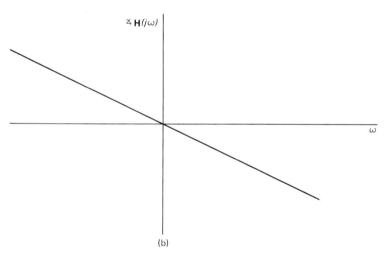

(b)

Fig. 5-9

Transfer functions of ideal low pass filters; (a) magnitude; (b) phase

Applying Euler's relation and eliminating the odd integrand, we obtain

$$h(t) = \frac{1}{\pi} \int_0^{\omega_c} \cos \omega(t - T)\, d\omega$$

Then,

$$h(t) = \frac{1}{\pi} \frac{\sin \omega_c(t - T)}{t - T} \qquad (5\text{--}137)$$

This is of the form (sin x)/x. Note that $h(t)$ is *not* zero for $t < 0$. Thus, the ideal low pass filter is *not* causal system. In general, it cannot be built. In Sections 5-5 and

5-6, we discussed that in causal systems the real and imaginary parts of the transfer function and the magnitude and phase of the transfer function were related. Here, we specified them independently. Thus, we really should not expect that the system should be causal. In the example of Section 5-6 (see Eq. 5–119), we considered a transfer function whose amplitude was

$$|H(j\omega)| = \begin{cases} 1, & -\omega_c \leq \omega \leq \omega_c \\ d, & |\omega| > \omega_c \end{cases} \tag{5–138a}$$

If we make $d$ arbitrarily small, this amplitude approaches that of the ideal low pass filter. The phase angle for a causal minimum phase-shift network is given in Eq. 5–122, it is

$$\phi(\omega) = \frac{\ln d}{\pi} \ln \left| \frac{\omega - \omega_c}{\omega + \omega_c} \right| \tag{5–138b}$$

which is considerably different from the linear phase shift we have considered.

**Linear Phase-Shift Networks.**   Now we shall adopt a different viewpoint. Assume that $H(j\omega)$ has a phase shift that varies linearly with frequency and let us see what characteristics $|H(j\omega)|$ must have if the system is to be causal. The derivation follows one given by the author [3].

In general, for a linear phase-shift system,

$$H(j\omega) = |H(j\omega)| e^{-j\omega T} \tag{5–139}$$

Then, the impulse response is

$$h(t) = \frac{1}{2\pi} \int_{-\infty}^{\infty} |H(j\omega)| e^{j\omega(t-T)} d\omega$$

However, $|H(j\omega)|$ is an even function of $\omega$. Hence, [if $H(j0)$ is bounded]

$$h(t) = \frac{1}{\pi} \int_0^{\infty} |H(j\omega)| \cos \omega(t - T) \, d\omega \tag{5–140}$$

Then,

$$h(t + T) = \frac{1}{\pi} \int_0^{\infty} |H(j\omega)| \cos \omega t \, d\omega \tag{5–141}$$

Then, since $\cos x$ is an even function of time, $h(t + T)$ is an even function of time for a linear phase system.

In a causal system, $h(t) = 0$ for $t < 0$. Using this and the evenness of $h(t + T)$, we obtain

$$h(t + T) = 0; \quad t < -T, \quad t > T \tag{5–142}$$

Note that Eq. 5–142 applies for a causal linear phase system.

The transfer function of a system is the Fourier transform of its impulse response. Then, in a causal linear phase system of phase shift $-jT\omega$, we have

$$H(j\omega) = \int_0^{2T} h(t)\, e^{-j\omega t}\, dt \qquad (5\text{--}143)$$

The upper limit of integration becomes $2T$ because of Eq. 5–142. Let $x = t - T$. Then, Eq. 5–143 becomes

$$H(j\omega) = \int_{-T}^{T} h(x + T)\, e^{-j\omega x}\, e^{-j\omega T}\, dx \qquad (5\text{--}144)$$

Then, since $h(x + T)$ is even and $e^{j\omega T}$ is a constant as far as the integration is concerned, we have

$$H(j\omega) = |H(j\omega)|\, e^{-j\omega T} = e^{-j\omega T} \int_{-T}^{T} h(x + T)\cos \omega x\, dx \qquad (5\text{--}145)$$

The integral is real, hence,

$$|H(j\omega)| = 2 \int_0^{T} h(x + T)\cos \omega x\, dx$$

Let us write $2h(x + T) = w(x)$; then,

$$|H(j\omega)||H(j\omega)| = \int_0^{T} w(x)\cos \omega x\, dx \qquad (5\text{--}146)$$

Consider the significance of Eq. 5–146. This equation shows that if a linear phase system of phase shift $-\omega T$ is to be causal, then the magnitude of the transfer function must be expressible as a function which has a bandlimited Fourier spectrum. (In this case, this is not a function of time.) Then, the discussions of Section 2-13, 2-14, and 2-17 are applicable. For instance, from Shannon's sampling theorem (see Section 2-17), we have that $|H(j\omega)|$ can only be specified at a set of points $\pi/T$ radians apart.

Note that $|H(j\omega)|$ as given by Eq. 5–146 may become negative. This can be considered to be a shift of $\pi$ radians in the phase angle of $H(j\omega)$. Thus, the phase shift may be linear plus or minus steps of $\pi$ radians.

In general, Eq. 5–146 indicates that we can come arbitrarily close to any desired $|H(j\omega)|$, if we make $T$ sufficiently large. However, this means that the time delay of the system is increased. Then, the output signal may have to be greatly delayed if certain $|H(j\omega)|$ are desired.

## 5-9. BAND PASS SYSTEMS—EQUIVALENT LOW PASS SYSTEMS

Very often, especially in communication systems, filters are built which are designed to pass a relatively narrow band of frequencies and to reject others. For instance, such filters are used to select a single radio or television signal and reject

all others. Let us study the response of these filters. We shall make some simplifying
approximations which are often justified in practice when the pass band bandwidth is
very much less than the center frequency of the pass band.

A typical transfer function of a band pass system is illustrated in Fig. 5–10.
All transfer functions of systems whose responses are real will have a transfer func-
tion $H(j\omega)$ such that $|H(j\omega)|$ is even and $\sphericalangle H(j\omega)$ is odd (see Section 2-6). That
is $H(j\omega) = H^*(-j\omega)$. Band pass systems often are designed to pass a narrow range

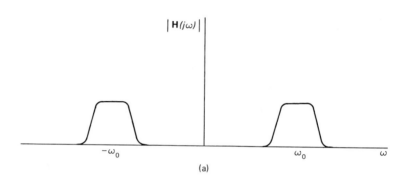

(a)

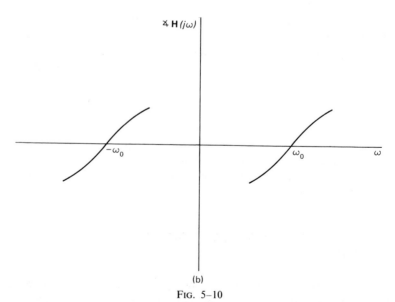

(b)

FIG. 5–10

Transfer function of a system having arithmetic symmetry about $\omega = \omega_0$,
(a) magnitude; (b) phase

of frequencies about some frequency $\omega_0$. In such cases, $H(j\omega)$ is often such that it can be approximately assumed to exhibit arithmetic symmetry about $\omega_0$ (see Fig. 5–10). We shall now express this mathematically. Let us write

$$H(j\omega) = H_+(j\omega) + H_-(j\omega) \tag{5–147}$$

with

$$H_+(j\omega) = 0, \qquad \omega < 0 \tag{5–148a}$$
$$H_-(j\omega) = 0, \qquad \omega > 0 \tag{5–148b}$$

where $H_+(j\omega)$ represents $H(j\omega)$ for positive $\omega$ and $H_-(j\omega)$ represents $H(j\omega)$ for negative $\omega$. Assume that these are symmetric about $\omega_0$ and $-\omega_0$, respectively; then

$$H_+(j\omega_0 + j\omega) = H_+^*(j\omega_0 - j\omega) \tag{5–149a}$$
$$H_-(-j\omega_0 - j\omega) = H_-^*(-j\omega_0 + j\omega) \tag{5–149b}$$

Equations 5–148 and 5–149 imply that $H_+(j\omega) = 0,\ \omega > 2\omega_0$. This is not the case in practice. However, in most practical (narrow) band pass systems, $|H(j\omega)|$ is so small and falls off so rapidly for $\omega > 2\omega_0$ that very little error is introduced by using this assumption.

Now let us obtain the impulse response of the system.

$$h(t) = \frac{1}{2\pi} \int_{-2\omega_0}^{0} H_-(j\omega)\, e^{j\omega t} d\omega + \frac{1}{2\pi} \int_{0}^{2\omega_0} H_+(j\omega)\, e^{j\omega t} d\omega \tag{5–150}$$

Since $H(j\omega) = H^*(-j\omega)$ in any system with a real time response, then $H_-(j\omega)$ and $H_+(j\omega)$ will be conjugates. Thus, the integrals of Eq. 5–150, when evaluated, will be conjugates of each other. The sum of two conjugates is twice the real part of one, hence,

$$h(t) = \frac{1}{\pi} \operatorname{Re} \int_{0}^{2\omega_0} H_+(j\omega)\, e^{j\omega t} d\omega \tag{5–151}$$

Let

$$y = \omega - \omega_0 \tag{5–152}$$

Thus, Eq. 5–151 becomes

$$h(t) = \frac{1}{\pi} \operatorname{Re} e^{j\omega_0 t} \int_{-\omega_0}^{\omega_0} H_+(jy + j\omega_0)\, e^{jyt} dy \tag{5–153}$$

Now let us define a new transfer function

$$H_{lo}(j\omega) = H_+(j\omega + j\omega_0) \tag{5–154}$$

where $H_{lo}(j\omega)$ represents $H_+(j\omega)$ which has been shifted in frequency by $\omega_0$ radians. For the $H(j\omega)$ of Fig. 5–10, $H_{lo}(j\omega)$ will be as shown in Fig. 5–11. Then, $H_{lo}(j\omega)$ has the form of a low pass function. It is called the *equivalent low pass transfer function* or the transfer function of the *equivalent low pass system*. Substituting Eq. 5–154 into Eq. 5–153, we obtain

$$h(t) = \frac{1}{\pi} \operatorname{Re} e^{j\omega_0 t} \int_{-\omega_0}^{\omega_0} H_{lo}(j\omega)\, e^{j\omega t} d\omega \tag{5–155}$$

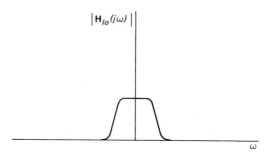

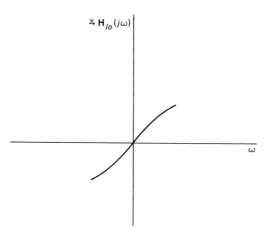

FIG. 5–11
Equivalent low pass transfer function for the transfer
function of Fig. 5–10

Now, let us define

$$h_{lo}(t) = \frac{1}{2\pi} \int_{-\omega_0}^{\omega_0} H_{lo}(j\omega) e^{j\omega t} d\omega \qquad (5\text{–}156)$$

Note that

$$H_{lo}(j\omega) = 0 \quad \text{for} \quad |\omega| > \omega_0 \qquad (5\text{–}157)$$

since $H_+(j\omega) = 0$ for $\omega > 2\omega_0$ or $\omega < 0$. Thus, $h_{lo}(t)$ represents the impulse response of the equivalent low pass system. Note that $h_{lo}(t)$ will be a real function of time because $H_{lo}(j\omega) = H_{lo}^*(-j\omega)$. This is due to the symmetry assumed in $H_+(j\omega)$. Substituting Eq. 5–156 into Eq. 5–155 and taking the real part, we have

$$h(t) = 2h_{lo}(t) \cos \omega_0 t \qquad (5\text{–}158)$$

Thus, the impulse response of the band pass system is an amplitude-modulated wave. The envelope of modulation is twice the impulse response of the equivalent low pass system. Thus, we need only compute $h_{lo}(t)$ to obtain the impulse response. This often reduces the amount of work required in obtaining the impulse response of a band pass system.

Very often, when we deal with band pass systems; we are interested in their response to an amplitude-modulated signal. That is, we wish to determine the response to an input $f(t)$ which is given by

$$f(t) = f_{lo}(t) \cos \omega_0 t \qquad (5\text{–}159)$$

Assume as before that the transfer function has arithmetic symmetry about $\omega = \omega_0$ and determine $g(t)$, the output of the system. (Note that the envelope of modulation of the input signal is $f_{lo}(t)$.)

Let us obtain the Fourier transform of $f(t)$. If

$$f_{lo}(t) \leftrightarrow F_{lo}(j\omega) \qquad (5\text{–}160)$$

then, from Eq. 2–180, we have

$$f(t) \leftrightarrow \frac{F_{lo}(j\omega - j\omega_0) + F_{lo}(j\omega + j\omega_0)}{2} \qquad (5\text{–}161)$$

We shall now make an approximation which shall be used later,

$$F_{lo}(j\omega) = 0, \qquad |\omega| > \omega_0 \qquad (5\text{–}162)$$

For most amplitude-modulated signals, $F_{lo}(j\omega)$ is usually so very small and falls off sufficiently fast for $|\omega| > \omega_0$, so this approximation is justified in practice, thus,

$$F_{lo}(j\omega - j\omega_0) = 0, \qquad \omega > 2\omega_0 \quad \text{or} \quad \omega < 0$$

$$\qquad (5\text{–}163)$$

$$F_{lo}(j\omega + j\omega_0) = 0, \qquad \omega > 0 \quad \text{or} \quad \omega < -2\omega_0$$

The Fourier transform of $g(t)$, the systems output, is $F(j\omega) H(j\omega)$. Substituting Eqs. 5–161 and 5–147 and noting Eqs. 5–148 and 5–163, we obtain

$$G(j\omega) = \tfrac{1}{2} \left[ F_{lo}(j\omega - j\omega_0) H_+(j\omega) + F_{lo}(j\omega + j\omega_0) H_-(j\omega) \right] \qquad (5\text{–}164)$$

Each term in the first expression is zero for negative $\omega$, while each term in the second is zero for positive $\omega$. Note that $F_{lo}(j\omega - j\omega_0)$ exhibits arithmetic symmetry about $\omega = \omega_0$, while $F_{lo}(j\omega + j\omega_0)$ exhibits arithmetic symmetry about $\omega = -\omega_0$. Then, taking the inverse Fourier transform and proceeding as in Eq. 5–151, we have

$$g(t) = \frac{1}{2\pi} \, \text{Re} \int_0^{2\omega_0} F_{lo}(j\omega - j\omega_0) H_+(j\omega) e^{j\omega t} d\omega \qquad (5\text{–}165)$$

Let

$$y = \omega - \omega_0$$

Then,

$$g(t) = \frac{1}{2\pi} \operatorname{Re} e^{j\omega_0 t} \int_{-\omega_0}^{\omega_0} F_{lo}(jy) H_+(jy + j\omega_0) e^{jyt} dy \qquad (5\text{-}166)$$

Substituting Eq. 5–154 yields

$$g(t) = \frac{1}{2\pi} \operatorname{Re} e^{j\omega_0 t} \int_{-\omega_0}^{\omega_0} F_{lo}(j\omega) H_{lo}(j\omega) e^{j\omega t} d\omega \qquad (5\text{-}167)$$

where we have replaced $y$ by $\omega$ as the variable of integration. Now let us define

$$g_{1o}(t) = \frac{1}{2\pi} \int_{-\omega_0}^{\omega_0} F_{lo}(j\omega) H_{lo}(j\omega) e^{j\omega t} d\omega \qquad (5\text{-}168)$$

As in the case of Eq. 5–156, this must be a real function of time. Substituting Eq. 5–168 into Eq. 5–167 and taking the real part, we have

$$g(t) = g_{lo}(t) \cos \omega_0 t \qquad (5\text{-}169)$$

Consider the physical significance of this expression. Equation 5–169 represents an amplitude-modulated wave. The envelope of modulation is $g_{lo}(t)$. From Eq. 5–168 we ascertain that $g_{lo}(t)$ represents the response of a low pass system whose transfer function is $H_{lo}(j\omega)$ to a signal $f_{lo}(t)$, whose Fourier spectrum is $F_{lo}(j\omega)$ (see Eq. 5–160). Thus, the response of a band pass filter with arithmetic symmetry to an amplitude-modulated signal is an amplitude-modulated signal. The envelope of modulation of the output is equal to the response of the equivalent low pass system (whose transfer function is $H_{lo}(j\omega)$) to an input which is equal to the envelope of modulation of the input.

The results of this section were derived using an arithmetic symmetry assumption. This is usually a very satisfactory approximation. If there is any question of the accuracy of the approximation, the results should be checked using the complete transfer function and transforms. Usually if $\omega_0$ is very much greater than the bandwidth of $f_{lo}(t)$, the results will be accurate.

## 5-10. BOUNDS ON SYSTEM RESPONSE

At times, we wish to obtain information about the response of a system without having to evaluate the transient response. In this section we shall determine some restrictions [4] on the transient response which can be readily determined. We shall also determine some restrictions on $F(j\omega)$.

**Bounds on Overshoot.** Let us restrict the overshoot of the unit step response of various classes of systems. If $a(t)$ is the unit step response, the overshoot is given by (see Eq. 5–49)

$$O_s = \frac{a(t)_{max} - a(\infty)}{a(\infty)} \qquad (5\text{-}170)$$

Assume that the systems which we deal with are causal. Therefore, we can use Eq. 2–164 to express the impulse response, hence,

$$h(t) = \frac{2}{\pi} \int_0^\infty R(\omega) \cos \omega t \, d\omega \qquad (5\text{–}171)$$

where $R(\omega)$ is the real part of the system's transfer function. Now, from Eq. 5–47, we can obtain the unit step response $a(t)$ from the unit impulse response

$$a(t) = \int_0^t h(y) \, dy \qquad (5\text{–}172)$$

Note that the lower limit of Eq. 5–47 is $-\infty$. We have changed it to zero here since $h(t) = 0$ for $t < 0$, i.e., the system is causal. Substituting Eq. 5–171 into Eq. 5–172 and assuming that $R(\omega)$ is such that the order of integration can be interchanged, we have

$$a(t) = \frac{2}{\pi} \int_0^\infty R(\omega) \int_0^t \cos \omega y \, dy \, d\omega$$

Integrating, we obtain

$$a(t) = \frac{2}{\pi} \int_0^\infty \frac{R(\omega) \sin \omega t}{\omega} \, d\omega \qquad (5\text{–}173)$$

(We shall use Eqs. 5–171 and 5–173 to obtain the results we desire.)

Let us impose general conditions on $R(\omega)$ and see how they affect the overshoot of the unit step response. Assume that

$$R(\omega) \geq 0 \qquad (5\text{–}174\text{a})$$

$$\frac{dR(\omega)}{d\omega} \leq 0 \qquad (5\text{–}174\text{b})$$

$$\frac{d^2 R(\omega)}{d\omega^2} \geq 0 \qquad (5\text{–}174\text{c})$$

Thus, $R(\omega)$ is never negative and monotonically decreases as $\omega$ increases (its derivative is nonpositive) and its rate of fall off monotonically decreases (the second derivative is nonnegative, while $dR(\omega)/d\omega \leq 0$).

The impulse response is given by Eq. 5–171. Integrating this equation by parts yields

$$h(t) = \frac{2}{\pi} \left[ \frac{R(\omega) \sin \omega t}{t} \right]_0^\infty - \frac{2}{\pi t} \int_0^\infty \frac{dR(\omega)}{d\omega} \sin \omega t \, d\omega \qquad (5\text{–}175)$$

Since $R(\omega) \geq 0$ and monotonically decreases, $R(\infty) = 0$. Thus, the bracketed expression is 0 for $t > 0$, hence,

$$h(t) = -\frac{2}{\pi t} \int_0^\infty \frac{dR(\omega)}{d\omega} \sin \omega t \, d\omega \qquad (5\text{–}176)$$

Note that $dR(\omega)/d\omega$ is negative and its magnitude is decreasing. (A negative quantity with a positive derivative has a decreasing magnitude.) Then, the integral of Eq. 5–176 is always positive. The discussion following Eq. 2–147 can be used to show this, thus,

$$h(t) \geq 0 \tag{5-177}$$

However, $h(t)$ is the derivative of $a(t)$ (see Eq. 5–48). Thus, $a(t)$ must be a monotonic increasing function of time. Hence, its maximum value must be $a(\infty)$. Therefore, $a(t)$ cannot overshoot. Thus, in any causal system, where the real part of its transfer function satisfies Eqs. 5–174, there will be no overshoot in the unit step response.

Now we relax the restrictions on $R(\omega)$ and see how this affects the overshoot. However, assume that the conditions of Eqs. 5–174a and 5–174b hold, but not that of Eq. 5–174c. Thus, we assume

$$R(\omega) \geq 0 \tag{5-178a}$$

$$\frac{dR(\omega)}{d\omega} \leq 0 \tag{5-178b}$$

We use Eq. 5–173 to express the unit step response. We break this equation into an infinite series of integrals as follows

$$a(t) = \frac{2}{\pi} \left[ \int_0^{\pi/t} R(\omega) \frac{\sin \omega t}{\omega} \, d\omega + \int_{\pi/t}^{3\pi/t} R(\omega) \frac{\sin \omega t}{\omega} \, d\omega + \ldots \right] \tag{5-179}$$

Note that the limits of integration are chosen so that each integrand contains one half cycle of $\sin \omega t$. The first integral consists of the area under the first positive loop of $\sin \omega t$ times $R(\omega)/\omega$ and the second integral consists of the area under the first negative loop of $\sin \omega t$ times $R(\omega)/\omega$. Note that $R(\omega)/\omega$ is positive and decreases monotonically with $\omega$. Then, using the arguments following Eq. 2–147, we determine the following. $a(t)$ is always positive and the first integral in the series of Eq. 5–179 is greater than the sum of all the integrals. Note that some of the integrals will be positive and others will be negative, hence,

$$a(t) < \frac{2}{\pi} \int_0^{\pi/t} R(\omega) \frac{\sin \omega t}{\omega} \, d\omega \tag{5-180}$$

From Eqs. 5–178, we have

$$R(\omega) \leq R(0) \tag{5-181}$$

Then, since $(\sin \omega t)/\omega \geq 0$ in the integrand of Eq. 5–180, we have

$$a(t) \leq \frac{2}{\pi} R(0) \int_0^{\pi/t} \frac{\sin \omega t}{\omega} \, d\omega \tag{5-182}$$

Now let $\omega t = x$, then, we have

$$a(t) < \frac{2}{\pi} R(0) \int_0^\pi \frac{\sin x}{x} dx \qquad (5\text{--}183)$$

but (see Eq. 2–88)

$$\int_0^\pi \frac{\sin x}{x} dx = Si(\pi) = 1.85194 \qquad (5\text{--}184)$$

Substituting Eq. 5–184 into Eq. 5–183, we obtain

$$a(t) \leqq \frac{2}{\pi} Si(\pi) R(0) = 1.179 R(0) \qquad (5\text{--}185)$$

We have bounded the maximum value of $a(t)$. Now let us determine the final value of $a(t)$ in terms of $R(0)$. From Eq. 5–172, we have

$$a(\infty) = \int_0^\infty h(y) dy \qquad (5\text{--}186)$$

Now take the Fourier transform of $h(t)$, this yields

$$H(j\omega) = \int_0^\infty h(t) e^{-j\omega t} dt$$

Let $\omega = 0$, then,

$$H(j0) = \int_0^\infty h(t) dt \qquad (5\text{--}187)$$

Comparing Eqs. 5–186 and 5–187, we have

$$a(\infty) = H(j0) \qquad (5\text{--}188)$$

Since the imaginary part of $H(j\omega)$ is an odd function of $\omega$, $H(j0)$ will be real, thus,

$$a(\infty) = R(0) \qquad (5\text{--}189)$$

Substituting Eqs. 5–185 and 5–189 into Eq. 5–170, we obtain

$$O_s \leqq \frac{2}{\pi} Si(\pi) - 1 = 0.179 \qquad (5\text{--}190)$$

Therefore, in a causal system, where the real part of the transfer function is positive and decreases monotonically, the overshoot of the unit step response cannot be greater than 0.179, or 17.9 percent of the final value.

**Bound on $F(j\omega)$.**   As another illustration of a bound, let us restrict the magnitude of $F(\omega)$, the Fourier transform of a given $f(t)$ [5]. Assume that $f(t)$ has the following properties.

$$\lim_{t \to \infty} f(t) = 0 \qquad (5\text{--}191a)$$

$$\lim_{t \to -\infty} f(t) = 0 \qquad\qquad (5\text{--}191\text{b})$$

We assume that the total variation of $f(t)$ for $-\infty \leq t \leq \infty$ is bounded; thus,

$$\overset{\infty}{\underset{-\infty}{V}}\,[f(t)] \leq N \qquad\qquad (5\text{--}192)$$

The total variation of a function of time is the sum of the magnitudes of all the differences of $f(t)$ between successive maxima and minima. Consider Fig. 5–12.

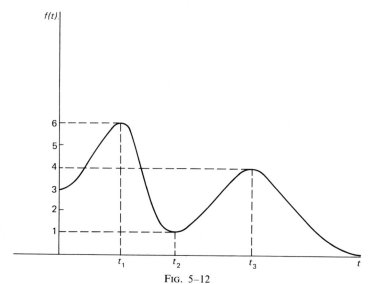

FIG. 5–12

Function of time used to illustrate the total variation of $f(t)$

There, $f(t) = 0$ for $t < 0$, varies for $t > 0$, and approaches 0 as $t$ approaches $\infty$. The maxima and minima of $f(t)$ occur at $t_1$, $t_2$, and $t_3$. The first variation is from 0 at $t = 0 -$ to 6 at $t = t_1$, i.e., $|f(0-) - f(t_1)|$. The next variation we have is $|f(t_1) - f(t_2)| = 6 - 1 = 5$. Then, we have $|f(t_2) - f(t_3)| = 4 - 1 = 3$. Finally, $|f(t_3) - f(t_\infty)| = 4$. Then, the total variation for the example is given by

$$\overset{\infty}{\underset{-\infty}{V}}\,[f(t)] = 6 + 5 + 3 + 4 = 18$$

Note that the endpoints, in this case $+\infty$ and $-\infty$, are included with the maxima and minima. In general, we have

$$\overset{t=t_{N+1}}{\underset{t=t_0}{V}}\,[f(t)] = |f(t_0) - f(t_1)| + |f(t_1) - f(t_2)|$$

$$+ |f(t_{N-1}) - f(t_N)| + |f(t_N) - f(t_{N+1})| \qquad (5\text{--}193)$$

where $f(t_i)$, $i = 1, 2, \ldots, N$ are the points of maxima and minima of $f(t)$, $f(t_0)$ and $f(t_{N+1})$ are the endpoints.

Now let us use the concept of a total variation to bound $F(j\omega)$. The Fourier transform of $f(t)$ is given by

$$F(j\omega) = \int_{-\infty}^{\infty} f(t) e^{-j\omega t} dt \qquad (5\text{--}194)$$

Integrating by parts and using Eq. 5–191, we obtain

$$F(j\omega) = \frac{1}{j\omega} \int_{-\infty}^{\infty} e^{-j\omega t} \frac{df(t)}{dt} dt \qquad (5\text{--}195)$$

Now break the integral up into a series of integrals in the following way

$$F(j\omega) = \frac{1}{j\omega} \sum_{i=0}^{K} \int_{t_i}^{t_{i+1}} e^{-j\omega t} \frac{df(t)}{dt} dt \qquad (5\text{--}196)$$

where $t_0 = -\infty$, $t_{K+1} = \infty$, and $t_{i+1} \geqq t_i$. Thus, Eq. 5–196 is equal to Eq. 5–195. The values of $t_i$ are chosen to be the values of $t$ where the maxima and minima of $f(t)$ occur. Thus, $df(t)/dt$ does not change sign for $t_{i+1} \leqq t \leqq t_i$; now

$$|F(j\omega)| < \frac{1}{\omega} \sum_{i=0}^{K} \left| \int_{t_i}^{t_{i+1}} e^{-j\omega t} \frac{df(t)}{dt} dt \right| \qquad (5\text{--}197)$$

In the range $t_i \leqq t \leqq t_{i+1}$, $df(t)/dt$ does not change sign. Also, $|e^{-j\omega t}| = 1$: hence,

$$\left| \int_{t_i}^{t_{i+1}} e^{-j\omega t} \frac{df(t)}{dt} dt \right| \leqq \left| \int_{t_i}^{t_{i+1}} \frac{df(t)}{dt} dt \right| \qquad (5\text{--}198)$$

Evaluating the right-hand integral, we obtain

$$\left| \int_{t_i}^{t_{i+1}} e^{-j\omega t} \frac{df(t)}{dt} dt \right| \leqq |f(t_{i+1}) - f(t_i)| = |f(t_i) - f(t_{i+1})| \qquad (5\text{--}199)$$

Substituting this into Eq. 5–197, we have

$$|F(j\omega)| < \frac{1}{\omega} \sum_{i=0}^{K} |f(t_i) - f(t_{i+1})| \qquad (5\text{--}200)$$

Since $t_i$, $i = 1, 2, \ldots K$ are the maxima and minima of $f(t)$, and $t_0 = 0$ and $t_{K+1} = \infty$, the summation of Eq. 5–200 is the total variation of $f(t)$ (see Eq. 5–193). Then, substituting Eq. 5–192, we have

$$|F(j\omega)| \leqq \frac{1}{\omega} \mathop{V}_{-\infty}^{\infty} [f(t)] = \frac{N}{\omega} \qquad (5\text{--}201)$$

Thus, we have obtained a readily evaluated bound on $|F(j\omega)|$. (A shorter derivation, based on the Stieltjes integral, is presented in [5].)

In the derivation, we have assumed that $f(t)$ is continuous so that $df(t)/dt$ exists. However, if $f(t)$ has jump discontinuities, we can use distribution theory and express the derivative in terms of $\delta(t)$. Thus, Eq. 5–201 is valid if $f(t)$ has jump discontinuities.

We can extend Eq. 5–201. For example, if we integrate Eq. 5–195 by parts a second time, we have

$$F(j\omega) = \frac{1}{\omega^2} \int_{-\infty}^{\infty} e^{-j\omega t} \frac{d^2f(t)}{dt^2} dt \qquad (5\text{–}202)$$

Now assume that the total variation of $df(t)/dt$ is bounded

$$\overset{\infty}{\underset{-\infty}{V}} \left[ \frac{df(t)}{dt} \right] \leqq N_1 \qquad (5\text{–}203)$$

Then, proceeding as in the derivation of Eq. 5–201, we obtain

$$|F(j\omega)| \leqq \frac{1}{\omega^2} \overset{\infty}{\underset{-\infty}{V}} \left[ \frac{df(t)}{dt} \right] \leqq \frac{N_1}{\omega^2} \qquad (5\text{–}204)$$

Here we must assume that $df(t)/dt$ is continuous or has jump discontinuities and that the $df(t)/dt = 0$ at $t = {}^{\pm}\infty$. In general, the results can be extended so that we have

$$|F(j\omega)| \leqq \frac{1}{\omega^{n+1}} \overset{\infty}{\underset{-\infty}{V}} \left[ \frac{d^nf(t)}{dt^n} \right] \qquad (5\text{–}205)$$

where all derivatives up the $n$th must be continuous. The $n$th derivative can have jump discontinuities.

## 5-11. EFFECTIVE BANDWIDTH OF A SIGNAL

Often when a signal is transmitted through a low pass system, we want the system output to be a constant times the input, with possibly some time delay (see Section 5-8). Thus, the transfer function of the system should be essentially constant with zero or linear phase shift for the bandwidth of the signal; that is for all frequencies contained in the Fourier transform of the signal. In theory, most signals encountered have infinite bandwidth. However, the contribution of those frequency components of $F(j\omega)$ for $\omega$ greater than some value, say $\omega_a$, is often so small that it can be neglected. In this case, we can say that $\omega_a$ is the effective bandwidth of the signal [5,6]. Thus, systems designed to pass these signals without distortion need only pass frequencies up to $\omega_a$.

The preceding statements provide some physical basis for the definition of an effective bandwidth. However, if the definition is to be useful, we must discuss it in mathematical terms. First we consider what it means when we say that the contribution of $F(j\omega)$ for $\omega > \omega_a$ is so small that it can be neglected. Suppose $f(t)$

has a Fourier transform $F(j\omega)$:

$$f(t) \leftrightarrow F(j\omega) \tag{5-206}$$

Now let us define a signal $f_a(t)$ with Fourier transform $F_a(j\omega)$, that is,

$$f_a(t) \leftrightarrow F_a(j\omega) \tag{5-207}$$

where $F_a(j\omega)$ is given by

$$F_a(j\omega) = \begin{cases} F(j\omega), & -\omega_a \leq \omega \leq \omega_a \\ 0, & |\omega| > \omega_a \end{cases} \tag{5-208}$$

Thus, $f_a(t)$ is a bandlimited approximation to $f(t)$. Now, we define an error

$$\varepsilon(t) = f(t) - f_a(t) \tag{5-209}$$

We must choose an error criterion which gives a single number based on $\varepsilon(t)$ (see Section 2-14). Let us call this number $\varepsilon$. Then, the effective bandwidth of $f(t)$ is the minimum value of $\omega_a$ which keeps $\varepsilon$ less than some specified value. That is, an error $\varepsilon$ is specified. Then, the effective bandwidth of $f(t)$ is the minimum $\omega_a$ that results in the actual error being less than or equal to $\varepsilon$.

It is, in general, tedious to find $\omega_a$. A value could be guessed at; $f_a(t)$ is then computed. This can be used to find $\varepsilon$. If it is too large (small), then a larger (smaller) value of $\omega_a$ must be tried. However, very easily applied bounds which have been developed by Giardina and Chirlian can be obtained [5, 6]. These bounds and the effective bandwidth vary with the error criterion used.

**Mean Square Error Criterion.**   We shall obtain a bound on $\omega_a$ based on a mean square error criterion. That is, we shall find an $\omega_a$ which will keep

$$\varepsilon_{MS} = \left\{ \int_{-\infty}^{\infty} [f(t) - f_a(t)]^2 \, dt \right\}^{1/2} \tag{5-210}$$

equal to or less than a specified value. We shall assume that $f(t)$ satisfies Eqs. 5–191 and 5–192, that is,

$$\lim_{t \to -\infty} f(t) = 0 \tag{5-211a}$$

$$\lim_{t \to \infty} f(t) = 0 \tag{5-211b}$$

$$\overset{\infty}{\underset{-\infty}{V}} \, [f(t)] < N \tag{5-211c}$$

and that $f(t)$ is continuous or has jump discontinuities. Note that Eq. 5–211c indicates that the total variation of $f(t)$ is bounded by $N$.

Applying Parseval's theorem (see Eq. 2–233) to Eq. 5–210 yields

$$\varepsilon_{MS}{}^2 = \frac{1}{2\pi} \int_{-\infty}^{\infty} |F(j\omega) - F_a(j\omega)|^2 \, d\omega \tag{5-212}$$

Substituting Eq. 5–208, we obtain

$$\varepsilon_{MS}{}^2 = \frac{1}{2\pi} \int_{-\infty}^{-\omega_a} |F(j\omega)|^2 \, d\omega + \frac{1}{2\pi} \int_{\omega_a}^{\infty} |F(j\omega)|^2 \, d\omega \qquad (5\text{–}213)$$

Thus,

$$\varepsilon_{MS}^2 = \frac{1}{\pi} \int_{\omega_a}^{\infty} |F(j\omega)|^2 \, d\omega \qquad (5\text{–}214)$$

Since Eqs. 5–211 are satisfied and $f(t)$ is continuous with possible jump discontinuities, Eq. 5–201 can be used. Substituting this equation into Eq. 5–214 yields

$$\varepsilon_{MS}^2 \leqq \frac{1}{\pi} \int_{-\omega_a}^{\infty} \frac{N^2}{\omega^2} \, d\omega \qquad (5\text{–}215)$$

Integrating, we obtain

$$\varepsilon_{MS}^2 \leqq N^2 / \pi\omega_a \qquad (5\text{–}216)$$

Now assume that $\varepsilon_{MS}$ is specified. Any value of $\omega_a$ that keeps $\varepsilon_{MS}$ less than the specified value will be a satisfactory one. The smallest value of $\omega_a$ which satisfies Eq. 5–216 is the one which satisfies it with an equals sign. Let us call this value $\omega_0$. Substituting into Eq. 5–216 and solving for $\omega_0$, we obtain

$$\omega_0 = N^2 / \pi\varepsilon_{MS}^2 \qquad (5\text{–}217)$$

Then, any value of

$$\omega_a > \omega_0 \qquad (5\text{–}218)$$

will keep $\varepsilon_{MS}$ less than its specified value. (Note that this is a bound. There *may* be values of $\omega_a$ smaller than $\omega_0$ which keep $\varepsilon_{MS}$ less than its specified value, however, *any* value of $\omega_a > \omega_0$ will keep $\varepsilon_{MS}$ equal to or less than its specified value.) Thus, $\omega_0$ given by Eq. 5–217 is a bound on the effective bandwidth of a signal based upon a mean square error requirement.

**Maximum Error Criterion.**   Now let us obtain a bound on $\omega_a$ based on a maximum error criterion. We shall define our criterion as

$$\varepsilon_{max} = |f(t) - f_a(t)|_{max} \qquad (5\text{–}219)$$

In this case, we shall impose different restrictions on $f(t)$. Assume that $f(t)$ is continuous and that, in addition to Eqs. 5–211a and 5–211b,

$$\lim_{t \to \infty} \frac{df(t)}{dt} = 0 \qquad (5\text{–}220a)$$

$$\lim_{t \to -\infty} \frac{df(t)}{dt} = 0 \qquad (5\text{–}220b)$$

and

$$\mathop{V}_{-\infty}^{\infty} \left[ \frac{df(t)}{dt} \right] \leqq N_1 \qquad (5\text{–}220c)$$

Also assume that $df(t)/dt$ is continuous or has jump discontinuities. (Thus, $f(t)$ is continuous.)

Then, expressing $f(t)$ and $f_a(t)$ as the inverse Fourier transforms of $F(j\omega)$ and $F_a(j\omega)$, respectively, we can write Eq. 5–219 in the following way:

$$\varepsilon_{max} = \left| \frac{1}{2\pi} \int_{-\infty}^{\infty} F(j\omega)\, e^{j\omega t} d\omega - \frac{1}{2\pi} \int_{-\omega_a}^{\omega_a} F_a(j\omega)\, e^{j\omega t} d\omega \right|_{max} \qquad (5\text{--}221)$$

Then, substituting Eq. 5–208 and manipulating, we obtain

$$\varepsilon_{max} = \left| \frac{1}{2\pi} \int_{-\infty}^{-\omega_a} F(j\omega)\, e^{j\omega t} d\omega + \frac{1}{2\pi} \int_{\omega_a}^{\infty} F(j\omega)\, e^{j\omega t} d\omega \right|_{max} \qquad (5\text{--}222)$$

Then, since $\left| e^{j\omega t} \right| = 1$ and $\left| F(j\omega) \right| = \left| F(-j\omega) \right|$,

$$\varepsilon_{max} \le \frac{1}{\pi} \int_{\omega_a}^{\infty} \left| F(j\omega) \right| d\omega \qquad (5\text{--}223)$$

The conditions imposed upon $f(t)$ guarantee that Eq. 5–204 is valid. Substituting this equation into Eq. 5–223 and integrating, we have

$$\varepsilon_{max} \le N_1/\pi\omega_a \qquad (5\text{--}224)$$

Then, proceeding as in the case of Eq. 5–218, we obtain

$$\omega_0 = \frac{N_1}{\varepsilon_{max}\pi} \qquad (5\text{--}225)$$

Thus, any value of $\omega_a$ such that

$$\omega_a > \omega_0 \qquad (5\text{--}226)$$

will guarantee that the error be less than $\varepsilon_{max}$.

These results for maximum error require that $f(t)$ be continuous. If it is discontinuous, then the bandlimited approximation will exhibit Gibbs phenomenon. Thus, in the neighborhood of the time when the discontinuity occurs, the maximum error will never be less than 8.95 percent of the jump (see Section 2-5). Note that the values of $\omega_0$ calculated in Eqs. 5–217 and 5–225 are different. This is because different error criteria were used. Usually, a maximum error criterion results in a larger bandwidth than does the mean square error criterion.

These results can be extended to the total variation of higher-order derivatives by using Eq. 5–205. This will be left to the reader.

## 5-12. THE RESPONSE OF MULTIPLE INPUT AND OUTPUT SYSTEMS

In this chapter have, thus far, we have been concerned with networks which have a single input and/or output. However, the theory can be extended to systems with multiple inputs and/or outputs.

Suppose the system has $k$ inputs and $n$ outputs and assume that we have

$$T\{f_m(t)\} = g_{im}(t); \qquad m = 1, 2, \ldots, k, \qquad i = 1, 2, \ldots, n \qquad (5\text{--}227)$$

in the linear system, a signal $f_m(t)$ applied at input $m$ produces an output $g_{im}(t)$ at output $i$. If the system is linear, we have

$$\sum_{m=1}^{K} T\{f_m(t)\} = \sum_{m=1}^{K} g_{im}(t), \qquad i = 1, 2, \ldots, n \qquad (5\text{--}228)$$

The response at any output to a set of inputs is the sum of the outputs due to each input alone. We assume that when one input acts alone, the others are replaced by zero signal, but all other conditions remain the same.

In an electric network, all voltage or current generators but the one in question are set equal to zero voltage or current. Hence, the generators are replaced by their internal impedances. The only "signal portion" of the generator is set equal to zero. Equation 5–228 can be considered to be a definition of linearity in a multiple input system.

Now let us define $h_{im}(t, T)$ as the response at output $i$ to a unit impulse applied at time $T$ to input $m$. Then, substituting Eq. 5–13 into Eq. 5–227 and then into Eq. 5–228, we have

$$g_i(t) = \sum_{m=1}^{K} T\{f_m(t)\} = \sum_{m=1}^{k} \int_{-\infty}^{\infty} f_m(y) h_{im}(t, y) \, dy, \qquad i = 1, 2, \ldots, n \qquad (5\text{--}229)$$

Thus, we have expressed the response to a sum of signals in terms of the sum of the responses to unit impulses applied at each input.

If the system is linear and time invariant, Eq. 5–229 becomes (see Eq. 5–17)

$$g_i(t) = \sum_{m=1}^{k} \int_{-\infty}^{\infty} f_m(y) h_{im}(t - y) \, dy, \qquad i = 1, 2, \ldots, n \qquad (5\text{--}230)$$

Interchanging the order of integration and summation, we have

$$g_i(t) = \int_{-\infty}^{\infty} \sum_{m=1}^{k} f_m(y) h_{im}(t - y) \, dy, \qquad i = 1, 2, \ldots, n \qquad (5\text{--}231)$$

We can obtain a similar result using transfer functions. For example, if

$$f_m(t) \leftrightarrow F_m(j\omega)$$
$$g_i(t) \leftrightarrow G_i(j\omega)$$

then, applying the time convolution theorem (see Eq. 2–209) to Eq. 5–231, we obtain

$$G_i(j\omega) = \sum_{m=1}^{K} F_m(j\omega) H_{im}(j\omega) \qquad (5\text{--}232)$$

where

$$h_{im}(t) \leftrightarrow H_{im}(j\omega) \qquad (5\text{--}233)$$

Then, $H_{im}(j\omega)$ is the *transfer function to output i from input m*.

If multiple input systems are analyzed using state variable procedures, then the results of Chapter 4 can be applied directly. That is, in that chapter, the state variable equations were formulated on the basis of multiple input and multiple output systems.

## PROBLEMS

**5-1.** The response of a linear, time-varying system to a delayed unit impulse input $\delta(t - T)$ is $e^{-(t-T)}u(t - T)$ if $T < 1$ and is $u(t - T)e^{-2(t-T)}$ if $T \geq 1$. What is the response to a signal $e^{-t}u(t)$?

**5-2.** The impulse response of a linear, time-invariant system is $e^{-t\sin 2t}u(t)$. What is the response to $\mu(t)\,te^{-t}$?

**5-3.** Repeat Problem 5-2 for a system whose impulse response is $u(t)$.

**5-4.** What is the transfer function of the system in Problem 5-2?

**5-5.** What is the response of the system of Problem 5-2 to a signal whose Fourier transform is

$$\frac{\pi}{2}[\delta(\omega - \omega_0) + \delta(\omega + \omega_0)] + \frac{j\omega}{\omega_0^2 - \omega^2}$$

Use Fourier transform techniques.

**5-6.** Repeat Problem 5-5 for the transfer function of Problem 5-3.

**5-7.** What is the response of the system of Problem 5-3 to a signal whose Laplace transform is

$$\frac{s}{(s^2 + \omega_0^2)}$$

Use Laplace transform techniques.

**5-8.** What is the sinusoidal steady-state transformed form of the transfer function of the system in Problem 5-2?

**5-9.** When an input of $e^{-t}u(t)$ is applied to a system, its output is $(e^{-2t}\sin t)u(t)$. What is the transfer function of the system?

**5-10.** Repeat Problem 5-9 for a system whose input is $e^{-t}u(t)$ and whose output is $[e^{-2(t-1)}\sin(t - 1)]u(t - 1)$.

**5-11.** Find the unit impulse response of the system of Problem 5-9.

**5-12.** Repeat Problem 5-11 for the system of Problem 5-10.

**5-13.** Find the unit step response for the system of Problem 5-9.

**5-14.** Repeat Problem 5-13 for the system of Problem 5-10.

**5-15.** Find the 10–90 percent rise time and overshoot of the unit step response of the network of Problem 5-9.

**5-16.** Repeat Problem 5-15 for the network of Problem 5-10.

**5-17.** Compare the results of Problems 5-15 and 5-16. Compare the use of systems with these transfer functions in digital systems.

**5-18.** Write a complete computer program which computes the 10–90 percent rise time and the overshoot of $a(t)$, the unit step response of a network. Assume that the data for $a(t)$ is to be enetered into an array by the user of the program.

**5-19.** Repeat Problem 5-18, but now assume that the data are to be entered from a FUNCTION.

**5-20.** Use the program of Problem 5-19 to compute the 10–90 percent rise time and the overshoot of

$$a(t) = (1 - e^{-3t}\cos 5t)u(t)$$

**5-21.** Repeat Problem 5-20 for

$$a(t) = (1 - e^{3t} \cos 5t + e^{-2t} \sin 3t) u(t)$$

**5-22.** Use the fast Fourier transform to obtain the unit impulse response of a network whose transfer function is $1/(1 + j10^{-2}\omega)(1 + j2 \times 10^{-2}\omega)$. Use 1024 samples with spacing $\Delta t = 0.01$ second.

**5-23.** Repeat Problem 5-22, but now obtain the response to $e^{-0.1t}$.

**5-24.** A network has a unit impulse response which is given by

$$h(t) = e^{-t}(\sin 2t) u(t)$$

Find $a(t)$ unit step response of the network. Then use $a(t)$ to find the response of the system to $f(t) = (1 - e^{-t}) u(t)$.

**5-25.** Repeat Problems 5-24 for

$$f(t) = e^{-t}u(t)$$

**5-26.** Prove that: if the unit step response of a system is 0 for $t < 0$, then the system is causal. Do not use the unit impulse response.

**5-27.** A causal system has a transfer function whose real part is

$$R(\omega) = \frac{5 - \omega^2}{\omega^4 - 6\omega^2 + 25}$$

Find the imaginary part of the transfer function $X(\omega)$.

**5-28.** Repeat Problem 5-27 for $R(\omega) = \delta(\omega)$.

**5-29.** A causal system has a transfer function whose imaginary part is

$$\frac{-2\omega}{(\omega^4 - 6\omega^2 + 25)}$$

Find the real part of the transfer function $R(\omega)$.

**5-30.** A minimum phase system has a transfer function whose magnitude is

$$|H(j\omega)| = \frac{1}{\sqrt{1 + \omega^2}}$$

Find the angle of the transfer function as a function of $\omega$.

**5-31.** A minimum phase system has a transfer function whose angle is

$$\theta = -\tan^{-1}\omega$$

Find the magnitude of the transfer function as a function of frequency.

**5-32.** Discuss how the specifications of the magnitude of the transfer function for $-\omega_0 \leq \omega \leq \omega_0$ and the angle of the transfer function for $|\omega| > \omega_0$ can be used to obtain the complete transfer function for a minimum phase system.

**5-33.** The transfer function of a system in Laplace transformed formed is

$$H(s) = \frac{3s^{10} + 2s^9 + 4s^6 + 2s^3 + s^2 + 1}{(s + 1)(s + 2)(s + 3)(s + 4)^2 (s + 5)^6}$$

Find $\int_0^\infty R(\omega) \, d\omega$, where $H(j\omega) = R(\omega) + jX(\omega)$.

**5-34.** Determine the unit step response of the ideal low pass filter whose transfer function is

$$F(\omega) = \begin{cases} 1e^{-j\omega T}, & -\omega_c \leq \omega \leq \omega_c \\ 0, & |\omega| > \omega_c \end{cases}$$

Can the system be causal, if $T$ is finite?

**5-35.** A system has a transfer function

$$H(j\omega) = (\sin \omega + \sin 3\omega + \sin 5\omega) e^{-\omega T}$$

If the system is to be causal, what is the minimum value that $T$ can have?

**5-36.** A band pass system has the response

$$H(j\omega) = \frac{1}{1 + j1000\left( \dfrac{\omega}{\omega_0} - \dfrac{\omega_0}{\omega} \right)}$$

where $\omega_0 = 2\pi \times 10^6$ radians/second. What is the unit impulse response of the system? Assume that $H(j\omega)$ approximates a function with arithmetic symmetry about $\omega = \omega_0$.

**5-37.** Find the response of the system of Problem 5-36 to an input

$$f(t) = e^{-t} \cos \omega_0 t \, \mu(t)$$

Assume that the Fourier transform of $e^{-t}\mu(t)$ can be considered zero for $\omega > \omega_0$.

**5-38.** The real part of the transfer function of a causal network has the following properties:

$$\frac{dR(\omega)}{d\omega} \geq 0, \qquad 0 \leq \omega \leq \omega_0$$

$$\frac{dR(\omega)}{d\omega} \leq 0, \qquad \omega > \omega_0$$

$$R(\omega) \geq 0$$

$$R(\omega_0) = R_{max}$$

Obtain a bound on the overshoot of the unit step response of the network.

**5-39.** Derive Eq. 5–205 including all the details.

**5-40.** Obtain a bound on the effective bandwidth of a signal $f(t)$ based upon a mean square error criterion and upon the total variation of the $n$th derivative of $f(t)$. Restrict $f(t)$ as necessary.

**5-41.** Repeat Problem 5-40, but now use a maximum error criterion.

**5-42.** Discuss the analysis of linear systems with multiple inputs and outputs in terms of the analysis of systems with a single input and output.

# REFERENCES

1. Papoulis, A. *The Fourier Integral and Its Applications.* New York: McGraw-Hill, 1962, p. 81.
2. Elmore, W. C. "The Transient Response of Damped Linear Networks with Particular Regard to Wideband Amplifiers." In *Journal of Applied Physics.* Vol. 19, 1948, pp. 55–63.
3. Chirlian, P. M. "The Physical Realizability and Realization of Linear Phase Shift Networks." In *Quart. of Applied Math.* Vol. 18, 1960, pp. 31–35.

4. Zemanian, A. H. "Bounds Existing on the Time and Frequency Response of Various Types of Networks." In *Proc. IRE*. Vol. 42, 1954, pp. 835–839.
———————— "Further Bounds Existing on the Transient Response of Various Types of Networks." In *Proc. IRE*. Vol. 43, 1955, pp. 322–326.
Chirlian, P. M. "Restrictions Imposed upon the Unit Step Response of Linear Phase Shift Networks." In *Quart. of Applied Math*. Vol. 17, 1959, pp. 225–230.
5. Giardina, C. R. "Bounds on the Effective Bandwidth of a Signal." *Ph. D. Dissertation*. Stevens Institute of Technology, 1970.
Giardina, C. R., and Chirlian, P. M. "Restrictions of the Effective Bandwidth of Signals." In IEEE Trans. on Circuit Theory. Vol. CT-18, 1971, pp. 422–425.
6. Chirlian, P. M. "The Effective Bandwidth of a System." In *Quart. of Applied Math*. Vol. 25, 1967, pp. 311–312.

## BIBLIOGRAPHY

Javid, M., and Brenner, E. *Analysis, Transmission, and Filtering of Signals*. Chap. 6. New York: McGraw-Hill, 1963.
Papoulis, A. *The Fourier Integral and Its Applications*. Chaps. 5–7. New York: McGraw-Hill, 1962.
Schwartz, M. *Information Transmission, Modulation, and Noise*. 2d ed. Chap. 2. New York: McGraw-Hill, 1970.

# CHAPTER 6

# Discrete Time Systems

There are many systems which operate by sampling signals at discrete time intervals. The signals are assumed to be constant between the sampled intervals. These systems are called *discrete time systems* or *sampled data systems*. There are many reasons why these discrete time systems are used. The samples may be the only signals that are available. For instance, consider a radar which continuously scans the sky over an airport. Assume that the reflection from each airplane constitutes a signal. Then, the signal from any one airplane is only available during the time that the radar beam scans it. This may be for only a 0.001 second per each second. The signal is assumed to be essentially constant during any one scan. Hence this is a discrete time signal. At times, information which is continuously available is only sampled at discrete intervals because this actually improves the properties of the system. Suppose that the system is a chemical plant which is controlled by an automatic control system. The chemical processes are studied by means of transducers which measure pressure, temperature, etc. If this were a continuous system, the control system would continuously modify operating conditions such as temperature. In a large plant, this could result in very expensive operation. For instance, an oil burner might constantly be turned on and off. Since the rate of change of such a process is usually slow, a more economical operation would result if the transducers are checked at discrete time intervals when suitable control action would be taken. This type of process is assumed to continue without change between samples. On the other hand, certain parameters change rapidly; hence, these should be checked continuously or sampled at frequent intervals.

Sampled data systems can include large digital computers. Since these systems are sampled, the computer can be timeshared. This can result in very economical use of the computer.

At times, digital computers are often used to simulate or calculate the response of continuous systems as well. We have already considered such an application. In Section 4-8, we discussed a numerical procedure for solving state variable equations. There, the $d\hat{q}(t)/dt$ matrix (i.e., the derivatives of the state variable) was assumed to be constant over intervals of time and to change at discrete sampled times. Thus, when this numerical solution is used, the set of state variable equations represents a discrete time system.

In general, discrete time systems are not represented by differential equations since their major parameters are assumed to be constant over time intervals. However, such systems can be represented by *difference equations*. We shall discuss the formulation of these equations and techniques for their solution in the remainder of this chapter.

## 6-1. DIFFERENCE EQUATIONS

In this section we shall consider the fundamental ideas of difference equations of linear systems. In the next section we shall discuss state variables and generalize these results to nonlinear and time-varying systems. Let us consider an application where difference equations would be used. For example, suppose that a radar system is used to land airplanes at an airport. The radar antenna rotates continuously. Assume that it makes one revolution per second. Now suppose that this radar is used by the ground controller (i.e., the man in the control tower who supplies the information to the plane's pilot). The airplane's position is determined once a second. Thus, the plane's position is known only when it is scanned. This is true of any other parameter, such as velocity. Assume that $x(t)$ represents the airplane's position. The ground controller does not know $x(t)$. He only knows the discrete quantities $x(t_0)$, $x(t_1)$, $x(t_2)$, .... Information is sent from the ground controller to the pilot, which causes him to alter the course of the plane. Thus, this is a feedback system. The radar information could be interpreted by a digital computer instead of a ground controller, and the pilot could be replaced by a radar controlled automatic pilot. A more conventional feedback system would then result. However, a system with human inputs will be superior under certain circumstances.

As far as the observer (ground controller or computer) is concerned, the system only changes in discrete steps. Analysis of a discrete system is often simpler using difference equations than it would be using differential equations. The actual system really is characterized by a differential equation. That is, the airplane does not jump in discrete steps, but moves continuously. In general, sampled systems are of this type. That is, they respond continuously, but are only observed at discrete times. Thus, we shall develop difference equations, which characterize the discrete observations of such systems, from their differential equations.

Let us start with a simple example and then generalize it. Consider the first-order differential equation

$$\frac{dx(t)}{dt} + x(t) = y(t) \tag{6-1}$$

where $y(t)$ is a known function of time. We can approximate $dx(t)/dt$ by

$$\frac{dx(t)}{dt} = \frac{x(t + T) - x(t)}{T} \tag{6-2}$$

Assume that $T$ is a short enough interval of time so that $dx(t)/dt$, $x(t)$, and $y(t)$ can be assumed to be constant over these intervals. In this case, the approximation in Eq. 6-2 is valid. Then, Eq. 6-1 can be written as

$$\frac{x(t + T) - x(t)}{T} + x(t) = y(t) \tag{6-3}$$

Since the variables are assumed constant over intervals of $T$, we need only sample at $t = 0$, $T$, $2T$, ... to obtain desired information. Let us use the following notation

$$x(rT) = x(r) \qquad (6\text{-}4a)$$

That is, $x(3)$ represents the value of $x$ at $t = 3T$, the third sample. Then, since $x(t)$ is constant between samples, let

$$x(t) = x(r), \qquad rT \leq t \leq (r + 1)\,T \qquad (6\text{-}4b)$$

where $r$ represents $rT$, an allowed sampling time of $x(t)$; that is, $r$ replaces $rT$. The notation of Eq. 6–4b might be confusing; i.e., if $T = 0.01$ Eq. 6–4b is written as $x(0.03) = x(3)$. However, in any one equation we shall be working with either discrete or continuous time systems, so that this problem should not arise. Note if $(t)$ appears then the independent variable is time; if $(r)$ appears, then it represents the $r^{th}$ sample time; i.e., the time is $rT$. Then, Eq. 6–3 can be written as

$$\frac{x(r + 1) - x(r)}{T} + x(r) = y(r) \qquad (6\text{-}5)$$

Now suppose the independent signal $y(r)$ is known; i.e., it is the value of $y(t)$ at each sample time. Then, to solve for $x(r)$, we proceed in the following way. Assume that $T$ has been specified and $x(0)$ is given as an initial condition. Then, from Eq. 6–5, we have

$$x(r + 1) = (1 - T)\,x(r) + Ty(r) \qquad (6\text{-}6)$$

Substituting $x(0)$ and $y(0)$, we obtain

$$x(1) = (1 - T)\,x(0) + Ty(0) \qquad (6\text{-}7a)$$

Thus, $x(1)$ is now known and it can be substituted into Eq. 6–6 to obtain

$$x(2) = (1 - T)\,x(1) + Ty(1) \qquad (6\text{-}7b)$$

This process can then be repeated until the desired values of $x(r)$ are obtained. Later we shall see that Eq. 6–6 is in state variable form which can readily be solved. However, now we are concerned with the formulation of classical difference equations.

We shall proceed by analogy with Eq. 6–1. Assume that $T$ is small enough so that we can accurately represent the second derivative by

$$\frac{d^2x(t)}{dt^2} = \frac{\left.\dfrac{dx(t)}{dt}\right|_{t=t+T} - \left.\dfrac{dx(t)}{dt}\right|_{t=T}}{T} \qquad (6\text{-}8)$$

Substituting Eq. 6–2, we obtain

$$\frac{d^2x(t)}{dt^2} = \frac{\dfrac{x(t+2T)-x(t+T)}{T} - \dfrac{x(t+T)-x(t)}{T}}{T}$$

Thus,

$$\frac{d^2x(t)}{dt^2} = \frac{x(t+2T)-2x(t+T)+x(t)}{T^2} \qquad (6\text{–}9)$$

Thus, a second derivative can be represented using the notation of Eq. 6–4b, as

$$\frac{d^2x(t)}{dt^2} = \frac{x(r+2)-2x(r+1)+x(r)}{T^2} \qquad (6\text{–}10)$$

where $(t)$ indicates a function of time and $(r)$ indicates a function of the sample number.

In general, if we have $d^n x(t)/dt^n$, we can approximate it by

$$\frac{d^n x(t)}{dt^n} = \sum_{k=0}^{n} \alpha_k x(r+k) \qquad (6\text{–}11)$$

where the $\alpha_k$ are appropriate constants. Then, if we have a linear differential equation

$$a_m \frac{dx^m(t)}{dt^m} + a_{m-1}\frac{dx^{m-1}(t)}{dt^{m-1}} + \cdots + a_1 \frac{dx(t)}{dt} + a_0 x(t)$$

$$= b_1 y_1(t) + b_2 y_2(t) + \cdots + b_k y_k(t) \qquad (6\text{–}12)$$

and $T$ is sufficiently small, we can represent it by the difference equation

$$\alpha_m(r+m) + \alpha_{m-1}(r+m-1) + \cdots + \alpha_1(r+1) + \alpha_0(r)$$

$$= \beta_1 y_1(r) + \beta_2 y_2(r) + \cdots + \beta_k y_k(r) \qquad (6\text{–}13)$$

It is assumed that the spacing $T$ between the samples is so short that the system can be represented accurately by Eq. 6–13, which is an *nth-order difference equation*.

Now assume that the system is continuous. Hence, it can be represented by the following set of linear differential equations:

$$a_{1m}\frac{d^m x_1(t)}{dt^m} + \cdots + a_{11}\frac{dx_1(t)}{dt} + a_{10}x_1(t) = b_{11}y_1(t) + \cdots + b_{1k}y_k(t)$$

$$\cdots \cdots \cdots \cdots \cdots \cdots \cdots \cdots \cdots \cdots \cdots \cdots \cdots \cdots \qquad (6\text{–}14)$$

$$a_{nm}\frac{d^m x_n(t)}{dt^m} + \cdots + a_{n1}\frac{dx_n(t)}{dt} + a_{n0}x_n(t) = b_{n1}y_1(t) + \cdots + b_{nk}y_k(t)$$

Then a set of difference equations corresponding to these is

$$\alpha_{1m}x_1(r+m) + \cdots + \alpha_{1n}x_1(r+1) + \alpha_{10}x_1(r) = \beta_{11}y_1(r) + \cdots + \beta_{1k}y_k(r)$$

$$\cdots \cdots \cdots \cdots \cdots \cdots \cdots \cdots \cdots \cdots \cdots \cdots \cdots \cdots \qquad (6\text{–}15)$$

$$\alpha_{nm}x_n(r+m) + \cdots + \alpha_{n1}x_n(r+1) + \alpha_{n0}x_n(r) = \beta_{nm}y_1(r) + \cdots + \beta_{nk}y_k(r)$$

Note that $(t)$ or $(r)$ indicates whether the continuous or sampled signal is being considered.

It is convenient to introduce operational notation [1]. We define the operator $E$ by the following:

$$Ex(r) = x(r + 1) \tag{6-16}$$

or, in general,

$$E^j x(r) = x(r + j) \tag{6-17}$$

Thus, we can write one of Eqs. 6–15 as

$$(\alpha_{jm} E^m + \cdots + \alpha_{j1} E_1 + \alpha_{j0}) x(r) = \sum_{v=1}^{k} \beta_{jv} y_v(r) \tag{6-18}$$

These equations may be generalized in that the right-hand side may contain differences of $y_v(r)$; i.e., $y(r + 1)$, etc. This corresponds to the right-hand sides of Eqs. 6–14 having derivatives of the $y_v(t)$.

As we have seen, difference equations can represent approximations of differential equations. In Section 6-5 we shall show that this is equivalent to the numerical approximation procedure presented in Section 4-8 for the solution of state variable equations. However, at times, the system can only be sampled at discrete intervals. Under these conditions, difference equations actually represent the measured response of the system.

Difference equations can be formulated so that they give *exact* results at each sample interval. Consider an example which illustrates this. We shall use the first-order differential equation

$$\frac{dx(t)}{dt} + a_1 x(t) = y(t) \tag{6-19}$$

Assume that $y(t)$ does actually change in discrete steps:

$$y(t) = y(t_r), \qquad t_r \leqq t \leqq t_{r+1} \tag{6-20a}$$

where

$$t_r = rT, \qquad r = 0, 1, 2, \ldots \tag{6-20b}$$

Then, for $t_r < t < t_{r+1}$, Eq. 6–19 becomes

$$\frac{dx(t)}{dt} + a_1 x(t) = y(rT), \qquad t_r < t \leqq t_{r+1} \tag{6-21}$$

Note that $y(rT)$ is constant. The initial condition at $t = t_r$ is $x(t) = x(rT)$. Then, the solution of Eq. 6–21 for $t_r < t \leqq t_{r+1}$ is

$$x(t) = \frac{y(rT)}{a_1} + \left[ x(rT) + \frac{y(rT)}{a_1} \right] e^{-a_1(t-rT)} \tag{6-22}$$

This can be verified by substituting Eq. 6–22 into Eq. 6–21 and verifying that the initial condition is satisfied. Now let $t = (r + 1) T$; then,

$$x[(r + 1) T] = \frac{y(rT)}{a_1} + \left[ x(rT) + \frac{y(rT)}{a_1} \right] e^{-a_1 T} \tag{6-23}$$

We shall now use the difference equation notation; that is, $x(rT)$ is replaced by $x(r)$; doing this and manipulating, we obtain

$$x(r + 1) = e^{-a_1 T} x(r) + \frac{1}{a_1}(1 - e^{-a_1 T}) y(r) \qquad (6\text{-}24)$$

Note that $e^{-a_1 T}$ and $(1/a_1)(1 - e^{-a_1 T})$ are constant. This is a first-order difference equation, which can be solved as Eq. 6–6. The values of $x(r)$ obtained from Eq. 6–24 will be exactly equal to the actual $x(t)$ at the sample instants.

## 6-2. BASIC STATE VARIABLE EQUATIONS FOR DISCRETE TIME SYSTEMS

In Chapter 4 we discussed the use of state variable equations and demonstrated that they are especially useful if computer solutions are desired and/or if nonlinear or time-varying systems are analyzed. The same advantages are present when sampled systems are encountered. The results of this section are analogous to those of Section 4-2, therefore basic details are not repeated here.

In general, the state variable equations will be written in the form

$$q_1(r + 1) = f_1[q_1(r), q_2(r), ..., q_n(r), y_1(r), y_2(r), ..., y_k(r), r]$$
$$q_2(r + 1) = f_2[q_1(r), q_2(r), ..., q_n(r), y_1(r), y_2(r), ..., y_k(r), r]$$
$$\cdot \quad \cdot \quad \cdot \quad \cdot \quad \cdot \quad \cdot \quad \cdot \quad \cdot \quad \cdot \quad \cdot \quad \cdot \quad \cdot \quad \cdot \quad \cdot \quad \cdot \quad \cdot \quad \cdot \quad \cdot \quad \cdot \qquad (6\text{-}25)$$
$$q_n(r + 1) = f_n[q_1(r), q_2(r), ..., q_n(r), y_1(r), y_2(r), ..., y_k(r), r]$$

Note that $q_i(r)$ represents the state variable in a sampled system, and is thus constant between samples. Also $q_i(r)$ is the value of $q_i(t)$ at the $r$th sample. The state variable equations are of the following form: *a single variable at sample $r + 1$ is equal to a function of all the other state variables at sample $r$, independent variables at sample $r$, and $r$.* We can write this in matrix form as

$$\hat{q}(r + 1) = \hat{f}[\hat{q}(r), \hat{y}(r), \hat{r}] \qquad (6\text{-}26)$$

The definitions of these matrices are analogous to those of Eqs. 4–13 through 4–16. The state variable equations of discrete time systems are difference equations.

As in the case of continuous systems, the variables of discrete time systems can be expressed in terms of the state variables, the known signals, and the sample in question:

$$\hat{x}(r) = \hat{h}[\hat{q}(r), \hat{y}(r), \hat{r}] \qquad (6\text{-}27)$$

where $\hat{x}(r)$ is the vector (column matrix) of the system. This is analogous to Eqs. 4–17 through 4–19.

The functions that we have discussed are general in that they apply to linear or nonlinear, time-varying, or time-invariant systems. However, let us now restrict ourselves to linear, time-invariant systems. Then, by analogy to Eq. 4–23, the state variable equations of a simple system can be written as

$$\hat{q}(r + 1) = \hat{a}\hat{q}(r) + \hat{b}\hat{y}(r) \tag{6-28}$$

where $\hat{a}$ is an $n \times n$ matrix of constants and $\hat{b}$ is an $n \times k$ matrix of constants. Similarly, Eq. 6–27 becomes

$$\hat{x}(r) = \hat{c}\hat{q}(r) + \hat{d}\hat{y}(r) \tag{6-29}$$

where $c$ is an $n \times n$ matrix of constants and $\hat{d}$ is an $n \times k$ matrix of constants.

Now let us show how a set of state variable difference equations for a linear, time-invariant system can be obtained from a set of difference equations of the form of Eqs. 6–15. We shall give a procedure that replaces each of Eqs. 6–15 by a set of state variable equations. The set of all these sets are the state variable equations for the system. One typical equation of Eqs. 6–15 is

$$\alpha_n x(r + n) + \alpha_{n-1} x(r + n - 1) + \cdots + \alpha_1 x(r + 1) + \alpha_0 x(r) = y(r) \tag{6-30}$$

where, for brevity, we have omitted the subscripts from the $x(r)$ and $y(r)$. Then, one possible choice of state variables is

$$\begin{aligned}
q_1(r) &= x(r) \\
q_2(r) &= x(r + 1) = q_1(r + 1) \\
q_3(r) &= x(r + 2) = q_2(r + 1) \\
&\ \ . \\
&\ \ . \\
&\ \ . \\
q_n(r) &= x(r + n - 1) = q_{n-1}(r + 1)
\end{aligned} \tag{6-31}$$

The first $n - 1$ state variable equations can be obtained directly from Eq. 6–31:

$$\begin{aligned}
q_1(r + 1) &= q_2(r) \\
q_2(r + 1) &= q_3(r) \\
&\ \ . \\
&\ \ . \\
&\ \ . \\
q_{n-1}(r + 1) &= q_n(r)
\end{aligned} \tag{6-32}$$

The $n$th equation is found by substituting Eq. 6–31 into Eq. 6–30; this yields

$$q_n(r + 1) = -\frac{\alpha_0}{\alpha_n} q_1(r) - \frac{\alpha_1}{\alpha_n} q_2(r) - \cdots - \frac{\alpha_{n-1}}{\alpha_n} q_n(r) + \frac{1}{\alpha_n} y(r) \tag{6-33}$$

Equations 6–32 and 6–33 are a set of state variable equations for the system characterized by Eq. 6–30.

Difference equations of the type of Eq. 6–30 may contain a linear combination of several independent variables $y_j(r)$ on its right-hand side. In this case, the right-hand side of Eq. 6–33 will contain a linear sum of the independent variables.

A somewhat more difficult problem occurs if the right-hand side of Eq. 6–30 contains samples other than the $r$th one. State variable equations should only contain functions of the $r$th sample on the right-hand side. Choosing state variables as in Eq. 6–32, in this case, leads to functions such as $y(r + b)$ on the right-hand side of the equation, which is not allowed. The problem can be resolved by redefining the choice of state variable equations. This development closely parallels that of Eqs. 4–39 through 4–42. Suppose the difference equation is of the form

$$\sum_{i=0}^{n} \alpha_i x(r + i) = \sum_{j=0}^{k} \sum_{i=0}^{n} \beta_{ij} y_j(r + i) \qquad (6\text{–}34)$$

This is similar to Eq. 6–30 except that now we have $k$ independent variables and that samples for the $r$th to the $(r + n)$th can appear on the right-hand side of the equation. Now we choose the state variables as follows:

$$x(r) = q_1(r) + \sum_{j=1}^{k} \gamma_{j1} y_j(r) \qquad (6\text{–}35)$$

where the $\gamma_{j1}$ are constants; we evaluate them in the following way. Substitute Eq. 6–35 into Eq. 6–34. Choose the set of $\gamma_{j1}, j = 1, 2, ..., k$ so that after combining terms, the coefficient of each $y_j(r + n)$ is set equal to zero. Then, the next state variable is defined by the equation

$$q_1(r + 1) = q_2(r) + \sum_{j=1}^{k} \gamma_{j2} y_j(r) \qquad (6\text{–}36)$$

This equation is substituted into the one that resulted when Eq. 6–35 was substituted into Eq. 6–34. Equation 6–36 is substituted there for all the $q_1(r + h), h \geq 1$. Then, the value $\gamma_{j2}$ is chosen so that the coefficients of $y_j(r + n - 1)$ become zero. This process then is repeated. In general, we define the state variables as

$$q_{i-1}(r + 1) = q_i(r) + \sum_{j=1}^{k} \gamma_{ji} y_j(r), \qquad i = 1, 2, ..., n \qquad (6\text{–}37)$$

where the $\gamma_{ji}$ are determined by substituting in successive equations and by cancelling the coefficient of the appropriate $y_j(r + h)$. Note that in Eq. 6–37, we define $q_0(r + 1)$ as $x(r)$ (see Eq. 6–35).

As an example, let us determine a set of state variable difference equations which can be used to represent the difference equation

$$x(r + 2) + 2x(r + 1) + x(r) = y(r + 2) + 3y(r + 1) + y(r) \qquad (6\text{–}38)$$

Then (see Eq. 6–35),

$$x(r) = q_1(r) + \gamma_{11} y(r) \qquad (6\text{–}39)$$

Substituting, we have

$$q_1(r + 2) + \gamma_{11}y(r + 2) + 2q_1(r + 1) + 2\gamma_{11}y(r + 1) + q_1(r) + \gamma_{11}y(r)$$

$$= y(r + 2) + 3y(r + 1) + y(r) \quad (6\text{-}40)$$

Rearranging, we have

$$q_1(r + 2) + 2q_1(r + 1) + q_1(r)$$
$$= (-\gamma_{11} + 1)y(r + 2) + (-2\gamma_{11} + 3)y(r + 1) + (-\gamma_{11} + 1)y(r) \quad (6\text{-}41)$$

Then, set $\gamma_{11} = 1$. This yields

$$q_1(r + 2) + 2q_1(r + 1) + q_1(r) = y(r + 1) \quad (6\text{-}42)$$

Now choose

$$q_1(r + 1) = q_2(r) + \gamma_{12}y(r) \quad (6\text{-}43)$$

Substituting in Eq. 6–42, we have

$$q_2(r + 1) + \gamma_{12}y(r + 1) + 2q_2(r) + 2\gamma_{12}y(r) + q_1(r) = y(r + 1)$$

Rearranging, we have

$$q_2(r + 1) + 2q_2(r) + q_1(r) = (-\gamma_{12} + 1)y(r + 1) - 2\gamma_{12}y(r) \quad (6\text{-}44)$$

Then set

$$\gamma_{12} = 1 \quad (6\text{-}45)$$

The equation then becomes

$$q_2(r + 1) + 2q_2(r) + q_1(r) = -2y(r) \quad (6\text{-}46)$$

Then, Eqs. 6–43, 6–45, and 6–46 yield the state variable equations

$$q_1(r + 1) = 0q_1(r) + q_2(r) + y(r) \quad (6\text{-}47a)$$
$$q_2(r + 1) = -q_1(r) - 2q_2(r) - 2y(r) \quad (6\text{-}47b)$$

The value of $x(r)$ can be obtained from the state variables and the known functions using Eq. 6–39 and the fact that $\gamma_{11} = 1$; thus,

$$x(r) = q_1(r) + y(r) \quad (6\text{-}48)$$

The procedure for obtaining a new set of state variables as linear combinations of the state variables (see Eqs. 4–43 through 4–45) can be applied to the state variable equations of linear discrete time systems.

**State Variable Operations for Discrete Time Electric Networks.** The basic ideas presented in Section 4–3 for the choice of state variables and their defining equations can be carried over to discrete time electric networks. If possible, all the capacitor voltages and all the inductor currents should be chosen as the state variables. Section 4-3 should be reviewed considering discrete time networks. In Section 6-1 a difference equation for an electric network was obtained.

## 6-3. STATE VARIABLE EQUATIONS FOR TIME-VARYING DISCRETE TIME SYSTEMS

In Section 4-4, we discussed the formulation of state variable equations for time-varying, continuous time systems. We shall apply much of this discussion to discrete time systems. First, consider an example. In Eqs. 4–73 through 4–76, the state variable equations for a time-varying electric network were obtained; these were

$$\frac{di_L(t)}{dt} = -\frac{1}{L(t)}\left[ R_1(t) + \frac{dL(t)}{dt} \right] i_L(t) - \frac{1}{L(t)} v_C(t) + \frac{1}{L(t)} v(t) \quad (6\text{–}49\text{a})$$

$$\frac{dv_C(t)}{dt} = \frac{1}{C(t)} i_L(t) - \frac{1}{C(t)}\left[ \frac{1}{R_2(t)} + \frac{dC(t)}{dt} \right] v_C(t) \quad (6\text{–}49\text{b})$$

The state variables are $i_L(t)$ and $v_C(t)$. The known signal is $v(t)$. Now choose a sample interval small enough so that all the time-varying quantities including the derivatives of $L(t)$ and $C(t)$ can be considered constant over each interval. Then, using Eq. 6–2 and discrete time notation, we have

$$i_L(r + 1) = -\frac{T}{L(r)}\left[ R_1(r) + \frac{dL(r)}{dt} - \frac{L(r)}{T} \right] i_L(r) - \frac{1}{L(r)} v_C(r) + \frac{1}{L(r)} v(r) \quad (6\text{–}50\text{a})$$

$$v_C(r + 1) = \frac{T}{C(r)} i_L(r) - \frac{T}{C(r)}\left[ \frac{1}{R_2(r)} + \frac{dC(r)}{dt} - \frac{C(r)}{T} \right] v_C(r) \quad (6\text{–}50\text{b})$$

Note that $i_L(r)$ is the value of $i_L$ at the $r$th sample etc. In forming the time-varying expressions, we first formulate the equations assuming that the parameters vary continuously and then consider that all pertinent quantities remain constant between sample times. For example, $dL(r)/dt$ is the value of $dL(t)/dt$ evaluated at $t = Lr$. If we assumed that $L$ remained constant between samples before formulating the equations, then $dL(t)/dt$ would consist of a series of impulses. Thus, it is probably desirable to formulate the equations on a continuous basis and then assume that all quantities are constant between samples.

We have discussed this example considering the discrete time equations to be an approximation of the continuous ones. However, this may not be the case. Suppose $i_L$ and $v_C$ are only sampled at discrete times, for any of the reasons discussed at the beginning of the chapter. Also, $v(t)$ may (or may not) vary in a discrete fashion. Thus, Eqs. 6–50 could actually represent a discrete time system. In general, the parameters of such a system (i.e., $L(t)$ and $C(t)$) might vary continuously with time. We have assumed that the time $T$ between samples was short.

If it is not, a set of difference equations can be obtained by following the basic procedures used to obtain Eq. 6–24. However, this involves solving time-varying differential equations.

Since we are considering linear systems, the state variable equations will be of the form of Eqs. 6–28 and 6–29, except that now the $\hat{a}$, $\hat{b}$, $\hat{c}$, and $\hat{d}$ matrices will be time varying. Thus, the general form of the state variable equations of the discrete time system will be

$$\hat{q}(r + 1) = \hat{a}(r)\,\hat{q}(r) + \hat{b}(r)\,\hat{y}(r) \tag{6–51}$$

Similarly, if we express the system quantities in terms of the state variables, then Eq. 6–29 becomes

$$\hat{x}(r) = \hat{c}(r)\,\hat{q}(r) + \hat{d}(r)\,\hat{y}(r) \tag{6–52}$$

Then, the general form of the state variable equations for linear, time-varying systems is similar to that for linear, time-invariant systems.


## 6-4. BASIC STATE VARIABLE EQUATIONS FOR NONLINEAR, DISCRETE TIME SYSTEMS

The basic state variable equations for discrete time systems as given in Eqs. 6–25 and 6–26 apply to nonlinear systems. In this case, the functions expressed in these equations are nonlinear. The ideas discussed in Section 4-5 which consider the basic ideas for the formulation of equations for nonlinear systems should be applied to discrete time systems also.

Suppose a system whose state variable equations are given in Eqs. 4–94 and 4–95 is a sampled system and that time $T$ between samples is sufficiently short so that the system's quantities can be considered constant over $T$. Then, using discrete time notation and applying Eqs. 6–2 to 4–94, and 4–95, we obtain

$$i_L(r + 1) = -\,T\,\frac{[i_T(r) + \alpha_2 i_L^2(r)]}{1 + 3\beta_3 i_L^2(r)} + i_L(r) - \frac{T v_C(r)}{1 + 3\beta_3 i_L^2(r)} + \frac{T v(r)}{1 + 3\beta_3 i_L^2(r)} \tag{6–53}$$

$$v_C(r + 1) = \frac{T i_L(r)}{1 + 4\gamma_4 v_C^3(r)} - \frac{v_C^3(r)}{1 + 4\gamma_4 v_C^3(r)} + v_C(r) \tag{6–54}$$

If the time between samples is not short, a set of difference equations can be obtained using the method for obtaining Eq. 6–24. However, this involves solving a differential equation to obtain the difference equation. In the case of nonlinear systems, this can be difficult.

## 6-5. SOLVING STATE VARIABLE EQUATIONS FOR LINEAR, NONLINEAR, TIME-INVARIANT, TIME-VARYING, AND NONLINEAR DISCRETE TIME SYSTEMS

The solution of state variable equations for linear discrete time systems is simpler than that for linear, continuous time systems. This is because difference, rather than differential equations, must be solved.

**Linear, Time-Invariant Systems.** Suppose we wish to solve the state variable difference equations for the linear, time-invariant system given in Eq. 6–28. These are

$$\hat{q}(r + 1) = \hat{a}\hat{q}(r) + \hat{b}\hat{y}(r) \tag{6-55}$$

Before solving this in general, consider a specific example

$$q_1(r + 1) = a_{11}q_1(r) + a_{12}q_2(r) + b_{11}y(r) \tag{6-56a}$$

$$q_2(r + 1) = a_{21}q_1(r) + a_{22}q_2(r) + b_{21}y(r) \tag{6-56b}$$

It is assumed that the initial state is known; thus $q_1(0)$ and $q_2(0)$ are known quantities and $y(r)$ represents a known signal. Thus, if $r = 0$, we have

$$q_1(1) = a_{11}q_1(0) + a_{12}q_2(0) + b_{11}y(0) \tag{6-57a}$$

$$q_2(1) = a_{21}q_1(0) + a_{22}q_2(0) + b_{21}y(0) \tag{6-57b}$$

Thus, we have determined $q_1(1)$ and $q_2(1)$ in terms of known quantities. Then, letting $r = 1$ in Eqs. 6–56, we can determine $q_1(2)$ and $q_2(2)$ in terms of the now known $q_1(1)$ and $q_2(1)$. Proceeding in this way, the values of desired $q_1(r)$ and $q_2(r)$ can be determined.

In general, setting $r = 1$ in Eq. 6–55, we have

$$\hat{q}(1) = \hat{a}\hat{q}(0) + \hat{b}\hat{y}(0) \tag{6-58}$$

Thus, the $\hat{q}(1)$ matrix has been determined. Substituting this into Eq. 6–55 we have

$$\hat{q}(2) = \hat{a}\hat{q}(1) + \hat{b}\hat{y}(1) \tag{6-59}$$

Proceeding in this way, we have

$$q(r) = \hat{a}\hat{q}(r - 1) + \hat{b}\hat{y}(r - 1) \qquad \qquad * \tag{6-60}$$

(We shall see in the next section that this form of the solution is ideally suited for computer solution.) However, it is sometimes useful to express $\hat{q}(r)$ in terms of $\hat{q}(0)$. Substituting Eq. 6–58 into Eq. 6–59, we have

$$q(2) = \hat{a}^2\hat{q}(0) + \hat{a}\hat{b}\hat{y}(0) + \hat{b}\hat{y}(1) \tag{6-61}$$

If we continue substituting in this way, we obtain,

$$\hat{q}(r) = \hat{a}^r\hat{q}(0) + \sum_{k=0}^{r-1} \hat{a}^{r-k-1}\hat{b}\hat{y}(k) \tag{6-62}$$

where

$$\hat{a}^0 = \hat{U} \tag{6–63}$$

Thus, we have obtained an expression for the state variables at any sample in terms of $\hat{q}(0)$. This equation is analogous to Eq. 4–127 for continuous time systems. In this case $\hat{a}^r$ is analogous to the state transition matrix. Equation 4–139 can be used to express $\hat{a}^r$ as a sum of $n$ matrices.

**Linear, Time-Varying Systems.**  The state variable equations for linear, time-invariant systems are very similar to Eq. 6–55 but now the $\hat{a}$ and $\hat{b}$ matrices are function of time; hence,

$$\hat{q}(r + 1) = \hat{a}(r)\,\hat{q}(r) + \hat{b}(r)\,\hat{y}(r) \tag{6–64}$$

Again, we assume that the initial state $\hat{q}(0)$ is specified; then,

$$\hat{q}(1) = \hat{a}(0)\,\hat{q}(0) + \hat{b}(0)\,\hat{y}(0) \tag{6–65}$$

Then, since $\hat{a}(r)$, $\hat{b}(r)$, and $\hat{y}(r)$ are known, we have determined $\hat{q}(1)$. Proceeding successively, we have,

$$\hat{q}(r) = \hat{a}(r - 1)\,\hat{q}(r - 1) + \hat{b}(r - 1)\,\hat{y}(r - 1), \qquad r = 1, 2, \dots \tag{6–66}$$

Thus, we have obtained the desired state variables; hence, have solved the equations.

Equation 6–66 is a complete solution of the state variable equation of linear, time-varying systems. (It is also well suited to computer solution.) However, let us obtain another form which expresses $\hat{q}(r)$ in terms of $\hat{q}(0)$ and no other state variables. For example, from Eq. 6–66, we have

$$\hat{q}(2) = \hat{a}(1)\,\hat{q}(1) + \hat{b}(1)\,\hat{y}(1) \tag{6–67}$$

Substituting Eq. 6–65, we have

$$\hat{q}(2) = \hat{a}(1)\,\hat{a}(0)\,\hat{q}(0) + \hat{a}(1)\,\hat{b}(0)\,\hat{y}(0) + \hat{b}(1)\,\hat{y}(1) \tag{6–68}$$

If we repeat this we have

$$\hat{q}(r) = \hat{a}(r - 1)\,\hat{a}(r - 2) \dots \hat{a}(0)\,\hat{q}(0)$$
$$+ \sum_{k=0}^{r-1} \hat{a}(r - 1)\,\hat{a}(r - 2) \dots \hat{a}(k + 1)\,\hat{b}(k)\,\hat{y}(k) \tag{6–69}$$

Note that if $k + 1 > r - 1$, then no $\hat{a}$ terms appear in that particular summation term. We have assumed that the occurrence of the initial state was $r = 0$. In a time-varying system, the time of application of the signal will have an effect on the results. In this case, $\hat{q}(r)$ corresponds to time $T_0 + rT$, where $T_0$ is the initial time and $T$ is the time between samples. Thus, the 0 sample occurs at time $T_0$.

**Nonlinear Systems.**  The general form of the state variable equations for nonlinear systems is Eq. 6–26:

$$\hat{q}(r + 1) = \hat{f}\left[\hat{q}(r), \hat{y}(r), \hat{r}\right] \tag{6–70}$$

Then, as before, if the initial state is known

$$\hat{q}(1) = \hat{f}\left[\hat{q}(0), \hat{y}(0), 0\right] \tag{6–71}$$

Thus, $\hat{q}(1)$ is expressed in terms of known quantities and can be evaluated. Hence, we can find $\hat{q}(2)$ from $\hat{q}(1)$. In general, we have

$$\hat{q}(r) = \hat{f}\left[\hat{q}(r-1), \hat{y}(r-1), r-1\right] \tag{6–72}$$

Thus, the nonlinear difference equations can be evaluated.

## 6-6. COMPUTER SOLUTION OF STATE VARIABLE EQUATIONS OF LINEAR, NONLINEAR, TIME-INVARIANT, AND TIME-VARYING DISCRETE TIME SYSTEMS

The solution of the difference state variable equations of discrete time systems is simpler than the solution of the differential equations of continuous time systems. The computer programs which implements the solution for discrete time systems are also somewhat simpler than those for continuous time systems. We shall illustrate this by considering the general form of the state variable equations. For continuous time systems, we have (see Eq. 4–16)

$$\frac{d\hat{q}(t)}{dt} = \hat{f}\left[\hat{q}(t), \hat{y}(t), \hat{t}\right] \tag{6–73}$$

The numerical solution (see Section 4-8) for this equation, as before, uses a discrete time approach. Again, time interval $T$ is chosen; then, $\hat{q}(0)$, $\hat{y}(0)$ are employed to compute $d\hat{q}(0)/dt$, using the equation

$$\frac{d\hat{q}(0)}{dt} = \hat{f}\left[\hat{q}(0), \hat{y}(0), 0\right] \tag{6–74a}$$

This and the time interval are used to compute $\hat{q}(T)$. Thus (see Eq. 4–167)

$$\hat{q}(T) = \hat{q}(0) + T\frac{d\hat{q}(0)}{dt} \tag{6–74b}$$

This equation is then used to compute $d\hat{q}(T)/dt$ which is employed to obtain $\hat{q}(2T)$, etc.

When difference equations are to be solved, the basic form of the state variable equations using difference equation notation is

$$\hat{q}(r+1) = \hat{f}\left[\hat{q}(r), \hat{y}(r), \hat{r}\right] \tag{6–75}$$

For example,

$$\hat{q}(1) = \hat{f}\left[\hat{q}(0), \hat{y}(0), 0\right] \tag{6–76}$$

Note that Eq. 6–75 is analogous to Eq. 6–73. However, Eq. 6–73 gives a derivative which is used to compute the state variable, while Eq. 6–75 gives the state variable itself.

**Linear, Time-Invariant Systems.** Let us now consider a specific program. The SUBROUTINE STATEL is listed in Fig. 4–12. This evaluates the difference equations of a linear, time-invariant system.

The DO loops of lines 130–230 compute the derivatives of the state variables. However, a comparison of Eqs. 6–73 and 6–75 indicates that the same computations would now calculate the values of $q(r)$ at the next sample point for a discrete time system. (Note that $q(0)$ is entered by the user of the program. When the SUB-ROUTINE is called, the new Q array is calculated and entered over the old one.) Thus, if line 250 is replaced by

$$Q(I) = DQ(I)$$

the program will now evaluate the discrete time state variable. Note that the DQ now does not give the derivative, but the actual value of Q. The reason for using two arrays is that *all the old* $Q(I)$, $I = 1, 2, ..n$ *are used in computing each new* $Q(I)$. Thus, we cannot write over the old ones until the new ones are all calculated. Hence, we need two arrays, one of which stores the new values. When all the new values are computed, these are written over the old ones.

In lines 80 and 90, $y_1(r)$ and $y_2(r)$ are computed, using discrete time notation. The variable TT is a function of the sample $r$ and is computed using $r$ (i.e., the number of times that the SUBROUTINE is called) and DELT, the spacing between samples. An alternative procedure for obtaining $y_1(r)$ and $y_2(r)$ is to enter them in an array.

**Linear, Time-Varying Systems.**  In general, all the comments made for linear, time-invariant systems also apply for the program for the time-varying system. The comments made about $\hat{y}$ now also apply to $\hat{a}$ and $\hat{b}$. Thus the SUBROUTINE STATET (see Fig. 4–14) can be applied to a specific discrete time system, if line 300 were changed to

$$Q(I) = DQ(I)$$

**Nonlinear Systems.**  Again the comments made for linear, time-invariant systems apply to the program for nonlinear systems. The SUBROUTINE STATEN of Fig. 4–15 could be used for a discrete time system of state variable equations by replacing line 120 by

$$Q(I) = DQ(I)$$

This would then solve the state variable difference equations

$$q_1(r + 1) = \frac{-q_1(r)}{1 + q_1^2(r)} - \frac{q_2(r)}{1 + q_1^2(r)} + \frac{y(r)}{1 + q_1^2(r)} \qquad (6\text{--}77a)$$

$$q_2(r + 1) = q_1(r) - q_2^3(r) \qquad (6\text{--}77b)$$

where

$$y(r) = 1 \qquad (6\text{--}77c)$$

## 6-7.  THE z-TRANSFORM

In this section we shall discuss a transform procedure which can be used to analyze discrete time or sampled data systems. This will be related to the Laplace transform and is only applicable to linear systems. First, consider the simple *sampler circuit* shown in Fig. 6–1. We shall use Fig. 6–2 to describe its operation. Assume

Fɪɢ. 6–1
Simple sampler

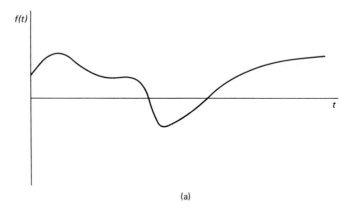

(a)

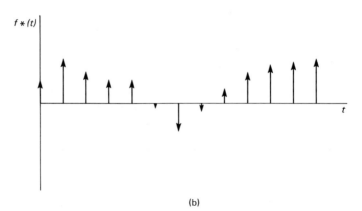

(b)
Fɪɢ. 6–2
(a) Input to sampler of Fig. 6–1; (b) output of sampler

that $f(t)$ is sampled at intervals of $T$ seconds. Once every $T$ seconds, the switch
closes for a very short fraction of $T$. Thus, a sample of $f(t)$ is obtained. The samples
have the form of extremely short pulses. If the duration of a pulse is very much
shorter than the response time of the system, then the response of the system to
the pulse is essentially the same as the response to a unit impulse whose "area"
is the same as that of the pulse. For example, a square pulse of height $h_1$ and width
$t_1$ occurring at time $t_2$ could be represented by $h_1 t_1 \delta(t - t_2)$. Thus, the output of

the sampler of Fig. 6–1 could be represented by a sequence of impulses as shown in Fig. 6–2b. If the sampling times are $T$ seconds apart, then we can write

$$f_*(t) = \sum_{k=0}^{\infty} f(kT)\,\delta(t - kT) \qquad (6\text{–}78)$$

(If we use discrete time notation, $f(rT)$ may be written as $f(r)$ and $f_*(t)$ as $f_*(r)$.) Note that we have omitted a constant which is proportional to the width of the pulse. This is done to avoid cluttering the notation. We shall assume that the sampler produces a signal given by Eq. 6–78 and all functions of time are zero for $t < 0$.

In the previous sections of this chapter, we have assumed that the sample signal remains constant at the sampled value until the next sample was taken. Here we have assumed that the samples are a train of impulses. However, later we shall show that we can apply the analysis based on a train of impulses to other forms of samplers.

Now let us take the Laplace transforms of $f(t)$ and $f_*(t)$. We define

$$f(t) \leftrightarrow F(s) \qquad (6\text{–}79a)$$

and

$$f_*(t) \leftrightarrow F_*(s) \qquad (6\text{–}79b)$$

Then, using Table 3-1 and Eq. 3–76, we obtain

$$F_*(s) = \sum_{k=0}^{\infty} f(kT)\,e^{-kTs} \qquad (6\text{–}80)$$

Now let us obtain the transform in a different form. From Eq. 2–174, we have

$$f(x)\,\delta(x - x_0) = f(x_0)\,\delta(x - x_0) \qquad (6\text{–}81)$$

Then, Eq. 6–78 can be written as

$$f_*(t) = \sum_{k=0}^{\infty} f(t)\,\delta(t - kT) = f(t)\sum_{k=0}^{\infty} \delta(t - kT) \qquad (6\text{–}82)$$

Thus, we can apply complex convolution (see Eq. 3–201) to obtain the Laplace transform of $f_*(t)$. First, we must obtain the Laplace transform of $\sum_{k=0}^{\infty} \delta(t - kT)$. Using Eq. 6–80 with $f(kT) = 1$, we have

$$\sum_{k=0}^{\infty} \delta(t - kT) \leftrightarrow \sum_{k=0}^{\infty} e^{-kTs} \qquad (6\text{–}83)$$

The summation can be expressed in closed form as

$$\frac{1}{1 - e^{-sT}} = \sum_{k=0}^{\infty} e^{-kTs} \qquad (6\text{–}84)$$

Hence,

$$\sum_{n=0}^{\infty} \delta(t - kT) \leftrightarrow \frac{1}{1 - e^{-sT}}, \qquad \mathrm{Re}\,s > 0$$

(Note that the poles of $1/(1 - e^{-sT})$ occur on the $j\omega$ axis.) Then, applying complex convolution to Eq. 6–82, we have

$$F_*(s) = \frac{1}{2\pi j}\,F(s) * \frac{1}{1 - e^{-sT}}$$

Assume that $F(s)$ has all its poles in the left half plane; i.e., Re $s > -\sigma_1$ where $\sigma_1 > 0$. Then, Eq. 3–202 yields

$$F_*(s) = \frac{1}{2\pi j} \int_{C-j\infty}^{C+j\infty} \frac{1}{1-e^{-yT}} F(s-y)\,dy;$$

$$\text{Re } s > -\sigma_1, \qquad 0 < C < \text{Re } s + \sigma_1$$

(6–85)

The poles of $1/(1-e^{-sT})$ lie at the points where $e^{-sT} = 1$, or

$$s = \pm j\frac{2\pi n}{T} = \pm j\omega_s n, \qquad n = 0, 1, 2, \dots$$

(6–86)

where $\omega_s$ is $2\pi$ times the sample frequency

$$\omega_s = \frac{2\pi}{T}$$

(6–87)

If the poles of $F(s)$ lie at $s = s'_n$, $n = 1, 2, \dots$, the poles of the integrand lie at

$$y = \pm j\omega_s n$$

(6–88a)

and at

$$y = s'_n + s, \qquad n = 1, 2, \dots$$

(6–88b)

where the $s'_n$ are the poles of $F(s)$. Since the contour of integration lies to the left of Re $s + \sigma_1$ (but greater than zero) the path of integration lies between the poles of $1/(1-e^{-yT})$ and those of $F(y-s)$. Then, proceeding as in Section 3-14, we obtain (if the integral vanishes on the infinite semicircle)

$$F_*(s) = \sum \left[ \text{Res at } y = \pm j\omega_s n \text{ of } \frac{F(s-y)}{1-e^{-yT}} \right]$$

(6–89a)

or

$$F_*(s) = \sum \left[ \text{Res at } y = s'_n \text{ of } \frac{F(s-y)}{1-e^{-sT}} \right]$$

(6–89b)

Using Eq. 6–89a, we have

$$F_*(s) = \frac{1}{T} \sum_{n=-\infty}^{\infty} F(s+j\omega_s n)$$

(6–90)

Thus, we have obtained an alternative expression for Eq. 6–80.

Then, in summation, if we have an $f(t)$ and it is sampled as indicated in Fig. 4–2, so that $f_*(t)$ results, then the Laplace transform of $f_*(t)$ is given by

$$F_*(s) = \sum_{n=0}^{\infty} f(nT) e^{-nTs}$$

(6–91)

or

$$F_*(s) = \frac{1}{T} \sum_{n=-\infty}^{\infty} F(s+j\omega_s n)$$

(6–92)

We shall use transforms of the form of Eq. 6–91. It is convenient to make the following substitution:

$$z = e^{sT} \tag{6-93}$$

Then Eq. 6–91 becomes

$$F(z) = \sum_{n=0}^{\infty} f(nT) z^{-n} \tag{6-94}$$

$F(z)$ is then called the *z-transform* of $f(t)$, where $F(z)$ represents Eq. 6–94, while $F(s)$ represents the Laplace transform of $f(t)$. If we adhere strictly to notation, the meaning of $F(z)$ is simply $F(s)$ with $s$ replaced by $z$. Of course, we do not mean this. In general, $F(z)$ represents the $z$-transform, whereas $F(s)$ represents the Laplace transform of $f(t)$. The $(s)$ or $(z)$ indicates which transform is used. (If there are specific instances where trouble can arise, then identifying subscripts will be used.) We shall also use the notation

$$f(t) \leftrightarrow F(z) \tag{6-95}$$

That, to obtain the $z$-transform of a sampled $f(t)$, where sampling is the type indicated in Fig. 6–2, we can use Eq. 6–94. Equivalently, we can obtain the Laplace transform of $f_*(t)$ and then substitute (see Eq. 6–93)

$$s = \frac{1}{T} \ln z \tag{6-96}$$

As an example, let us obtain the $z$-transform of

$$f(t) = u(t) e^{-at} \tag{6-97}$$

We use Eq. 6–94 to obtain the $z$-transform

$$F(z) = \sum_{n=0}^{\infty} e^{-anT} z^{-n} \tag{6-98}$$

This summation can be written in closed form as

$$F(z) = \frac{1}{1 - e^{-aT} z^{-1}}$$

Then,

$$F(z) = \frac{z}{z - e^{-aT}} \tag{6-99}$$

Alternatively, we could obtain this using the convolution (see Eq. 6–85). The Laplace transform of $u(t) e^{-at}$ is $1/s + a$, $\mathrm{Re}\, s > -a$. The sampled function produces the sequence $1, e^{-T}, e^{-2T}, \dots$. The inverse Laplace transform of $1/(s + a)$ yields $u(t) e^{-at}$. At $t = 0$, this yields $\frac{1}{2}[f(0-) + f(0+)] = \frac{1}{2}$ not 1. To correct this discrepancy, assume that we advance the time response by $\varepsilon$, where $\varepsilon \to 0$. That is, we consider

$u(t + \varepsilon) e^{-a(t+\varepsilon)}$. Then, $f(0-) = 1$. This eliminates the problem. Thus, the Laplace transform that we use is

$$F(s) = \frac{e^{\varepsilon s}}{s + a}$$

The integrand then is

$$F_*(s) = \frac{1}{2\pi j} \int_{C-j\infty}^{C+j\infty} \frac{1}{1 - e^{-yT}} \frac{e^{\varepsilon(s-y)}}{s - y + a} \, dy;$$

$$\mathrm{Re}\, s > -a, \qquad 0 < C < \mathrm{Re}\, s + a$$

The path of integration lies between the singularities of $1/(1 - e^{-yT})$ and those of $1/(s - y + a)$. The factor $e^{\varepsilon(s-y)}$ causes the integral to vanish if we close the path of integration to the right. If this factor were not included, the integral over that infinite semicircle would not be zero. Then, using Eq. 6–89b to evaluate the integral, we have

$$F_*(s) = \lim_{\varepsilon \to 0} [\mathrm{Res}\ \mathrm{at}\ y] = s + a$$

$$F_*(s) = \lim_{\varepsilon \to 0} \frac{e^{\varepsilon aT}}{1 - e^{-sT}e^{-aT}} = \frac{1}{1 - e^{-sT}e^{-aT}}$$

Then, let $z = e^{sT}$ and we obtain Eq. 6–99.

Consider the region of analyticity of the z-transform. In general,

$$F(z) = \sum_{n=0}^{\infty} f(nT) z^{-n} \tag{6–100}$$

Then, this is a power series in $1/z$. Thus, it is a *Laurent* series (see Section B-8), which will converge for large $|1/z|$. Then, we should state that

$$F(z) = \sum_{n=0}^{\infty} f(nT) z^{-n}, \qquad |z| > z_0 \tag{6–101}$$

In general, it can be shown that if the series converges absolutely for $|z| > z_0$, then $F(z)$ will be analytic in the region for $|z| > z_0$. That is, $F(z)$ is analytic in a region outside of a circle of radius $z_0$ which is centered at $z = 0$. This is shown in Fig. 6–3.

We shall use the z-transform to solve difference equations. Using difference equation notation, $f(rT)$ becomes $f(r)$. Since we only are considering $f(t)$ at its sample times, we do not know its values between samples. For example, if $f(t) = u(t) e^{-at}$ at $t = rT, r = 1, 2, \ldots$, and $f(t) = u(t) t \sin t$ at all other times, its z-transform is still given in Eq. 6–99, since at the sampled instants, it appears to be $u(t) e^{-at}$. Thus, it is more realistic to speak of $f(r)$, since this emphasizes the sampled nature of the signal.

Table 6-1 lists a table of z-transforms of common functions.

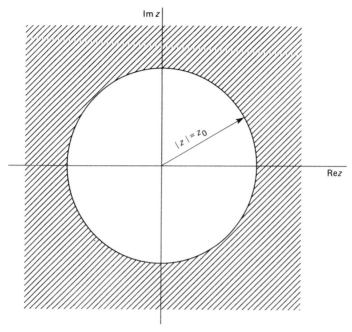

FIG. 6–3
Region of analyticity of the z-transform lies outside of circle

TABLE 6-1

| $f(r) \longleftarrow \longrightarrow F(z)$ | | $z_0$ |
|---|---|---|
| $u(r)$ | $\dfrac{z}{z-1}$ | $1$ |
| $u(r)\,rT$ | $\dfrac{Tz}{(z-1)^2}$ | $1$ |
| $u(r)\,(rT)^2$ | $T^2\dfrac{z(z+1)}{(z-1)^3}$ | $1$ |
| $u(r)\,e^{-arT}$ | $\dfrac{z}{z-e^{-aT}}$ | $e^{-aT}$ |
| $u(r)\sin \omega_0 rT$ | $\dfrac{z\sin \omega_0 T}{z^2-2z\cos \omega_0 T+1}$ | $1$ |
| $u(r)\,e^{-arT}\sin \omega_0 rT$ | $\dfrac{e^{aT}z\sin \omega_0 T}{e^{2aT}z^2-2e^{aT}z\cos \omega_0 T+1}$ | $e^{-aT}$ |

(Note that the sampled notation can be such that the $T$ can be omitted from the terms in the first column, if desired.)

Problems occur if we attempt to obtain the $z$-transform of an impulse. For example (see Fig. 6–2), if the sampler produced impulses upon sampling a bounded $f(t)$, what does it produce when it samples an impulse? One interpretation is that it just produces an impulse when it samples an impulse. This can lead to great difficulty. A train of impulses occurring at the sample time would produce the same output as a constant signal. This can lead to confusion. If, in a practical case, the samples of a train of impulses do actually approximate a train of approximate impulses (e.g., the sampler is nonlinear and saturates at some maximum output), this may be a valid representation. Mathematically, the output of the sampler is not clearly defined.

**The Inverse $z$-Transform.** Let us now see how we can obtain $f(t)$ from $F(z)$. Of course, if we have computed $F(z)$ from $f(t)$ and tabulated the transforms, then the table can be used to obtain the inverse transform. However, now let us see if we can evaluate it directly. In general (see Eq. 6–100), where $f(rT)$ is replaced by the discrete notation $f(r)$,

$$F(z) = \sum_{r=0}^{\infty} f(r) z^{-r} \tag{6-102}$$

This is of the form of a Laurent series. Then the coefficients of the Laurent series (see Eq. B-58), in this case, $f(r)$, are given by

$$f(r) = \frac{1}{2\pi j} \oint_C F(z) z^{r-1} dz, \qquad |C| > z_0 \tag{6-103}$$

where $C$ is a circle about the origin whose radius is greater than $z_0$; that is, the path lies in the region where $F(z)$ is analytic. The $z$-transform pair is given by Eqs. 6–102 and 6–103. We repeat them here

$$F(z) = \sum_{r=0}^{\infty} f(r) z^{-r}, \qquad |z| > z_0 \tag{6-104}$$

$$f(r) = \frac{1}{2\pi j} \oint_C F(z) z^{r-1} dz, \qquad |C| > z_0 \tag{6-105}$$

We now consider an example of the procedure for obtaining the inverse $z$-transform. Evaluate the inverse $z$-transform of $z/(z - e^{-aT})$, $|z| > e^{-aT}$; then,

$$f(r) = \frac{1}{2\pi j} \oint_C \frac{z^r}{z - e^{-aT}} dz, \qquad |z| > e^{aT}$$

Thus,

$$f(r) = \left[ \text{Res} \frac{z^r}{z - e^{-aT}} \text{ at } z = e^{-aT} \right]$$

Evaluating the residue, we obtain

$$f(r) = (e^{-aT})^r = e^{-aTr}, \qquad r > 0$$

This checks with Table 6-1.

If the $z$-transform can be expressed in a Laurent series in $z$, Eq. 6–104 can be used to obtain $f(r)$ directly. Often, division can be used to determine the Laurent series. For example,

$$\boldsymbol{F}(z) = \frac{z}{z - e^{-aT}} = \frac{1}{1 - z^{-1}e^{-aT}}$$

Now perform the division:

$$
\begin{array}{r}
1 + z^{-1}e^{-aT} + z^{-2}e^{-2aT} + \cdots \\[4pt]
1 - z^{-1}e^{-aT} \overline{\big)\, 1 \phantom{aaaaaaaaaaaaaaaaaaaa}} \\
\underline{1 - z^{-1}e^{-aT}} \phantom{aaaaaaaaaaaa} \\
z^{-1}e^{-aT} \phantom{aaaaaaaaa} \\
\underline{z^{-1}e^{-aT} - z^{-2}e^{-2aT}} \phantom{aa} \\
z^{-2}e^{-2aT} \phantom{aa} \\
\underline{z^{-2}e^{-2aT} - z^{-3}e^{-3aT}} \\
z^{-3}e^{-3aT} \\
\vdots \\
\vdots
\end{array}
$$

Thus,

$$\boldsymbol{F}(z) = 1 + e^{-aT}z^{-1} + e^{-2aT}z^{-2} + \cdots$$

Then, from Eq. 6–104, we obtain $f(r)$ as

$$f(0) = 1$$
$$f(1) = e^{-aT}$$
$$f(2) = e^{-2aT}$$
$$\vdots$$
$$\vdots$$

# 6-8. SOLVING DIFFERENCE EQUATIONS USING THE z-TRANSFORM

We begin by determining the $z$-transform of $f(r + n)$ in terms of the $z$-transform of $f(r)$. Suppose (using discrete notation) we have a function $f(r)$ whose $z$-transform is $F(z)$:

$$f(r) \leftrightarrow \boldsymbol{F}(z) \qquad\qquad (6\text{--}106)$$

Now let us determine the $z$-transform of $f(r + 1)$. From Eq. 6–104, we have

$$f(r) \leftrightarrow \sum_{r=0}^{\infty} f(r) z^{-r}, \qquad |z| > z_0 \qquad\qquad (6\text{--}107)$$

Then,
$$f(r) \leftrightarrow f(0) + f(1) z^{-1} + f(2) z^{-2} + f(3) z^{-3} + \dots \qquad (6\text{--}108)$$

Hence,
$$f(r+1) \leftrightarrow f(1) + f(2) z^{-1} + f(3) z^{-3} + \dots$$

We can write this as
$$f(r+1) \leftrightarrow -zf(0) + z[f(0) + f(1) z^{-1} + f(2) z^{-2} + f(3) z^{-3} + \dots]$$

Comparing this with Eqs. 6–108 and 6–106, we have
$$f(r+1) \leftrightarrow zF(z) - zf(0) \qquad (6\text{--}109)$$

Now let us compute the $z$-transform of $f(r+2)$. Let $F_1(z)$ be the $z$-transform of $f(r+1)$. Then, using Eq. 6–109
$$f(r+2) \leftrightarrow zF_1(z) - zf(1)$$

Substituting Eq. 6–109, we have
$$f(r+2) \leftrightarrow z^2 F(z) - z^2 f(0) - zf(1) \qquad (6\text{--}110)$$

In general, we can repeat this procedure and obtain
$$f(r+n) \leftrightarrow z^n \left[ F(z) - \sum_{i=0}^{n-1} f(i) z^{-i} \right] \qquad (6\text{--}111)$$

Let us see how this can be used to solve a difference equation. Suppose we have
$$f(r+2) + 2f(r+1) + f(r) = u(r) \qquad (6\text{--}112)$$

Then,
$$f(r) \leftrightarrow F(z)$$

Taking the $z$-transform of both sides of the equation yields
$$z^2 F(z) - z^2 f(0) - zf(1) + 2zF(z) - 2zf(0) + F(z) = \frac{z}{z-1}$$

Assume that
$$f(0) = 0$$
$$f(1) = 1$$

Then, we obtain
$$(z^2 + 2z + 1) F(z) = \frac{z}{z-1} + z = \frac{z^2}{z-1}$$

$$F(z) = \frac{z^2}{(z-1)(z^2 + 2z + 1)} = \frac{z^2}{z^3 + z^2 - z - 1}$$

We can write this as
$$F(z) = \frac{1}{z + 1 - \dfrac{1}{z} - \dfrac{1}{z^2}}$$

Finally, carrying out the division outlined at the end of the last section, we have

$$f(0) = 0$$
$$f(1) = 1$$
$$f(2) = -1 \qquad\qquad (6\text{-}113)$$
$$f(3) = 2$$
$$f(4) = -2$$
$$\vdots$$

Substituting into the difference equation will verify this result.

A solution in closed form can be obtained by evaluating the inverse $z$-transform integral. From Eq. 6–105, we have

$$f(r) = \frac{1}{2\pi j} \oint_C \frac{z^{r+1}}{(z-1)(z+1)^2}\,dz, \qquad |C| > 1$$

Using residues, we obtain

$$f(r) = \frac{1}{4} + \left[ \frac{(z-1)(r+1)z^r - z^{r+1}}{(z-1)^2} \right]_{z=-1}$$

$$f(r) = \tfrac{1}{4}[1 - 2(r+1)(-1)^r + (-1)^r] = \tfrac{1}{4}[1 - (2r+1)(-1)^r] \quad (6\text{-}114)$$

If this is substituted, the difference equation is checked. Thus, the $z$-transform greatly simplifies the solution of difference equations.

Often simultaneous difference equations must be solved. If their $z$-transforms are taken, they become simultaneous algebraic equations. Then, sets of $z$-transformed equations, each having one unknown can be obtained by applying the usual procedures for the solution of simultaneous equations, and each of these can be solved by the procedures outlined in this section.

A quantity that is sometimes defined is the *forward difference* $\Delta f(r)$

$$\Delta f(r) = f(r+1) - f(r)$$

Similarly, we can define

Hence,
$$\Delta^2 f(r) = \Delta[\Delta f(r)] = \Delta f(r+1) - \Delta f(r)$$
$$\Delta^2 f(r) = f(r+2) - f(r+1) - [f(r+1) - f(r)]$$
$$\Delta^2 f(r) = f(r+2) - 2f(r+1) + f(r)$$

The $z$-transform of the forward difference can be found from the $z$-transform of $f(r+n)$. The details will be left to the reader.

## 6-9. SOLVING STATE VARIABLE EQUATIONS OF LINEAR TIME-INVARIANT DISCRETE TIME SYSTEMS USING THE $z$-TRANSFORM

The $z$-transform can be used to solve the state variable equations of linear, time-invariant systems. These equations are of the form (see Eq. 6–28):

$$\hat{q}(r + 1) = \hat{a}\hat{q}(r) + \hat{b}\hat{y}(r) \tag{6–115}$$

Using Eq. 6–109, we obtain

$$z\hat{Q}(z) - z\hat{q}(0) = \hat{a}\hat{Q}(z) + \hat{b}\hat{Y}(z) \tag{6–116}$$

where

$$\hat{q}(r) \leftrightarrow \hat{Q}(z) \tag{6–117a}$$

and

$$\hat{y}(r) \leftrightarrow \hat{Y}(z) \tag{6–117b}$$

(Note that the $z$-transform of a matrix is the $z$-transform of each element in the matrix.) Then, rearranging, we have

$$(z\hat{U} - \hat{a})\,\hat{Q}(z) = \hat{b}\hat{Y}(z) + z\hat{q}(0) \tag{6–118}$$

where $\hat{U}$ is a unit matrix of order $n$ (there are $n$ state variables). Then, if $(z\hat{U} - \hat{a})$ possesses an inverse, we have

$$\hat{Q}(z) = (z\hat{U} - \hat{a})^{-1}\left[\hat{b}\hat{Y}(z) + z\hat{q}(0-)\right] \tag{6–119}$$

Thus, we have obtained a solution of the desired equations. We shall not give an example of a $z$-transform solution here, since one was given in the last section.

## 6-10. CONVOLUTION THEOREM APPLIED TO $z$-TRANSFORMS

Convolution theorems exist for the $z$-transform and they are just as powerful and useful as they are for the Laplace and Fourier transforms. Before discussing them, we begin by defining *convolution of discrete signals*. To do this, we use the notation for the convolution of two discrete time signals as $f_1(r)$ and $f_2(r)$; then,

$$f(r) = f_1(r) * f_2(r) \tag{6–120}$$

The convolution is defined as

$$f(r) = \sum_{k=-\infty}^{\infty} f_1(k)f_2(r - k) \tag{6–121}$$

Then, this is analogous to the convolution of two continuous time signals. Note that Eq. 6–121 is written assuming that $f_1(r)$ and $f_2(r)$ are nonzero for positive, as well as for negative, $r$. If this is not the case and they are nonzero only for positive $r$, if we wish we can restrict the limits

$$f(r) = \sum_{k=0}^{r} f_1(k)f_2(r - k) \tag{6–122}$$

Note that we can write the upper limit as $\infty$ since $f_2(r - k) = 0$ for $k > r$.
    In this section, we shall use the notation

$$f(r) \leftrightarrow F(z) \qquad |z| > z_0$$

$$f_1(r) \leftrightarrow F_1(z) \qquad |z| > z_1$$

$$f_2(r) \leftrightarrow F_2(z) \qquad |z| > z_2$$

**Sample Convolution Theorem.**   Now let us derive the convolution theorem. Use
Eq. 6–104 to take the z-transform of both sides of Eq. 6–122. This yields

$$f(r) \leftrightarrow \sum_{r=0}^{\infty} f(r) z^{-r} = \sum_{r=0}^{\infty} z^{-r} \sum_{k=0}^{\infty} f_1(k) f_2(r - k) \qquad (6\text{--}123)$$

Now assume that the functions are such that the order of summation can be interchanged; hence,

$$f(r) \leftrightarrow \sum_{k=0}^{\infty} f_1(k) \sum_{r=0}^{\infty} f_2(r - k) z^{-r} \qquad (6\text{--}124)$$

The second summation is just the z-transform of $f_2(r - k)$. Then, following a development similar to that of Eq. 6–111, we obtain

$$f_2(r - k) \leftrightarrow F_2(z) z^{-k}$$

Hence,

$$f(r) \leftrightarrow \sum_{k=0}^{\infty} f_1(k) z^{-k} F_2(z) \qquad (6\text{--}125)$$

Note that the $f(i)$, corresponding to those in Eq. 6–111, refer to negative values
for the $i$. Thus, the $f(i)$ are zero. Removing $F_2(z)$ from the summation, we are left
with the z-transform of $f_1(r)$; hence,

$$f(r) \leftrightarrow F_1(z) F_2(z) \qquad (6\text{--}126)$$

Or, equivalently,

$$\sum_{k=0}^{\infty} f_1(k) f_2(r - k) \leftrightarrow F_1(z) F_2(z) \qquad (6\text{--}127)$$

which is the sample convolution theorem.

**Complex Convolution Theorem.**   The results we obtain here are, strictly speaking,
not in the form of a convolution. However, we call it complex convolution by analogy
with the Laplace transform.
    We wish to determine the z-transform of the product $f_1(r) f_2(r)$. Assume that

$$f_1(r) \leftrightarrow F_1(z), \qquad |z| > z_1 \qquad (6\text{--}128a)$$

$$f_2(r) \leftrightarrow F_2(z), \qquad |z| > z_2 \qquad (6\text{--}128b)$$

Then, using Eq. 6–104, we have

$$f_1(r)f_2(r) \leftrightarrow \sum_{r=0}^{\infty} f_1(r)f_2(r)\, z^{-r}, \qquad |z| > z_0 \tag{6–129}$$

where $z_0$ is such that the $z$-transform exists. Then, using Eq. 6–105, we have

$$f_1(r) = \frac{1}{2\pi j} \oint_C \frac{F_1(z)}{z}\, z^r\, dz, \qquad |C| > z_1 \tag{6–130}$$

Substituting in Eq. 6–129 and assuming that the functions are such that the order of summation and integration can be interchanged, we have

$$f_1(r)f_2(r) \leftrightarrow \frac{1}{2\pi j} \oint_C \frac{F_1(y)}{y} \sum_{r=0}^{\infty} f_2(r)\, y^r z^{-r}\, dy \tag{6–131}$$

where we have changed the variable of integration from $z$ to $y$ to avoid confusion. We can write the inner summation as

$$\sum_{r=0}^{\infty} f_2(r)\, (z/y)^{-r}$$

Thus, if we consider $z/y$ as a variable, then this summation has the form of Eq. 6–104. Hence, it is the $z/y$-transform of $f_2(r)$; therefore,

$$\sum_{r=0}^{\infty} f_2(r)\, (z/y)^{-r} = F_2(z/y), \qquad |z/y| > z_2 \tag{6–132}$$

The condition $|z/y| > z_2$ is equivalent to $|y| < |z/z_2|$. Substituting in Eq. 6–131, we obtain

$$f_1(r)f_2(r) \leftrightarrow \frac{1}{2\pi j} \oint_C \frac{F_1(y)\, F_2(z/y)}{y}\, dy;$$

$$|C| > z_1, \qquad |y| < |z/z_2|, \qquad |z| > z_0 \tag{6–133}$$

The contour of integration will be circular and $|y|$ is given by the radius of the circle which is $|C|$; hence, Eq. 6–133 becomes

$$f_1(r)f_2(r) \leftrightarrow \frac{1}{2\pi j} \oint_C \frac{F_1(y)\, F_2(z/y)}{y}\, dy; \qquad \frac{|z|}{z_2} > |C| > z_1, \qquad |z| > z_0 \tag{6–134}$$

As an example of this theorem, let us obtain the $z$-transform of $r^2 u(r)$. We write this as

$$r^2 u(r) = r u(r)\, r u(r)$$

We wish to determine $F(z)$, $|z| > z_0$; then (see Table 6-1),

$$F_1(z) = \frac{Tz}{(z-1)^2}, \qquad |z| > 1$$

$$F_2(z) = \frac{Tz}{(z-1)^2}, \qquad |z| > 1$$

Substituting in Eq. 6–134, we have

$$f(r) \leftrightarrow \frac{T^2}{2\pi j} \oint_C \frac{y(z/y)}{(y-1)^2 (z/y-1)^2} \frac{1}{y} dy, \qquad |z| > |C| > 1$$

Rearranging, we obtain

$$f(t) \leftrightarrow \frac{T^2}{2\pi j} \oint_C \frac{yz}{(y-1)^2 (z-y)^2} dy \qquad (6\text{--}135)$$

The singularities occur at $y = 1$ and $y = z$. The contour $C$ must be such that $|C| > 1$ and $|C| < |z|$. Then, choose $|z|$ large enough so that $|z| > z_0$. We do not know $|z_0|$; however, $z$ can be made as large as desired without affecting the relative position of the path and the poles (see Fig. 6–4); then,

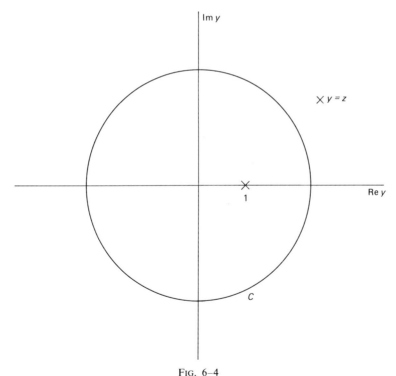

FIG. 6–4
Illustration of the contour of integration of Eq. 6–135

$$f(r) \leftrightarrow T^2 \left[ \text{Res at } y = 1 \text{ of} \frac{yz}{(y-1)^2(z-y)^2} \right]$$

Thus,

$$f(t) \leftrightarrow T^2 \frac{d}{dy} \frac{yz}{(z-y)^2} \bigg|_{y=1}$$

Evaluating, we have

$$f(t) \leftrightarrow \frac{T^2 z(z+1)}{(z-1)^3}$$

This is correct (see Table 6-1).


## 6-11. DISCRETE TIME SYSTEM RESPONSE—TRANSFER FUNCTIONS

Let us assume that a signal $f(t)$ is sampled and then applied to a linear, time-invariant system. The system output is then sampled. This entire system is illustrated in schematic form in Fig. 6–5. This is typical of many sampled systems. They are continuous, but their inputs are sampled and their outputs are only measured at discrete times.

FIG. 6–5
Linear, time-invariant system with sampled input and output

The system contained within the box is linear. For the moment let it be time varying. Its impulse response is $h(t, T)$ (see Eq. 5–6). If

$$f_*(t) = \delta(t - T) \tag{6–136}$$

then

$$g(t) = h(t, T) \tag{6–137}$$

Note that $h(t, T)$ is not the response to a sampled impulse, but the response of the continuous portion of the system to an impulse directly applied at its input.

Now suppose that a signal $f(t)$ is applied, as shown, and the sampler produces $f_*(t)$, a train of impulses (see Fig. 6–2). Then, since the system is linear, the response $g(t)$ is the sum of the individual impulse responses; hence (see Eq. 6–78),

$$f_*(t) = \sum_{k=0}^{\infty} f(kT)\,\delta(t - kT) \tag{6–138}$$

Then,

$$g(t) = \sum_{k=0}^{\infty} f(kT)\,h(t, kT) \tag{6–139}$$

Assume that the system is time invariant, as well as linear; then (see Eq. 5–16),

$$h(t, T) = h(t - T) \tag{6-140}$$

For a linear, time-invariant system, Eq. 6–139 becomes

$$g(t) = \sum_{k=0}^{\infty} f(kT) h(t - kT) \tag{6-141}$$

The output of the system is sampled. Thus, we only wish $g(t)$ at intervals of $rT$ seconds. Then, using discrete time notation (i.e., $g(r)$ replaces $g(rT)$ and $f(r)$ replaces $f(rT)$), we have

$$g(r) = \sum_{k=0}^{\infty} f(k) h(r - k) \tag{6-142}$$

Note that $h(r - k)$ is the value of $h(t - kT)$ at $t = rT$. Thus (see Eq. 6–121) $g(r)$ is the convolution of $f(r)$ and $h(r)$.

The output of the system is $g_*(r)$. By analogy with $f(r)$, this is (in discrete time notation)

$$g_*(r) = \sum_{k=0}^{\infty} g(k) \delta(r - k) \tag{6-143}$$

Thus, we need only find $g(r)$ to determine the system output.

Now let us express the system response in terms of $z$-transforms; let

$$h(t) \leftrightarrow H(z) \tag{6-144}$$

That is, $H(z)$ is the $z$ transform of the impulse response of the box; also let

$$f(t) \leftrightarrow F(z) \tag{6-145a}$$

$$g(t) \leftrightarrow G(z) \tag{6-145b}$$

Then, applying the sample convolution theorem (see Eq. 6–127), to Eq. 6–142, we obtain

$$G(z) = H(z) F(z) \tag{6-146}$$

The result is analogous to Eq. 5–21 for continuous time systems. It states that *the z-transform of the output of a sampled system is equal to the z-transform of the input times the z-transform of the impulse response of the unsampled parts of the system.* Then, $H(z)$ is called the *transfer function of the sampled system.* It is important to remember that $H(z)$ is obtained from the unsampled impulse response.

Consider the network of Fig. 6–6a as an example of this procedure. It has a unit step input which is sampled. The samplers are not just switches, but they produce the impulse train of Fig. 6–2b. Let us determine $v_{2*}(r)$, the sampled output. This is given by

$$v_{2*}(r) = \sum_{k=0}^{\infty} v_2(r) \delta(r - k) \tag{6-147}$$

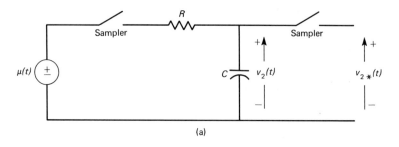

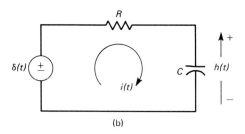

FIG. 6–6

(a) Simple sampled network; (b) network used to calculate $H(z)$

Thus, we must determine $v_2(r)$. Let us find the transfer function of the system. We use Fig. 6–6b for this. Then, using the Laplace transform to obtain the impulse response, we have

$$1 = \left( R + \frac{1}{Cs} \right) I(s)$$

$$H(s) = \frac{I(s)}{Cs}$$

Then, solving, we obtain

$$H(s) = \frac{1}{1 + RCs} = \frac{1}{RC} \frac{1}{s + 1/RC}$$

Taking the inverse Laplace transform, we have

$$h(t) = \frac{1}{RC} e^{-t/RC} u(t) \tag{6–148}$$

At the sampled intervals this is

$$h(rT) = \frac{1}{RC} e^{-rT/RC} u(rT), \qquad r = 0, 1, 2, \ldots$$

Then, taking the $z$-transform of $h(r)$, as a sampled function, we have (see Table 6-1)

$$H(z) = \frac{1}{RC} \frac{z}{z - e^{-T/RC}} \tag{6-149}$$

where $T$ is the interval between samples. From Table 6-1, we have

$$u(r) \leftrightarrow \frac{z}{z - 1}$$

Hence,

$$V_2(z) = H(z) F(z)$$

$$V_2(z) = \frac{1}{RC} \frac{z}{z - e^{-T/RC}} \frac{z}{z - 1}$$

The inverse $z$-transform is given by (see Eq. 6–105)

$$v_2(r) = \frac{1}{RC} \frac{1}{2\pi j} \oint_C \frac{z^{r+1}}{(z - e^{-T/RC})(z - 1)} dz$$

where $C$ encloses all the poles. These occur at $z = 1$ and $z = e^{T/RC}$. Evaluating the residues, we have

$$v_2(r) = \frac{1}{RC} \frac{1 - e^{-(r+1)T/RC}}{1 - e^{-T/RC}}, \qquad r = 0, 1, \ldots$$

Thus, we have obtained the output at the sample intervals. Note that at $r = 0$, $v_2(0) = 1/RC$. It seems strange to have a unit step response change its value instantaneously. However, remember that the sampler actually generates impulses which are applied to the circuit.

Let us consider another example. The block diagram of Fig. 6–7 represents a sampled feedback system. Let us obtain its transfer function. The sampled input to the $A(z)$ block is the sampled $f(t)$ plus the output of the $\beta$ block. Thus this input is

$$F(z) - \beta(z) G(z)$$

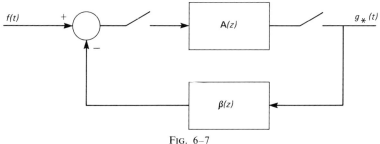

FIG. 6–7
Sampled feedback system

The output $G(z)$ is $A(z)$ times the input; hence,

$$[F(z) - \beta(z)\,G(z)]\,A(z) = G(z)$$

Thus, the transfer function of this system is given by

$$H(z) = \frac{G(z)}{F(z)} = \frac{A(z)}{1 + A(z)\,\beta(z)} \qquad (6\text{–}150)$$

This result is similar to that for an ordinary feedback system.

The location of the sampler can greatly affect the transfer function. Consider the feedback system of Fig. 6–8, where the sampler has been shifted. In this case, the input to the $\beta$ network is not a sequence of impulses, but the response of the $A$ network to such a sequence. In order to obtain the output of the $\beta$ network, we shall work with the transfer functions on a Laplace transformed basis; i.e., on a continuous basis. We shall call these transfer function $A_s(s)$ and $\beta_s(s)$.

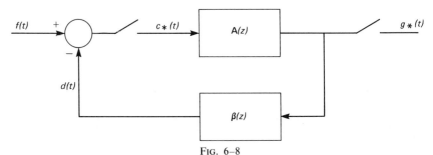

FIG. 6–8
Another sampled feedback system

Now let us obtain the transfer function from $c$ to $d$. We proceed as in Eqs. 6–148 and 6–149. The transfer function is $A_s(s)\,\beta_s(s)$. Take the inverse Laplace transform: call this $h_{A\beta}(t)$. Now form $h_{A\beta}(rT)$ and take its $z$-transform: call this $\overline{A\beta}(z)$. It is important to note that

$$\overline{A\beta}(z) \neq A(z)\,\beta(z)$$

Then, on a $z$-transform basis, we have

$$C(z) = F(z) - C(z)\,\overline{A\beta}(z)$$

Solving for $C(z)$ and noting that $G(z) = C(z)\,A(z)$, we obtain the transfer function

$$H(z) = \frac{G(z)}{F(z)} = \frac{A(z)}{1 + \overline{A\beta}(z)}$$

Note that this relation is *not* the same as Eq. 6–150.

**Boxcar Hold Circuit.** Consider another example. Suppose the sampler does not produce impulses, but just remains constant at the last sampled value of $f(r)$. That is, the output of the new sampler is $f'_*(t)$ where

$$f'_*(t) = f(rT), \qquad rT \le t < (r + 1) T \qquad (6\text{–}151)$$

We need not actually specify a new sampler but only consider the standard one in cascade with a circuit which converts the impulses into flat-topped pulses of duration $T$. Thus we desire a network whose impulse response is

$$h(t) = u(t) - u(t - T) \qquad (6\text{–}152)$$

Hence, its response to a unit impulse is a unit pulse of duration $T$. Using Table 3-1 and Eq. 3–76, we have

$$H(s) = \frac{1}{s}(1 - e^{-sT}) \qquad (6\text{–}153)$$

This system can be placed in cascade with the system input to produce the desired form of sampled input. The circuit produces square pulses and is called a *boxcar hold circuit*.

**An Alternative Procedure for Determining $H(z)$.** In the analyses of this section, we obtain $H(z)$ by determining the Laplace transform of the impulse response and then taking the inverse Laplace transform. This time function is used to obtain the $z$-transform (see Eqs. 6–147 through 6–149).

Now consider another procedure which does not require the inverse Laplace transform. If $h(t)$ is the unit impulse response (see Eq. 6–104), its $z$-transform is

$$H(z) = \sum_{k=0}^{\infty} h(r) z^{-r} \qquad (6\text{–}154)$$

Consider a sampled form of the impulse response.

$$h_*(t) = \sum_{k=0}^{\infty} h(kT) \delta(t - kT) \qquad (6\text{–}155)$$

Then, the Laplace transform of this is given by

$$H_{*L}(s) = \sum_{k=0}^{\infty} h(kT) e^{-kTs} \qquad (6\text{–}156)$$

Comparing Eqs. 6–154 and 6–156, we determine that $H(z)$ can be obtained from $H_L(s)$ by replacing $e^{Ts}$ with $z$. Using Eq. 2–174, we can write Eq. 6–155 as

$$h_*(t) = h(t) \sum_{k=0}^{\infty} \delta(t - kT) \qquad (6\text{–}157)$$

Let us obtain the Laplace transform of the terms on the right-hand side of Eq. 6–157:

$$h(t) \leftrightarrow H(s), \qquad \text{Re } s > \sigma_0$$

$$\sum_{k=0}^{\infty} \delta(t - kT) \leftrightarrow \frac{1}{1 - e^{-sT}}, \qquad \text{Re } s > 0$$

(see Eq. 6–85.) Then, the Laplace transform of $h_*(t)$ can be expressed as the complex convolution of the two quantities (see Eq. 3–202); hence,

$$H_{*L}(s) = \frac{1}{2\pi j} \int_{C-j\infty}^{C+j\infty} \frac{H_L(y)}{1 - e^{-(s-y)T}} \, dy; \qquad \text{Re } s > \sigma_0, \qquad \sigma_0 < C < \text{Re } s \qquad (6\text{–}158)$$

We can obtain $H(z)$ by replacing $e^{-sT}$ with $1/z$; thus,

$$H(z) = \frac{1}{2\pi j} \int_{C-j\infty}^{C+j\infty} \frac{H_L(y)}{1 - \dfrac{e^{yT}}{z}} \, dy \qquad (6\text{–}159)$$

It is inconvenient to express the location of $C$ in terms of $z$. However (see Eq. 6–158), the path of integration lies to the right of the rightmost singularity of $H_L(y)$, but to the left of the roots of $1 - (e^{-yT}/z)$. This integral is evaluated as the usual convolution. For example, suppose we consider

$$H(s) = \frac{1}{(s + a)(s + b)} = \frac{1}{b - a}\frac{1}{s + a} + \frac{1}{a - b}\frac{1}{s + b}$$

Then,

$$h(t) = \left( \frac{1}{b - a} e^{-at} + \frac{1}{a - b} e^{-bt} \right) u(t)$$

Using Table 6-1, we have

$$H(z) = \frac{1}{b - a}\frac{z}{z - e^{-aT}} + \frac{1}{a - b}\frac{z}{z - e^{-bT}}$$

Let us use Eq. 6–159 and work with $H(s)$ directly; then,

$$H(z) = \frac{1}{2\pi j} \int_{C-j\infty}^{C+j\infty} \frac{1}{(y + a)(y + b)} \frac{1}{1 - \dfrac{e^{yT}}{z}} \, dy \qquad (6\text{–}160)$$

The contour of integration is as shown in Fig. 6–9. The integral vanishes on the infinite semicircle; hence,

$$H(z) = [\text{Res at } y = a] + [\text{Res at } y = b]$$

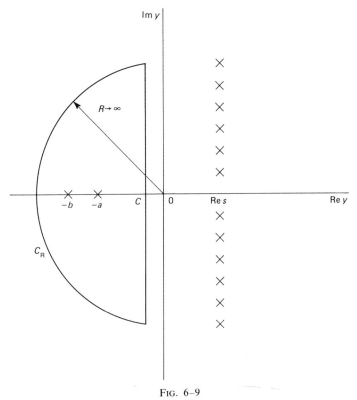

Fɪɢ. 6–9
Contour of integration used to evaluate Eq. 6–160

Evaluating the residues we have

$$H(z) = \frac{1}{b-a} \frac{1}{1 - \dfrac{e^{-aT}}{z}} + \frac{1}{a-b} \frac{1}{1 - \dfrac{e^{-bT}}{z}}$$

$$H(z) = \frac{1}{b-a} \frac{z}{z - e^{-aT}} + \frac{1}{a-b} \frac{z}{z - e^{-bT}}$$

There are times when the integral over the infinite semicircle does not vanish; e.g., $H(s) = 1/(s + a)$. In such cases, the value of $h(0)$ may cause problems. For the Laplace transform, $h(0) = \frac{1}{2}[h(0-) + \frac{1}{2}h(0+)]$, but this is not how $h(0)$ is defined for the z-transforms (see the discussion following Eq. 6–99). To resolve this difficulty, when Eq. 6–159 is used, $H(s)$ can be multiplied by $e^{\varepsilon s}$. This will cause the integral to vanish on the infinite contour. After $H(z)$ is obtained, let $\varepsilon$ approach 0. This procedure is illustrated following Eq. 6–99.

## PROBLEMS

**6-1.** Obtain a difference equation which corresponds to the differential equation

$$\frac{d^2x(t)}{dt^2} + 2\frac{dx(t)}{dt} + x(t) = y(t)$$

**6-2.** A system is characterized by the differential equation

$$\frac{d^2x(t)}{dt^2} + 3\frac{dx(t)}{dt} + 2x(t) = y(t)$$

The output is sampled at intervals of $T$ seconds, $y(t)$ changes discretely, $y(t) = y(rT)$, $rT \leq t < r(T+1)$. Determine the difference equation for this system.

**6-3.** A system is characterized by the difference equation

$$x(r+2) + 3x(r+1) + x(r) = y(t)$$

Obtain a set of state variable equations which characterize the system.

**6-4.** Repeat Problem 6-3 for the difference equations

$$x_1(r+3) + 2x_1(r+2) + x_1(r+1) + x_1(r) = y_1(r) + 2y_2(r)$$
$$x_2(r+3) + 4x_2(r+2) + x_2(r+1) + 4x_2(r) = y_1(r) - 3y_2(r)$$

**6-5.** Repeat Problem 6-3 for the difference equation

$$x(r+4) + 4x(r+3) + 2x(r+2) + 7x(r+1) + 3x(r) = y(r+1) + y(r)$$

**6-6.** A system is characterized by the differential equation

$$a_2(t)\frac{d^2x(t)}{dt^2} + a_1(t)\frac{dx(t)}{dt} + a_0(t)x(t) = y(t)$$

where $a_k(t)$, $k = 0, 1, 2$ and $y(t)$ are known functions of time; $y(t)$ is such that $y(t) = y(rT)$, $rT \leq t \leq (r+1)T$; $x(t)$ is sampled. The sampling interval is $T$. Obtain a difference equation that characterizes the system. Assume that $T$ is so short that no function changes by important amounts in an interval of $T$ seconds.

**6-7.** Indicate the changes that occur in Problem 6-6 if $T$ is not short.

**6-8.** A system is characterized by the differential equation

$$x(t)\frac{d^2x(t)}{dt^2} + 2x^2(t)\frac{dx(t)}{dt} + x^2(t) = y(t)$$

where $y(t)$ is as in Problem 6-6 and $x(t)$ is to be sampled every $T$ seconds. Obtain a difference equation that characterizes the system. Assume that the sampling interval is short enough so that $x(t)$ and its derivatives do not change substantially in any interval of $T$ seconds.

**6-9.** Indicate how the solution to Problem 6-8 would be modified if $T$ is long.

**6-10.** Solve the state variable difference equations for the first 5 sample times

$$\hat{q}(r+1) = \hat{a}\hat{q}(r) + \hat{b}\hat{y}(r)$$

where

$$\hat{q}(0) = \begin{bmatrix} 1 \\ 1 \end{bmatrix}$$

$$\hat{a} = \begin{bmatrix} 1 & 4 \\ 1 & 1 \end{bmatrix}$$

$$\hat{b} = \begin{bmatrix} 1 \\ 2 \end{bmatrix}$$

$$\hat{y}(r) = [r]$$

**6-11.** Repeat Problem 6-10, but now obtain the solution in closed form.

**6-12.** Repeat Problem 6-10 for the matrices

$$\hat{q}(0) = \begin{bmatrix} 1 \\ 0 \\ 1 \end{bmatrix}$$

$$\hat{a} = \begin{bmatrix} 1 & 2 & 3 \\ 1 & 1 & 1 \\ 1 & 2 & 1 \end{bmatrix}$$

$$\hat{b} = \begin{bmatrix} 1 \\ 1 \\ 2 \end{bmatrix}$$

$$\hat{y}(r) = [r]$$

**6-13.** Repeat Problem 6-10 for the matrices

$$\hat{q}(0) = \begin{bmatrix} 0 \\ 0 \end{bmatrix}$$

$$\hat{a}(r) = \begin{bmatrix} r & 2r^2 \\ 1 & r \end{bmatrix}$$

$$\hat{b}(r) = \begin{bmatrix} r \\ 1 \end{bmatrix}$$

$$\hat{y}(r) = [r]$$

**6-14.** Solve the following state variable difference equations for the first 3 sample times:

$$q_1(r + 1) = q_1(r) q_2(r) + q_1^2(r) + y(r)$$
$$q_2(r + 1) = q_1(r) + q_2^2(r) + y(r)$$

where

$$y(r) = r$$

$$\hat{q}(0) = \begin{bmatrix} 1 \\ 2 \end{bmatrix}$$

**6-15.** Write a computer program to solve the state variable equations of Problem 6-10.
**6-16.** Repeat Problem 6-15 for the equations of Problem 6-12.
**6-17.** Repeat Problem 6-15 for the equations of Problem 6-13.
**6-18.** Repeat Problem 6-15 for the equations of Problem 6-14.
**6-19.** Obtain the z-transform of

$$f(r) = u(r) \cos \omega_0 r$$

The sample interval is *T* seconds.

**6-20.** Repeat Problem 6-19 for

$$f(r) = u(r) e^{-ar} \cos \omega_0 r$$

**6-21.** Repeat Problem 6-20 for

$$f(r) = re^{-r}u(r)$$

**6-22.** Obtain the inverse $z$-transform of

$$F(z) = \frac{1}{(z+1)(z-2)}, \qquad |z| > 2$$

**6-23.** Repeat Problem 6-22 for

$$F(z) = \frac{1}{z^3(z+1)(z^2+1)}, \qquad |z| > 1$$

**6-24.** Find the inverse $z$-transform of

$$F(z) = \frac{1}{z^2+z+1}, \qquad |z| > z_0$$

Assume that $z_0$ is such that $F(z)$ is analytic for $|z| > z_0$. Find $z_0$.

**6-25.** Use the $z$-transform to solve the difference equation

$$x(r+2) + 3x(r+1) + 2x(r) = u(r)$$

Assume that $x(1) = x(0) = 0$.

**6-26.** Repeat Problem 6-25 for

$$x(r+2) - 3x(r+1) + 2x(r) = u(r) e^{-r}$$

**6-27.** Use the $z$-transform to solve the state variable difference equation of Problem 6-12.

**6-28.** Use the $z$-transform to solve the equations

$$x_1(r+1) + x_2(r) = u(r)$$
$$x_1(r) + x_2(r+1) = 2u(r)$$

where

$$x_1(0) = x_2(0) = 0$$

**6-29.** Obtain the inverse $z$-transform of

$$F(z) = \frac{z}{z-1} \cdot \frac{z}{z - e^{-aT}}$$

**6-30.** Obtain the $z$-transform of

$$f(r) = u(r) re^{-ar}$$

Use the convolution theorem to obtain the result.

**6-31.** The box of Fig. 6–5 has an impulse response given by

$$h(t) = e^{-t}u(t)$$

The input signal is

$$f(t) = e^{-2t}u(t)$$

Find the sampled output signal. What is the transfer function of the system on a $z$-transformed basis?

**6-32.** Repeat Problem 6-31 for

$$h(t) = e^{-t} \cos \omega_0 t \, u(t)$$

$$f(t) = e^{-2t} u(t)$$

**6-33.** The box of Fig. 6–5 has a transfer function whose Laplace transform is

$$F(s) = \frac{s - 1}{(s + 1)(s + 2)(s + 3)}$$

Determine the transfer function of the system on a $z$-transformed basis. Compute the sampled output signal if

$$f(t) = u(t)$$

**6-34.** Repeat Problem 6-33 for

$$F(s) = \frac{1}{s^2 + s + 1}$$

## REFERENCES

1. Schwarz, R. J., and Friedland, B. *Linear Systems.* New York: McGraw-Hill, 1965, p. 57.

## BIBLIOGRAPHY

Cadzow, J. A., and Martens, H. R. *Discrete Time and Computer Control Systems.* Englewood Cliffs, N.J.: Prentice-Hall, 1970.
Freeman, H. *Discrete Time Systems: An Introduction to the Theory.* New York: Wiley, 1965.
Schwartz, R. J., and Friedland, B. *Linear Systems.* pp. 95–96. New York: McGraw-Hill, 1965.
Truxal, J. G. *Control System Synthesis.* Chap. 9. New York: McGraw-Hill, 1955.

# CHAPTER 7

# System Stability

All systems are either *passive* or *active*. A passive system is one which contains no energy sources. Since we assume that all systems satisfy the law of conservation of energy, a passive system can only obtain energy from its applied signals. Thus, the output signal of a passive system can contain no more energy than that supplied by the input signals.

An active system contains energy sources within it. There may be a battery or power supply connected to a 60 Hz power line. The connection to the power line is not usually considered an input signal. Hence, the power supplied by the power supply is considered to be from an internal source. For example most amplifiers and control systems are active devices.

Active systems may *oscillate*; that is, they may produce output signals even when there is no input. Systems are sometimes deliberately constructed so that they generate signals. In these cases, oscillation is desirable. However, in many cases, oscillation destroys the operation of the system. For example, when a public address system howls, there is oscillation and the system cannot be used properly. If a system oscillates, it is said to be *unstable*. A system can be unstable even if it does not oscillate. For instance, if a finite or zero input signal produces an output of the form $e^{2t}$, the system is said to be unstable since the output builds up without limit. In this chapter we shall develop formal definitions of unstable systems. If a system is not unstable, it is *stable*. Since very many practical systems are active, it is extremely important to be able to determine if the system is stable. In this chapter we shall shall consider system stability in detail.

We shall start with a discussion of linear, time-invariant systems and then extend our discussion to other systems.

## 7-1. GENERAL DISCUSSION OF LINEAR, TIME-INVARIANT SYSTEM STABILITY

We are going to study the stability of systems in this chapter. Thus, at the start, we should consider a fundamental definition of stability. However, we shall see that there are several somewhat different definitions of stability.

We begin by considering an example of an unstable system and discuss its disadvantages. This will suggest some possible definitions of stability. We shall, for the next few sections, restrict ourselves to linear, time-invariant continuous time systems.

Suppose such a system has a transfer function given by

$$H(s) = \frac{1}{s+1} + \frac{0.001}{s-2} \tag{7-1}$$

The Laplace transform response of the system to a unit step input is (see Eq. 5–42)

$$A(s) = \frac{1}{s(s+1)} + \frac{0.001}{s(s-2)} \tag{7-2a}$$

Rearranging, we have

$$A(s) = \frac{1}{s} - \frac{1}{s+1} - \frac{0.0005}{s} + \frac{0.0005}{s-2} \tag{7-2b}$$

Then, taking the inverse Laplace transform and considering that $1 \gg 0.005$, we obtain

$$a(t) = [1 - e^{-t} + 0.0005e^{2t}]u(t) \tag{7-3}$$

The first two terms are typical of the unit step response of systems. However, there is an additional term with a *positive* exponent. This can be ignored for small time; however, eventually this term will become arbitrarily large and override the others. Since no system is completely linear, such a large signal will cause the device to operate nonlinearly. In an amplifier, the transistors will saturate or become cut off; a mechanical system will reach its limit stops, etc.

Suppose we have a linear, time-invariant system such as that characterized by the box in Fig. 7–1.

FIG. 7–1
Linear, time-invariant system

Let $f(t)$ be its input signal and $g(t)$ its output signal; also,

$$f(t) \leftrightarrow F(s) \tag{7-4a}$$

$$g(t) \leftrightarrow G(s) \tag{7-4b}$$

where $F(s)$ and $G(s)$ are the Laplace transforms of $f(t)$ and $g(t)$, respectively, and $H(s)$ is the Laplace transform of the impulse response; that is (see Eq. 5–42), it is the transfer function in Laplace transformed form; thus,

$$G(s) = F(s)H(s) \tag{7-5}$$

Now consider the evaluation of the inverse Laplace transform using residues (see Eq. 3–146). There will be a term in $g(t)$ corresponding to each pole of $F(s)H(s)$. Poles in the left half plane lead to exponentially damped functions of time, while those in the right half place increase exponentially. Simple poles on the $j\omega$ axis lead to sinusoids whose maximum value is constant. Multiple poles on the $j\omega$ axis lead to functions of time which increase as $t^n$, $n > 0$.

Suppose we apply an $f(t)$ to test if the system is stable; that is, we determine $g(t)$ in response to $f(t)$. But $g(t)$ should not increase without limit. In this case, $f(t)$ should also not increase without limit, since we would not be able to determine if the unbounded output is due to the system or the excitation. Note that if the input to an ideal system increases, the output (within the practical limits of the system) should also increase. This is proper behavior. However, if a bounded signal causes an infinite output, then the device will operate improperly. For this reason, we restrict $f(t)$ to those functions whose Laplace transforms have all their poles in the left-half plane.

Now $G(s)$ will contain poles which are those of $F(s)$ and of $H(s)$. Assume that a zero of $F(s)$ does not cancel a pole of $H(s)$, etc. Then, $g(t)$ will contain one component corresponding to *each* pole of $F(s)$ and $G(s)$. The components which correspond to $H(s)$ are *natural frequencies* of the system. Note that they may be complex. For example, the inverse transform of $1/[(s + 1)^2 + 9]$ is $(1/3)e^{-t}\sin 3tu(t)$, so we can speak of a frequency $-1 \pm j3$ here.

Then, in an unrigorous sense, if the poles of the system's transfer function lie in the right-half plane or on the $j\omega$ axis, the system will be unstable. If all the poles lie in the left-half plane, the system will be stable. (Simple poles may, in some definitions of stability, be allowed on the $j\omega$ axis.)

Now let us consider one rigorous definition of stability. It is: *A system is stable if its response to any bounded input is bounded*; that is, if for *all*

$$|f(t)| \le M_f \qquad (7\text{–}6a)$$

the response

$$|g(t)| \le M_g \qquad (7\text{–}6b)$$

then the system is said to be stable and $M_f$ and $M_g$ are finite positive numbers.

This appears to be a very tedious definition to test because the response to every possible bounded input must be found and checked. However, this is not the case. A criterion for stability is equivalent to the following: *a system is stable if*

$$\int_{-\infty}^{\infty} |h(t)|\, dt \le M \qquad (7\text{–}7)$$

where $M$ is a finite positive number. The system is stable if the integral of the magnitude of its impulse response is bounded. Let us show the equivalence of these definitions. From Eq. 5–17, we have

$$g(t) = \int_{-\infty}^{\infty} f(y)h(t - y)\, dy \qquad (7\text{–}8)$$

Letting $t - y = x$, Eq. 7-8 becomes

$$g(t) = \int_{-\infty}^{\infty} f(t - x) h(x) \, dx \qquad (7-9)$$

The magnitude of $g(t)$ is limited by the expression

$$|g(t)| \leq \int_{-\infty}^{\infty} |f(t - x)| \, |h(x)| \, dx$$

Substituting Eq. 7-6a, we have

$$|g(t)| \geq M_f \int_{-\infty}^{\infty} |h(x)| \, dx$$

Then, substituting Eq. 7-7, we obtain

$$|g(t)| \leq M_f M \qquad (7-10)$$

Thus, $g(t)$ will be bounded for any finite input if relation 7-7 is true.

Now let us show that if $\int_{-\infty}^{\infty} |h(x)| \, dx$ is unbounded. there is at least one $f(t)$ which results in an unbounded $g(t)$. Choose $f(t)$ in the following way

$$f(t_0 - t) = \operatorname{sgn} h(t) \qquad (7-11)$$

That is, choose a $t_0$. Then, if $h(t) > 0$, $f(t_0 - t) = 1$; if $h(t) < 0$, $f(t_0 - t) = -1$; thus, $f(t_0 - x) h(x) = |h(x))|$.

Substituting in Eq. 7-9, we have

$$g(t_0) = \int_{-\infty}^{\infty} |h(x)| \, dx \qquad (7-12)$$

However, we hypothesized that $\int_{-\infty}^{\infty} |h(x)| \, dx$ was unbounded. Hence, $g(t_0)$ is unbounded.

Thus, we have shown that the criterion for stability, which states that the response to any bounded input is bounded, is equivalent to stating that the system is stable if $\int_{-\infty}^{\infty} |h(t)| \, dt$ exists.

Let us see how the criterion relates to the transfer function $H(s)$. If $H(s)$ contains poles in the right-half plane, then $h(t)$ will contain components of the form $e^{at}$, $e^{at} \cos \omega_0 t$, $e^{at} \sin \omega_0 t$, $e^{at} t^n \cos \omega_0 t$, etc., where $t > 0$ and $a > 0$. The absolute integral of these functions becomes infinite. Poles on the $j\omega$ axis result in functions of the form $t^n \cos \omega_0 t$ or $t^n \sin \omega_0 t$, or $t^n$; $n \geq 0$, $t > 0$. The absolute values of all the integrals of these functions is infinite. Thus, if $H(s)$ has poles in the right-half plane or on the $j\omega$ axis, the system is unstable. On the other hand, if all the poles lie in the left-half plane, then the components will be exponentially damped and the absolute integral will be bounded. In this case, the system will be stable.

Using the definition of stability just discussed, simple poles on the $j\omega$ axis lead to instability. This is usually a satisfactory definition for amplifiers or control systems, since we do not want a system to excite a sinusoidal component and not have it decay. Also, any slight change in system characteristics could cause the poles to shift into the right-half plane. Thus, slight changes in operation could cause the system to become unstable. Thus, in a practical sense, simple poles on the $j\omega$ axis are undesirable. However, when networks are studied, transfer functions with simple poles on the $j\omega$ axis can be obtained using passive resistors, inductors and capacitors. Consider Fig. 7–2. Here

$$\frac{G(s)}{F(s)} = \frac{1}{LCs^2 + 1} \tag{7-13}$$

The poles occur at $s = \pm j/\sqrt{LC}$.

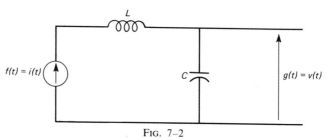

FIG. 7–2

Network whose transfer function has poles at $s = \pm j\omega_0 = \pm j1/\sqrt{LC}$

It is often convenient to consider that all passive networks be stable. In this case, it is desirable to allow simple poles on the $j\omega$ axis in stable systems. A definition of stability which allows simple poles on the $j\omega$ axis is: *The response to any bounded input of finite duration is bounded.* Any $f(t)$ which is of finite duration and bounded will have a Laplace transform all of whose poles lie in the left half plane. (Note that its Fourier transform will exist and be bounded.) Then, if $H(s)$ has a simple pole on the $j\omega$ axis, $g(t)$ will contain sinusoids which do not build up with time, and the network will be stable. Note that, if the duration of $f(t)$ is not restricted, then $F(s)$ can have poles on the $j\omega$ axis. These can be chosen to coincide with a $j\omega$ axis pole of $H(s)$. Then, $G(s)$ will have a double pole on the $j\omega$ axis and $g(t)$ will be unbounded. In general, the definition of stability that we shall use for linear, time-invariant systems is the first one that we discussed; that is, the response to any bounded input must be bounded. Thus simple poles on the $j\omega$ axis are not allowed in a stable system.

Now let us discuss another aspect of stability. Consider the system shown in Fig. 7–3. The system is comprised of two subsystems in cascade, which are such that the overall transfer function is the product of the individual transfer functions. This is typical of cascaded amplifiers. We assume that $H_1(s)$ has all its poles in the left-half plane. Thus, the overall system as illustrated in Fig. 7–3b is stable.

Suppose a signal $f(t)$ is applied. Then, in general, $g_1(t)$ will contain a term of the form $Ke^{at}$, where $a > 0$. Thus, $g_1(t)$ will increase without limit. The response of the

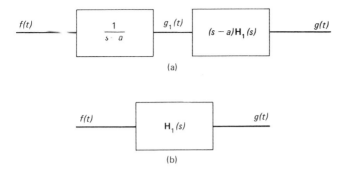

FIG. 7–3
(a) System composed of the cascade of two systems; (b) an alternate
representation of this system which is equivalent in some sense

second system will be such that $g(t)$ is bounded, even though $g_1(t)$ is not. Actually, if
the system were truly linear, and could work with infinite signals, there would be no
problem. However, all practical systems saturate, cut off, or become nonlinear as the
signals become large. Then, as $g_1(t)$ increases, nonlinear operation results. Thus
the system will fail to operate properly. Hence, this system suffers from all the
difficulties of an unstable one, even though a linear analysis of the input and output
signals indicate that the system is stable. Such a system should be classified as
unstable even though we cannot observe the instability.

The problem, in this case, is that the system has a natural frequency $e^{at}$ which
cannot be observed in the output. If all the natural frequencies of a system can be
observed in the output, the system is said to be *observable*. Thus, care should be taken
when stability measurements are made to insure that the system is observable, or
that all the natural frequencies can be determined. Note that if a *complete nonlinear*
analysis of the system of Fig. 7–3 were made, the instability would be determined
because the extreme nonlinearity of operation would be established. However,
if the system usually operates in a linear fashion, it is desirable, if possible, to use
linear analysis, which is much simpler than nonlinear analysis.

Let us now discuss another problem. Consider the balanced bridge in Fig. 7–4a.
Then, in response to the current $f(t)$

$$i_b(t) = 0 \qquad\qquad (7-14)$$

Hence,

$$v(t) = Ri(t) \qquad\qquad (7-15)$$

The transfer function of this network, considering $v(t)$ as the output and $i(t)$ as the
input, is

$$H(s) = R \qquad\qquad (7-16)$$

This has no poles in the right-half plane. Then, the system appears to be stable.
However, consider the circuit as viewed from the detector branch (note the negative

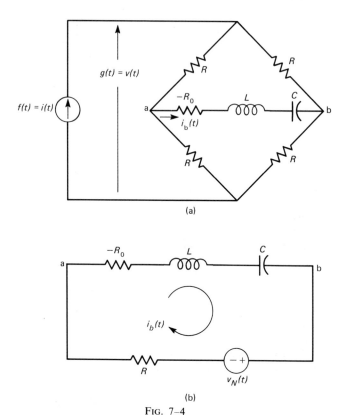

FIG. 7–4

(a) Balanced bridge network; (b) equivalent network as viewed from detector arm

resistor). The current generator appears as as open circuit. Thus, the circuit can be represented as shown in Fig. 7–4b. We have added the generator $v_v(t)$, which can be considered an extremely small voltage set up by the random motion of the electrons in the circuit; that is, it is a noise voltage. Let us determine the response $i_b(t)$ to this equivalent noise voltage. In Laplace transformed form, we have

$$I_b(s) = \cfrac{V_n(s)}{R - R_0 + Ls + \cfrac{1}{Cs}} = \cfrac{V_n(s)\,(s/L)}{s^2 + \cfrac{1}{L}(R - R_0)\,s + \cfrac{1}{LC}} \qquad (7\text{–}17)$$

The transfer function for the "noise" system is

$$H_n(s) = \cfrac{s/L}{s^2 + \cfrac{1}{L}(R - R_0)s + \cfrac{1}{LC}} \qquad (7\text{–}18)$$

We have assumed that the resistance of the detector arm is negative. This would be impossible in a passive system, but it can easily be obtained using amplifiers. If $R_0 > R$, then $H_n(s)$ will have poles in the right half plane.

The system will operate in the following way. Let us assume that $i(t)$ is applied and that the response $v(t)$ is measured. Now assume that a small noise voltage will excite $i_b(t)$. This will start as a very small value, but will build up exponentially. The current will be in the resistors R as well as in the detector branch. In this case, the component of voltage across the upper and lower resistors will exactly cancel, so they will not affect $v(t)$. However, when $i_b(t)$ becomes sufficiently large, the resistors, and other circuit elements, will operate nonlinearly, and improper operation will result. Then, $v(t)$ will no longer equal $i(t)$ R since the value of R will change with $i_b(t)$. Thus, even though the transfer function has no poles in the right half plane or on the $j\omega$ axis, the system is unstable. In this case, the system input does not excite all the natural frequencies of the system; i.e., those corresponding to the poles of $H_n(s)$ (see Eq. 7–18).

If the input to a time-invariant, linear system excites all the natural frequencies of the system, then the system is said to be *controllable*. Thus, when system stability is studied on the basis of response to an input (i.e., the transfer function) care should be taken to see that it is controllable.

The stability of time-invariant, linear systems is often determined by studying the transfer function. If this study is to be valid, the system must be both observable and controllable. Very many linear, time-invariant systems are both observable and controllable. In the next section, we shall consider procedures which can be used to study the stability of such linear, time-invariant systems.

## 7-2. ROUTH-HURWITZ ALGORITHMS

Let us now determine if a linear, time-invariant, controllable and observable system is stable. We do this by investigating the transfer function $H(s)$ of the system, where $H(s)$ is the ratio of two polynomials in $s$:

$$H(s) = \frac{N(s)}{D(s)} \qquad (7\text{–}19)$$

Assume that $N(s)$ and $D(s)$ have no common roots. Then, the system will be stable if $H(s)$ has no poles on the $j\omega$ axis or in the right-half plane. This is equivalent to stating that $D(s)$ has no roots on the $j\omega$ axis or in the right-half plane.

We can determine if $D(s)$ has no roots on the $j\omega$ axis or in the right half plane by solving for all the roots. However, if the degree of the $D(s)$ polynomial is large, this is a very tedious procedure. Actually, we do not need the exact location of the roots; we just must know if *any* of them lie on the $j\omega$ axis or in the right-half plane. In this section we shall develop procedures which can supply the information without factoring $D(s)$. If the system is to be stable, then $D(s)$ must have all of its roots in the left-half plane. A polynomial which has all its roots in the left-half plane is called a *Hurwitz* polynomial.

Now let us consider $D(s)$ and see what characteristics it must have if it is to be a Hurwitz polynomial:

$$D(s) = s^n + a_{n-1}s^{n-1} + \cdots + a_1 s + a_0 \qquad (7\text{--}20)$$

If *any* of the coefficients are zero or are negative, then $D(s)$ must have right-half plane or $j\omega$ axis roots. This can be seen by combining factors of the form $(s + a)$ and $[(s + \alpha)^2 + \beta^2]$. If $\alpha > 0$, all coefficients will be present. Thus, if any

$$a_k \leqq 0, \qquad k = 0, 1, 2, ..., n - 1 \qquad (7\text{--}21)$$

then the polynomial will not be Hurwitz and we need proceed no further. However, $D(s)$ can have roots on the $j\omega$ axis or in the right-half plane, even if all the $a_k$ are positive. Thus, further testing is required.

As an aid in the development of tests, we shall develop other functions. Let us define

$$F(s) = \frac{D(s) + D(-s)}{D(s) - D(-s)} \qquad (7\text{--}22)$$

The numerator of $F(s)$ is an even polynomial which is comprised of all the even powers of $F(s)$. The denominator of $F(s)$ is an odd polynomial which is comprised of all the odd polynomials. From Eq. 7-20 we have, if $n$ is even,

$$F(s) = \frac{s^n + a_{n-2}s^{n-2} + \cdots + a_2 s^2 + a_0}{a_{n-1}s^{n-1} + a_{n-3}s^{n-3} + \cdots + a_1 s} \qquad (7\text{--}23a)$$

and for odd $n$,

$$F(s) = \frac{s^n + a_{n-2}s^{n-2} + \cdots + a_1 s}{a_{n-1}s^{n-1} + a_{n-3}s^{n-3} + \cdots + a_0} \qquad (7\text{--}23b)$$

Note that the highest powers of the numerator and denominator of $F(s)$ differ by unity.

Now consider the behavior of $F(s)$ on the $j\omega$ axis. If $n$ is even,

$$F(j\omega) = \frac{(-1)^{n/2}\omega^n + \cdots - a_2\omega^2 + \omega_0}{j\omega[a_{n-1}(-1)^{(n-2)/2} + \cdots - a_3\omega^2 + a_1]} \qquad (7\text{--}24)$$

Thus, $F(j\omega)$ will be an odd function of $\omega$, which is purely imaginary. Note that $F(s)$ will have either a simple pole or a simple zero at $s = 0$ and also will have either a simple pole or a simple zero at $s = \infty$.

We now define a new function $W(s)$ as follows:

$$W(s) = \frac{D(s)}{D(-s)} \qquad (7\text{-}25)$$

Rearranging Eq. 7–22, we have

$$F(s) = \frac{W(s) + 1}{W(s) - 1} \qquad (7\text{-}26)$$

Now we shall prove the following: *If $D(s)$ is a Hurwitz polynomial, then it is necessary and sufficient that*

$$|W(s)| \begin{cases} > 1, & \operatorname{Re} s > 0 \\ = 1, & \operatorname{Re} s = 0 \\ < 1, & \operatorname{Re} s < 0 \end{cases} \qquad (7\text{-}27)$$

To show this consider the following. Let us write $D(s)$ in factor form:

$$D(s) = (s + s_1)(s + s_2) \ldots (s + s_n) \qquad (7\text{-}28)$$

where

$$s = -s_i, \qquad i = 1, 2, \ldots, n \qquad (7\text{-}29)$$

are the roots of $D(s)$. Assume that the coefficients of $D(s)$ are real. Then, any complex roots occur in conjugate form. Let

$$s_i = \sigma_i + j\omega_i \qquad (7\text{-}30)$$

Then,

$$W(s) = \frac{(s + s_1)(s + s_2) \ldots (s + s_n)}{(-s + s_1)(-s + s_2) \ldots (-s + s_n)} \qquad (7\text{-}31)$$

Let us write

$$W(s) = W_1(s) W_2(s) \ldots W_n(s) \qquad (7\text{-}32a)$$

where

$$W_i(s) = \frac{s + s_i}{-s + s_i^*} \qquad (7\text{-}32b)$$

where $W_i(s)$ consists of one factor of the numerator and the factor of the denominator that corresponds to the conjugate of $s_i$. Note that if $s_i$ is real, $s_i^* = s_i$. Using Eq. 7–30 and writing $s = \sigma + j\omega$, we have

$$|W_i(s)|^2 = \frac{|s + s_i|^2}{|-s + s_i^*|^2} = \frac{(\sigma + \sigma_i)^2 + (\omega + \omega_i)^2}{(\sigma - \sigma_i)^2 + (\omega + \omega_i)^2} \qquad (7\text{-}33)$$

Now assume that $D(s)$ is a Hurwitz polynomial. Then, since all the roots lie in the left-half plane,

$$\sigma_i > 0, \qquad i = 1, 2, \ldots, n \qquad (7\text{-}34)$$

Let us see how this affects $|W_i(s)|$. If $\sigma = 0$ (i.e., on the $j\omega$ axis),

$$|W_i(s)|^2 = \frac{\sigma_i^2 + (\omega + \omega_i)^2}{\sigma_i^2 + (\omega + \omega_i)^2} = 1 \qquad (7\text{--}35)$$

In the right-half plane, $\sigma > 0$; then,

$$(\sigma + \sigma_i)^2 > (\sigma - \sigma_1)^2 \qquad (7\text{--}36)$$

Hence,

$$|W_i(s)|^2 > 1$$

Finally, in the left-half plane $\sigma < 0$; thus;

$$|W_i(s)|^2 < 1 \qquad (7\text{--}37)$$

Since this is true for each factor of $|W(s)|^2$ (see Eq. 7–32), we have verified that Eq. 7–27 is valid if $D(s)$ is a Hurwitz polynomial.

Now let us consider the converse; that is, if Eq. 7–27 is satisfied, then $D(s)$ is a Hurwitz polynomial. We prove this by contradiction. Assume that $D(s)$ has a right-half plane zero. Then, $D(-s)$ has a left half plane root. Therefore, $W(s)$ must have a left-half plane pole. Then, near the pole, $|W(s)|^2 > 1$. This violates our assumption that Eq. 7–27 is satisfied. Thus, if Eq. 7–27 is satisfied, $D(s)$ must be a Hurwitz polynomial. Hence, Eq. 7–27 is a necessary and sufficient condition that $D(s)$ be a Hurwitz polynomial.

Now let us establish another condition for $D(s)$ to be a Hurwitz polynomial. If $D(s)$ is a Hurwitz polynomial, it is necessary and sufficient that $F(s)$ have simple poles which lie on the $j\omega$ axis and have real positive residues. We prove this by working with Eq. 7–26; that is,

$$F(s) = \frac{W(s) + 1}{W(s) - 1} \qquad (7\text{--}38)$$

We write $W(s)$ in polar form:

$$W(s) = |W(s)| \, e^{j\theta(s)} \qquad (7\text{--}39a)$$

or, equivalently,

$$W(s) = |W(s)| \cos \theta + j |W(s)| \sin \theta \qquad (7\text{--}39b)$$

Substituting in Eq. 7–38, we have

$$F(s) = \frac{|W(s)| \cos \theta + 1 + j |W(s)| \sin \theta}{|W(s)| \cos \theta - 1 + j |W(s)| \sin \theta} \qquad (7\text{--}40)$$

Multiplying numerator and denominator by $|W(s)| \cos \theta - 1 - j |W(s)| \sin \theta$ and manipulating, we obtain

$$F(s) = \frac{|W(s)|^2 - 1 - j2 |W(s)| \sin \theta}{|W(s)|^2 + 1 - 2 |W(s)|^2 \cos \theta} \qquad (7\text{--}41)$$

The real part of $F(s)$ is

$$\text{Re } F(s) = \frac{|W(s)|^2 - 1}{|W(s)|^2 + 1 - 2|W(s)| \cos \theta} \tag{7-42}$$

Therefore, if $|W(s)| = 1$

$$\text{Re } F(s) = 0 \tag{7-43}$$

The denominator of $\text{Re } F(s)$ will never be negative, since it can be written as $(|W(s)| \cos \theta - 1)^2 + |W(s)|^2 \sin^2 \theta$; hence,

$$\text{Re } F(s) \begin{cases} < 0, & |W(s)| < 1 \\ > 0, & |W(s)| > 1 \end{cases} \qquad \begin{array}{l} (7\text{-}44\text{a}) \\ (7\text{-}44\text{b}) \end{array}$$

Combining Eqs. 7-43 and 7-44 with Eq. 7-27, we obtain: If $D(s)$ is a Hurwitz polynomial, then it is necessary and sufficient that

$$\text{Re } F(s) \begin{cases} > 0, & \text{Re } s > 0 \\ = 0, & \text{Re } s = 0 \\ < 0, & \text{Re } s < 0 \end{cases} \tag{7-45}$$

Now assume that $F(s)$ has a pole of multiplicity $k$ at $s = s_0$. In the neighborhood of $s_0$ we can approach $F(s)$ arbitrarily closely by

$$F(s) = \frac{Ke^{j\alpha}}{(s - s_0)^k} \tag{7-46}$$

where $K$ and $\alpha$ are real constants and $H$ is positive. We now consider $F(s)$ on a circle of radius $\rho$ centered at $s_0$:

$$s - s_0 = \rho e^{j\phi} \tag{7-47}$$

Then

$$F(s) = \frac{K}{\rho^k} e^{j(\alpha - k\phi)} \tag{7-48}$$

Hence,

$$\text{Re } F(s) = \frac{K}{\rho^k} \cos(\alpha - k\phi) \tag{7-49}$$

On the circle about $s_0$, $\phi$ will vary from 0 to $2\pi$ radians. For any $k > 0$, $\cos(\alpha + k\phi)$ will change sign as $s$ varies around the circle. Thus, on the circle, $\text{Re } F(s)$ must be both positive and negative. However (see Eq. 7-45), $\text{Re } F(s) > 0$ for $\text{Re } s > 0$ and $\text{Re } F(s) < 0$ for $\text{Re } s < 0$. Therefore, if $D(s)$ is a Hurwitz polynomial, $\text{Re } F(s)$ *cannot* change sign in the left-half plane or in the right-half plane. Hence, $s_0$ cannot lie in the left-or right-half plane. Thus, $F(s)$ cannot have poles in the left or right-half plane.

Now consider poles on the $j\omega$ axis and assume that $s_0$ (see Eq. 4-76) lies on the

$j\omega$ axis. Thus, using the notation of Eq. 7–47, Eq. 7–45 becomes

$$\text{Re } F(s) \begin{cases} > 0, & -\pi/2 < \phi < \pi/2 \\ < 0, & \pi/2 < \phi < 3\pi/2 \end{cases} \qquad (7\text{–}50)$$

If, in Eq. 7–49, $k > 1$, then Re $F(s)$ will change sign at least 4 times on the circle, so Eq. 7–50 must be violated. Therefore, multiple $j\omega$ axis poles are not allowed. If $k = 1$, the only value of $\alpha$ which allows Eq. 7–50 to be satisfied is

$$\alpha = 0 \qquad (7\text{–}51)$$

If $F(s)$ has a simple pole, then $Ke^{j\alpha}$ is its residue. Hence, if $D(s)$ is a Hurwitz polynomial, then the only poles that $F(s)$ can have are simple ones which lie on the $j\omega$ axis with real positive residues.

Now let us prove the converse: *if $F(s)$ has only simple poles which lie on the $j\omega$ axis and have real positive residues, then $D(s)$ is a Hurwitz polynomial.* Functions which are the ratio of two polynomials with simple poles may be expressed in a partial fraction expansion of the form

$$F(s) = K_\infty s + \sum_{i=1}^{n'} \frac{K_i}{s + s_i} \qquad (7\text{–}52)$$

where the $K_i$ are the residues of the poles. Since, $F(s)$ only has $j\omega$ axis poles Eq. 7–52 will be of the form

$$F(s) = K_\infty s + \sum_{i=1}^{n} K_i \left( \frac{1}{s + j\omega_1} + \frac{1}{s - j\omega_1} \right); \qquad i = 1, 2, ..., \infty \quad (7\text{–}53)$$

If $s = \sigma + j\omega$, then

$$\text{Re } F(s) = K_\infty \sigma + \sigma \sum_{i=1}^{n} K_i \left[ \frac{1}{\sigma^2 + (\omega + \omega_i)^2} + \frac{1}{\sigma^2 + (\omega - \omega_i)^2} \right] \qquad (7\text{–}54)$$

Each term in the summation will be positive and $K_\infty$ is positive. Thus, Eq. 7–54 can be written as $\sigma$ times a positive quantity. Hence, Eq. 7–45 is satisfied. Therefore, Eq. 7–27 is also satisfied and we have established that: A necessary and sufficient condition that $D(s)$ be a Hurwitz polynomial is that $F(s)$ have only simple poles which lie on the $j\omega$ axis and have real positive residues.

This condition can be used as the basis of a test. That is, construct $F(s)$ and determine the location of its poles. They must all be simple and lie on the $j\omega$ axis. Then verify that the residues are positive. The disadvantage of the test is that the denominator of $F(s)$ must be factored. This can be tedious, although it will contain only even or only odd powers of $s$. Hence, it will be easier to factor than would be $D(s)$.

As an example, suppose

$$D(s) = s^3 + 6s^2 + 2s + 1$$

Then,

$$F(s) = \frac{6s^2 + 1}{s^3 + 2s} = \frac{6s^2 + 1}{s(s^2 + 2)}$$

The poles are simple and lie at $s = 0$, $\pm j\sqrt{2}$. Thus, they lie on the $j\omega$ axis. The residues are

$$[\text{Res at } s = 0] = 1/2$$

$$[\text{Res at } s = j2] = 11/4$$

$$[\text{Res at } s = -j2] = 11/4$$

All the residues are positive. Thus, $D(s)$ is a Hurwitz polynomial. If the order of $D(s)$ is large, then factoring the denominator of $F(s)$ is tedious. We shall now develop a test which does not require factoring.

First we must extend the results developed for $F(s)$ to $1/F(s)$. Let us consider the real part of

$$\frac{1}{F(s)} = \frac{1}{\text{Re } F(s) + j \text{Im } F(s)} = \frac{\text{Re } F(s) - j \text{Im } F(s)}{\text{Re}^2 F(s) + \text{Im } F^2(s)} \qquad (7\text{-}55)$$

If $\text{Re } F(s) > 0$, then $\text{Re } 1/F(s) > 0$; if $\text{Re } F(s) < 0$, then $\text{Re } 1/F(s) < 0$; if $\text{Re } F(s) = 0$, then $\text{Re } 1/F(s) = 0$. Thus, the previously developed results which apply to $\text{Re } F(s)$ also apply to $\text{Re } 1/F(s)$. Hence, we can now state: *A necessary and sufficient condition that $D(s)$ be a Hurwitz polynomial is that $F(s)$ and/or $1/F(s)$ have only* simple poles which lie on the $j\omega$ axis and have real positive residues.

Now we are in a position to develop a test which does not require factoring. The highest power of the numerator and denominator of $F(s)$ differs by unity (see Eq. 7–23). Now construct $G(s)$ such that

$$G(s) = \begin{cases} F(s), & n \text{ even} \\ 1/F(s), & n \text{ odd} \end{cases} \qquad (7\text{-}56)$$

Then, $G(s)$ will always have a pole at $s = \infty$. Then, if $D(s)$ is a Hurwitz polynomial, this must be a simple pole with a real positive residue. Hence, we can write $G(s)$ in a partial fraction expansion (see Eq. 7–53),

$$G(s) = \alpha_1 s + G_1(s) \qquad (7\text{-}57)$$

where $\alpha_1$ must be real and positive. Now $G_1(s)$ will have only finite poles, and the residues of these poles will be the same as those of $G(s)$. (In the vicinity of the poles, $G_1(s)$ and $G(s)$ must behave in the same way.) Thus, if $D(s)$ is a Hurwitz polynomial, $G_1(s)$ must have only simple poles which lie on the (finite) $j\omega$ axis with real positive residues. Thus, it satisfies the condition we have established. In addition,

$$G_1(s) = \sum_{i=1}^{n-1} \frac{K_i}{s - s_i}$$

Hence, $\lim_{s \to \infty} G_1(s) = 0$. Thus, if $G_1(s)$ is written as the ratio of two polynomials, the denominator polynomial must be *one* degree higher than the numerator. Note that it cannot be more than one since we have demonstrated that $1/G_1(s)$ must have only simple poles on the $j\omega$ axis.

Proceeding as in the case of Eq. 7–57, we obtain

$$\frac{1}{G_1(s)} = \alpha_2 s + G_2(s)$$

where $\alpha_2$ must be real and positive if $D(s)$ is a Hurwitz polynomial. Then, we have

$$\frac{1}{G_2(s)} = \alpha_3 s + G_3(s), \qquad 0 < \alpha_3$$

$$\vdots$$

$$\frac{1}{G_{n-1}(s)} = \alpha_n s, \qquad 0 < \alpha_n$$

All these conditions must be met if $D(s)$ is a Hurwitz polynomial. Note that $G(s)$ is expressed in the form of a Stieltjes continued fraction: that is

$$G(s) = \alpha_1(s) + \cfrac{1}{\alpha_2 s + \cfrac{1}{\alpha_3 s + \cfrac{\phantom{1}}{\ddots \cfrac{1}{\alpha_{n-1}s + \cfrac{1}{\alpha_n}}}}} \qquad (7\text{–}58)$$

If $D(s)$ is a Hurwitz polynomial, it is necessary and sufficient that all $\alpha_k > 0$, $k = 1, 2, ..., n$. Also, if any $\alpha$ are 0, then $D(s)$ is *not* a Hurwitz polynomial.

The continued fraction can be easily generated by dividing the denominator of $G(s)$ into the numerator *once*. Then, the remainder is divided into the divisor, etc. Consider an example. Determine if

$$D(s) = s^5 + s^4 + 2s^3 + s^2 + 3s + 1$$

is a Hurwitz polynomial. For this function,

$$G(s) = \frac{s^5 + 2s^3 + 3s}{s^4 + s^2 + 1}$$

Then, performing the long division

$$
\begin{array}{r}
s \\
s^4 + s^2 + 1\,\overline{\big)\,s^5 + 2s^3 + 3s} \\
s^5 + s^3 + s
\end{array}
$$

$$
\begin{array}{r}
s \\
s^3 + 2s\,\overline{\big)\,s^4 + s^2 + 1} \\
s^4 + 2s^2
\end{array}
$$

$$
\begin{array}{r}
-s \\
-s^2 + 1\,\overline{\big)\,s^3 + 2s} \\
s^3 - s
\end{array}
$$

$$
\begin{array}{r}
-\tfrac{1}{3}s \\
3s\,\overline{\big)\,-s^2 + 1} \\
s^2
\end{array}
$$

$$
\begin{array}{r}
3s \\
1\,\overline{\big)\,3s} \\
3s \\
\hline
0
\end{array}
$$

The values of the $\alpha$'s are

$$
\begin{aligned}
\alpha_1 &= 1 \\
\alpha_2 &= 1 \\
\alpha_3 &= -1 \\
\alpha_4 &= -\tfrac{1}{3} \\
\alpha_5 &= 3
\end{aligned}
$$

Then, $D(s)$ is not a Hurwitz polynomial since all the $\alpha$'s were not positive.
Consider another example:

$$
D(s) = s^4 + 2s^3 + 3s^2 + 2s + 2
$$

Then, the long division is

$$
\begin{array}{r}
\tfrac{1}{2}s \\
2s^3 + 2s\,\overline{\big)\,s^4 + 3s^2 + 2} \\
s^4 + s^2
\end{array}
$$

$$
\begin{array}{r}
s \\
2s^2 + 2\,\overline{\big)\,2s^3 + 2s} \\
2s^3 + 2s \\
\hline
0
\end{array}
$$

The values of the $\alpha$'s are

$$\alpha_1 = \tfrac{1}{2}$$
$$\alpha_2 = 1$$

However, four values of $\alpha$ are expected, so the test terminates prematurely. Thus, $D(s)$ is not a Hurwitz polynomial.

Now consider an algorithm called Routh's algorithm which carries out division, but does not require as much writing. Let us examine one step in the division where, for convenience, we have written the coefficients as $a$'s and $b$'s.

$$\frac{a_1}{b^1} s$$

$$b_1 s^{k-1} + b_2 s^{k-3} + b_3 s^{k-5} + \cdots \left| \overline{a_1 s^k + \qquad a_2 s^{k-2} + \qquad a_3 s^{k-4} + \cdots} \right.$$

$$a_1 s^k + \qquad \frac{a_1 b_2}{b_1} s^{k-2} + \qquad \frac{a_1 b_3}{b_1} s^{k-4} + \cdots$$

$$\frac{b_1 a_2 - a_1 b_2}{b_1} s^{k-2} + \frac{b_1 a_3 - a_1 b_3}{b_1} s^{k-4} + \cdots$$

Let us write $G(s)$ in the following way

$$G(s) = \frac{a_1 s^k + a_2 s^{k-2} + a_3 s^{k-4} + \cdots}{b_1 s^{k-1} + b_2 s^{k-3} + b_3 s^{k-5} + \cdots} \tag{7-59}$$

Now form the following array:

$$
\begin{array}{cccc}
a_1 & a_2 & a_3 & \cdots \\
b_1 & b_2 & b_3 & \cdots \\
c_1 & c_2 & c_3 & \cdots \\
d_1 & d_2 & d_3 & \cdots \\
\multicolumn{4}{c}{\cdots\cdots\cdots\cdots\cdots}
\end{array}
$$

where the first two rows are obtained from $G(s)$ and the subsequent ones are obtained from the two proceeding rows in the following way:

$$c_j = \frac{b_1 a_{j+1} - a_1 b_{j+1}}{b_1}$$

$$d_j = \frac{c_1 b_{j+1} - b_1 c_{j+1}}{c_1}$$

$$\begin{array}{c} \cdot \\ \cdot \\ \cdot \end{array}$$

Compare this with the general form of the division. The array is generated by the operation of long division; that is, the third row contains the third remainder, the fourth row the fourth remainder, etc. If any of the $\alpha_1$ are negative, the first term in the preceding remainder must be negative. Thus, an equivalent criterion for the $\alpha_1$'s is that all the coefficients of the first terms of the array (or remainders) must be positive.

For instance, consider one of the previous examples. Let us determine if $D(s)$ is a Hurwitz polynomial where

$$D(s) = s^5 + s^4 + 2s^3 + s^2 + 3s + 1$$

Then, form the array:

|  |  |  |
|---|---|---|
| 1 | 2 | 3 |
| 1 | 1 | 1 |
| 1 | 2 |  |
| $-1$ | 1 |  |
| 3 |  |  |
| 1 |  |  |

(Note that a blank space is treated as a zero.)

**Computer Implementation.** The operations of the Routh test easily can be programmed. We shall list a program segment here, since many of the ideas have been discussed in previous programs. Assume that the appropriate DIMENSION statements have been written and the A and B arrays entered. A number K, equal to the desired number of rows to be calculated (i.e., the highest power minus one), is also assumed to have been entered. We also assume that the maximum number of coefficients in the A array is entered as N. The B array can have one term less than the A array. For convenience, we make them the same size and enter the last term as zero. Then, a program segment is

```
        DO 50   J = 1, K
        JJ = (J - 1)/2
        M = N - 1 + JJ
        DO 10 I = 1, M
        C(I) = (B(1)*A(I + 1) - A(1)*B(I + 1))/B(1)
        IF (C(1).LE.0) GO TO 500
10      CONTINUE
        MM = M + 1
        C(MM) = 0
        DO 20 L = 1, MM
        A(L) = B(L)
        B(L) = C(L)
20      CONTINUE
50      CONTINUE
           .
           .
           .
500     CONTINUE
```

The first DO loop just cycles the operation, each value of J corresponding to one remainder. The number of terms in each row diminishes by 1 in pairs of rows. The constant JJ accomplishes this. Since JJ is an intiger, it will be 0 for $J = 1, 2$; 1 for $J = 3, 4$; etc. Thus, $N - 1 - JJ$ represents the number of terms to be calculated in a row. The C(I) are then calculated in the first internal DO loop. If $C(1) \leq 0$, the procedure terminates. Line 500 is outside of the range of the main DO loop. After the C row is calculated, the B array replaces the A array and the C array replaces the B array. This is done in the second internal DO loop. The procedure is then repeated. The details of the output statements will be left to the reader.

The Routh algorithm is a convenient one to use if $D(s)$ is given and we wish to determine if it is a Hurwitz polynomial. However, at times, one or more of the coefficients of $D(s)$ can be varied and we wish to determine the range of values that they can have if $D(s)$ is to be a Hurwitz polynomial. The Routh algorithm can be used here, but it is awkward. The Hurwitz algorithm is better for this case. We shall state it without proof.

Construct $G(s)$ as given in Eq. 7–59. Then, form the following array

$$\hat{M} = \begin{bmatrix} b_1 & b_2 & \cdots & 0 & 0 \\ a_1 & a_2 & \cdots & 0 & 0 \\ 0 & b_1 & b_2 & \cdots & 0 & 0 \\ 0 & a_1 & a_2 & \cdots & 0 & 0 \\ 0 & 0 & b_1 & b_2 & \cdots & 0 \\ 0 & 0 & a_1 & a_2 & \cdots & 0 \\ \cdots & & & & & \\ 0 & 0 & & \cdots & b_{n-1} & 0 \\ & & & \cdots & a_{n-2} & a_n \end{bmatrix} \qquad (7\text{--}60)$$

The first row contains all the denominator's coefficients and the second all the numerator's coefficients. The next two rows are the same as the first two, except that they are shifted to the right by one column. Repeat this process until M is a $k \times k$ matrix, where $k$ is the highest power of $D(s)$. Note that the last row may be an $a$ row or a $b$ row. Any blank spaces are entered as zero. Consider this example:

$$G(s) = \frac{a_1 s^6 + a_2 s^4 + a_3 s^2 + a_4}{b_1 s^5 + b_2 s^3 + b_3 s} \qquad (7\text{--}61)$$

then

$$\hat{M} = \begin{bmatrix} b_1 & b_2 & b_3 & 0 & 0 & 0 \\ a_1 & a_2 & a_3 & a_4 & 0 & 0 \\ 0 & b_1 & b_2 & b_3 & 0 & 0 \\ 0 & a_1 & a_2 & a_3 & a_4 & 0 \\ 0 & 0 & b_1 & b_2 & b_3 & 0 \\ 0 & 0 & a_1 & a_2 & a_3 & a_4 \end{bmatrix} \qquad (7\text{--}62)$$

Similarly, if

$$G(s) = \frac{a_1 s^7 + a_2 s^5 + a_3 s^3 + a_4 s}{b_1 s^6 + b_2 s^4 + b_3 s^2 + b_4} \qquad (7\text{--}63)$$

then

$$\hat{M} = \begin{bmatrix} b_1 & b_2 & b_3 & b_4 & 0 & 0 & 0 \\ a_1 & a_2 & a_3 & a_4 & 0 & 0 & 0 \\ 0 & b_1 & b_2 & b_3 & b_4 & 0 & 0 \\ 0 & a_1 & a_2 & a_3 & a_4 & 0 & 0 \\ 0 & 0 & b_1 & b_2 & b_3 & b_4 & 0 \\ 0 & 0 & a_1 & a_2 & a_3 & a_4 & 0 \\ 0 & 0 & 0 & b_1 & b_2 & b_3 & b_4 \end{bmatrix} \qquad (7\text{--}64)$$

The necessary and sufficient condition for $D(s)$ to be a Hurwitz polynomial is that the determinant of $\hat{M}$ and all its principal minors are positive. For instance, in Eq. 7–64, the conditions are

$$b_1 > 0$$

$$\begin{vmatrix} b_1 & b_2 \\ a_1 & a_2 \end{vmatrix} > 0$$

$$\begin{vmatrix} b_1 & b_2 & b_3 \\ a_1 & a_2 & a_3 \\ 0 & b_1 & b_2 \end{vmatrix} > 0 \qquad (7\text{--}65)$$

$$\vdots$$

$$|\hat{M}| > 0$$

Consider an example which illustrates this procedure. Suppose

$$D(s) = s^3 + as^2 + 3s + 1$$

and we wish to find the allowable values of $a$ for which $D(s)$ is a Hurwitz polynomial. Form the Hurwitz array:

$$\hat{M} = \begin{bmatrix} a & 1 & 0 \\ 1 & 3 & 0 \\ 0 & a & 1 \end{bmatrix}$$

Then,

$$a > 0$$

$$\begin{vmatrix} a & 1 \\ 1 & 3 \end{vmatrix} = 3a - 1 > 0$$

and

$$\begin{vmatrix} a & 1 & 0 \\ 1 & 3 & 0 \\ 0 & a & 1 \end{vmatrix} = 1 \begin{vmatrix} a & 1 \\ 1 & 3 \end{vmatrix} = 3a - 1 > 0$$

Thus, $D(s)$ will be a Hurwitz polynomial if

$$a > \tfrac{1}{3}$$

## 7-3. NYQUIST CRITERION

The Routh and Hurwitz algorithms indicate if a system is stable or, possibly, the range of values that a parameter can have if the system is stable. However, these algorithms do not show how to modify the system if it is unstable. In this section we shall develop a procedure which will indicate how the $j\omega$ axis behavior should be modified to stabilize an unstable system. That is, it indicates how the sinusoidal steady-state response should be modified. Since the procedure is based upon the sinusoidal steady-state response of elements of the system, data can easily be measured or computed.

In this section we shall restrict ourselves to a very common form of system whose block diagram is given in Fig. 7–5. This block diagram is in transformed form with $F(s)$ the input and $G(s)$ the output. Note that some of the output signal is returned to the input through the $\beta(s)$ block. The transfer function of the blocks are $A(s)$ and $\beta(s)$. The input to the $A(s)$ block is

$$F(s) - G(s)\,\beta(s)$$

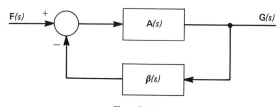

Fig. 7–5
Block diagram of single loop feedback system

Thus

$$G(s) = A(s)\left[F(s) - G(s)\,\beta(s)\right] \tag{7–66}$$

Solving for $G(s)$, we have

$$G(s) = \frac{A(s)}{1 + A(s)\,\beta(s)}\,F(s) \tag{7–67}$$

Thus, the transfer function of the system is

$$H(s) = \frac{A(s)}{1 + A(s)\,\beta(s)} \qquad (7-68)$$

We assume that the system is observable and controllable (see Section 7-1), and we wish to determine if it is stable.

The system is called a *feedback* system since a portion of the output signal is returned, or fed back, to the input. (Any system which oscillates must have some form of feedback.)

Now consider the stability of the overall system. If $H(s)$ is to be stable, then all of its poles must lie in the left-half plane. The poles of $H(s)$ are either poles of $A(s)$ or zeros of $1 + A(s)\,\beta(s)$. Suppose each of the subsystems of Fig. 7–5 are stable. (They can be evaluated by the methods of the previous section.) In many systems, $A(s)$ and $\beta(s)$ represent relatively simple subsystems whose stability can be easily discerned.

If $A(s)$ is stable, all of its poles lie in the left-half plane. Thus, the overall system will be stable if all the zeros of $1 + A(s)\,\beta(s)$ also lie in the left-half plane. There is one exception to this statement: if $1 + A(s)\,\beta(s)$ and $A(s)$ *both* have a zero (or zeros) in the right-half plane at the same point $s$, then they will cancel. In this case, $1 + A(s)\,\beta(s)$ can have zeros in the right-half plane and the system will still be stable. If $1 + A(s)\,\beta(s)$ has zero in the right-half plane, it must be verified that they are not zeros of $A(s)$. Fortunately, many systems are such that $A(s)$ does not have zeros in the right-half plane. We shall assume that $A(s)$ has no zeros in the right-half plane or, at least, there is no zero in the right-half plane in common with those of $1 + A(s)\,\beta(s)$. Now let us write

$$U(s) = 1 + A(s)\,\beta(s) \qquad (7-69)$$

We wish to investigate $U(s)$ to determine if it has zeros in the right-half plane. Therefore, we will now develop a theorem which will aid us in doing this: *If the only singularities that* $U(s)$ *and* $1/U(s)$ *have within a closed contour C are poles, and* $U(s)$ *is analytic and not zero on C, then*

$$\frac{1}{2\pi j} \oint_C \frac{1}{U(s)} \frac{dU(s)}{ds}\, dz = Z - P \qquad (7-70)$$

*where Z and P are numbers of zeros and poles, respectively, of* $U(s)$ *within C.*

Each pole or zero is counted in order of its multiplicity. We shall now derive this theorem. Assume that $U(s)$ has a pole of multiplicity $n$ at $s = s_0$. Then, near the pole we can expand $U(s)$ in a Laurent series:

$$U(s) = \frac{K_m}{(s - s_0)^n} + \frac{K_{m-1}}{(s - s_0)^{n-1}} + \cdots \qquad (7-71)$$

Then,

$$\frac{dU(s)}{ds} = \frac{-K_m n}{(s - s_0)^{n+1}} + \cdots \tag{7-72}$$

Therefore,

$$\frac{1}{U(s)} \frac{dU(s)}{ds} = \frac{-n}{s - s_0} + \cdots \tag{7-73}$$

Therefore, $[1/U(s)] \, dU(s)/ds$ has a simple pole whose residue is $-n$ at $s = s_0$, if $U(s)$ has a pole of multiplicity $n$ at $s = s_0$.

Now suppose $U(s)$ has a zero of multiplicity $n$ at $s = s_0$. Then, in the neighborhood of $s_0$ we can expand $U(s)$ in a Taylor's series:

$$U(s) = K_n(s - s_0)^n + K_{n-1}(s - s_0)^{n-1} + \cdots \tag{7-74}$$

Differentiating, we obtain

$$\frac{dU(s)}{ds} = nK_n(s - s_0)^{n-1} + \cdots \tag{7-75}$$

Then,

$$\frac{1}{U(s)} \frac{dU(s)}{ds} = \frac{n}{s - s_0} + \cdots \tag{7-76}$$

Then, if $U(s)$ has a zero of multiplicity $n$ at $s = s_0$, $[1/U(s)] \, dU(s)/ds$ will have a simple pole of residue $n$ at $s = s_0$. Since $U(s)$ is analytic except at its poles, $dU(s)/ds$ will be analytic, except at the poles of $U(s)$; $1/U(s)$ is analytic at all points within $C$ except at those where $U(s)$ has zeros. Thus, at those points where $U(s)$ has poles or zeros, $[1/U(s)] \, dU(s)/ds$ will have simple poles with real residues. The magnitudes of the residues are equal to the multiplicity of the pole or zero in question. The residues are positive at zeros of $U(s)$ and negative at poles of $U(s)$. Now apply residue theory, (see Eq. B–69) to Eq. 7–70. This yields

$$\frac{1}{2\pi j} \oint_C \frac{1}{U(s)} \frac{dU(s)}{ds} \, ds = \sum [\text{residues of all poles within } C]$$

Hence,

$$\frac{1}{2\pi j} \oint_C \frac{1}{U(s)} \frac{dU(s)}{ds} \, ds = Z - P \tag{7-77}$$

and the theorem is proved. Note that each pole and zero is counted in order of its multiplicity.

Let us now investigate the integral of this theorem. We can write

$$\frac{1}{U(s)} \frac{dU(s)}{ds} = \frac{d \ln U(s)}{ds} \tag{7-78}$$

Now let us put $U(s)$ in polar form

$$U(s) = r(s) e^{j\phi(s)} \qquad (7\text{-}79)$$

where $r(s)$ is the magnitude of $U(s)$; then,

$$\ln U(s) = \ln r(s) + j\phi(s) \qquad (7\text{-}80)$$

Now substitute Eq. 7–78 into the right-hand side of Eq. 7–70. This yields

$$\frac{1}{2\pi j} \oint_C \frac{d \ln U(s)}{ds} ds = \frac{1}{2\pi j} \oint_C d[\ln U(s)]$$

$$= \frac{1}{2\pi j} \oint_C d[\ln r(s)] + \frac{1}{2\pi} \oint_C d\phi(s) \qquad (7\text{-}81)$$

Now consider the contour C. Assume that we start at $s_0$ and travel around it until we return to $s_0$ (see Fig. 7–6a). Let us now look at the path that $U(s)$ takes in the $U(s)$ plane as s traverses C. A typical plot is shown in Fig. 7–6b. We start at $U(s_0)$ and traverse some path. Since $U(s)$ is a function (thus, it is single valued), we return to the same point that we started from; i.e., $U(s_0)$. Now consider the integrals on the right-hand side of Eq. 7–81. We shall write the integral(s) as open integral(s).

$$\int_{s=-a}^{b} d[\ln r(s)] = \ln r(b) - \ln r(a)$$

For the closed contour, points a and b are the same. Thus, $r(b) = r(a)$; hence,

$$\oint d[\ln r(s)] = 0 \qquad (7\text{-}82)$$

Now consider the second integral

$$\frac{1}{2\pi} \int_{s=a}^{b} d\phi(s) = \frac{1}{2\pi} [\phi(b) - \phi(a)] \qquad (7\text{-}83)$$

Even though $U(a) = U(b)$ when points a and b coincide, the angle of $U(a)$ minus the angle of $U(b)$ need not be zero. (The angles of $U(a)$ and $U(b)$ may differ by an integral multiple of $2\pi$ radians.) In Fig. 7–6b, the curve of $U(s)$ circles the origin twice. Consider a radius vector drawn from the origin to the contour. Now trace out the complete circle, starting at $U(s_0)$ and return to $U(s_0)$. The radius vector will make two complete revolutions. This means that the angle of $U(s)$ will be increased by $2(2\pi) = 4\pi$ radians. In general, if the contour of $U(s_0)$ circles the origin $N$ times, the angle of $U(s_0)$ will have increased by $2\pi N$ radians as the contour is traversed from $s_0$ back to $s_0$. Thus, the evaluation of Eq. 7–83 yields

$$\frac{1}{2\pi} \oint_s d\phi(s) = N \qquad (7\text{-}84)$$

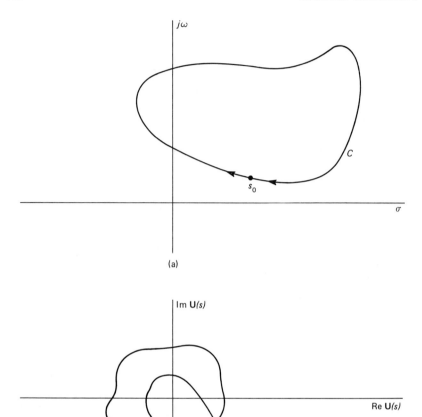

FIG. 7-6
(a) Illustration of a closed contour in the $s$ plane; (b) variation of $U(s)$ in the $U(s)$ plane

Again, $N$ is the number of times a radius vector (drawn from the origin of the $U(s)$ plane to the $U(s)$ curve) encircles the origin as $s$ traverses the closed contour $C$. Note that positive (clockwise) encirclings of the origin are substracted from the counterclockwise ones to obtain $N$. Then, substituting Eqs. 7-84, 7-82, and 7-81 into Eq. 7-77, we have

$$N = Z - P \qquad (7\text{-}85)$$

To obtain the number of zeros minus the number of poles that $U(s)$ has within a closed contour $C$, plot $U(s)$ for all points on $C$ and count the number of times the plot of $U(s)$ encircles the origin.

We wish to investigate a function in the entire right-half plane. Thus, we wish the region enclosed by the contour $C$ to be the entire right-half plane. A contour which accomplishes this is shown in Fig. 7–7. Remember that $U(s)$ must be analytic and nonzero on $C$. Assume that the poles and zeros of $U(s)$ lie within a bounded distance from the origin. Thus, for sufficiently large radius $R$, all the singularities of $U(s)$ will be enclosed. For any practical system, $|U(s)|$ usually approaches zero as $|s|$ approaches infinity. However, this does not introduce a problem since it can be assumed that $R$ is arbitrarily large, but finite. Hence, $U(s)$ is not zero on the "infinite" semicircle, but will, in general, be arbitrarily small. Thus, if we plot $U(j\omega)$, for $-\infty \le \omega < \infty$, the net number of times that $U(j\omega)$ encircles the origin in the $U(s)$ plane is the number

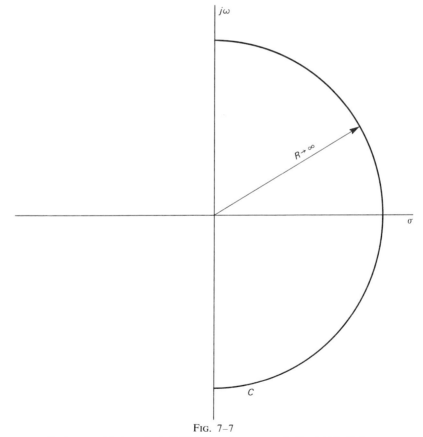

FIG. 7–7
Contour used to investigate if $U(s)$ has poles or zeros in the right-half plane

of zeros minus the number of poles of $U(s)$ in the right-half plane. If $U(s)$ has zeros on the $j\omega$ axis, then the contour should be indented around them by taking small semicircles to the right of the $j\omega$ axis.

Now let us return to the problem of the system stability. From Eq. 7–69, we have

$$U(s) = 1 + A(s)\beta(s) \tag{7-86}$$

We have assumed that $A(s)$ and $\beta(s)$ are both stable. Hence, they do not have poles on the $j\omega$ axis or in the right-half plane, so $A(s)$ will not have poles in the right-half plane. Thus, if we plot $1 + A(j\omega)\beta(j\omega)$, $-\infty \leq \omega \leq \infty$, and count the number of times it circles the origin, this will yield the number of zeros that $1 + A(s)\beta(s)$ has in the right-half plane. We have assumed that $A(s)$ has no zeros in the right-half plane, which cancel those of $1 + A(s)\beta(s)$. We can state that: *The system will be stable if and only if the plot of $1 + A(s)\beta(s)$ does not encircle the origin.*

The quantity $A(j\omega)\beta(j\omega)$ can usually be measured or calculated easily. For example, in Fig. 7–5, if we break the connection to the summer, the diagram of Fig. 7–8 results. So $A(s)\beta(s)$ represents the transfer function of the $A(s)$ system in cascade with the $\beta(s)$ system.

Suppose $F(s)$ is the system input and $F_1(s)$ is its output, then the transfer function of the open loop system is $L(s) = F_1(s)/F(s)$, or

$$L(s) = A(s)\beta(s) \tag{7-87}$$

where $L(s)$ is called the *open loop gain* or the *open loop transfer function*. Note that it is measured by opening the feedback loop. $L(j\omega)$ is the open loop gain on a sinusoidal steady-state basis. In general, we can easily calculate or measure $L(j\omega)$ Often, instead of plotting $1 + L(j\omega)$, we plot $L(j\omega)$. The previous discussion is valid, except that now we must consider the encircling of the point $-1$. That is, we take $1 + L(j\omega)$ and substract 1 from it. This test that we have derived is called the *Nyquist criterion* and the plot of $L(j\omega)$ is the *Nyquist diagram*.

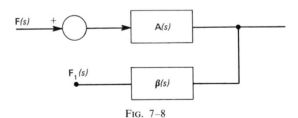

FIG. 7–8
Illustration of the measurement of open loop gain

Let us consider an example of this procedure. Suppose the open loop gain of a system is given by

$$L(j\omega) = \frac{K}{\left(1 + j\dfrac{\omega}{\omega_0}\right)^3} \tag{7-88}$$

What is the largest value that $K$ can have if the system is to be stable? A plot of $L(j\omega)$

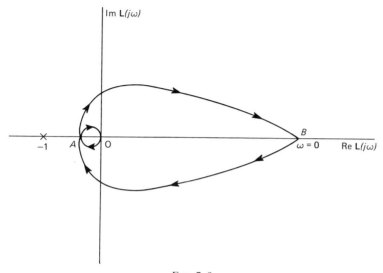

FIG. 7–9
Plot of the open loop gain of Eq. 7–88

is shown in Fig. 7–9. The origin corresponds to $\omega = \pm \infty$. The *critical point* (the point that must not be encircled) is $(-1, 0)$. If the line $\overline{OA}$ has a magnitude of 1 or greater, then the system will be unstable.

At $\omega = 0$,

$$L(j0) = K \tag{7–89}$$

Thus, the line $\overline{OB}$ corresponds to $K$. Now let us determine the maximum value that $K$ can have. At point $A$, $L(j\omega)$ is real and negative. Let us call the frequency where this occurs $\omega_c$; then,

$$3 \tan^{-1} \frac{\omega_c}{\omega_0} = \pi$$

and

$$\frac{\omega_c}{\omega_0} = \tan \frac{\pi}{3} = \sqrt{3}$$

Hence,

$$|L(j\omega_c)| = \frac{K}{[1 + (\sqrt{3})^2]^{3/2}} = \frac{K}{8}$$

Thus,

$$\overline{OA} = \frac{K}{8}$$

$$\overline{OB} = K$$

Hence, $\overline{OB}$ is 8 times as large as $\overline{OA}$ and the maximum value that $\overline{OA}$ can have, if the system is stable, is 1; hence,

$$K_{max} = 8 \tag{7–90}$$

Two other typical forms of the Nyquist diagrams are illustrated in Fig. 7–10. Both represent stable systems. Figure 7–10a is *unconditionally stable*, since $L(j\omega)$ can be multiplied by any positive constant and the system will still be stable. Figure 7–9 is the Nyquist diagram for a *stable* system. If the constant multiplier of $L(j\omega)$ is increased sufficiently, the system becomes unstable. Figure 7–10b represents a *conditionally stable system*. As drawn, the diagram represents a stable system. However, if the constant multiplier of $L(j\omega)$ *decreases* so that the critical point lies in the leftmost shaded area, the system becomes *unstable*. A stable system which becomes unstable when its open loop gain decreases is called conditionally stable. Of course, if the gain of the system represented in Fig. 7–10b increases so that the critical point lies in the rightmost shaded area, the system will also be unstable.

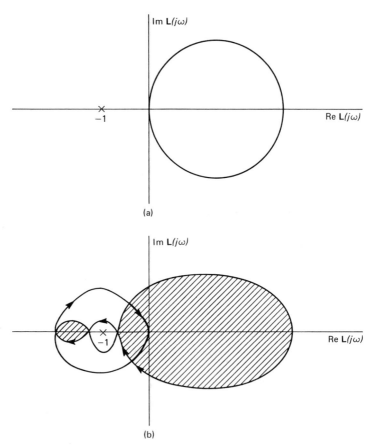

(a)

(b)

Fig. 7–10

Nyquist diagram s of stable systems; (a) unconditionally stable system; (b) conditionally stable system

When systems are initially started, their open loop gains build up from a zero, or small values. In the case of conditional stability, a system will be unstable during this start up period. At times, the oscillation builds up so rapidly that the system is driven into nonlinear regions before the oscillation stops. In this case, the gain may never increase enough to stop the oscillation. In such cases switches are provided to open the feedback loop until the open loop gain has built up sufficiently to prevent oscillation. Once the open loop gain has built up, the switches are closed. Momentary oscillation in conditionally stable amplifiers is usually not objectionable. However, in a control system, where large components may be moved about, this condition can be dangerous.

Often, the Nyquist diagram of an unstable system can be studied and then corrective networks can be added which modify the value of $L(j\omega)$ in order to make the system stable. Such procedures are discussed in the design and synthesis texts cited in the bibliography at the end of this chapter.

## 7-4. SYSTEM STABILITY USING STATE VARIABLES

If nonlinear systems are considered, the problem of stability becomes complex. To illustrate this we consider an unstable linear system, such as that characterized by Eq. 7-1, and then a nonlinear one. If there is no input to the system of Eq. 7-1, there will be no output. Thus, zero output can be said to be an equilibrium point of the system. However, if there is *any* input signal of finite duration, the output will have a term with an exponential build up and, thus, approach infinity asymptotically. This is characteristic of linear unstable systems. Thus, we can easily apply a definition of stability: *A system is stable if its response to any bounded input is bounded* (see Section 7-1). If the system is stable then it will eventually return to its equilibrium point, provided the signal is of finite duration.

Now consider a nonlinear system. If no signal is applied, there may be an equilibrium condition which results in zero output. However, if the system is unstable, an input signal usually results in a signal which grows in amplitude until the nonlinearity of the system limits its value. For instance, a transistor amplifier which is unstable operates linearly at small signal levels. However, as the signal level increases, the device becomes nonlinear. At large enough signal levels, the transistor either saturates or cuts off and the signal levels are limited. Since the amplifier is unstable, a small signal will initiate the oscillation which typically builds up as $e^{at}\cos\omega_0 t$, $a > 0$. However, when the signal level becomes sufficiently large, the nonlinearities will limit the build up and the output will approach a finite (distorted) sinusoid. In this case, the trajectory of the state variables in the state space is called a *limit cycle*. Thus, the system is unstable, but its response is bounded. Hence, we must develop new criteria for stability for nonlinear systems.

We shall study systems in general using their state variables. This has several advantages. State variables are a superior means of evaluation when nonlinear or time-varying systems are used. A system may not be observable (see Section 7-1) because one of the natural frequencies does not appear in the output. However, that natural frequency will often show up as a component of one of the state variables.

Consider a linear system that is at an equilibrium point and suppose we change one of the state variables of the system. In an amplifier, put an initial charge on one of the capacitors; in a mechanical system, displace one of the components.

The response of the system will be its natural nodes or natural frequencies. If the system is stable, it will return to the equilibrium point and its motion will be characterized by damped exponentials; that is, the state (state variables) will return to the original equilibrium value. If the system is unstable, then one or more of the natural frequencies will be characterized by an exponential build up and the response will be unbounded. In this case, the state (i.e., the value of some, or all, of the state variables) will build up exponentially.

If a nonlinear system is displaced from its equilibrium point, the situation is more complex. Three possibilities can occur: (1) the state $\hat{g}(t)$ can return to values which are arbitrarily close to the original ones, (2) the state will not return to the original condition, but will always remain a finite distance from it (that is, all the state variables are bounded, but they do not approach their initial values), and (3) the state variables $\hat{q}(t)$ increase without limit.

In the first case, the equilibrium state is stable. In a linear system, this corresponds to a stable system since the system returns to its initial value. An example of the second case is nonlinear oscillation which we used as an example earlier. The device is unstable, but all the variables are bounded. This case is said to be [1] *bounded but unstable.*

The third case corresponds to instabilities in a linear system. Such a system neither bounded nor stable or, equivalently, it is *unbounded and unstable.*

We have described stability in terms of a small disturbance from an equilibrium state. In the case of linear systems, this is usually sufficient. However, in the case of nonlinear systems, we may have to generalize this. Consider a rock in stable equilibrium near the edge of a cliff. If we push the rock by a small amount, it will return to its original position which implies stability. However, a large displacement causes the rock to fall off the edge of the cliff. Hence, we have a bounded but unstable situation.

If we are to mathematically describe stability, then we must include some standard mathematical terminology here. Consider a matrix $\hat{q}(t)$

$$\hat{q}(t) = \begin{bmatrix} q_1(t) \\ q_2(t) \\ \cdot \\ \cdot \\ \cdot \\ q_n(t) \end{bmatrix} \qquad (7\text{--}91)$$

We define the *Tchebycheff norm,* or simply the *norm* of the matrix, as

$$\|\hat{q}(t)\| = \max|q_i(t)| \tag{7-92}$$

That is, at any time $t$, the norm of $\hat{q}(t)$ is the magnitude of its largest component. For example, if

$$\hat{q} = \begin{bmatrix} 1 \\ 2 \\ -6 \\ -9 \\ 4 \end{bmatrix}$$

then

$$\|\hat{q}\| = 9$$

This definition of a norm can apply to a general $n \times m$ matrix as well as to a vector. There are other definitions of norms. However, all the definitions satisfy the following three conditions

(1) $$\|\hat{q}\| = 0, \qquad \text{if and only if } \hat{q} = 0 \tag{7-93}$$

(That is, a norm of a vector is zero if and only if every element of the vector is zero.)

(2) $$\|\hat{q}_a + \hat{q}_b\| \leq \|\hat{q}_a\| + \|\hat{q}_b\| \tag{7-94}$$

(The norm of the sum of two vectors is less than the sum of their norms.) This is called the *triangle inequality*. It can be demonstrated by considering the components of the vectors: $|q_i + q_j| \leq |q_i| + |q_j|$.

(3) $$\|\alpha\hat{q}\| = |\alpha|\,\|\hat{q}\| \tag{7-95}$$

where $\alpha$ is a constant which may be complex. Note that Eq. 7–92 satisfies this since

$$|\alpha q_i| = |\alpha|\,|q_i|$$

There are definitions of norms other than that given in Eq. 7–92: one is designated by $L_2$ (*mean square* or *Euclidean norm*). This is defined by

$$\|\hat{q}\|_2 = (\hat{q}\,\hat{q}^T)^{1/2} = \left(\sum_{i=1}^{n} q_i^2\right)^{1/2} \tag{7-96}$$

The norm that we shall specifically discuss is that given in Eq. 7–92, although many of our discussions will apply to other norms as well.

*Neighborhood*: Consider a constant matrix $\hat{q}_e$. A neighborhood is the set of all states which are less than $\varepsilon$ from $\hat{q}_e$ on a normal basis. Then, the neighborhood $N(\hat{q}_e, \varepsilon)$ is the set of all $\hat{q}$ which satisfy

$$\|\hat{q} - \hat{q}_e\| < \varepsilon \tag{7-97}$$

That is, we are given $\hat{q}_e$ and $\varepsilon$. To see if $\hat{q}$ is in $N(\hat{q}_e, \varepsilon)$, compare each component $q_i$ of $\hat{q}$ with the corresponding component $q_{ei}$ of $\hat{q}_e$ such that

$$|\hat{q}_i - \hat{q}_{ei}| \leq \varepsilon, \qquad i = 1, 2, ..., n$$

Then $\hat{q}$ lies in $N(\hat{q}_e, \varepsilon)$. Thus, if $\hat{q}$ is in $N(\hat{q}_e, \varepsilon)$ then $\hat{q}$ is "close enough" to $\hat{q}_e$.

We shall consider stability in the sense that the system is at an equilibrium state $\hat{q}_e$ and then it is *perturbed* from it. This can be most easily specified by assuming that the initial state $\hat{q}(t_0)$ of the system is different from the equilibrium state. An electric network might be in a stable state when all the state variables are zero; i.e., the voltages across all the capacitors and the currents through all the inductors are zero. Then, $\hat{q}(t_0)$ would make one or more of these voltages or currents nonzero.

*Bounded* [1]: An equilibrium state $\hat{q}_e$ is bounded if and only if a neighborhood $N(\hat{q}_e, \delta)$ exists about $\hat{q}_e$, such that if $\hat{q}(t_0)$ lies in $N$. Then $\|\hat{q}(t) - \hat{q}_e\|$ is bounded for all $t > t_0$. If the state is bounded, then we say that $\hat{q}_e$ is bounded; if $\hat{q}_e = 0$, then we say that the origin is bounded.

Let us consider the meaning of this definition. The equilibrium state is *perturbed* to $q(t_0)$ such that

$$\|\hat{q}(t_0) - \hat{q}_e\| < \delta \qquad (7\text{-}98)$$

That is, each

$$|q_i(t_0) - q_{ei}| < \delta$$

The resulting trajectory of the system for all time is then $\hat{q}(t)$. If

$$\|\hat{q}(t) - \hat{q}_e\| < M \qquad (7\text{-}99)$$

where $M$ is an arbitrary positive constant, then the system is said to be bounded. In a bounded system, the state variables remain within a finite amount of their equilibrium values, provided the equilibrium is not perturbed by more than $\delta$. All practical systems are limited by their nonlinearities. Thus all practical systems are bounded. If a system is not bounded, it is *unbounded*.

*Liapunov stability*: A system in equilibrium state is *Liapunov stable* if and only if there exists a $\delta$ for every $\varepsilon$ such that for every $\hat{q}(t_0)$ which lies in $N(\hat{q}, \delta)$, then $\|\hat{q}(t) - \hat{q}_e\| < \varepsilon$, $t > t_0$. The point $\hat{q}_e$ in state space is then Liapunov stable. If $\hat{q}_e = 0$, we say that the *origin is Liapunov stable*.

Let us consider this definition. If a system is Liapunov stable, then for every $\varepsilon > 0$, we find a $\delta$ such that, for every initial perturbation, $\hat{q}(t_0)$, which is close enough to $\hat{q}_e$ so that $\|\hat{q}(t_0) - \hat{q}_e\| < \delta$, then $\hat{q}(t)$ will remain close enough to $\hat{q}_e$, for all time so that $\|\hat{q}(t) - \hat{q}_e\| < \varepsilon$, $t > t_0$. That is, in a Liapunov stable system the response $\hat{q}(t)$ will always remain close (within $\varepsilon$) to its equilibrium value, provided the perturbation is smaller than $\delta$. In general, if $\varepsilon$ is specified, smaller, $\delta$ must become smaller, so that a smaller perturbation is placed on the system.

Let us now consider a linear system. If its transfer function has simple poles on the $j\omega$ axis, then $\hat{q}(t)$ will have elements which vary sinusoidally about the final value. As $\delta$ is decreased, then $\|\hat{q}(t) - \hat{q}_e\|$ will also decrease and the system will be Liapunov stable. If any poles lie in the right half plane, then the system will be Liapunov unstable since some components of $q(t)$ will build up exponentially. Similar arguments can be applied to nonlinear systems.

Since $\varepsilon \neq 0$, a very low level of oscillation might persist in a Liapunov stable system. In a linear system, this permits simple poles on the $j\omega$ axis. Now consider a definition of stability which does not allow small, persistent oscillation.

*Asymptotic stability*: A system in equilibrium state is *asymptotic stable* if it is Liapunov stable and if, for any $\hat{q}(t_0)$ in $N(\hat{q}_0, \delta)$, $\|\hat{q}(t) - \hat{q}_e\|$ approaches zero as

$t$ approaches infinity. In such a case, we say that $\hat{q}_e$ is an *asymptotic stable point* or that $\hat{q}_e$ is asymptotic stable.

Asymptotic stability includes all the characteristics of Liapunov stability. In addition, each state variable must approach its equilibrium value as $t$ approaches infinity. Then, the small oscillations discussed in conjunction with Liapunov stability cannot occur. In a linear, time-invariant system, this corresponds to requiring that all the poles of the transfer function lie in the left half plane.

The definitions of stability depend upon the neighborhood $N(\hat{q}_e, \delta)$ which restricts $\hat{q}(t_0)$. In some systems, $\delta$ is limited, while in others it is unbounded; that is $\delta$ can be chosen arbitrarily large and the system is still stable. If $\delta$ is unbounded, the system is said to be *globally stable*, or *stable in the large*. Consider the example of the rock on the cliff. It was asymptotic stable for sufficiently small $\delta$, but not for large $\delta$. Thus, it was not globally asymptotic stable. A linear, time-invariant system, all of whose poles lie in the left half plane, will, in general, be globally asymptotic stable, since the effects of *any* perturbation will be exponentially damped.

Although we shall use state variables for nonlinear systems, let us, in the remainder of this section, consider some results which apply to linear, time-invariant systems. These are characterized by state variable equations of the form (see Eq. 4–96)

$$\frac{d\hat{q}(t)}{dt} = \hat{a}\hat{q}(t) = \hat{b}\hat{y}(t) \tag{7–100}$$

The solution to these equations is given by (see Eq. 4–127)

$$\hat{q}(t) = e^{t\hat{a}}\hat{q}(0-) + e^{t\hat{a}}\int_{0-}^{t} e^{-\tau\hat{a}}\hat{b}\hat{y}(\tau)\,d\tau \tag{7–101}$$

where we assume that the initial time is $t = 0-$.

The equilibrium state is that of an unexcited system with zero initial conditions; that is,

$$\hat{q}_e = 0 \tag{7–102}$$

This is called the origin. That is, it is the origin of the state space.

Now we can develop the following theorem: *The origin of a linear system is bounded if and only if $e^{t\hat{a}}$ is bounded for all $t > 0$.* Let us consider the proof of this theorem. Since we are considering systems without excitation

$$\hat{y}(t) = 0 \tag{7–103}$$

Thus, Eq. 7–101 becomes

$$\hat{q}(t) = e^{t\hat{a}}\hat{q}(0-)$$

Then, from Eq. 7–102

$$\|\hat{q}(t) - \hat{q}_e\| = \|\hat{q}(t)\| = \|e^{t\hat{a}}\hat{q}(0-)\| \tag{7–104}$$

We must look at the norm of the product of two matrices. Consider $\|\hat{A}\hat{B}\|$, where $\hat{A}$ is a square matrix and $\hat{B}$ is a column matrix. The product is a column matrix. Each element is given by

$$AB_{ij} = \sum_{j=1}^{n} a_{ij}b_j \tag{7–105}$$

If $\|A\| = M$ and $\|B\| = N$, then

$$\sum_{j=1}^{n} a_{ij}b_{ij} \leqq nMN \tag{7-106}$$

Hence,

$$\|AB\| \leqq n \|A\| \|B\| \tag{7-107}$$

If the norm of $\|e^{t\hat{a}}\|$ is bounded,

$$\|e^{t\hat{a}}\| < M$$

Then

$$\|\hat{q}(t)\| \leqq nM \|\hat{q}(0-)\| \tag{7-108}$$

Thus, if the norm of $e^{t\hat{a}}$ is bounded, the origin will be bounded for bounded $\|\hat{q}(0-)\|$.

Now consider the converse; that is, if $\|e^{t\hat{a}}\|$ is unbounded, let us show that we can find a $\hat{q}(0-)$ with a bounded norm which causes the $\|\hat{q}(t)\|$ to be unbounded. If $\|e^{ta}\|$ is unbounded at least one element of $e^{t\hat{a}}$ is unbounded. Then, we can choose a $\hat{q}(0-)$ such that at least one element of $e^{ta}\hat{q}(0-)$ is unbounded. Thus, we have proved the theorem.

Let us discuss a theorem which states: *If the origin of a linear, time-invariant system is bounded, then the origin is Liapunov stable.* Thus, we must show that for every $\varepsilon$ we can find a $\delta$ such that the definition of Liapunov stability holds; that is, if for *every* $\hat{q}(0-)$ which satisfies

$$\|\hat{q}(0-)\| < \delta \tag{7-109a}$$

we have

$$\|\hat{q}(t)\| < \varepsilon \tag{7-109b}$$

Let us consider the proof. Since the system is bounded,

$$\|e^{t\hat{a}}\| < M$$

Then, using Eq. 7-108 and manipulating, we have

$$\|\hat{q}(t)\| \leqq nM\delta \tag{7-110}$$

Thus $\|\hat{q}(t)\|$ is restricted. Substitute Eq. 7-109 to obtain the restriction on $\delta$:

$$\delta \leqq \frac{\varepsilon}{nM} \tag{7-111}$$

Thus, if $\delta$ satisfies relation 7-111, Eq. 7-109b will also be satisfied. Hence, the theorem is proved. Thus, in a linear, time-invariant system, boundedness implies Liapunov stability.

If $\|e^{t\hat{a}}\|$ is not only bounded, but also approaches zero as $t$ approaches infinity, the system will also be asymptotic stable. This can be seen from Eq. 7-108. Now, $M$ is a function of time which is bounded and approaches zero as $t$ approaches infinity. Hence, $\|\hat{q}(t)\|$ approaches 0 and the desired result is obtained.

We have thus far considered systems without input signals. Now let us discuss the definition of stability in terms of the input signal. In Section 7-1, we said that a system is stable if the response to any bounded input was bounded. We shall now consider a definition based on state variables. *A linear, time-invariant system is stable with respect to a set of inputs $\hat{y}(t)$ if, for any $\hat{y}(t)$ with bounded norms, the norm of $\hat{g}(t)$ is bounded for all $t > 0$.* That is, given any $\hat{y}(t)$ such that $\|\hat{y}(t)\| < M$, then, if the system is stable, $\|\hat{g}(t)\| < Q$, where $M$ and $Q$ are real positive constants.

It appears as though this definition is very difficult to test since we must obtain the response to *every* bounded $\hat{y}(t)$. However (see Section 7-1 for an analogy), we can show that we need only test the appropriate impulse responses. Accordingly, let $h_{ij}(t)$ be the response of state variable $q_i(t)$ when

$$y_j(t) = \delta(t) \tag{7-112}$$

with all other $y_i(t)$ zero; $i = 1, 2, ..., k, i \neq j$ The response of $q_i(t)$ to an arbitrary $y_j(t)$ is given by (see Eq. 5-17)

$$q_i(t) = \int_{-\infty}^{\infty} y_j(x) h_{ij}(t - x) dx \tag{7-113}$$

Now assume that all the $y_j(t)$ are applied. The system is l near; hence, the response of $q_i(t)$ to all the $y_j(t)$ is

$$q_i(t) = \sum_{j=1}^{k} \int_{-\infty}^{\infty} y_j(x) h_{ij}(t - x) dx, \qquad i = 1, 2, ..., n \tag{7-114}$$

We assume that $h_{ij}(t)$ and $y_j(t)$ are such that the order of summation and integration can be interchanged.

$$q_i(t) = \int_{-\infty}^{\infty} \sum_{j=1}^{k} y_j(x) h_{ij}(t - x) dx, \qquad i = 1, 2, ..., n \tag{7-115}$$

In matrix form, these equations become

$$\hat{g}(t) = \int_{-\infty}^{\infty} \hat{h}(t - x) \hat{y}(x) dx \tag{7-116}$$

where

$$\hat{h}(t) = [h_{ij}(t)] \tag{7-117}$$

is an $n \times k$ matrix.

Now let us assume that the integral of the absolute value of every impulse response is bounded; then,

$$\int_{-\infty}^{\infty} |h_{ij}(t)| dt \leq M \tag{7-118}$$

Also assume that

$$\|\hat{y}(t)\| < N \tag{7-119}$$

Then, proceeding as in Eqs. 7-9 and 7-10,

$$q_i(t) \leq kMN, \qquad i = 1, 2, ..., n \tag{7-120}$$

Therefore,

$$\|\hat{g}(t)\| \leq kMN \tag{7-121}$$

Thus, we have proved that if every integral of the absolute value of the impulse response is bounded, all the state variables will be bounded for any bounded input.

Let us now show that if *any*

$$\int_{-\infty}^{\infty} |h_{ij}(t)| \, dt$$

is unbounded, we can find a $\|y(t)\| < N$ such that $\|q(t)\|$ is unbounded. For the $h_{ij}(t)$ whose absolute integral is unbounded, choose

$$y_k(t_0 - t) = 0, \qquad k \neq j$$
$$y_j(t_0 - t) = \text{sgn } h_{ij}(t) \tag{7-122}$$

Then, by analogy, using Eq. 7–12, we have

$$q_i(t_0) = \int_{-\infty}^{\infty} |h_{ij}(y)| \, dy$$

We have hypothesized that the integral is unbounded; thus, $q_i(t)$ is unbounded. Hence, $\|\hat{g}\|$ is unbounded.

We have shown that an equivalent definition of stability in a linear, time-invariant system is: *A necessary and sufficient condition that a linear, time-invariant system be stable is that*

$$\int_{-\infty}^{\infty} |h_{ij}(t)| \, dt \leq M; \qquad i = 1, 2, ..., n, \qquad j = 1, 2, ..., k \tag{7-123}$$

## 7-5. OBSERVABILITY AND CONTROLLABILITY IN LINEAR SYSTEMS

In Section 7-1, we discussed observability and controllability qualitatively; now we consider these concepts quantitatively.

Let us begin by considering the state variable equations in Laplace transformed form (see Eq. 4–156):

$$(s\hat{U} - \hat{a})\hat{Q}(s) = \hat{b}Y(\hat{s})$$

where we have assumed zero initial conditions. With no excitation $\hat{Y}(s) = 0$. Then, we are left with the homogeneous differential equation

$$(s\hat{U} - \hat{a})Q(\hat{s}) = 0 \tag{7-124}$$

Thus, the natural frequencies of the system are the roots of

$$|s\hat{U} - \hat{a}| = 0 \tag{7-125}$$

Let us call the roots $s_1, s_2, ..., s_n$. (Note, the *vertical bars* about a matrix signify the determinant of the matrix.)

We shall now discuss some mathematics which shall allow us to formalize our discussion of observability and controllability. Let us *diagonalize* the $\hat{a}$ matrix (see Section C-3). First we must obtain the eigenvalues. These are the roots of the characteristic equations (see Eq. C–25),

$$|\hat{a} - \lambda \hat{U}| = 0 \tag{7–126}$$

Thus (see Eq. 7–125), the natural frequencies are the eigenvalues of the system. We shall assume that they are distinct. Let

$$\hat{s}_n = \begin{bmatrix} s_1 & 0 & \cdots & 0 \\ 0 & s_2 & \cdots & 0 \\ \cdots & \cdots & \cdots & \cdots \\ 0 & 0 & \cdots & s_n \end{bmatrix} \tag{7–127}$$

be the diagonal matrix of eigenvalues. Now suppose we have obtained $\hat{\eta}$, the matrix of eigenvectors (see Section C-3). Thus, we can write (see Eq. C–34)

$$\hat{a} = \hat{\eta}\hat{s}_n\hat{\eta}^{-1} \tag{7–128}$$

We assume that $\eta^{-1}$ exists. It will always exist if the eigenvalues are distinct. Note that $\hat{a}$ is a matrix of real constants even though $\hat{\eta}$ and $\hat{s}_n$ may contain complex numbers. Now let us write the state variable equations in differential equation form

$$\frac{d\hat{q}(t)}{dt} = \hat{a}\hat{q}(t) + \hat{b}\hat{y}(t) \tag{7–129}$$

Substituting Eq. 7–128 into Eq. 7–129 yields

$$\frac{d\hat{q}(t)}{dt} = \eta s_n \eta^{-1}\hat{q}(t) + \hat{b}\hat{y}(t) \tag{7–130}$$

Now let us define a new matrix $\hat{q}_d(t)$ in the following way:

$$\hat{\eta}^{-1}\hat{q}(t) = \hat{q}_d(t) \tag{7–131a}$$

or, equivalently,

$$\hat{q}(t) = \hat{\eta}\hat{q}_d(t) \tag{7–131b}$$

Note that $\hat{\eta}$ and $\hat{\eta}^{-1}$ are arrays of (possibly complex) constants. Then, substituting in Eq. 7–130, we have

$$\hat{\eta}\frac{d\hat{q}_d(t)}{dt} = \hat{\eta}\hat{s}_n\hat{q}_d(t) + \hat{b}\hat{y}(t) \tag{7–132}$$

Now premultiplying by $\eta^{-1}$ yields

$$\frac{d\hat{q}_d(t)}{dt} = \hat{s}_n\hat{q}_d(t) + \hat{\eta}^{-1}\hat{b}\hat{y}(t) \tag{7–133}$$

Let us consider each differential equation that Eq. 7–133 represents. (Note that $\hat{s}_n$ is a diagonal matrix.) Thus, a single scalar equation is

$$\frac{d\hat{q}_{di}}{dt} = s_i q_{di}(t) + \sum_{k=1}^{n} \alpha_{ik} y_k(t), \qquad i = 1, 2, ..., n \tag{7–134}$$

where $\alpha_{ik}$ is a constant determined from $\boldsymbol{\eta}^{-1}b$ (see Eq. 7–136). The natural frequency of the equation is $s_t$ Thus, each natural frequency occurs in *one and only one* of the elements of $\hat{q}_d(t)$.

Now let us study controllability. If all the $q_{di}$ are nonzero, then (see Eq. 7–131b) since $\hat{\boldsymbol{\eta}}$ will be a nonzero matrix of the eigenvectors, all the natural frequencies will occur in each element of $\hat{q}(t)$.

Let us now determine the conditions that cause each $q_{di}(t)$, $i = 1, 2, ..., n$ to be nonzero. Rewrite Eq. 7–134 as

$$\frac{dq_{di}(t)}{dt} - s_i q_{ki}(t) = \sum_{k=1}^{n} \alpha_{ik} y_k(t), \qquad i = 1, 2, ..., n \qquad (7\text{–}135)$$

where

$$\boldsymbol{\eta}^{-1}\hat{b} = \hat{\alpha} = [\alpha_{ik}] \qquad (7\text{–}136)$$

We assume that $\hat{q}(0-) = 0$. Thus, if $q_{di}(t)$ is not to be zero, the right-hand side of Eq. 7–135 must not be zero. Let us define *controllability with respect to a given input*: A system is controllable with respect to an input $y_j(t)$, if, when $y_i(t) \neq 0$ ($i = 1, 2, ...,$ $k, j \neq i$), then $y_j(t)$ induces *all* the natural frequencies of the system in each $\hat{q}(t)$. This requires that no element of $\hat{q}_d(t)$ be zero. Then (see Eq. 7–135), if $q_{di}(t)$ is not zero, then $\hat{\alpha}$ must not be zero. If $y_j(t)$ is to excite *all* the natural frequencies, then

$$\alpha_{ij} \neq 0, \qquad i = 1, 2, ..., n$$

Thus, to determine if the network is controllable with respect to $y_j(t)$, we form the matrix $\hat{\boldsymbol{\eta}}^{-1}\hat{b}$ and inspect its $j$th column. All of its elements should be nonzero.

As an example, let us consider the system characterized by the state variable equations

$$\frac{dq_1(t)}{dt} = q_1(t) + 6q_2(t) + b_1 y_1(t) \qquad (7\text{–}137\text{a})$$

$$\frac{dq_2(t)}{dt} = q_1(t) + 2q^2(t) + b_2 y_1(t) \qquad (7\text{–}137\text{b})$$

Let us determine the conditions on $b_1$ and $b_2$ such that the system is controllable. That is, all the natural frequencies be excited in both $q_1(t)$ and $q_2(t)$. The $\hat{a}$ matrix is

$$\hat{a} = \begin{bmatrix} 1 & 6 \\ 1 & 2 \end{bmatrix}$$

Thus, the eigenvalues are found by solving

$$\begin{vmatrix} 1 - \lambda & 6 \\ 1 & 2 - \lambda \end{vmatrix} = \lambda^2 - 3\lambda - 4 = (\lambda + 1)(\lambda - 4) = 0$$

Then the eigenvalues are $\lambda = -1, 4$. To obtain the eigenvectors, we solve

$$\begin{bmatrix} 1 - \lambda_j & 6 \\ 1 & 2 - \lambda_j \end{bmatrix} \begin{bmatrix} q_{d1j} \\ q_{d2j} \end{bmatrix} = \begin{bmatrix} 0 \\ 0 \end{bmatrix}$$

With $\lambda = -1$, we obtain $q_{d11} + 3q_{d21} = 0$. Let $q_{d11} = 3$, then $q_{d21} = -1$. With $\lambda = 4$, we have $q_{d12} = 2q_{d22}$. Let $q_{d12} = 2$. Then $q_{d22} = 1$; therefore, the matrix of eigenvalues is

$$\eta = \begin{bmatrix} 3 & 2 \\ -1 & 1 \end{bmatrix} \tag{7-138}$$

The inverse matrix is

$$\eta^{-1} = \frac{1}{5}\begin{bmatrix} 1 & -2 \\ 1 & 3 \end{bmatrix}$$

Then,

$$\eta^{-1}\hat{b} = \frac{1}{5}\begin{bmatrix} 1 & -2 \\ 1 & 3 \end{bmatrix}\begin{bmatrix} b_1 \\ b_2 \end{bmatrix} = \frac{1}{5}\begin{bmatrix} b_1 - 2b_2 \\ b_1 + 3b_2 \end{bmatrix}$$

If all the natural frequencies are to be excited,

$$b_1 - 2b_2 \neq 0$$

and

$$b_1 + 3b_2 \neq 0$$

**Observability.** Assume that the outputs of the system are given by

$$\hat{x}(t) = \hat{c}\hat{q}(t) + \hat{d}\hat{y}(t) \tag{7-139}$$

The natural frequencies will not be a function of $\hat{y}(t)$ in the equation. However, we assume that the $\hat{y}(t)$ excites them in the state variables. Hence, we need only consider

$$\hat{x}(t) = \hat{c}\hat{q}(t) \tag{7-140}$$

Then, using Eqs. 7-131, we have

$$\hat{x}(t) = \hat{c}\hat{\eta}\hat{q}_d(t) \tag{7-141}$$

Let us write

$$\hat{\gamma} = \hat{c}\hat{\eta} = [\gamma_{ij}] \tag{7-142}$$

Then, Eq. 7-141 expresses the set of equations

$$x_i(t) = \sum_{j=1}^{n} \gamma_{ij}q_{dj}(t), \qquad i = 1, 2, \dots \tag{7-143}$$

Each $q_d(t)$ contains one and only one natural frequency. If all the natural frequencies are to be observable in the output $x_1(t)$, then all $\gamma_{ij}, j = 1, 2, \dots, n$ must be nonzero. Thus, to determine if the network is observable, we need only study the $\hat{\gamma}$ matrix. If all the natural frequencies are to be present in $x_i$, then the $i$th row of $\hat{\gamma}$ must have no zero elements. If all the natural frequencies are to be present in all the outputs $\hat{x}(t)$, then no element of $\hat{\gamma}$ can be zero.

Consider an example of this procedure. Let us assume that the state variable equations are given by Eqs. 7-137 and, in addition, the output signal in terms of the state variables is

$$x(t) = c_1q_1(t) + c_2q_2(t) + 3y(t)$$

Let us determine the conditions on

$$\hat{c} = [c_1 \; c_2]$$

such that all the natural frequencies are observable in the output. From Eq. 7–138, we have

$$\eta = \begin{bmatrix} 3 & 2 \\ -1 & 1 \end{bmatrix}$$

Thus, from Eq. 7–142

$$\gamma = \hat{c}\eta = [c_1 \; c_2] \begin{bmatrix} 3 & 2 \\ -1 & 1 \end{bmatrix} = [(3c_1 - c_2)(2c_1 + c_2)]$$

Then, if all the natural frequencies are to appear in the output,

$$3c_1 - c_2 \neq 0$$
$$2c_1 + c_2 \neq 0$$

## 7-6. LIAPUNOV STABILITY CRITERIA

General (nonlinear) system stability is a far more complex topic than is linear, time-invariant system stability. Contrast the definitions of stability introduced in Section 7-4 with those of Section 7-1. Accordingly, stability criteria become much more complex.

One general concept that we can use to define a stable system is: *In a stable system, the total energy decreases with time.*

Consider a passive series RLC circuit with some initial charge on the capacitor. The current in the circuit for $t > 0$ will be a damped sinusoid. The current through the resistor causes power to be dissipated as heat. Thus, the net stored energy decreases with time. If the system were unstable (e.g., if the resistance were negative), then power would be supplied by the negative resistor and the energy would increase.

A borderline case is a conservative system. Here the total energy remains constant. A lossless LC would constitute such a system. Using the definition of stability given in Section 7-1, this would be an unstable system.

In general, we shall characterize the system by a set of state variable equations. Since state variables can represent many different properties, energy cannot be easily expressed in terms of state variables. Thus, it appears as though a stability criterion based on energy would not be very useful. Liapunov showed that a large class of functions of the state variables which behave in a fashion similar to an energy expression, can be used in place of the energy in determining system stability. This then provides a useful criterion for the study of system stability.

Before we study Liapunov's stability criteria, we must discuss some definitions. Consider a *scalar function of a matrix* $V(\hat{q})$; that is, $V$ is a number which is a function of all the elements of $\hat{q}$. For example, if

$$\hat{q} = \begin{bmatrix} q_1 \\ q_2 \end{bmatrix}$$

then a possible $V(\hat{q})$ is

$$V(\hat{q}) = q_1^2 + q_2^2 \tag{7-144}$$

If every element of $\hat{q} = 0$, then we write $V(\hat{0})$.

A scalar function $V(\hat{q})$ is *positive definite* if and only if

$$V(\hat{0}) = 0 \tag{7-145}$$

and

$$V[\hat{q}(t)] > 0, \qquad \hat{q}(t) \neq 0 \tag{7-146}$$

that is, $V(\hat{q})$ is positive definite if it is zero when *all* the elements of $\hat{q}$ are zero and it is *positive* if *any* of the elements of $\hat{q}$ are not zero. If $q_1$ and $q_2$ are real, Eq. 7–144 represents a positive definite function. If Eq. 7–146 is replaced by

$$V(\hat{q}) < 0 \tag{7-147}$$

the function is said to be *negative definite*.

Suppose $V$ is an explicit function of not only state variables, but also of time. We write this as $V[\hat{q}(t), t]$. In general, state variables are functions of time. However, in $V(\hat{q})$, time does not appear explicitly (see Eq. 7–144). On the other hand, in $V[\hat{q}(t), t]$ time can appear explicitly; e.g., $V = a_1^2 + q_2^2 t^2$. A $V[\hat{q}(t), t]$ is positive definite if there is a positive definite function $W(\hat{q})$ in which time does not appear explicitly such that

$$V[\hat{q}(t), t] \geq W[\hat{q}(t)], \qquad t > t_0 \tag{7-148a}$$

and

$$V[\hat{0}, t] = 0 \tag{7-148b}$$

Similarly, it is negative definite if Eq. 7–148a is replaced by

$$V[\hat{q}(t), t] \leq -W(\hat{q}), \qquad t > t_0 \tag{7-149}$$

Consider an $n$-dimensional state space whose coordinates are state variables. Let $D$ be a region in the state space which contains the origin; i.e., the point where $\hat{q} = 0$. Suppose we can find a function $V[\hat{q}(t), t]$ of state variables, and possibly also of time, which is positive definite and satisfies

$$-\frac{dV[\hat{q}(t), t]}{dt} \geq 0 \tag{7-150}$$

along trajectories which lie in $D$. Then $V(\hat{q}, t)$ is a *Liapunov function*. It is important to realize that $V[\hat{q}(t), t]$ need not be any specific function. It must only be a positive definite function of $\hat{q}$ and $t$ and its derivative must satisfy Eq. 7–150. We shall present some stability theorems on the basis of Liapunov functions. The form of Liapunov functions is not specified. For any specific system, we must try to find a Liapunov function if it exists. In a sense, it is an advantage that the form is not given since it provides us with some freedom. However, it is also a disadvantage since a general procedure for finding the function is not known. We shall perform examples which illustrate these ideas after we present some stability theorems.

We can state the following theorem: *The origin of a system is Liapunov stable if we can find a Liapunov function $V[\hat{q}(t), t]$ in a region D which contains $\hat{q} = 0$;* i.e., the origin of the state space. That is, a system is Liapunov stable if we can find a positive definite function $V[\hat{q}(t), t]$ which can be differentiated with respect to all the state variables and time and satisfies

$$\frac{dV[\hat{q}(t), t]}{dt} = \frac{\partial V[\hat{q}(t), t]}{\partial t} + \sum_{i=1}^{n} \frac{\partial V[\hat{q}(t), t]}{\partial q_i(t)} \frac{\partial q_i(t)}{\partial t} \leqq 0 \qquad (7\text{–}151)$$

To prove the theorem we must show that for every $\varepsilon$ there exists a $\delta$ such that if $\hat{q}(t_0)$ lies in the neighborhood $N(\hat{q}_e, \delta)$, then

$$\|\hat{q}(t) - \hat{q}_e\| \leqq \varepsilon, \qquad t > t_0 \qquad (7\text{–}152)$$

where

$$\hat{q}_e := \hat{0} \qquad (7\text{–}153)$$

since we are considering stability of the origin. Also, since $V[\hat{q}(t), t]$ possesses a derivative, we can write

$$V[\hat{q}(t), t] = \int_{t_0}^{t} \frac{dV[\hat{q}(y), y]}{dy} \, dy + V[\hat{q}(t_0), t_0] \qquad (7\text{–}154)$$

In the region D, Eq. 7–151 is negative. Thus, the integrand of Eq. 7–154 is never positive, Therefore, the integral is equal to or less than zero; hence,

$$V[\hat{q}(t_0), t_0] > V[\hat{q}(t), t], \qquad t > t_0 \qquad (7\text{–}155)$$

Since $V[\hat{q}(t), t]$ is a positive definite function of time, there must exist another positive definite function $W[\hat{q}(t)]$ such that

$$V[\hat{q}(t), t] > W[\hat{q}(t)], \qquad t > t_0 \qquad (7\text{–}156)$$

Now let us look at a geometric interpretation which will aid us in the proof. We shall consider a diagram using only one state variable (since we are restricted to 2-dimensional plots). However, this can be carried over to multidimensional space. The first diagram we consider is Figure 7–11a which shows a typical $W(\hat{q})$. Since it is positive definite, $W(\hat{0}) = 0$. For the moment, assume that $W[\hat{q}(t)]$ is such that if the magnitude of any element of $\hat{q}(t)$ increases, with all other elements remaining constant, $W[\hat{q}(t)]$ increases. Thus, the bowl-shaped region of Fig. 7–11a results. Corresponding to $\|q\| = \varepsilon$, there is a *minimum* value of $W(\hat{q})$ which we shall call $W_{max}$. This notation seems confusing. Let us explain it. Here we assume that $W$ has the bowl shape of Fig. 7–11a. We restrict $\hat{q}(t)$ so that $\|\hat{q}(t)\| \leqq \varepsilon$. As we increase $\varepsilon$, then $W$ can have *larger* values. Hence, $W_{max}$ represents the *smallest* value of $W[\hat{q}(t)]$ for which $\|q\| = \varepsilon$. For example, in Fig. 7–11a, $W(+\varepsilon) > W(-\varepsilon)$. Thus, we use $W(-\varepsilon) = W_{max}$.

Also $V[\hat{q}(t), t]$ will be a continuous function of $\hat{q}(t)$ and $t$. In addition, $V[\hat{0}, t] = 0$. Thus, we can always find a $\hat{q}(t_0)$ such that

$$V[\hat{q}(t_0), t_0] < W_{max} \qquad (7\text{–}157)$$

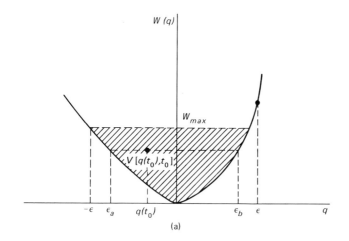

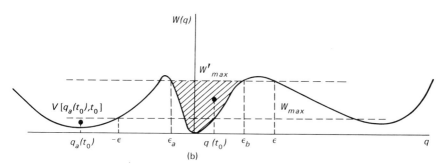

Fig. 7–11

(a) Monotonically increasing $W(q)$, $[V(\hat{q}(t_0), t_0]$ can be chosen to be any point in the shaded region; (b) nonmonotonically increasing $W(q)$, $V[\hat{q}(t_0, t_0)]$ can be chosen to be any point in the shaded region.

From Eq. 7–155, we have

$$V[\hat{q}(t), t] < W_{max}, \qquad t > t_0 \tag{7–158}$$

However,

$$V[\hat{q}(t), t] > W(q) \tag{7–159}$$

Thus, as $\hat{q}(t)$ and $t$ vary, $V[\hat{q}(t), t]$ is restricted to the shaded area of Fig. 7–11a. Then, Eq. 7–159 and the discussion of $W_{max}$ indicates that in this area

$$\|\hat{q}(t)\| < \varepsilon \tag{7–160}$$

Thus, if $\hat{q}(t_0)$ is chosen so that $V[\hat{q}(t_0), t_0] < W_{max}$, then Eq. 7–160 will be satisfied. Hence, the system will be stable since the norm of $\hat{q}(t)$ is restricted. Note that if $V[\hat{q}(t_0), t_0]$ is chosen to be less than $W_{max}$, then $\|\hat{q}(t)\|$ will be less than $\varepsilon$. For example, in Fig. 7–11a, $\|\hat{q}(t)\| \leq \varepsilon_b$.

Now assume that $W(\hat{q})$ does not increase monotonically (see Fig. 7–11b). For the value of $\varepsilon$ given on the diagram, $W_{max}$ is as shown. We choose $\hat{q}(t)$ such that $V[\hat{q}(t_0), t_0] < W_{max}$. Then, we will not necessarily obtain stability. Suppose $\hat{q}(t_0)$ is $\hat{q}_a(t_0)$, as illustrated in Fig. 7–11b. At no time can $\|\hat{q}(t)\|$ be less than $\varepsilon$. However, we shall now show that a suitable choice of $\hat{q}(t_0)$ can be found so that $\|\hat{q}(t)\| < \varepsilon$, $t > t_0$, $W(\hat{0}) = 0$, and $W(\hat{q}) > 0$. Thus, there must always be some (possibly very small) region about the origin where $W(\hat{q})$ increases monotonically along any straight line path drawn from the origin; i.e., a bowl shaped region in $n$-dimensions results. Choose a value $W'_{max}$ such that if $W$ increases from zero and $W < W_{max}$, then $\hat{q}$ is restricted to the bowl shaped region. Also choose $W'_{max}$ small enough so that $\|q\| < \varepsilon$. A typical $W'_{max}$ is illustrated by the shaded area of Fig. 7–11b. Now choose $\hat{q}(t_0)$ such that $V[\hat{q}(t_0), t_0] < W'_{max}$ and that $\|\hat{q}(t_0)\| < \varepsilon_r$, where $\varepsilon_r = \delta$ keeps $\hat{q}(t_0)$ in the allowable region. The proof proceeds exactly as before. This completes the proof.

If we can find a positive definite function of state variables and time $V[\hat{q}(t), t]$ such that $V[\hat{q}(t), t] > W[\hat{q}(t)]$ and $dV[\hat{q}(t), t]/dt < 0$, the origin will be Liapunov stable.

In the preceding theorem, we allowed $dV[\hat{q}(t), t]/dt$ to be zero. If we further restrict it so that it is never zero, except when $\hat{q} = 0$, then the origin will be *asymptotic stable*. The proof follows that of the previous one, except that now

$$\frac{dV[\hat{q}(t), t]}{dt} < 0 \tag{7–161}$$

Hence, $V[\hat{q}(t), t]$ approaches 0 as $t$ approaches infinity. We restrict $V[\hat{q}(t_0), t_0]$ to an allowable region (see Fig. 7–11) in which $W(\hat{q})$ only becomes zero at $\hat{q} = 0$. Then, since

$$V[\hat{q}(t), t] > W[\hat{q}(t)] \tag{7–162}$$

and

$$\lim_{t \to \infty} V[\hat{q}(t), t] = 0$$

We have $\lim_{t \to \infty} \hat{q}(t) = 0$. Hence, the origin is asymptotic stable.

Note that these conditions are sufficient. If we can find an appropriate Liapunov function, then the system will be stable. However, if we cannot find the function, we can make no definite statement. (Note that these theorems apply to nonexcited systems.)

Let us now illustrate the procedure with some examples. Suppose that the state variable equations for a (nonexcited) nonlinear system are

$$\frac{dq_1(t)}{dt} = -4q_1(t) - 3q_2(t) \tag{7–163a}$$

$$\frac{dq_2(t)}{dt} = 3q_1(t) - 2q_2(t) - \sinh q_2(t) \tag{7–163b}$$

Let us determine if the origin is stable. We must guess at a possible positive definite function. Let us choose a very simple one as a trial

$$V[\hat{q}(t), t] = \tfrac{1}{2} q_1^2(t) + \tfrac{1}{2} q_2^2(t) \tag{7-164}$$

(Note that $t$ does not appear explicitly, however this is allowed.) This equation is positive for all $\hat{q}$; we can write

$$W[\hat{q}(t)] = \tfrac{1}{3} q_1^2(t) + \tfrac{1}{3} q_2^2(t)$$

Then,

$$\frac{dV[\hat{q}(t), t]}{dt} = q_1(t) \frac{dq_1(t)}{dt} + q_2(t) \frac{dq_2(t)}{dt} \tag{7-165}$$

Note that total derivatives are used since the left-hand side of Eq. 7–165 actually is $dV/dt$ since $t$ does not appear explicitly. Then, substituting Eqs. 7–163, we have

$$\frac{dV[\hat{q}(t), t]}{dt} = -4q_1^2(t) - 2q_2^2(t) - q_2(t) \sinh q_2(t) \tag{7-166}$$

where $q_1^2(t)$, $q_2^2(t)$, and $q_2(t) \sinh q_2(t)$ are nonnegative; thus,

$$\frac{dV[\hat{q}(t), t]}{dt} \leqq 0 \tag{7-167}$$

Hence, the origin is stable. Note that Eq. 7–166 will not be zero unless $\hat{q}(t) = 0$. Equation 7–161 is also satisfied; thus, the stability is asymptotic.

Consider the following: $W[\hat{q}(t)]$ monotonically increases as $q_1(t)$ and $q_2(t)$ increase for all $q_1(t)$ and $q_2(t)$. This is analogous to Fig. 7–11a for all $\hat{q}$. In addition, $dV[\hat{q}(t), t]/dt < 0$, except when $\hat{q} = 0$. Thus, we can choose any initial condition (with an appropriate $\varepsilon$) and the origin will be asymptotic stable. Thus, the origin is *globally* asymptotic stable.

Consider the feedback system which is characterized by the block diagram of Fig. 7–12. Since we are considering the stability of the origin, we assume that the input $y(t) = 0$. The state variables which characterize this system are

$$\frac{dq_1(t)}{dt} = -4q_1(t) - 3q_2(t) \tag{7-168a}$$

$$\frac{dq_2(t)}{dt} = 3q_1(t) - 2q_2(t) + 2q_2^3(t) \tag{7-168b}$$

Again we shall try to use the simple, positive, semidefinite function

$$V[\hat{q}(t), t] = \tfrac{1}{2} q_1^2(t) + \tfrac{1}{2} q_2^2(t) \tag{7-169}$$

Thus,

$$\frac{dV[\hat{q}(t), t]}{dt} = -4q_1^2(t) - 2q_2^2(t) + 2q_2^4(t) \tag{7-170}$$

This will be negative for all $q_1(t)$ for those values of $q_2$ which satisfy

$$q_2^2(t) > q_2^4(t) \tag{7-171}$$

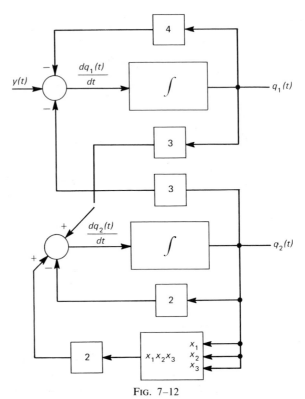

FIG. 7–12

Block diagram for state variables of the feedback system of Eqs.
7–168 (Note multiplier whose output is the product of its inputs.)

where, if $|q_2(t)| < 1$, then $V[\hat{q}(t), t]$ satisfies all the criteria for asymptotic stability. Thus, we must choose $|q_2(t_0)| < 1$. Then, using the Liapunov function of Eq. 7–169, we cannot state that the origin is globally asymptotic stable, but we can state that the origin is asymptotic stable for $|q_2(t)| < 1$. If we can find other Liapunov functions, we might be able to extend this region.

The theorems we have discussed here are *sufficient* to guarantee stability; however, they are not *necessary*. No necessary and sufficient conditions for stability are known. We can also obtain some sufficient conditions for instability. If we find a positive definite $V[\hat{q}(t), t]$ such that $V[\hat{q}(t), t] > W[\hat{q}(t)]$ and a positive definite $W_1[\hat{q}(t)]$ exists such that

$$W_1[\hat{q}(t)] > V[\hat{q}(t), t]$$

where both $W$ and $W_1$ are characterized by Fig. 7–11a and if $dV[\hat{q}(t), t]/dt > 0$, except that $dv[\hat{q}(0), 0]/dt = 0$, then the origin will be unstable. The proof of this follows the previous theorem and will be left to the reader.

The sufficient conditions are not necessary. Then, if we cannot find Liapunov functions to satisfy them, it may mean that the system is not stable (as in the case of the stability theorems) or it may just mean that we are not able to find an appropriate Liapunov function.

## 7-7.  COMPUTER INVESTIGATION OF INSTABILITY

If we cannot find Liapunov functions for a nonlinear system to demonstrate that a system is either stable or unstable, then we do not know if the system is stable. In this case, the following procedure may be tried. Form the state variable equations and solve them on computers (see Section 4-9). Various initial conditions can be tried. By studying the state variables $\hat{q}(t)$ for large $t$, some knowledge of the system stability can be obtained.

If a small displacement from the origin causes $\hat{q}(t)$ to approach a limit cycle and not return to the origin, then we can state the origin is unstable. Similarly, we can introduce input signals $\hat{y}(t)$ which are of finite duration and see if $\hat{q}(t)$ approaches the desired final value or oscillates about it.

If the procedure indicates that the system is unstable, then a definite result is obtained. Since computer solutions are approximate, it is possible that after sufficiently long time, the apparent limit cycle actually is not *one* and the system is actually stable. However, if a system appears to oscillate for a long period of time, it is unstable in a practical sense. Consider an audio amplifier that "howls" for 5 minutes and then stops whenever a signal is applied or changes rapidly. In theory, this is stable, but in practice, the device would be rejected. Therefore, if the computer solution indicates that the device is unstable, a definite answer is obtained. However, if each trial input yields a satisfactory $\hat{q}(t)$ for all $t$ up to the last value calculated, there is no guarantee, if $\hat{q}(t)$ were calculated for larger $t$, that $\hat{q}(t)$ would not become unstable. Also, a different input might have an output which is unstable.

We can study $d\hat{q}(t)/dt$, as well as $\hat{q}(t)$. If $dq_i(t)/dt$ and $q_i(t)$ are of opposite signs, then $|q_i(t)|$ will decrease. If $\hat{q}(t)$ approaches zero and all

$$q_i(t) \frac{dq_i(t)}{dt} < 0$$

for large $t$, then this is another indication that the origin is stable. Again it is only an indication and not definite. Great care should be taken here. For example an automatic pilot may appear to be stable for most inputs. However, if, in flight, an improbable input, such as an extremely strong and turbulent gust of wind, occurs and the response to it is unstable, the results may be catastrophic.

Many systems behave properly for all practical inputs if their response to some typical inputs is satisfactory. However, in nonlinear systems, unexpected things can happen.

## 7-8. STABILITY OF SAMPLED SYSTEMS

At the start of this discussion we shall restrict ourselves to linear, time-invariant sampled systems which are characterized by Fig. 7–13. Thus (see Eq. 6–146) the $z$-transformed form of the output in terms of the $z$-transformed form of the input is

$$G(z) = H(z) F(z) \tag{7–172}$$

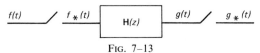

FIG. 7–13

Linear, time-invariant system with sampled input
and output

Now consider the $z$-transform (see Table 6-1). If all the poles of $G(z)$ are inside the unit circle in the $z$-plane, then $g(t)$ will be comprised of damped exponentials. Poles outside of the unit circle lead to exponential build up. Simple poles on the unit circle lead to sinusoids or constants, while multiple poles on the unit circle lead to functions of time multiplied by $t^n$, $n > 1$. Thus, the unit circle in the $z$-plane plays the same role as does the $j\omega$ axis in the $s$-plane. Similarly, the right half $s$-plane corresponds to the exterior of the unit circle in the $z$-plane and the left half $s$-plane corresponds to the interior of the unit circle in the $z$-plane. From Eq. 6–93, we have

$$z = e^{sT} \tag{7–173}$$

Let $s = j\omega$; then,

$$z = e^{j\omega T}$$

which characterizes the unit circle. If $\mathrm{Re}\ s \leq 0$, then $|z| < 1$ and if $\mathrm{Re}\ s > 0, |z| > 1$. Thus, the previous discussion is substantiated.

A linear, time-invariant sampled system will be stable if all the poles of its transfer function in $z$-transformed form lie within the unit circle. If we can write $H(z)$ as the ratio of two polynomials in $z$:

$$H(z) = \frac{N(z)}{D(z)} \tag{7–174}$$

then we must investigate $D(z)$ to see if there are poles outside of the unit circle. Accordingly, $D(z)$ can be factored to accomplish this. However, this is tedious and the Routh-Hurwitz algorithms and the Nyquist criterion can be modified to eliminate obtaining the roots of $D(z)$.

**Routh-Hurwitz Algorithms.**  The Routh-Hurwitz algorithms can most easily be applied by transforming $D(z)$ into a new polynomial $D_1(p)$, so that the roots of $D(z)$ inside the unit circle lie in the left-half $p$-plane, while those roots of $D(z)$ outside the unit circle are transformed into the right-half $p$-plane. We start by considering $D(z)$:

$$D(z) = a_n z^n + a_{n-1} z^{n-1} + \cdots + a_1 z + a_0 \qquad (7\text{--}175)$$

Now make the substitution

$$p = \frac{z+1}{z-1} \qquad (7\text{--}176a)$$

or, equivalently,

$$z = \frac{p+1}{p-1} \qquad (7\text{--}176b)$$

Then (see Eqs. 7–38 through 7–45) this is the desired transform. Substituting Eq. 7–176a into Eq. 7–175, we have

$$D_1(p) = a_n \left( \frac{p+1}{p-1} \right)^n + a_{n-1} \left( \frac{p+1}{p-1} \right)^{n-1} + \cdots + a_1 \left( \frac{p+1}{p-1} \right) + a_0 \qquad (7\text{--}177)$$

Rearranging, we have

$$D_1(p) = \frac{a_n(p+1)^n + a_{n-1}(p+1)^{n-1}(p-1) + \cdots + a_0(p-1)^n}{(p-1)^n} \qquad (7\text{--}178)$$

Now we apply the Hurwitz test to the polynomial

$$D_2(p) = a_n(p+1)^n + a_{n-1}(p+1)^{n-1}(p-1) + \cdots + (p-1)^n \qquad (7\text{--}179)$$

If the test fails, then $D(z)$ has poles outside of the unit circle.

For example, suppose

$$D(z) = 5z^2 + z + 1$$

then form

$$D_2(p) = 5(p+1)^2 + (p+1)(p-1) + (p-1)^2$$

$$D_2(p) = 7p^2 + 8p + 7$$

The Routh test yields

$$\begin{array}{cc} 7 & 7 \\ 8 & \\ 7 & \end{array}$$

Since all the coefficients in the first column are positive, the system is stable.

The use of the Routh algorithm can be tedious when $z$ transforms are investigated, because we must make the substitution of Eq. 7–176b and then form the polynomial $D_z(z)$. There is a procedure due to Jurey [2] which modifies the results of Marden [3] in which we can work directly with the polynomial $D(z)$ (see Eq. 7–175) and test to see if all its roots lie within the unit circle. Consider this test. Let $D(z)$ be given by

$$D(z) = a_n z^n + a_{n-1} z^{n-1} + \cdots + a_1 z + a_0$$

We then form the following stability test table.

STABILITY TEST TABLE

| Row | | | | | | | |
|-----|------|---------|---------|-----|----------|----------|-------|
| 1   | $a_n$ | $a_{n-1}$ | $a_{n-2}$ | $\cdots$ | $a_2$ | $a_1$ | $a_0$ |
| 2   | $a_0$ | $a_1$ | $a_2$ | $\cdots$ | $a_{n-2}$ | $a_{n-1}$ | $a_n$ |
| 3   | $b_{n-1}$ | $b_{n-2}$ | $b_{n-3}$ | $\cdots$ | $b_1$ | $b_0$ | |
| 4   | $b_0$ | $b_1$ | $b_2$ | | $b_{n-2}$ | $b_{n-1}$ | |
| 5   | $c_{n-2}$ | $c_{n-3}$ | $c_{n-4}$ | $c_0$ | | | |
| 6   | $c_0$ | $c_1$ | $c_2$ | $c_{n-2}$ | | | |
| .   | .    | .       | .       | | | | |
| .   | .    | .       | .       | | | | |
| .   | .    | .       | .       | | | | |
| $2n-3$ | $r_2$ | $r_1$ | $r_0$ | | | | |

The rows of the table are separated into pairs. The first row consists of the coefficients of $D(z)$; the second consists of the coefficients written in reverse order. Row three is generated in accordance with the following scheme:

$$b_{n-1} = \begin{vmatrix} a_n & a_0 \\ a_0 & a_n \end{vmatrix}$$

$$b_{n-2} = \begin{vmatrix} a_n & a_1 \\ a_0 & a_{n-1} \end{vmatrix}$$

$$b_{n-3} = \begin{vmatrix} a_n & a_2 \\ a_0 & a_{n-2} \end{vmatrix}$$
$$\vdots$$

The fourth row is obtained from the third row by writing it in reverse order. Each pair of rows is determined from the preceding pair in a similar way; for example,

$$c_{n-2} = \begin{vmatrix} b_{n-1} & b_0 \\ b_0 & b_{n-1} \end{vmatrix}$$

$$c_{n-3} = \begin{vmatrix} b_{n-1} & b_1 \\ b_0 & b_{n-2} \end{vmatrix}$$
$$\vdots$$

Note that each pair of rows has one less term than the preceding pair. Generate the table until the $(2n-3)$th row is obtained. Then, the following are the necessary and sufficient conditions that $D(z)$ have all its roots within the unit circle

$$D(1) > 0$$

$$(-1)^n D(-1) > 0$$

$$a_n > |a_0|$$

$$b_{n-1} > |b_0|$$

$$c_{n-2} > |c_0|$$

$$\vdots$$

$$r_2 > |r_0|$$

The conditions on the coefficients can be stated in the following way. Inspect each odd-numbered row. The first coefficient must be greater than the magnitude of the last coefficient.

Let us consider an example of this procedure.

$$D(z) = 2z^5 + 2z^4 + 3z^3 + 4z^2 + 4z + 1$$

Then, $D(1) > 0$ and $(-1)D(-1) = (-1)(-2 + 2 - 3 + 4 - 4 + 1) = 2 > 0$. Now form a table (see Table 7-1):

| Row | | | | | | |
|---|---|---|---|---|---|---|
| 1 | 2 | 2 | 3 | 4 | 4 | 1 |
| 2 | 1 | 4 | 4 | 3 | 2 | 2 |
| 3 | 3 | 0 | 2 | 5 | 6 | |
| 4 | 6 | 5 | 2 | 0 | 3 | |
| 5 | −27 | −30 | −6 | 15 | | |
| 6 | 15 | −6 | −30 | −27 | | |

We have not proceeded further since the test fails. (Actually, we could have stopped at row 3 since $6 > 3$; rows 5 and 6 were calculated as examples.) Thus, $D(z)$ has roots which line within the unit circle.

**Nyquist Criterion.** A single loop sampled feedback system will have a $z$-transformed gain which corresponds to Eq. 7–68. In $z$-transformed form, we have

$$H(z) = \frac{A(z)}{1 + A(z)\,\beta(z)} \qquad (7\text{--}180)$$

We assume (see Section 7-3) that $A(z)$ has no poles outside of the unit circle. We wish to determine if $1 + A(z)\,\beta(z)$ has any zeros outside of the unit circle. Thus, the procedure is essentially the same as for a continuous time system, except that now we cannot use the contour of Fig. 7–7. Since we wish to investigate the exterior of the unit circle, the contour of Fig. 7–14a can be used. This contour consists of the unit

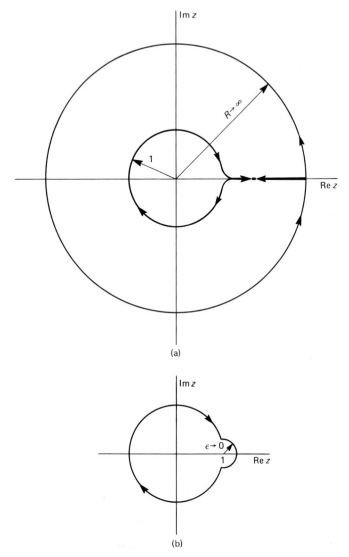

FIG. 7–14

(a) A path in the $z$-plane used to obtain the Nyquist criteria for a discrete
time system; (b) simplification of this path

circle, except for a small region: the "upper" Re $z$ axis for $z > 1$, the infinite circle, and the "lower" Re $z$ axis; for $z > 1$. In general, most practical systems are such that

$$\lim_{|z| \to 0} A(z)\,\beta(z) = 0 \tag{7-181}$$

Also, $A(z)\,\beta(z)$ is single valued so that the plot of $1 + A(z)\,\beta(z)$ as $z$ varies along the Re $z$ axis is just a straight line which juts out of the plot of $1 + A(z)\,\beta(z)$. Thus, it does not affect the curve's enclosure of the origin. Hence, this part of the curve can be omitted. Therefore, we can use the contour of Fig. 7–13b to obtain the Nyquist plot. Note that the curve is indented around $z = 1$.

**Observability and Controllability.** The concepts of observability and controllability apply to sampled, as well as, to discrete systems. In fact, the results developed in Section 7-5 can usually be applied to sampled systems. The development of the proofs are very similar and the details will be left to the reader.

**Stability in General Sampled Systems.** If we consider stability in general sampled systems, which may be nonlinear, we must use definitions similar to those given in Section 7-4. In this case, $t$ is replaced by the sample number $r$. We cannot obtain any general necessary and sufficient conditions for stability. The results are analogous to continuous time systems. Let us determine some sufficient conditions for stability. Again, we use positive definite functions. Equations 7–145 and 7–146 define a positive definite discrete time function if we replace $t$ with $r$. We shall also work with $V[\hat{q}(r), r]$ as a positive definite function of $q$ and the sample number $r$. In this case, $r$ replaces $t$ in Eqs. 7–148. For example,

$$V[\hat{q}(r), r] = \tfrac{1}{2}\,q_1^2(r) + \tfrac{1}{2}\,q_2^2(r) \tag{7-182}$$

Note that this is a continuous function of $\hat{q}(r)$ even though $\hat{q}(r)$ is not a continuous function of $r$.

A sampled function $V[\hat{q}(r), r]$ is called a *Liapunov function* if it satisfies

$$V[\hat{q}(r), r] \geqq W[q(r)] \tag{7-183}$$

where $W[\hat{q}(r)]$ is a positive definite function of $\hat{q}(r)$, and

$$V[\hat{q}(r+1), r+1] - V[\hat{q}(r), r] \leqq 0 \tag{7-184}$$

Equation 7–184 is the sampled equivalent of Eq. 7–150.

Now we can state the following theorem: *The origin of a sampled system is Liapunov stable if we can find a Liapunov function for contours in a region D which contains the origin.* The proof essentially follows that of the continuous system. Equation 7–151 was used to show that

$$V[\hat{q}(t_0), t_0] \geqq V[\hat{q}(t), t]$$

Similarly, Eq. 7–184 can be used to show that

$$V[\hat{q}(0), 0] \geqq V[\hat{q}(r), r], \qquad r > 0 \tag{7-185}$$

The proof of this theorem essentially follows that for the continuous time system. The details will be left to the reader.

Again, proceeding as in the continuous time case, if Eq. 7–184 is replaced by

$$V[\hat{q}(r + 1), r + 1] - V[\hat{q}(r), r] < 0, \qquad \hat{q}(r) \neq r \qquad (7\text{--}186)$$

then the origin will by asymptotic stable.

We shall apply this procedure to the stability of a nonlinear sampled feedback system whose difference equations are

$$q_1(r + 1) = \sqrt{\tfrac{1}{2} q_1^2(r) + \tfrac{1}{4} q_2^2(r)} \qquad (7\text{--}187a)$$

$$q_2(r + 1) = \sqrt{\tfrac{1}{3} q_1^2(r) + \tfrac{1}{2} q_2^2(r)} \qquad (7\text{--}187b)$$

Let us attempt to use the Liapunov function

$$V[\hat{q}(r), r] = q_1^2(r) + q_2^2(r) \qquad (7\text{--}188)$$

Then, substituting Eqs. 7–187, we obtain

$$V[\hat{q}(r + 1), r + 1] - V[\hat{q}(r), r] = -\tfrac{1}{6} q_1^2(r) - \tfrac{1}{4} q_2^2(r) \qquad (7\text{--}189)$$

Thus,

$$V[\hat{q}(r + 1), r + 1] - V[\hat{q}(r), r] \leqq 0, \qquad \hat{q}(r) \neq 0$$

Thus, the origin is globally asymptotic stable.

## PROBLEMS

**7-1.** A linear, time-invariant system has an impulse response given by

$$h(t) = (e^{-at} \sin t) u(t), \qquad a > 0$$

Demonstrate that the system is stable.

**7-2.** A linear, time-invariant system has an impulse response which is given by

$$h(t) = (e^t \sin 2t) u(t)$$

Find a bounded input signal which will produce an unbounded output.

**7-3.** Prove that the following two statements are equivalent for a linear, time-invariant system. (1) A system is stable if its response to any bounded input is bounded and (2)

$$\int_{-\infty}^{\infty} \left| \frac{da(t)}{dt} \right| dt$$

is bounded, where $a(t)$ is the unit step response.

**7-4.** Discuss the part that observability and controllability play in studies of the stability of linear, time-invariant systems.

**7-5.** Use the test on the poles and residues of $F(s)$ (see Eq. 7–22) to determine if

$$D(s) = s^4 + 2s^3 + 3s^2 + s + 1$$

is a Hurwitz polynomial.

**7-6.** Use the Routh algorithm to test if

$$D(s) = s^4 + 2s^3 + 3s^2 + s + 1$$

is a Hurwitz polynomial.

**7-7.** Repeat Problem 7 6 for

$$D(s) = s^9 + s^8 + 2s^7 + 3s^6 + 3s^5 + 5s^4 + 2s^3 + 3s^2 + 2s + 1$$

**7-8.** Repeat Problem 7-6 for

$$D(s) = s^4 + 3s^3 + 3s^2 + 3s + 2$$

**7-9.** Use the Hurwitz algorithm to determine if the polynomial of Problem 7-6 is a Hurwitz polynomial.

**7-10.** Repeat Problem 7-9 for the polynomial of Problem 7-7.

**7-11.** Repeat Problem 7-9 for the polynomial of Problem 7-8.

**7-12.** Find the range of $K$ for which

$$D(s) = s^3 + Ks^2 + 2s + 1$$

is a Hurwitz polynomial.

**7-13.** The feedback system of Fig. 7–5 is characterized by the following functions

$$A(j\omega) = \frac{A_0}{(j\omega + 1)\left(j\dfrac{\omega}{2} + 1\right)^2}$$

$$\beta = \tfrac{1}{10}$$

Use a Nyquist criterion to find the maximum value that $A_0$ can have if the system is to be stable.

**7-14.** Repeat Problem 7-13 if

$$A(j\omega) = \frac{A_0}{(j\omega + 1)\left(j\dfrac{\omega}{100} + 1\right)^2}$$

**7-15.** A feedback system is characterized by Fig. 7–5. Discuss stability of the system in terms of the amplitude and phase of $A(\omega)\beta(\omega)$. Consider the Bode relations here.

**7-16.** Repeat Problem 7-13 for

$$A(j\omega) = \frac{A_0}{\left(1 + \dfrac{1}{j\omega}\right)^4 (j\omega + 1)^3}$$

**7-17.** Using the definition of a norm given in Eq. 7–92, find the norm of

$$\hat{a} = \begin{bmatrix} 1 & 2 \\ -6 & -8 \end{bmatrix}$$

**7-18.** Find the $L_2$ norm of the matrix of Problem 7-17.

**7-19.** Find the norm (see Eq. (7–92)) of the matrix $\hat{a}$, where

$$\hat{a} = \begin{bmatrix} 1 & 2 \\ 7 & 9 \end{bmatrix} \begin{bmatrix} 6 & 4 \\ 3 & 1 \end{bmatrix}$$

**7-20.** A linear, time-invariant system is such that

$$\|e^{t\hat{a}}\| < Me^{-2t}$$

where $M$ is a positive constant. Show that the response to any $\hat{y}(t)$ of bounded norm and finite duration is bounded.

**7-21.** A linear, time-invariant system has two input signals $y_1(t)$ and $y(t)$, and three state variables $q_1(t)$, $q_2(t)$, and $q_3(t)$. If $y_1(t) = \delta(t)$ and $y_2(t) = 0$, then

$$q_1(t) = e^{-t}u(t)$$

$$q_2(t) = e^{-2t}u(t)$$

$$q_3(t) = (e^{-t}\sin t)u(t)$$

If $y_2(t) = \delta(t)$ and $y_1(t) = 0$, then

$$q_1(t) = e^{-3t}u(t)$$

$$q_2(t) = (e^{-3t}\sin 2t)u(t)$$

$$q_3(t) = e^{-t}u(t)$$

Show that any output of the system will be bounded, if the system is observable and controllable.

**7-22.** A system is characterized by the state variable equations

$$\frac{d\hat{q}(t)}{dt} = \hat{a}\hat{q}(t) + \hat{b}\hat{y}(t)$$

$$\hat{x}(t) = c\hat{q}(t) + d\hat{y}(t)$$

where

$$\hat{a} = \begin{bmatrix} 1 & 1 \\ -2 & 4 \end{bmatrix}$$

$$\hat{b} = \begin{bmatrix} b_{11} & b_{12} \\ b_{21} & b_{22} \end{bmatrix}$$

$$c = \begin{bmatrix} c_{11} & c_{12} \\ c_{21} & c_{22} \end{bmatrix}$$

Determine the conditions on $\hat{b}$ if the system is to be controllable with respect to $\hat{y}_1$; repeat this for $y_2$. Determine the restrictions on $c$ if all the natural frequencies appear in $x_1(t)$; repeat this for $x_2(t)$.

**7-23.** A system is characterized by the state variable equations

$$\frac{dq_1(t)}{dt} = -4q_1(t) - 2q_2(t)$$

$$\frac{dq_2(t)}{dt} = +2q_1(t) - 4q_2(t) - \tanh q_2(t)$$

Investigate the stability of the system.

**7-24.** Repeat Problem 7-23 for

$$\frac{dq_1(t)}{dt} = -4q_1(t) - q_2(t)$$

$$\frac{dq_2(t)}{dt} = 3q_1(t) - 4q_2(t) - q_2^3(t)$$

**7-25.** Repeat Problem 7-23 for

$$\frac{dq_1(t)}{dt} = -4q_1(t) - q_2(t) - q_3(t) + q_1^3(t)$$

$$\frac{dq_2(t)}{dt} = q_1(t) - 3q_2^3(t) - q_3^2(t)q_2(t)$$

$$\frac{dq_3(t)}{dt} = q_1(t) - \frac{q_1^2(t)}{q_3(t)} + q_3(t)$$

**7-26.** Use computer techniques to investigate the stability of the system given below for various inputs

$$\frac{dq_1(t)}{dt} = -4q_1(t) - q_2(t) + y_1(t)$$

$$\frac{dq_2(t)}{dt} = 3q_1(t) - 4q_2(t) - q_2^3(t) + 2y_1(t)$$

**7-27.** Write a computer program which investigates the stability of the origin. Determine if all

$$q_i(t)\frac{dq_i(t)}{dt} < 0, \qquad i = 1, 2, ..., n$$

Assume that $q_i(t)$ and $dq_i(t)/dt$ are entered from subroutines.

**7-28.** Determine if

$$D(z) = z^4 + 2z^3 + 3z^2 + 2z + 1$$

has any roots outside of the unit circle.

**7-29.** Repeat Problem 7-28, for

$$D(z) = z^6 + 2z^5 + 3z^4 + 2z^3 + 2z^2 + z + 1$$

**7-30.** Investigate the stability of a sampled function system whose open loop gain is

$$A(z)\beta(z) = \frac{2z}{z^3 + 2z^2 + 1}$$

Use the Nyquist criterion.

**7-31.** A sampled system is characterized by the following state variable difference equations:

$$q_1(r + 1) = \sqrt{\tfrac{1}{2}q_1^2(r) + \tfrac{1}{2}q_2^2(r)}$$

$$q_2(r + 1) = \sqrt{\tfrac{1}{4}q_1^2(r) + \tfrac{1}{4}q_2^2(r)}$$

Investigate the stability of the origin of this system.

# REFERENCES

1. Schwarz, R. J., and Friedland, B. *Linear Systems.* New York: 1965, pp. 371, 372.
2. Jury, E. I., and Blanchard, J. "A Stability Test for Linear Discrete Systems in Table Form." In *Proc. IRE.* Vol. 49, 1961, pp. 1947, 1948.
3. Marden, M. "The Geometry of the Zeros of Polynomial in a Complex Variable." In *Proc. American Math. Soc.,* 1949, pp. 148–161.

# BIBLIOGRAPHY

Balabanian, N., Bickart, T. A., and Seshu, S. *Electrical Network Theory.* Chaps. 9 and 10. New York: Wiley, 1969.
Schwarz, R. J., and Friedland, B. *Linear Systems.* Chaps. 11 and 12. New York: McGraw-Hill, 1965.

# CHAPTER 8

# Statistical Processes—Noise

In previous chapters we have discussed procedures for obtaining the response of a system to known signals. However, there are circumstances where the total signal is not exactly known at every instant.

Let us consider an example of this. Because of thermal agitation, the free electrons of all materials are in random motion. This results in random voltages and currents. In an amplifier, these voltages and currents are added to the signal voltages and currents. Thus, any signal will have an unknown component called *noise*. Signals may be so much larger than the noise that the noise can be ignored. However, sometimes the noise is so large that the desired signal may be obscured. Thus, it is often necessary to consider means of reducing the noise. Since noise is random, it cannot be expressed as an exact function of time.

A radio receiver will not only produce the type of noise which we have discussed, but there will also be interference which results from sources external to the receiver, such as lightening or electric motors. These "signals" can also be classified as interfering noise.

Noise need not be electric. Suppose an airplane flies through turbulent air. The airplane is a system with its position the output signal. The gusts of wind perturb the output signal just as thermal agitation of the electrons perturbed the output of the radio. Thus, the wind can be thought of as a noise signal.

If noise generated in a radio receiver could be predicted, a signal equal to the magnitude of the noise signal could be introduced to cancel the noise. Unfortunately, we cannot predict the values of noise signals, so they must be treated as *random signals*.

This does not mean that we know nothing about noise signals. Suppose we take a simple resistance and observe the voltage due to the random motion of the free electrons across it as a function of time using a sensitive voltmeter or oscilloscope. After a long time, we can determine data such as the following: The noise voltage remains less than 0.001 volt for 90 percent of the time, the voltage lies between 0.0005 and 0.001 volt for 40 percent of the time, and the voltage is less than 1.0 volt for 99.99999 percent of the time. At any instant, we cannot exactly determine what the voltage will be at the next instant. However, we can make some statements about the *probability* of the value of the voltage. On the basis of the previous data, if very many measurements are made, then 90 percent of them will be less than 0.001 volt. If measurements are made at only 10 instants, we cannot definitely state that 9 of these will be 0.001 volt, or less. However, if very many measurements are made; say $10^6$, then approximately $0.9 \times 10^6$ of them will be 0.001 volt, or less. We shall be concerned with random noise signals on a probabilistic basis. We have discussed probability in a very general way in this introduction. In the subsequent sections of this chapter, we shall formalize our discussion. We shall introduce probabilistic concepts and illustrate them with examples. Alternatively, we could take an axiomatic approach (i.e., state a series of axioms and then develop the theory). This is somewhat more rigorous. However, the approach we use is more understandable. The subsequent discussion will be rigorous. After probability is introduced and formalized we shall then study random noise on the basis of probability. In the next chapter we shall discuss the transmission of signals in the presence of noise. Procedures for reducing the effect of the noise will be considered there.

## 8-1. SOME BASIC IDEAS OF PROBABILITY

In general, we shall be concerned with continuous systems. However, to simplify the discussion we shall begin by considering discrete activities, such as tossing a coin or casting a pair of dice, and later, we shall generalize our results for continuous systems.

Suppose a coin is tossed. There are only two possible outcomes "heads" or "tails." Each of these is termed an *event*. Thus, when the coin is tossed, there are two possible events. Now let us assume that we toss the coin $N$ times and $N_H$ heads occur. We define the probability that a head occurs by the following notation,

$$P(H) = \lim_{N \to \infty} \frac{N_H}{N} \qquad (8-1)$$

We perform the experiment very many times and take the ratio of the number of heads occurring to the total number of tosses. If the coin is unbiased (i.e., neither side is weighted more heavily than the other), then

$$P(H) = \tfrac{1}{2} \qquad (8-2)$$

If the experiment is performed a few times, this does *not* mean that half of the results will be heads. In general, only when a very large number of tosses are made will $N_H/N \approx 0.5$.

Now, suppose a single unbiased die (one of a pair of dice) is tossed. Then the numbers 1, 2, 3, 4, 5, or 6 can result. Since the die is unbiased, on the average, each number will result 1/6 of the times that the die is tossed. Then, the probability that any one number will result is given by

$$P(1) = P(2) = P(3) = P(4) = P(5) = P(6) = \tfrac{1}{6} \qquad (8-3)$$

There are six possible results. Since the likelihood of any one occurring is equal, then the probability that any one will occur is 1/6. Now suppose that the die is weighted so that the occurrence of a 3 is twice as great as that of any other number (assuming that the likelihood of any of the other numbers occurring is equal). Now, *all* the probabilities are not equal. Thus, we have

$$P(3) = 2P(1) = 2P(2) = 2P(4) = 2P(5) = 2P(6) \tag{8-4}$$

Let us determine the probabilities. If we perform $N$ experiments, where $N$ is very large and $N_k$ is equal to the number of times that a $k$ results ($N_3$ is the number of times that a 3 results, etc.),

$$P(k) = \lim_{N \to \infty} \frac{N_k}{N} \tag{8-5}$$

Hence,

$$P(1) + P(2) + P(3) + P(4) + P(5) + P(6)$$

$$= \lim_{N \to \infty} \left[ \frac{N_1}{N} + \frac{N_2}{N} + \frac{N_3}{N} + \frac{N_4}{N} + \frac{N_5}{N} + \frac{N_6}{N} \right] \tag{8-6}$$

However, the only possible outcomes from tossing a die are 1, 2, 3, 4, 5, or 6, and one and only one number results each time that the die is tossed, hence,

$$N_1 + N_2 + N_3 + N_4 + N_5 + N_6 = N \tag{8-7}$$

Then,

$$P(1) + P(2) + P(3) + P(4) + P(5) + P(6) = 1 \tag{8-8}$$

Let us consider the significance of this. The $P(1) + P(2) + P(3) + P(4) + P(5) + P(6)$ represents the probability of obtaining a 1, 2, 3, 4, 5, or 6. Since these are the only possibilities, it is certain that one of them will result. Hence, the probability of this occurrence is 1, i.e., $(N_1 + N_2 + N_3 + N_4 + N_5 + N_6)/N = 1$. Solving Eqs. 8–4 and 8–8, we obtain

$$P(1) = P(2) = P(4) = P(5) = P(6) = \tfrac{1}{7} \tag{8-9a}$$
$$P(3) = \tfrac{2}{7} \tag{8-9b}$$

Now let us generalize these results. Suppose an experiment can have outcomes $A_1, A_2, ..., A_n$. If we perform the experiment $N$ times and $N_k$ is the number of times that $A_k$ results, then the probability of the occurrence of the event $A_k$ is defined as

$$P(A_k) = \lim_{N \to \infty} \frac{N_k}{N} \tag{8-10}$$

Let us discuss some limiting cases. If it is *impossible* for an event to occur, then $N_k = 0$. In this case, Eq. 8–10 yields

$$P(A_k) = 0 \tag{8-11a}$$

Thus, *an impossible event has zero probability of occurring.*

If it is *certain* that an event $A_k$ will occur, then the outcome of the experiment will always be $A_k$. Hence, $N_k = N$ and Eq. 8–10 yields

$$P(A_k) = 1 \qquad\qquad (8\text{–}11\text{b})$$

Hence. *a certain event will have unity probability of occurring.*

In general,

$$0 \leqq P(A_k) \leqq 1 \qquad\qquad (8\text{–}12)$$

The number of occurrences of an event cannot be more than the number of experiments and it cannot be negative.

Now let us obtain the probability that either $A_j$ or $A_k$ can occur. For example, what is the probability of tossing a single die and obtaining a 1 or a 3? The possible outcomes are 1, 2, 3, 4, 5, or 6. If the die is unbiased, then each of these has equal probability. If many tosses are made, a 1 will occur (on the average) $1/6$ of the time. Similarly (on the average), a 3 will occur $1/6$ of the time. Thus, the probability of obtaining either a 1 or a 3 is $1/6 + 1/6 = 1/3$. In general (see Eq. 8–10), we have

$$P(A_k \text{ or } A_j) = \lim_{N \to \infty} \frac{N_j + N_k}{N}$$

Hence,

$$P(A_k \text{ or } A_j) = P(A_k) + P(A_j) \qquad\qquad (8\text{–}13)$$

If events $A_1$, $A_2$, ..., $A_n$ are *mutually exclusive*, the occurrence of $A_j$ precludes the occurrence of any other $A_k$, $k \neq j$ in the same experiment. If a die is tossed and a 4 results, then a 1, 2, 3, 5, or 6 *cannot also result.*

The set of events $A_1$, $A_2$, ..., $A_n$ is said to be *completely exhaustive* if some $A_j$, $j = 1, 2, ..., n$ must result each time that the experiment is performed. If the experiment consists of tossing a single die, then 1, 2, 3, 4, 5, and 6 represent a completely exhaustive set, while 1, 2, 4, 5, and 6 is not a completely exhaustive set.

If $A_1$, $A_2$, ..., $A_n$ forms both a mutually exclusive set and a completely exhaustive set, then

$$P(A_1) + P(A_2) + \cdots + P(A_n) = 1 \qquad\qquad (8\text{–}14)$$

Since the events are mutually exclusive, only one $A_j$ can result for each experiment. Also, since the set is completely exhaustive, then only $A_1$, $A_2$, ..., or $A_n$ can result. Hence, it is certain that the outcome of the experiment will be one and only one of the $A_1$, $A_2$, ..., $A_n$. Then, applying an extention of Eq. 8–13, Eq. 8–14 results.

At times, we wish to perform successive experiments. If we know the outcome of one experiment, then it may affect the probability of succeeding ones. Suppose there are two red balls and two blue balls in a box. The probability of picking a blue ball from the box is 0.5 (i.e., $2/4$). If a blue ball is picked and removed from the box, then the next time that the experiment is performed, the bog will contain only three balls, one blue and two red. Now, the probability of picking a blue ball is $1/3 = 0.3333$. In this case, the knowledge of the first event changes the probability of the occurrence of the second event.

For convenience in working with such information, we define *conditional probability* $P(A_k|A_j)$. This is the probability that event $A_k$ occurs if we know that event $A_j$ has occurred. If the events are *independent* of each other, then

$$P(A_k|A_j) = P(A_k) \tag{8-15}$$

For example, if, in the toss of a die, a 3 results, this will *not* affect any subsequent toss of the die.

As another example, let us consider the probability of the occurrence of the letter $u$ in the English language. It is much less than 0.25. However, if we know that the letter preceding the $u$ is a $q$, then the probability of the $u$'s occurring is unity. In this case, we have $P(u|q) = 1$.

Suppose we perform an experiment which requires two events as its result; e.g., tossing two dice or picking two colored balls from a box. Let the experiment be performed $N$ times and let $N_{kj}$ be the number of times that event $A_k$ results after event $A_j$ has resulted. In the experiment of drawing the balls from the box, $N_{kj}$ could be the number of times a blue ball was picked on the second draw, if a blue ball were also picked on the first. Also let $N_j$ be the number of times event $j$ occurs on the first pick (e.g., the number of times that a blue ball is picked on the first draw), then

$$P(A_k|A_j) = \lim_{N \to \infty} \frac{N_{kj}}{N_j} \tag{8-16}$$

Note that the denominator of Eq. 8–16 is $N_j$ and not $N$, since $P(A_k|A_j)$ is the probability that $A_k$ occurs if we know that $A_j$ has previously occurred.

Now let us determine the probability of two successive events occuring. For instance, for the previous example what is the probability of drawing two blue balls from a box? This is called a *joint probability* and is written as $P(A_k, A_j)$, where $P(A_k, A_j)$ represents the probability of the sequence $A_k A_j$ resulting. Using the definitions preceding Eq. 8–16, we have

$$P(A_k, A_j) = \lim_{N \to \infty} \frac{N_{kj}}{N} \tag{8-17}$$

Note that now the denominator is $N$, the *total* number of trials, since we wish to determine the ratio of the number of times that the sequence occurs to the total number of trials; thus, we can rewrite Eq. 8–17 as

$$P(A_k, A_j) = \lim_{N \to \infty} \frac{N_{kj}}{N_j} \frac{N_j}{N} \tag{8-18}$$

Assuming that all ratios remain bounded (i.e., $N_j \neq 0$), we have

$$P(A_k, A_j) = \left( \lim_{N \to \infty} \frac{N_{kj}}{N_j} \right) \left( \lim_{N \to \infty} \frac{N_j}{N} \right) \tag{8-19}$$

Substituting Eqs. 8–10 and 8–16 we obtain

$$P(A_k, A_j) = P(A_j) P(A_k | A_j) \qquad (8\text{–}20a)$$

Proceeding in an analogous fashion, we obtain

$$P(A_k, A_j) = P(A_k) A(A_j | A_k) \qquad (8\text{–}20b)$$

The joint probability of two occurrences is the probability of one occurrence times the conditional probability of the other, knowing that the first has occurred.

As an example, let us determine the probability of drawing two blue balls from a box containing two red balls and two blue balls. The probability of drawing a blue ball from the box is $P(B) = 1/2$. Then, the probability of drawing another blue ball from the remaining three if a blue ball has already been drawn is $P_B(B) = 1/3$. Hence, the probability of drawing both blue balls is

$$P(B, B) = \tfrac{1}{2}(\tfrac{1}{3}) = \tfrac{1}{6}$$

Let us show that this is correct. Let us list all possible pairs of drawings. To differentiate, let us call the four balls $B_1$, $B_2$, $R_1$, and $R_2$, where $B_1$ and $B_2$ are blue, etc. All possible pairs of drawings are: $B_1 B_2$, $B_1 R_1$, $B_1 R_2$, $B_2 R_1$, $B_2 R_2$, $B_2 B_1$, $R_1 B_1$, $R_1 B_2$, $R_1 R_2$, $R_2 B_1$, $R_2 B_2$, and $R_2 R_1$. Thus, there are *twelve* possible drawings. Only two of these $B_1 B_2$ or $B_2 B_1$ represent a choice of two blue balls. Hence, the result of $1/6$ is verified.

If the two events are independent of each other, then knowledge of the first does not affect the second. Thus, the conditional probability becomes the ordinary problem. Hence, if $A_k$ and $A_j$ are independent, then

$$P(A_k, A_j) = P(A_k) P(A_j) \qquad (8\text{–}21)$$

For example, the probability of tossing two heads in series is

$$P(H, H) = \tfrac{1}{2} \cdot \tfrac{1}{2} = \tfrac{1}{4}$$

**Mean Value–Expected Value.** Suppose we have an experiment that yields a numerical value; e.g., casting a die. The outcome of the experiment is a set of $n$ discrete numbers $x_1, x_2, ..., x_n$. In this case, we can state that $x$ is the outcome of the experiment and $x$ is called a *chance variable*, a *random variable*, or a *stochastic variable*. We shall assume that the probability of $x$'s assuming the values $x_1, x_2, ..., x_n$ are

$$P(x_1), P(x_2), ..., P(x_n)$$

respectively.

Now suppose the experiment is repeated many times. Let us determine the average of all the outcomes. That is we shall determine the *mean value* of the stochastic variable $x$. We shall define the result and then justify it.

$$E[x] = \bar{x} = P(x_1) x_1 + P(x_2) x_2 + \cdots + P(x_n) x_n \qquad (8\text{–}22)$$

where $E[x] = \bar{x}$ is called the *mean value* of the stochastic variable $x$. Alternatively, $E[x] = \bar{x}$ is called the *expected value* of $x$. The reader should note that the expected value is *not* the value most often expected, but the mean (or average) value of many experiments.

If a die is tossed very many times, then 1, 2, 3, 4, 5, and 6 will all result about an equal number of times. Thus, the mean value will be

$$E[x] = \bar{x} = \tfrac{1}{6}(1) + \tfrac{1}{6}(2) + \tfrac{1}{6}(3) + \tfrac{1}{6}(4) + \tfrac{1}{6}(5) + \tfrac{1}{6}(6) = \tfrac{21}{6} = 3.5$$

Of course, 3.5 is *not* the value most often expected to occur.

Let us justify the choice of Eq. 8–22 as the definition of the mean value. Suppose any value of $x$ were equally probable. Then, if a great many experiments were performed, each value would occur (approximately) an equal number of times. Then, the average value would be

$$\bar{x} = E[x] = \frac{x_1 + x_2 + \cdots + x_n}{N} \tag{8–23}$$

If the probability of each variable occurring is equal, then

$$P(x_1) = P(x_2) = \ldots = P(x_n) = \frac{1}{N} \tag{8–24}$$

Thus, Eq. 8–22 would yield the proper value.

Now let us discuss a case where the probabilities are unequal. Suppose the probability of $x_2$'s occurring is $b$ times that of any of the other values. Then,

$$\bar{x} = E[x] = \frac{x_1 + bx_2 + x_3 + \cdots + x_n}{N + b - 1} \tag{8–25}$$

Note that we have divided by $N + b - 1$ because there are now $N + b - 1$ terms in the numerator (i.e., there are $b$ $x_2$'s). The probabilities are given by

$$\frac{1}{b}P(x_2) = P(x_1) = P(x_3) = \cdots = P(x_n)$$

Using this equation and Eq. 8–14, we obtain

$$P(x_2) = \frac{b}{N + b - 1} \tag{8–26a}$$

$$P(x_1) = P(x_3) = \cdots = P(x_n) = \frac{1}{N + b - 1} \tag{8–26b}$$

Substituting Eqs. 8–26 into Eq. 8–22, we obtain Eq. 8–25. Thus, we have again verified Eq. 8–22. We can proceed in this way for an arbitrary set of probabilities. So Eq. 8–22 is justified.

The mean value $\bar{x}$ is the average value of the stochastic variable $x$. Suppose, for example, $x$ represents a sample of a continuous function of time. The $\bar{x}$ would correspond to its zero frequency, or direct value, i.e., the average value is the zero frequency value. For example, if $x_1, x_2, ..., x_n$ represented samples of a current, then (on the average) $\bar{x}$ would be the direct-current component. In Section 8-3 we shall note that, at times, this concept must be modified. It is included here to provide some physical feel for the ideas discussed.

Now let us introduce a new variable $x'$, where

$$x' = x - \bar{x} \tag{8-27}$$

To obtain $x'$, we subtract $\bar{x}$ from the outcome of the experiment. From Eq. 8–22, we have

$$E[x'] = \bar{x}' = \bar{x} - \bar{x} = 0 \tag{8-28}$$

Thus, the expected value of $x'$ is zero. That is, $x'$ represents the value of $x$ with the zero frequency component removed. Many systems remove the zero frequency component from the signal.

Very often, when we deal with systems, we wish to know the average power supplied by a signal. This is proportional to the average value of the signal squared. This is also called the *mean square value* of the signal. Hence, we wish to obtain the average or the expected value of the square of the signal, which is

$$E[x^2] = \bar{x}^2 = P(x_1)\,x_1^2 + P(x_2)\,x_2^2 + \cdots + P(x_n)\,x_n^2 \tag{8-29}$$

This definition follows that of Eq. 8–22. Note that the probabilities are not squared since the probability of $x_j$'s occurring is what determines the *weight* to be given to $x_j^2$ in Eq. 8–29.

In general, Eqs. 8–22 and 8–29 can be generalized and we can write the expected value of the stochastic variable $x$ raised to any power as

$$E[x^k] = \overline{x^k} = \sum_{j=1}^{n} P(x_j)\,x_j^k \tag{8-30}$$

where $E[x^k]$ is called the $k$th *moment* of the stochastic variable $x$.

In many systems, the mean, or average, value is removed from the signal. In this case, the signal $x'$, defined in Eq. 8–27, results. Moments defined in terms of such a stochastic variable are called the *central moments*:

$$E[(x - \bar{x})^k] = \overline{(x - \bar{x})^k} = \sum_{j=1}^{n} P(x_j)(x_j - \bar{x})^k \tag{8-31}$$

If $k = 1$, the central moment is zero (see Eq. 8–28); if $k = 2$, the central moment is especially important. In many systems, this yields a value proportional to the average power since the zero frequency component is removed. This central moment is called the *variance* and is usually denoted by $\sigma^2$, hence,

$$\sigma^2 = E[(x - \bar{x})^2] = \overline{(x - \bar{x})^2} = \sum_{j=1}^{n} P(x_j)(x_j - \bar{x})^2 \tag{8-32}$$

We can write Eq. 8–32 as

$$\sigma^2 = \sum_{j=1}^{n} P(x_j)\, x_j^2 - 2\bar{x} \sum_{j=1}^{n} P(x_j)\, x_j + \bar{x}^2 \sum_{j=1}^{n} P(x_j) \tag{8–33}$$

Substituting Eqs. 8–29, 8–22, and 8–14, we have

$$\sigma^2 = \overline{x^2} - \bar{x}^2 \tag{8–34}$$

The variance is the difference between the second moment and the square of the first moment. Alternatively, we can state that *the variance is the difference between the mean square value and the square of the mean value.* Note that in the notation used here $\overline{x^2}$ is the mean of the squared value while $\bar{x}^2$ is the square of the expected, or mean value.

Another commonly used definition is the (nonnegative) square root of the variance $\sqrt{\sigma^2} = \sigma$. This is called the *standard deviation*, which can be only positive or zero.

## 8-2. RANDOM SIGNALS

The output signals of a system are often represented by continuous functions. In general, this output will usually consist of a nonrandom (desirable) signal and random noise. For the time being, let us ignore the nonrandom signal and concentrate on the random one. Statistical processes will be used to describe the random signal.

Suppose we have a system with no nonrandom input signal such that the output consists entirely of noise. For example, such a system could be a sensitive radio receiver which is not tuned to a station. The output of the receiver could be $x_1(t)$ of Fig. 8–1. Now suppose several receivers are built, which have the *same* schematic diagram and components and operate at the same temperature, line voltage, etc. The noise outputs of each receiver will be statistically identical to the first. However, at any instant, their actual outputs will be different. Three such functions are shown in Fig. 8–1.

Now suppose there are a very large number of systems and the output of each is given by $x_1(t)$, $x_2(t)$, $x_3(t)$, .... The entire set of these $x_i(t)$ is said to be a *random process*, or *ensemble*, which we shall write as $\{x(t)\}$, Note that $\{x(t)\}$ consists of the set $x_1(t)$, $x_2(t)$, .... A single member of the ensemble, e.g., $x_2(t)$ is called a *sample function*. The value of a sample function at a fixed time is called a *random variable*, e.g., $x_3(t)$. Since we do not know the sample functions exactly, but can only specify them on a statistical basis, we sometimes do not designate the particular sample function being discussed. In such cases, the sample function will be written as $X(t)$.

Let us discuss the concept of an ensemble in greater detail. Suppose we have a very large number of radio receivers which are *identical*. This is an *ensemble of radio receivers.* The noise output of each receiver can be discussed on a probabilistic basis. In order to obtain the statistical data at time $t_1$, the noise outputs of all the receivers of the ensemble are measured at time $t_1$. Thus, a measurement on the ensemble of these receivers provides stochastic data. The reader may ask why we do not make measurements on one system at many different times to obtain data. At times, this will provide the same data as that obtained from the ensemble. However, in cases such as time-varying systems, data for the system at $t = t_1$ cannot be obtained from measurements made at other times.

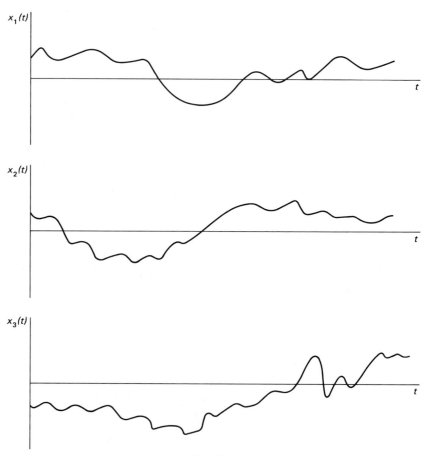

Fig. 8–1

Three sample functions from the ensemble $\{x(t)\}$

**Distribution Functions.** Let us assume that $X(t)$ is a random variable, that is, it is a value of one of the sample functions at time $t$. Then, we define the following as a *probability distribution*.

$$P(x_1, t) = \text{Probability} \left[ X(t) \leq x_1 \right] \qquad (8\text{--}35)$$

where $P(x_1 t)$ is the probability that, at time $t$, a sample function will be equal to or less than $x_1$. To obtain this, in theory, the value of each $X(t)$ of the ensemble is studied at time $t$. The ratio of the number of sample functions equal to or less than $x_1$ to the total number of sample functions is equal to $P(x_1, t)$. If the random process is independent of time, the parameter $t$ will be omitted; e.g., $P(x_1)$.

Even though we are considering continuous functions, let us use a discrete function for an illustration. Suppose the system output is the number resulting from the toss of a single die. Since there is equal probability of all integers from 1 to 6 inclusive, we have $P(x) = 0$, $x < 1$; $P(x) = 1/6$, $1 \leq x < 2$; $P(x) = 2/6$, $2 \leq x < 3$; $P(x) = 3/6$, $3 \leq x < 4$; $P(x) = 4/6$, $4 \leq x < 5$; $P(x) = 5/6$, $5 \leq x < 6$; $P(x) = 1$, $6 \leq x$. (We have assumed that the random process is independent of time.) Note that $P(x)$ continuously increases. For instance, $P(1)$ is the probability that the output be 1, while $P(2)$ is the probability that it be 2 or less; e.g., in the discrete case, that it is either 1 or 2.

Let us consider some properties of probability distribution functions; first

$$0 \leq P(X, t) \leq 1 \qquad (8\text{--}36)$$

where the probability that $X(t) \leq x$ cannot be less than zero (an impossibility) or greater than 1 (a certainty). The value of $P(x, t)$ cannot decrease as $x$ increases; that is $\partial P(x, t)/\partial x$ is nonnegative. This is true for the reasons discussed above.

Now consider the value of $P(x, t)$ at its endpoints.

$$P(-\infty, t) = 0 \qquad (8\text{--}37a)$$

$$P(\infty, t) = 1$$

For all practical processes, the output will never be $-\infty$, and it will always be between $-\infty$ and $+\infty$.

Two simple probability distributions are i'.ustrated in Fig. 8–2. The first is for the discrete example of tossing the die which we have presented. The second is for a continuous function. Note that it satisfies all the conditions we have discussed.

As an example, let us determine the probability that, at a given time $t$, the output of a sample function lies between $x_1$ and $x_2$, that is,

$$x_1 \leq X(t) \leq x_2 \qquad (8\text{--}38)$$

The probability that $X(t)$ is less than $x_2$ at time $t$ is $P(x_2, t)$. However, if $X(t)$ is to be in the range of Relation 8–38, then this probability must be diminished by the probability that $X(t)$ is less than $x_1$, thus,

$$\text{Prob}\left[x_1 \leq X(t) \leq x_2, t\right] = P(x_2, t) - P(x_1, t) \qquad (8\text{--}39)$$

**Probability Density Functions.**  We shall now discuss another function which describes random variables. This is the derivative of the probability distribution function. We call this new function the *probability density, p(x, t)*, where

$$p(x, t) = \frac{\partial P(x, t)}{\partial x} \tag{8-40}$$

At a fixed time, we can write

$$P(x_2, t) - P(x_1, t) = \int_{x_1}^{x_2} p(x, t)\, dx \tag{8-41}$$

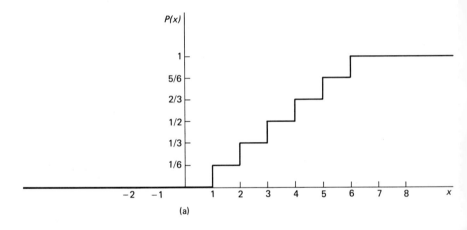

(a)

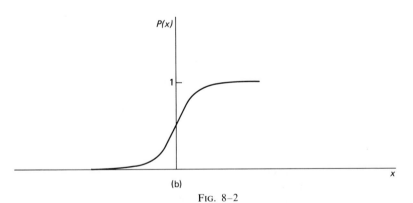

(b)

FIG. 8–2

Typical probability distribution functions; (a) for tossing a single die; (b) for a typical continuous system, independent of time

This follows from the definition of the derivative. Thus, at a fixed time, the area under the probability density curve for $x_1 < x < x_2$ is the probability that $X(t)$ lies between $x_1$ and $x_2$. Thus, $p(x, t)\,dx$ is the probability that the variable $X(t)$ lies between $x$ and $x + dx$. If $p(x, t)$ is bounded, then the probability that $X(t)$ lies in this differentially small range is itself differentially small.

If the lower limit of Eq. 8–41 becomes $-\infty$, then using Eqs. 8–37a and 8–35, we have

$$P(x_1, t) = \int_{-\infty}^{x_1} p(x, t)\,dx \qquad (8\text{–}42)$$

Let us now consider other properties of the probability density. Since $P(x, t)$ is a nondecreasing function of $x$, then

$$p(x, t) \geq 0 \qquad (8\text{–}43)$$

Also, from Eq. 8–37b we have, for all $t$,

$$\int_{-\infty}^{\infty} p(x, t)\,dt = 1 \qquad (8\text{–}44)$$

As an example in Fig. 8–3 we have illustrated the probability density functions for probability distribution functions of Fig. 8–2. For the discrete stochastic variable, $p(x)$ becomes a series of impulse functions.

Another example of a probability density function is the noise produced by the random motion of electrons in a resistor. The probability that a particular level of noise voltage occurs decreases as the voltage increases. Thus, the probability density will fall off with voltage level.

**Functions of Random Variables.** At times, we deal with known functions of a random variable. Consider $f(x)$, where $x$ is a random variable. Then, $f(x)$ will have a random output. As an example, let

$$Y = f(X) = e^{-X} \qquad (8\text{–}45)$$

where the probability distribution of $x$ is given by

$$p(x) = \begin{cases} 0, & x < 0 \\[2mm] \dfrac{1}{b}, & 0 \leq x \leq b \\[2mm] 0, & x > b \end{cases} \qquad (8\text{–}46)$$

That is, $X$ is never less than zero or greater than $b$ and it takes on any value between zero and $b$ with equal likelihood.

Now let us find the probability that $Y$ be less than some value $y$. If $Y \leq y$, then $x \geq -\ln Y$. If $y < 0$, then $P(y) = 0$, since $Y = f(X)$ cannot be negative. The smallest value that $Y$ can have is $e^{-b}$. Thus, if $y < e^{-b}$, then $P(y) = 0$.

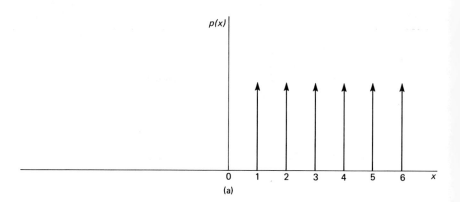

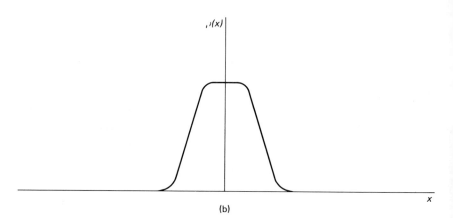

FIG. 8–3

Probability density functions for the probability distribution functions of Fig. 8–2

Now suppose $y$ lies between 1 and $e^{-b}$. If $e^{-b} \leq Y \leq y$, then $x$ must lie between $b$ and $-\ln y$, hence,

$$P(y) = \int_{-\ln y}^{b} \frac{1}{b} \, dx = \frac{b + \ln y}{b}$$

If $y > 1$, then $P(y) = 1$, since all values of $Y$ must be equal to or less than 1, hence,

$$P(y) = \begin{cases} 0, & y < e^{-b} \\ \dfrac{b + \ln y}{b}, & e^{-b} \leq y \leq 1 \\ 1, & y > 1 \end{cases}$$

Then, differentiating, we obtain the probability density of $Y$:

$$p(y) = \begin{cases} 0, & y < e^{-b} \\ \dfrac{1}{by}, & e^{-b} \leq y \leq 1 \\ 0, & y > 1 \end{cases} \qquad (8\text{--}47)$$

Then, in the range $e^{-b} \leq y \leq 1$, the function is more likely to take on the smaller values (i.e., close to $e^{-b}$) even though the probability of $x$ taking on any value in the range $0 \leq x \leq b$ is uniform.

**Joint and Conditional Probability Density Functions.**   We shall now assume that we have two random variables $X$ and $Y$. These can come from two different processes or can be determined from one process at different times. Again suppose we have an ensemble of random sample functions for each process. Often, we are interested in systems that interact. In such cases, a knowledge of one random variable will affect the probability of the other.

Suppose $X$ represents the noise input of an amplifier, while $Y$ represents its output. The amplifier not only amplifies the input signal, but also adds noise to it. If the amplifier noise is negligible, then a knowledge of the input signal uniquely determines the output signal. As the amplifier noise increases, the uncertainty in the output signal increases even if the input signal is known. However, a knowledge of the input signal still provides some information about the probable value of the output signal. To express the probability of such systems mathematically, we define a conditional probability distribution $p = (x|y, t)$. This is defined as the probability that $x \leq X \leq x + dx$, when the value of $Y$ is fixed at $y$. Thus, $p(x|y, t)$ is the probability density for $X$, knowing that $Y$ is fixed at $y$ at time $t$, then,

$$\text{Prob}\left[x_1 \leq X(t) \leq x_2, Y = y, t\right] = \int_{x_1}^{x_2} p(x|y, t)\, dx \qquad (8\text{--}48)$$

This equation is exactly analogous to Eqs. 8–39 and 8–41.

Another quantity of interest is the *joint probability density*. This is given by

$$p(x, y, t)\, dx\, dy = \text{Prob}\left[x \leq X \leq x + dx, y \leq Y \leq y + dy, t\right] \qquad (8\text{--}49)$$

The joint probability density is the probability that, at a given time $t$, $X$ lies between $x$ and $x + dx$ and $Y$ lies between $y$ and $y + dy$, thus,

$$\text{Prob}\left[x_1 \leq X(t) \leq x_2, y_1 \leq Y \leq y_2, t\right] = \int_{x_1}^{x_2} \int_{y_1}^{y_2} p(x, y, t)\, dx\, dy \qquad (8\text{--}50)$$

Conditional and joint probabilities are analogous to the probabilities for discrete systems (see Section 8-1). The relation between conditional and joint probabilities can be obtained from the development of Eq. 8–20 for discrete systems by assuming that the number of discrete events increases so that the discrete system approaches a continuous system, thus,

$$p(x, y, t) = p(x, t) p(y|x, t) \qquad (8\text{--}51a)$$

and

$$p(x, y, t) = p(y, t) p(x|y, t) \qquad (8\text{--}51b)$$

If the two processes are unrelated, a knowledge of one will not affect the other's probability, hence,

$$p(x|y, t) = p(x, t) \qquad (8\text{--}52)$$

Also, in an unrelated case,

$$p(x, y, t) = p(x, t) p(y, t) \qquad (8\text{--}53)$$

Let us consider some other relations for joint and conditional probabilities:

$$p(x, y, t) \geq 0 \qquad (8\text{--}54a)$$
$$p(x|y, t) \geq 0 \qquad (8\text{--}54b)$$

The reasons for this are analogous to those given for Eq. 8–43, also,

$$\int_{-\infty}^{\infty} \int_{-\infty}^{\infty} p(x, y, t)\, dx\, dy = 1 \qquad (8\text{--}55)$$

This is analogous to Eq. 8–44.

Suppose we are given the joint probability density $p(x, y, t)$ and wish to determine the probability density $p(x, t)$. First, determine the probability that $X$ lies in the range

$$-\infty \leq X \leq x \qquad (8\text{--}56)$$

for *all* possible $y$. This is $P(x, t)$, the probability distribution of $x$; it is given by

$$P(x, t) = \int_{-\infty}^{\infty} \int_{-\infty}^{x} p(x_1, y, t)\, dx_1\, dy \qquad (8\text{--}57)$$

Note that the integration with respect to $y$ is from $-\infty$ to $\infty$. Thus (see Eq. 8–50) we are determining Prob $[-\infty \leq X \leq x, t]$ for all possible $y$. Therefore, we obtain the probability distribution of $x$ independent of $y$. From Eq. 8–40, we have

$$p(x, t) = \frac{\partial}{\partial x} \int_{-\infty}^{\infty} \int_{-\infty}^{x} p(x_1, y, t)\, dx_1\, dy \qquad (8\text{--}58)$$

We assume that $p(x, y, t)$ is such that the order of differentiation and integration can be interchanged; doing this and differentiating, we have

$$p(x, t) = \int_{-\infty}^{\infty} p(x, y, t)\, dy \qquad (8\text{--}59a)$$

Similarly,

$$p(y, t) = \int_{-\infty}^{\infty} p(x, y, t)\, dy \qquad (8\text{--}59b)$$

We have assumed here that there are two random processes. Actually, there can be an arbitrary number of processes. Thus, the previous concepts can be extended to the general case. For instance, conditional probability density, in these cases, expresses a probability density for one variable assuming that the others are known. Similarly, a joint probability density for many variables could be defined.

**Mean Value-Expected Value.** Now let us obtain the mean, or the expected, value of a continuous random variable. This is defined in the following way:

$$\bar{x}(t) = E[x(t)] = \int_{-\infty}^{\infty} xp(x, t)\,dx \qquad (8\text{–}60)$$

Let us consider the physical significance of this expression. At a time $t$, $p(x, t)\,dx$ is the probability that $X$ lies between $x$ and $x + dx$. The integral of Eq. 8–60 is equivalent to the summation of Eq. 8–22 for discrete random variables. Each value of $x$ is weighted in accordance with its probability $p(x, t)\,dx$ and then "summed" in a Riemann integral. This infinite sum in the limit is the definition of the Riemann integral. Since $X(t)$ is the general variable representation of any element of the ensemble, the mean value is, at times, written as $E[X(t)] = \bar{X}(t)$. However, it is often conventional to use the lower-case letter. We shall do this here. Note that the expected value represents an average taken over the ensemble at a fixed time $t$. That is, $p(x, t)$ is a probability density determined from the ensemble at a particular time. $t$. Thus, $\bar{x}(t)$ represents the following. At time $t$, each $x(t)$ is determined for each of the elements of the ensemble. $\bar{x}(t)$ is the mean of these values. This is called an *ensemble average*. Note that the expected value is not the most probable value, but is a weighted average (see Section 8-1).

As an example let us obtain the expected value of the stochastic variable whose probability density is given by Eq. 8–46, thus,

$$\bar{x} = E(x) = \int_{0}^{b} \frac{x}{b}\,dx = \frac{1}{2b} \qquad (8\text{–}61)$$

Since Eq. 8–46 indicates that all values of $x$ between 0 and $b$ are equally likely, it is reasonable to obtain $1/2b$ as the average value.

**Time Average.** We have just discussed the ensemble average. That is at a fixed time $t$, we consider the value of each element in the ensemble and average them. Now let us consider a different calculation. Suppose we observe $x(t)$ for one element of the ensemble and average its value over all time. This is called the time average $\langle x(t) \rangle$, then,

$$\langle x_i(t) \rangle = \lim_{T \to \infty} \frac{1}{2T} \int_{-T}^{T} x_i(t)\,dt \qquad (8\text{–}62)$$

Note that $x_i(t)$ represents the $i$th element of the ensemble. In the next section, we shall discuss possible relations between the time average and the ensemble average. In general, they are different quantities calculated in different ways.

**Expected Value of a Function.**    Suppose we have a known function of a random variable $f(x)$. Let us obtain the expected value of $f(x)$. That is, we "average" all possible values of $f(x)$ corresponding to all possible values of $x$. Each $f(x)$ is weighted in accordance with the probability of occurrence of the corresponding $x$. This is similar to Eq. 8–60, except that now $x$ is replaced by $f(x)$, hence,

$$\overline{f(x)} = E[f(x)] = \int_{-\infty}^{\infty} f(x)\, p(x, t)\, dx \tag{8–63}$$

As an example, let us obtain the expected value of the function of Eq. 8–45, using the probability distribution of Eq. 8–46, then,

$$E[f(x)] = \int_{0}^{b} \frac{1}{b} e^{-x} dx = \frac{1 - e^{-b}}{b} \tag{8–64}$$

We can compute this in another way. The probability distribution of $f(x)$ is given in Eq. 8–47. Let us compute its expected value. Then, from Eq. 8–60, we have

$$\bar{y} = E[f(x)] = \int_{-\infty}^{\infty} y\, p(y)\, dy$$

Substituting Eq. 8–47 yeidls

$$\bar{y} = E[f(x)] = \int_{e^{-b}}^{1} \frac{1}{b} dy = \frac{1 - e^{-b}}{b} \tag{8–65}$$

Equations 8–64 and 8–65 give the same results, as they should.

**Moments–Variance.**    If, in Eq. 8–63, we replace $f(x)$ by $x^k$, we obtain the expected value of $x^k$, the $k$th moment, which is

$$E[x^k(t)] = \overline{x^k(t)} = \int_{-\infty}^{\infty} x^k\, p(x, t)\, dx \tag{8–66}$$

When $k = 2$, this is the second moment, which is also called the *mean square value* of the random value.

Let us now obtain the *central moments* (see Section 8-1). We subtract the mean value $\bar{x}$ from the random variable and then obtain the moments of the resulting random variable; thus,

$$E[(x(t) - \bar{x}(t))^k] = \overline{[x - \bar{x}(t)]^k} = \int_{-\infty}^{\infty} (x - \bar{x})^k\, p(x, t)\, dx \tag{8–67}$$

The first central moment (i.e., $k = 0$) is zero. The second the *variance* and is usually written as $\sigma^2$ (see Sec. 8-1), where

$$\sigma^2(t) = \int_{-\infty}^{\infty} [x - \bar{x}(t)]^2\, p(x, t)\, dt \tag{8–68}$$

Rearranging, we have

$$\sigma^2(t) = \int_{-\infty}^{\infty} x^2 p(x, t)\, dt - 2\bar{x} \int_{-\infty}^{\infty} x p(x, t)\, dt + \bar{x}^2 \int_{-\infty}^{\infty} p(x, t)\, dt$$

Substituting Eqs. 8–66, 8–60, and 8–44, we obtain

$$\sigma^2 = \overline{x^2} - \bar{x}^2 \qquad (8\text{–}69)$$

Thus, as in the discrete case, *the variance is the difference between the mean of the squared value and the square of the mean value of the random variable.* The positive square root of the variance $\sigma$ is the *standard deviation.*

To provide some physical feel for the variance and mean value, we shall derive a useful inequality. Let us start with the variance of a random variable. At a fixed time $t$, we have

$$\sigma^2(t) = \int_{-\infty}^{\infty} [x - \bar{x}(t)]^2\, p(x, t)\, dx$$

Let $y = x - \bar{x}(t)$; then,

$$\sigma^2(t) = \int_{-\infty}^{\infty} y^2 p[y + \bar{x}(t), t]\, dy$$

Now choose a positive constant $b$. Since the integrand is everywhere positive, if we eliminate any of the range of integration, the value of the integral will be reduced. Thus, we obtain the bound,

$$\sigma^2(t) \geq \int_{-\infty}^{-b} y^2 p[y + \bar{x}(t), t]\, dy + \int_{b}^{\infty} y^2 p[y + \bar{x}(t), t]\, dy$$

In the range of both integrands $y^2 > b^2$. Then, since each term of the integrand is positive, we have

$$\sigma^2(t) \geq b^2 \left( \int_{-\infty}^{-b} p[y + \bar{x}(t), t]\, dy + \int_{b}^{\infty} p[y + \bar{x}(t), t]\, dy \right)$$

Replacing $y + \bar{x}(t)$ by $x$, we obtain

$$\sigma^2(t) \geq b^2 \left[ \int_{-\infty}^{-b + \bar{x}(t)} p(x, t)\, dx + \int_{b + \bar{x}(t)}^{\infty} p(x, t)\, dx \right] \qquad (8\text{–}70)$$

The first integral is the probability that $X$ lies in the range $-\infty \leq X \leq \bar{x}(t) - b$, while the second is the probability that $X$ lies in the range $\bar{x}(t) + b \leq x \leq \infty$. Their sum is the probability that $X$ does not lie within $b$ units of $\bar{x}(t)$. Thus, Eq. 8–70 can be written as

$$\frac{\sigma^2(t)}{b^2} \geq \text{Prob}\left[ |X(t) - \bar{x}(t)| \geq b \right] \qquad (8\text{–}71)$$

Now let $b = k\sigma$, where $k$ is a positive constant; then

$$\frac{1}{k^2} \geq \text{Prob}\left[|X(t) - \bar{x}(t)| \geq k\sigma\right] \tag{8-72}$$

The probability that $|X| \geq a$ is one minus the probability that $|X| < a$. That is, if $\alpha$ is the probability that an event will occur, then $1 - \alpha$ is the probability that it will not occur; e.g., if there are three chances in ten that an event will occur, then there must be seven chances in ten that it will not. If $|X(t) - \bar{x}(t)| \geq k\sigma$ then $X(t)$ does not lie within $k\sigma$ of $\bar{x}(t)$. Hence, $1 - 1/k^2$ is a bound on the probability that $X(t)$ lies within $k\sigma$ of $\bar{x}(t)$, or equivalently, that $|X - \bar{x}(t)| \leq k\sigma(t)$; thus,

$$\text{Prob}\left[|X - \bar{x}(t)| < k\sigma(t)\right] \geq 1 - \frac{1}{k^2} \tag{8-73}$$

Since the probability cannot be negative, we require that $k \geq 1$. (Note the reversal of the inequality sign.) If the probability of an event's occurring is less than $1/k^2$, the probability of its not occurring must be more than $1 - 1/k^2$. Equation 8–73 is called *Tchebycheff's inequality*. Note that it is not an equation but just gives a lower bound on the probability. Let us consider the significance of Tchebysheff's inequality. It gives the probability that the random variable $X$ lies within $k$ standard deviation $(k\sigma)$ of its mean value. Consider some typical values of $k$

$$\text{Prob}\left[|X - \bar{x}(t)| < 2\sigma(t)\right] \geq 0.75 \tag{8-74a}$$
$$\text{Prob}\left[|X - \bar{x}(t)| < 10\sigma(t)\right] \geq 0.99 \tag{8-74b}$$

Thus, regardless of the form of $p(x, t)$, the probability that $X$ lies within 2 standard deviations of the mean value is 0.75 and that $X$ lies within 10 standard deviations of the mean value is 0.99. Therefore, in a large ensemble, at time $t$, it is likely that at least $3/4$ of the $x_i(t)$ lie within $2\sigma$ of the expected values. Also, 99 percent of the $x_i(t)$ on the average, will lie within $10\sigma$ of $\bar{x}(t)$. Note that Eq. 8–74 does not depend upon the form of $p(x, t)$. If the form of $p(x, t)$ is known, then these probabilities can be calculated exactly.

As an example, consider a random variable whose probability distribution is

$$p(x) = \begin{cases} ae^{-ax}, & x \geq 0 \tag{8-75a} \\ 0, & x < 0 \tag{8-75b} \end{cases}$$

Then, the mean value is given by

$$\bar{X} = \int_0^\infty ax\, e^{-ax}dx = \frac{1}{a}$$

The variance is

$$\sigma^2 = \int_0^\infty ax^2\, e^{-ax}dx = \frac{2}{a^2}$$

Then, the standard deviation is

$$\sigma = \sqrt{2}/a$$

As the value of $a$ is increased, the probability distribution becomes smaller for all $x > 0$. Thus, as $a$ is increased, it is to be expected that more and more values of $x$ will be in the vicinity of $x = 0$. As $a$ increases, $\bar{x}$ decreases, and approaches zero as $1/a$. The standard deviation falls off as $1/a$. Then, the Tchebycheff inequality indicates that

$$\text{Prob}\left[\left|X - \frac{1}{a}\right| < \frac{\sqrt{2k}}{a}\right] \geq 1 - \frac{1}{k^2}$$

Hence, as $a$ increases, the likelihood of $X$'s being found close to the origin increases.

Let us exactly compute the probability that $|X - 1/a| < \sqrt{2k}/a$. We can do this, since we know the form of $p(x)$. It is given by Eq. 8–75; hence,

$$\text{Prob}\left[\left|X - \frac{1}{a}\right| \leq \frac{\sqrt{2k}}{a}\right] = \int_0^{\sqrt{2k/a}} ae^{-ax}dx$$

$$\text{Prob}\left[\left|X - \frac{1}{a}\right| < \frac{\sqrt{2k}}{a}\right] = 1 - e^{-\sqrt{2k}}$$

This is more exact than the Tchebycheff inequality. However, the Tchebycheff inequality can be used, if the exact form of $p(x)$ is not known.

In this section we considered that the probability density could vary with time. In many systems, this is not the case. The parameter $t$ can then be dropped from the equations. This will be discussed in the next section.

## 8-3. RANDOM PROCESSES

Physical systems impose restrictions on the types of random processes which can exist. These restrictions often simplify the analysis of the system. In this section, we shall discuss some commonly encountered restrictions on random processes.

**Stationary Processes.** In the last section we assumed that the random process could be time dependent. In many cases, this time dependence is not present. Suppose we measure the noise voltage across a resistor. Let us call some time $t = 0$ and record the output $X(t)$ from an ensemble of resistors. These data can then be used to determine a probability density $p(x, t)$ and all the possible joint probability densities $p(x|y, t)$ etc. If we choose a different time for the origin of the measurements, we obtain another $p(x, t)$ etc. If all of the probability densities determined are independent of the choice of the time origin, then $p(x, t)$, $p(x|y, t)$, etc. will be independent of $t$. The process is then said to be *stationary*. In this case, the probability density is written as $p(x)$, $p(x|y)$, etc.

Let us consider an example of a stationary and nonstationary process. The thermal excitation of the free electrons produces the noise voltage of a resistor. Thus, this noise is a function of the temperature. If the resistor is kept at a constant temperature, the process will be stationary. However, if the temperature of the resistor is varied as a function of time, the process will be nonstationary.

In general, when we deal with stationary processes, the parameter $t$ will be omitted from the expression. For example, the expected value (see Eq. 8–60) will be written as

$$\bar{x} = E[x] = \int_{-\infty}^{\infty} x \, p(x) \, dx \qquad (8–76)$$

and the variance (see Eq. 8–68) is

$$\sigma^2 = \int_{-\infty}^{\infty} (x - \bar{x})^2 \, p(x) \, dx \qquad (8–77)$$

If a process is to be stationary, it must have started at $t = -\infty$ and not end until $t = +\infty$. Of course, we do not work with such processes. Thus, there are no practical stationary random processes. However, if all data taken over a finite time interval indicate that the process is stationary, we often can assume that, for all practical purposes, the process is stationary. This assumption often introduces negligible error. Consider the resistor noise just discussed. If its temperature remains constant for several hours, then, during much of the time we can, to a high degree of accuracy, assume that the process is stationary.

**Ergodic Processes.**   Some stationary processes exhibit the property that statistical data, obtained by observing an entire ensemble at a fixed time, are identical with the data obtained by observing one sample function for all time. Processes which have this property are *ergodic*. Statistical data can be obtained by making a measurement on an entire ensemble of resistors at a fixed time. However, the same statistical data will be obtained by observing a single resistor for a long time. As another example of an ergodic process, assume that an ensemble of identical dice are cast. The statistical information obtained from observing the ensemble for one cast is the same as that obtained from studying one die cast many times.

If a process is ergodic, the ensemble averages will be equal to the corresponding time averages. For instance, for the moments (see Eq. 8–66), we have

$$\int_{-\infty}^{\infty} x^k p(x) \, dx = \lim_{T \to \infty} \frac{1}{2T} \int_{-T}^{T} x_i^k(t) \, dt \qquad (8–78)$$

where $x_i(t)$ is one member of the ensemble. Alternatively, we can write

$$\overline{x^k} = E[x^k] = \langle x^k \rangle \qquad (8–79)$$

A process cannot be ergodic unless it is also stationary. If a process changes with time, then we cannot expect statistics determined from the ensemble at one instant of time to be the same as that determined from a single sample function for all time. However, if a process is stationary, it need not necessarily be ergodic. Let us consider an example which illustrates this. Suppose each sample function of an ensemble $x_i(t)$ has a probability density given by $(1/\sqrt{2\pi}\sigma) e^{-x^2/2\sigma_i^2}$, where the $\sigma_i$ varies for each sample function. The process will be stationary, but the data obtained from one sample function $x_i(t)$ over all time will not be the same as the data obtained from the ensemble at a fixed time, since the $\sigma_i$ vary from sample to sample. Another example of a stationary process which is not ergodic can be obtained from an ensemble of dice. If some, but not all, of the dice are weighted (e.g., so that a 6 always results), the ensemble averages will not be the same as the time averages for a single die.

In general, most of the processes we shall deal with will be stationary ergodic processes. Let us consider some physical aspects of these systems. For example, from Eq. 8–78, if $k = 1$,

$$\int_{-\infty}^{\infty} x\, p(x)\, dx = \lim_{T \to \infty} \int_{-T}^{T} x(t)\, dt \tag{8–80}$$

The right-hand side of this equation is the time average, or the direct value. Thus, in an ergodic system, the ensemble average which yields the expected value $\bar{x} = E[x]$ is also the direct value. Also, $\bar{x}^2$, the square of the expected value, is now proportional to the power supplied by the direct component. From Eq. 8–78, we have

$$\int_{-\infty}^{\infty} x^2 p(x)\, dx = \lim_{T \to \infty} \int_{-T}^{T} x_i^2(t)\, dt \tag{8–81}$$

Thus, the ensemble average which is the mean square value $\bar{x}^2$, or the expected value of $x^2$, is also proportional to the average power of the signal. Similarly, the variance $\sigma^2$ is proportional to the power supplied by the varying portion of the signal; that is, by the signal with the direct component removed. Also note that the standard deviation is proportional to the rms value (effective value) of the signal component of $x(t)$, and that the relations between ensemble averages and time averages are only valid for ergodic processes. However, many of the systems with which we shall deal are ergodic.

**Markov Processes.** Consider a process sampled at discrete times. In practice, even if we have a continuous system, we may only sample it at discrete times. Even if we read the signal from an oscilloscope, we can only practically work with a finite number of points. We have considered joint probabilities where a knowledge of one or more values can affect the probability of another. In general, if we sample a variable at $n - 1$ times and we know $x_1(t_1), x_2(t_2), \ldots, x_{n-1}(t_{n-1})$, then the probability of the sample, $x_n(t_n)$ can depend upon all of these. If the process is such that the probability $p(x_n, t_n)$ depends only upon $x_{n-1}(t_{n-1})$ (i.e., the sample immediately preceding the one in question), then the process is called a *Markov process*. Knowledge of $x_1(t_1) \ldots x_{n-2}(t_{n-2})$ does not affect the probability $p(x_n, t_n)$ in a Markov process.

**Deterministic Processes.** If a process can be predicted on the basis of past data, then it is said to be *deterministic*. In general, the random processes that we discussed are *nondeterministic*. It seems as though a random process cannot be deterministic by definition. However, consider the following. Suppose there is a process given by the ensemble $\{x(t)\}$ where each member of the ensemble is given by

$$x_i(t) = A_i, \qquad i = 1, 2, \ldots \tag{8-82}$$

where each $A_i$ is a constant. Thus, if a particular $A_i$ is known at one time, it is known for all time. However, the $A_i$ may be random variables. That is, until the $A_i$ are measured, their values can only be predicted on a probabilistic basis. Hence, this is a deterministc random process. However, in general, we shall be concerned with nondeterministic random processes.

## 8-4. SOME COMMON PROBABILITY DENSITIES AND DISTRIBUTIONS—THE CENTRAL LIMIT THEOREM

Any function satisfying the requirements of Section 8-2 can be a probability density or distribution. However, the physical characteristics of a system determine the proper probability function. The probability of very large noise voltages appearing across a resistor falls off as the amplitude of the voltage is increased. A probability that does not reflect this would not be a suitable one to use. Of course, not all probability densities which fall off as the amplitude of the variable increases are suitable for describing resistor noise. The random process must be studied on either a theoretic or an experimental basis to obtain the correct distribution.

In this section we shall discuss some probability densities that are used to describe certain physical processes. In general, the densities which we present here will be for stationary processes. Thus, they will not be expressed as a function of time.

**Gaussian Density.** The Gaussian, or normal, probability density is given by

$$p(x) = \frac{1}{\sqrt{2\pi}\,\sigma} e^{-(x-\bar{x})^2/2\sigma^2} \tag{8-83}$$

This is illustrated in Fig. 8–4. It is called a "bell shaped" curve since it has the shape of a bell. In Eq. 8–83, we have used the symbols $\bar{x}$ and $\sigma$, which are used to represent mean and standard deviation, respectively. Let us show that it is proper to use them

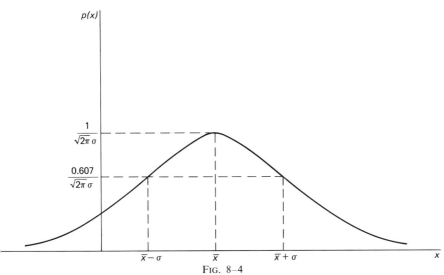

FIG. 8-4

Gaussian probability density

$$p(x) = \frac{1}{\sqrt{2\pi}\sigma} e^{-(x-x^2)/2\sigma^2}$$

here. The expected or mean value is (see Eq. 8-60)

$$E[x] = \frac{1}{\sqrt{2\pi}\,\sigma} \int_{-\infty}^{\infty} x e^{-(x-\bar{x})^2/2\sigma^2} dx \qquad (8-84)$$

Let

$$x - \bar{x} = y \qquad (8-85)$$

Then

$$E[x] = \frac{1}{\sqrt{2\pi}\,\sigma} \int_{-\infty}^{\infty} (y + \bar{x}) e^{-y^2/2\sigma^2} dy \qquad (8-86)$$

Evaluating the integral [1], we have

$$E[x] = \bar{x} \qquad (8-87)$$

Thus, it is proper to use $\bar{x}$ in Eq. 8-83.

Now let us compute the variance of Eq. 8-83. This is given by (see Eq. 8-68)

$$E[(x - \bar{x})^2] = \frac{1}{\sqrt{2\pi}\,\sigma} \int_{-\infty}^{\infty} (x - \bar{x})^2 e^{-(x-x)^2/2\sigma^2} dx \qquad (8-88)$$

Substituting Eq. 8-85, we obtain

$$E[(x - \bar{x})^2] = \frac{1}{\sqrt{2\pi}\,\sigma} \int_{-\infty}^{\infty} y^2 e^{-y^2/2\sigma^2} dy$$

Integrating yields [1]

$$E[(x - \bar{x})^2] = \sigma^2 \tag{8-89}$$

Thus, it is correct to use $\sigma$ in Eq. 8–83. The Tchebycheff inequality (see Eq. 8–73) can be used to bound the probability so that the random variable $X(t)$ lies within $k$ standard deviations of the mean value. However, the Tchebycheff inequality is just a bound which indicates that $X(t)$ lies within $k\sigma$ of $\bar{x}$ and is *greater than* $1 - 1/k^2$. This is valid for all probability densities, but when we work with a known probability density, we can compute the value directly, that is, we wish to obtain

$$\text{Prob}\left[|x - \bar{x}| \leq k\sigma\right]$$

The Gaussian density is symmetric about $x = \bar{x}$, hence, we can state that

$$\text{Prob}\left[|x - \bar{x}| \leq k\sigma\right] = 2\,\text{Prob}\left[\bar{x} \leq x \leq \bar{x} + k\sigma\right] \tag{8-90}$$

Using Eqs. 8–39 and 8–41, we obtain

$$\text{Prob}\left[|x - \bar{x}| \leq k\sigma\right] = \frac{2}{\sqrt{2\pi}\,\sigma} \int_{\bar{x}}^{\bar{x}+k\sigma} e^{-(x-x)^2/2\sigma^2} dx \tag{8-91}$$

The integral cannot be solved in closed form. However, a similar integral has been solved by numerical methods and the results have been tabulated [2]. It is called the *normal curve of error* and is given by

$$\Phi(y) = \frac{1}{\sqrt{2\pi}} \int_0^y e^{-x^2/2}\, dx \tag{8-92}$$

Substituting

$$y = \frac{x - \bar{x}}{\sigma}$$

into Eq. 8–91 and manipulating, we obtain

$$\text{Prob}\left[|x - \bar{x}| \leq k\sigma\right] = \frac{2}{\sqrt{2\pi}} \int_0^k e^{-y^2/2} dy$$

Thus,

$$\text{Prob}\left[|x - \bar{x}| \leq k\sigma\right] = 2\Phi(k) \tag{8-93}$$

Let us compare this probability with the bound given by the Tchebycheff inequality for various values of $k$, if $k = 1$, $2\phi(k) = 0.683$, $1 - 1/k^2 = 0.0$; if $k = 2$, $2\phi(k) = 0.955$, $1 - 1/k^2 = 0.75$; if $k = 3$, $2\phi(k) = 0.997$, $1 - 1/k^2 = 0.889$. Two things should be noted. First, as expected, the Tchebycheff inequality is simply a lower bound and the probabilities are actually higher than that given by $1 - 1/k^2$. Second, almost all of the random variables will be within two standard deviations of the mean if the probability density is Gaussian.

**The Central Limit Theorem.**   At times, a random process is composed of the sum of very many very small independent random processes. For instance, the noise produced in a resistor is due to the motion of very many individual electrons. Each electron's motion is essentially independent, hence the total noise can be considered as the sum of many independent terms. In such cases, *where the random process is composed of the sum of small independent processes, the probability density of the over-all process will approach a Gaussian one as the number of individual processes approaches infinity; this is independent of the probability densities of the individual processes.* This statement is the *central limit theorem.*

We shall develop the central limit theorem. (This derivation will not be completely rigorous but will provide the reader with a feel for the theorem.)

Let us begin by assuming that we have a process composed of $n$ independent stationary random variables $x_1, x_2, ..., x_n$. Their probability densities are $p_1(x)$, $p_2(x), ..., p_n(x)$. We form another random process which is defined as

$$x = \frac{x_1 + x_2 + \cdots + x_n}{\sqrt{n}} \tag{8-94}$$

To keep the process bounded, we have divided by $\sqrt{n}$. However, this is a constant. Thus, it will not change the form of the probability density. We will now show that as $n$ approaches $\infty$, the probability density of $x$ approaches a Gaussian one independent of $p_1(x)$, $p_2(x)$.... To simplify the analysis, we shall assume that the expected values of $x_1, x_2, ..., x_n$ are zero. A change here will only change the expected value of the final $x$, but will not change the form of the density. Now let us form the expected value of the function $e^{j\alpha x}$. Substituting in Eq. 8–63, we have

$$E[e^{j\alpha x}] = \int_{-\infty}^{\infty} e^{j\alpha x} p(x) \, dx \tag{8-95}$$

where $\alpha$ is a parameter. Note that in Eq. 8–63, $f(x)$ can be a complex function. For brevity, let us write

$$\phi(\alpha) = E[e^{j\alpha x}] \tag{8-96}$$

Hence,

$$\phi(\alpha) = \int_{-\infty}^{\infty} p(x) e^{j\alpha x} dx \tag{8-97}$$

This has essentially the same form as the inverse Fourier transform. Thus (see Eqs. 2–61 and 2–62), we can write

$$p(x) = \frac{1}{2\pi} \int_{-\infty}^{\infty} \phi(\alpha) e^{-j\alpha x} dx \tag{8-98}$$

Substituting Eq. 8–94 into Eq. 8–96, we obtain

$$\phi(\alpha) = E[e^{j\alpha(x_1 + x_2 + \cdots + x_n)/\sqrt{n}}] \tag{8-99}$$

Thus,

$$\phi(\alpha) = E\left[\prod_{i=1}^{n} e^{j\alpha x_i/\sqrt{n}}\right] \tag{8-100}$$

Let us determine what is meant by the expected value of a function of many variables. Suppose that we have $f(x_1, x_2, ..., x_n)$ and desire its expected value. The probability that $x_1 \leq X_1 \leq x_1 + dx_1, \quad x_2 \leq X_2 \leq x_2 + dx_2, ..., x_n \leq X_n \leq x_n + dx_n$ is $p(x_1, x_2, ..., x_n)\,dx_1\,dx_2\,...\,dx_n$. Then (see Section 8-2) the expected value is given by

$$E[f(x_1, x_2, ..., x_n)] = \int_{-\infty}^{\infty}\int_{-\infty}^{\infty}\cdots\int_{-\infty}^{\infty} f(x_1, x_2, ...,$$

$$x_n)\,p(x_1, x_2, ..., x_n)\,dx_1\,dx_2\,...\,dx_n \tag{8-101}$$

We have assumed that the functions are all independent, hence (see Eq. 8–53),

$$p(x_1, x_2, ..., x_n) = p(x_1)\,p(x_2)\ldots p(x_n) \tag{8-102}$$

Then, substituting Eqs. 8–100 and 8–102 into Eq. 8–101, we have

$$\phi(\alpha) = \int_{-\infty}^{\infty}\int_{-\infty}^{\infty}\cdots\int_{-\infty}^{\infty} \prod_{i=1}^{n} e^{j\alpha x_i/\sqrt{n}} p(x_i)\,dx_i \tag{8-103}$$

Since the variables are all independent, the multiple integral of the product is just the product of the single integrals, thus

$$\phi(\alpha) = \prod_{i=1}^{n}\int_{-\infty}^{\infty} p(x_i)\,e^{j\alpha x_i/\sqrt{n}}dx_i \tag{8-104}$$

Note that each integral of the product is the expected value of $e^{j\alpha x_i/\sqrt{n}}$, therefore,

$$\phi(\alpha) = \prod_{i=1}^{n} E\left[e^{j\alpha x_i/\sqrt{n}}\right]$$

Expanding the exponential in a Taylor's series, we obtain

$$\phi(\alpha) = \prod_{i=1}^{n} E\left[1 + \frac{j\alpha x_i}{\sqrt{n}} - \frac{\alpha^2 x_i^2}{2!\,n} - j\frac{\alpha^3 x_i^3}{3!\,(n)^{3/2}} - \cdots\right] \tag{8-105}$$

Since $\alpha$ and $n$ are parameters independent of $x$

$$E\left(\frac{j\alpha}{n}x_i\right) = \frac{j\alpha}{n} E[x_i]$$

$$E\left(\frac{\alpha^2 x_i^2}{2!\,n}\right) = \frac{a^2}{2!\,n} E[x_i^2],$$

$$\vdots$$

(see Eq. 8–63). Hence,

$$\phi(\alpha) = \prod_{i=1}^{n}\left[1 + \frac{j\alpha}{n} E(x_i) - \frac{\alpha^2}{2n} E(x_i^2) - j\frac{\alpha^3}{6(n)^{3/2}} E(x_i^3) + \cdots\right] \tag{8-106}$$

We have assumed that each $x_i$ has zero expected value. Therefore, $E(x_i) = 0$. We also assume that all the expected values are bounded; then, as $n$ becomes large, the higher-order terms can be neglected. Therefore, in the limit, as $n$ approaches infinity,

$$\phi(\alpha) = \prod_{i=1}^{n} \left( 1 - \frac{\alpha^2}{2n} E[x_i^2] \right) \tag{8-107}$$

Now take the natural logarithm of both sides of this expression.

$$\ln \phi(\alpha) = \sum_{i=1}^{n} \ln \left( 1 - \frac{\alpha^2}{2n} E[x_i^2] \right)$$

The Taylor series for $\ln(1 + x)$ is

$$\ln(1 + x) = x - \frac{x^2}{2} + \frac{1}{3}x^3 - \frac{1}{4}x^4 + \cdots \quad -1 < x < 1$$

In this case, $x = -(\alpha^2/2n) E[x_i^2]$. We assume that $n$ is large enough so that we can neglect the higher powers of $1/n$, and so that $|x| < 1$, hence,

$$\ln \phi(\alpha) = \sum_{i=1}^{n} \left( -\frac{\alpha^2}{2n} E[x_i^2] \right) \tag{8-108}$$

Let

$$\sigma^2 = \frac{1}{n} \sum_{i=1}^{n} E[x_i^2] \tag{8-109}$$

Then,

$$\ln \phi(\alpha) = -\frac{\alpha^2}{2} \sigma^2 \tag{8-110}$$

or

$$\phi(\alpha) = e^{-\alpha^2\sigma^2/2} \tag{8-111}$$

Now, substituting this result into Eq. 8–98, we obtain

$$p(x) = \frac{1}{2\pi} \int_{-\infty}^{\infty} e^{-\alpha^2\sigma^2/2} e^{-j\alpha x} d\alpha \tag{8-112}$$

Rearranging, we have

$$p(x) = \frac{e^{-x^2/2\sigma^2}}{2\pi} \int_{-\infty}^{\infty} \exp\left[ -\frac{\sigma^2}{2}\mu^2 \right] d\mu \tag{8-113}$$

where

$$\mu = \alpha + \frac{jx}{\sigma^2} \tag{8-114}$$

Integrating [1], we have

$$p(x) = \frac{1}{\sqrt{2\pi}\,\sigma} e^{-x^2/2\sigma^2} \tag{8-115}$$

Thus (see Eq. 8–83) we have demonstrated that $p(x)$ approaches a Gaussian density independent of the densities $p(x_1), p(x_2), \ldots$

**Uniform Density.** At times, a random variable has equal probability of assuming any value within a given range and zero probability of taking of any value outside of that range. In this case, the probability density is *uniform* and is given by

$$p(x) = \begin{cases} \dfrac{1}{x_2 - x_1}, & x_1 \leq x \leq x_2 \\ \\ 0, & x > x_2 \quad \text{or} \quad x < x_1 \end{cases} \qquad (8\text{--}116)$$

Let us obtain the expected value and the variance for this density

$$\bar{x} = \int_{-\infty}^{\infty} x p(x)\, dx = \int_{x_1}^{x_2} \frac{x}{x_2 - x_1}\, dx = \frac{x_2^2 - x_1^2}{2(x_2 - x_1)}$$

Hence,

$$\bar{x} = \frac{x_2 + x_1}{2} \qquad (8\text{--}117)$$

Thus, the mean value lies midway between $x_1$ and $x_2$. This is to be expected since all values between $x_1$ and $x_2$ are equally likely. The variance is given by Eq. 8–69 as

$$\sigma^2 = \overline{x^2} - \bar{x}^2$$

Substituting Eq. 8–116 into Eq. 8–66, and integrating, we obtain for $\overline{x^2}$

$$\overline{x^2} = \int_{x_1}^{x_2} x^2 \frac{1}{x_2 - x_1}\, dx = \frac{x_2^3 - x_1^3}{3(x_2 - x_1)} = \frac{x_2^2 + x_1 x_2 + x_1^2}{3}$$

Hence,

$$\sigma^2 = \frac{(x_2 - x_1)^2}{12} \qquad (8\text{--}118)$$

Note that the variance decreases as $x_2$ approaches $x_1$.

**Rayleigh Density.** Another probability density which is often encountered in the *Rayleigh density* which is

$$p(x) = \begin{cases} \dfrac{x e^{-x^2/2\alpha^2}}{\alpha^2}, & 0 \leq x \leq \infty \\ \\ 0, & x < 0 \end{cases} \qquad (8\text{--}119)$$

Here note that the values of $x$ are always positive. The mean value is given by

$$\bar{x} = \int_0^{\infty} \frac{x^2 e^{-x^2/2\alpha^2}}{\alpha^2}\, dx = \sqrt{\frac{\pi}{2}}\, \alpha \qquad (8\text{--}120)$$

We shall obtain the variance using Eq. 8–69. The mean square value is

$$\bar{x}^2 = \int_0^\infty \frac{x^3 e^{-x^2/2\alpha^2}}{\alpha^2}\, dx = 2\alpha^2$$

Then, Eq. 8–69 yields

$$\sigma^2 = \left( 2 - \frac{\pi}{2} \right)\alpha^2 \qquad (8\text{–}121)$$

**Binomial Distribution.**   Suppose we have an expression which is discrete and has two possible choices. For instance, consider tossing a coin, there are two possible outcomes, heads or tails. Another example is a digital system used to transmit information. Here, the transmission consists of a sequence of pulses. All pulses are of equal height and duration. The presence or absence of a pulse constitutes one part of a signal. When a pulse is present, it is often represented by a one, while the absence of a pulse is a zero. Thus, a sequence 11001101001000111 could constitute a message. If there is noise present, a one could be received as a zero and vice versa. It is important to know the probable number of errors that can result in a message (sequence of pulses) in terms of the probability of an error occurring in one symbol. We shall now develop a result that will enable us to determine this probability.

Let us assume that we perform an experiment which has two possible outcomes $A$ and $B$, where the probability that $A$ occurs is $p$ while the probability that $B$ occurs is $q$. Since $A$ and $B$ are the only possible outcomes

$$p + q = 1 \qquad (8\text{–}122)$$

Now we wish to determine the probability of having $A$ occur $n$ times, if we perform the experiment $m$ times. Suppose $n = 2$ and $m = 3$. If $A$ occurs twice then the sequence can be $AAB$, $ABA$, or $BAA$. The probability of the occurrence of *each* sequence is given by the product of the probabilities of each individual occurrence. For each one of the sequences, the probability is $p^2 q$. In general, the probability of any *one* sequence's containing $n$ $A$'s and $m - n$ $B$'s is $p^n q^{m-n}$. To obtain the probability that $n$ $A$'s occur in a sequence of $m$ terms, we must multiply this probability by the total number of sequences containing $n$ $A$'s and $m-n$ $B$'s. This number is the number of ways that $n$ $A$'s and $m-n$ $B$'s can be arranged which is given by the binomial coefficient $\binom{m}{n}$, where

$$\binom{m}{n} = \frac{m!}{n!(m - n)!} \qquad (8\text{–}123)$$

Thus, the probability that there are $n$ $A$'s in a sequence of $m$ experiments is

$$P_m(n) = \frac{m!}{n!(m - n)!}\, p^n q^{(m-n)} \qquad (8\text{–}124)$$

This is called a *binomial* distribution.

Let us again consider the case of the transmission of digital data. We wish to determine the probability of having $n$ errors in a message $m$ units long. If $p$ is the probability of a single error (i.e., a one received as a zero or vice versa) then $P_m(n)$ is the probability of having $n$ errors in a message of $m$ terms. In general, we do not want to know if there will be exactly $n$ errors in a message of $m$ units. We would like to know if there will be $r$ or *fewer* errors. The probability of this is given by $P_m(1) + P_m(2) + \cdots + P_m(r)$, that is, the sum of the probabilities of having 1 error, 2 errors, $\cdots$, $r$ errors. Hence, $B_m(r)$, the probability of having $r$ errors or less in a message of $m$ digits is

$$B_m(r) = \sum_{i=1}^{r} P_m(i) \qquad (8\text{-}125)$$

**Poisson Distribution.** In certain discrete random processes characterized by binomial distributions $m$ the number of experiments, becomes very large, while $p$ becomes small. We assume that $mp$ remains bounded. In such cases, Eq. 8–124 can be tedious to use. However, as $m$ approaches infinity, the distribution approaches

$$P_m(n) = \frac{e^{-mp}(mp)^n}{n!} \qquad (8\text{-}126)$$

Equation 8–126 is called a Poisson distribution. This distribution is often used to approximate the binomial distribution if $m$ is very large and $mp$ is small. For certain random processes, the Poisson distribution is exact.

## 8-5. NOISE-SPECTRAL DENSITY

Let us now consider the probability density of resistor noise. The noise voltage across a resistor is due to the motion of the (very many) free electrons. At any instant, the total noise is the sum of many components. Each one is produced by an individual free electron. Thus, the noise can be thought of as the sum of very many random processes.

In any practical resistance, there will be an extremely large number of free electrons and the contribution of any one electron will be extremely small. Thus, resistor noise satisfies the conditions of the central limit theorem. So resistor noise will have a *Gaussian probability density*. Such noise is called *Gaussian noise*.

In general, a random noise signal will be some function of time $f(t)$. Thus, it will have a Fourier transform $F(j\omega)$. We cannot predict the form of $f(t)$ exactly. Hence, we cannot predict $F(j\omega)$. However, we can often predict the amount of power contained in a band of frequencies. From Eq. 2–233 we have that the total energy contained in a signal is given by

$$W = \int_{-\infty}^{\infty} f^2(t)\, dt = \frac{1}{2\pi} \int_{-\infty}^{\infty} |F(j\omega)|^2\, d\omega$$

The power is equal to $dW/dt$; that is, the energy per unit time. To study this let us divide both sides of the above equation by $2T$:

$$\frac{1}{2T} \int_{-\infty}^{\infty} f^2(t)\, dt = \frac{1}{4\pi T} \int_{-\infty}^{\infty} |F(j\omega)|^2\, d\omega$$

Assume for the moment that $f(t)$ is zero, except in the range $-T \leq t \leq T$. Then, the left-hand integral represents the average power supplied in the interval; i.e., the total energy divided by the duration of the signal. Now let $T$ approach $\infty$. In this case, $f(t)$ can exist for all time. The left-hand integral will now represent the average power, i.e., the power averaged over all time; hence,

$$P_{ave} = \lim_{T \to \infty} \frac{1}{2T} \int_{-T}^{T} f^2(t)\, dt = \lim_{T \to \infty} \frac{1}{4\pi T} \int_{-\infty}^{\infty} |F(j\omega)|^2\, d\omega \qquad (8\text{–}127)$$

If $f(t)$ falls off sufficiently fast, the average power will approach zero.

Suppose $f(t)$ consist of a short pulse. Then, the total power supplied will be finite for a short duration and zero for the remainder of the time. Hence, the average overall time will be zero. On the other hand, the average power of a signal which does not fall off with time, e.g., a stationary noise signal, or a periodic signal, will have finite average power.

From Eq. 8–127 we can *define* the average power per unit bandwidth as

$$S(\omega) = \lim_{T \to \infty} \frac{1}{2T} |F(j\omega)|^2 \qquad (8\text{–}128)$$

where $S(\omega)$ is called the *spectral density*. In general, since we deal with real time functions, $S(\omega)$ will be an even function. The total average power contained in the signal can then be written as

$$P_{ave} = \frac{1}{2\pi} \int_{-\infty}^{\infty} S(\omega)\, d\omega = \frac{1}{2\pi} \int_{0}^{\infty} 2S(\omega)\, d\omega$$

The *power spectrum* is defined to be a quantity which is assumed to exist only for nonnegative $\omega$ and is equal to $2S(\omega)$. (Note that $S(\omega)$ is a *real* function of $\omega$.)

Let us now consider resistor noise. Suppose a resistor is connected to an ideal band pass filter, as shown in Fig. 8–5. The filter has the transfer function

$$H(j\omega) = \begin{cases} 1, & \omega_1 \leq \omega \leq \omega_2 \quad \text{or} \quad -\omega_1 \geq \omega \geq -\omega_2 \\ 0, & \text{otherwise} \end{cases}$$

That is, it passes frequencies between $\omega_1$ and $\omega_2$ without attenuation and rejects all others. Physical studies which we shall not consider here indicate that the mean square value of the output noise voltage $v$ is given by

$$\langle v^2 \rangle = 4kTR \frac{\omega_2 - \omega_1}{2\pi}$$

FIG. 8–5

Resistor connected to a filter network

where $k$ is Boltzmann's constant $1.380 \times 10^{-23}$ joule/$^\circ K$, $R$ is the resistance in ohms, and $T$ is the temperature in $^\circ K$. It is important to note that the mean square voltage is proportional to the *difference* between $\omega_1$ and $\omega_2$, but does not depend upon their values directly. We call $(\omega_2 - \omega_1)/2\pi$ the *bandwidth B*,

$$B = \frac{\omega_2 - \omega_1}{2\pi} \qquad (8\text{–}129)$$

Thus, we have

$$\langle v^2 \rangle = 4kTRB \qquad (8\text{–}130)$$

The mean square voltage is proportional to the bandwidth $B$ regardless of its central frequency. Therefore, the power supplied in any equal bandwidth must be the same. Thus, for the noise voltage, the spectral density is given by (the power per unit bandwidth):

$$G(\omega) = \frac{\langle v^2 \rangle}{2B} \qquad (8\text{–}131)$$

Note that we divide by $2B$ since there is a bandwidth both above and below $\omega = 0$. Substituting Eq. 8–130, we have

$$G(\omega) = 2kTR \qquad (8\text{–}132)$$

This is a constant independent of frequency.

In general, resistor noise represents a stationary ergodic process if the temperature $T$ is constant. Hence, time and ensemble averages are equal. Therefore, Eq. 8–130 can be written as

$$\overline{v^2} = \langle v^2 \rangle = 4kTRB \qquad (8\text{–}133)$$

The spectral density of resistor noise is constant over all frequencies. In those cases where the noise spectral density is constant over all frequencies, it is referred to as *white noise*. (This is analogous to white light which contains equal quantities of all visible light components.) If noise is white and has a Gaussian distribution, it is called *white Gaussian noise*.

Detailed measurements of resistor noise were first performed by J. B. Johnson. For this reason, resistor noise is often called *Johnson noise*.

Resistor noise is only approximately white noise. If power supplied in any unit bandwidth is constant and not differentially small, the energy contained in an infinite bandwidth will be infinite. Thus, in any practical system, all noise spectra must fall off with frequency. However, it has been found that resistor noise is essentially constant over an extremely wide bandwidth. If the bandwidths of a system lie well within the frequency region where the noise spectral density can be considered to be constant, the noise can be considered to be white. This is the case for most systems except those that use extremely high frequencies.

One fact should be noted. If $f(t)$ represents a white noise signal, then its spectral density is constant. Thus, $|F(j\omega)|^2$, the Fourier transform of $f(t)$, is constant (see Eq. 8–129). However, this does not mean that $F(j\omega)$ is constant since the phase of $F(j\omega)$ is now a random variable. If $F(j\omega)$ is a real constant, $f(t)$ will be an impulse function (see Table 2-1). This is, of course, not true in the case of random noise.

When we consider noise in general, it may not be white. In this case, the total average power contained in the signal is given by (see Eqs. 8–127 and 8–128):

$$N = \lim_{T \to \infty} \frac{1}{4\pi T} \int_{-T}^{T} |F(j\omega)|^2 \, d\omega = \lim_{T \to \infty} \frac{1}{2T} \int_{-T/2\pi}^{T/2\pi} |F(j\omega)|^2 \, df$$

$$= \int_{-\infty}^{\infty} G(\omega) \, df \qquad (8\text{–}134)$$

**Signal-to-Noise Ratio.** Noise is undesirable in communication systems because it obscures a desired signal. The output signal usually consists of a desired signal plus noise. A figure of merit of the noisiness of a signal is the ratio of the signal to the noise. This can be expressed as a power ratio. If $\langle v_s \rangle$ is the mean square signal voltage and $\langle v_n \rangle$ is the mean square noise voltage, then the power signal-to-noise ratio is

$$S_p = \frac{\langle v_s^2 \rangle}{\langle v_n^2 \rangle} \qquad (8\text{–}135a)$$

At times, this is expressed as a voltage ratio rather than a power ratio; That is,

$$S_v = \frac{\langle v_s \rangle}{\langle v_n \rangle} \qquad (8\text{–}135b)$$

Many times, a system receives an input signal and then amplifies it. It is desirable that the system add as little noise as possible to the signal, and, if possible, that the system reduce the noise. If the desired signal has a bandlimited spectrum, while the noise is white, then by filtering the overall signal properly, the noise power can be reduced, while the signal power is unchanged. A noise figure of merit for systems compares the input and output signal to noise ratios. Such a figure of merit is called the *noise figure*. It is usually expressed in decibels and is given by

$$NF = 10 \log_{10} \frac{S_{pi}}{S_{po}} = 20 \log_{10} \frac{S_{vi}}{S_{vo}} \qquad (8\text{–}136)$$

where $S_{pi}$ and $S_{po}$ are the input and the output power signal-to-noise ratios, respectively, and $S_{vi}$ and $S_{vo}$ are the corresponding voltage signal-to-noise ratios.

## 8-6. FILTERED NOISE

Most communication systems filter their input signals to isolate the desired signal from unwanted signals. For instance, a radio is tuned, so that one desired signal can be received without hearing all the other signals that are simultaneously broadcast. This filtering often improves the signal-to-noise ratio. Consider the block diagram of Fig. 8–6. The input signal consists of a signal part and a noise part $f_{Si}(t)$ and $f_{Ni}(t)$, respectively. Similarly, the output consists of signal and noise components. Their Fourier spectra are given by $F_{Si}(j\omega)$, $F_{Ni}(j\omega)$, $F_{So}(j\omega)$, and $F_{No}(j\omega)$. We shall assume that $F_{Si}(j\omega)$ is a known quantity, while the noise Fourier transform $F_{Ni}(j\omega)$ is not known. However, we shall also assume that the spectral density $G_{Ni}(\omega)$, which is proportional to $|F_{Ni}(j\omega)|^2$, is a known quantity.

Now assume that $F_{Si}(j\omega)$ satisfies

$$F_{Si}(j\omega) = 0; \qquad \omega < \omega_2, \qquad -\omega_1 < \omega < \omega_1, \qquad \omega > \omega_2$$

Then, $F_{Si}(j\omega)$ only consists of frequencies in the range $\omega_1 \leq \omega \leq \omega_2$ and in the corresponding negative band; thus, $F_{Si}(j\omega)$ is bandlimited.

$$f_{Si}(t) + f_{Ni}(t) \qquad\qquad \boxed{H(j\omega)} \qquad\qquad f_{So}(t) + f_{No}(t)$$

FIG. 8–6
Signal and noise passed through filter

Suppose that the noise is white and results from a stationary ergodic process. The noise power is proportional to the bandwidth (see Eq. 8–130). Thus, it is desirable to restrict the bandwidth as much as possible without affecting the signal. If the filter has a transfer function which is given by

$$H(j\omega) = \begin{cases} 1, & \omega_1 \leq \omega \leq \omega_2, \qquad -\omega_2 \leq \omega \leq -\omega_1 \\ 0, & \text{otherwise} \end{cases} \qquad (8\text{–}137)$$

then the signal will pass through the filter unchanged, while the noise is attenuated. Thus, the filter will improve the signal-to-noise ratio. The transfer function of Eq. 8–137 is called an *ideal band pass filter*. Its amplitude is illustrated in Fig. 8–7.

An ideal band pass filter is not causal (see Sections 5-8 and 5-9). Thus, conventional filters will not usually have the transfer function of Eq. 8–137. A typical simple band pass filter characteristic, which can be easily built is shown in Fig. 8–8.

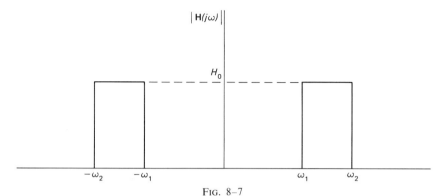

FIG. 8–7
Magnitude of the transfer function of an ideal band pass filter

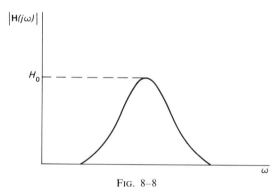

FIG. 8–8
Magnitude of the transfer function of a simple band pass
filter

Let us determine the noise power contained in the output of general filters. We assume that the input noise is white. Thus, the power spectrum is given by

$$G(\omega) = \frac{\eta_o}{2} \qquad (8\text{–}138)$$

where $\eta_o$ is a constant. The factor of $1/2$ is arbitrary. It is conventional to include it, since there are both positive and negative values of $\omega$. Thus, the power contained in a differentially small bandwidth $df$ is $(\eta_o/2)\,df = (\eta_o/2)\,d\omega/2\pi$. Hence, the total input noise power is

$$N_i = \frac{1}{2\pi} \int_{-\infty}^{\infty} \frac{\eta_o}{2}\,d\omega = \int_{-\infty}^{\infty} \frac{\eta_o}{2}\,df \qquad (8\text{–}139)$$

This represents infinity energy. However (see Section 8-5) in practical cases, $G(\omega)$ does fall off for sufficiently large $\omega$. In this case, we shall ignore this since we assume that the filter's bandwidth lies well within the flat portion of the noise spectrum. Then, the average noise power at the output of an ideal band pass filter is

$$N_o = \frac{1}{2\pi} \int_{\omega_1}^{\omega_2} H_o^2 \eta_o d\omega = \eta_o H_o^2 \frac{(\omega_2 - \omega_1)}{2\pi} \tag{8-140}$$

We have eliminated the factor of $1/2$ since the frequencies for $-\omega_2 \leqq \omega \leqq -\omega_1$ are not included in the integral; then (see Eq. 8–129)

$$N_o = \eta_o B H_o^2 \tag{8-141}$$

where $H_0$ is the magnitude of the transfer function in the pass band.

Now let us assume that the noise is sent through an arbitrary filter of transfer function $H(j\omega)$. The output noise power will be

$$N_o = \frac{1}{2\pi} \int_0^\infty \eta_o |H(j\omega)|^2 \, d\omega \tag{8-142}$$

or, equivalently,

$$N_o = \frac{\eta_o}{2\pi} \int_0^\infty |H(j\omega)|^2 \, d\omega \tag{8-143}$$

It is conventional to define an *equivalent noise bandwidth*. This is the bandwidth of an ideal band pass filter, whose magnitude $H_0$ is equal to the maximum magnitude of $H(j\omega)$, and which results in the same noise power output. Equating Eqs. 8–141 and 8–143 and manipulating, we have

$$B_{Neq} = \frac{1}{2\pi} \int_0^\infty \frac{|H(j\omega)|^2}{H_o^2} \, d\omega \tag{8-144}$$

where $B_{Neq}$ is such that the area under the curve of the ideal band pass filter of bandwidth $B_{Neq}$ is equal to the area under the $|H(j\omega)|$ curve.

**Narrow Band Filtering.** Assume that white noise is passed through a narrow band, band pass filter of the type discussed in Section 5-9. Let us determine the probability distribution of the output and relate it to the output of an amplitude modulation detector. We assume that the noise is generated from a stationary ergodic process. To obtain the desired result, we shall approximate the continuous spectrum of signals by a set of discrete sinusoids spaced $\Delta\omega$ apart. This is illustrated in Fig. 8–9. In the limit, as $\Delta\omega$ approaches zero, the results will become exact. We shall choose the coefficients of each sinusoid so that the correct power is contained in each $\Delta\omega$. Since the input noise is white, the output spectral density will be

$$G(\omega) = \frac{\eta_o}{2} |H(j\omega)|^2 \tag{8-145}$$

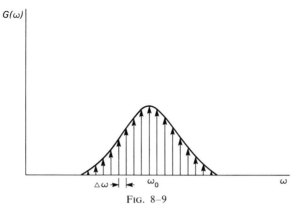

FIG. 8–9

Power spectrum of noise signal passed through a narrow band
filter. The spectrum is represented by a set of discrete frequency
terms. Only positive values of $\omega$ are drawn here

where $H(j\omega)$ is the transfer function of the filter. We shall assume that $H(j\omega)$ is
such that $G(\omega)$ falls to zero before $\omega$ reaches zero or $2\omega_0$. This is the same narrow
band approximation as that made in Section 5-9. Thus, the entire bandwidth for
positive $\omega$ lies between $\omega_0 - M\Delta\omega \leq \omega \leq \omega_0 + M + \Delta\omega$, where $M$ is a constant
which depends on $\Delta\omega$; i.e., $M < \omega_0/\Delta\omega$. In most systems $M \ll \omega_0/\Delta\omega$; that is,
the bandwidth is much less then $\omega_0$.

The power contained in a sinusoid should be equal to the power in the corresponding bandwidth $\Delta\omega$. This power is

$$\frac{1}{2\pi} \int_{\omega_0 + k\Delta\omega}^{\omega_0 + (k+1)\Delta\omega} G(\omega)\, d\omega \approx \frac{1}{2\pi} G(\omega_0 + k\,\Delta\omega)\,\Delta\omega \qquad (8\text{--}146)$$

Note that it is assumed that $\Delta\omega$ is small enough so that in any $\Delta\omega$, $G(\omega)$ can be
considered constant. If the sinusoid of frequency $\omega_0 + k\,\Delta\omega$ has a peak value $A_k$,
then the power contained in it is $A_k^2/2$. We assume, as in the case of the Fourier
series, that only positive frequency terms are present. Thus, the power given by
Eq. 8–146 should be multiplied by 2. Hence, we set $A_k^2/2$ equal to twice Eq. 8–146.
Therefore,

$$A_k = \sqrt{2G(\omega + k\,\Delta\omega)\,\Delta\omega/\pi} = \sqrt{4G(\omega + k\,\Delta\omega)\,\Delta f} \qquad (8\text{--}147)$$

Then, the $k$th sinusoidal term can be written as

$$\sqrt{4G(\omega + k\,\Delta\omega)\,\Delta f} \cos\left[(\omega_0 + k\,\Delta\omega)\,t + \phi_k\right]$$

This is a cosinusoid of amplitude $A_k$ and the angular frequency $\omega_0 + k\,\Delta\omega$. Since
the spectral density provides no information about the phase, we have included
$\phi_k$, which is a random variable lying in the range $-\pi \leq \phi_k \leq \pi$.

Because of the bandlimiting assumption, $A_k$ will be zero if $\omega > \omega_0 + M\Delta\omega$ or $\omega < \omega - M\Delta\omega$. Then, the value of the noise voltage can be written as

$$n(t) = \sum_{k=-M}^{M} A_k \cos\left[(\omega_0 + k\,\Delta\omega)\,t + \phi_k\right] \qquad (8\text{--}148)$$

Using the identity

$$\cos(a + b) = \cos a \cos b - \sin a \sin b \qquad (8\text{--}149)$$

we obtain

$$\cos\left[(\omega_0 + k\Delta\omega)t + \phi_k\right] = \cos\omega_0 t \cos(k\Delta\omega t + \phi_k)$$
$$- \sin\omega_0 t \sin(k\Delta\omega t + \phi_k) \qquad (8\text{--}150)$$

Thus, Eq. 8–148 can be written as

$$n(t) = \sum_{k=-M}^{M} A_k \left[\cos(k\Delta\omega t + \phi_k)\cos\omega_0 t - \sin(k\Delta\omega t + \phi_k)\sin\omega_0 t\right] \quad (8\text{--}151)$$

Let us write

$$x(t) = \sum_{k=-M}^{M} A_k \cos(k\Delta\omega t + \phi_k) \qquad (8\text{--}152a)$$

$$y(t) = \sum_{y=-M}^{M} A_k \sin(k\Delta\omega t + \phi_k) \qquad (8\text{--}152b)$$

Then,

$$n(t) = x(t)\cos\omega_0 t - y(t)\sin\omega_0 t \qquad (8\text{--}153)$$

Let us consider $x(t)$ and $y(t)$. In general, $k\Delta\omega$ will be much less than $\omega_0$. Thus, $x(t)$ and $y(t)$ represent functions of time which vary slowly in comparison with $\cos\omega_0 t$ or $\sin\omega_0 t$.

We can write Eq. 8–153 as

$$n(t) = r(t)\cos\left[\omega_0 t + \theta(t)\right] \qquad (8\text{--}154)$$

where

$$r(t)\ x^2(t) + y^2(t) \qquad (8\text{--}155a)$$

and

$$\theta(t) = \tan^{-1}\frac{y(t)}{x(t)} \qquad (8\text{--}155b)$$

Thus (see Section 5-9) the noise voltage can be represented as a cosinusoid whose amplitude varies as $r(t)$; that is, $r(t)$ is the *envelope* of $n(t)$. A typical $n(t)$ is shown in Fig. 8–10. Note that the phase angle $\theta(t)$ is also a random variable. Thus, the instantaneous frequency of $n(t)$ can also be said to vary. Note that both $r(t)$ and $\theta(t)$ vary slowly in comparison with $\cos\omega_0 t$.

Each term in the summation of Eq. 8–152a is independent of all the others. Thus, $x(t)$ can be considered to be made up of independent random variables. Note

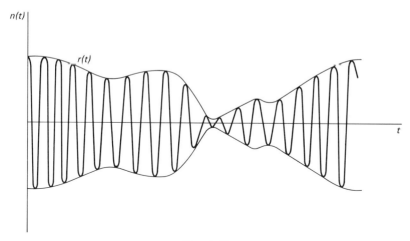

FIG. 8–10
Typical $n(t)$

that, in the limit, as $\Delta\omega$ approaches zero, $M$ will approach infinity. (This keeps the bandwidth constant.) Also, $A_k$ varies as $\sqrt{\Delta\omega}$. Thus, $A_k$ becomes very small in the limit. Hence Eq. 8–152a, and similarly, Eq. 8–152b satisfy the conditions of the central limit theorem. Therefore, $x(t)$ and $y(t)$ are Gaussian random variables. We assume that the signals are of zero mean value; i.e., their direct components have been removed. Then, the only unknown in the Gaussian probability density (see Eq. 8-83) is the variance $\sigma$. Thus, to determine the probability density, we need only determine the variance; that is, we must obtain $\overline{x^2(t)}$ and $\overline{y^2(t)}$. One way of doing this is to take the time averages, since the system is ergodic (see Eq. 8-81); thus,

$$\overline{x^2(t)} = \lim_{T \to \infty} \frac{1}{2T} \int_{-T}^{T} \left[ \sum_{k=-M}^{M} A_k \cos(k\,\Delta\omega t + \phi_k) \right]^2 dt \qquad (8–156)$$

When the series is squared it will contain terms of the form $\cos\omega_1 t \cos\omega_2 t$ and $\cos^2\omega_1 t$, $\omega_1 \neq \omega_2$. If $\omega_1 \neq \omega_2$, the result will be zero. This is because

$$\cos\omega_1 t \cos\omega_2 t = \tfrac{1}{2}\left[\cos(\omega_1 + \omega_2)t + \cos(\omega_1 - \omega_2)t\right]$$

Thus,

$$\int_{-T}^{T} \cos\omega_1 t \cos\omega_2 t \, dt$$

will always be bounded; i.e., the integral of the cosine is the sine. Since we divide by $1/2T$ in Eq. 8–156, as $T$ approaches infinity, the contribution of this term will approach zero. (The inclusion of the random $\phi_k$ variables complicates the matter somewhat. However, the basic idea is given here.) Hence, we are left with

$$\overline{x^2(t)} = \lim_{T \to \infty} \frac{1}{2T} \int_{-T}^{T} \sum_{k=-M}^{M} A_k^2 \cos^2(k\,\Delta\omega t + \phi_k) \, dt \qquad (8–157)$$

where
$$\cos^2(k\,\Delta\omega t + \phi_k) = \tfrac{1}{2} + \tfrac{1}{2}\cos 2(k\,\Delta\omega t + \phi_k)$$

The contribution of the $\cos^2(k\,\Delta\omega t + \phi_k)$ terms will be zero in the limit; thus, we have
$$\overline{x^2(t)} = \sum_{k=-M}^{M} \frac{A_k^2}{2}$$

Then (see the discussion following Eq. 8–146 the power of each sinusoid is $A_k^2/2$. Equation 8–146 is the sum of all the individual powers. Hence, it is the total noise power
$$\overline{x^2(t)} = N_o \tag{8–158a}$$

Similarly,
$$\overline{y^2(t)} = N_o \tag{8–158b}$$

Note that $x^2(t)$ does not represent the power of $x(t)\cos\omega_o t$. On the average, $x^2(t)$ will be twice this power. We have determined that $x(t)$ and $y(t)$ are Gaussian random variables with zero mean and variance $N_o$.

In general, $x(t)$ and $y(t)$ are independent. Therefore a knowledge of one does not change the probability of the other. Thus (see Eqs 8–51 through 8–53) we can write the joint probability as
$$p(x, y) = p(x)\,p(y) = \left(\frac{1}{\sqrt{2\pi N_o}}\, e^{-x^2/2N_o}\right)\left(\frac{1}{\sqrt{2\pi N_o}}\, e^{-y^2/2N_o}\right)$$

or
$$p(x, y) = \frac{1}{2\pi N_o}\, e^{-(x^2+y^2)/2N_o} \tag{8–159}$$

Now let us obtain the probability distribution of $r(t)$ and $\theta(t)$. Note that $r(t)$ and $\theta(t)$ are the polar coordinates which are equivalent to the rectangular coordinates $x(t)$ and $y(t)$. Let us consider some fundamental definitions (see Eq. 8–49).
$$p(x, y)\,dx\,dy = \text{Prob}[x \leq X \leq x + dx,\, y \leq Y \leq y + dy] \tag{8–160a}$$

Then we can write
$$q(r, \theta)\,dr\,d\theta = \text{Prob}[r \leq R \leq r + dr,\, \theta \leq \Theta \leq \theta + d\theta] \tag{8–160b}$$

Equations 8–160a and 8–160b express equivalent probabilities, one in rectangular coordinates, the other in polar coordinates; hence,
$$p(x, y)\,dx\,dy = q(r, \theta)\,dr\,d\theta \tag{8–161}$$

The equivalent differential areas in rectangular and polar coordinates are
$$dx\,dy = r\,dr\,d\theta \tag{8–162}$$

Substituting Eqs. 8–162, 8–159, and 8–155a into the left hand side of Eq. 8–161, we have
$$q(r, \theta) = \frac{r\,e^{-r^2/2N_o}}{2\pi N_o} \tag{8–163}$$

Let us now obtain the probability densities or $r$ and $\theta$, where $-\pi \leq \theta \leq \pi$. Applying Eq. 8–59, we obtain

$$q(r) = \int_{-\pi}^{\pi} \frac{re^{-r^2/2N_o}}{2\pi N_o}\, d\theta \qquad (8-164)$$

The integrand is constant with respect to $\theta$; integrating yields

$$q(r) = \frac{re^{-r^2/2N_o}}{N_o} \qquad (8-165)$$

This is the Rayleigh distribution (see Eq. 8–119). The mean and variance are given in Eqs. 8–120 and 8–121, respectively.

Now let us determine $q(\theta)$, where

$$q(\theta) = \int_{0}^{\infty} \frac{re^{-r^2/2N_o}}{2\pi N_o}\, dr, \qquad 0 \leq r < \infty \qquad (8-166)$$

Let

$$\mu = r^2/2N_o$$

Then, the integral becomes

$$q(\theta) = \frac{1}{2\pi} \int_{0}^{\infty} e^{-\mu}d\mu$$

Integrating, we obtain

$$q(\theta) = \frac{1}{2\pi}, \qquad -\pi \leq \theta \leq \pi \qquad (8-167)$$

Note that the angle of $\theta$ was initially restricted to lie between $-\pi$ and $\pi$. Thus, $q(\theta)$ has a uniform distribution. Thus, the noise output of a narrow band, band pass filter, with white noise input, is a waveform whose envelope has a Rayleigh probability density and whose phase angle has a uniform probability density.

The noise waveform is of the form of Eq. 8–154, which we repeat here:

$$n(t) = r(t) \cos[\omega_0 t + \theta(t)]$$

A typical function having this waveform is shown in Fig. 8–10. If this waveform were detected by the usual amplitude-modulated detector, called a *linear detector*, the output signal would have the same waveform as $r(t)$. The direct component might possibly be removed. Thus, the noise output of an amplitude-modulated detector would have a Rayleigh probability density.

A frequency-modulated system would produce a very different signal. The signal would be filtered and then passed through a limiter which would clip it. Hence, the positive and negative values of the waveform would not be allowed to exceed specified magnitudes. The resultant signal would be passed through additional tuned band pass filters and limiters, and then applied to a frequency-modulation detector. Such a detector produces an output which is proportional to $\omega_i - \omega_o$, where $\omega_i$ is the instantaneous frequency of the signal. The value of $\omega_i$ depends upon $\theta(t)$ and, to a lesser extent, upon $r(t)$. This dependence is complex and depends upon nonlinear circuits. Thus, no simple statement can be made about the probability density of the noise output of a frequency-modulated detector.

## 8-7. CORRELATION FUNCTIONS

*Correlation functions* will not only provide us with information about the behavior of random variables, but are a means of determining their spectral density and extracting certain signals from noisy ones. At the start we shall define correlation functions and discuss their properties. A computer program for their evaluation will also be considered. A correlation function provides a means of determining to what degree two functions are (correlated) related. Suppose that we have two functions $x(t)$ and $y(t)$. Their correlation function $R_{xy}(\tau)$ is defined as

$$R_{xy}(\tau) = \lim_{T \to \infty} \frac{1}{2T} \int_{-T}^{T} x(t)\, y(t + \tau)\, dt \qquad (8\text{–}168)$$

This function is actually called the *crosscorrelation* of $x(t)$ and $y(t)$. The crosscorrelation is actually the *time average* of $x(t)\, y(t + \tau)$, as a function of the parameter $\tau$.

Let us consider several types of functions and look at the way in which $R_{xy}(\tau)$ gives a measure of the degree to which they are related. Suppose $x(t)$ and $y(t)$ are random variables. (We shall assume that the processes which generate them are stationary and ergodic.) Then, the time average can be obtained from the ensemble average; hence,

$$R_{xy}(\tau) = \int_{-\infty}^{\infty} \int_{-\infty}^{\infty} xyp(x, y)\, dx\, dy \qquad (8\text{–}169)$$

Now let us assume that $x(t)$ and $y(t)$ are independent processes; then (see Eq. 8–53)

$$p(x, y) = p(x)\, p(y)$$

Substituting, we obtain

$$R_{xy}(\tau) = \int_{-\infty}^{\infty} \int_{-\infty}^{\infty} xp(x)\, yp(y)\, dx\, dy \qquad (8\text{–}170)$$

Since $xp(x)$ is independent of $yp(y)$, the double integral becomes the product of two single integrals

$$R_{xy}(\tau) = \left( \int_{-\infty}^{\infty} xp(x)\, dx \right) \left( \int_{-\infty}^{\infty} yp(y)\, dy \right) \qquad (8\text{–}171)$$

Each of the integrals is the mean or expected value; hence,

$$R_{xy}(\tau) = \bar{x}\bar{y} \qquad (8\text{–}172)$$

Thus, if two functions are independent of each other (i.e., unrelated), their cross-correlation is the product of their mean values. Note that in ergodic systems, the mean values are the direct values. The direct component of two signals can, in a sense, be thought of as correlated, since they are the same waveforms.

In most communication systems, the direct values are removed from the signal. Thus, we deal with signals of zero mean value. Therefore, two stationary, ergodic random variables of zero mean will have a zero crosscorrelation function if they are unrelated; hence,

$$R_{xy}(\tau) = 0 \qquad (8\text{--}173)$$

Now let us consider some other signals and determine their crosscorrelation. Suppose $x(t)$ and $y(t)$ are both cosinusoids

$$x(t) = \cos \omega_1 t \qquad (8\text{--}174a)$$
$$y(t) = \cos \omega_2 t \qquad (8\text{--}174b)$$

Then, their crosscorrelation is

$$R_{xy}(\tau) = \lim_{T \to \infty} \frac{1}{2T} \int_{-T}^{T} \cos \omega_1 t \cos \omega_2 (t + \tau) \, d\tau \qquad (8\text{--}175)$$

Using Eq. 8–149, we obtain

$$R_{xy}(\tau) = \lim_{T \to \infty} \frac{1}{4T} \int_{-T}^{T} \cos \left[ (\omega_1 + \omega_2) t + \omega_2 \tau \right]$$
$$+ \cos \left[ (\omega_1 - \omega_2) t - \omega_2 \tau \right] dt \qquad (8\text{--}176)$$

If $\omega_1 \neq \omega_2$, then

$$R_{xy}(\tau) = \lim_{T \to \infty} \left[ \frac{\dfrac{\sin \left[ (\omega_1 + \omega_2) t + \omega_2 \tau \right]}{\omega_1 + \omega_2} + \dfrac{\sin \left[ (\omega_1 - \omega_2) t - \omega_2 \tau \right]}{\omega_1 - \omega_2}}{4T} \right]_{t = -T}^{T} \qquad (8\text{--}177)$$

As $T$ approaches infinity, the expression becomes zero.

$$R_{xy}(\tau) = 0, \qquad \omega_1 \neq \omega_2 \qquad (8\text{--}178)$$

Thus, if the frequency of $x(t)$ and $y(t)$ are different, their crosscorrelation is zero. In a sense, if their frequencies are different, we can say that the signals are uncorrelated.

Now let us consider the case where $\omega_1 = \omega_2 = \omega_0$. Then, Eq. 8–176 becomes

$$R_{xy}(\tau) = \lim_{T \to \infty} \frac{1}{4T} \int_{-T}^{T} \left[ \cos (2\omega_0 t + \omega_0 \tau) + \cos \omega_0 \tau \right] dt$$

Integrating, and noting that $\cos \omega_0 \tau$ is a constant with respect to $t$, we obtain

$$R_{xy}(\tau) = \tfrac{1}{2} \cos \omega_0 \tau \qquad (8\text{--}179)$$

In this case, the correlation function is a nonzero periodic function of $\tau$. Note that when related signals are correlated, their crosscorrelation is not zero for all $\tau$.

**Autocorrelation.** Very often, we deal with a special case of correlation function. In this case (see Eq. 8–168) $x(t)$ and $y(t)$ are the same function; that is, we have

$$R_x(\tau) = \lim_{T \to \infty} \frac{1}{2T} \int_{-T}^{T} x(t)\, x(t + \tau)\, dt \qquad (8–180)$$

Note that we have only used a single subscript. Alternatively, we could call this $R_{xx}(\tau)$. $R_x(\tau)$ is called the *autocorrelation* of $x(t)$. In this case, we test to see how $x(t)$ is correlated with itself as a function of $\tau$. Hence, we compare the correlation of $x(t)$ and $x(t + \tau)$. If $\tau = 0$, then $x(t) = x(t + \tau)$ and *both* signals are closely correlated. However, if $x(t)$ represents a random variable, such as resistor noise, then as $\tau$ increases, the correlation between $x(t)$ and $x(t + \tau)$ will, in general, decrease. We shall show next that the autocorrelation in many such cases will approach zero as $\tau$ approaches infinity if $\overline{x(t)} = 0$.

When a system is ergodic, the ensemble and time averages are equal; thus,

$$R_x(\tau) = \overline{x(t)\, x(t + \tau)} \qquad (8–181)$$

The autocorrelation can then be obtained from Eq. 8–169:

$$R_x(\tau) = \int_{-\infty}^{\infty} \int_{-\infty}^{\infty} x_1 x_2 p(x_1, x_2, t)\, dx_1 dx_2 \qquad (8–182)$$

where $x_1$ and $x_2$ represent the variables $x(t)$ and $x(t + \tau)$, respectively. If $x(t)$ represents a variable which is such that, for sufficiently large $\tau$ (i.e., $\tau > \tau_0$), $x_1(t)$ is unrelated to $x(t + \tau)$, then we can use Eq. 8–171 to express the correlation. In this case, $p(x) = p(y)$; therefore,

$$R_x(\tau) = \left( \int_{-\infty}^{\infty} x p(x)\, dx \right)^2, \qquad \tau > \tau_0 \qquad (8–183)$$

Hence, in this case

$$R_x(\tau) = \bar{x}^2, \qquad \tau > \tau_0 \qquad (8–184)$$

If the signal has zero mean value, then

$$R_x(\tau) = 0, \qquad \tau > \tau_0 \qquad (8–185)$$

Let us now consider the autocorrelation of a periodic function of time $f(t)$. Suppose $f(t)$ is represented by a Fourier series (see Eq. 2–291b); that is,

$$f(t) = \sum_{n=-\infty}^{\infty} C_n e^{jn\omega_0 t} \qquad (8–186)$$

Then, the autocorrelation of this function is

$$R_x(\tau) = \lim_{T \to \infty} \frac{1}{2T} \int_{-T}^{T} \left( \sum_{n=\infty}^{\infty} C_n e^{jn\omega_o t} \right) \left( \sum_{k=-\infty}^{\infty} C_n e^{jk\omega_o(t+\tau)} \right) dt \quad (8\text{--}187)$$

The product of the summation will contain terms of the form:

$$C_n^2 e^{jn\omega_o(2t+\tau)}, \qquad C_n C_{-n} e^{\pm jn\omega_o\tau}, \qquad C_n C_k e^{jn\omega_o t} e^{jk\omega_o(t+\tau)}$$

The first and third of these lead to sinusoids and cosinusoids which vary with time. Hence (see Eqs. 8–175 through 8–178) their contribution will be zero. The $C_n C_{-n} e^{jn\omega_o t}$ terms are constants as far as the integral is concerned; thus, we have

$$R_x(\tau) = \lim_{T \to \infty} \frac{1}{2T} \sum_{n=-\infty}^{\infty} C_n C_{-n} e^{jn\omega_o \tau} \int_{-T}^{T} dt \quad (8\text{--}188)$$

Hence,

$$R_x(\tau) = \sum_{n=-\infty}^{\infty} C_n C_{-n} e^{jn\omega_o \tau} \quad (8\text{--}189)$$

This is also in the form of a Fourier series of a periodic function whose period is the same as that of $f(t)$. Therefore, the autocorrelation of a periodic function is periodic. The period of the autocorrelation will be the same as that of the original signal. In general (see Eq. 2–293 and the equation following it),

$$C_{-n} = C_n^* \quad (8\text{--}190)$$

Hence, Eq. 8–189 can be written as

$$R_x(\tau) = \sum_{n=-\infty}^{\infty} |C_n|^2 e^{jn\omega_o \tau} \quad (8\text{--}191)$$

Alternatively, we have

$$R_x(\tau) = C_0^2 + 2 \sum_{n=1}^{\infty} |C_n|^2 \cos n\omega_0 \tau \quad (8\text{--}192)$$

Let us consider some other properties of the autocorrelation. If $\tau = 0$, we have (see Eq. 8–180)

$$R_x(0) = \lim_{T \to \infty} \frac{1}{2T} \int_{-T}^{T} x^2(t) \, dt = \langle x^2(t) \rangle \quad (8\text{--}193)$$

That is, $R_x(0)$ is the time average of $x^2(t)$. If the system is ergodic, then

$$R_x(0) = \overline{x^2} \quad (8\text{--}194)$$

Let us now prove that no value of the correlation function will be greater than $R_x(0)$. We start by considering the time average of the function $[x(t) \pm x(t + \tau)]^2$.

$$\langle [x(t) \pm x(t + \tau)]^2 \rangle$$

$$= \lim_{T \to \infty} \frac{1}{2T} \int_{-T}^{T} [x^2(t) \pm 2x(t)\, x(t + \tau) + x^2(t + \tau)] \, dt \quad (8\text{--}195)$$

Consider each part of this integral

$$\lim_{T \to \infty} \frac{1}{2T} \int_{-T}^{T} x^2(t)\, dt = R_x(0) \tag{8-196a}$$

(See Eq. 8–180.) Now consider the last term of Eq. 8–195. In general, since we integrate over all time

$$\lim_{T \to \infty} \frac{1}{2T} \int_{-T}^{T} x^2(t + \tau)\, dt = \lim_{T \to \infty} \frac{1}{2T} \int_{-T}^{T} x^2(t)\, dt = R_x(0) \tag{8-196b}$$

Then, substituting Eqs. 8–196 and 8–180 into Eq. 8–195, we have

$$\langle [x(t) + x(t + \tau)]^2 \rangle = 2R_x(0) \pm 2R_x(\tau) \tag{8-197}$$

The value of a real number squared is never negative. Thus, the time average $\langle [x(t) + x(t + \tau)]^2 \rangle$ must be nonnegative; therefore,

$$2R_x(0) \pm 2R_x(\tau) \geq 0$$

Hence,

$$R_x(0) \geq |R_x(\tau)| \tag{8-198}$$

Thus, the autocorrelation function achieves its maximum magnitude at $\tau = 0$. There may be values of $\tau$ where $|R_x(\tau)| = R_x(0)$, but $|R_x(\tau)|$ will never exceed $R_x(0)$. Let us now investigate $R_x(-\tau)$. From Eq. 8–180, we have

$$R_x(-\tau) = \lim_{T \to \infty} \frac{1}{2T} \int_{-T}^{T} x(t)\, x(t - \tau)\, dt$$

Letting $z = t - \tau$ and substituting and manipulating, we obtain

$$R_x(-\tau) = \lim_{T \to \infty} \frac{1}{2T} \int_{-T-\tau}^{T-\tau} x(z)\, x(z + \tau)\, dz$$

Comparing this with Eq. 8–180 and noting that the limits of integration approach plus or minus infinity in each case, we have

$$R_x(\tau) = R_x(-\tau) \tag{8-199}$$

Thus, the autocorrelation function is an even function of $\tau$.

Let us assume that we have a random process which is composed of the sum of two other random processes:

$$z(t) = x(t) + y(t) \tag{8-200}$$

We can express the autocorrelation of $z(t)$ in terms of the correlation functions of $x(t)$ and $y(t)$;

$$R_z(\tau) = \lim_{T \to \infty} \frac{1}{2T} \int_{-T}^{T} [x(t) + y(t)]\, [x(t + \tau) + y(t + \tau)]\, dt \tag{8-201}$$

Multiplying the integrand and comparing the results with Eqs. 8–168 and 8–180, we obtain

$$R_z(\tau) = R_x(\tau) + R_{xy}(\tau) + R_{yx}(\tau) + R_y(\tau) \qquad (8\text{–}202)$$

This is the sum of all possible autocorrelation and crosscorrelation functions of $x(t)$ and $y(t)$.

In general, if $z(t)$ were composed of the sum of more than two processes, the same statement would apply. If $x(t)$ and $y(t)$ are uncorrelated and have zero mean, then (see Eq. 8–173) Eq. 8–202 becomes

$$R_z(\tau) = R_x(\tau) + R_y(\tau) \qquad (8\text{–}203)$$

In this section, we have studied some of the properties of the autocorrelation function. In subsequent sections we shall discuss that the spectral density can be obtained from the autocorrelation function. In addition, we shall demonstrate in Section 8-9 that if a signal contains a periodic component and a great deal of noise, then autocorrelation can often be used to extract the signal from the noise. In such case, when signals are to be detected, they are usually sampled at a large set of points equidistant in time. Let us see how the autocorrelation can be approximated from such a set of points. When we deal with practical signals, they start at some time which we shall call $t = 0$; thus,

$$x(t) = 0, \qquad t < 0 \qquad (8\text{–}204)$$

Then, Eq. 8–180 becomes

$$R_x(\tau) = \lim_{T \to \infty} \frac{1}{2T} \int_0^T x(t)\, x(t + \tau)\, d\tau \qquad (8\text{–}205)$$

We cannot integrate to $T = \infty$ in a numerical analysis or computer program. Thus, let us choose some large time $T_0$ and integrate to this value; that is, we approximate Eq. 8–205 by

$$R_x(\tau) = \frac{1}{2T_0} \int_0^{T_0} x(t)\, x(t + \tau)\, dt \qquad (8\text{–}206)$$

To determine if the value of $T_0$ is sufficiently large, the discussion of Section 2-18 should be considered. To evaluate the integral, we shall use the integration procedure of Section 2-18. If the reader is not familiar with this, this section should be reviewed. Let us assume that we wish to evaluate $R_x(\tau)$ for $0 \le \tau \le \tau_0$, and that we wish to evaluate $R_x(\tau)$ from discrete values of $\tau$ spaces $\Delta\tau$ seconds apart. The input signal $x(t)$ should be sampled at times $\Delta t$ apart, where $\Delta t = \Delta\tau$.

Let us assume that $N$ samples have been obtained and we wish to have $K$ values of $R(\tau)$; i.e., we calculate $R(0)$, $R(\Delta\tau)$, $R(2\Delta\tau)$, ..., $R(K - 1)\,\Delta\tau$. Corresponding to $T_0$ in Eq. 8–206, we must have a sufficient number of terms in the summation that approximate the integral. Suppose $N_T$ terms are sufficient. Then, we must have enough samples so that

$$N \ge N_T + K \qquad (8\text{–}207)$$

Note that $N_T$ must be an integer which satisfies $N_T \geq (T_0/\Delta t) + 1$.

Now assume that we have sampled a sequence of $N$ values of $x$: $x_1, x_2, ..., x_N$. Then, using Eq. 2–324, we can approximate Eq. 8–206 by

$$R_x(k\Delta\tau) = \left[ \frac{1}{2T_0} \sum_{n=1}^{N_T} x_n x_{n+k} \Delta t - \frac{x_1 x_{k+1} + x_{N_T} x_{N_T+k}}{2} \Delta t \right] \qquad (8\text{–}208)$$

Now let us consider a computer program that implements this. It is important to use a computer here since, in general, a great many points will be required. The SUBROUTINE AUTCOR shown in Fig. 8–11 will be used.

Common storage is used to enter data from the main program and to transfer the answer from the SUBROUTINE. The array of input samples of $x(t)$ is represented by $X$. The program is dimensioned for up to 1000 samples. However, this number can be increased by simply changing the dimension assignments in the common statements in the subroutine and in the main program. The total number of terms in the summations is $NT$. It corresponds to $N_T$ in Eq. 8–208. Then $K$ corresponds to $k$ in Eq. 8–208. A DO loop in the main program increases the value of $K$ by one starting with zero. Each time the DO loop is cycled a different $R(k\Delta\tau)$ is obtained until the desired number of $R(\tau)$ are calculated. Note that each value of $K$ corresponds to a different $\tau = k\Delta\tau$.

Let us consider the details of the program. In line 40, the value of R is set equal to 0. Then, in lines 50 and 60 $KJ = K + 1$ and $JJ = K + NT$ are determined. Note that $K + 1$ is used since $x_1$ and not $x_0$ is the first term in the array. (Remember that the array index starts with 1 and not 0.) This corresponds to Eq. 8–208. In line 70, B, which is equal to $(x_1 x_{k+1} + x_{N_T} x_{N_T+k})/2$, is determined. Each time

```
00010              SUBRØUTINE AUTCØR
00020      C       PRØGRAM TAKES AUTØCØRRELATIØN
00030              CØMMØN X(1000),R,NT,K
00040              R=0.
00050              KJ=K+1
00060              JJ=K+NT
00070              B=(X(1)*X(KJ)+X(JJ)*X(NT))/2.
00080              DØ 500 J=1,NT
00090              JM=J+K
00100              R=R+X(J)*X(JM)
00110      500     CØNTINUE
00120              ANT=NT
00130              R=(R-B)/(2.*ANT-2.)
00140              RETURN
00150              END
```

FIG. 8–11
SUBROUTINE AUTCOR that is used to calculate the auto-correlation function

the DO loop of lines 80–110 is cycled, R is increased by $X(J) * X(J + K)$. This is done $N_T$ times. In line 120, we obtain ANT a real value of $N_T$. In line 130, B is subtracted from R and the result is divided by $2 * (ANT - 1) = 2 * (N_T - 1)$ to obtain the final value of R. Note the following, the expression $(R - B)$ should be multiplied by $\Delta t / 2T_0$, see Eq. 8–208. Let us consider this $T_0 \approx \Delta t (N_T - 1)$; hence,

$$\frac{\Delta t}{2T_0} = \frac{1}{2 * (NT - 1)} = \frac{1}{2 * NT - 2}$$

The value of R is returned to the main program by the common statement. This value is printed and the DO loop in the main program is cycled to obtain a new value of K, which is then used to compute a new value for R.

A similar program could be used to obtain the crosscorrelation. In this case, two arrays X and Y must be entered. Then, in line 70, $X(KJ)$ and $X(JJ)$ are replaced by $Y(KJ)$ and $Y(NT)$, respectively. Also, in line 100, $X(JM)$ is replaced by $Y(JM)$. A function can be used at times to obtain the Y terms. In this case, storage of an array would not be necessary. The crosscorrelation can then be computed.

## 8-8. RELATION BETWEEN AUTOCORRELATION FUNCTIONS AND SPECTRAL DENSITY— WEINER-KINCHINE THEOREM

We begin with the fundamental definition of the autocorrelation (see Eq. 8–180):

$$R_x(\tau) = \lim_{T \to \infty} \frac{1}{2T} \int_{-T}^{T} x(t)\, x(t + \tau)\, dt \qquad (8\text{–}209)$$

Now replace $t$ by $-t$; then,

$$R_x(\tau) = \lim_{T \to \infty} \frac{1}{2T} \int_{-T}^{T} x(-t)\, x(\tau - t)\, dt \qquad (8\text{–}210)$$

Assume that we have another function $x_1(t)$ which is such that $x_1(t) = x(-t)$. Substituting in Eq. 8–210, we obtain

$$R_x(\tau) = \lim_{T \to \infty} \frac{1}{2T} \int_{-T}^{T} x_1(t)\, x(\tau - t)\, dt \qquad (8\text{–}211)$$

Equation 8–211 represents the convolution of $x_1(t)$ and $x(t)$ (see Eq. 2–202). We shall now use the time convolution theorem. This involves working with Fourier transforms. Let the Fourier transform of $x(t)$ be $X(j\omega)$:

$$x(t) \leftrightarrow X(j\omega) \qquad (8\text{–}212)$$

Proceeding in a manner similar to the derivation of Eq. 2–232, we obtain

$$x(-t) = x_1(t) \leftrightarrow X(-j\omega)$$

Then, applying Eq. 2–209 to Eq. 8–211, we have

$$R_x(\tau) \leftrightarrow \lim_{T \to \infty} \frac{1}{2T} X(-j\omega) X(j\omega) \qquad (8\text{–}213)$$

Since $x(t)$ is real,

$$X(-j\omega) = X^*(j\omega) \qquad (8\text{–}214)$$

(See discussion preceding Eq. 2–228.) Substituting Eq. 8–214 into Eq. 8–213 yields

$$R_x(\tau) \leftrightarrow \lim_{T \to \infty} \frac{1}{2T} |X(j\omega)|^2$$

The right-hand side of the expression is the spectral density (see Eq. 8–128); hence,

$$R_x(\tau) \leftrightarrow S(\omega) \qquad (8\text{–}215)$$

*Thus, the autocorrelation and spectral density are a Fourier transform pair.* This is called the *Weiner-Kinchine theorem.*

This is a very useful theorem. For instance, suppose a random signal is sampled and its correlation function determined (see Section 8-7). Then, the spectral density can be found using Eq. 8–215. Conversely, the autocorrelation can be determined from the spectral density.

Let us determine the correlation function of white noise. On a normalized basis

$$S(\omega) = 1 \qquad (8\text{–}216)$$

To obtain the autocorrelation, we take the inverse Fourier transform of $S(\omega)$. Thus (see Table 2-1) we have

$$R_x(\tau) = \delta(\tau) \qquad (8\text{–}217)$$

If $x(t)$ represents white noise, $x(t)$ and $x(t + \tau)$ are uncorrelated provided $\tau \neq 0$.

It may seem strange to have no correlation between $x(t)$ and $x(t + \tau)$ even for extremely small values of $\tau$. However, this is due to the assumption that the bandwidth is infinite. Consider a case in which the spectral density falls off as $\omega$ is increased. Suppose

$$S(\omega) = \frac{1}{1 + \left(\dfrac{\omega}{\omega_0}\right)^2} \qquad (8\text{–}218)$$

This spectral density is shown in Fig. 8–12a. The inverse Fourier transform of $S(\omega)$ is

$$R_x(\tau) = \frac{1}{2\pi} \int_{-\infty}^{\infty} \frac{1}{1 + \left(\dfrac{\omega}{\omega_0}\right)^2} e^{j\omega\tau} d\omega = \frac{1}{\pi} \int_{0}^{\infty} \frac{\cos \omega\tau}{1 + \left(\dfrac{\omega}{\omega_0}\right)^2} d\omega$$

Integrating, we have [1]

$$R_x(\tau) = \frac{\omega_0}{2} e^{-|\omega_0\tau|} \qquad (8\text{–}219)$$

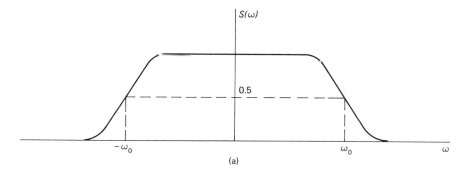

(a)

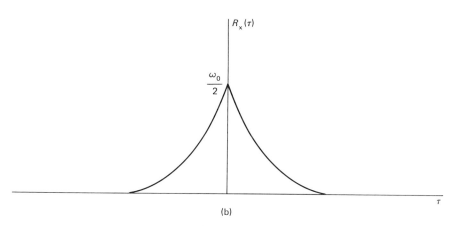

(b)

FIG. 8–12

(a) Spectral density $S(\omega) = \dfrac{1}{1 + \dfrac{\omega^2}{\omega_0^2}}$ : (b) autocorrelation of this function $R_x(\tau) = \dfrac{\omega_0}{2} e^{-|\omega_0 \tau|}$

This correlation falls off exponentially with $\tau$ and is illustrated in Fig. 8–12b. Note that as $\omega_0$ increases, the rate of fall off and the amplitude of $R_x(0)$ both increase. In the limit $R_x(\tau)$ approached $\delta(\tau)$.

The autocorrelation of many functions will approach zero as $\tau$ approaches infinity. Let us investigate this. From Eqs. 8–215 and 2–62 we have

$$R_x(\tau) = \frac{1}{2\pi} \int_{-\infty}^{\infty} S(\omega)\, e^{j\omega\tau} d\omega \qquad (8\text{–}220)$$

Now assume that $S(\omega)$ is bounded, continuous, and possesses all its derivatives, and falls to zero as $t$ approaches infinity at least as fast as $1/|\omega|^n$, where $n > 1$. Thus, we can use the Riemann-Lebesgue lemma (see Eq. 2–41); hence,

$$\lim_{\tau \to \infty} R_x(\tau) = 0 \qquad (8\text{–}221)$$

Thus, for a very large class of functions, their autocorrelations will approach zero as $\tau$ approaches infinity.

Equation 8–221 does not apply for periodic signals, because $S(\omega)$ will not satisfy the conditions imposed (impulses will be present in the Fourier transform). The properties of the autocorrelation discussed here will enable us to use it to extract certain signals from noise. We shall discuss this in the next section.

## 8-9. USE OF CORRELATION FUNCTIONS FOR DETECTING SIGNALS IN THE PRESENCE OF NOISE— ELEMENTARY NOISE FILTERING

A very common problem is the detection of a signal in the presence of noise. Suppose the desired signal is a very weak radar signal, such as one reflected from a distant planet. The desired signal often consists of a periodic waveform or one that repeats itself for a very long time so that it can be considered to be periodic for all practical purposes. However, it is often so weak that the signal-to-noise ratio is very small. In such cases, if the waveform of signal plus noise is inspected by ordinary means, one cannot tell whether or not the signal is present since the noise obscures it. Correlation techniques can be used to determine if the periodic signal is present. Accordingly, we can say that the signal has been *extracted* from the noise.

Let us consider the procedure. Suppose we receive a signal $x(t)$, which is composed of a desired periodic signal $f(t)$ and noise $n(t)$; then,

$$x(t) = f(t) + n(t) \tag{8–222}$$

The receiver will, in general, remove the direct component from the signal. Hence, we shall assume that $f(t)$ and $n(t)$ both have zero mean value. We shall also assume that $f(t)$ and $n(t)$ are generated by ergodic processes, and $x(t)$ is received for a long time and is recorded. Then the computer technique of Section 8-7 can be used to obtain the autocorrelation function. The autocorrelation of $x(t)$ is given by Eq. 8–203, since $f(t)$ and $n(t)$ are uncorrelated; hence,

$$R_x(\tau) = R_f(\tau) + R_n(\tau) \tag{8–223}$$

where $R_f(\tau)$ is the autocorrelation function of the signal and $R_n(\tau)$ is the autocorrelation function of the noise. In general (see Section 8-8), the autocorrelation of the noise will fall off to zero as $\tau$ approaches infinity, while that of the signal will repeat itself periodically. For example, if

$$f(t) = C_0\cos \omega_0 t \tag{8–224}$$

then (see Eq. 8–192)

$$R_f(\tau) = 2C_0^2\cos \omega_0^2 \tag{8–225}$$

A typical noise autocorrelation function is illustrated in Fig. 8–12b. The value of $R_x(\tau)$ will be the sum of these two correlation functions $R_f(\tau)$ and $R_x(t)$. This

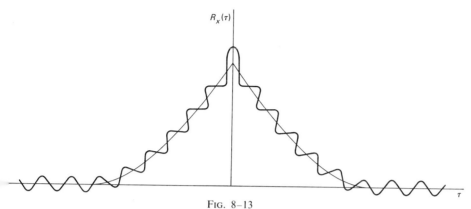

FIG. 8–13

Autocorrelation of a sinusoidal function plus noise

summation is illustrated in Fig. 8–13. After $|\tau|$ becomes sufficiently large, the waveform becomes that of cos $\omega_0 t$. Thus, the presence of $f(t)$ can be detected. The correlation function is inspected for large values of $\tau$. If $R_x(\tau)$ is periodic, of period $2\pi/\omega_0$, then the signal is present. If $R_x(\tau)$ does not have the periodic component, then the desired signal is absent.

Figure 8–13 seems to indicate that we do not have to use large values of $\tau$ to determine if the periodic component is present. The presence of the periodic component is obvious for small $\tau$ also. In theory, if $R_n(\tau)$ is a smooth curve, large values of $\tau$ may not be needed to the signal. However, in practice, this is usually not true. The autocorrelation is approximated by an equation, such as Eq. 8–208. Since this is only approximate, the autocorrelation of the noise will not be a smooth curve, but will have some *random* variations. If the magnitude of the noise is very large in comparison with the signal, then the randomness can obscure the periodic component of $R_x(\tau)$. If $\tau$ is increased, the noise autocorrelation will decrease. This will also decrease the "random" component of $R_n(\tau)$. Thus, large values of $\tau$ may be required before the presence or absence of the periodic component is clear. In general, if the signal is such that the signal-to-noise ratio is extremely small, very large values of $\tau$ must be used. This requires the sampling of many points (see Eq. 8–207).

**Use of Crosscorrelation.** If we know the form of the periodic waveform that we wish to detect, then autocorrelation detection procedures can be improved upon by using crosscorrelation. We use the received signal $x(t)$ and the periodic signal $f(t)$ in the crosscorrelation. Thus, the crosscorrelation is

$$R_{xf}(\tau) = R_{ff}(\tau) + R_{nf}(\tau) \qquad (8-226)$$

$R_{ff}(\tau)$ is the same as the autocorrelation of the signal. However, now the noise is crosscorrelated with the periodic waveform. Since these two signals are uncorrelated, and we assume, of zero mean, then (see Eq. 8–173)

$$R_{nf}(\tau) = 0 \qquad\qquad (8\text{–}227)$$

Thus, if the signal is present,

$$R_{xf}(\tau) = R_f(\tau) \qquad\qquad (8\text{–}228a)$$

while if the signal is not present,

$$R_{xf}(\tau) = 0 \qquad\qquad (8\text{–}228b)$$

Thus, we can use crosscorrelation to determine if the signal is present.

Equation 8–227 indicates that $R_{nf}(\tau)$ is zero for all $\tau$. Then, the computation becomes much simpler since large values of $\tau$ are not required. In practice, we may still have to use very many points in a calculation. When the actual computation is performed, the results only approximate the theoretical ones. Thus, the calculated $R_{nf}(\tau)$ will not be zero. However, it will, in general, fall off as the accuracy of computation is increased. Thus, if the signal-to-noise ratios are very low, a large number of sample points may have to be used, even with crosscorrelation, to reduce $R_{nf}(\tau)$ to sufficiently small values. (Note that $R_f(\tau)$ will be small if the signal is small.) Less computation is usually required with crosscorrelation than with autocorrelation.

**Frequency Domain Filtering for Detecting Signals in the Presence of Noise.** We have discussed the use of correlation functions to extract a signal from the noise. In general, we have been processing the signal in the time domain. That is, $x(t)$ was used to compute an autocorrelation or a crosscorrelation function. Actually, if the desired signal waveform is known so that crosscorrelation techniques can be used, then we can also filter in the frequency domain. That is, we can obtain the same result as with crosscorrelation by filtering the signal $x(t) = f(t) + n(t)$. The transfer function of the filter must be the appropriate $H(j\omega)$. If $x(t)$ is the input to the filter, then $R_{xf}(t)$ should be the output.

Let us determine the proper $H(j\omega)$ to use. Suppose the desired signal is $f(t)$. Then, the crosscorrelation between the received signal and $f(t)$ is

$$R_{xf}(\tau) = \lim_{T \to \infty} \frac{1}{2T} \int_{-T}^{T} f(t)\, x(t + \tau)\, dt \qquad\qquad (8\text{–}229)$$

Proceeding as in Eqs. 8–209 through 8–215, we obtain

$$R_{xf}(\tau) \leftrightarrow X(j\omega)\, F(-j\omega) \qquad\qquad (8\text{–}230)$$

where $X(j\omega)$ is the Fourier transform of $x(t)$ and $F(j\omega)$ is the Fourier transform of $f(t)$.

The Fourier transform of the crosscorrelation function is given by Relation 8–230. Let us see how we can generate a function whose Fourier transform is $X(j\omega)\, F(-j\omega)$. If (see Section 5-1) a signal $f_1(t)$, whose Fourier transform is $F_1(j\omega)$, is applied to a network whose transfer function is $H(j\omega)$, the Fourier transform of the output will be $F_1(j\omega)\, H(j\omega)$. Thus (see Eq. 8–230) we can achieve the desired

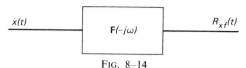

FIG. 8–14

Block diagram of frequency domain filter whose
output is the crosscorrelation function

output if we apply a signal, whose Fourier transform is $X(j\omega)$, to a filter whose transfer function is $F(-j\omega)$. The signal, whose Fourier transform is $X(j\omega)$, is the input signal $x(t)$. Such a filter is shown in Fig. 8–14.

Now suppose the desired output signal $f(t)$ is a periodic function with period $T_0$. Then (see Eq. 2–289)

$$f(t) \leftrightarrow \frac{2\pi}{T_0} \sum_{n=-\infty}^{\infty} F_0(jn\omega_0)\,\delta(\omega - n\omega_0) \tag{8-231}$$

where the $F_0(jn\omega_0)$ are constant. The desired filter should then have a transfer function

$$H(j\omega) = \frac{2\pi}{T_0} \sum_{n=-\infty}^{\infty} F(jn\omega_0)\,\delta(\omega + n\omega_0) \tag{8-232}$$

(Note that $\delta(x) = \delta(-x)$.)

This filter cannot be achieved in practice. However, it can be approximated. Notice that $H(j\omega)$ is zero except when $\omega = n\omega_0$, $n = \pm 1, \pm 2 \dots$. Thus, we can approximate this by the filter characteristics of Fig. 8–15. The width of each isolated pass band should be as narrow as possible. All should be of equal width. The transfer

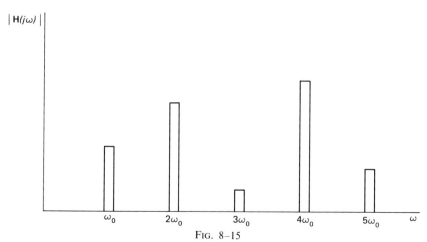

FIG. 8–15

Magnitude of the transfer function of a filter which approximates the transfer function of Eq. 8–232. Only positive frequency values are shown

function of each pass band is proportional to $F(jn\omega_0)$. Such a filter is not physically realizable. However, it can be approximated.

If the desired signal $f(t)$ is characterized by relation 8–231, the filters will pass all the harmonics of $f(t)$ and reject all other frequencies. The signal component will not be rejected, although its waveform will be altered to produce the convolution. Noise spectral density will, in general, be distributed over all frequencies. Thus, the filter will reject almost all of the noise. Hence, the noise components of the output will be greatly attenuated. In the ideal case, the pass bands of the filter will be zero and the noise will be zero. We thus obtain the desired crosscorrelation.

If the transfer function of Fig. 8–15 is modified so that the response at each harmonic frequency is constant at unity then, as before, almost all of the noise will be rejected and the signal will be unchanged. In this case, the filter's output is no longer the crosscorrelation, but the signal itself. This is an alternative way of detecting the signal. Crosscorrelation techniques can be used if the desired signal is not periodic. Then, there will be a large output at only one $\tau$.

In this section we have discussed some basic ideas of extracting a signal from noise. In the next chapter we shall discuss additional ones.

## PROBLEMS

**8-1.** A single die is weighted so that a 3 results five times as often as any other possible number; the numbers 1, 2, 4, 5, and 6 occur with equal frequency. Determine the probability of each number's occurring.

**8-2.** If a single unbiased die is tossed, what is the probability of obtaining a number greater than 2 on a single toss?

**8-3.** Repeat Problem 8-2, but now use the die of Problem 8-1.

**8-4.** A single unbiased coin is tossed four times. What is the probability that four heads result?

**8-5.** Repeat Problem 8-4, but now determine the probability that three heads and one tail will result.

**8-6.** Repeat Problem 8-5, but now determine the probability that three heads and one tail *or* four heads will result.

**8-7.** A box contains two each of red, blue, and green balls. Determine the probability of drawing a red ball from the box.

**8-8.** Repeat Problem 8-7, but now determine the probability of drawing a green ball from the box after drawing a red one.

**8-9.** Repeat Problem 8-7, but now determine the probability of drawing two red balls and a green ball from the box.

**8-10.** A very large set of dice are all identical. They are weighted so that $P(1) = 0.3$, $P(2) = 0.2$, $P(3) = 0.2$, $P(4) = 0.1$, $P(5) = 0.1$, and $P(6) = 0.1$. Let $x_j$ be the number appearing on the $j$th die. Find $E[x] = \bar{x}$, the expected value, when this ensemble of dice is cast.

**8-11.** Repeat Problem 8-10, but now find the first three moments.

**8-12.** Repeat Problem 8-10, but now find the variance and standard variation.

**8-13.** A certain random variable $X$ has a probability distribution given by

$$P(x) = \begin{cases} 0, & x < 0 \\ 1 - e^{-x}, & x > 0 \end{cases}$$

Determine the probability that $X < 2$.

**8-14.** Repeat Problem 8-13, but now determine the probability that $1 \leq X \leq 2$.

**8-15.** A random variable has a probability density given by

$$p(x) = \begin{cases} 0, & x < -1 \\ 1/2, & -1 \leq x \leq 1 \\ 0, & x > -1 \end{cases} ,$$

What is the probability that $0 \leq x \leq 1/2$?

**8-16.** A random variable has a probability density function given by

$$p(x) = Ae^{-2|x|}$$

Find the value of $A$.

**8-17.** A random variable has a probability density function

$$p(x) = e^{-x}, \qquad x > 0$$

Determine the probability density function for $x < 0$.

**8-18.** For the probability density function of Problem 8-17, determine the probability that $0.5 \leq x \leq 1$.

**8-19.** A random variable has a probability density function

$$p(x) = \begin{cases} e^{-x}, & x > 0 \\ 0, & x < 0 \end{cases}$$

A function of the random variable is

$$Y = f(x) = 2x + 3$$

**8-20.** A random variable $X$ has a conditional probability density

$$p(x|y) = \begin{cases} |y| e^{-x|y|}, & x \geq 0 \\ 0, & x < 0 \end{cases}$$

If $y = 3$, what is the probability that $1 \leq X \leq 2$?

**8-21.** Two random variables $X$ and $Y$ have a joint probability density

$$p(x, y) = \begin{cases} ye^{-y}e^{-xy}; & x \geq 0, \quad y \geq 0 \\ 0, & \text{elsewhere} \end{cases}$$

Find the probability that $1 \leq X \leq 2, 0 \leq Y \leq 1$.

**8-22.** Two random variables are characterized by the following probability distribution functions

$$p(x|y) = \begin{cases} |y| e^{-x|y|}, & x \geq 0 \\ 0, & x < 0 \end{cases}$$

$$p(y) = \begin{cases} 0, & y < 0 \\ 1, & 0 \leq y \leq 1 \\ 0, & y < 1 \end{cases}$$

Find the joint probability density $p(x, y)$.

**8-23.** For the random variables of Problem 8-21, find $p(x)$ and $p(y)$.

**8-24.** Repeat Problem 8-23 for the random variable of Problem 8-22.

**8-25.** A random variable has a probability density

$$p(x) = \tfrac{1}{2} e^{-|x|}$$

Find the expected value of $x$.

**8-26.** Repeat Problem 8-25, but now use the probability density

$$p(x) = \begin{cases} e^{-x}, & x \geq 0 \\ 0, & x < 0 \end{cases}$$

**8-27.** Find the expected value of the function

$$y = x^2 + x$$

if $x$ is a random variable whose probability density is given in Problem 8-25.

**8-28.** Repeat Problem 8-27 for the probability density of Problem 8-26.

**8-29.** Find the mean square value of the random variable of Problem 8-25.

**8-30.** Repeat Problem 8-29 for the random variable of Problem 8-26.

**8-31.** Find the variance and standard deviation of the random variable of Problem 8-25.

**8-32.** Repeat Problem 8-31 for the function of Problem 8-19.

**8-33.** Verify Tchebycheff's inequality for the random variable of Problem 8-25.

**8-34.** Discuss why an ergodic process must be stationary, but that a stationary process need not be ergodic.

**8-35.** A function of a random variable is given by

$$f(x) = x^2 + 2x$$

Determine its expected value if $x$ has a Gaussian probability density. Assume that $\bar{x} = 0$.

**8-36.** Why do you expect that resistor noise will have a Gaussian probability density?

**8-37.** What is the probability of tossing six heads when a coin is tossed ten times.

**8-38.** Verify (numerically) the relationship between the binomial and Poisson distributions for small $mp$.

**8-39.** A function $z$ is composed of the sum of two independent Gaussian random variables. Find the variance and mean of $z$. Assume that the two variables have zero mean.

**8-40.** What is the mean square noise voltage per unit bandwidth produced across a 10 ohm resistor operating at $300° K$?

**8-41.** Resistor noise is passed through an ideal band pass filter whose bandwidth is $B_1 = \omega_2 - \omega_1$. This is then added to a sinusoidal signal. The noise and signal are such that the power signal-to-noise ratio is 0.1. The composite signal is then passed through a second ideal band pass filter whose pass band lies in the range $\omega_1 \leq \omega \leq \omega_2$. Neither filter attenuates the signal. The bandwidth of the second filter is $0.01B_1$. What is the signal-to-noise ratio of the output signal?

**8-42.** What is the noise figure of the second filter of Problem 8-41.

**8-43.** Find the equivalent noise bandwidth of a filter whose transfer function is given by

$$|H(j\omega)| = \frac{1}{1 + \left(\dfrac{\omega}{\omega_0}\right)^2}$$

**8-44.** White noise is passed through a narrow band, band pass filter. The power spectrum of the output is given by

$$G(\omega) = \begin{cases} 2 \text{ watts/herz}, & 10^6 \leq \omega \leq 10^6 + 1000 \\ 2 \text{ watts/hertz}, & -(10^6 + 1000) \leq \omega \leq -10^6 \\ 0, & \text{elsewhere} \end{cases}$$

This noise is detected by a linear amplitude-modulated detector. Determine the probability density of the output waveform.

**8-45.** Repeat Problem 8-44, but now assume that the output of the detector has zero mean value; i.e., the direct component is removed.

**8-46.** Find the crosscorrelation of

$$x(t) = t$$
$$y(t) = e^{-t}$$

**8-47.** Repeat Problem 8-46 for

$$x(t) = \cos 2t$$
$$y(t) = e^{-t} + \cos 2t$$

**8-48.** Repeat Problem 8-46 for

$$x(t) = 1 + \cos 2t$$
$$y(t) = 2 + \sin 3t$$

**8-49.** Find the autocorrelation of

$$f(x) = \begin{cases} 1, & 0 \le x \le 0.5 \\ -1, & 0.5 < x < 1.0 \end{cases}$$

$$f(x + 1) = f(x)$$

where $f(x)$ is a square wave that has a period of 1 second.

**8-50.** An ergodic random process has an autocorrelation function

$$R_x(\tau) = 5e^{-|\tau|}$$

What are the values of the mean, mean square, and variance?

**8-51.** A process has an autocorrelation function given by

$$R_x(\tau) = 5e^{-\tau^2} + 9 \cos 2\tau$$

Determine any periodic components present in $x(t)$.

**8.52.** Two independent ergodic processes have an autocorrelation function given by

$$R_x(\tau) = 5e^{-\tau^2} + 1$$
$$R_y(\tau) = e^{-\tau^2} \cos 2\tau + 3$$

Assume that $x(t)$ and $y(t)$ are uncorrelated except for their direct values. A process is characterized by

$$z(t) = x(t) + y(t)$$

Determine the autocorrelation function $R_z(\tau)$.

**8-53.** Write a computer program that determines the expected value, mean square value, variance, and standard deviation for an array of data.

**8-54.** Write a complete computer program that can be used to evaluate the autocorrelation function. Do not refer to Fig. 8–11.

**8-55.** Repeat Problem 8-54, but do not use a trapazoidal integration procedure.

**8-56.** Verify the programs of Problems 8-54 and 8-55 using the subroutine of Fig. 8–11.

**8-57.** A function has a spectral density

$$S(\omega) = \frac{1}{\left[1 + \left(\dfrac{\omega}{\omega_a}\right)^2\right]\left[1 + \left(\dfrac{\omega}{\omega_b}\right)^2\right]}$$

Determine its autocorrelation function.

**8-58.** Repeat Problem 8-57 for

$$S(\omega) = e^{-|\omega|}$$

**8-59.** A signal consists of noise whose spectral density is given by

$$S(\omega) = 10^4 e^{-|\omega|}$$

and a desired signal cos $t$. Determine and plot the autocorrelation function of the composite signal. Discuss how the autocorrelation may be used to extract signal from noise.

**8-60.** Repeat Problem 8-59, but now use crosscorrelation. Use the function $f(t) = \cos t$ in the crosscorrelation with the composite signal.

**8-61.** Determine the transfer characteristic of a frequency domain filter which can be used to accomplish the crosscorrelation of Problem 8-60.

**8-62.** A signal consists of

$$x(t) = 1000 \cos t + \cos 2t$$

The 1000 cos $t$ is used to simulate an interference signal. Thus, the function cos $2t$ is to be detected by means of crosscorrelation; that is, we use cross correlation with

$$y(t) = \cos 2t$$

Modify SUBROUTINE AUTCOR (see Fig. 8–11) so that it can perform the crosscorrelation. (Note that the data can be obtained from built in FORTRAN SUBROUTINES.) Determine the minimum value of NT and K and the maximum spacing between samples that can be used if the cos $2t$ component of the crosscorrelation is to be 100 times greater than any interference; i.e., the cos $t$ component.

## REFERENCES

1. Pierce, B. O. *A Short Table of Integrals*. 3d ed. Boston: Ginn, 1929, Section IV.
2. Selby, S. M., and Girling, B. *Standard Mathematical Tables*. 14th ed. pp. 258–267. Cleveland, Ohio: The Chemical Rubber Co., 1965.

## BIBLIOGRAPHY

Bennett, W. R. *Introduction to Signal Transmission*. Chap. 2. New York: McGraw-Hill, 1970.
Carlson, A. B. *Communication System*. Chap. 4. New York: McGraw-Hill, 1968.
Cooper, G. R. and McGillem, C. D. *Methods of Signal and System Analysis*. Chaps. 9–11. New York: Holt, 1967.
Lathi, B. P. *Signals, Systems and Communication*. Chaps. 12 and 13. New York: Wiley, 1965.
Schwartz, M. *Information Transmission, Modulation and Noise*. 2d ed. Chaps. 5–7. New York: McGraw-Hill, 1970.
Schwarz, R. J., and Friedland, B. *Linear Systems*. Chap. 9. New York: McGraw-Hill, 1965.

# CHAPTER 9

# Signal Transmission

In many systems the transmission of information is of prime importance. For instance, in radio or television, the information consists of the sound and/or the picture. In radar, the information is the location of an object. In this chapter, we shall discuss the transmission of information. A mathematical definition of information will be given and the transmission of information will be discussed. We shall begin by assuming that signals containing information are not obscured by noise, then, we shall consider signals with noise and procedures for extracting signals from noise.

## 9-1. INFORMATION CONTENT OF SIGNALS—ENTROPY

In order to study the transmission of information, we must have a mathematical definition of what is meant by information. In this section we shall discuss such a definition. In developing a definition we should take our intuitive feel for information into account. Let us discuss an ordinary situation where some messages are transmitted and consider the content of information in each.

Suppose a man approaches an information desk at an airport inquiring about a certain flight. He is answered by one of the following statements.

1. The flight will be affected by gravity.
2. The flight has been delayed 15 minutes by head winds.
3. The flight has been delayed 24 hours by very severe head winds.

Statement 1 provides no information while statements 2 and 3 do provide information. Let us consider why. Statement 1 provides no information because the plane must be affected by gravity: the probability of this occurring is unity. Since the observer knows that this is a certainty, no information is conveyed by telling him it has occurred.

Statement 2 provides information because the probability of the plane's being delayed is not unity. That is, we are not certain that the airplane will be delayed. Thus, when he is told that the airplane is delayed, he has received information.

Statement 3 provides the same type of information as statement 2. However, it provides much more information since it describes that a near impossible event has occurred. The wind must have been such that the plane was supported without using its engines since, under ordinary circumstances, a fuel supply would not last 24 hours. This event is extremely unlikely. Note that when we are told that such an event has occurred, this implies a great deal of information has been presented.

The information content of a message should be zero when the probability of the event's occurring is unity and it should increase as the probability of the event's occurring decreases. Let us now formalize the discussion of the transmission of information. We shall start by assuming that we can obtain information by asking a series of questions which can be answered by yes or no. For instance, if we wish to know when a flight will arrive, we could ask the following series of questions which call for yes or no answers. (The answers are given in parentheses.)

Is the flight on time? (No.)
Is the flight early? (No.)
Is the flight more than 20 minutes late? (No.)
Is the flight more than 10 minutes late? (Yes.)

This sequence of questions determines that the flight is between 10 and 20 minutes late.

Suppose the plane was actually 24 hours late. Many more questions would have to be asked, not only because the time was long, but also because the questioner would not consider the probability of the occurrence of such an improbable happening. In the above sequence of questions, he would not be likely to change the third question to, "Is the plane more than 12 hours late?"

Now let us formulate a mathematical definition of information. We shall base our definition on the idea that information can be conveyed by a sequence of questions which have yes or no answers. We must name a unit of information. It is conventional to call this a *bit*. A bit is defined as *the amount of information provided by determining that one of two equally likely events has occurred*. The word, *bit*, is the contraction of *binary digit*. In many pulse systems, information is conveyed by the presence or absence of a pulse. Thus, a sequence of pulses and blank spaces are transmitted. The presence of a pulse is analogous to a yes while the absence is analogous to a no. This is one reason why we use the two choices, yes and no. A pulse does not always transmit 1 bit of information, see Section 9-3.

If the probability of either a yes or a no answer is equally likely, then 1 bit of information is provided by the answer to the question. However, as we have seen, if the probability of an occurrence of an event is 1, then no information is transmitted if we receive a yes answer. If event $A$ has the probability $P_A$ of occuring, then the information that $A$ *has* occurred is given by

$$I(A) = -\log_2 P_A = \log_2 \frac{1}{P_A} \text{ bits} \qquad (9\text{--}1)$$

This is a logarithm to the base 2 of $1/P_A$. A plot of this function is given in Fig. 9–1. It is always positive and becomes infinite as the probability of the event's occurring approaches zero. That is, if we are told that a very unlikely event has occurred, the information content is high. If $P_A = 1/2$ (i.e., equal likelihood of occurring or not) then $I(A) = 1$, but if $P_A = 1$, then $I_A = 0$. That is, no information is conveyed if we are told that a certain event has occurred.

Let us consider an example. Suppose we transmit a message using an alphabet. For simplification, assume that there are only three letters, $A$, $B$, and $C$ and that

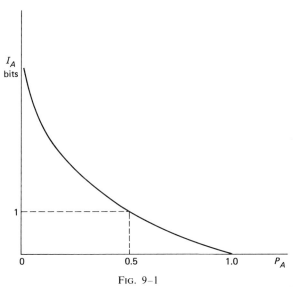

FIG. 9–1

Information in a message that an event has occurred in terms
of the probability that the event occurred

their probabilities of occurrence are

$$P(A) = 0.5 \qquad (9\text{–}2\text{a})$$

$$P(B) = 0.4 \qquad (9\text{–}2\text{b})$$

$$P(C) = 0.1 \qquad (9\text{–}2\text{c})$$

Now assume that we receive a message consisting of a sequence of these three
letters. What is the information conveyed, when we receive the sequence *AAB*?
The probability that this occurs is

$$P(AAB) = P(A)\,P(B)\,P(B) = 0.1 \qquad (9\text{–}3)$$

Thus, the information content is

$$I(AAB) = -\log_2 0.1 = \log_2 10 = 3.322 \text{ bits} \qquad (9\text{–}4)$$

Let us consider this in detail.

$$I(AAB) = -\log_2 \left[ P(A)\,P(A)\,P(B) \right]$$

$$= -\log_2 P(A) - \log_2 P(A) - \log_2 P(B). \qquad (9\text{–}5)$$

Then, the information content of the message is the sum of the information contents of the individual characters. Note that this is true, in general, if the probabilities are independent, because of the nature of the logarithm. When we receive a character it is equivalent to having received a yes answer to a question asking if the character had been sent.

Now let us determine the information content of the message $AAC$.

$$I(AAC) = -\log_2\left[(0.5)(0.5)(0.1)\right]$$
$$= -\log_2 0.025 = \log_2 40 = 5.322 \text{ bits}$$

The message $AAC$ has a higher information content than the message $AAB$, since $AAB$ is more likely.

We shall now obtain an expression for the average information content of a symbol. Suppose we have an alphabet of $K$ characters and we transmit a long message of $N$ characters. If $I_N$ is the information content of the message, then the average information content per character, which we call the *entropy* denoted by $H$, is given by

$$H = \lim_{N \to \infty} \frac{I_N}{N} \tag{9-7}$$

(Note that we let $N$ approach infinite to generalize the average.)

Let us express this in terms of the probability of occurrence. The likelihood of any sumbol's occrring is $P_i$. Thus, when the $i$th symbol is transmitted $-\log_2 P_i$ is added to $I_N$. In computing the average information transmitted, by a symbol, we can average the information transmitted by all symbols. This average must be weighted in accordance with the probability of that symbol's being sent. Hence, the entropy can be expressed as

$$H = \sum_{k=1}^{K} P_k I(k)$$

where $I(k)$ and $P_k$ are the information and probability of the $k$th symbol of the alphabet, respectively. There are $K$ symbols in the alphabet. Substituting Eq. 9-1, we have

$$H = \sum_{k=1}^{K} -P_k \log_2 P_k = \sum_{k=1}^{K} P_k \log_2 \frac{1}{P_k} \tag{9-8}$$

Note that $K$ represents the total number of symbols in the alphabet, not the number of symbols in a message. The unit of entropy is bits/symbol. (The word, *entropy*, is used because of the similarity of some of the equations to those of thermodynamic entropy.)

As an example, let us compute the entropy of the source characterized by Eqs.

9-2. The average information per symbol of this source is

$$H = -0.5 \log_2 0.5 - 0.4 \log_2 0.4 - 0.1 \log_2 0.1 = 1.361 \text{ bits/symbol}$$

As a final example, consider a system which has two possible outputs: one has probability $P$ of occurring, and the other, probability $1 - P$ of occurring. Then, the entropy of this source is given by

$$H = -P \log_2 P - (1 - P) \log_2 (1 - P) \qquad (9-9)$$

A plot of this entropy is given in Fig. 9-2. where $H = 0$ if $P = 0$ or $P = 1$. Note that

$$\lim_{P \to 0} P \log_2 P = 0$$

This can be obtained by applying L'Hopital's rule. The result agrees with our previous discussion of information content. For instance, suppose a system produces two symbols, $A$ or $B$. If the probability of an $A$'s occurring is 1, then we know that the symbol will be an $A$ and no information is conveyed by telling us that it has occurred. As $P$ approaches zero, the entropy $P \log_2 P$ also approaches zero. If we are told that a very low probability event has occurred, then much information has been conveyed. However, entropy is the average information per symbol. Since the likelihood of a very low probability event's occurring is low, then the low probability event does not contribute substantially to the entropy. In the limit, as $P$ approaches zero, it does not contribute at all.

This result can be generalized. Suppose a source transmits $K$ symbols. The entropy is given by Eq. 9-8. What should be the values of the $P_k$ if $H$ is to be maximized? It can be shown that $H$ is maximized when all $P_k$ are equal, that is,

$$P_0 = P_1 = P_2 = \ldots = P_k = \frac{1}{K}$$

$$H_{max} = -\log \frac{1}{K} = \log K \qquad (9-10)$$

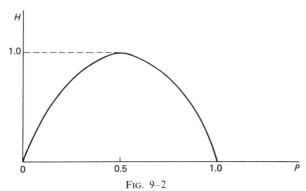

FIG. 9-2

Plot of entropy for a system with two possible events. The probability
of one event is $P$

**Conditional Entropy.** We have assumed that the probability of an event's occurring was not related to the occurrence of a previous event, that is, each event is unrelated. However, this is often not the case. Consider an information source which produces English text. If we have no other information, the probability that the next letter be a $U$ is approximately 0.02 On the other hand, if the preceding letter is a $Q$, the probability that the next letter be a $U$ is 1.0. In such cases, it is conventional to define a *conditional entropy* as

$$H_c = - \sum_{i=1}^{M} \sum_{j=1}^{M} P(i) P(j|i) \log_2 P(j|i) \tag{9-11}$$

where $P(i)$ is the probability of the occurrence of the $i$th symbol and $P(j|i)$ is the probability of occurrence of the $j$th symbol if it is known that the $i$th symbol has just occurred; e.g., $P(A)$ is the probability of an $A$, $P(U|Q)$ is the probability that a $u$ occurs after a $q$, etc.

The relation between the conditional entropy $H_c$ and the entropy $H$ of a source gives some measure of the *redundance* of the source, where redundance is a measure of the repetitiveness of the content. The $U$ following a $Q$ supplies no information because we know that it must occur.

Suppose we could predict each letter from the preceding one. Then (see Eq. 9–11) $H_c$ would be zero. Of course, then, each message sequence could be predicted from its first letter. In general, because of redundance,

$$H_c \leq H \tag{9-12}$$

The equality will only result when the symbols are independent; in this case, $P(j|i) = P(j)$ and Eq. 9–11 becomes

$$H_c = - \sum_{i=1}^{M} \sum_{j=1}^{M} P(i) P(j) \log_2 P(j) \tag{9-13}$$

But (see Eq. 8–14)

$$\sum_{i=1}^{M} P(i) = 1 \tag{9-14}$$

Hence,

$$H_c = \sum_{j=1}^{M} P(j) \log_2 P(j) = H \tag{9-15}$$

If $H = H_c$, a system is completely *nonredundant*, that is, no symbol can be predicted from the preceding one. In a sense, redundance implies inefficiency since more symbols must be transmitted than are needed. However, it can also be an advantage, since, in a redundant system, messages can be understood even if errors occur. For example, TYE BYOK IS OB TME TABLY can easily be understood as THE BOOK IS ON THE TABLE. In fact, we shall see that redundance can be used to transmit messages reliably in the presence of noise, regardless of how small the signal-to-noise ratio is.

Some measure of the redundancy of a system is given by $H_c/H$, which is called the *relative entropy*. In addition, we mathematically define *redundancy* as

$$\mathcal{R} = 1 - \frac{H_c}{H} \qquad (9\text{--}16)$$

(Note that in a nonredundant system $\mathcal{R} = 0$.)

We have assumed that the probability of one symbol's occurring depends only upon the previous symbol, i.e., a Markov process. These results can be extended to systems where the joint probabilities depend upon two or more of the previous characters.

These results can be applied to continuous systems in a variety of ways. One way is to *quantitize* a continuous signal that is, to represent it by a set of discrete levels, e.g., if $0 \leq f(t) \leq 0.1$, $f = 0$; if $0.1 < f(t) \leq 0.2$, $f = 0.1$; The system is now discrete so the previous results can be used. In the limit, as we approach an infinite number of levels, the approximation becomes exact. Continuous systems will be discussed subsequently.

## 9-2. CHANNEL CAPACITY

In this section we shall consider the rate at which information can be transmitted and discuss some results which are fundamental to the transmission of information.

We shall first study the rate of transmission of information. Suppose an information source has an entropy $H$, that is, on the average, each symbol transmits $H$ bits of information. Now suppose, on the average, the source produces $r$ symbols per second. We state that the *entropy rate $H_r$* of the information source is

$$H_r = rH \text{ bits/sec.} \qquad (9\text{--}17)$$

We are, in general, concerned with the transmission from an information source to an information receiver. In a radio signal, the information source may be the announcer speaking into the microphone. The information receiver is the listener. The source and receiver are connected by a *communication channel*, or simply, *channel*. In radio transmission, the channel could consist of the microphone, radio transmitter, sending antenna, space between antennas, receiving antenna, radio receiver, and loudspeaker. Often, we shall concentrate our attention on only one part of the channel.

Let us consider an example of transmission. Suppose we have an alphabet consisting of three symbols $A$, $B$, and $C$. We can transmit these in various ways. Suppose we transmit a sequence of pulses so that each pulse is transmitted at 1 second intervals from some specified starting time $t = 0$. (The pulse duration is much shorter than 1 second.) If a pulse is present, at the integral second, we call this a "1". If, on the integral second time, the pulse is absent, we call this a "0." Now suppose we use the following code: transmit 0 for *A*, 10 for *B*, and 11 for *C*. Then, the sequence *BAC* would be 10011. Such a sequence of pulses is shown in Fig. 9–3. The information source produces symbols, e.g., *A*, *B*, *C*. The pulses used in the code are called *binary digits* or *pulses*. Note the distinction between the words symbols, and binary digits or pulses.

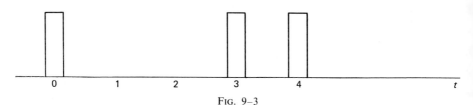

Fig. 9–3

A sequence of pulses which transmite the pulse sequence 10011

An alternative form of coding would be to transmit pulses of different amplitudes for *A*, *B*, or *C*. For instance, *A* could be represented by a 1 volt pulse, *B* by a 2 volt pulse, and *C* by a 3 volt pulse.

In these examples, the pulses arrive once per second, which is a very slow rate. Usually, pulses are transmitted at much faster rates. The number of binary digits per second is called the *pulse rate*. The faster the pulse rate, the faster will be the entropy rate; i.e., the bits per second that can be transmitted. The maximum pulse rate is limited by the bandwidth of a channel over which the pulses are transmitted.

Let us consider an ideal case. Assume that a channel has a transfer function

$$(j\omega) = \begin{cases} 1, & -2\pi B \leqq \omega \leqq 2\pi B \\ 0, & |\omega| > 2\pi B \end{cases} \tag{9-18}$$

That is, the system has the characteristics of an ideal low pass filter of bandwidth *B*. Before proceding, let us clarify some notation. $\boldsymbol{H}(j\omega)$ is used as the transfer function of a device while *H* is the entropy of a source. These notations are the conventional ones to use. There should be no confusion since the transfer function will always have the $(j\omega)$ present while the entropy will not. The transfer function will also be written in boldface type, and the entropy will be in italic type.

Now let us consider the bandlimited channel and see how it limits the rate at which pulses are transmitted. The ideal low pass filter will cause the pulses to become rounded and spread in time. If the pulses are not sufficiently separated, they will overlap. If the overlap is severe, we cannot determine if a pulse is present or absent when the coding scheme of Fig. 9–3 is used. If the amplitude of the pulse is used to transmit the information, then the overlap can obscure the level of the pulses.

Let us determine the maximum rate of transmission of the pulses *r* in terms of the bandwidth $B$, which allows detection of pulses without error. For example, $r$ must be small enough so that we can distinguish whether successive pulses are 0s or 1s. We shall use Shannon's sampling theorem to do this. This theorem (see Section 2-17) states that, if a system is bandlimited with bandwidth $2\pi B = \omega_a$, then its output $f(t)$ can be completely specified by sampling $f(t)$ at points spaced

$$t = \frac{\pi}{\omega_a} = \frac{1}{2B} \text{ sec.} \tag{9-19}$$

apart. Alternatively, this theorem indicates that we can specify a signal of bandwidth $B$ at points $1/2B$ seconds apart and the resulting signal will pass through these points. In order to obtain rectangular pulses as shown in Fig. 9–3, we require infinite bandwidth. However, if we bandlimit a signal, then we can make it pass through a set of points $t = \pi/\omega_a$ seconds apart (see Eq. 2–319). If a system has bandwidth $B$, we can always transmit a signal through it such that at points $1/2B$ seconds apart, the output will be the correct; i.e., 0 or 1. Suppose we want to transmit the sequence of pulses of Fig. 9–3. The output of a bandlimited channel, where $2B = 1$, would be such that, at $t = 0$, the output will be 1; at $t = 1$ and $t = 2$, the output will be 0; and at $t = 3$ and $t = 4$, the output will be 1. In general, the pulses will be rounded and there will be oscillation about the 0 axis, but at $t = 0, 1, 2, 3,$ and 4, the output will be correct. This is illustrated in Fig. 9–4.

We shall state that the bandwidth must be such that we can specify the amplitude exactly at the center of each pulse. Thus, the time between pulses $T$ must be equal to or greater than that given by Eq. 9–19; hence,

$$T \geq \frac{1}{2B} \tag{9-20}$$

Conversely, the rate of repetition of pulses $r = 1/T$ must be such that

$$r \leq 2B \tag{9-21}$$

Thus, *if a channel has an ideal bandwidth $B$, then pulses can be transmitted at a rate $r \leq 2B$. The rate cannot exceed $2B$ if there are to be no errors.* If $r$ is only slightly greater than $2B$, then most pulses will be received correctly. This equation was first

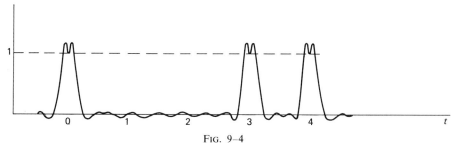

FIG. 9–4
Sequence of pulses after they have passed through a bandlimited system where $B \geq 1/2$

developed by H. Nyquist. Thus, we see that the channel can limit the rate at which information is transmitted.

**Channel Capacity.** Channel capacity is the maximum rate at which information can be transmitted through a channel. Suppose we can determine the total number of messages which can be transmitted *without error* through a channel in time $T$. Let us call this $N(T)$. Then the channel capacity $C$ is defined as

$$C = \lim_{T \to \infty} \frac{1}{T} \log_2 N(T) \text{ bits/sec.} \tag{9-22}$$

We let $T$ become arbitrarily large to obtain a representative average.

Let us consider an example which illustrates an alternative interpretation of channel capacity. Suppose we have an information source which produces $n$ symbols at an arbitrary rate. We wish to test the channel to see what maximum entropy rate can be achieved at its output. The transmission is to be without errors. We shall adjust the probabilities of the symbols so that the entropy of the information source is maximized. This is done so that a low entropy rate of the source is not charged to the channel. To do this (see Eq. 9–10), the probability of each symbol should be equal and given by $P = 1/n$. Thus, the entropy of the source is given by

$$H = -\log_2 \frac{1}{n} = \log_2 n \tag{9-23}$$

Now assume that the channel has a bandwidth $B$, $-B < \omega < B$. Then (see Eq. 9–21) the maximum rate at which pulses can be transmitted through the channel is $r$ pulses per second where

$$r = 2B \tag{9-24}$$

Let us assume that we require only one pulse to transmit each symbol. For instance, the amplitude of a pulse can represent the symbol. Thus, the maximum entropy rate at the output of the channel is

$$H_{r,max} = 2B \log_2 n \tag{9-25}$$

Now let us compute the channel capacity of a channel of bandwidth $B$. In time $T$, the source can produce $rT$ symbols. Assume that each symbol is represented by one pulse. Since there are $n$ different symbols, the number of different messages that can be sent in time $T$ is

$$N(T) = n^{rT} \tag{9-26}$$

(We can transmit $r$ pulses per second.) If noise were present, $N(T)$ would be less than $n^{rT}$, since some of the messages would be received with errors. Hence, they would not be counted in $N(T)$. Thus, in the noiseless case the channel capacity is given by

$$C = \lim_{T \to \infty} \frac{1}{T} \log_2 n^{rT} = \lim_{T \to \infty} r \log_2 n \tag{9-27}$$

Substituting Eq. 9–24, we have

$$C = 2B \log_2 n \qquad (9\text{--}28)$$

Comparing this with Eq. 9–25, we obtain

$$C = H_{r,max} \qquad (9\text{--}29)$$

Thus, this channel capacity is equal to the maximum entropy rate that can be transmitted through a channel. That is, if the channel is supplied with an information source which has the following properties: (1) it can produce symbols at an arbitrary rate and (2) the symbol probabilities are such that its entropy is maximized. Then the channel capacity is the maximum entropy rate which can be transmitted over the channel. For this example we encoded the signal using the amplitude of the pulses. Actually, coding procedures exist such that we can encode using binary digits and still transmit at the maximum rate, see Section 9-3.

Now suppose we have a communication channel whose channel capacity is $C$ and we wish to transmit information over this channel using an information source with information rate $H_r$. If the information source transmits at a $r$ symbols/second, which is greater than that defined by Eq. 9–21, errors will result. In general, the faster $r$ is, the greater will be the number of errors. However, we can use encoding to improve the situation. It will be discussed in the next section that an encoding scheme always exists which can be used to transmit messages over a channel with an arbitrarily small frequency of errors providing

$$H_r \leqq C \qquad (9\text{--}30)$$

That is, *an information source of information rate $H_r$ can always be encoded in such a way that the information can be transmitted over a channel of capacity C with arbitrarily small error provided that $H_r \leqq C$. If $H_r > C$, then some errors will always result.* This is a fundamental theorem concerned with the transmission of information and is valid even if a channel introduces noise. However, noise can reduce channel capacity. We shall discuss this theorem in greater detail in subsequent sections. We have not considered noise, to any great extent, in this section. In the next one we shall again consider noise free channels and then, in subsequent sections, shall finally discuss the effects of noise and procedures for reducing these effects.

The pulses we have considered need not be exactly as pictured in Fig. 9–3 or 9–4. When radio transmission is used, pulses are transmitted using amplitude, frequency, or phase modulation.

Other coding schemes besides the presence or absence of a pulse exist. For instance one of two different sinusoidal frequencies may be transmitted. One of these could correspond to a 0, and the other, to a 1. The basic ideas of information transmission apply no matter what transmission system is used. For example, let a 0 be represented by a 1000 Hz sinusoid, and a 1, by a 1200 Hz sinusoid. If we switch rapidly from 0s to 1s, more than 200 Hz of bandwidth is required. If this is not available, then it will not be possible to properly identify the sinusoids.

## 9-3. ENCODING

When information is transmitted over a channel, the transmission should result in a minimum number of errors and utilize a minimum amount of time. Information is usually coded in some form before it is transmitted. The coding can take many forms. For instance, telegraph signals are transmitted using Morse code. Here pulses and spaces of different lengths are transmitted. In a simple audio amplifier, sound pressure is encoded into voltage, where the voltage is proportional to the sound pressure. More complex coding schemes also exist. Some basic ideas of these coding procedures were discussed in the last chapter. That is, each symbol from the information source can be represented by a sequence of binary digits (zeros or ones). Remember that our termonology is: the information source produces symbols (i.e., *A*, *B*, *C*, ...) while the binary digits are zeros or ones. Each symbol may be represented by more than one binary digit. This form of coding can be used not only to represent discrete things such as an alphabet but also continuous quantities. For instance, consider a continuous $f(t)$ which is sampled at discrete times $t_0$ apart. Then, we have a sequence of points $f_0, f_1, f_2, ...,$ where

$$f_k = f(kt_0) \tag{9-31}$$

Now we quantize these levels. That is, suppose we set up a set of $N$ discrete levels $g_0, g_1, g_2, ..., g_N$, where

$$g_n = nK \tag{9-32}$$

and $K$ is a constant. If the input signal $f(t)$ is a voltage which varies between 0 and 1 volt, then $N$ could be 101 and $K$ would be 0.01 volt, so that the $g_N$ are 0, 0.01, 0.02,..., 0.99, 1.00 volt, respectively. The input signal is then quantized; that is, if $nK \leq f_k \leq (n+1)K$, then $f_k$ is replaced by $g_n$. If a sample is 0.516 volt, it is quantized as 0.51. Thus, the voltage $f(t)$ can now be represented by an alphabet of 101 characters. This alphabet can be encoded, transmitted, and decoded.

There are many reasons why we use codes. For one thing, coding enables us to transmit signals over a channel at close to the maximum rate. The number of errors due to noise can often be made arbitrarily small by the proper use of coding. In some communication systems, a signal must be amplified by many amplifiers. For instance, in a transcontinental telephone system, there are amplifiers placed about every 50 miles. These amplifiers introduce nonlinear distortion. The cumulative distortion produced by these amplifiers can be severe; however, if we transmit binary digits, we are only interested in the presence or absence of a signal. Thus, the nonlinear distortion will not affect the signal. Excellent telephone and television signals have been transmitted using these coding procedures.

Let us now discuss the encoding and decoding of a set of symbols. Suppose we have an alphabet of three symbols, *A*, *B*, and *C*, and we use the following code:

For $A$ we transmit 0, for $B$ we transmit 1, and for $C$ we transmit 10. This code is not a good one since a code must be decodable. In general, long sequences of symbols will be transmitted. We should be able to decode continuously. Suppose we receive the sequence 101010.... This could be the sequence $C\ C\ C$ or $BABABA$. A device which produces the code is called an *encoder* and a device which reconstructs the symbols from the code is called a *decoder*. If a code is such that the message can be uniquely recovered by a decoder, then the coder or code is said to be *nonsingular*, otherwise it is *singular*.

Now consider a nonsingular code. Suppose we use the following code

| Symbol | Code | |
|--------|------|---|
| A | 0 | |
| B | 10 | |
| C | 11 | (9–33) |

Now consider a sequence 01011100011. The first letter must be an $A$, since no other code symbol starts with 0. The next letter must be a $B$, since any code starting with 1 must be either 10 or 11. Similarly, the next letter must be a $C$, etc. Then, the sequence we have is $ABCBAAC$.

We must consider a general procedure for obtaining nonsingular codes. However, before we do so, let us discuss another idea which will influence the selection of these codes. In the above code, only one binary digit is required to transmit an $A$, while two binary digits are required to transmit a $B$ or a $C$. Suppose the probability of an $A$ occurring is much greater than that of a $B$ or a $C$; e.g., $P(A) = 0.8$, $P(B) = 0.1$, $P(C) = 0.1$. Then, in an average message, a minimal number of binary digits would be used, since the most probable symbol $A$ is represented by the fewest binary digits. On the other hand, if $P(A) = 0.1$, $P(B) = 0.4$, and $P(C) = 0.5$, the average message would use many more binary digits since the symbol with the lowest probability is assigned the least number of binary digits. Note that in Morse code, the letter $E$, which has the greatest probability of occurring, is given the shortest code, a single dot, while those letters which occur infrequently are given long codes.

To express these ideas mathematically, let us determine the average number of binary digits (i.e., zeros or ones) required to transmit a symbol. The average is weighted in accordance with the probability of occurrence of the symbol. This average is given by

$$A_c = \sum_{i=1}^{N} P(i) N_B(i) \qquad (9-34)$$

where $P(i)$ is the probability of occurrence of the $i$th symbol and $N_B(i)$ is the number of binary digits representing the $i$th symbol. In the code of Eq. 9–33, if $P(A) = 0.8$, $P(B) = 0.1$, and $P(C) = 0.1$, then

$$A_c = 0.8(1) + 0.1(2) + 0.1(2) = 1.2 \text{ binary digits/symbol}$$

On the other hand, if $P(A) = 0.1$, $P(B) = 0.4$, and $P(C) = 0.5$, then

$$A_c = (.1)\,1 + 0.4(2) + 0.5(2) = 1.9 \text{ binary digits/symbol}$$

Then, to minimize the number of binary digits transmitted, we must consider the probabilities of occurrence of the symbols. Since the bandwidth limits the maximum rate of transmission of binary digits, we desire to make $A_c$ as small as possible.

**Fano's Procedure for Encoding.** We shall now discuss a method developed by R.M. Fano, which forms a nonsingular code and assigns the least number of binary digits to the high probability symbols. Suppose we have characters $x_1, x_2, x_3,..., x_N$ with respective probabilities $P_1, P_2,..., P_N$ that we wish to encode. Let us assume that these characters have been numbered in order of their probabilities, that is,

$$P_1 \geq P_2 \geq ... \geq P_N \tag{9-35}$$

Now divide the symbols into two groups. Let the first group consist of $x_1, x_2,..., x_K$ and the second group of $x_{K+1}, x_{K+2},..., x_N$. The choice of $K$ should be such that

$$P_1 + P_2 + \cdots + P_K \approx P_{K+1} + P_{K+2} + \cdots + P_N \tag{9-36}$$

That is, we divide the group into two groups of approximately equal probabilities. Then, assign a 0 to each symbol of the first group and a 1 to each symbol of the second. Repeat the procedure using the first group as a new group and do the same with the second group. Repeat this procedure until each symbol is given a unique code.

Let us illustrate this procedure. To be concise we shall do this in tabular form. Suppose we have 10 symbols $x_1, x_2,..., x_{10}$ with the probabilities shown in Table 9-1.

TABLE 9-1.

| Symbol | Proba-bility | first step | second step | third step | fourth step | fifth step | sixth step = code |
|---|---|---|---|---|---|---|---|
| $x_1$ | 0.49 | $a\underline{0}$ | $\underline{0}$ | $\underline{0}$ | $\underline{0}$ | $\underline{0}$ | $\underline{0}$ |
| $x_2$ | 0.15 | 1 | 10 | $c_1\underline{100}$ | 100 | 100 | 100 |
| $x_3$ | 0.15 | 1 | $b\underline{10}$ | 101 | 101 | 101 | 101 |
| $x_4$ | 0.06 | 1 | 11 | 110 | $d_1\underline{1100}$ | 1100 | 1100 |
| $x_5$ | 0.06 | 1 | 11 | $c_2\underline{110}$ | 1101 | 1101 | 1101 |
| $x_6$ | 0.03 | 1 | 11 | 111 | 1110 | $e_1\underline{11100}$ | 11100 |
| $x_7$ | 0.02 | 1 | 11 | 111 | $d_2\underline{1110}$ | 11101 | 11101 |
| $x_8$ | 0.02 | 1 | 11 | 111 | 1111 | 11110 | 11110 |
| $x_9$ | 0.015 | 1 | 11 | 111 | 1111 | 11111 | 111110 |
| $x_{10}$ | 0.005 | 1 | 11 | 111 | 1111 | 11111 | 111111 |

The first step of the procedure is shown in the third column. Here $x_1$ is put into the first group and the remaining symbols in the second group. The first group is assigned a 0, while the second is assigned a 1. The groups are divided at $a$, where a horizontal line is drawn. Now we perform the second step. The first group cannot be subdivided further. Thus, no new binary digits are assigned to it.

The second group is divided at $b$, and 0 and 1 are assigned, as before. This is indicated in the fourth column. Note that the new and old division lines are drawn here. The third step is indicated in the fifth column. The first part of the second group (i.e., $x_2$, and $x_3$) is divided into two parts at $c_1$, and 0 and 1 are assigned. Similarly, the second group (i.e., $x_4$ through $x_{10}$) is divided at $c_2$, and 0 and 1 are assigned, as before.

The process is repeated in the sixth through eighth columns. The divisions are indicated by the horizontal lines. Note that once a sequence of binary digits is divided so that each of its numbers is isolated above and below by horizontal lines, it is no longer worked with. When all groups of binary digits have been separated by horizontal lines, the procedure stops. The final code is given by the last column. For example, $x_1$ is represented by 0, $x_3$ by 101, $x_7$ by 11101, and $x_{10}$ by 111111. Each symbol is given a different sequence of binary digits and the low probability symbols receive more binary digits than the high probability ones.

The code derived by Fano's procedure is a nonsingular one. Consider $x_{10}$. The only way that a sequence of six 1s can be generated is by $x_{10}$. No sequence of symbols can generate six 1s in sequence. Thus, if six 1s appear, regardless of what appears before or after them, $x_{10}$ must have been transmitted. Similarly, consider $x_9$. If a sequence of five 1s is followed by a zero, there is no ambiguity as to the 0, it must belong with the five 1s. Again no sequence of symbols (excluding $x_9$) can generate 111110. Proceding in this way, we can show that each symbol can be uniquely decoded. This procedure has been illustrated with ten symbols, but it can be applied to any number of symbols.

**Multiple Symbol Coding.**    Fano's procedure is desirable for encoding symbols. However, we can extend it so that the average number of binary digits per symbol is reduced. This can be accomplished by encoding groups of symbols rather than just one symbol at a time. Suppose we have a two-symbol alphabet. We can encode just the two symbols $A$ and $B$. However, we can also consider all possible pairs of letters. That is, any message could be sent by sending these pairs, $AA$ $AB$ $BA$ $BB$. Now there are four characters, each one of these can be encoded. Let us show that the average number of binary digits per symbol is reduced by this process. The case will be illustrated in Tables 9-2 and 9-3, respectively.

TABLE 9-2

| Symbol | Probability | Code |
|--------|-------------|------|
| $A$ | 0.8 | 0 |
| $B$ | 0.2 | 1 |

Then (see Eq. 9–34)

$$A_c = 0.8(1) + 0.2(1) = 1 \text{ binary digit/symbol}$$

Thus, we transmit one binary digit for each symbol. Now let us consider the case of the groups of two symbols.

In this case, the average number of binary digits per pair of symbols is

$$A_c = 0.64(1) + 0.16(2) + 0.16(3) + 0.04(3) = 1.56 \text{ binary digit/symbol pair}$$

TABLE 9-3

| Multiple Symbol | Probability | Code |
|:---:|:---:|:---:|
| *AA* | 0.64 | 0 |
| *AB* | 0.16 | 10 |
| *BA* | 0.16 | 110 |
| *BB* | 0.04 | 111 |

Two single symbols are transmitted each time a binary digit code is sent; i.e., 10 transmits both *A* and *B*. Thus, the number of binary digits per single symbol is given by

$$A_{c2} = \frac{A_c}{2} = 0.78 \text{ binary digits/symbol}$$

The subscript 2 indicates that the symbols are encoded in groups of 2. Thus, by encoding groups of symbols, we have reduced the number of binary digits per symbol from 1 to 0.78.

We can extend this further. For example, we can consider groups of three symbols i.e., *AAA*, *AAB*, *ABA*, *ABB*, *BAA*, *BAB*, *BBA*, and *BBB*. Computation of the code indicates that this further reduces the number of binary digits per symbol. Formation of this code will be left as an exercise for the reader.

In general, as the number of symbols in the group increases, the number of binary digits per symbol decreases. It can be shown that if the entropy of the source is $H$, then the minimum value of $A_{cn}$ (i.e., the average binary digits/symbol with groups of $n$ symbols) is $H$; that is,

$$A_{cn} \geqq H \qquad (9\text{-}37\text{a})$$

In addition as $n$, the number of symbols in a group, increases, $A_{cn}$ approaches $H$; thus,

$$\lim_{n \to \infty} A_{cn} = H \qquad (9\text{-}37\text{b})$$

It is desirable to make $A_{cn}$ as small as possible. Thus, we define an efficiency of a code as the ratio of $H$ to $A_{cn}$; hence,

$$\eta_c = \frac{H}{A_{cn}} \times 100 \text{ percent} \qquad (9\text{-}38)$$

For example, for the signal source of Table 9-3,

$$H = -0.8 \log_2 0.8 - 0.2 \log_2 0.2 = 0.722.$$

Thus, for the single group $\eta_c = (0.722/1) = 72.2$ percent, while for the two group code $\eta_c = (0.722/0.78) = 92.6$ percent. In general, as $n$ approaches infinity, $\eta_c$ approaches 100 percent.

In order to encode groups of symbols, the encoder must be able to store the symbols until an entire group is received. This increases the complexity of an encoder and also delays the transmission of symbols. For instance, suppose 20 symbols are encoded in each group. All 20 symbols must be entered and stored before they can be transmitted. If multiple symbol encoding were not used, then each symbol could be transmitted immediately. Thus, it may not be desirable to multiple encode very

many symbols in a group. In the previous example, encoding in groups of two resulted in a coding efficiency of 92.6 percent. It may not pay to increase the size of the
group further since very little increase in efficiency can be obtained.

In the last section we considered a fundamental theorem which states that if the
entropy rate $H_r$ of a source is equal to or less than the channel capacity $C$, we can
transmit with an arbitrarily small number of errors. In addition, the theorem states
that if $H > C$, we cannot transmit without error. Let us derive these results using
encoding. These statements will not constitute a rigorous proof but will provide a
physical basis for the fundamental theorem.

Suppose are transmitting with binary digits and have no way of determining
beforehand if the next pulse will be a 0 or 1. Thus, the probability of the occurrence
of a binary digit is 0.5, since there are only two possible choices. Thus, each binary
digit transmits one bit. Therefore, if the average number of binary digits per symbol
of the code is $A_{cn}$, then the number of symbols (*not* binary digits) per second, which
can be transmitted through a channel of capacity $C$ bits/sec, is

$$r_c = \frac{C}{A_{cn}} \text{ symbols/sec} \tag{9-39}$$

Note that each binary digit transmits one bit of information. Then, in a channel with a
capacity of $C$ bits/sec., the rate of transmission of symbols must be $C$ divided by
the (average) number of binary digits per symbol.

Now the source has an entropy rate of $H_r$ bits/sec and an entropy of $H$ bits/
symbol, hence, it produces

$$r = \frac{H_r}{H} \text{ symbols/sec} \tag{9-40}$$

If the channel transmits without error, then

$$r_c \geq r \tag{9-41}$$

We assume that

$$C \geq H_r \tag{9-42}$$

Then, Relation 9-41 can always be satisfied if a code exists such that $A_{cn} = H$.
In our previous discussion of coding, we stated that (see Eq. 9-37b)

$$\lim_{n \to \infty} A_{cn} = H \tag{9-43}$$

Thus, a code such that $A_{cn} = H$ does exist. Hence, Relation 9-41 can be satisfied
and we can transmit with no error. Note that if $C > H_r$, then Relation 9-41 can
be satisfied using $A_{cn} > H$. In this case, encoding groups of an infinite number
of symbols is not necessary. On the other hand, if $C = H_r$, we must encode groups
of infinite size to transmit with zero error. Of course, this is theoretically possible,
but practically it can only be approached. Now suppose

$$H_r \geq C \tag{9-44}$$

Since $A_{cn} \geq H$, we have (see Eqs. 9–39 and 9–40)

$$r > r_c \tag{9-45}$$

Thus, we must transmit at a rate faster than that which can be accepted by the channel, so some error must result. Thus, we have demonstrated the fundamental theorem.

## 9-4. TRANSMISSION OF INFORMATION OVER NOISY CHANNELS—NOISE REDUCING CODES

In this section we shall discuss the transmission of information over channels which introduce noise. We shall consider how the noise probability density affects error rate. It will be shown that, regardless of the signal-to-noise ratio, we can always encode in such a way that the transmitted information can be received with an arbitrarily small rate of error.

Suppose we encode information as a sequence of binary digits (see Section 9-3). If the channel is noisy, then the received signal may not be the same as the transmitted one. For instance, noise may cause a transmitted "1" to be received as a "0" or vice versa. In general, if we encode using Fano's procedure, any sequence of 1s and 0s can be decoded into a message. Thus, if any binary digit is in error, the received message will be in error.

Let us represent the effect of noise quantitatively. To do this we introduce a *foward transition probability matrix:*

$$\hat{P}^+ = [P_{ij}^+] \tag{9-46}$$

where $P_{ij}^+$ represents the probability that if the input symbol to a channel is $x_i$, then the output will be $x_j$. (The subscripts $i$ and $j$ also indicate the row and column of $P_{ij}^+$ in the matrix.)

Suppose we have three symbols $x_1$, $x_2$, and $x_3$. Then, in a noiseless channel,

$$\hat{P}^+ = \begin{bmatrix} 1 & 0 & 0 \\ 0 & 1 & 0 \\ 0 & 0 & 1 \end{bmatrix} \tag{9-47}$$

That is, if $x_j$ is transmitted, then $x_j$ and nothing else will be received. In a noisy channel, we might have

$$\hat{P}^+ = \begin{bmatrix} 0.9 & 0.05 & 0.05 \\ 0.1 & 0.8 & 0.1 \\ 0.1 & 0.2 & 0.7 \end{bmatrix} \tag{9-48}$$

In this case, if $x_1$ is transmitted, the probability is 0.9 that it will be correctly received, 0.05 that it will be received as $x_2$, and 0.05 that it will be received as $x_3$. Similarly, if $x_3$ is transmitted, the probability is 0.7 that it will be received correctly, 0.2 that it will be received as $x_2$, and 0.1 that it will be received as $x_1$. This is diagrammatically illustrated in Fig. 9–5.

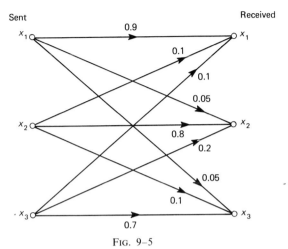

FIG. 9–5
Diagrammatic representation of the matrix of Eq. 9–48

We can consider the probability from an alternative viewpoint. Suppose an $x_3$ is received at the channel output, what is the probability that an $x_3$ (or $x_2$ or $x_1$) is the channel input? To represent this we can introduce a *reverse transition probability matrix*.

$$\hat{P}^- = [P_{ij}^-] \qquad (9\text{–}49)$$

where $P_{ij}^-$ represents the probability that $x_j$ is transmitted if $x_i$ is received. Either Eq. 9–46 or 9–49 can be used to characterize the noisy channel. Note that, in each case, if the channel is noiseless (and $H_r < C$), then all symbols will be transmitted with zero error and

$$\hat{P}^+ = \hat{P}^- = \hat{U} \qquad (9\text{–}50)$$

where $\hat{U}$ is the unit matrix.

Let us determine the matrix $P^+$ when a system is transmitting binary digits. For simplification, let us consider a transition probability matrix of the binary digits (not the symbols):

$$\hat{B}^+ = \begin{bmatrix} B_{00}^+ & B_{01}^+ \\ B_{10}^+ & B_{11}^+ \end{bmatrix} \qquad (9\text{–}51)$$

where $B_{ij}^+$ is the probability that if an $i$ is sent, a $j$ will be received. For example, $P_{01}$ is the probability that if a 0 is sent, a 1 will be received.

Suppose we have a narrow band channel which is perturbed by Gaussian noise. We shall assume that the signals are detected by an amplitude-modulated detector so that all the signals are positive and the noise output has a Rayleigh distribution (see Section 8-6).

In the ideal case, if there is no noise, a "0" would be received as 0 volt, while a "1" would be received as $X_1$ volts, where $X_1$ is some arbitrary reference value. In the noisy case, we do not have any ideal situation, hence we adjust the detector so that a 0 is received if the signal at the appropriate time of detection is between 0 and $(1/2) X_1$ volts and a 1 is received if the output is greater than $(1/2) X_1$ volts. The output noise signal will have a probability distribution given by (see Eq. 8–165)

$$p(x) = \frac{xe^{-x^2/2N_0}}{N_0} \tag{9-52}$$

where $N_0$ is the total noise power.

Now let us assume that a 0 is transmitted, and determine the probability that it be received correctly. If the 0 is received correctly, then the output voltage must be between 0 and $(1/2) X_1$ volts, thus,

$$B_{00}^+ = \frac{1}{N_0} \int_0^{X_1/2} xe^{-x^2/2N_0}\, dx \tag{9-53}$$

Let $y = x^2/2N_0$. Substituting, we obtain

$$B_{00}^+ = \int_0^{(1/8)X_1^2/N_0} e^{-y}\, dy = 1 - e^{-(1/8)X_1^2/N_0} \tag{9-54}$$

The probability that a transmitted 0 be received as a 1 is

$$B_{01}^+ = \frac{1}{N_0} \int_{(1/2)X_1}^{\infty} e^{-x^2/2N_0}\, dx \tag{9-55}$$

Substituting as in Eq. 9–54, we have

$$B_{01}^+ = \int_{(1/8)X_1^2/N_0}^{\infty} e^{-y}\, dy = e^{-(1/8)X_1^2/N_0} \tag{9-56}$$

The probability of transmitting and receiving a 1 will now be considered. At first glance, it may appear as though a 1 could never be received in error since the noise output is always positive. Hence, it always seems to make the positive output signal larger. However, this is *not* the case. We assume that the output of an amplitude-modulated detector is the envelope of modulation of an amplitude-modulated sinusoid (see Section 8-6). The sinusoid is an alternating signal. A typical amplitude-modulated sinusoid transmitting 1s and 0s is shown in Fig. 9–6. Before detection, the noise can take on positive and negative values. Thus, at times, a noise component will add to the envelope while, at other times, it will subtract from it. Hence, any noise signal whose output magnitude is greater than $(1/2) X_1$ can potentially produce an error. We shall consider a worst possible case and assume that any output noise signal greater in magnitude than $(1/2) X_1$ will produce an

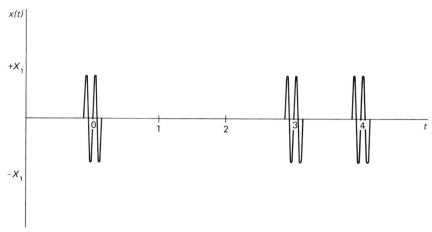

FIG. 9–6
Amplitude-modulated signal transmitting the sequence 10011

error. In this case, the probability that an error results when a 1 is transmitted is
the same as that for an error resulting when a 0 is transmitted, therefore,

$$B_{10}^+ = B_{01}^+ \tag{9–57}$$

Hence,

$$B_{11}^+ = B_{0}^+ \tag{9–58}$$

Thus, the foward transition probability matrix is

$$\hat{B}^+ = \begin{bmatrix} 1 - e^{-X_1^2/(8N_0)} & e^{-X_1^2/(8N_0)} \\ e^{-X_1^2/(8N_0)} & 1 - e^{-X_1^2/(8N_0)} \end{bmatrix} \tag{9–59a}$$

Let us interpret this physically. Since $X_1$ represents the maximum sinusoidal signal,
the power is $X_1^2/2$. Let us assume that the binary pulses occupy one half of the time.
That is, if a continuous sequence of 1's are transmitted, then the average power
would be $X_1^2/4$. On the average, half the pulses transmitted are 0's. In this case,
the average signal power is $S = X_1^2/8$. Thus, Eq. 9–59 can be written as

$$\hat{B} = \begin{bmatrix} 1 - e^{-S/N_0} & e^{-S/N_0} \\ e^{-S/N_0} & 1 - e^{-S/N_0} \end{bmatrix} \tag{9–59b}$$

Therefore, the probability of error falls off as the exponential of the signal-to-noise ratio. Hence, the frequency of errors decreases rapidly as the signal-to-noise ratio increases.

**Reduction of the Effects of Noise.** We shall now consider a procedure whereby the error due to noise can be reduced to arbitrarily small values. Let us assume that we are transmitting binary digits and have a transition probability matrix

$$\hat{B} = \begin{bmatrix} 1-q & q \\ q & 1-q \end{bmatrix} \tag{9-60}$$

For simplicity, we have made the error probability of a 0 and that of a 1 both equal to $q$. Now let us show that the value of $q$ will be less than 0.5.

$$q < 0.5 \tag{9-61}$$

If the signal-to-noise ratio approaches zero, then 1s and 0s will be generated in a random fashion. In this case, the probability of error will be exactly one half. That is, we would not need the communication channel, but could just guess if a 1 or 0 had been transmitted. Since 0s and 1s occur with equal probability, our guess would be (on the average) correct half the time. Since the signal-to-noise ratio will be greater than zero, $q$ must be greater than 0.5.

Let us introduce redundancy (see Section 9-1). Suppose we repeat each binary digit an odd number of times. As an example, assume that each binary digit is repeated 5 times. Then, the sequence 10110100 would be sent as

$$1111100000111111111100000111110000000000$$

The receiver inspects each group of five binary digits and uses a majority rule to determine which signal has been sent. That is, if a majority (three or more) of the received binary symbols is 1's, the receiver indicates that a 1 has been transmitted. This is called a *received binary digit*. Similarly, if a majority of symbols is 0's, the receiver indicates that a 0 has been sent. Thus, the sequence

$$1110100110111001000101010100110000000011$$

will be received as 10100100. Compare this with the first sequence of binary digits given above. Even though there are many errors in the total sequence, after the majority rule is applied, there is only one error in the received binary digits.

If sufficient redundance is introduced, the number of errors can be made arbitrarily small. Let us consider this. Suppose $q$ is the probability of an error in a single binary digit and we repeat each binary digit $N$ times, where $N$ is odd. That is, each binary digit is transmitted as a sequence of $N$ binary digits. If an error results in the received binary digit, there must be

$$\frac{N+1}{2} \quad \text{or} \quad \frac{N+3}{2}, \ldots, \quad \text{or } N$$

errors in the received group of $N$ binary digits. Let us consider the probability of this occurring. If a sequence of $N$ 1's is transmitted, then the probability of having exactly $k$ 0's occurring at the output of the sequence is (see Eq. 8–124)

$$q_k' = \frac{N!}{k!(N-k)!} q^k (1-q)^{N-k}$$

Thus, the probability that a 1 be received as a 0 is

$$q_N = \sum_{k=(N+1)/2}^{N} q_k' \qquad (9\text{--}62)$$

Let us illustrate this with an example. Suppose the transition probability matrix is given by

$$\hat{B}^+ = \begin{bmatrix} 0.8 & 0.2 \\ 0.2 & 0.8 \end{bmatrix} \qquad (9\text{--}63)$$

That is, without redundance, there is a 20 percent probability of error. Now we shall introduce redundance. Let us assume that $N = 5$; i.e., each binary digit is repeated five times. Thus, there must be three or more errors in a redundant group before an error results in the received binary digit. Now let us compute the $q_k'$ for $k = 3, 4, 5$, these are

$$q_3' = \frac{5!}{3!(2!)} (0.2)^3 (0.8)^2 = 0.0512$$

$$q_4' = \frac{5!}{4!} (0.2)^4 (0.8) = 0.0064$$

$$q_5' = (0.2)^5 = 0.00032$$

Thus,

$$q_5 = q_3' + q_4' + q_5' = 0.0579$$

Hence,

$$\hat{B}_5^+ = \begin{bmatrix} 0.9421 & 0.0579 \\ 0.0579 & 0.9421 \end{bmatrix}$$

Thus the probability of error has been greatly reduced. In general, by increasing the number of redundant terms in a group, we can reduce the probability of error to arbitrarily small values.

We have considered redundancy by repeating binary digits. Actually, we can also repeat the symbols themselves. For instance, the sequence $ABC$ could be transmitted as $AAABBBCCC$, where the symbols are encoded as in Section 9-3. The basic ideas are the same as the previous ones and the numbers of errors can be reduced to arbitrarily small values.

Let us consider a segment of a FORTRAN program which will take binary digits which have been transmitted using redundance and convert them on a majority choice basis to a nonredundant sequence. If each binary digit is repeated 5 times then 111110000011111 would be given as 101.

Let NT be the total number of binary digits (in the example just cited, NT = 15) and let J be the number of times that the binary digit is repeated in the group (in this example J = 5). Also let F(I) be the array containing the input (redundant) binary digits; that is, each of its elements is 0 or 1. This represents the received binary digits. Now let us consider the program sequence. We will not list input, output, or dimension statements, etc. here. We shall assume that the arrays F(I) and G(I) have been specified to be integers. Alternatively they can be replaced by the arrays KF(I) and KG(I).

```
          JJ = J/2
          JM = JJ + 1
          NN = NT/J
          DO 100 I = 1, NN
          KB = 0
          DO 50 K = 1, J
          KI = J * (I − 1) + K
          KB = KB + F(KI)
    50    CONTINUE
          G(I) = 0
          IF(KB.GE.JM) G(I) = 1
    100   CONTINUE
```

In the first two lines, the number of terms necessary for a majority is calculated. Note that J/2 is an integer. Thus, any fractional part will be discarded. Note that we choose J odd. For instance, if J = 5, then J/2 = 2 and JM = 1 + J/2 = 3. Thus, 3 or more constitutes a majority. In the third line, the number of received binary digits is calculated. That is, the total number of symbols is divided by the number of symbols in each group.

Each cycle of the outer DO loop works with a group of (redundant) binary digits. In the inner DO loop, the sum of the terms in a single redundant group is obtained. If the sum is greater than JM, then G(I) = 1, otherwise G(I) = 0. If J = 5, then if the sum of the 1's and 0's (on an ordinary arithmetic basis) is 3 or more, the group is considered to represent a 1. If the sum is less than 3, the group represents a 0. After cycling the outer DO loop NN times the G array will contain the non-redundant binary digits.

This program can be modified so that input data and the output are continuously transmitted. That is, data are fed to the computer from the channel directly. In this case, NT is not known. However, this is only used to control the number of times that the outer DO loop is cycled. Thus, NN can be replaced by a sufficiently large number. The input and output of the program must be such that continuous data can be entered and extracted. The operating manual of the computer should be consulted for this information.

## 9-5. CHANNEL CAPACITY OF NOISY CHANNELS

We can use redundance to reduce the error of transmission of signals contaminated with noise to arbitrarily small values. However, since redundancy requires repetition, we must transmit more binary digits per symbol in the redundant case. Thus, the rate of transmission of information is reduced by redundancy. The fundamental theorem, which states that we can transmit without error if $H_r < C$ (see Sections 9-2 and 9-3), still applies even in a noisy channel. However, the presence of noise reduces the channel capacity $C$. The fundamental definition of channel capacity requires the transmission of signals without error (see Eq. 9–22). In general, for most noise probabilities (e.g., Gaussian) there is some finite, but usually very small probability of having extremely large noise signals. Thus, the only time that we are certain of having zero error in a message of length $T$, where $T$ approaches $\infty$, is when the signal-to-noise ratio or the redundancy is infinite. Hence, if we strictly adhere to the definition of channel capacity, the value of $C$ becomes zero if any noise is present. However, in a practical case, if the signal-to-noise ratio and/or the redundancy is made sufficiently large, the transmission can be considered errorless. Thus, if the rate of errors is sufficiently small we shall assume that the transmission is errorless (for the computation of $C$).

We shall discuss a general case and not just work with binary digits. To do this we shall assume that we are transmitting pulses of different amplitudes. We can include binary digits as a special case by allowing only two levels, 0 and 1. We can also approach the continuous case by allowing the levels to become arbitrarily close.

Now suppose the average signal power is $S$, while the average noise power is $N$. We wish to transmit signals with a very small rate of error. Assume that the pulse amplitudes are quantized into discrete levels. These levels cannot be spaced too closely together if we do not wish to cause the noise to produce errors. It has been found by experiment that if the levels are spaced in voltage by an amount proportional to $\sqrt{N}$ (i.e., equal to the rms noise voltage), an acceptably small number of errors occurs. The total power at the output of the channel is

$$P_T = S + N \tag{9–64}$$

The maximum rms voltage of the channel is, on the average proportional to $\sqrt{S + N}$. This voltage can be divided into levels (proportional to $\sqrt{N}$ apart. Thus, the maximum number of voltage levels is

$$N_{max} = \sqrt{\frac{S + N}{N}} = \sqrt{1 + \frac{S}{N}} \tag{9–65}$$

In a binary channel, there are two levels 0 and 1. Thus, we can have $N_{max} = 2$. In this case, $S/N = 3$. Let us see what sort of error rate results. Substitute $S/N = 3$ into Eq. 9–59b, which gives the foward transition probability matrix for amplitude-modulated binary digits. This yields a probability of error of $e^{-3} = 0.05$. Thus, we have about 5 percent error. In many cases, this can be considered a sufficiently low error rate.

Let us assume that this frequency of error is sufficiently small and we can compute the channel capacity on the basis of Eq. 9–65. We shall use the number of allowed levels given by Eq. 9–65. This is the maximum number of different symbols that can be transmitted if each pulse transmits one symbol. (Note that the same rate of transmission using binary digits can be obtained by using proper coding.) Substituting in Eq. 9–28, which gives channel capacity in terms of number of symbols, yields

$$C = 2B \log_2 \sqrt{1 + S/N} \tag{9-66a}$$

This can be written as

$$C = B \log_2 \left( 1 + \frac{S}{N} \right) \tag{9-66b}$$

This is called the *Hartley-Shannon law*. It relates the bandwidth $B$ and signal-to-noise ratio to channel capacity. Increasing $B$ and/or increasing $S/N$ increases channel capacity. Let us relate $S/N$ to $B$. Suppose $B_1$ and $S_1/N_1$ yield the same channel capacity as $B_2$ and $S_2/N_2$, then,

$$B_1 \log_2 \left( 1 + \frac{S_1}{N} \right) = B_2 \log_2 \left( 1 + \frac{S_2}{N_2} \right)$$

Hence,

$$\frac{B_2}{B_1} = \frac{\log_2 \left( 1 + \frac{S_1}{N} \right)}{\log_2 \left( 1 + \frac{S_2}{N_2} \right)} \tag{9-67}$$

If $S_1/N_1 = 1$, while $S_2/K_2 = 10$, then $B_2/B_1 = 0.289$. Thus, an improvement in signal-to-noise ratio from 1 to 10 allows the bandwidth to be reduced by a factor of 0.289, if the same channel capacity is desired.

## 9-6. USE OF FILTERS TO EXTRACT SIGNALS FROM NOISE

In this section we shall discuss filters which minimize the effects of noise on a continuous signal. In Section 8-9 we discussed some filtering techniques; in this section we shall consider alternative procedures. The original results in this area were obtained by Weiner [1]. Much additional work on noise-reducing filters was obtained by Kalman [2]. Some of the basic results were simplified by Bode and Shannon [3].

Let us now formulate characteristics of a practical noise-reducing filter. Assume that we have a signal $x(t)$ which consists of a desired signal $f(t)$ and a noise signal $n(t)$; then,

$$x(t) = f(t) + n(t) \qquad (9\text{--}68)$$

The output of the filter will be a signal $g(t)$, (see Fig. 9–7). Ideally, $g(t)$ will be of the form

$$g(t) = f(t + \alpha) \qquad (9\text{--}69)$$

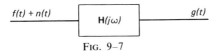

FIG. 9–7
Representation of a noise-reducing filter

The filter should completely remove the noise without distorting the signal, although it may delay it ($\alpha$ may be positive or negative).

In general, a filter will not behave in this ideal way. Thus, there will be an error between the actual output and the desired one; hence,

$$\varepsilon(t) = g(t) - f(t + \alpha) \qquad (9\text{--}70)$$

where $\alpha$ is adjusted to minimize the error. That is, time delay in the filter should not be charged against its performance.

In order to minimize the error, we must choose an error criterion which yields a single number and minimizes it. This idea and error criteria are discussed in detail in Section 2-14. We shall use a mean square error criterion here; that is, we wish to minimize

$$\varepsilon_{MS} = \int_{-\infty}^{\infty} \varepsilon^2(t)\, dt = \int_{-\infty}^{\infty} [g(t) - f(t + \alpha)]^2 dt \qquad (9\text{--}71)$$

We must determine a transfer function $H(j\omega)$ which minimizes $\varepsilon_{MS}$. Note that for each $H(j\omega)$ we must use a value of $\alpha$ which minimizes the error. We shall use the following notation for the Fourier transform of various quantities.

$$f(t) \leftrightarrow F(j\omega) \qquad (9\text{--}72\text{a})$$
$$n(t) \leftrightarrow N(j\omega) \qquad (9\text{--}72\text{b})$$
$$g(t) \leftrightarrow G(j\omega) \qquad (9\text{--}72\text{c})$$
$$h(t) \leftrightarrow H(j\omega) \qquad (9\text{--}72\text{d})$$

Note that $n(t)$ and $N(j\omega)$ are unknown quantities.

Now let us obtain the Fourier transform of $\varepsilon(t)$. The Fourier transform of the output of the filter is given by

$$G(j\omega) = [F(j\omega) + N(j\omega)]\, H(j\omega) \qquad (9\text{--}73)$$

Then,

$$\varepsilon(t) \leftrightarrow [F(j\omega) + N(j\omega)]\, H(j\omega) - F(j\omega)\, e^{j\alpha\omega}$$

We can write this as

$$\varepsilon(t) \leftrightarrow F(j\omega)\left[H(j\omega) - e^{j\alpha\omega}\right] + N(j\omega)H(j\omega) \tag{9-74}$$

Now apply Parseval's theorem (Eq. 2–233) to Eq. 9–74. This yields

$$\varepsilon_{MS} = \frac{1}{2\pi} \int_{-\infty}^{\infty} \left| F(j\omega)\left[H(j\omega) - e^{j\alpha\omega}\right] + N(j\omega)H(j\omega) \right|^2 d\omega \tag{9-75}$$

We wish to determine $H(j\omega)$ and $\alpha$ which minimize the relation. However, $N(j\omega)$ is an unknown quantity, that is, we do not know the Fourier transform of the noise. Thus, we cannot proceede further. However, we usually do know the spectral density of the noise.

Let us see if we can obtain a relation which expresses $\varepsilon_{MS}$, or something equivalent to it, in terms of the spectral densities. We shall write $S_f(\omega)$ and $S_n(\omega)$ as the spectral density of the signal and noise, respectively.

Now consider the right-hand side of relation 9–74. We could assume that this Fourier transform were obtained in the following way: the signal $f(t)$ is applied to a filter whose transfer function is $H(j\omega) - e^{j\alpha\omega}$ and the noise $n(t)$ is applied to a filter whose transfer function is $H(j\omega)$; the output of these two filters are then added; the right-hand side of relation 9-74 yields the Fourier transform of the output of this ficticious pair of filters.

If $S_1(\omega)$ is the spectral density of the input to a filter of transfer function $H(j\omega)$, then $|H(j\omega)|^2 S_1(j\omega)$ will be the spectral density of the output. In addition, the spectral density of the sum of two functions is the sum of their spectral densities. Hence, the spectral density of the sums of the outputs of these two ficticious filters is

$$S_f(\omega)\left|H(j\omega) - e^{j\alpha\omega}\right|^2 + S_n(\omega)\left|H(j\omega)\right|^2$$

The integrand of Eq. 9–75 is proportional to the spectral density of $\varepsilon(t)$ (see Section 8–5). Thus, if we minimize

$$\varepsilon_1 = \frac{1}{2\pi} \int_{-\infty}^{\infty} \left[ S_f(\omega)\left|H(j\omega) - e^{j\alpha\omega}\right|^2 + S_n(\omega)\left|H(j\omega)\right|^2 \right] d\omega \tag{9-76}$$

with respect to $\alpha$ and $H(j\omega)$, we shall have minimized $\varepsilon_{MS}$ to the best of our ability. Note that if we actually know $N(j\omega)$, then $n(t)$ is known and we could generate a signal $- n(t)$ to cancel the noise. Of course, we do not know $N(j\omega)$ or $n(t)$. Hence, Eq. 9–76 is a realistic one with which to work. The spectral densities of the signal and noise $S_f(\omega)$ and $S_n(\omega)$ are assumed to be known quantities. In practical cases, this is usually true. Let us write

$$H(j\omega) = \left|H(j\omega)\right| \varepsilon^{j\theta(\omega)} \tag{9-77}$$

Then, Eq. 9–76 can be written as

$$\varepsilon_1 = \frac{1}{2\pi} \int_{-\infty}^{\infty} \left[ \left|H(j\omega)\right|^2 S_n(\omega) + S_f(\omega) \left| \left|H(j\omega)\right| \cos\theta(\omega) - \cos\alpha\omega \right.\right.$$
$$\left.\left. + j\left|H(j\omega)\right|\sin\theta(\omega) - \sin\alpha\omega \right|^2 \right] d\omega$$

Rearranging, we have

$$\varepsilon_1 = \frac{1}{2\pi} \int_{-\infty}^{\infty} \left\{ |H(j\omega)|^2 S_n(\omega) + S_f(\omega)[|H(j\omega)|\cos\theta(\omega) - \cos\alpha\omega]^2 \right.$$

$$\left. + S_f(\omega)[|H(j\omega)|\sin\theta(\omega) - \sin\alpha\omega]^2 \right\} d\omega$$

Therefore, we have

$$\varepsilon_1 = \frac{1}{2\pi} \int_{-\infty}^{\infty} \left( [|H(j\omega)|^2 S_n(\omega) \right.$$

$$\left. + \left\{ |H(j\omega)|^2 + 1 - 2|H(j\omega)|\cos[\theta(\omega) - \alpha\omega] \right\} S_f(\omega) \right) d\omega \qquad (9\text{-}78)$$

We wish to find $|H(j\omega)|$ and $\theta(\omega)$, which minimize $\varepsilon_1$. Note that $|H(j\omega)|$, $S_f(\omega)$, and $S_n(\omega)$ are all positive quantities. (The spectral density is defined as positive.) In addition, the term included in the braces is positive since it represents the sum of two real quantities which have been squared. Thus, if we choose $\theta(\omega)$ to minimize

$$|H(j\omega)|^2 + 1 - 2|H(j\omega)|\cos[\theta(\omega) - \alpha\omega]$$

we will have chosen a $\theta(\omega)$ which minimizes $\varepsilon_1$. In general, $a^2 + 1 - 2a = (a - 1)^2 \geqq 0$; then,

$$|H(j\omega)|^2 + 1 \geq 2|H(j\omega)|$$

Thus, the above expression is minimized if we set $\cos[\theta(\omega) - \alpha\omega] = 1$ or, equivalently,

$$\theta(\omega) = \alpha\omega \qquad (9\text{-}79)$$

Thus, Eq. 9-78 becomes

$$\varepsilon_1 = \frac{1}{2\pi} \int_{-\infty}^{\infty} [|H(j\omega)|^2 [S_n(\omega) + S_f(\omega)] - 2|H(j\omega)|S_f(\omega) + S_f(\omega)] d\omega \qquad (9\text{-}80)$$

We must now choose $|H(j\omega)|$ that minimizes this expression. Let us rewrite Eq. 9-80 as

$$\varepsilon_1 = \frac{1}{2\pi} \int_{-\infty}^{\infty} \left[ \left( |H(j\omega)|\sqrt{S_n(\omega) + S_f(\omega)} - \frac{S_f(\omega)}{\sqrt{S_n(\omega)S_f(\omega)}} \right)^2 \right.$$

$$\left. + S_f(\omega) - \frac{S_f^2(\omega)}{S_f(\omega) + S_n(\omega)} \right] d\omega$$

Combining the last two terms, we have

$$\varepsilon_1 = \frac{1}{2\pi} \int_{-\infty}^{\infty} \left[ \left( |H(j\omega)|\sqrt{S_n(\omega) + S_f(\omega)} - \frac{S_f(\omega)}{\sqrt{S_n(\omega) + S_f(\omega)}} \right)^2 \right.$$

$$\left. + \frac{S_n(\omega)S_f(\omega)}{S_n(\omega) + S_f(\omega)} \right] d\omega \qquad (9\text{-}81)$$

Both terms of the integrand are positive. However, only the first contains $|H(j\omega)|$. Thus, the value of $|H(j\omega)|$ which causes the first term to be zero is the one which minimizes $\varepsilon_1$. This value of $|H(j\omega)|$ is

$$|H(j\omega)| = \frac{S_f(\omega)}{S_f(\omega) + S_n(\omega)} \qquad (9\text{-}82)$$

Combining this with Eq. 9–79, we obtain the transfer function of the noise-reducing filter as

$$H(j\omega) = \frac{S_f(\omega)}{S_f(\omega) + S_n(\omega)} e^{j\alpha\omega} \qquad (9\text{-}83)$$

Note that $\alpha$ is arbitrary since changing it would just vary the time delay of the filter.

The error $\varepsilon_1$ that results when the filter is used, can be obtained by substituting Eq. 9–82 into Eq. 9–81; this yields

$$\varepsilon_1 = \frac{1}{2\pi} \int_{-\infty}^{\infty} \frac{S_n(\omega)\, S_f(\omega)}{S_n(\omega) + S_f(\omega)}\, d\omega \qquad (9\text{-}84a)$$

Or, alternatively,

$$\varepsilon_1 = \frac{1}{2\pi} \int_{-\infty}^{\infty} \frac{S_n(\omega)/S_f(\omega)}{1 + S_n(\omega)/S_f(\omega)}\, d\omega \qquad (9\text{-}84b)$$

If the ratio $S_n(\omega)/S_f(\omega)$ is decreased over any $\omega$, the error will decrease.

Equation 9–83 provides a simple procedure for obtaining the transfer function of the noise reducing filter. However, the filter will usually not be causal (see Section 5-4). We have shown that a causal filter would have a unit impulse response which is zero for $t < 0$. In this case, the impulse response is

$$h(t) = \frac{1}{2\pi} \int_{-\infty}^{\infty} \frac{S_f(\omega)}{S_f(\omega) + S_n(\omega)} e^{j\omega(\alpha + t)}\, d\omega \qquad (9\text{-}85)$$

In general, this will be nonzero for $t < 0$. Thus, the filter is not causal.

**Noise Filtering with a Causal Filter.** Here, the results will not be as good as those obtained with a noncausal filter; that is, $\varepsilon_1$ will be greater than the value given in Eq. 9–84. However, a physically realizable filter will be obtained.

Let us consider the noncausal filter. Its response to the input signal $x(t)$ is given by (see Eq. 5–52)

$$g(t) = \int_{-\infty}^{\infty} h(y)\, x(t - y)\, dy \qquad (9\text{-}86)$$

If the filter is such that $h(y)$ contributes a negligible amount to the integrand for $y \leqq -T (h(y)$ is small for $y < -T$ and falls off sufficiently fast as the magnitude of $-t$ increases), then we can approximate the filter by one whose impulse response is

$$h_1(t) = \begin{cases} h(t), & t \geq -T \\ 0, & t < -T \end{cases}$$

(9–87a)
(9–87b)

This filter is not causal since $h(t) \neq 0$ for $t < 0$. However, if we delay the output of the filter by $T$ seconds, it will be causal; then, if

$$h_1(t) \leftrightarrow H_1(j\omega)$$

(9–88)

a filter which is causal, and whose output approximates the desired one, has the transfer function and impulse response given by

$$h_1(t - T) \leftrightarrow H_1(j\omega) e^{-j\omega T}$$

(9–89)

The filters we have discussed (causal or noncausal) can remove random variations of noise. Thus, they are called *smoothing filters*. Now consider the noncausal filter. From Eq. 9–86, in order to compute $g(t)$ at time $t$, we must know all values of $x(t)$ from $t = -\infty$ to $t = +\infty$. Thus, a noncausal filter must be able to predict the future values of its input signal. For this reason, a noncausal filter is called a *predicting filter*. If a noncausal filter has a transfer function such as that given in Eq. 9–87 then it need only predict $T$ seconds into the future. Of course, the causal filter does not predict at all; its response depends only upon present and past values of its input.

Let us take another point of view. Again consider Eq. 9–86 and suppose we cannot approximate $h(t)$ by Eq. 9–87. However, we wish to use a causal filter which minimizes the mean square error. Let us now obtain the best possible causal filter which does not use time delay. We start with $S_f(\omega)$ and $S_n(\omega)$, the signal and noise spectral densities, respectively. Then $S_x(\omega)$, the spectral density of the total signal is given by

$$S_x(\omega) = S_f(\omega) + S_n(\omega)$$

(9–90)

Now suppose we pass this through a filter whose transfer function has a magnitude given by

$$|H_w(j\omega)|^2 = \frac{1}{S_x(\omega)}$$

(9–91)

The response of this filter to the signal plus noise will have a power spectrum given by

$$|H_w(j\omega)|^2 S_x(\omega) = 1$$

(9–92)

Thus, this filter produces a white noise spectral density from the input signal plus noise.

Since we intend to use some properties of white noise in our derivation, we require the spectral density of white noise. The introduction of the filter $H_w(j\omega)$ allows us to do this. (Since $H_w(j\omega)$ is known, we can always reconstruct its input from its output so that no data are lost by including this filter.)

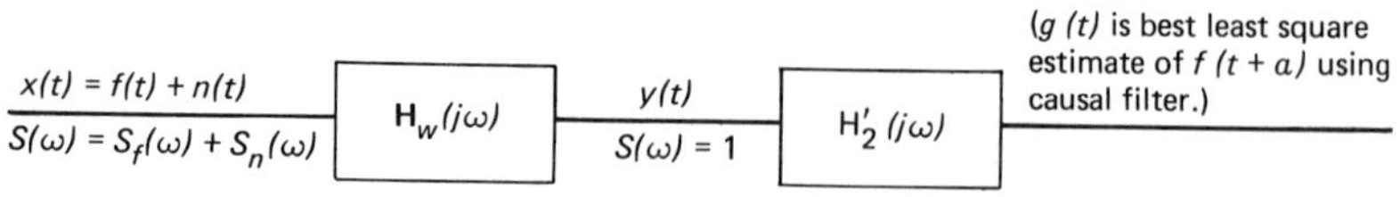

FIG. 9–8
Causal noise-reducing filter

The final filter will be causal and it will consist of $H_w(j\omega)$ in cascade with another filter. This is shown in Fig. 9–8. Thus, it is desirable if both of these filters are causal. We can obtain a causal filter for $H_w(j\omega)$ since only its magnitude is specified. In this case, we can obtain a causal filter if the phase angle satisfies the Bode equation (see Eq. 5–117). Thus, we can use this equation to obtain a physically realizable $H_w(j\omega)$. We assume that this is done.

The output of $H_w(j\omega)$ has a spectral density $S(\omega) = 1$. Thus, the autocorrelation of this signal is an impulse (see Eqs. 8–216 and 8–217), that is, if $y(t)$ is the output of this filter, $y(t)$ is uncorrelated with $y(t + T)$, $T \neq 0$.

The ideal noise reducing filter has a transfer function given by Eq. 9–83. Now assume that we cascade $H_w(j\omega)$ with a filter which is such that the transfer function of the combination is given by Eq. 9–83. Thus, if $H_2(j\omega)$ is the transfer function of the second filter in the cascade, then

$$H_w(j\omega)\, H_2(j\omega) = \frac{S_f(\omega)}{S_f(\omega) + S_n(\omega)}\, e^{j\alpha\omega}$$

Hence,

$$H_2(j\omega) = \frac{1}{H_w(j\omega)}\, \frac{S_f(\omega)}{S_f(\omega) + S_n(\omega)}\, e^{j\alpha\omega} \qquad (9\text{–}93)$$

This will, in general, be a noncausal filter.

Consider approximating this filter by a causal filter. Let us call $h_2(t)$ the impulse response of the second (noncausal) filter, thus,

$$h_2(t) \leftrightarrow H_2(j\omega) \qquad (9\text{–}94)$$

We shall write the impulse response as

$$h_2(t) = h_-(t) + h_+(t) \qquad (9\text{–}95)$$

where

$$h_-(t) = 0, \qquad t \geq 0 \qquad (9\text{–}96a)$$
$$h_+(t) = 0, \qquad t < 0 \qquad (9\text{–}96b)$$

If we replace $H_2(j\omega)$ by a filter whose impulse response is $h_+(t)$, then a causal filter will result.

We now must determine if the error at the output of the filter can be reduced by modifying $h_+(t)$ for $t > 0$. Let us call the input to the second filter whose transfer function is $H_2(j\omega)$, $y(t)$. Then, the output $g(t)$ is

$$g(t) = \int_{-\infty}^{\infty} y(z) h(t - z) \, dz \qquad (9\text{--}97)$$

This can be written as

$$g(t) = \int_{t}^{\infty} y(z) h_-(t - z) \, dz + \int_{-\infty}^{t} y(z) h_+(t - z) \, dz \qquad (9\text{--}98)$$

The first integral uses future values of $y(z)$. This is a predictor and uses $h_-(t)$. The second integral represents the response of the causal filter. Let us write the response as

$$g(t) = g_-(t) + g_+(t) \qquad (9\text{--}99)$$

where $g_-(t)$ corresponds to the first integral of Eq. 9–98.

Now let us replace $H_2(j\omega)$ by another filter $H'_2(j\omega)$ which is causal:

$$h'_2(t) \leftrightarrow H'_2(j\omega) \qquad (9\text{--}100)$$

Since the filter is causal

$$h'_2(t) = 0, \qquad t < 0 \qquad (9\text{--}101)$$

The response of this filter to the impulse $y(t)$ is

$$g'(t) = \int_{-\infty}^{t} y(z) h'_2(t - z) \, dz \qquad (9\text{--}102)$$

Now let us determine the $h'_2(t)$ which minimizes the mean square error. The minimum mean square error is obtained when we use the noncausal $H_2(j\omega)$ as the transfer function. This filter has the response $g(t)$. We wish $g'(t)$ to approximate it as closely as possible. Let us use the criterion that we wish to minimize the mean square value of $g(t) - g'(t)$; that is, we wish to obtain the $g'(t)$ that minimizes

$$\varepsilon' = \int_{-\infty}^{\infty} [g(t) - g'(t)]^2 dt \qquad (9\text{--}103)$$

Substituting Eq. 9–99 and manipulating, we have

$$\varepsilon' = \int_{-\infty}^{\infty} [g_+(t) - g'(t)]^2 dt$$

$$- 2 \int_{-\infty}^{\infty} g_-(t) [g_+(t) - g'(t)] \, dt + \int_{-\infty}^{\infty} g_-^2(t) \, dt \qquad (9\text{--}104)$$

The second integral represents the crosscorrelation of $g_-(t)$ with $g_+(t) + g'(t)$ (see Section 8-7). However, $g_-(t)$ represents the response of the filter $H_2(j\omega)$ to future values of the input $y(t)$, while $g_+(t)$ and $g'(t)$ represent the response to past and present values of $y(t)$. We discussed earlier that $y(t)$ had a white noise spectrum so that its past and present values are uncorrelated with its future values. The response of the filter to these uncorrelated values will be uncorrelated. Thus, the second integral is zero. Hence, we wish to choose $g'(t)$ such that we minimize

$$\varepsilon' = \int_{-\infty}^{\infty} [g_+(t) - g'(t)]^2 dt + \int_{-\infty}^{\infty} g_-^2(t)\, dt \qquad (9\text{–}105)$$

Both integrands are positive and the second is not a function of $g'(t)$. Thus, $\varepsilon'$ is minimized if

$$g'(t) = g_+(t) \qquad (9\text{–}106)$$

Thus, the response of the noncausal and causal filters are the same for positive time. Hence, to minimize the mean square error using a causal filter, we calculate $H_2(j\omega)$ and obtain its impulse response. The causal filter has an impulse response equal to $h_+(t)$; i.e., the impulse response of $H_2(j\omega)$ for $t > 0$. This causal filter is used as $H_2'(j\omega)$ in Fig. 9–8.

In summary, the total causal filter has a transfer function $H_w(j\omega) H_2'(j\omega)$, where $H_w(j\omega)$ has a magnitude given by Eq. 9–91 and a phase angle calculated from the Bode relation. $H_2'(j\omega)$ is calculated from $H_2(j\omega)$ (see Eq. 9–93) as follows: its impulse response $h_2'(t)$ is zero for $t < 0$ and equal to the impulse response of $H_2(j\omega)$ for $t > 0$.

Let us illustrate noise reducing filter design with an example. Suppose we have a signal $f(t)$ whose spectral density is given by

$$S_f(\omega) = \frac{1}{\omega^2 + 4} \qquad (9\text{–}107)$$

and it is transmitted through a channel which introduces white noise; thus,

$$S_n(\omega) = 1$$

We wish to filter this using a causal filter which minimizes the mean square error of the output. The spectrum of the composite signal is given by (see Eq. 9–90)

$$S_x(\omega) = \frac{1}{\omega^2 + 4} + 1 = \frac{\omega^2 + 5}{\omega^2 + 4} \qquad (9\text{–}108)$$

We now must find a causal filter whose transfer function has a magnitude given by

$$|H_w(j\omega)|^2 = \frac{\omega^2 + 4}{\omega^2 + 5} \qquad (9\text{–}109)$$

When $S_x(\omega)$ is expressed as the ratio of two polynomials, we need not use the Bode relation to find the phase angle of $H_w(j\omega)$. Let us illustrate this. We can write Eq. 9–109 as

$$|H_w(j\omega)|^2 = \frac{(2 + j\omega)(2 - j\omega)}{(\sqrt{5} + j\omega)(\sqrt{5} - j\omega)} \qquad (9\text{–}110)$$

This is of the form

$$|H_w(j\omega)|^2 = H_w(j\omega) H_w^*(j\omega) = H_w(j\omega) H_w(-j\omega) \qquad (9\text{–}111)$$

where

$$H_w(j\omega) = \frac{2 + j\omega}{\sqrt{5} + j\omega} \tag{9-112}$$

Note that the magnitude of $(2 + j\omega)/(\sqrt{5} + j\omega)$ is the same as that of $(2 - j\omega)/(\sqrt{5} - j\omega)$. Thus, $H_w(j\omega)$ has the proper magnitude.

We can show that the impulse response is causal in the following way. Replace $j\omega$ by $s$, the Laplace transform variable; thus,

$$H_w(s) = \frac{s + 2}{s + \sqrt{5}}$$

The impulse response will be zero for $t < 0$ (see Section 3-11), so the network is causal.

If $|H_w(j\omega)|^2$ is expressed as the ratio of two polynomials in $s$, we can always factor it as $H_w(s) H_w(-s)$, where $H_s(s)$ contains no right-half plane poles. Now $S(\omega)$ is an even function of $\omega$. Thus, it only contains even powers of $\omega$. If we replace $j\omega$ by $s$, then $S(s)$ will be an even function of $s$. Then, if $s_0$ is a pole or zero of $S(s)$, so $-s_0$ will also be a root. Since complex roots occur in conjugate pairs, the pole zero pattern of $S(s)$ will have the form shown in Fig. 9-9. Thus, if we use all the left-half plane poles and zeros to form $H_w(s)$ (note that $|H_w(j\omega)|^2 = 1/S(\omega)$ so that zeros become poles) we will obtain a causal transfer function. Note that we will have

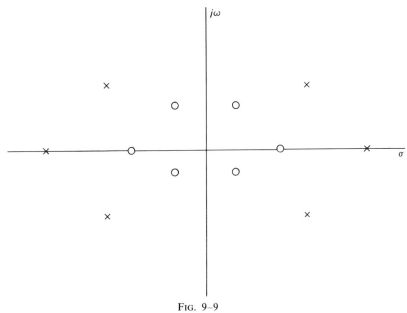

FIG. 9-9
Typical pole-zero plot of $S(s)$

factored $|H_w(j\omega)|^2 = |H_w(j\omega)| |H_w(-j\omega)|$. If poles or zeros of $S(s)$ lie on the $j\omega$ axis, they must be of even multiplicity, since $S(\omega)$ is always positive. (It would change signs at a root of odd multiplicity.) Thus, "half" of these roots should be alloted to $H_w(j\omega)$.

Now let us continue with the example. If we were to use a noncausal filter, its transfer function would be (see Eq. 9–83)

$$H(j\omega) = \frac{1/(\omega^2 + 4)}{[1/(\omega^2 + 4)] + 1} e^{-\alpha\omega} = \frac{1}{\omega^2 + 5} e^{-\alpha\omega}$$

Then, from Eq. 9–93, we have

$$H_2(j\omega) = \frac{j\omega + \sqrt{5}}{j\omega + 2} \cdot \frac{1}{\omega^2 + 5} e^{-\alpha\omega} = \frac{1}{(j\omega + 2)(\sqrt{5} - j\omega)} e^{-\alpha\omega}$$

If we make $\alpha$ positive, we introduce a time delay into the filter. This can be used to reduce the error. The use of time delay is equivalent to the discussion of Eqs. 9–87 through 9–89. Such time delay is often difficult to achieve in practice, or it involves cumbersome storage of data. To simplify the filter we have assumed that there is no such time delay. Hence, let us assume that $\alpha = 0$. Then, taking the inverse transform, we obtain the unit impulse response

$$h_2(t) = \begin{cases} \dfrac{1}{(2 + \sqrt{5})} e^{-2t}, & t > 0 \\[2ex] -\dfrac{1}{(2 + \sqrt{5})} e^{\sqrt{5}t}, & t < 0 \end{cases}$$

Then, the causal filter $H'_2(j\omega)$ has an impulse response

$$h'(t) = \frac{1}{(2 + \sqrt{5})} u(t) e^{-2t}$$

Hence,

$$H'_2(j\omega) = \frac{1}{2 + \sqrt{5}} \cdot \frac{1}{j\omega + 2}$$

The overall transfer function of the filter is given by

$$H_T(j\omega) = H_w(j\omega) H'_2(j\omega)$$

Therefore, the transfer function of the causal filter is

$$H_T(j\omega) = \frac{1}{(2 + \sqrt{5})(j\omega + \sqrt{5})}$$

## PROBLEMS

**9-1.** Eight cards numbered from 1 to 8, are placed in a box. One card is drawn from the box. What is the information content of the message stating which card is drawn from the box?

**9-2.** An information source transmits the symbols $A$, $B$, $C$, and $D$ with probabilities $P(A) = 0.5$, $P(B) = 0.3$, $P(C) = 0.1$, and $P(D) = 0.1$. What is the entropy of the source?

**9-3.** Repeat Problem 9-2, but now assume that each symbol has an equal probability of occurring.

**9-4.** Suppose the information source of Problem 9-2 is such that the probability of occurrence of a symbol is a function of the previous symbol, in particular,

$$
\begin{array}{llll}
P(A|A) = 0.0, & P(B|A) = 0.5, & P(C|A) = 0.2, & P(D|A) = 0.3 \\
P(A|B) = 1.0, & P(B|B) = 0.0, & P(C|B) = 0.0, & P(D|B) = 0.0 \\
P(A|C) = 0.0, & P(B|C) = 0.4, & P(C|C) = 0.3, & P(D|C) = 0.3 \\
P(A|D) = 0.0, & P(B|D) = 0.1, & P(C|D) = 0.5, & P(D|D) = 0.4
\end{array}
$$

Compute the conditional entropy of the source.

**9-5.** Find the redundance of the source of Problem 9-4.

**9-6.** The source of Problem 9-2 produces 20 symbols per second. What is its entropy rate?

**9-7.** A channel has an ideal low pass filter characteristic. Its pass band is from $-2\pi \times 10^6 \leq \omega \leq 2\pi \times 10^6$. How many binary digits (pulses) per second can this channel transmit?

**9-8.** The channel of Problem 9-7 is to transmit information contained in 100 symbols. What is the channel capacity?

**9-9.** A signal source transmits symbols $x_1$, $x_2$, $x_3$, $x_4$, and $x_5$ with probabilities $P(x_1) = 0.4$, $P(x_2) = 0.3$, $P(x_3) = 0.15$, $P(x_4) = 0.1$, and $P(x_5) = 0.05$. Use Fano's procedure to encode this using binary digits.

**9-10.** Compute the average number of binary digits/symbol for the code of Problem 9-9.

**9-11.** Repeat Problem 9-9, but now encode in groups of two.

**9-12.** Repeat Problem 9-10 for the code of Problem 9-11.

**9-13.** Repeat Problem 9-9, but now encode in groups of three.

**9-14.** Repeat Problem 9-10 for the code of Problem 9-13.

**9-15.** Obtain and compare the efficiency of the codes of Problems 9-9, 9-11, and 9-13.

**9-16.** The source of Problem 9-9 produces 100 symbols per second. It is to transmit information over a channel which is such that $0.9C = H_r$, where $C$ is the channel capacity and $H_r$ is the entropy rate of the source. Determine a code which will allow the transmission to take place with zero error.

**9-17.** Binary digits are transmitted over a noisy channel using amplitude modulation. If a sequence of 1s is transmitted, the output is 0 for half of the time; i.e., a 1 occupies 50 percent of the time. It is desired that only one in every 100 binary digits has an error. What should the signal-to-noise ratio of the channel be?

**9-18.** Repeat Problem 9-17, but now assume that a sequence of 1s results in transmission for 10 percent of the time.

**9-19.** A noisy channel is such that the foward transition matrix for binary digits is

$$
\hat{B} = \begin{bmatrix} 0.7 & 0.3 \\ 0.3 & 0.7 \end{bmatrix}
$$

It is desired to transmit binary digits with a frequency of error of less than one in every 100. Redundancy is to be used to accomplish this. How many times should each binary digit be repeated to accomplish this?

**9-20.** Obtain a complete FORTRAN program which obtains a nonredundant sequence of binary digits from a redundant one using the sequence of Section 9-4; that is, write input, output, dimension statements, etc.

**9-21.** A communication channel passes all frequencies from $-2\pi \times 10^6 \leqq \omega \leqq 2\pi \times 10^6$ with zero attenuation and rejects all others. The power signal-to-noise ratio of this channel is 10. What is the channel capacity?

**9-22.** A noisy channel has a channel capacity $C$. The signal power $S$ is increased so that the channel capacity is doubled. Express the new signal-to-noise ratio in terms of the old signal-to-noise ratio.

**9-23.** A signal whose spectral density is

$$S_f(\omega) = \frac{1}{1 + \omega^2}$$

is transmitted through a channel which introduces white noise. Determine an optimum (non-causal) filter which extracts the signal from the noise with minimum mean square error.

**9-24.** Repeat Problem 9-23, but now restrict the filter to be causal.

**9-25.** Repeat Problem 9-23, but now assume that the noise has a spectral density

$$S_n(\omega) = \frac{1}{1 + \omega^2}$$

**9-26.** Repeat Problem 9-25, but now restrict the filter to be causal.

**9-27.** Repeat Problem 9-23, but now use

$$S_f(\omega) = \frac{1 + \omega^2}{(4 + \omega^2)(9 + \omega^2)}$$

and

$$S_n(\omega) = \frac{1}{2 + \omega^2}$$

**9-28.** Repeat Problem 9-24 for the spectral densities of Problem 9-27.

# REFERENCES

1. Weiner, N. *The Extrapolation, Interpolation, and Smoothing of Stationary Time Series.* New York: Wiley, 1949. (This was published as a report in 1942.)
2. Kalman, R. E. "A New Approach to Linear Filtering and Prediction Problems." In *Trans. ASME.* Series D, Vol. 82, 1960, pp. 35–45.
   Kalman, R. E., and Bucy, R. S. "New Results in Linear Filtering and Prediction Theory." In *Trans. ASME.* Series D, Vol. 83, 1961, pp. 95–108.
3. Bode, H. W., and Shannon, C. E. "A Simplified Derivation of Linear Least Square Smoothing and Prediction Theory." In *Proc. IRE.* Vol. 38, 1950, pp. 417–425.

# BIBLIOGRAPHY

Brown, W. M., and Palermo, C. J. *Random Processes, Communications and Radar.* Chaps. 4–7. New York: McGraw-Hill, 1969.

Carlson, A. B. *Communications Systems.* Chap. 8. New York: McGraw-Hill, 1968.

Cooper, G. R., and McGillem, C. D. *Methods of Signsl and System Analysis.* Chap. 12. New York: Holt, 1967.

Lathi, B. P. *Signals, Systems and Communication.* Chap. 14. New York: Wiley, 1965.

Schwarz, R. J., and Friedland, B. *Linear Systems.* Chap. 10. New York: McGraw-Hill, 1965.

# CHAPTER 10

# Distributed Systems

All systems consist of elements which are spatially distributed. Consider an actual electric resistor. It is not simply a resistance, but it incorporates inductance. This is because any closed loop must have an inductance. Also, there is capacitance from each part of the resistor to other parts of the circuit and to other parts of the resistor. If we wish to describe these effects exactly, an infinite number of resistances, inductances, and capacitances are required. In many circumstances, such a detailed description is not necessary. Many circuits are very accurately represented by a few discrete elements. However, there are circumstances when more accurate modeling is necessary. We then must consider the elements of the system not as discrete entities, but as distributed in space throughout the system. In electric circuits, this usually occurs when the size of the system is comparable to, or greater than, the wavelength of the highest frequency present.

Distributed systems are encountered in applications other than simple electric networks. The motion of the charge carriers in the base of a transistor should be solved by distributed system procedures. Another example of a distributed system is a string under tension. It can be represented by masses and springs distributed throughout the space of the string. Another example of a distributed system is a heat exchanger. For instance, consider a transitor in the center of a large heat sink.

In general, all systems are distributed. Of course, we can often approximate them by nondistributed (lumped) systems. However, the study of distributed systems is an important one.

Lumped systems (e.g., electric networks containing resistance, inductance and capacitance) are characterized by differential equations. Distributed systems are characterized by *partial* differential equations. In this chapter, the formulation and solution of partial differential equations shall be discussed, where the Laplace transform procedure shall be emphasized. We shall usually describe distributed electric networks here; however, the discussions can be applied to other systems, such as heat flow, thin film networks, and diffusion of charge in a semiconductor. The basic concepts discussed here can be used in the study of all distributed parameter systems.

## 10-1. VOLTAGE AND CURRENT RELATIONS IN A TRANSMISSION LINE

As an example of a general distributed system, we shall investigate a two-wire electrical transmission line, shown in Fig. 10–1a, which consists of two wires in space.

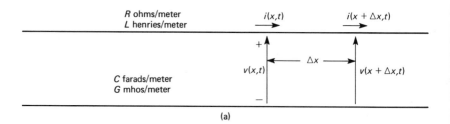

(a)

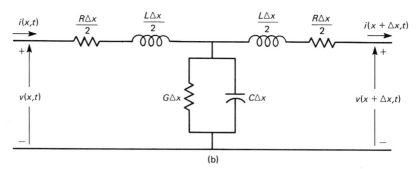

(b)

FIG. 10–1

(a) Electrical transmission line; (b) lumped parameter approximation of a short length of this line

The wires possess a resistance of $R$ ohms per meter and an inductance of $L$ henries per meter. For instance, if a 1-meter length of the transmission line is short circuited at one end and the input resistance could be measured ignoring any shunt conductance, the series resistance of both wires is $R$ ohms. There also is a capacitance between the wires of $C$ farads per meter. We also assume that the dielectric between the wires is not perfect and that there is a conductance of $G$ mhos per meter between the wires. Now, let us consider a short length $\Delta x$ of the transmission line. We can approximate it by the model shown in Fig. 10–1b. (Note that, for convenience, all the resistances and inductances have been put in the upper wire.) In the limit as $\Delta x$ approaches zero, this becomes an exact model for a differential length of transmission line.

Now let us consider equations for the model of Fig. 10–1b.

$$v(x + \Delta x, t) - v(x, t) = -\left[\frac{R\Delta x}{2} + \frac{L\Delta x}{2}\frac{\partial}{\partial t}\right][i(x, t) + i(x + \Delta x, t)] \quad (10\text{–}1)$$

In the limit, as $\Delta x$ approaches zero, $i(x, t)$ approaches $i(x + \Delta x, t)$; that is,

$$i(x, t) = \lim_{\Delta x \to 0} i(x + \Delta x, t) \quad (10\text{–}2)$$

Thus, Eq. 10–1 can be written as

$$\lim_{\Delta x \to 0} \frac{[v(x + \Delta x, t) - v(x, t)]}{\Delta x} = -\left( R + \frac{L\partial}{\partial t} \right) i(x, t) \tag{10-3}$$

The left-hand side of this equation is just the definition of the partial derivative of $v$ with respect to $x$; thus, we have

$$\frac{\partial v(x, t)}{\partial x} = -Ri(x, t) - L\frac{\partial i(x, t)}{\partial t} \tag{10-4}$$

Similarly, we can write

$$\lim_{\Delta x \to 0} \frac{i(x + \Delta x, t) - i(x, t)}{\Delta x} = -Gv(x, t) - C\frac{\partial v(x, t)}{\partial t} \tag{10-5}$$

Taking the limit, we obtain

$$\frac{\partial i(x, t)}{\partial x} = -Gv(x, t) - C\frac{\partial v(x, t)}{\partial t} \tag{10-6}$$

Equations 10–4 and 10–6 are fundamental equations which characterize a transmission line. We repeat them here

$$\frac{\partial v(x, t)}{\partial x} = -Ri(x, t) - L\frac{\partial i(x, t)}{\partial t} \tag{10-7a}$$

$$\frac{\partial i(x, t)}{\partial x} = -Gv(x, t) - C\frac{\partial v(x, t)}{\partial t} \tag{10-7b}$$

There are many techniques which can be used to solve these partial differential equations. We shall use the Laplace transform to solve these partial differential equations. The following notation for the Laplace transform shall be used

$$v(x, t) \leftrightarrow V(x, s) \tag{10-8a}$$
$$i(x, t) \leftrightarrow I(x, s) \tag{10-8b}$$

The derivation of the Laplace transform of the partial derivative with respect to time is the same as that of the total derivative (see Section 3-5). Thus, the expression for the Laplace transform of the partial derivative with respect to time is the same as that given in Eq. 3–57.

Let us now consider the Laplace transform of $\partial f(x, t)/\partial x$. Substituting in Eq. 3–10, we have

$$\frac{\partial f(x, t)}{\partial x} \leftrightarrow \int_0^\infty \frac{\partial f(x, t)}{\partial x} e^{-st} dt \tag{10-9}$$

We assume that $f(x, t)$ is such that the order of differentiation and integration can be interchanged; then,

$$\frac{\partial f(x, t)}{\partial x} \leftrightarrow \frac{\partial}{\partial x} \int_0^\infty f(x, t) e^{-st} dt \tag{10-10}$$

The integral is just $F(x, s)$, the Laplace transform of $f(x, t)$; thus,

$$\frac{\partial f(x, t)}{\partial x} \leftrightarrow \frac{\partial F(x, s)}{\partial x} \tag{10–11}$$

Now let us take the Laplace transform of both sides of Eq. 10–7a. This yields

$$\frac{\partial V(x, s)}{\partial x} = -RI(x, s) - LsI(x, s) + Li(x, 0-) \tag{10–12}$$

where $i(x, 0-)$ is the current at all points of the transmission line at $t = 0_-$. Thus, it is an initial condition. A derivative with respect to $s$ does not appear in Eq. 10–12. In fact, this equation can be solved by assuming that $s$ is a constant (for each value of $s$). Thus, the partial derivative can be replaced by a total derivative. Doing this and proceeding similarly with Eq. 10–7b, we obtain

$$\frac{dV(x, s)}{dx} = -RI(x, s) - LsI(x, s) + Li(x, 0) \tag{10–13a}$$

$$\frac{dI(x, s)}{dx} = -GV(x, s) - CsV(x, s) + Cv(x, 0) \tag{10–13b}$$

These are the fundamental equations for a transmission line, in Laplace transformed form and they have the same form as the basic linear, time-invariant state variable equations (see Eq. 4–20). In this case, the variable is $x$ rather than $t$. Note that $s$ can be treated as a parameter. Thus, the techniques of Section 4-6 can be used to solve the equations.

Let us define the matrices.

$$\hat{Q}(x, s) = \begin{bmatrix} V(x, s) \\ I(x, s) \end{bmatrix} \tag{10–14a}$$

$$\hat{A} = \begin{bmatrix} -R & -Ls \\ -G & -Gs \end{bmatrix} \tag{10–14b}$$

$$\hat{B} = \begin{bmatrix} L \\ C \end{bmatrix} \tag{10–14c}$$

$$\hat{y} = \begin{bmatrix} i(x, 0-) \\ v(x, 0-) \end{bmatrix} \tag{10–14d}$$

Thus, the solution to the set of equations is given by (see Eq. 4–127)

$$\hat{Q}(x, s) = e^{x\hat{A}}\hat{Q}(0-, s) + e^{x\hat{A}} \int_{0_-}^{x} e^{-z\hat{A}}\hat{B}\hat{y}(z) \, dz \tag{10–15}$$

The details of evaluation will be left to the reader, see Section 4-6.

Now we shall consider an important example. When electrical transmission lines are used, the initial conditions are often zero. That is, the line is initially at rest when a signal is applied to the input; the signal propagates down the transmission line to the output. Let us consider this case. We can use Eq. 10–15 here with $\hat{y} = 0$. However, we can use Eq. 10–13 directly. Let us do this. Setting the initial conditions

$$i(x, 0_-) = 0$$

$$v(x, 0_-) = 0$$

Eqs. 10–13 become

$$\frac{dV(x, s)}{dx} = -(R + Ls)\,I(x, s) \tag{10–16a}$$

$$\frac{dI(x, s)}{dx} = -(G + Cs)\,V(x, s) \tag{10–16b}$$

Differentiating Eq. 10–16a with respect to $x$ and substituting Eq. 10–16b for $dI(x, s)/dx$, we obtain

$$\frac{d^2 V(x, s)}{dx^2} = (R + Ls)(G + Cs)\,V(x, s) \tag{10–17a}$$

Similarly,

$$\frac{d^2 I(x, s)}{dx^2} = (R + Ls)(G + Cs)\,I(x, s) \tag{10–17b}$$

These are both linear differential equations, with constant coefficients. Their solutions are

$$V(x, s) = A_1 e^{-\gamma x} + A_2 e^{\gamma x} \tag{10–18a}$$

$$I(x, s) = B_1 e^{-\gamma x} + B_2 e^{\gamma x} \tag{10–18b}$$

where $A_1$, $A_2$, $B_1$, and $B_2$ are constants with respect to $x$ (they may be functions of $s$) and

$$\gamma(s) = \sqrt{(R + Ls)(G + Cs)} \tag{10–19}$$

where $\gamma(s)$ is called the *propagation constant* or the *propagation function* of the transmission line.

The constants $A_1$, $A_2$, $B_1$, and $B_2$ depend upon the boundary conditions of the transmission line; that is, they are functions of the connections made to the input and termination of the line. We shall now determine these constants for several special cases.

**Semi-infinite Transmission Line.** A simple, but informative example, is one where a transmission line has a generator at its input and extends an infinite distance from the input. This is diagrammatically indicated in Fig. 10–2. We shall determine

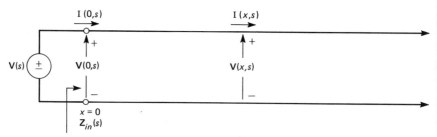

Fɪɢ. 10–2
Semi-infinite transmission line

the voltage and current, in Laplace transformed form, for this transmission line. Thus, we must evaluate the constants of Eqs. 10–18. In a semi-infinite line, $x$ can increase without limit. Thus, in general, the magnitude of $e^{\gamma x}$ will also increase without limit. Such an operation violates the law of conservation of energy since $V$ and $I$ would also become infinite. Hence, in a semi-infinite transmission line,

$$A_2 = 0 \qquad\qquad (10\text{–}20a)$$

$$B_2 = 0 \qquad\qquad (10\text{–}20b)$$

Then, Eq. 10–18a becomes

$$V(x, s) = A_1 e^{-\gamma x}$$

Let $x = 0$; then,

$$V(0, s) = A_1 \qquad\qquad (10\text{–}21)$$

The input voltage to the transmission line is equal to the voltage $V(s)$ of the input generator; thus,

$$A_1 = V(s) \qquad\qquad (10\text{–}22)$$

The voltage along the transmission line is, therefore,

$$V(x, s) = V(s)\, e^{-\gamma x} \qquad\qquad (10\text{–}23)$$

Let us consider a specific example. Suppose a transmission line is *lossless*; that is, the dissipative elements are zero. In this case, $R = 0$ and $G = 0$ (see Eq. 10–19), hence,

$$\gamma(s) = s\sqrt{LC} \qquad\qquad (10\text{–}24)$$

Substituting in Eq. 10–23, we have

$$V(x, s) = V(s)\, e^{-s\sqrt{LC}\, x} \qquad\qquad (10\text{–}25)$$

That is, (see Eq. 3–76), the voltage at any point along the transmission line has the same form as the input voltage, but is delayed by $x\sqrt{LC}$ seconds and the signal travels down the transmission line with a *velocity of propagation*,

$$v_p = \frac{1}{\sqrt{LC}} \qquad (10\text{–}26)$$

In a distributed system, we often find that signals are propagated with a finite velocity in contrast with lumped systems, where the signal can appear at all points simultaneously.

Now let us determine the current, in Laplace transformed form, for the general semi-infinite line. From Eq. 10–16a, we have

$$I(x, s) = -\frac{1}{R + Ls}\frac{dV(x, s)}{dx}$$

Substituting Eq. 10–23, we obtain

$$I(x, s) = \frac{\gamma}{R + Ls} V(s)\, e^{-\gamma x}$$

Then substituting Eq. 10–19, we have

$$I(x, s) = \sqrt{\frac{G + Cs}{R + Ls}}\, V(s)\, e^{-\gamma x} \qquad (10\text{–}27)$$

we define $\sqrt{(R + Ls)/(G + Cs)}$ by a special name. It is called the *characteristic impedance* of the transmission line and is denoted by $\mathbf{Z}_0(s)$; thus,

$$\mathbf{Z}_0(s) = \sqrt{\frac{R + Ls}{G + Cs}} \qquad (10\text{–}28)$$

(Note that this has the dimension of an impedance.) If the line is lossless, then

$$\mathbf{Z}_0 = \sqrt{L/C} \qquad (10\text{–}29)$$

The characteristic impedance is a pure resistance, which is often called the *characteristic resistance*. Note that in the lossless line, the current, as well as the voltage can be considered to propagate along a transmission line with the velocity $v_p$ (see Eq. 10–26). We shall discuss lossless transmission lines in greater detail in the next section.

Now let us determine the input impedance of the general semi-infinite transmission line. The input impedance is the ratio of the input voltage to the input current (in Laplace transformed form); then, $\mathbf{Z}_{in}(s) = V(0, s)/I(0, s)$. Substituting Eqs. 10–27 and 10–23, with $x = 0$, we have

$$\mathbf{Z}_{in}(s) = \sqrt{\frac{R + Ls}{G + Cs}} = \mathbf{Z}_0(s) \qquad (10\text{–}30)$$

Hence the input impedance of a semi-infinite transmission line is equal to the characteristic impedance. This is a physical significance of the characteristic impedance.

**Finite Transmission Line with Arbitrary Termination.** Now suppose we have a finite transmission line of length $D$ meters, which is terminated in an impedance $Z_L(s)$. This is illustrated in Fig. 10–3. In this case, the boundary conditions are

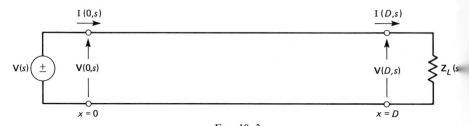

FIG. 10–3
Finite transmission line of arbitrary termination

and
$$V(0, s) = V(s) \qquad (10\text{–}31\text{a})$$

$$\frac{V(D, s)}{I(D, s)} = Z_L(s) \qquad (10\text{–}31\text{b})$$

Then, substituting in Eqs. 10–18, we have

$$V(s) = A_1 + A_2 \qquad (10\text{–}32\text{a})$$

$$V(D, s) = A_1 e^{-\gamma D} + A_2 e^{\gamma D} \qquad (10\text{–}32\text{b})$$

$$I(0, s) = B_1 + B_2 \qquad (10\text{–}32\text{c})$$

$$I(D, s) = B_1 e^{-\gamma D} + B_2 e^{\gamma D} \qquad (10\text{–}32\text{d})$$

Note that not all the quantities on the left-hand side of the equations are known. There are four unknown constants. Let us express $B_1$ and $B_2$ in terms of $A_1$ and $A_2$. From Eq. 10–16, we have

$$I(x, s) = -\frac{1}{R + Ls}\frac{dV(x, s)}{dx}$$

Substituting Eqs. 10–18 and 10–19 yields

$$I(x, s) = \sqrt{\frac{G + Cs}{R + Ls}}\, A_1 e^{-\gamma x} - \sqrt{\frac{G + Cs}{R + Ls}}\, A_2 e^{\gamma x} \qquad (10\text{–}33)$$

Substituting Eq. 10–28, we have

$$I(x, s) = \frac{A_1}{Z_0} e^{-\gamma x} - \frac{A_2}{Z_0} e^{\gamma x} \qquad (10\text{–}34)$$

Comparing this with Eq. 10–18b and noting that $A_1$, $A_2$, and $Z_0$ are independent of $x$, we obtain

$$B_1 = \frac{A_1}{Z_0}(s) \tag{10–35a}$$

$$B_2 = -\frac{A_2}{Z_0}(s) \tag{10–35b}$$

Then, substituting in Eqs. 10–31 and using Eqs. 10–32, we obtain for the boundary conditions

$$V(s) = A_1 + A_2 \tag{10–36a}$$

$$Z_L(s) = \frac{A_1 e^{-\gamma D} + A_2 e^{\gamma D}}{\dfrac{1}{Z_0(s)}[A_1 e^{-\gamma D} - A_2 e^{\gamma D}]} \tag{10–36b}$$

Thus, we have two linear simultaneous equations for the unknowns $A_1$ and $A_2$. Solving these, we have

$$A_1 = \frac{V(s)}{1 + e^{-2\gamma D}\left[\dfrac{Z_L(s) - Z_0(s)}{Z_L(s) + Z_0(s)}\right]} \tag{10–37a}$$

$$A_2 = \frac{V(s)\left[\dfrac{Z_L(s) - Z_0(s)}{Z_L(s) + Z_0(s)}\right] e^{-2\gamma D}}{1 + e^{-2\gamma D}\left[\dfrac{Z_L(s) - Z_0(s)}{Z_L(s) + Z_0(s)}\right]} \tag{10–37b}$$

We now define a quantity $\rho(s)$, which is called the *reflection coefficient* (We shall discuss the reason for this name subsequently.):

$$\rho(s) = \frac{Z_L(s) - Z_0(s)}{Z_L(s) + Z_0(s)} \tag{10–38}$$

Then, substituting Eqs. 10–37, 10–38, and 10–35 into Eqs. 10–18, we have

$$V(x, s) = \frac{V(s)}{1 + e^{-2\gamma D}\rho(s)}\left[e^{-\gamma x} + \rho(s) e^{\gamma(x - 2D)}\right] \tag{10–39a}$$

$$I(x, s) = \frac{V(s)/Z_0(s)}{1 + e^{-2\gamma D}\rho(s)}\left[e^{-\gamma x} - \rho(s) e^{\gamma(x - 2D)}\right] \tag{10–39b}$$

Let us consider the physical significance of these equations. For expedience, we shall discuss lossless lines; then (see Eq. 10–24) $\gamma = s\sqrt{LC}$. The term $e^{-\gamma x}$ represents a time delay which increases with $x$; that is, the $e^{-\gamma x}$ term can be considered to indicate that a signal is traveling from the input ($x = 0$) of the transmission line.

Now consider the term $e^{\gamma(x-2D)}$. Suppose $x = 0$. This represents a time delay equal to twice the time it takes the signal to travel from $x = 0$ to the end of the transmission line at $x = D$. If a signal travels down the line and part of it is reflected *back* from the termination, it would take a time corresponding $e^{-2\gamma D}$ to return to the input. Now suppose $x = 1/4\ D$. A reflected signal would have to travel from the input to the end and then be reflected back $3/4$ of the length of the line. Note that $e^{\gamma(\frac{1}{4}D - 2D)} = e^{-\gamma 1\frac{3}{4}D}$. (This is a delay time exactly corresponding to the time it would take a signal to travel the 1 and $3/4$ lengths.) Proceeding in this way we can see that the $e^{\gamma(x-2D)}$ term represents a signal reflected back from the termination $Z_L(s)$. Note that $x - 2D$ decreases as we approach the end of the line at $x = D$. Again, this indicates that there is propagation back from the end of the line. Thus $\rho(s)$ is the ratio of the reflected signal to the incident signal.

Now let us consider the case where

$$Z_L(s) = Z_0(s) \tag{10--40a}$$

Then (see Eq. 10--38)

$$\rho(s) = 0 \tag{10--40b}$$

In this case, Eqs. 10--39 become

$$V(x, s) = V(s)\, e^{-\gamma x}, \qquad 0 \le x \le D \tag{10--41a}$$

$$I(x, s) = \frac{V(s)}{Z_0}\, e^{-\gamma x}, \qquad 0 \le x \le D \tag{10--41b}$$

Note that the reflection terms are absent. In fact, they are the same as the equations for the semi-infinite lines (see Eqs. 10--25 and 10--27). Thus, if the load impedance is equal to the characteristic impedance, no reflection takes place; i.e., the $e^{\gamma(x-2D)}$ terms are missing. We previously demonstrated that the characteristic impedance was the input impedance of a semi-infinite transmission line. Therefore, if a transmission line is terminated in its characteristic impedance, it *appears* to be terminated in a semi-infinite transmission line. Thus, the line appears to continue and there should be no reflection. When a line is terminated in its characteristic impedance, it acts as though it is semi-infinite in that no signal is reflected from the termination. When the reflection coefficient is zero, there are no reflection terms. This is why $\rho(s)$ is called the reflection coefficient. Note that $\rho(s)$ is only zero when $Z_L(s) = Z_0(s)$.

Specific examples of reflected signals will be discussed in the next section. **Coaxial Cable.** We have considered two-wire parallel transmission lines. However, another configuration is often used. It consists of two concentric cylindrical conductors. The inner cylinder is a wire of circular cross section and the outer cylinder is often made of braided wire to make it flexible. The space between the inner and outer conductors is usually filled with a flexible dielectric. Because of its construction, this is called a *coaxial cable*.

The outer conductor is placed at ground potential. Since this conductor completely surrounds the inner one, it tends to shield it from stray fields. Thus, coaxial cable is used when it is desirable to shield a transmission line from picking up stray signals. It is also used when it is desirable to prevent the field of a signal from interfering with other devices. For instance, a radio transmitter often is connected to its antenna by coaxial cable to reduce the interference caused by the transmitted radio signals on nearby equipment.

## 10-2. TRANSIENT RESPONSE OF TRANSMISSION LINES—DISTORTIONLESS TRANSMISSION—RC TRANSMISSION LINES—GENERAL TRANSMISSION LINES

In the last section we obtained the Laplace transform of the voltage and current of a transmission line as a function of distance. We shall now obtain these voltages and currents as a function of time (and distance).

**Lossless and Distortionless Transmission Lines.** Very often, we use transmission lines to transmit signals from one point to another. In this case, the output of a transmission line should be an exact replica of the input, except possibly for a delay in time. In these cases a transmission line usually terminates in an impedance equal to the characteristic impedance; thus, Eqs. 10–41 apply. Hence, the factor $e^{\gamma x}$ (see Eqs. 10–41) should be of the form $f(x) e^{-K_1 x s}$, where $f(x)$ is a real function and $K_1$ is a constant. Let us see what conditions we can impose upon a transmission line to obtain the desired form for $\gamma(s)$. From Eq. 10–19, we have

$$\gamma(s) = \sqrt{(R + Ls)(G + Cs)} \tag{10-42}$$

Now, suppose the transmission line is such that

$$R + Ls = K^2(G + Cs) \tag{10-43}$$

where $K$ is a constant. In this case,

$$\frac{R}{G} = \frac{L}{C} = K^2 \tag{10-44}$$

Thus, $\gamma$ becomes

$$\gamma = \frac{1}{K}(R + Ls) \tag{10-45}$$

Alternatively, we can write

$$\gamma = \sqrt{RG} + s\sqrt{LC} \tag{10-46}$$

Substituting in Eq. 10–41a, we have

$$V(x, s) = V(s) e^{-x\sqrt{RG}} e^{sx\sqrt{LC}} \tag{10-47}$$

Taking the inverse Laplace transform of this equation yields

$$v(x, t) = e^{-x\sqrt{RG}} v(t - x\sqrt{LC}) \tag{10-48}$$

where $v(t) \leftrightarrow V(s)$.

The voltage waveform at any point on the transmission line is an exact replica of the voltage of the input generator, except that it has been delayed by $x\sqrt{LC}$ seconds, and the amplitude has been reduced by $e^{-x\sqrt{RG}}$. This is termed *distortionless transmission* and a line whose parameters satisfy Eq. 10–44 is a *distortionless* transmission line. The signal at point $x$ occurs $x\sqrt{LC}$ seconds later than the input signal; that is, it takes $x\sqrt{LC}$ seconds for the signal to traverse $x$ meters. Hence, the signal travels at a velocity of propagation

$$v_p = \frac{1}{\sqrt{LC}} \text{ meters/sec} \tag{10–49}$$

It can be shown that this velocity is equal to the velocity of light in the dielectric of the transmission line. Thus, energy is sent down the line at this velocity. This is consistent with the theory of special relativity.

Now suppose the input voltage is $u(t)$, the unit step. Then, the voltage along the transmission line is given by

$$v(x, t) = e^{-x\sqrt{RG}}u(t - x\sqrt{LC}) \tag{10–50}$$

This is illustrated by a series of diagrams in Fig. 10–4, where, for simplicity, we assume that a semi-infinite transmission line is used. The input voltage as a function of time is shown in Fig. 10–4a.

Now suppose at a fixed time $t$ we plot the voltage drop across the line as a function of distance. (This is shown in Fig. 10–4b.) Note that the voltage falls off exponentially with distance from the input. However, since the voltage travels with finite velocity, the voltage is zero for $x > x_1$, where $x_1 = v_p t_1$, since the signal has not reached there yet. The arrow indicates the direction of propagation with increasing time.

A different form of graph is shown in Fig. 10–4c. Here, the voltage at a fixed point $x_1$ is plotted as a function of time. The voltage is zero until $t = t_1$, since this is the length of time required for the signal to travel to point $x_1$. For $t > t_1$, the voltage has the same waveform as the input signal delayed by $t_1$ seconds, except that it is decreased in magnitude by $e^{-x\sqrt{RG}}$.

Let us determine the characteristic impedance for a distortionless line. Substituting Eqs. 10–43 and 10–44 into Eq. 10–28 yields

$$Z_0(s) = \sqrt{R/G} = \sqrt{L/C} = R_0 \tag{10–51}$$

Then, the distortionless line has a purely resistive characteristic impedance.

A special case of a distortionless transmission line is the lossless transmission line (see Section 10-1) in which

$$R = G = 0 \tag{10–52}$$

The reader may ask how a lossless transmission line can have a resistive characteristic impedance. Remember that $Z_0(s)$ represents the input impedance of a semi-infinite transmission line. Even though the transmission line is lossless, energy

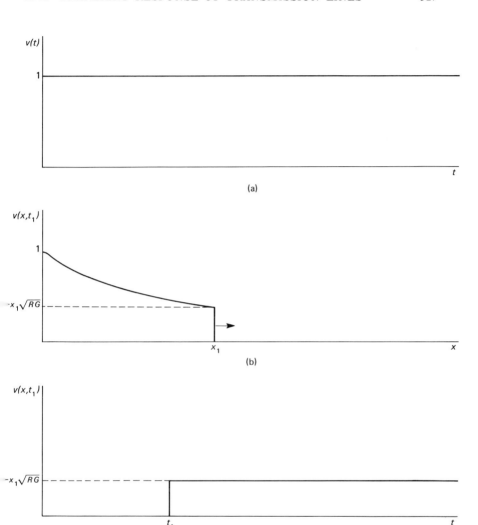

FIG. 10–4

Voltage waveforms on a distortionless, semi-infinite transmission line; (a) input voltage; (b) voltage at a fixed time $t_1$, as a function of distance; (c) voltage at a fixed distance $x_1$, as a function of time

can be propagated down it. If the line is semi-infinite, this propagation will continue indefinitely. Thus in this sense energy is absorbed by the line, so its input impedance can be resistive.

Now let us consider a lossless transmission line of length $D$ (see Fig. 10–3) and determine its voltage and current. We shall consider the voltage first. To simplify the discussion, we shall assume that the load impedance is a pure resistance. Then, from Eq. 10–39a, we have

$$V(x, s) = \frac{V(s)}{1 + e^{-2Ds\sqrt{LC}}\rho(s)} \left[e^{-xs\sqrt{LC}} + \rho(s)\, e^{s\sqrt{LC}(x-2D)}\right] \qquad (10\text{–}53)$$

where, for the case of a real load impedance

$$\rho(s) = \frac{R_L - R_0}{R_L + R_0} \qquad (10\text{–}54)$$

is a real number. Now let us assume that the transmission line is open circuited. In this case, $R_L = \infty$ and $\rho(s) = 1$, so Eq. 10–53 becomes

$$V(x, s) = V(s)\left[\frac{e^{-xs\sqrt{LC}} + e^{s\sqrt{LC}(x-2D)}}{1 + e^{-2sD\sqrt{LC}}}\right] \qquad (10\text{–}55)$$

Expanding the denominator, we have

$$\frac{1}{1 + e^{-2sD\sqrt{LC}}} = 1 - e^{-2sD\sqrt{LC}} + e^{-4sD\sqrt{LC}} - e^{-6sD\sqrt{LC}} + \cdots$$

and substituting in Eq. 10–55, we obtain

$$V(x, s) = V(s)\left[e^{-xs\sqrt{LC}} + e^{-s\sqrt{LC}(x-2D)} - e^{-s\sqrt{LC}(x+2D)} - e^{s\sqrt{LC}(x-4D)} + \cdots\right] \qquad (10\text{–}56)$$

Thus, we can express the voltage using the infinite series

$$v(x, t) = v(t + x\sqrt{LC}) + v[t - \sqrt{LC}(x - 2D)]$$
$$- v[t - \sqrt{LC}(x + 2D)] + \cdots \qquad (10\text{–}57)$$

Let us consider a specific waveform. Suppose $v(t)$, the input signal, is the unit step. Then,

$$v(x, t) = u(t - x\sqrt{LC}) + u[t - \sqrt{LC}(x - 2D)]$$
$$- u[t - \sqrt{LC}(x + 2D)] - \cdots \qquad (10\text{–}58)$$

Various voltage waveforms are shown in Fig. 10–5. Let us discuss these waveforms. To facilitate this, let us determine $T$, the time required for the signal to travel the total length of the transmission line (see Eq. 10–49)

$$T = D/v_p = D\sqrt{LC}$$

In Fig. 10–5a, the voltage as a function of distance is plotted for a fixed time $t_1$, where $0 < t_1 < T$. The unit step is propagated down the line. At $t = t_1$ it has just reached $x_1$. In Fig. 10–5b, $T < t_2 < 2T$. When the voltage reaches the termination, it is reflected. Since $\rho = +1$, the reflected waveform is in phase with the incident waveform, and the two voltages add to produce 2 volts. Note that the first reflected signal is represented by $e^{-s\sqrt{LC}(x-2D)}$.

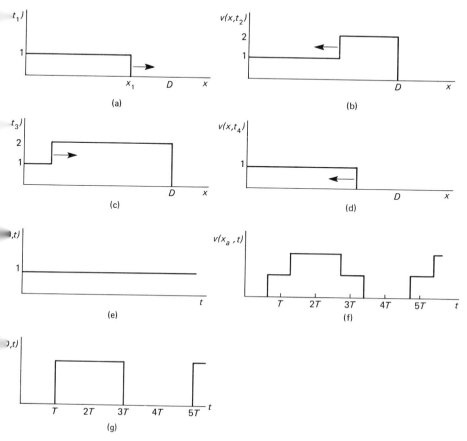

FIG. 10–5

Voltage waveform on a finite, lossless transmission line terminated in an open circuit with unit step voltage input $T = D/v_p = D\sqrt{LC}$; (a) voltage at fixed time $t_1 < T$ as a function of $x$; (b) voltage at a fixed time $t_2$, $T < t_2 < 2T$, as a function of $x$; (c) voltage at a fixed time $t_3$, $2T < t_3 < 3T$, as a function of $x$; (d) voltage at a fixed time $t_4$, $3T < t_4 < 4T$, as a function of $x$; (e) input voltage, as a function of time; (f) voltage at point $x$, as a function of time; (g) receiving end voltage, as a function of time.

As $t_2$ increases, this voltage moves back towards the input. This is indicated by the arrow of Fig. 10–5b. The input generator keeps the input voltage constant at 1 volt, while the reflected voltage would tend to make it two volts. Thus, something must offset the effect of the reflected waveform. (We can consider the impedance at the input to be zero.) Thus, the reflection coefficient there is minus one. Hence, a voltage waveform of $-1$ volt (i.e., the negative of the one arriving at the input) will be reflected from the input end. This is shown in Fig. 10–5c, which plots voltage as a function of position for a fixed time $t_3$, where $2T < t_3 < 3T$.

In Fig. 10–5d, the voltage wave of $-1$ volt is reflected from the output end (with the same sign since $\rho = 1$ at the output). Thus, the voltage becomes zero and travels backward along the line for a fixed time $t_4$, where $3T < t_4 < 4T$. These graphs repeat every $4T$.

Graphs of voltage as function of time for three representative values of $x$ are shown in Figs. 10–5e through g. The explanation of these is the same as that for the preceding graphs.

Now let us consider the current waveform. From Eq. 10–39b, we have

$$I(x, s) = \frac{V(s)/R_0}{1 + e^{-2Ds\sqrt{LC}}\rho(s)} \left[ e^{-sx\sqrt{LC}} - \rho(s) e^{s\sqrt{LC}(x - 2D)} \right] \qquad (10\text{–}59)$$

Manipulating this equation in the same way as we did Eq. 10–53 to obtain Eq. 10–56 (if $\rho(s) = 1$) yields

$$I(x, s) = \frac{V(s)}{R_0} \left[ e^{sx\sqrt{LC}} - e^{s\sqrt{LC}(x - 2D)} - e^{-s\sqrt{LC}(x + 2D)} + \cdots \right] \qquad (10\text{–}60)$$

Thus, if $v(0, t) = u(t)$, we have

$$i(x, s) = \frac{1}{R_0} \left[ u(t - x\sqrt{LC}) - u[t - \sqrt{LC}(x - 2D)] \right.$$
$$\left. - u[t - \sqrt{LC}(x + 2D)] + \cdots \right] \qquad (10\text{–}61)$$

Some plots of typical waveforms are shown in Fig. 10–6. The basic explanations are the same as for the voltage graphs of Fig. 10–5. However, note that a minus sign appears in Eq. 10–39b, while a plus sign appears in Eq. 10–39a. Then, whenever a voltage is reflected with the same polarity as the incident wave, the current will be reflected with the reverse polarity of the incident and vice versa. Note that the voltage at the input to the line is always constant at a positive value, while the input current alternates. Thus, the power into the line is positive and negative, alternately. That is, at times, the line takes power from the generator, and, at other times, it supplies it back. Thus, the net energy taken from the generator is zero.

We just considered the lossless case. If the distortionless line is not lossless, then there will be attenuation as the signal propagates down the line. Thus, the reflections will be smaller. Also, these reflections will be attenuated. After sufficient time has elapsed, the reflection will become negligible. If the termination impedance is an open circuit and the input is a unit step voltage generator, then the voltage at any fixed $x$ will eventually approach a constant value as a function of time. (It will fall off with distance from the input.) The current waveform will be a constant function of time at any fixed $x$. Note that the current will be zero at the open-circuit end.

Now let us again consider the general case of the distortionless line. If it is ter-

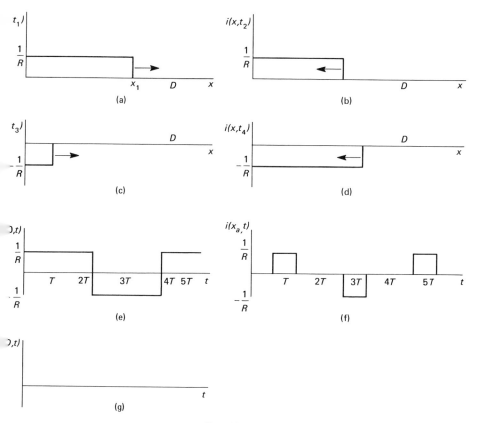

FIG. 10–6

Current waveforms on a finite lossless transmission line terminated in an open circuit, $T = D/V_p = D\sqrt{LC}$ where the input voltage is a unit step; (a) current at a fixed time $t_1 < T$, as a function of $x$; (b) current at a fixed time $t_2$, $T_1 < t_2 < 2T$, as a function of $x$; (c) current at a fixed time $t_3$, $2T < t_3 < 3T$, as a function of $x$; (d) current at a fixed time $t_4$, $3T < t_4 < 4T$, as a function of $x$; (e) input current, as a function of time; (f) current at point $x = x_a$, as a function of time; (g) load current, as a function of time

minated in its characteristic resistance, then $\rho(s) = 0$; thus,

$$V(x, s) = V(s)\,e^{-x\sqrt{RG}}\,e^{-xs\sqrt{LC}} \qquad (10\text{–}62)$$

Then the output signal will be a replica of the input signal delayed by $D\sqrt{RC}$ seconds and reduced in magnitude by $e^{-D\sqrt{RG}}$. Thus, distortionless transmission will have been achieved. It is, therefore, desirable to construct transmission lines so that they are distortionless; i.e., so that Eq. 10–44 is satisfied.

In general, most transmission lines can be constructed with very small $G$ so that

$$\frac{R}{G} > \frac{L}{C} \tag{10-63}$$

To achieve distortionless transmission, the "greater than" sign must be replaced by equals. One way to obtain this would be to use a poor dielectric so that $G$ becomes larger. This will make the transmission distortionless. However, it will also increase attenuation. (Note that the signal at the output is reduced by a factor of $e^{-D\sqrt{RG}}$.) The other alternative is to increase $L$. This is often accomplished by placing small inductances in series with the transmission line. These inductances are distributed uniformly throughout the line. Let us designate such inductance $L_c$. If $d_1$ is the distance between inductors and $L$ is the inductance per meter of the transmission line, then the inductance should be such that the overall inductance per unit length; i.e., $(Ld_1 + L_c)/d_1$ satisfies Eq. 10–44. If inductors are used in pairs (one in the upper wire and one in the lower one), each inductance should be $L_c/2$ henries (see Fig. 10–1). The spacing of the inductors should be much less than the smallest wavelength of the signals transmitted (wavelength is discussed in Section 10-4).

*RC* **Transmission Line.**   Now let us consider a transmission line whose series resistance $R$ per unit length is very much larger than the series inductance $L$ per unit length. Often, a satisfactory approximation can be obtained by assuming that $L$ is zero. Also, the conductance of the dielectric between transmission lines is often so low that it can be ignored (i.e., $G = 0$). The equations used for the study of heat flow are often the same as the equations of a transmission line with $L = 0, G = 0$. Another application is in distributed integrated circuits. They are often composed of distributed resistances and capacitances. Hence, the approximation that $L = 0$ and $G = 0$ are good here. We assume that

$$L = 0 \tag{10-64a}$$

$$G = 0 \tag{10-64b}$$

Then, Eqs. 10–19 and 10–28 become

$$\gamma(s) = \sqrt{RCs} \tag{10-65}$$

$$Z_0(s) = \sqrt{R/Cs} \tag{10-66}$$

Let us consider the case of the semi-infinite transmission line; then (see Eqs. 10–23 and 10–27)

$$V(x, s) = V(s)\, e^{-x\sqrt{RCs}} \tag{10-67a}$$

$$I(x, s) = V(s)\, \sqrt{Cs/R}\ e^{-x\sqrt{RCs}} \tag{10-67b}$$

Let us assume that the input voltage is a unit step; thus,

$$V(s) = \frac{1}{s} \tag{10-68}$$

We shall determine $i(x, t)$ and $v(x, t)$. Let us determine $i(x, t)$ first. Then, substituting in Eq. 3–11, we have

$$i(x, t) = \sqrt{\frac{C}{R}} \frac{1}{2\pi j} \int_{C-j\infty}^{C+j\infty} \frac{e^{-x\sqrt{RCs}+st}}{\sqrt{s}} \, ds, \qquad C > 0 \qquad (10\text{–}69)$$

The integral was (essentially) evaluated in the example of Eqs. 3–158 through 3–168. Following this example, we obtain

$$i(x, t) = u(t) \sqrt{\frac{C}{\pi Rt}} e^{-x^2 RC/4t} \qquad (10\text{–}70)$$

Before discussing the form of the current, let us determine the transmission line voltage. Substituting Eq. 10–68 into Eq. 10–67a, we have

$$V(x, s) = \frac{e^{-x\sqrt{RCs}}}{s} \qquad (10\text{–}71)$$

We could evaluate this using the inverse Laplace transform integral directly. However, there is a simple procedure in this case. To evaluate the current, we obtain the inverse Laplace transform of

$$I(x, s) = \sqrt{\frac{C}{R}} \frac{e^{-x\sqrt{RCs}}}{\sqrt{s}} \qquad (10\text{–}72)$$

Compare Eqs. 10–71 and 10–72. This indicates that

$$V(x, s) = \sqrt{\frac{C}{R}} R \int_{x}^{\infty} \frac{e^{-y\sqrt{RCs}}}{\sqrt{s}} \, dy = R \int_{x}^{\infty} I(y, s) \, ds \qquad (10\text{–}73)$$

Now suppose

$$f(x, t) \leftrightarrow F(x, s) \qquad (10\text{–}74)$$

Let us determine the inverse Laplace transform of $\int_{x}^{\infty} F(y, s) \, dy$. We shall call this $f_1(x, t)$; then,

$$f_1(x, t) = \frac{1}{2\pi j} \int_{C-j\infty}^{C+j\infty} e^{st} \int_{x}^{\infty} F(y, s) \, dy \, ds \qquad (10\text{–}75)$$

Now assume that the functions are such that the order of integration can be interchanged; then,

$$f_1(x, t) = \int_{x}^{\infty} \frac{1}{2\pi j} \int_{C-j\infty}^{C+j\infty} F(y, s) \, ds \, dx = \int_{x}^{\infty} f(y, t) \, dy \qquad (10\text{–}76)$$

Hence, we have

$$\int_{x}^{\infty} f(y, t) \, dy \leftrightarrow \int_{x}^{\infty} F(y, s) \, dy \qquad (10\text{–}77)$$

That is, if a function of time is a continuous function of a parameter and we integrate the time function with respect to this parameter, the Laplace transform of this integrated function is just the integral of the Laplace transform of the original function with respect to the parameter. Then, applying Eqs. 10–77 through 10–73, we obtain

$$v(x, t) = R \int_x^\infty i(y, t)\, dy \tag{10-78}$$

Substituting Eq. 10–70, we have

$$v(x, t) = u(t)\sqrt{\frac{RC}{\pi t}} \int_x^\infty e^{-y^2 RC/4t}\, dy$$

Let $z = y\sqrt{RC/4t}$; then, substituting, we obtain

$$v(x, t) = u(t)\, \frac{2}{\sqrt{\pi}} \int_{(x/2)\sqrt{RC/t}}^\infty e^{-z^2}\, dz \tag{10-79}$$

This integral cannot be evaluated in closed form. However, there are functions which have been numerically integrated and tabulated which can be used numerically to express $v(x, t)$. One is the *error function* [1]. This is written as

$$erf(x) = \frac{2}{\sqrt{\pi}} \int_0^x e^{-z^2}\, dz \tag{10-80}$$

where $erf(x)$ is the error function of $x$. If $x = \infty$, then

$$erf(\infty) = \frac{2}{\sqrt{\pi}} \int_0^\infty e^{-z^2}\, dz = 1 \tag{10-81}$$

Thus, we can express $v(x, t)$ in terms of the tabulated error function as

$$v(x, t) = u(t)\left[ 1 - erf\left(\frac{x}{2}\right)\sqrt{\frac{RC}{t}} \right] \tag{10-82}$$

It is conventional to write

$$erf_c(x) = 1 - erf(x) \tag{10-83}$$

where $erf_c$ is the *complementary error function*; then,

$$v(x, t) = u(t)\, erf_c\left(\frac{x}{2}\right)\sqrt{\frac{RC}{t}} \tag{10-84}$$

The current $i(x, t)$ is given by Eq. 10–70. Let us repeat it here:

$$i(x, t) = u(t)\sqrt{\frac{C}{\pi R t}}\, e^{-x^2 RC/4t} \tag{10-85}$$

Plots of $v(x, t)$ and $i(x, t)$ are given in Fig. 10–7.

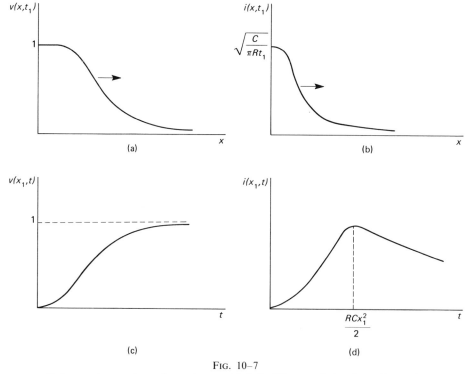

FIG. 10–7

Voltage and current waveforms in a semi-infinite RC transmission line with a unit step voltage input; (a) voltage vs distance at a fixed time $t_1$; (b) current vs distance at a fixed time $t_1$; (c) voltage vs time at a fixed distance $x_1$; (d) current vs time at a fixed distance $x_1$

Consider Fig. 10–7a where $v(x, t_1)$ versus $x$ is plotted. At any time $t_1$, the voltage is not zero at any point, no matter how large $x$ is. This indicates that the signal propagates down the transmission line at infinite velocity. This waveform violates the physical principle that energy cannot be transmitted at more than the velocity of light. Paradoxes, such as this, can occur in electric circuits when inductance and/or capacitance are ignored. However, this does not mean that the equations do not yield valid approximations. If the small values of $v(x, t)$ are assumed to be zero, this waveform acts as a signal transmitted down the line. The difference between an actual and an approximated signal is often small for all values of $x$, and, in that sense, the approximations made are valid.

Figure 10–7b is a plot of current versus distance at a fixed time. Again the curve indicates that the current is nonzero at all points on the line.

Figures 10–7c and d are plots of voltage and current versus time at a fixed point on the transmission line. Note that there is no time delay, but the waveforms become nonzero instantly. (This is equivalent to our discussion of infinite velocity of propagation.) Note, however, that both $v(x, t)$ and $i(x, t)$ remain small for small $t$. This approximates time delay which would be calculated if we had considered small inductances of the transmission line. We shall next consider general transmission lines and demonstrate that a time delay corresponding to a finite velocity of propagation does occur.

**General *RLGC* Transmission Lines.** We have, thus far, considered some special transmission lines. Now let us analyze the time domain response of a general transmission line. First, let us consider a semi-infinite transmission line. We shall introduce some parameters which will be useful in describing the performance of such a line. From Eq. 10–19, the propagation constant is

$$\gamma(s) = \sqrt{(R + Ls)(G + Cs)}$$

This can be written as

$$\gamma(s) = \sqrt{LC}\sqrt{\left(s + \frac{R}{L}\right)\left(s + \frac{G}{C}\right)} \qquad (10\text{–}86)$$

Now let us define two constants $\alpha$ and $d$, where

$$\alpha + d = \frac{R}{L} \qquad (10\text{–}87a)$$

$$\alpha - d = \frac{G}{C} \qquad (10\text{–}87b)$$

Thus,

$$\alpha = \frac{1}{2}\left(\frac{R}{L} + \frac{G}{C}\right) \qquad (10\text{–}88a)$$

$$d = \frac{1}{2}\left(\frac{R}{L} - \frac{G}{C}\right) \qquad (10\text{–}88b)$$

Note that if the line is distortionless (see Eq. 10–44), then $d = 0$. For this reason, $d$ is called the *generalized distortion constant* and $\alpha$ is the *generalized attenuation constant*. Note that if the line is lossless, then signals can be propogated without attenuation and $\alpha = 0$. Substituting of Eqs. 10–88 into Eq. 10–86 yields

$$\gamma(s) = \sqrt{LC}\sqrt{(s + \alpha)^2 - d^2} \qquad (10\text{–}89)$$

We can also express the characteristic impedance in terms of these constants. Comparing Eqs. 10–19 and 10–28, we have

$$Z_0 = \frac{\gamma}{G + Cs} = \sqrt{LC}\,\frac{\sqrt{(s + \alpha)^2 - d^2}}{G + Cs} \qquad (10\text{–}90)$$

Now let us assume that a semi-infinite transmission line is driven by a voltage generator (see Fig. 10–2). We also assume that the input generator supplies a unit step of voltage. Then (see Eqs. 10–23 and 10–27) we have

$$V(x, s) = \frac{1}{s}e^{-x\sqrt{LC}\sqrt{(s + \alpha)^2 - d^2}} \qquad (10\text{–}91a)$$

$$I(x, s) = \frac{C + G/s}{\sqrt{LC}\sqrt{(s + \alpha)^2 - d^2}} e^{-x\sqrt{LC}\sqrt{(s+\alpha)^2 - d^2}} \tag{10–91b}$$

Note that, as we have seen, if $d = 0$, the voltage wave will propagate down the line with attenuation, but with no distortion.

Obtaining the inverse of these Laplace transforms is an involved procedure. Therefore, let us consider one term (which is a part of $I(x, s)$):

$$\frac{e^{x\sqrt{LC}\sqrt{(s+\alpha)^2 - d^2}}}{\sqrt{(s + \alpha)^2 - d^2}}$$

If the factor $s + \alpha$ is replaced by $s$, the time function will be unchanged except that a factor $e^{-\alpha t}$ will be omitted (see Eq. 3–77). Thus, we need only obtain the inverse Laplace transform of a function of the form

$$\frac{e^{-a\sqrt{s^2 - d^2}}}{\sqrt{s^2 - d^2}}$$

Hence, we wish to evaluate

$$f(t) = \frac{1}{2\pi j} \int_{C-j\infty}^{C+j\infty} \frac{e^{-a\sqrt{s^2 - d^2}}}{\sqrt{s^2 - d^2}} e^{st} \, ds$$

This integral has a pair of branch points $s = \pm d$. The evaluation of the integral follows the procedures of Section 3-12. The integral cannot be evaluated in closed form. However, proper substitutions can be made [2] so that the integral can be related to some integrals whose solutions can be expressed in terms of modified Bessel functions; that is, the solution is expressed in terms of a tabulated infinite series. (Note that a table of Laplace transforms commonly occurring in transmission line problems is given in [2].)

Alternatively, the function $e^{a\sqrt{s^2 - d^2}}/\sqrt{s^2 - d^2}$ can be expanded in a Taylor's series. The inverse transform of this can be taken term by term. The resulting series will be that of a modified Bessel function. If either of these procedures is used, we find the desired inverse transform is given by

$$I_0(d\sqrt{t^2 - a^2})\, u(t - a) \leftrightarrow \frac{e^{-a\sqrt{s^2 - d^2}}}{\sqrt{s^2 - d^2}} \tag{10–92}$$

where $I_0(y)$ is a modified Bessel function of order zero. A plot of this function is given in Fig. 10–8a. Using Eq. 3–77, we obtain

$$\frac{e^{x\sqrt{LC}\sqrt{(s+\alpha)^2 - d^2}}}{\sqrt{(s + \alpha)^2 + d^2}} \leftrightarrow u(t - x\sqrt{LC})\, e^{-\alpha t} I_0(d\sqrt{t^2 - x^2 LC}) \tag{10–93}$$

Then, applying Eq. 3–65, assuming zero initial conditions, we have, for the inverse

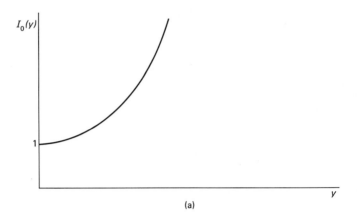

(a)

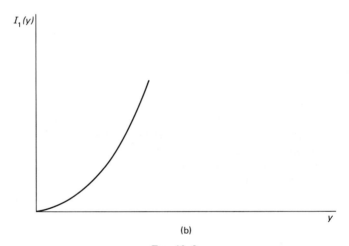

(b)

FIG. 10–8
Plots of modified Bessel functions; (a) order zero; (b) order one

Laplace transform of Eq. 10–91b,

$$i(x, t) = \sqrt{\frac{C}{L}}\, u(t - x\sqrt{LC})\,\big[e^{-\alpha t}I_0(d\sqrt{t^2 - x^2 LC})$$

$$+ \frac{G}{C}\int_{x\sqrt{LC}}^{t} e^{-\alpha y}I_0(d\sqrt{y^2 - x^2 LC})\,dy\big] \qquad (10\text{–}94)$$

Note that the lower limit of integration is $x\sqrt{LC}$ and not zero, since the integrand is zero for $t < x\sqrt{LC}$; i.e., $u(t - xLC)$ is omitted from the integrand.

Let us now obtain the inverse Laplace transform of $V(x, s)$. We can write this in the form

$$V(x, s) = \frac{e^{-x\sqrt{LC}\sqrt{(s+\alpha)^2 - d^2}}}{s} = -\frac{1}{s\sqrt{LC}}\frac{d}{dx}\frac{e^{-x\sqrt{LC}\sqrt{(s+\alpha)^2 - d^2}}}{\sqrt{(s+\alpha)^2 - d^2}} \quad (10\text{--}95)$$

Proceeding as in Eqs. 10–74 through 10–77, we can show that if we differentiate a function of $s$ with respect to a parameter, we then can obtain the inverse transform of the differentiated function by differentiating the inverse transform (of the original function of $s$) with respect to the parameter. Then, using Eq. 10–93 and 3–65, we have (note that $v(x, t)$ is the inverse Laplace transform of $V(x, s)$)

$$v(x, t) = -\frac{1}{\sqrt{LC}}\int_0^t \frac{d}{dx}\left[I_0(d\sqrt{y^2 - x^2LC})\, e^{-\alpha y} u(y - x\sqrt{LC})\right] dy \quad (10\text{--}96)$$

Observe that the lower limit is zero since we have included the unit step in the integrand. The function has a discontinuity at $y = x\sqrt{LC}$. Thus, the derivative has an impulse there; that is

$$\frac{d}{dx}u(y - x\sqrt{LC}) = -\sqrt{LC}\,\delta(y - x\sqrt{LC})$$

Hence,

$$v(x, t) = -\frac{1}{\sqrt{LC}}\int_0^t \left[-\sqrt{LC}\,\delta(y - x\sqrt{LC})\, I_0(0)\, e^{-\alpha x\sqrt{LC}}\right.$$

$$\left. -\frac{dxLC\, u(y - x\sqrt{LC})}{\sqrt{y^2 - x^2LC}}\, I_0'(d\sqrt{y^2 - x^2LC})\right] dy \quad (10\text{--}97)$$

Note that $I_0(0) = 1$. The derivative of $I_0(y)$ is given by

$$I_1(y) = \frac{d}{dy}I_0(y) = I_0'(y) \quad (10\text{--}98)$$

where $I_1(y)$ is the modified Bessel function of the first kind and is plotted in Fig. 10–8b; then,

$$v(x, t) = u(t - x\sqrt{LC})\left[e^{-\alpha x\sqrt{LC}}\right.$$

$$\left. + dx\sqrt{LC}\int_{x\sqrt{LC}}^t \frac{I_1(d\sqrt{y^2 - x^2LC})}{\sqrt{y^2 - x^2LC}}\, dy\right] \quad (10\text{--}99)$$

This integral can be evaluated using numerical means. Plots of the voltage and current are given in Fig. 10–9. The final values of the current and voltage can be

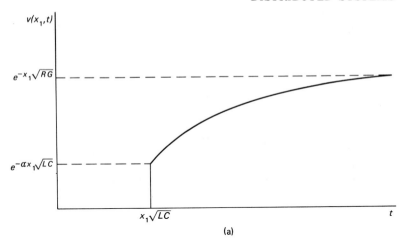

(a)

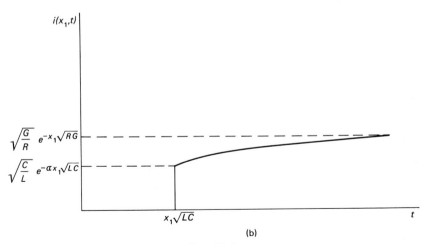

(b)

Fig. 10–9

Voltage and current vs time on a general semi-infinite transmission line, in response to a unit step of voltage; (a) voltage vs time; (b) current vs time

obtained from the final value theorem (see Section 3-10). Applying this theorem to Eqs. 10–91, we obtain

$$v(x, \infty) = \lim_{s \to 0} e^{-x\sqrt{LC}\sqrt{(s+a)^2 - d^2}} = e^{-x\sqrt{RG}} \qquad (10\text{–}100a)$$

$$i(x, \infty) = \sqrt{\frac{G}{R}}\, e^{-x\sqrt{RG}} \qquad (10\text{–}100b)$$

Consider the plot of $v(x, t)$. Equation 10–99 consists of two parts. The first is $u(t - x\sqrt{LC})\, e^{-ax\sqrt{LC}}$. This represents distortionless transmission. It is just a square wave that propagates with attenuation along the transmission line. The second term represents the distortion component. Note that, in a distortionless case, $d = 0$ and the second term vanishes. Then, the ideal output is just a delayed unit step. The departure from the delayed unit step is the distortion term.

Notice in the general transmission line, where inductance and capacitance are considered, that there is a finite velocity of propagation of the signal. This is in contrast to the RC line, where this type of propagation did not result. As was mentioned in the discussion (in this section) of the RC transmission line, this paradox occurs because inductance is ignored.

The current waveform is similar to the voltage waveform. It is illustrated in Fig. 10–9b. It is possible that $\sqrt{G/R}\, e^{-x_1\sqrt{RG}} < \sqrt{C/L}\, e^{-ax_1\sqrt{LC}}$. In this case, the response falls instead of rising, for $t > x_1\sqrt{LC}$.

Now let us consider another example. Suppose we have a general finite RL CG transmission line of length $D$, (see Fig. 10–3). Assume that this line is terminated in an open circuit; then,

$$Z_L(s) = \infty \tag{10–101}$$

The reflection coefficient (see Eq. 10–38) is

$$\rho(s) = +1$$

Then (see Eq. 10–39) the voltage of the line is

$$V(x, s) = \frac{V(s)}{1 + e^{-2\gamma D}} \left[ e^{-\gamma x} + e^{\gamma(x - 2D)} \right] \tag{10–102}$$

where $\gamma$ is given by Eq. 10–89. Let us assume that the input voltage is a unit step. Then, substituting $V(s) = 1/s$ and manipulating, we have

$$V(x, s) = \frac{1}{s} \frac{e^{-\gamma(x - D)} + e^{\gamma(x - D)}}{e^{\gamma D} + e^{-\gamma D}} \tag{10–103}$$

$$V(x, s) = \frac{1}{s} \frac{\cosh \gamma(x - D)}{\cosh \gamma D} \tag{10–104}$$

Taking the inverse Laplace transform of this function is essentially the same as that done in the example of Eq. 3–154. The poles occur at $s = 0$ and the roots of $\cosh \gamma D = 0$. That is where

$$\gamma D = j(2n - 1) \frac{\pi}{2}$$

Substituting Eq. 10–89, we obtain

$$\sqrt{LC}\, \sqrt{(s_n + \alpha)^2 - d^2} = \pm j(2n - 1) \frac{\pi}{2} \tag{10–105}$$

Solving for $s$ yields

$$(s_n + \alpha)^2 - d^2 = -(2n - 1)\frac{\pi^2}{4LC}$$

$$s_n = -\alpha \pm \sqrt{d^2 - (2n - 1)^2 \frac{\pi^2}{4LC}} \qquad (10\text{–}106)$$

Let us write this as

$$s_n = -\alpha + j\omega_k \qquad (10\text{–}107)$$

where

$$\omega_k = \sqrt{(2n - 1)^2 \frac{\pi^2}{4LC} - d^2} \qquad (10\text{–}108)$$

(Note that some of the $s_n$ can consist of *real* negative numbers. However, for sufficiently large $n$, $s_n$ becomes a complex number.) Then, using residues, we obtain

$$v(x, t) = \left.\frac{\cosh \gamma(x - D)}{\cosh \gamma D} e^{st}\right|_{s=0} + \sum_{n=-\infty}^{\infty} \left.\frac{e^{st}}{s}\frac{\cosh \gamma(x - D)}{\frac{d}{ds}\cosh \gamma D}\right|_{s=s_n} \qquad (10\text{–}109)$$

Manipulating, we have

$$v(x, t) = \frac{\cosh \sqrt{RG}(x - D)}{\cosh \sqrt{RG}\, D} + \sum_{n=-\infty}^{\infty} \left.\frac{e^{st}}{s}\frac{\cosh \gamma_n(x - D)}{\dfrac{\sqrt{LC}(s + \alpha)}{\sqrt{(s + \alpha)^2 - d^2}}\sinh \gamma_n D}\right|_{s=s_n} \qquad (10\text{–}110)$$

where $\gamma_n$ is evaluated with $s = s_n$. The details of the substitution are left to the reader.

In the previous analysis, we have assumed that a generator is connected directly to the input of the transmission line. However, there may also be some impedance in series with the generator (see Fig. 10–10).

In order to use the previous results to determine the transmission line voltage and current, we must determine $V(0, s)$. To do this we shall evaluate $Z_{in}(s)$, the

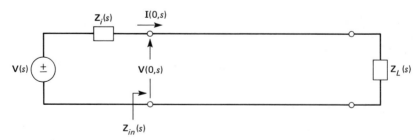

FIG. 10–10
Transmission line whose input voltage generator has a series impedance $Z_i(s)$

input impedance of the transmission line. This is given by

$$Z_{in}(s) = V(0, s)/I(0, s) \tag{10-111}$$

Substuting Eqs. 10–39, we obtain

$$Z_{in}(s) = Z_0(s) \frac{\left[1 + \rho(s) e^{-2\gamma D}\right]}{1 - \rho(s)^{-2\gamma D}} \tag{10-112}$$

Then,

$$V(0, s) = \frac{V(s) Z_{in}(s)}{Z_i(s) + Z_{in}(s)} \tag{10-113}$$

This relation gives the Laplace transform of the voltage at the transmission line input in terms of the generator voltage, series impedance, characteristic impedance, transmission line length, and transmission line termination. The inclusion of a series impedance can greatly complicate the solution for the voltages and currents.

## 10-3. SINUSOIDAL STEADY-STATE RESPONSE OF TRANSMISSION LINES

Very often, transmission lines are supplied with a single-frequency sinusoid, or a group of sinusoids, all of whose frequencies lie close to a central frequency. For instance, transmission lines are used to connect radio transmitters to antennas. The signals carried by the transmission line are the sinusoidal carrier and the sidebands. For such signals, a study of the sinusoidal steady-state response can supply much information about the behavior of the transmission lines. We assume that the input generators are sinusoidal and we are interested in the sinusoidal components of the currents and voltages. In Section 5-1, we saw that sinusoidal steady-state response could be obtained from the Laplace transformed form of the transfer function by replacing $s$ by $j\omega$. We shall now do this using the results of Section 10-1. The expression for the propagation constant, characteristic impedance, and reflection coefficient becomes (see Eqs. 10–19, 10–28, and 10–38)

$$\gamma(j\omega) = \sqrt{(R + j\omega L)(G + j\omega C)} \tag{10-114}$$

$$Z_0(j\omega) = \sqrt{\frac{R + j\omega L}{G + j\omega C}} \tag{10-115}$$

$$\rho(j\omega) = \frac{Z_L(j\omega) - Z_0(j\omega)}{Z_L(j\omega) + Z_0(j\omega)} \tag{10-116}$$

Then, from Eqs. 10–39 we have, for a transmission line of length $D$ with termination impedance $Z_L(j\omega)$ (see Fig. 10–3)

$$V(x, j\omega) = \frac{V(j\omega)}{1 + e^{-2\gamma D}\rho(j\omega)} \left[e^{-\gamma x} + \rho(j\omega) e^{\gamma(x - 2D)}\right] \tag{10-117a}$$

$$I(x, j\omega) = \frac{V(j\omega)/Z_0(j\omega)}{1 + e^{-2\gamma D}\rho(j\omega)}\left[e^{-\gamma x} - \rho(j\omega)\,e^{\gamma(x - 2D)}\right] \qquad (10\text{--}117\text{b})$$

where $V(j\omega)$ is the phasor representation of the input generator. (Remember that these are phasors, hence their magnitude represents the maximum (rms) value of the sinusoid and their phase angle represents the phase angle of the sinusoid.) Thus $V(j\omega) = 10e^{j\pi/4}$ represents a voltage $v(t) = 10\sin(\omega t + \pi/4)$. The impedance, viewed into the input of the transmission line, is given by $V(0, j\omega)/I(0, j\omega)$; hence,

$$Z_{in}(j\omega) = Z_0\frac{[1 + \rho(j\omega)\,e^{-\gamma 2D}]}{[1 - \rho(j\omega)\,e^{-\gamma 2D}]} \qquad (10\text{--}118)$$

These expressions can be used to find the voltage and current at all points along the transmission line.

## 10-4. LOSSLESS TRANSMISSION LINE—STANDING WAVES

Now we shall obtain the sinusoidal steady-state response for a lossless transmission line. In this case,

$$R = G = 0 \qquad (10\text{--}119)$$

Then, the propagation constant and characteristic impedance are (see Eqs. 10–114 and 10–115)

$$\gamma(j\omega) = -j\omega\sqrt{LC} = -j\beta \qquad (10\text{--}120)$$

$$Z_0 = \frac{R}{L} = R_0 \qquad (10\text{--}121)$$

where $\beta$ is called the *phase constant* and $R_0$ is the *characteristic resistance*. Thus, the expressions for voltage and current (see Eqs. 10–117) for a transmission line $D$ meters long (see Fig. 10–11) are

$$V(x, j\omega) = \frac{V(j\omega)}{1 + e^{-2j\beta D}\rho(j\omega)}\left[e^{-j\beta x} + \rho(j\omega)\,e^{j\beta(x - 2D)}\right] \qquad (10\text{--}122\text{a})$$

$$I(x, j\omega) = \frac{V(j\omega)/R_0}{1 + e^{-2j\beta D}\rho(j\omega)}\left[e^{-j\beta x} - \rho(j\omega)\,e^{-j\beta(x - 2D)}\right] \qquad (10\text{--}122\text{b})$$

Let us consider $V(x, j\omega)$. Rearranging Eq. 10–122a, we have

$$V(x, j\omega) = V(j\omega)\left[\frac{e^{-j\beta(x - D)} + \rho(j\omega)\,e^{j\beta(x - D)}}{e^{j\beta D} + \rho(j\omega)\,e^{-j\beta D}}\right] \qquad (10\text{--}123)$$

We introduce the following substitution

$$y = D - x \qquad (10\text{--}124)$$

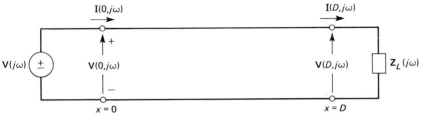

Fig. 10–11

Finite transmission line of arbitrary termination (voltages and currents are expressed in terms of phasors)

That is, $y$ represents distance measured from the *load end* of the transmission line. This substitution is made to put the relations in a simpler form; then,

$$V(y, j\omega) = V(j\omega) \left[ \frac{e^{+j\beta D} + \rho(j\omega) e^{-j\beta y}}{e^{j\beta D} + \rho(j\omega) e^{-j\beta D}} \right] \qquad (10\text{--}125a)$$

Is a similar way, we can write

$$I(y, j\omega) = \frac{V(j\omega)}{R_0} \left[ \frac{e^{j\beta y} - \rho(j\omega) e^{-j\beta y}}{e^{j\beta D} + \rho(j\omega) e^{-j\beta D}} \right] \qquad (10\text{--}125b)$$

For purposes of brevity, let us define the constant (with respect to $y$)

$$K(j\omega) = \frac{V(j\omega)}{e^{j\beta D} + \rho(j\omega) e^{-j\beta D}} \qquad (10\text{--}126)$$

Then,

$$V(y, j\omega) = K(j\omega) \left[ e^{j\beta y} + \rho(j\omega) e^{-j\beta y} \right] \qquad (10\text{--}127a)$$

$$I(y, j\omega) = \frac{K(j\omega)}{R_0} \left[ e^{j\beta y} - \rho(j\omega) e^{-j\beta y} \right] \qquad (10\text{--}127b)$$

As we have seen (see Section 10-1 and 10-2) there is an incident wave which travels from the input end ($x = 0$) to the receiving end ($x = D$) (see Fig. 10–11). This is represented by the $e^{j\beta y}$ term. There is a component reflected back from the termination which is represented by the $e^{-j\beta y}$ term. Thus, the reflection coefficient $\rho(j\omega)$ is the ratio of the reflected and incident components.

Suppose we have a semi-infinite transmission line or one terminated in its characteristic resistance so that $\rho(j\omega) = 0$. Then, Eq. 10–127a becomes

$$V(y, j\omega) = K(j\omega) e^{j\beta y} \qquad (10\text{--}128)$$

where (see Eq. 10–126)

$$K(j\omega) = V(j\omega) e^{-j\beta D} \qquad (10\text{--}129)$$

For simplicity, let us assume that $V(j\omega)$ is such that $K(j\omega) = V_0$. Then,

$$V(y, j\omega) = V_0 e^{j\beta y} \qquad (10\text{–}130)$$

This phasor represents a sinusoidal function of time given by

$$v(y, t) = V_0 \sin(\omega t + \beta y) \qquad (10\text{–}131)$$

At any fixed time $t_1$, voltage varies sinusoidally with distance along the transmission line. A *wavelength* $\lambda$ is defined as the length (distance) of one period; that is, $\lambda$ is the amount $y$ has to be varied so that $\omega t_1 + \beta y$ is increased by $2\pi$ radians; this is

$$\omega t_1 + \beta(y + \lambda) = \omega t_1 + \beta y + 2\pi \qquad (10\text{–}132)$$

Then, rearranging, we obtain

$$\lambda = \frac{2\pi}{\beta} \qquad (10\text{–}133)$$

Substituting Eqs. 10–120 and 10–26, we have

$$\lambda = 2\pi/\omega\sqrt{LC} = 1/f\sqrt{LC} = v_p/f$$

equivalently,

$$\lambda f = v_p \qquad (10\text{–}134)$$

This states that the product of frequency and wavelength is equal to the velocity of propagation of the signal.

Now let us express distance on transmission lines in terms of wavelength. Substituting Eq. 10–133 into Eq. 10–127, we obtain

$$V(y, j\omega) = K(j\omega)\left[e^{j2\pi(y/\lambda)} + \rho(j\omega)e^{-j2\pi(y/\lambda)}\right] \qquad (10\text{–}135a)$$

$$I(y, j\omega) = \frac{K(j\omega)}{R_0}\left[e^{j2\pi(y/\lambda)} - \rho(j\omega)e^{-j2\pi(y/\lambda)}\right] \qquad (10\text{–}135b)$$

Let us consider a specific example. Suppose a transmission line is open circuited; then (see Eq. 10–116) $\rho(j\omega) = 1$. Therefore, Eq. 10–135a becomes

$$V(y, j\omega) = K(j\omega)\left[e^{j2\omega y/\lambda} + e^{-j2\pi y/\lambda}\right] \qquad (10\text{–}136)$$

or equivalently

$$V(y, j\omega) = 2K(j\omega)\cos 2\pi y/\lambda \qquad (10\text{–}137)$$

Thus, the magnitude of the maximum value of the sinusoidal signal varies cosinusoidally along the transmission line. For example, suppose $2K(j\omega) = V_0$. Then, Eq. 10–137 is a phasor which represents the sinusoid

$$v(y, t) = V_0 \cos(2\pi y/\lambda)\sin \omega t = V_{max}\sin \omega t \qquad (10\text{–}138)$$

The peak value of the sinusoid is given by

$$V_{max} = V_0 \cos 2\pi y/\lambda \qquad (10\text{–}139)$$

This varies cosinusoidally with position, but it is not a function of time. As we have defined it, $V_{max}$ can be negative. This represents a 180° phase reversal. Plots of various waveforms are given in Fig. 10–12. In Fig. 10–12a, $V_m$ is plotted. Note that

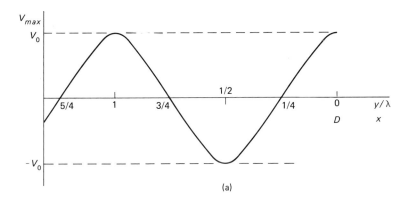

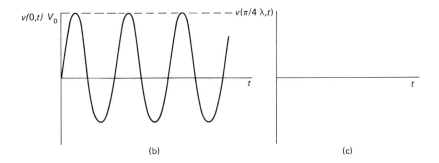

FIG. 10–12

Waveforms on a lossless line terminated in an open circuit; (a) $V_{max}$ vs distance. Note that $V_{max}$ can take on negative as well as positive values; (b) $v(t)$ measured at the end of the line; (c) $v(t)$ measured 1/4 wavelength from the end of the line

$V_{max}$ repeats itself periodically each $\lambda$. Remember that $V_{max}$ represents plus or minus the maximum value of the voltage sinusoid.

Waveforms of voltage versus time are shown for two representative positions. One is at the end of the line where a sinusoid results, the other is 1/4 wavelength from the end of the line. The voltage is zero. Thus, it is a sinusoid of zero amplitude.

Let us consider the reason for this behavior. A sinusoid of voltage propagates down a transmission line. It is reflected from the termination. At some points ($y = 0$, $\lambda/2, \lambda, 3\lambda/2, ...$), the incident and reflected waves add in phase and produce a maximum signal. At other points ($y = \lambda/4, 3\lambda/4, ...$) the incident and reflected waves are 180° out of phase so they cancel. At other points, the phase differences are neither $0°$ or $180°$, but some intermediate value. Thus, the maximum voltage has a magnitude which lies between zero and $V_0$.

The wavelength of Fig. 10–12a is called a *standing wave*. This is a waveform whicn is a function of position, but not of time. Note that the standing wave is not a waveform which actually exists in space or time; it represents the maximum value of the sinusoid at the point in question. Another type of waveform is the *traveling wave*. This actually represents a signal propagating along a transmission line.

Now let us return to the case of a general termination; in this case,

$$\rho(j\omega) = \frac{Z_L(j\omega) - Z_0(j\omega)}{Z_L(j\omega) + Z_0(j\omega)} \tag{10–140}$$

Let us write this as

$$\rho(j\omega) = |\rho(j\omega)| \, e^{j\phi(\omega)} \tag{10–141}$$

Substituting in Eq. 10–135a, we obtain

$$V(y, j\omega) = K(j\omega) \left[ e^{j2\pi y/\lambda} + |\rho(j\omega)| \, e^{-j[2\pi(y/\lambda) - \phi]} \right] \tag{10–142}$$

Manipulation yields

$$V(y, j\omega) = K(j\omega) \left[ \cos 2\pi y/\lambda + j\sin 2\pi y/\lambda \right.$$

$$\left. + |\rho(j\omega)| \cos\left( \frac{2\pi y}{\lambda} - \phi \right) - j|\rho(j\omega)| \sin\left( \frac{2\pi y}{\lambda} - \phi \right) \right]$$

Manipulating, we obtain

$$V(y, j\omega) = K(j\omega) \sqrt{1 + |\rho(j\omega)|^2 + 2|\rho(j\omega)| \cos\left( \frac{4\pi y}{\lambda} - \phi \right)} \, e^{j\theta} \tag{10–143a}$$

where

$$\theta = \tan^{-1} \frac{\sin \dfrac{2\pi y}{\lambda} - |\rho(j\omega)| \sin\left( \dfrac{2\pi y}{\lambda} - \phi \right)}{\cos \dfrac{2\pi y}{\lambda} + |\rho(j\omega)| \cos\left( \dfrac{2\pi y}{\lambda} - \phi \right)} \tag{10–143b}$$

As we proceed back along the transmission line, the magnitude and phase of the phasor $V(y, j\omega)$ changes. The magnitude of $V(y, j\omega)$ is given by

$$|V(y, j\omega)| = |K(j\omega)| \sqrt{1 + |\rho(j\omega)|^2 + 2|\rho(j\omega)| \cos\left( \frac{4\pi y}{\lambda} - \phi \right)} \tag{10–144}$$

Remember that the phasor $V(y, j\omega)$ represents a sinusoid; hence,

$$v(y, t) = |V(y, j\omega)| \sin(\omega t + \theta')$$

where $\theta'$ is the angle of $V(y, j\omega)$.

The maximum value of $|V(y, j\omega)|$ occurs when $\cos\left( \dfrac{4\pi y}{\lambda} - \phi \right) = 1$; thus,

$$|V(y, j\omega)|_{max} = |K(j\omega)| \sqrt{1 + |\rho(j\omega)|^2 + 2|\rho(j\omega)|}$$

$$= |K(j\omega)| \left[ 1 + |\rho(j\omega)| \right] \tag{10–145a}$$

The minimum value of $|V(y, j\omega)|$ occurs when $\cos\left(\dfrac{4\pi y}{\lambda} - \phi\right) = -1$; therefore,

$$|V(y, j\omega)|_{min} = |K(j\omega)|\sqrt{1 + |\rho(j\omega)|^2 - 2|\rho(j\omega)|}$$

$$= |K(j\omega)|\left[1 - |\rho(j\omega)|\right] \qquad (10\text{--}145b)$$

Note that $1 + |\rho(j\omega)|^2 - 2|\rho(j\omega)| = [1 - |\rho(j\omega)|]^2$, which is always positive. The position of the maxima and minima are given by

$$\left(\frac{y}{\lambda}\right)_{max} = \frac{k}{2} + \frac{\phi}{4\pi} \qquad k = 0, 1, 2, \ldots$$

$$\left(\frac{y}{\lambda}\right)_{min} = \frac{2k - 1}{4} + \frac{\phi}{4\pi}, \qquad k = 0, 1, 2, \ldots$$

The variation of $|V(y, j\omega)|$ with position is a consequence of the reflection of the signal from the termination. If there were no reflection (i.e., if $Z_L(j\omega) = R_0$ so that $\rho(j\omega) = 0$) then $|V(y, j\omega)|$ would be independent of $y$.

A quantity used to express the amount of reflection is called the *voltage standing wave ratio* (VSWR). It is the ratio of the maximum value of $|V(y, j\omega)|$ to its minimum value. The VSWR is given by

$$N_v = \frac{|V(y, j\omega)|_{max}}{|V(y, j\omega)|_{min}}$$

$$N_v = \frac{1 + |\rho(j\omega)|}{1 - |\rho(j\omega)|} \qquad (10\text{--}146)$$

At high frequencies, ordinary impedance measurement becomes difficult. However, it is relatively simple to measure the *magnitude* of voltage across a transmission line. Thus, the VSWR and the locations of the maxima and minima can be found. These can be used to determine the impedance terminating the transmission line. For this reason, impedance at high frequencies is often measured by placing the unknown impedance at the end of a transmission line.

Let us express this impedance in terms of measurements of the magnitude of transmission line voltages. Rearranging Eq. 10–146, we have

$$|\rho(j\omega)| = \frac{N_v - 1}{N_v + 1} \qquad (10\text{--}147)$$

The angle of $\rho(j\omega)$ (i.e., $\phi$) can be determined in the following way. Measure the distance of the closest minimum of $|V(y, j\omega)|$ from the end of the transmission line. Call this distance $y_0$. Then (see Eq. 10–144)

$$\cos\left(\frac{4\pi y_0}{\lambda} - \phi\right) = -1 \qquad (10\text{--}148)$$

Since this is the closest minimum

$$\frac{4\pi y_0}{\lambda} - \phi = \pi$$

$$\phi = \frac{4\pi y_0}{\lambda} - \pi \tag{10-149}$$

Thus, $\rho(j\omega)$ can be determined. Then, substituting in Eq. 10–140, we have

$$Z_L(j\omega) = Z_0(j\omega) \frac{1 + \rho(j\omega)}{1 - \rho(j\omega)} \tag{10-150}$$

Thus, the termination impedance can be found just by making measurements of the magnitude of the voltage along the transmission line. Special transmission lines called *slotted lines* are constructed to facilitate these measurements. Note that we measure the distance to the first minimum of voltage. In theory, the same information can be obtained by measuring the distance from the first maximum. However, nulls can usually be located with more accuracy than maxima. Thus, the distance from the minimum voltage is usually measured.

We have written the previous results in terms of the voltage. We can also work in terms of the current. Manipulating Eq. 10–135b, we have

$$I(y, j\omega) = \frac{K(j\omega)}{R_0} \left[ \cos 2\pi \frac{y}{\lambda} + j\sin 2\pi \frac{y}{\lambda} - |\rho(j\omega)| \cos \left( 2\pi \frac{y}{\lambda} - \phi \right) \right.$$

$$\left. + j|\rho(j\omega)| \sin \left( 2\pi \frac{y}{\lambda} - \phi \right) \right] \tag{10-151}$$

Hence,

$$I(y, j\omega) = \frac{K(j\omega)}{R_0} \sqrt{1 + |\rho(j\omega)|^2 - 2|\rho(j\omega)| \cos \left( 4\pi \frac{y}{\lambda} - \phi \right)} \, e^{j\theta_1} \tag{10-152a}$$

where

$$\theta_1 = \tan^{-1} \frac{\sin \frac{2\pi y}{\lambda} + |\rho(j\omega)| \sin \left( \frac{2\pi y}{\lambda} - \phi \right)}{\cos \frac{2\pi y}{\lambda} - |\rho(j\omega)| \cos \left( \frac{2\pi y}{\lambda} - \phi \right)} \tag{10-152b}$$

Then,

$$|I(y, j\omega)| = \frac{|K(j\omega)|}{R_0} \sqrt{1 + |\rho(j\omega)|^2 - 2|\rho(j\omega)| \cos \left( \frac{4\pi y}{\lambda} - \phi \right)} \tag{10-153}$$

The phasor represents the sinusoid

$$i(y, t) = |I(y, j\omega)| \sin (\omega t + \theta_1') \tag{10-154}$$

where $\theta'$ is the angle of $I(y, j\omega)$. Compare Eqs. 10–153 and 10–144. The value of $|I(y, j\omega)|$ and that of $|V(y, j\omega)|$ vary in the same way except that a maximum of $|V(y, j\omega)|$ occurs when

$$\cos\left(\frac{4\pi y}{\lambda} - \phi\right) = 1$$

while a maximum of $|I(y, j\omega)|$ occurs when

$$\cos\left(\frac{4\pi y}{\lambda} - \phi\right) = -1$$

Thus, the values of $|V(y, j\omega)|$ and $|I(y, j\omega)|$ are very similar. However, the values of $y$ which correspond to maxima of $|V(y, j\omega)|$ correspond to minima of $|I(y, j\omega)|$ and vice versa.

We can also define a current standing wave ratio (ISWR); this is

$$N_i = \frac{|I(y, j\omega)|_{max}}{|I(y, j\omega)|_{min}} = \frac{\sqrt{1 + |\rho(j\omega)|^2 + 2|\rho(j\omega)|}}{\sqrt{1 + |\rho(j\omega)|^2 - 2|\rho(j\omega)|}}$$

Thus,

$$N_i = \frac{1 + |\rho(j\omega)|}{1 - |\rho(j\omega)|} \tag{10–155}$$

Note (see Eq. 10–146) that the VSWR and ISWR are equal. Since these are equal, they are both often referred to as the *standing wave ratio* (SWR). However, it is important to note which has been measured when they are used for impedance measurements since the maxima of current and voltage occur at different points.

We have just treated the $K(j\omega)$ term as a constant. Now let us determine it. From Eq. 10–126, we have

$$K(j\omega) = \frac{V(j\omega)}{e^{j\beta D} + \rho(j\omega) e^{-j\beta D}} \tag{10–156}$$

Substituting Eqs. 10–133 and 10–141, we obtain

$$K(j\omega) = \frac{V(j\omega)}{e^{j2\pi D/\lambda} + |\rho(j\omega)| e^{-j(2\pi D/\lambda - \phi)}} \tag{10–157}$$

Comparing this with Eqs. 10–142 and 10–143, we have

$$K(j\omega) = \frac{V(j\omega)}{\sqrt{1 + |\rho(j\omega)|^2 + 2|\rho(j\omega)| \cos\left(\dfrac{4\pi D}{\lambda} - \phi\right)}} \, e^{-j\theta} \tag{10–158}$$

where $\theta$ is given by Eq. 10–143b if $y$ is replaced by $D$. The voltage at the maxima along the transmission line is given by Eq. 10–145a. Substituting Eq. 10–158 yields

$$|V(y, j\omega)|_{max} = \frac{|V(j\omega)| [1 + |\rho(j\omega)|]}{\sqrt{1 + |\rho(j\omega)|^2 + 2|\rho(j\omega)| \cos\left(\dfrac{4\pi D}{\lambda} - \phi\right)}} \tag{10–159}$$

It is possible that, at a maximum, the voltage is greater than the input voltage. From Eq. 10–153, we see that a similar effect can occur for current. This may appear strange at first. However, it is analogous to a series resonant circuit where the voltage across the capacitor or inductor can be greater than the input voltage. At a maximum voltage, the current is minimum, so that the power transmitted is never greater than the input power.

Now let us consider a special case. Suppose a transmission line is terminated in an open circuit; then, $\rho(j\omega) = 1$ and Eq. 10–159 yields

$$|V(y, j\omega)|_{max} = \frac{\sqrt{2}\,|V(j\omega)|}{\sqrt{1 + \cos \dfrac{4\pi D}{\lambda}}} \tag{10-160}$$

If $D = \lambda/4$, then $|V(y, j\omega)|$ becomes infinite. This again is equivalent to the series resonant circuit with zero loss.

If we consider losses, then the output voltage may be greater than the input voltage, but it will never be infinite. If the transient behavior of the quarter wavelength lossless transmission line excited by a sinusoid is analyzed, it is found that the output voltage consists of a sinusoid whose peak value increases continuously with time. (Again, this is analogous to the series resonant circuit.) The phenomenon whereby the output voltage of a transmission line may be greater than its input voltage on a sinusoidal steady-state basis is called the *Ferranti effect*. The output signal only can exceed the input signal when a periodic signal is transmitted. If the signals are nonperiodic, this increase will not occur for all time. The Ferranti effect can be considered to be due to reflection. If a signal is transmitted along a line, it is reflected from both ends of the line. In addition, new signals are being sent along the line by a generator. If the line length is $\lambda/4$, then all of these signals keep adding up in phase at the output. Thus, the signal continuously builds up.

## 10-5.  TRANSMISSION LINE IMPEDANCE AND ADMITTANCE—THE SMITH CHART

Lengths of transmission lines are often used in place of inductances and capacitances at high frequencies. At such frequencies (e.g., above 100 MHz) it becomes difficult to construct circuit elements which behave as inductances or capacitances using conventional coils or capacitors. However, we can utilize transmission lines for this purpose.

The input impedance of a transmission line of length $D$ is given by (see Eq. 10–118)

$$Z_{in}(j\omega) = Z_0(j\omega)\frac{1 + \rho(j\omega)\,e^{-2\gamma D}}{1 - \rho(j\omega)\,e^{-2\gamma D}} \tag{10-161}$$

Now let us assume that the transmission line is lossless. Substituting Eqs. 10–120, 10–121, and 10–133, we obtain

$$Z_{in}(j\omega) = R_0 \frac{1 + \rho(j\omega)\,e^{-j4\pi D/\lambda}}{1 - \rho(j\omega)\,e^{-j4\pi D/\lambda}} \tag{10-162}$$

Manipulating, we have

$$Z_{in}(j\omega) = R_0 \frac{e^{j2\pi D/\lambda} + \rho(j\omega)\,e^{-j2\pi D/\lambda}}{e^{j2\pi D/\lambda} - \rho(j\omega)\,e^{-j2\pi D/\lambda}} \tag{10-163}$$

Now let us express $\rho(j\omega)$ in polar form:

$$\rho(j\omega) = |\rho(j\omega)|\,e^{j\phi(\omega)} \tag{10-164}$$

Then,

$$Z_{in}(j\omega) = R_0 \frac{e^{j2\pi D/\lambda} + |\rho(j\omega)|\,e^{-j(2\pi D/\lambda - \phi)}}{e^{j2\pi D/\lambda} - |\rho(j\omega)|\,e^{-j(2\pi D/\lambda - \phi)}} \tag{10-165}$$

Let us consider some special cases. Suppose the termination impedance is an open circuit. Then $Z_L(j\omega) = \infty$ and $\rho(j\omega) = 1$. Then, Eq. 10–163 becomes

$$Z_{inoc}(j\omega) = R_0 \frac{e^{j2\pi D/\lambda} + e^{-j2\pi D/\lambda}}{e^{j2\pi D/\lambda} - e^{-j2\pi D/\lambda}} \tag{10-166}$$

Manipulating, we have

$$Z_{inoc}(j\omega) = -jR_0 \frac{\cos 2\pi D/\lambda}{\sin 2\pi D/\lambda}$$

$$Z_{inoc}(j\omega) = \frac{-jR_0}{\tan 2\pi D/\lambda} \tag{10-167}$$

This impedance is expressed in terms of $D/\lambda$, which is the ratio of the length of the transmission line to the wavelength. Note that $\lambda$ is a function of $\omega$. Let us express the impedance as a function of $\omega$ directly. Substituting Eq. 10–134, we have

$$Z_{inoc}(j\omega) = \frac{-jR_0}{\tan \omega D/v_p} \tag{10-168}$$

where $v_p$ is the velocity of propagation (see Eq. 10–26) given by $v_p = 1/\sqrt{LC}$. Note that $Z_{inoc}(j\omega)$ is a pure reactance which is given by

$$X(\omega) = \frac{R_0}{\tan 2\pi D/\lambda} \tag{10-169}$$

A plot of this reactance versus $D/\lambda$ is given in Fig. 10–13.

If we express the impedance as a function of $s$, the Laplace transform variable, we have

$$Z_{inoc}(s) = \frac{R_0 \cosh sD/v_p}{\sinh sD/vp} \tag{10-170}$$

The impedance has an infinite number of poles and zeros.

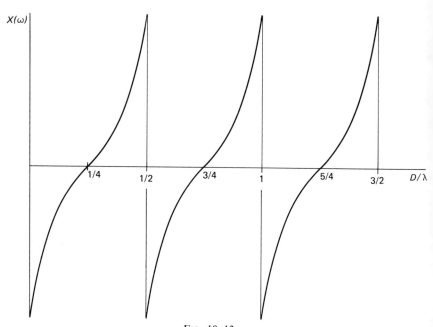

Fɪɢ. 10–13

Plot of the input reactance of an open circuited lossless transmission line, as a function of $D/\lambda$

Now consider the reactance of Fig. 10–13. By proper adjustment of the length of the transmission line, we can obtain any value of reactance (both positive and negative). The impedance also passes through poles and zeros. Thus, an open circuited transmission line can at times replace a series *or* parallel resonant circuit.

Now let us consider the input impedance of a short circuited line. In this case, $Z_L(j\omega) = 0$ and $\rho(j\omega) = -1$. Manipulation of Eq. 10–163 yields

$$Z_{insc}(j\omega) = jR_0 \tan 2\pi D/\lambda \qquad (10\text{–}171)$$

This is a pure reactance. Its value is plotted in Fig. 10–14. This curve is essentially the same as that of Fig. 10–13 for the short circuited transmission line, except that the horizontal axis is displaced by $\lambda/4$. This is to be expected since the input impedance of a quarter wave long short circuited line is an open circuit. Thus, a short circuited line should act as an open circuited line which is one quarter wavelength shorter than it actually is. Similar statements can be made about open circuited transmission lines. It is often desirable to use short, rather than open, circuited lines. At high frequencies energy can be radiated from the open end of a transmission line. Thus, the load impedance does not appear infinite. However, it is relatively easy to obtain a good short circuit.

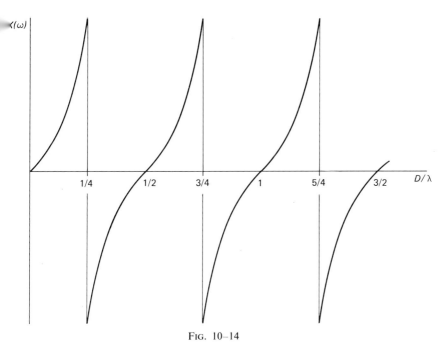

FIG. 10–14

Plot of the input reactance of a short circuited lossless transmission line, as a function of $D/\lambda$

**Quarter Wavelength Transmission Lines.** Now let us consider another special example. Suppose a transmission line, one-quarter wavelength long, is terminated in an arbitrary impedance $Z_L(j\omega)$. Let us determine its input impedance. From Eq. 10–162, we have

$$Z_{in}(j\omega) = R_0 \frac{1 + \rho(j\omega) e^{-j\pi}}{1 - \rho(j\omega) e^{-j\pi}} = R_0 \frac{1 - \rho(j\omega)}{1 + \rho(j\omega)}$$

Substituting Eq. 10–116 and manipulating, we obtain

$$Z_{in}(j\omega) = \frac{R_0^2}{Z_L(j\omega)} \qquad (10\text{–}172)$$

Thus, the input impedance of a quarter wavelength transmission line is the *reciprocal* of the load impedance multiplied by $R_0^2$.

**Half-Wavelength Transmission Lines.** We shall obtain the input impedance of a transmission line a half-wavelength long. Substituting in Eq. 10–162 yields

$$Z_{in}(j\omega) = R_0 \frac{1 + \rho(j\omega)\,e^{-j2\pi}}{1 - \rho(j\omega)\,e^{-j2\pi}} = R_0 \frac{1 + \rho(j\omega)}{1 - \rho(j\omega)}$$

Substituting Eq. 10–116 gives

$$Z_{in}(j\omega) = Z_L(j\omega) \tag{10–173}$$

Thus, the input impedance of a one half wavelength transmission line is equal to the load impedance.

**General Impedance Expressions–Smith Chart.** Thus far we have considered specific examples in computing the input impedance of a transmission line. Now let us assume that we have a lossless transmission line of arbitrary length and termination, and compute its input impedance. From Eq. 10–162, we have

$$Z_{in}(j\omega) = R_0 \frac{1 + \rho(j\omega)\,e^{-j4\pi D/\lambda}}{1 - \rho(j\omega)\,e^{-j4\pi D/\lambda}} \tag{10–174}$$

This expression is simple but can be tedious to use. Let us perform some manipulations which result in graphical procedures which greatly reduce the tedium. It is convenient to normalize $Z_{in}(j\omega)$; that is, let us use $Z_{in}(j\omega)/R_0$. We express the real and imaginary components of this as

$$\frac{Z_{in}(j\omega)}{R_0} = R_i + jX_i \tag{10–175}$$

Let us also express $\rho(j\omega)\,e^{-j4\pi D/\lambda}$ by a single variable.

$$\rho(j\omega)\,e^{-j4\pi D/\lambda} = W = u + jv \tag{10–176}$$

Substituting Eqs. 10–175 and 10–176 into Eq. 10–174, we obtain

$$R_i + jX_i = \frac{1 + u + jv}{1 - u - jv} \tag{10–177}$$

Multiplying the numerator and denominator of the right-hand side of Eq. 10–177 by $1 - u - jv$ and equating the real and imaginary parts of the equation yields

$$R_i = \frac{1 - (u^2 + v^2)}{(1 - u)^2 + v^2} \tag{10–178a}$$

$$X_i = \frac{2v}{(1 - u)^2 + v^2} \tag{10–178b}$$

Rearranging these expressions, we obtain

$$\left(u - \frac{R_i}{1 + R_i}\right)^2 + v^2 = \frac{1}{(1 + R_i)^2} \tag{10–179a}$$

$$(u - 1)^2 + \left(v - \frac{1}{X_i}\right)^2 = \frac{1}{X_i^2} \tag{10–179b}$$

Now let us consider plots of these two curves in the $W = u + jv$ plane for constant $R_i$ or constant $X_i$. Each of the curves represents a circle. Equation 10–179a represents a circle centered at

$$u = \frac{R_i}{1 + R_i} \tag{10–180a}$$

$$v = 0 \tag{10–180b}$$

with radius

$$r = \frac{1}{1 + R_i} \tag{10–180c}$$

Equation 10–179b represents a circle whose center is at

$$u = 1 \tag{10–181a}$$

$$v = \frac{1}{X_i} \tag{10–181b}$$

with radius

$$r = \frac{1}{X_i} \tag{10–181c}$$

Plots of these curves in the $W$-plane are shown in Fig. 10–15. This plot, called the *Smith chart*, was developed by P.H. Smith. The chart is useful for impedance calculations on transmission lines.

The Smith chart represents a plot of the normalized impedance $Z_{in}(j\omega)/R_0$ versus $W = \rho(j\omega) e^{-j4\pi D/\lambda}$. Suppose we have a transmission line of zero length. Then (see Eq. 10–176)

$$W_0 = \rho(j\omega) \tag{10–182}$$

Thus, the point representing the normalized load impedance

$$\frac{Z_L(j\omega)}{R_0} = R_{L0} + jX_{L0} \tag{10–183}$$

can be plotted on the Smith chart. (The constant $R_i$ and $X_i$ circles are used to plot this point.) The $u$ and $v$ coordinates of this point yield the reflection coefficient

$$\rho(j\omega) = u_0 + jv_0 \tag{10–184}$$

Now assume that $Z_L(j\omega)$ is used to terminate a transmission line $D$ meters long. At the input to the transmission line (i.e., $D$ meters from the termination)

$$W_{in} = \rho(j\omega) e^{-j4\pi D/\lambda} = W_0 e^{-j4\pi D/\lambda} \tag{10–185}$$

Thus, $W_{in}$ can be obtained from $W_0$ by multiplying it by $e^{-j4\pi D/\lambda}$. On the Smith chart this corresponds to a phasor whose magnitude is the same as $W_0$, but which has been rotated by $4\pi D/\lambda$ radians in the clockwise direction. Thus, $W_{in}$ can be easily obtained by graphic methods.

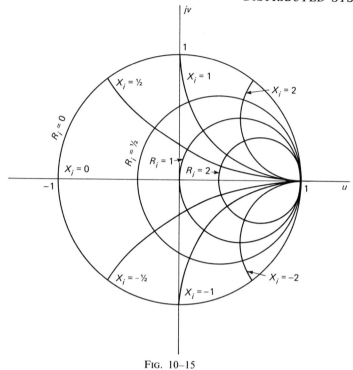

FIG. 10–15
Smith chart: a plot of the constant $R_i$ and $X_i$ curves in the $W$ plane

The $R_i$ and $X_i$ (circular) coordinates can be used to read the values of $R_i$ and $X_i$ which correspond to $W_{in}$. These values of $R_i$ and $X_i$ give the normalized input impedance; thus,

$$\mathbf{Z}_{in}(j\omega) = R_0(R_i + jX_i) \tag{10–186}$$

Hence, we have simplified the impedance calculations to a graphic operation.

The Smith chart is often supplied commercially printed in great detail (see Fig. 10–16). Note the great number of $R_i$ and $X_i$ circles. The outer edge is labelled in degrees. This can be used to measure the rotation of $W$ or to read the angle of $\rho$. There is also a scale labelled wavelength toward generator. This can be used in the same way as the degree scale. A rotation of the $W$ vector of $2\pi$ radians corresponds to a change of $D$ of one half-wavelength. The zero on the wavelength scale is arbitrarily placed. Since the scale is linear, the *difference* between two points on the scale is used. This corresponds to the length of the transmission line.

Let us illustrate this with an example. Suppose a transmission line whose characteristic resistance is $R_0 = 300$ ohms is terminated in an impedance $\mathbf{Z}_L(j\omega) = 600 - j300$ ohms. The transmission line length is $0.3\lambda$.

Let us determine the input impedance of this transmission line. The normalized

**IMPEDANCE OR ADMITTANCE COORDINATES**

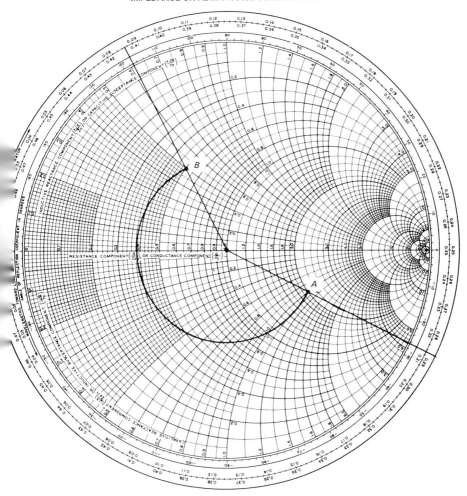

Fig. 10–16

A commercial Smith chart. The circle indicates the calculation of input impedance for a normalized load impedance of $2 - j1$ and a transmission line $0.3\lambda$ long

load impedance is

$$\frac{\mathbf{Z}_L(j\omega)}{R_0} = 2 - j1$$

This is plotted on point $A$ in Fig. 10–16. We must rotate through an angle corresponding to $0.3\lambda$; thus,

$$e^{-j4\pi D/\lambda} = e^{-j4\pi 0.3/\lambda} = e^{-j1.2\pi}$$

Thus, we rotate through $-1.2\pi$ radians or $216°$. We can use the degree scale around the perimeter of the Smith chart to obtain the $216°$ rotation.

Alternatively, the wavelength scale can be used. Point $A$ corresponds to a reading on this scale of $0.287\lambda$. (Note that this is a relative reading.) Add $0.3\lambda$ and we have $0.587\lambda$. This corresponds to point $B$. (Note that the wavelength scale reads $0.087$ since the scale increases to $0.5$ and then repeats itself.) Thus, point $B$ corresponds to $W_{in} = \rho(j\omega)\,e^{-j4\pi D/\lambda}$. From this point we can read the normalized impedance as

$$\frac{Z_{in}(j\omega)}{R_0} = 0.5 + j0.5$$

Thus, the input impedance is

$$Z_{in} = 150 + j150 \text{ ohms}$$

Point $A$ represents the reflection coefficient of the load. Reading this point in polar coordinates, we have

$$\rho = 0.39 \,\angle\,(-26.5°) = 0.39e^{-0.147\pi}$$

Thus, the Smith chart can greatly reduce the tedium involved in transmission line calculations.

**Using the Smith Chart on an Admittance Basis.**   At times it is desirable to deal with admittance rather than with impedance in transmission line calculations. Let us see how this affects Smith chart calculations. The following definitions will be used for the load admittance, input admittance, and characteristic admittance:

$$Y_L(j\omega) = \frac{1}{Z_L}(j\omega) \tag{10–187a}$$

$$Y_{in}(j\omega) = \frac{1}{Z_{in}}(j\omega) \tag{10–187b}$$

$$G_0 = \frac{1}{R_0} \tag{10–187c}$$

Now we shall define a reflection coefficient on an admittance basis:

$$\rho_y(j\omega) = \frac{Y_L(j\omega) - Y_0(j\omega)}{Y_L(j\omega) + Y_0(j\omega)} \tag{10–188}$$

Let us relate this to the reflection coefficient that we have been using. Substituting Eq. 10–187, we have

$$\rho_y(j\omega) = \frac{\dfrac{1}{Z_L(j\omega)} - \dfrac{1}{Z_0(j\omega)}}{\dfrac{1}{Z_L(j\omega)} + \dfrac{1}{Z_0(j\omega)}} = \frac{Z_0(j\omega) - Z_L(j\omega)}{Z_L(j\omega) + Z_0(j\omega)}$$

Comparing this with Eq. 10–116, we obtain

$$\rho_y(j\omega) = -\rho(j\omega) \tag{10–189}$$

The input admittance of the transmission line is (see Eq. 10–162)

$$Y_{in}(j\omega) = G_0 \frac{1 - \rho(j\omega)\,e^{-j4\pi D/\lambda}}{1 + \rho(j\omega)\,e^{-j4\pi D/\lambda}} \tag{10-190}$$

Substituting Eq. 10–189 yields

$$Y_{in}(j\omega) = G_0 \frac{1 + \rho_y(j\omega)\,e^{-j4\pi D/\lambda}}{1 - \rho_y(j\omega)\,e^{-j4\pi D/\lambda}} \tag{10-191}$$

Compare this with Eq. 10–162. These expressions have the same form, except that $Y_{in}(j\omega)$ replaces $Z_{in}(j\omega)$, $G_0$ replaces $R_0$, and $\rho_y(j\omega)$ replaces $\rho(j\omega)$. Thus, what we have said about the input impedance can now be applied to the input admittance if we make the substitutions: $Y_{in}(j\omega)$ for $Z_{in}(j\omega)$, $G_0$ for $R_0$, and $\rho_y(j\omega)$ for $\rho(j\omega)$. Hence, we can apply the Smith chart directly to admittance calculations.

For example, suppose we have a transmission line whose characteristic admittance is $G = 300$ mhos, which is $0.3\lambda$ and is terminated in an admittance $Y_L(j\omega) = 600 - j300$ mhos. Let us determine its input admittance. Point $A$ on the Smith chart of Fig. 10–16 represents the normalized load admittance and point $B$ represents the normalized input admittance, just as in the previous example. Thus, the input admittance is $Y_{in}(j\omega) = 150 + j150$ mhos. This exactly follows the previous example using impedance. Note that the two examples are *not* the same. In the previous example there was a load impedance of 600 ohms in series with a reactance of $-300$ ohms. In this example, the load consists of 600 mhos in parallel with a susceptance of $-300$ mhos. The characteristic impedance of both transmission lines are different etc. This example shows that the Smith chart can readily be used for admittance problems.

In Section 10-4 we saw that the SWR and the location of the first minimum of voltage (or current) could be used to calculate the load impedance. The Smith chart can aid in these calculations. At a voltage minimum, the impedance viewed toward the end of the line is purely resistive and equal to $R_0/N_v$, where $R_0$ is the characteristic resistance and $N_v$ is the SWR. This can be determined by substituting the expression $(y/\lambda)_{min}$ (following Eq. 10–145b) in the impedance expression. This establishes the point $1/N_v$ on the Smith chart. Then, rotating counterclockwise an amount corresponding to the distance from the minimum to the end of the line, we obtain the normalized load impedance. The wavelength toward load scale can be used here. Details of this operation will be left to the reader.

## 10-6. IMPEDANCE MATCHING—USE OF STUBS— SMITH CHART CALCULATIONS—COMPUTER CALCULATIONS

If the load impedance of a transmission line is not equal to the characteristic impedance, reflection takes place from the termination. This is usually undesirable, since reflection reduces efficiency in transmission of energy. An actual transmission line will have losses; that is, $R$ and $G$ will not be zero. Thus, when there is current through or voltage across the transmission line, power will be dissipated. Each time a signal is reflected, it traverses the transmission line, resulting in the dissipation of more energy.

Reflections are also undesirable, since the voltage across a transmission line, at maximum points of the standing wave, will be greater than if the transmission line were terminated with its characteristic impedance. In many cases, such as when a transmission line connects a high power transmitter to an antenna, transmission line voltages may be very large. Thus, if there are reflections, the maximum voltage rating of the transmission line will have to be greater than if there were no reflections. This can require the use of a larger, more expensive transmission line.

The $I^2R$ loss will be greatest at the point of current maxima. At times, when the standing wave ratio is high and very high powers are transmitted, the transmission line actually breaks down, either because of arcing or heating at the points of voltage and or current maxima.

Reflections on transmission lines can be undesirable for reasons other than efficiency. Suppose a television signal is brought from an antenna to a receiver using a transmission line and some reflection takes place from both the input and output ends. A signal will be reflected up and back along the transmission line. This will lead to multiple images or blurring of the picture.

Therefore, we desire to eliminate reflections. However, in many situations, we cannot set the load impedance equal to the characteristic impedance of the transmission line. The load may be some specified device such as an antenna, so that load impedance is fixed. This may not be equal to the characteristic impedance of any available transmission line. Thus, another procedure must be used to eliminate reflection. We shall show that a reactance can be placed in shunt with the transmission line at some point $P$ near the load such that the impedance viewed toward the load from point $P$ will be equal to the characteristic impedance. Thus, reflection will be eliminated from most of the transmission line.

Let us consider an impedance matching procedure. We shall work on the basis of admittance here. In Fig. 10–17, a simplified Smith chart is plotted on the basis of admittance. The normalized load admittance is assumed to lie at some point on the dashed circle. As we travel back from the termination along the transmission line, the locus of admittance, looking down the transmission line toward the load, will lie on the dashed circle. No matter what the radius of this circle it *must* cross the unit circle. Then, no matter what the terminating admittance, at some distance $D_0$ from the end of the transmission line, will be

$$Y_{in} = G_0 + jB \qquad (10\text{–}192)$$

Note that $G_0$ is the characteristic conductance (the reciprocal of the characteristic resistance) of a lossless transmission line. This is illustrated in Fig. 10–18a.

Now suppose we place an admittance equal to

$$Y_{sh} = -jB \qquad (10\text{–}193)$$

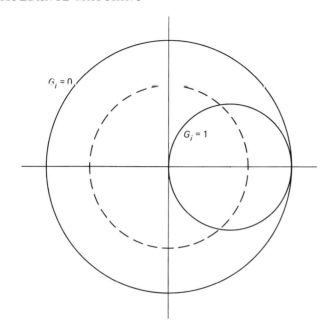

FIG. 10–17

Simplified Smith chart plotted on an admittance basis. The dashed circle
represents the locus of admittance viewed toward the load

in parallel with the transmission line $D_0$ meters from its end (see Fig. 10–18b) where
the admittance used is actually a short-circuited transmission line called a *short-
circuited stub*. The net admittance $Y_i$, looking down the transmission line to the right
of $P$, where the stub is connected, is

$$Y_i = Y_{in} + Y_{sh} = G_0 \qquad (10\text{–}194)$$

Thus, it appears as though an admittance equal to the characteristic admittance is connected at $P$. If we consider that the transmission line ends at a point $D_1$ meters from its
input (see Fig. 10–18b), then the load is equal to the characteristic resistance. The load
consists of a length of transmission line $D_0$ meters long terminated in $Y_L$ and a shunt
admittance which is called a *matching stub*. In general, $D_0$ will be less than $\lambda/2$, so
that in many cases, $D_1 \gg D_0$. Thus, standing waves will not appear on the transmission line, for most of its length.

Let us now consider an example of this procedure. Suppose that a lossless
transmission line whose characteristic resistance is 50 ohms is terminated in an
impedance of $12.5 - j12.5$ ohms. We wish to place a short-circuited stub as close as
possible to the end of a transmission line, so that the line is matched; i.e., in Fig.
10–18b, $Y_i = G_0$. We must work on an admittance basis. Then, the load admittance is

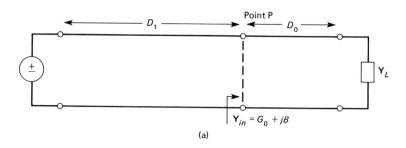

(a)

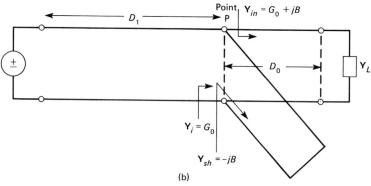

(b)

FIG. 10–18

Impedance matching using shunt stubs; (a) transmission line showing a point $D_0$ meters from the end of the line where $Y_{in} = G_0 + j\beta$; (b) matched transmission line where a parallel stub of admittance $-j\beta$ is placed $D_0$ meters from the end of the transmission line

$$Y_L = \frac{1}{12.5 - j12.5} = \frac{1}{25} + j\frac{1}{25}$$

The characteristic conductance is $G_0 = 1/R_0 = 1/50$. Thus, on a normalized basis $Y_L/G_0 = 2 + j2$. This is plotted as point $A$ on the Smith chart of Fig. 10–19. The admittance viewed into the line, as we proceed backward from the termination, lies on a circle which is centered at the origin and passes through $A$. This is drawn in Fig. 10–19. At point $B$, the circle intersects the $G_i = 1$ curve. Thus, at point $B$ the input admittance is $Y_{in}/G_0 = 1 - j1.6$. The susceptance $(-j1.6)$ is obtained from the Smith chart coordinates of point $B$. Using the wavelength scale, we see that point $B$ is a distance of $D = (0.321 - 0.208)\lambda = 0.113\lambda$ from the end of the trans-

**IMPEDANCE OR ADMITTANCE COORDINATES**

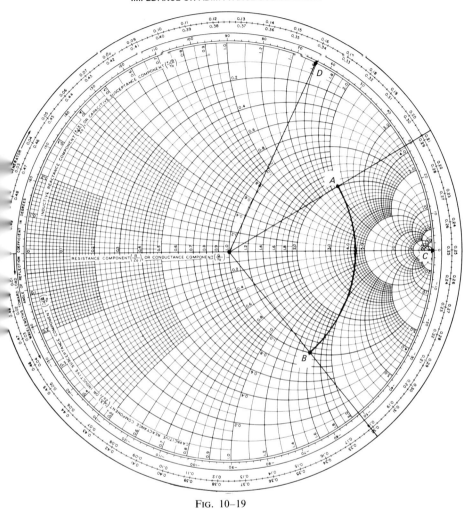

Fig. 10–19

Use of the Smith chart to determine location and admittance of matching stub

mission line. Thus, to achieve the desired impedance match, we must place a stub of normalized admittance $-(-j1.6)$ which is $Y_{sh}/G_0 = +j1.6$ at this point. From Eq. 10–171, we obtain

$$Y_{in,sc} = \frac{-jG_0}{\tan\dfrac{2\pi D}{\lambda}}$$

Hence,

$$\tan \frac{2\pi D}{\lambda} = -j \frac{G_0}{Y_{sh}}$$

In this case, we have

$$\tan \frac{2\pi D}{\lambda} = -1/1.6 = -.625$$

Solving, we obtain $D/\lambda = 0.411$. Thus, the short circuited stub should be 0.411 wavelengths long.

Alternatively, we can use the Smith chart to calculate this. A line terminated in a short circuit has infinite input admittance. This corresponds to point $C$ in Fig. 10–19. The desired normalized susceptance is $+j1.6$, which corresponds to point $D$. The locus of admittance of a short-circuited stub lies on the outer circle ($G = 0$). Thus, proceeding clockwise around the chart from $C$ to $D$ and reading the wavelength scale, we have $D = (0.25 + 0.161)\lambda = 0.411\lambda$. Thus, the Smith chart can be used for all calculations of the impedance matching. In this case, we place a short-circuited stub of length $0.411\lambda$ at a distance of $0.113\lambda$ from the end of the transmission line to achieve a match.

Now let us consider a computer program which implements the impedance matching. We shall use SUBROUTINE STUB shown in Fig. 10–20. We shall discuss the basic ideas used in this program before considering the steps of the program itself.

Assume that the normalized impedance at the end of a transmission line is $G_L + jB_L$, where $G_L > 1$. We then proceed backward from the end of the line in predetermined steps (we shall use steps of $0.01\lambda$). Compute $G_{in}$ at each step. Do this for each step until a value of $G_{in} \leq 1$ is obtained. Thus, we know that between the last two points $G_{in} = 1$, so the stub should be placed between these *two* points. The region between the last two points is then subdivided to determine more accurately the location of the stub.

In the program we shall not compare $G_{in}$ with 1 because $G_L$ may be less than one *or* greater than one. Thus, we would have to write different IF statements for $G_L < 1$ and $G_L > 1$. Therefore, we compute $G_{in}$, the input conductance, at each point, and then calculate $A = 1 - G_{in}$ and compare $A$'s at two adjacent points. If the stub location lies between two successive points, then $A$ will change sign. Then, we need only test to see if $A$ changes sign.

The subroutine is called STUB (YL, RO, D, DS). The characteristic *resistance* RO and the load *admittance* YL are entered and the stub location D and stub length DS are calculated by the SUBROUTINE. In line 30, the complex variables YL, RHO, and Y are declared. The reflection coefficient $\rho$ is computed in line 40. We can express $\rho$ as

$$\rho = \frac{\dfrac{1}{Y_L} - R_0}{\dfrac{1}{Y_L} + R_0} = \frac{1 - R_0 Y_L}{1 + R_0 Y_L} \tag{10–195}$$

This expression is used to compute RHO.

```
00010    C         SUBRØUTINE FØR CALC MATCHING STUB
00020              SUBRØUTINE STUB(YL,RO,D,DS)
00030              CØMPLEX YL,RHØ,Y
00040              RHØ=(1.-RO*YL)/(1.+RO*YL)
00050              DØ 100 I=1,100
00060              AI=I
00070              D1=0.01*(AI-1.)
00080              D2=0.01*AI
00090              A=1.-REAL(Y(D1,RHØ))
00100              IF(A.EQ.0.)GØ TØ 800
00110              B=1.-REAL(Y(D2,RHØ))
00120              IF(B.EQ.0.)GØ TØ 1000
00130              IF(A*B.LT.0.)GØ TØ 200
00140    100       CØNTINUE
00150    200       CØNTINUE
00160              DELT=(D2-D1)/2.
00170              D3=D1+DELT
00180              DØ 500 I=1,10
00190              A=1.-REAL(Y(D1,RHØ))
00200              B=1.-REAL(Y(D3,RHØ))
00210              IF(A*B)600,1200,550
00220    550       CØNTINUE
00230              D1=D3
00240              D3=D3+DELT
00250    600       CØNTINUE
00260              DELT=DELT/2.
00270              D3=D1+DELT
00280    500       CØNTINUE
00290    1200      CØNTINUE
00300              D=D3
00310              GØ TØ 1500
00320    800       CØNTINUE
00330              D=0.
00340              GØ TØ 1500
00350    1000      CØNTINUE
00360              D=D2
00370    1500      CØNTINUE
00380              X=AIMAG(Y(D,RHØ))
00390              DS=ATAN(1./X)/(2.*3.14159)
00400              IF(DS.LT.0.)DS=.5+DS
00410              RETURN
00420              END
00430              CØMPLEX FUNCTION Y(D,RHØ)
00440              CØMPLEX RHØ,CD,CE
00450              DX=-1.*4.*3.14159*D
00460              CD=CMPLX(0.,DX)
00470              CE=CEXP(CD)
00480              Y=(1.-RHØ*CE)/(1.+RHØ*CE)
00490              RETURN
00500              END
```

FIG. 10–20

SUBROUTINE STUB which is used to compute the position and length of a short-circuited matching stub

In lines 430–480, a COMPLEX FUNCTION Y (D, RHO) is computed. This gives the input impedance at a distance $D/\lambda$ from the end of the transmission line in terms of the reflection coefficient RHO. In the program, we set $\lambda = 1$. Then, $D$ is actually expressed in fractions of a wavelength. The data supplied to the FUNCTION are the distance D and RHO. Equation 10–162 is used to compute $Y_{in}$. Taking the reciprocal of this equation we have

$$\frac{Y_{in}(j\omega)}{G_0} = \frac{1 - \rho(j\omega)\,e^{-j4\pi D/\lambda}}{1 + \rho(j\omega)\,e^{-4j\pi D/\lambda}} \tag{10-196}$$

In line 450, $-4j\pi D/\lambda$ is calculated. (Note that $\lambda = 1$ so that $D$ will be in fractions of a wavelength.) In line 460, $CD = -j4\pi D/\lambda$ is obtained. Line 470 yields $e^{-j4\pi D/\lambda}$. Note that CEXP is a built-in FORTRAN SUBROUTINE to obtain $e$ to a complex power. Finally, Y is calculated in line 480.

Now let us return to the SUBROUTINE. In the DO loop of lines 50–140, the stub location is determined to within $0.01\lambda$. The value of Re $Y_{in}$ will be computed at steps $0.01\lambda$ apart and compared. Let us consider the reason for this step size. Within $0.5\lambda$ from the end of the transmission line, there are always two possible stub locations. This is shown in Fig. 10–17, where the $G_i = 1$ circle is intersected twice by the locus of admittance. In general, we desire to locate the stub as close as possible to the end of the transmission line. Also, for purposes of computation, we do not wish to have a single step include the two allowable locations; e.g., if $G_L/G_0 = 0.8 + j50$, the two stub locations will be very close. Thus, a relatively small step $(0.01\lambda)$ must be chosen. In this case, almost every value that can practically be read on the Smith chart can be used as a $Y_L$ without the possibility of having two stub locations included in one step. There are cases when $0.01\lambda$ may be too large. This occurs if the normalized susceptance of the load is very large and the normalized resistance of the load is less than one. Then, smaller steps sizes should be used.

In line 60, $AI = 1$ is obtained as a floating point number. The distance $D_1 = 0.01*(AI - 1)$ and $D_2 = 0.1*AI$ are computed in lines 70 and 80. In line 90, $A = 1 - \text{Re }Y(D1)$ is obtained. The FORTRAN notation for this operation is given in line 90. If the normalized load is of the form $Y_L(G_0 = 1 + jB$, then the stub should be located at the end of the line. The IF statement of line 100 transfers control to line 320, if $A = 0$. Then, in line 330, we set $D = 0$ and transfer to line 370.

If $A \neq 0$, then, in line 110, we compute $B = 1 - \text{Re }Y(D2)$. If $B = 0$, then D2 is the stub location. The IF statement of line 120 and the subsequent operations of lines 350–360 yield this value of D.

If the stub location lies between $D_1$ and $D_2$, then the value of B will be negative. Otherwise, it will be positive. If $A*B$ is negative, the IF statement of line 130 terminates the operation of the DO loop. If $A*B$ is positive, the DO loop is cycled again with values of D1 and D2 each increased by $0.1\lambda$. This is repeated until the product $A*B$ is negative (or zero). The DO loop then terminates. We have now determined that the stub location is between the two points D1 and D2.

We could repeat the procedure using steps of $0.001\lambda$ or smaller. However, once the approximate location is determined, we can use a procedure which converges more rapidly. Here each cycle of the DO loop divides the existing range by one half. Let us consider this. In line 160, we compute DELT = (D2 − D1)/2, and, in line 170, we compute D3 = D1 + DELT. Now we enter the DO loop of lines 180–280. A and B are now computed using the distances D1 and D3, respectively, in lines 190 and 200. The product A ∗ B is then tested by the IF statement of line 210. If A ∗ B = 0, D3 must be the stub location. (Note that A ≠ 0, since this was tested previously.) Control is then transferred to line 290 and then we set D = D3. If A ∗ B > 0, then the stub location must be in the next half of the range; D1 and D3 are each increased by DELT in lines 230 and 240. (Note that line 240 can be omitted, since D3 will be changed in line 270. Line 240 is included only to explain the program.) Since it is known that the root is within this range, it need not be tested. The range is then divided in half. In line 260, DELT = DELT/2 is computed. A new D3 is obtained in line 270. The DO loop is cycled again. If the original A ∗ B is negative, the operation of lines 230 and 240 is omitted. Each cycle of the DO loop reduces the uncertainty of the stub location by 1/2. Thus, in ten cycles, the range is divided into $2^{10} = 1024$ parts. It would take 1024 cycles to do this on a linear basis. (The linear procedure was used in the first DO loop, since we had to guarantee that two stub locations did not lie within one step.) The appropriate value of D is obtained in lines 280–370.

The stub location is computed in lines 380–400. The susceptance of Y at point D is computed in line 380. Then, from Eq. 10–171, we have

$$DS/\lambda = \frac{1}{2\pi} \tan^{-1}(1/X)$$

This is computed in line 390. Note that the minus sign which would be obtained from Eq. 10–171 is omitted since the susceptance of the stub should be the negative of the input susceptance of the transmission line. (We have used $1/X$ and not $-1/X$ so that the minus sign is omitted from the expression for $DS/\lambda$.)

If $1/X$ is negative, then $\pi/2 \leq \tan^{-1}(1/X) \leq \pi$. However, the computer calculates it in the range, $0 \leq \tan^{-1}(1/X) \leq -\pi/2$. The IF statement of line 400 corrects this. The values of D and DS are then returned to the main program to be printed.

## PROBLEMS

**10-1.** Discuss the basic differences between distributed and lumped systems.

**10-2.** The transmission line of Fig. 10–1 has the following parameters

$$R = 16 \times 10^{-3} \text{ ohm/meter}$$
$$G = 20 \times 10^{-9} \text{ mho/meter}$$
$$L = 10 \times 10^{-6} \text{ henry/meter}$$
$$C = 50 \text{ pf/meter}$$

Compute the characteristic impedance and propogation constant for this transmission line as a function of $s$.

**10-3.** The transmission line of Problem 10-2 is connected as shown in Fig. 10–2. If $V(s)$ represents a generator, whose voltage as a function of time, and

$$v(t) = u(t) \sin 1000t$$

determine $V(x, s)$ and $I(x, s)$ for this semi-infinite transmission line.

**10-4.** Repeat Problem 10-3 for the transmission line of Fig. 10–3, where $D = 3000$ meters and $Z_L = 447$ ohms (pure) resistance.

**10-5.** Repeat Problem 10-4, but now assume that $R = G = 0$.

**10-6.** A transmission line is $D$ meters long and is not lossless; i.e., $R \neq 0$ and/or $G \neq 0$. Show that as $D$ approaches infinity, the input impedance of the transmission line approaches the characteristic impedance, regardless of the terminating impedance of the transmission line.

**10-7.** Assume that the value of $L$ for the transmission line of Problem 10-2 can be adjusted. What value of $L$ should be used if the transmission line is to be distortionless?

**10-8.** A distortionless transmission line has the value of propogation constant $\gamma$ given by

$$\gamma = 10^{-8} + j0.334 \times 10^{-8}$$

The voltage of Fig. 10–21 is applied to the input of the transmission line. If the line is infinitely long, sketch curves of voltage and current versus position for $t = 0$, $10^{-6}$ sec., $10^{-3}$ sec., and curves of voltage and current versus time for $x = 0$, $D = 100$ meters, and $D = 10^{10}$ meters, where $x$ is distance measured from the input to the transmission line.

**10-9.** Repeat Problem 10-8 for the voltage of Fig. 10-22.

**10-10.** The voltage of Fig. 10–21 is applied to a lossless transmission line $D$ meters long. The length of the line is given by

$$\frac{D}{v_p} = 10^{-3} \text{ sec.}$$

where $v_p = 1/\sqrt{LC}$. The line is terminated in a short circuit. Plot curves of $v(x_1, t)$ and $i(x_1, t)$ for $x_1/v_p = 0, 0.5 \times 10^{-3}$ and $10^{-3}$. Then plot curves of $v(x, t_1)$ and $i(x, t_1)$ for $t_1 = 0.0, 10^{-3}$, and $2 \times 10^{-3}$.

**10-11.** Repeat Problem 10-10 for the voltage of Fig. 10–22.

**10-12.** How will the result of Problem 10-10 change if the pulse length increases to $10^{-2}$ sec.?

**10-13.** If the transmission line of Problem 10-10 becomes lossy, but remains distortionless, how would the results change?

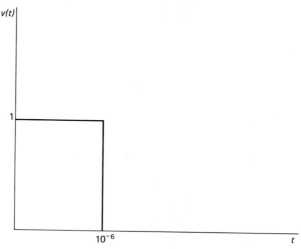

FIG. 10–21

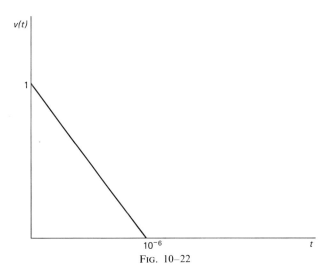

FIG. 10–22

**10-14.** Compute the input impedance of the transmission line of Problem 10-10.

**10-15.** Repeat Problem 10-10, but now assume that the transmission line is terminated in an open circuit.

**10-16.** Repeat Problem 10-10, but now assume that the transmission line is terminated in its characteristic impedance.

**10-17.** A transmission line is such that $L = 0$ and $G = 0$. The line is $D$ meters long and is terminated in a short circuit; the input voltage is the unit step. Determine $v(x, t)$ and $i(x, t)$ for the transmission line. The answer should be expressed in a series form.

**10-18.** Repeat Problem 10-17, but now assume that the transmission line is terminated in an open circuit.

**10-19.** Repeat Problem 10-17, but now assume that the transmission line is terminated in its characteristic impedance.

**10-20.** Repeat Problem 10-17, but do not assume that $L = 0$ and $G = 0$.

**10-21.** Repeat Problem 10-17, but now assume that an impedance of $2Z_0$ is in series with the voltage generator.

*Problems 10-22 through 10-50 are to be calculated on a sinusoidal, steady-state basis.*

**10-22.** Obtain the characteristic impedance and propagation constant of the transmission line of Problem 10-2.

**10-23.** The transmission line of Problem 10-2 is 1000 meters long and is terminated in an impedance consisting of a 10 ohm resistance and a 0.03 henry inductance in series. Determine the input impedance of the transmission line.

**10-24.** A lossless transmission line is such that $1/\sqrt{LC} = 2.997 \times 10^{-8}$ meters/sec. and $\sqrt{LC} = 50$ ohms. The input signal is $v(0, t) = 10 \sin 2\pi \times 10^9 t$. The transmission line is 100 meters long and is terminated in a short circuit. Determine $V(y, j\omega)$ and $I(y, j\omega)$ for the line. Plot $v(y, t)$ and $i(y, t)$ for $y = 0$, 10 meters, and 30 meters. Note that $y$ is distance measured from the termination end of the transmission line.

**10-25.** A lossless transmission line is such that $v_p = 1/\sqrt{LC} = 2.997 \times 10^8$ meters/sec. What is the wavelength if the frequency of the input signal is $10^6$ Hz?

**10-26.** Repeat Problem 10-25 for $f = 30 \times 10^6$ Hz.

**10-27.** A lossless transmission line is $2.5\lambda$ long. Its characteristic impedance is 300 ohms. It is terminated in a 50 ohm pure resistance. Plot the standing waves of voltage and current for this line. What is the reflection coefficient?

**10-28.** Repeat Problem 10-27, but now assume that the termination impedance is $j50$ ohms.

**10-29.** Determine the input impedance for the transmission line of Problem 10-27.

**10-30.** Repeat Problem 10-29 for the termination of Problem 10-28.

**10-31.** What is the standing wave ratio for the transmission line of Problem 10-27?

**10-32.** Repeat Problem 10-31 for the termination of Problem 10-28.

**10-33.** A certain lossless transmission line has a standing wave ratio of $N_v = 5.0$. The first minimum of voltage is located $0.16\lambda$ from the end of the transmission line. The characteristic impedance of the transmission line is 50 ohms. Determine the termination impedance.

**10-34.** Repeat Problem 10-33, but now assume that the first minimum of current lies $0.16\lambda$ from the end of the transmission line.

**10-35.** A lossless transmission line is terminated in a resistance equal to $3R_0$ ($R_0$ is the characteristic resistance). Calculate the input impedance of the transmission line if it is $0.25\lambda$

**10-36.** Repeat Problem 10-35, but assume that the transmission line length is $1.25\lambda$.

**10-37.** A lossless transmission line whose characteristic impedance is 300 ohms is terminated in an impedance of $200 + j100$ ohms. The transmission line is $0.167\lambda$ long. What is the input impedance?

**10-38.** Repeat Problem 10-37, but now assume that the characteristic admittance is 300 mhos and the termination admittance is $200 + j100$ mhos.

**10-39.** Compare Problems 10-37 and 10-38.

**10-40.** Repeat Problem 10-35, but now use a Smith chart.

**10-41.** Repeat Problem 10-36, but now use a Smith chart.

**10-42.** Repeat Problem 10-37, but now use a Smith chart.

**10-43.** Repeat Problem 10-38, but now use a Smith chart.

**10-44.** Repeat Problem 10-33, but now use a Smith chart.

**10-45.** Repeat Problem 10-34, but now use a Smith chart.

**10-46.** A transmission line has a characteristic resistance of 50 ohms. It is terminated in an impedance of $100 + j50$ ohms. Determine the location and length of a short circuit matching stub for the transmission line. (The impedance viewed from the stub location is to be 50 ohms.)

**10-47.** Repeat Problem 10-46 for a termination admittance of $100 + j50$ mhos and a characteristic admittance of 50 mhos.

**10-48.** Use SUBROUTINE STUB to solve Problem 10-47. The input and output statements must be written in a main program.

**10-49.** Write a computer program which calculates the location and length of a short circuited matching stub. Do not refer to Fig. 10–20 when you do this.

**10-50.** Modify SUBROUTINE STUB so that load impedance, rather than load admittance, can be entered.

## REFERENCES

1. Pierce, B. O. *A Short Table of Integrals.* Boston: Ginn, 1929, pp. 116–120.

2. Weber, E. *Linear Transient Analysis.* Vol. II. New York: Wiley, 1956, Sections 8.2 and 8.3.

## BIBLIOGRAPHY

Chirlian, P. M. *Integrated and Active Network Analysis and Synthesis.* Chap. 4. Englewood Cliffs, New Jersey: Prentice-Hall, 1967.

Guillemin, E. A. *Communication Networks.* Vol. II. Chaps. 1–3. New York: Wiley, 1935.

Karakash, J. J. *Transmission Lines and Filter Networks.* Sec. 1. New York: Macmillan, 1950.

Lathi, B. P. *Signals, Systems and Communications.* Chap. 9. New York: Wiley, 1965.

Schwarz, R. J., and Friedland, B. *Linear Systems.* Chap. 13. New York: McGraw-Hill, 1965.

Ware, L. A., and Reed, H. R. *Communication Circuits.* 3d ed. Chaps. 1, 5–8. New York: Wiley, 1949.

Weber, E. *Linear Transient Analysis.* Vol. II. Chaps. 6–8. New York: Wiley, 1956.

# Orthogonal Functions

## A-1. ORTHOGONAL FUNCTIONS

It is often desirable to represent a function of time $f(t)$ as an expansion of some elementary functions. That is, we write

$$f(t) = \sum_{n=0}^{\infty} a_n \phi_n(t), \qquad t_1 \leq t \leq t_2 \tag{A-1}$$

The $a_n$ are constants and the $\phi_n(t)$ are the elementary functions. We shall assume that the $\phi_n(t)$ are real. In general, the expansion is only valid for $t_1 \leq t \leq t_2$. The $\phi_n(t)$ are called the *basis functions*. For instance, in a Fourier series, they are sines and cosines.

Now let us consider the choice of $\phi_n(t)$. We wish the $\phi_n(t)$ to be such that the $a_n$ can be easily evaluated. In practice, this means that we must be able to determine any one $a_n$ without having to know the others. The coefficients will have this property if the basis functions satisfy a property known as *orthogonality*. Two functions are *orthogonal* in the range $t_1 \leq t \leq t_2$ with respect to the *weight function* $w(t)$, if

$$\int_{t_1}^{t_2} w(t)\, \phi_n(t)\, \phi_k(t)\, dt = 0, \qquad k \neq n \tag{A-2}$$

$$= \lambda_k, \qquad k = n$$

The weight function $w(t)$ is a positive function of time which is independent of $n$ and $k$. Functions which satisfy Eq. A-2 with $\lambda_k = 1$ are called *orthonormal*.

Now let us use Eq. A-2 to obtain the coefficients of the series of Eq. A-1. Multiply both sides of Eq. A-1 by $w(t)\,\phi_j(t)\, dt$ and integrate from $t_1$ to $t_2$. Assume that $a_n$ and $\phi_n(t)$ are such that the order of summation and integration can be interchanged; hence,

$$\int_{t_1}^{t_2} w(t)\, \phi_j(t)\, f(t)\, dt = \sum_{n=0}^{\infty} a_n \int_{t_1}^{t_2} w(t)\, \phi_n(t)\, \phi_j(t)\, dt \tag{A-3}$$

Equation A-2 indicates that the integral on the right-hand side is zero, unless $n = j$. Substituting Eq. A-2 and manipulating, we have

$$a_j = \frac{1}{\lambda_j} \int_{t_1}^{t_2} w(t)\, \phi_j(t)\, f(t)\, dt \tag{A-4}$$

Thus, each $a_j$ can be obtained without considering the others.

As an example of orthogonal function expansion (see Eqs. 2–290 through 2–295) we have the Fourier series. Here, the weight function is $w(t) = 1$ and the range of orthogonality is from $t = -T/2$ to $t = T/2$. In the case of the Fourier series, if $f(t)$ is periodic, the expression is also valid outside of the range.

If a set of functions $\phi_n(t)$ satisfy Eq. A–2, then they are orthogonal. However, this does not mean that they can be used in Eq. A–1 to represent all $f(t)$. In general, $f(t)$ must be continuous or have jump discontinuities. In addition, the basis functions $\phi_n(t)$ must be sufficiently general to represent all such $f(t)$. In general, an infinite set of $\phi_n(t)$ is required. Additional generality is also required. For instance, if $\phi_n(t)$ are polynomials, it must be possible to express all possible powers of $t$ with independent coefficients. Sets of orthogonal functions which are usable in these expansions are called *complete orthogonal sets*. Some typical ones are given at the end of this section.

Equation A–1 is, in general, an infinite series. However, practical considerations usually require that we work with a finite series. (e.g., we cannot sum an infinite number of terms on a computer) Thus, we truncate the series and an error results. We now ask the following question. If $f(t)$ is given by Eq. A–1 and we wish to represent it by a series of $N$ terms, what should be the value of the coefficients to minimize the error? That is, if we approximate $f(t)$ by

$$f_a(t) = \sum_{n=0}^{N} \alpha_n \phi_n(t) \tag{A–5}$$

then the error is

$$\varepsilon(t) = f(t) - f_a(t) \tag{A–6}$$

What should be the $\alpha_n$ if the error is to be minimized? Since $\varepsilon(t)$ is a function of time, a change in $\alpha_n$ may decrease the error for one time, but increase it for another time. Thus, we must choose an error criteria that gives a single number based on $\varepsilon(t)$ and then minimize that number. Various error criteria are discussed in Section 2-14. We shall not repeat the discussion here. We assume that the reader is familiar with it. However, it is important to note that the application usually determines which error criterion is best. We shall choose the weighted mean square criterion, which is defined as

$$\varepsilon = \int_{t_1}^{t_2} w(t) [f(t) - f_a(t)]^2 \, dt \tag{A–7}$$

We choose the criterion not because it is best for all applications, but simply because we can obtain some general results using it. The weight function is always positive. Also, $[f(t) - f_a(t)]^2 \geq 0$. Thus, $\varepsilon$ gives a measure of the error. As $\varepsilon(t)$ approaches zero for all $t$, $\varepsilon$ becomes zero and as $|\varepsilon(t)|$ becomes large, $\varepsilon$ tends to increase.

Now let us determine the value of $\alpha_i$ that minimizes $\varepsilon$. From Eqs. A–7 and A–5, we have

$$\varepsilon = \int_{t_1}^{t_2} w(t) [f(t) - \sum_{n=1}^{N} \alpha_n \phi_n(t)]^2 \, dt \tag{A–8}$$

Manipulating, we obtain

$$\varepsilon = \int_{t_1}^{t_2} w(t) \left[ f^2(t) - 2 \sum_{n=0}^{N} \alpha_n \phi_n(t) f(t) + \sum_{\substack{n=0 \\ k=0}}^{N} \alpha_k \alpha_n \phi_n(t) \phi_k(t) \right] dt \quad \text{(A–9)}$$

where the double index of summation implies a double summation. This equation can be rewritten as

$$\varepsilon = \int_{t_1}^{t_2} w(t) f^2(t) dt - 2 \sum_{n=0}^{N} \alpha_n \int_{t_1}^{t_2} w(t) \phi_n(t) f(t) dt$$

$$+ \sum_{\substack{n=0 \\ k=0}}^{N} \alpha_k \alpha_n \int_{t_1}^{t_2} w(t) \phi_n(t) \phi_k(t) dt \quad \text{(A–10)}$$

We have assumed that the functions are such that the order of integration and summation can be interchanged.

We wish to minimize $\varepsilon$ with respect to the $\alpha$'s. The first integral is independent of $\alpha$. Thus, let us write this integral as a constant

$$K = \int_{t_1}^{t_2} w(t) f^2(t) dt \quad \text{(A–11)}$$

The second integral of Eq. A–10 is just that given in Eq. A–4 and the last integral can be evaluated using Eq. A–2. Thus Eq. A–10 becomes

$$\varepsilon = K - 2 \sum_{n=0}^{N} \lambda_n a_n \alpha_n + \sum_{n=0}^{N} \alpha_n^2 \lambda \quad \text{(A–12)}$$

Note that the last summation is now a single summation since the last integral of Eq. A–10 is zero, unless $n = k$. Add and substract $\sum_{n=0}^{N} \lambda_n a_n^2$ from the right-hand side of Eq. A–12. Thus, we can write

$$\varepsilon = K - \sum_{n=0}^{N} \lambda_n a_n^2 + \sum_{n=0}^{N} \lambda_n (a_n - \alpha_n)^2 \quad \text{(A–13)}$$

The first summation is independent of $\alpha_n$. The only place that $\alpha_n$ appears is in the last summation as $(a_n - \alpha_n)^2$. The $\lambda$'s are always positive since (see Eq. A–2)

$$\lambda_n = \int_{t_1}^{t_2} w(t) \phi^2(t) dt$$

Thus, each $\lambda_n(a_n - \alpha_n)^2$ is positive. Thus we minimize the magnigude of the summation by minimizing the magnitude of each term. The smallest value that each term in the summation can have is zero. This occurs when

$$\alpha_n = a_n, \quad n = 0, 1, 2, ..., N \quad \text{(A–14)}$$

Hence, we minimize the weighted mean square when the coefficients of the truncated series of Eq. A-5 are those obtained by A-4. The weighted mean square error in this case is given by

$$\varepsilon = \int_{t_1}^{t_2} w(t) \, f^2(t) \, dt - \sum_{n=0}^{N} \lambda_n a_n \tag{A-15}$$

Let us unrigorously discuss the significance of Eq. A-7. The weighting function $w(t)$ tends to emphasize the error in regions where it is large and de-emphasize it in regions where it is small. Since we have minimized $\varepsilon$ we would, all other things being equal, assume that $f_a(t)$ should provide the best approximation to $f(t)$ for those values of $t$ where $w(t)$ is large. This statement may not always be valid. For instance, if $f(t)$ is discontinuous where $w(t)$ is large, and continuous where $w(t)$ is small, the error might well be smallest in the region of continuity of $f(t)$.

We have discussed the Fourier series as an example of orthogonal functions. We shall now list some others.

**Legendre Polynomials.**

$$\phi_n(t) = \frac{1}{2^n n!} \frac{d^n (t^2 - 1)^n}{dt^n}, \qquad n = 0, 1, \ldots \tag{A-16}$$

$$\phi_0(t) = 1$$

$$\phi_1(t) = t$$

$$\phi_2(t) = \tfrac{3}{2} t^2 - \tfrac{1}{2}$$

$$\phi_3(t) = (\tfrac{5}{2} t^3 - \tfrac{3}{2} t)$$

$$\phi_4(t) = \tfrac{35}{8} t^4 - \tfrac{15}{4} t^2 + \tfrac{3}{8}$$
$$\vdots$$

The weight function is

$$w(t) = 1 \tag{A-17}$$

The range of orthogonality is $-1 \leq t \leq 1$.

$$\int_{-1}^{1} \phi_m(t) \, \phi_n(t) \, dt = \begin{cases} 0, & m \neq n \\[2mm] \dfrac{2}{2n+1}, & n = m \end{cases} \tag{A-18}$$

**Tchebycheff Polynomials.**

$$\phi_n(t) = \cos(n \cos^{-1} t) = \operatorname{Re}\left[(t + j\sqrt{1 - t^2})^n\right] \tag{A-19}$$

$$\phi_0(t) = 1$$

$$\phi_1(t) = t$$

$$\phi_2(t) = 2t^2 + 1$$

$$\phi_3(t) = 4t^3 - 3t$$

$$\phi_4(t) = 8t^4 - 8t^2 + 1$$

The weight function is

$$w(t) = 1/(\sqrt{1 + x^2}) \qquad\qquad (A-20)$$

The range of orthogonality is $-1 \leq t \leq 1$.

$$\int_{-1}^{1} \phi_m(t)\, \phi_n(t)\, \frac{1}{\sqrt{1 + x^2}}\, dx = \begin{cases} 0 \quad, & m \neq n \\ \dfrac{\pi}{2^{2n-1}}, & m = n \end{cases} \qquad (A-21)$$

**Hermite Polynomials.**

$$\phi_n(t) = (-1)^n\, e^{t^2}\, \frac{d^n e^{-t^2}}{dt^n} \qquad\qquad (A-22)$$

$$\phi_0(t) = 1$$

$$\phi_1(t) = 2t$$

$$\phi_2(t) = 4t^2 - 2$$

$$\phi_3(t) = 8t^3 - 12t$$

$$\phi_4(t) = 16t^4 - 48t^2 + 12$$

The weight function is

$$w(t) = e^{-t^2} \qquad\qquad (A-23)$$

The range of orthogonality is $-\infty \leq t \leq \infty$.

$$\int_{-\infty}^{\infty} \phi_m(t)\, \phi_n(t)\, e^{-t^2}\, dt = \begin{cases} 0 \quad, & m \neq n \\ 2^n n!\, \sqrt{\pi}, & m = n \end{cases} \qquad (A-24)$$

**Laguerre Polynomials.**

$$\phi_n(t) = e^t\, \frac{d^n (t^n e^{-t})}{dt^n} \qquad\qquad (A-25)$$

$$\phi_0(t) = 1$$

$$\phi_1(t) = -t + 1$$

$$\phi_2(t) = t^2 - 4t + 2$$

$$\phi_3(t) = -t^3 + 9t^2 - 18t + 6$$

$$\phi_4(t) = t^4 - 16t^3 + 72t^2 - 96t + 24$$

The weight function is

$$w(t) = e^{-t} \qquad\qquad (A-26)$$

The range of orthogonality is $0 \leq t \leq \infty$.

$$\int_0^\infty \phi_m(t)\,\phi_n(t)\,e^{-t}\,dt = \begin{cases} 0, & m \neq n \\ (p!)^2, & m = n \end{cases} \tag{A-27}$$

There are other orthogonal functions than those which were listed here for purpose of example.

## BIBLIOGRAPHY

Guillemin, E. A. *The Mathematics of Circuit Analysis.* pp. 439–448. New York: Wiley, 1949.
Hildebrand, F. B. *Advanced Calculus for Engineers.* Chap. 5. Englewood Cliffs, N.J.: Prentice-Hall, 1949.

# Functions of a Complex Variable

Often in the study of systems or network response, functions of complex variables (i.e., functions where arguments have both a real and an imaginary part) are encountered. For instance, the Laplace transform of a time function is a function of a complex variable, We shall consider fundamental aspects of such functions. Most of this discussion will concern itself with the calculus of complex functions. It is assumed that the reader is familiar with the basic operations with complex numbers.

## B-1. FUNCTIONS OF A COMPLEX VARIABLE

A complex variable is one which can take on complex as well as real values; for example,

$$s = \sigma + j\omega \tag{B-1a}$$

This can also be written in polar form as

$$s = |s|\, e^{j\theta} \tag{B-1b}$$

where $j = \sqrt{-1}$. The value of the variable is often represented on a 2-dimensional set of coordinates called the $s$-plane (see Fig. B-1). Note that there is an axis of real numbers ($\sigma$ axis) and an axis of imaginary numbers ($j\omega$ axis).

Functions of complex variables are usually complex themselves. A function can be thought of mapping a set of points in the $s$-plane into another plane. (Complex functions will be represented by boldface quantities.) Consider the function

$$\boldsymbol{F}(s) = s^2 \tag{B-2}$$

We can write

$$\boldsymbol{F}(s) = U(s) + jV(s) \tag{B-3}$$

where $U(s)$ and $V(s)$ are the real and imaginary parts of $\boldsymbol{F}(s)$, respectively. Substituting Eq. B-1a into Eq. B-3 and manipulating, we obtain

$$U(s) = \sigma^2 - \omega^2 \tag{B-4a}$$

$$V(s) = 2\sigma\omega \tag{B-4b}$$

or, equivalently

$$\boldsymbol{F}(s) = |s|^2\, e^{j2\theta} \tag{B-4c}$$

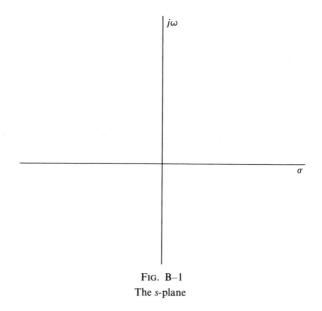

Equations (B–4) represent the mapping of points in the s-plane into points in the $F(s)$ plane. That is, each point in the s-plane maps into a point in the $F(s)$ plane whose distance from the origin is the square of the distance from the origin in the s-plane and whose angle is twice that of the s-plane angle.

If $F(s)$ is a function of a complex variable, then, for every s in a given set, there corresponds one value of $F(s)$. If more than one point corresponds to each s (e.g., $F_1(s) = s^{1/3}$) then this is, strictly speaking, not a function. However, it is often called a *multivalued function* of s. We shall consider in a subsequent section how such functions can be treated.

Usually, functions of a complex variable are defined so that when the variable takes on real values, the definition of a function is compatible with that of a real-valued function. For example,

$$F_1(s) = e^s = 1 + s + \frac{s^2}{2!} + \frac{s^3}{3!} + \cdots \tag{B–5a}$$

or

$$F_2(s) = \sin s = \frac{e^{js} - e^{-js}}{2j} \tag{B–5b}$$

or

$$F_3(s) = \cosh s = \frac{e^s + e^{-s}}{2} \tag{B–5c}$$

**Principal Value.**   The variable s is given in polar form in Eq. B–1b. If an integral multiple of $2\pi$ radians is added to $\theta$, the location of s in the s-plane is unchanged.

Thus, we can write

$$s = |s| e^{j\phi_k} \tag{B-6a}$$

where

$$\phi_k = \theta + 2k\pi, \qquad k = 0, \pm1, \pm2, ... \tag{B-6b}$$

Often, the mapping of a function of $s$ is independent of $k$. For example,

$$F_1(s) = s^2 = |s|^2 e^{2j\phi} = |s|^2 e^{j(2\theta + 2k\pi)} = |s|^2 e^{j2\theta}e^{j4k\pi}, \qquad k = 0, \pm1, \pm2, ... \tag{B-7}$$

However, at times, this is not true. Consider

$$F_2(s) = \ln s = \ln |s| + j\phi = \ln |s| + j(\theta + 2k\pi), \qquad k = 0, \pm1, \pm2, ... \tag{B-8}$$

The value of $k$ now affects both the magnitude and angle of $F_2(s)$. Often to avoid confusion, $\phi_k$ is restricted to lie between $-\pi$ and $\pi$; Thus,

$$-\pi \leqq \phi_k \leqq \pi \tag{B-9}$$

(i.e., $k = 0$ and $-\pi \leqq \theta \leqq \pi$.) In this range, the value of the function is called the *principal value*. Unless otherwise specified, the values of a function will be principal values.

## B-2. LIMITS, CONTINUITY, DERIVATIVES

A function $F(s)$ may only exist for certain values of $s$: for instance it may only exist for $s$ within some region of the $s$-plane. As an example, consider the power series expansion of $1/(1 - s)$ (see Section B-8).

$$F(s) = \sum_{n=0}^{\infty} s^n$$

This converges (exists) for $|s| < 1$ and does not exist elsewhere. The region $R$ of convergence is the unit circle in the $s$-plane. Similarly, functions may only exist in an arbitrary region $R$ (see Fig. B-2). Now assume that $s_0$ is some point within the region $R$, where $F(s)$ exists. We then define $F_0$ as the limit of $F(s)$ as $s$ approaches $s_0$, if, for any arbitrary real positive number $\varepsilon$, there exists another real positive number $\delta$ such that

$$|F(s) - F_0| < \varepsilon \tag{B-10a}$$

whenever

$$|s - s_0| < \delta \tag{B-10b}$$

That is, no matter how small we choose the difference $\varepsilon$ between $F(s)$ and $F_0$, there is a circular region about $s_0$ (defined by $\delta$) which maps into a region in the $F(s)$ plane, lying within $\varepsilon$ distance of $F_0$. When the limit exists we write

$$\lim_{s \to s_0} F(s) = F_0 \tag{B-11}$$

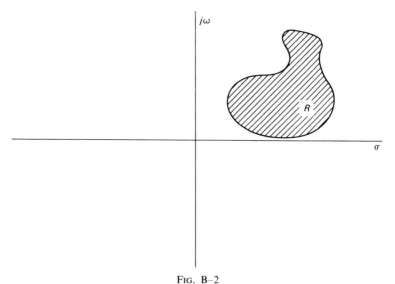

Fig B-2
The $s$-plane. The region where a certain $F(s)$ exists is shown shaded

**Continuity.**   A function of a complex variable is *continuous* at the point $s_0$ if $F(s_0)$ exists and if, for every real positive $\varepsilon$ there exists a real positive $\delta$ such that

$$|F(s) - F(s_0)| < \varepsilon \qquad\qquad \text{(B–12a)}$$

for all $s$ which satisfy

$$|s - s_0| < \delta \qquad\qquad \text{(B–12b)}$$

This definition agrees with the usual concepts of continuity: *A continuous function cannot change by a finite amount for a differentially small change in $s$*, since, for a discontinuous function, a finite $\varepsilon$ can exist for which no nonzero $\delta$ can be found.

**Derivatives.**   The derivative of a function of a complex variable is defined in a manner similar to that for a real variable:

$$\left.\frac{dF(s)}{ds}\right|_{s=s_0} = \lim_{\Delta s \to 0} \frac{F(s_0 + \Delta s) - F(s_0)}{\Delta s} \qquad\qquad \text{(B–13)}$$

For convenience, we shall, at times, use the somewhat incorrect notation

$$\left.\frac{dF(s)}{ds}\right|_{s=s_0} = \frac{dF(s_0)}{ds} = F'(s_0)$$

If the derivative exists, then $dF(s_0)/ds$ must exist *and* be independent of the direction from which $\Delta s_0$ is taken. For example, consider the function

$$F(s) = s^2$$

Then,

$$\frac{dF(s_0)}{ds} = \lim_{\Delta s \to 0} \frac{(s_0 + \Delta s)^2 - s^2}{\Delta s} = \lim_{\Delta s \to 0} 2s_0 - \Delta s = 2s_0$$

Note that, this is independent of the direction from which $s_0$ is approached. Thus, the derivative exists for *all* values of $s$. Hence, we say it exists in the *entire* $s$-plane. On the other hand, consider

$$F(s) = s^* = \sigma = j\omega$$

(The * superscript indicates conjugate.) Then write

$$F_1(s_0) = \lim_{\substack{\Delta\sigma_0 \to 0 \\ \Delta\omega_0 \to 0}} \frac{(\sigma_0 + \Delta\sigma) - j(\omega_0 + \Delta\omega) - (\sigma_0 - j\omega_0)}{\Delta\sigma_0 + j\Delta\omega_0} = \lim_{\substack{\Delta\sigma_0 \to 0 \\ \Delta\omega_0 \to 0}} \frac{\Delta\sigma_0 + j\Delta\omega_0}{\Delta\sigma_0 - j\Delta\omega_0}$$

Now let us assume that $s_0$ is approached along a line parallel to the $\sigma$ axis (i.e., $\Delta\omega_0 = 0$); then, $F_1(s_0) = 1$.

On the other hand, if $s_0$ is approached along a line parallel to the $j\omega$ axis (i.e., $\Delta\sigma = 0$), then $F_1(s_0) = -1$. These two values of $F_1(s_0)$ are different. Hence, we cannot say that $F_1(s_0)$ is the derivative of $F(s)$ at $s = s_0$. In fact, we can state that the derivative of $F(s)$ does not exist at $s = s_0$. In the above relation, $s_0$ could take on any value. Thus, the derivative of $F(s)$ does not exist at any point in the entire $s$-plane.

As a further example, consider the function $F(s) = 1/s$. Let us determine its derivative, if it exists:

$$\lim_{\Delta s \to 0} \frac{\dfrac{1}{s_0 + \Delta s} - \dfrac{1}{s_0}}{\Delta s} = -\frac{1}{s_0^2}$$

This is independent of the direction of $\Delta s$ and exists at all points in the $s$-plane except $s_0 = 0$.

Therefore,

$$\left. \frac{dF(s)}{ds} \right|_{s = s_0} = -\frac{1}{s_0^2}$$

and exists at all points in the $s$-plane except the origin.

## B-3. ANALYTIC FUNCTIONS—CAUCHY-RIEMANN EQUATIONS

Let us now consider a fundamental definition. A function which is single valued and possesses a derivative at all points within a region of the $s$-plane is said to be *analytic* in that region. (Note that, in general, a function is, by definition, single valued. In the next section we shall see that certain "multiple valued functions" can be restricted in such a way that they become "single valued.") A function is said to be analytic at a point if that point lies within a region where the function is analytic. For example, the function $F(s) = 1/s$ is analytic at all points except $s = 0$.

**Cauchy-Riemann Equations.**   We shall now develop a test which can be applied to determine if a function is analytic. Let us consider a function of a complex variable and write it as the sum of its real and imaginary parts:

$$F(s) = F(\sigma, \omega) = U(\sigma, \omega) + jV(\sigma, \omega) \tag{B-14}$$

Now let us assume that the derivative exists in some region and then evaluate the derivative at a point of that region in two ways. The first will assume that $\Delta s$ is parallel to the $\sigma$ axis and the second, that it is parallel to the $j\omega$ axis. (For convenience, we shall omit the subscript 0 from $s$. However, these derivatives are evaluated at a particular point in the $s$-plane.) Then,

$$\frac{dF(s)}{ds} = \lim_{\Delta\sigma \to 0} \frac{F(s + \Delta\sigma) - F(s)}{\Delta\sigma}$$

or, equivalently,

$$\frac{dF(s)}{ds} = \lim_{\Delta\sigma \to 0} \frac{U(\sigma + \Delta\sigma, \omega) - U(\sigma, \omega)}{\Delta\sigma} + j \lim_{\Delta\sigma \to 0} \frac{V(\sigma + \Delta\sigma, \omega) - V(\sigma, \omega)}{\Delta\sigma} \tag{B-15}$$

Each of these terms is just the definition of the partial derivative; thus

$$\frac{dF(s)}{ds} = \frac{\partial U(\sigma, \omega)}{\partial\sigma} + j\frac{\partial V(\sigma, \omega)}{\partial\sigma} \tag{B-16}$$

Similarly, considering $j\Delta\omega$, we have

$$\frac{dF(s)}{ds} = \lim_{\Delta\omega \to 0} \frac{V(\sigma, \omega + \Delta\omega) + V(\sigma, \omega)}{\Delta\omega}$$

$$- j \lim_{\Delta\omega \to 0} \frac{U(\sigma, \omega + \Delta\omega) - U(\sigma, \omega)}{\Delta\omega} \tag{B-17}$$

Hence,

$$\frac{dF(s)}{ds} = \frac{\partial V(\sigma, \omega)}{\partial\omega} - j\frac{\partial U(\sigma, \omega)}{\partial\omega} \tag{B-18}$$

Since the function is assumed to be analytic in a region containing the point $s$ where the derivative is evaluated, Eqs. B-16 and B-18 must yield the same result. Equating the real and imaginary parts of these equations, we have

$$\frac{\partial U(\sigma, \omega)}{\partial\sigma} = \frac{\partial V(\sigma, \omega)}{\partial\omega} \tag{B-19a}$$

and

$$\frac{\partial V(\sigma, \omega)}{\partial \sigma} = -\frac{\partial U(\sigma, \omega)}{\partial \omega} \tag{B–19b}$$

Equations B–19 are called the *Cauchy-Riemann equations*. They are derived by assuming that $dF(s)/ds$ exists. Hence, they are *necessary conditions* that the derivative exists. Thus, a necessary condition that $F(s)$ be analytic in a region is that it be single valued and satisfy the Cauchy-Riemann equations.

The Cauchy-Riemann equations are not *sufficient conditions* for the function to be analytic in a region. However, if the function is single valued and the partial derivatives $\partial U/\partial \sigma$, $\partial U/\partial \omega$, $\partial V/\partial \sigma$, and $\partial V/\partial \omega$ exist, are continuous, and satisfy the Cauchy-Riemann equations, then the function will be analytic in the region. This can be demonstrated in the following way. Suppose $s$ is a fixed point in a region where all four partial derivatives exist, are continuous, and satisfy Eqs. B–19. Then, since the partial derivatives exist and are continuous, we can write

$$dU(\sigma, \omega) = \frac{\partial U(\sigma, \omega)}{\partial \sigma} d\sigma + \frac{\partial U(\sigma, \omega)}{\partial \omega} d\omega \tag{B–20a}$$

and

$$dV(\sigma, \omega) = \frac{\partial V(\sigma, \omega)}{\partial \sigma} d\sigma + \frac{\partial V(\sigma, \omega)}{\partial \omega} d\omega \tag{B–20b}$$

However,

$$dF(\sigma, \omega) = dU(\sigma, \omega) + jdV(\sigma, \omega)$$

Hence, substituting Eqs. B–29, we have

$$dF(\sigma, \omega) = \left[ \frac{\partial U(\sigma, \omega)}{\partial \sigma} + j\frac{\partial V(\sigma, \omega)}{\partial \sigma} \right] d\sigma + \left[ \frac{\partial U(\sigma, \omega)}{\partial \omega} + j\frac{\partial V(\sigma, \omega)}{\partial \omega} \right] d\omega$$

Substituting Eqs. B–19 and manipulating, we have

$$dF(\sigma, \omega) = \left[ \frac{\partial U(\sigma, \omega)}{\partial \sigma} - j\frac{\partial U(\sigma, \omega)}{\partial \omega} \right] (d\sigma + jd\omega) \tag{B–21}$$

But,

$$ds = d\sigma + jd\omega \tag{B–22}$$

Therefore,

$$\frac{dF(\sigma, \omega)}{ds} = \frac{\partial U(\sigma, \omega)}{\partial \sigma} - j\frac{\partial U(\sigma, \omega)}{\partial \omega} \tag{B–23}$$

This is evaluated at the point in question and is independent of the direction of $ds$; the partial derivatives exist. Hence, the derivative exists and is independent of direction. Then, since the function is "single valued" it is analytic.

We can now state that the *necessary and sufficient conditions* for a (single-valued) function to be analytic in a region are: *Its four partial derivatives exist, are continuous, and satisfy the Cauchy-Riemann conditions in the region.* An interesting fact that can be proven about analytic functions is that they possess not only their first derivative, but all derivatives.

## B-4. SINGULARITIES

If a function $F(s)$ is analytic at all points in the $s$-plane except for a set of isolated points, then these points are termed *isolated singularities* or *singular points.*

**Poles.** If $F(s)$ is such that $(s - s_0)^n F(s)$ is analytic in some region of the $s$-plane which contains $s_0$, and $(s - s_0)^n F(s)$ is *not* zero at $s = s_0$, then $F(s)$ is said to have a *pole of order $n$* at $s = s_0$. Let us consider an example of this:

$$F(s) = \frac{1}{(s - 3)^2}$$

has a pole of order 2 at $s = 3$. Note that $F(s)$ and its derivatives do not exist at $s = 3$. However, it can be shown (see Section B-3) that $F(s)$ is analytic elsewhere.

If $F(s)$ is the ratio of two polynomials, then

$$F(s) = \frac{a_n s^n + a_{n-1} s^{n-1} + a_1 s + a_0}{b_m s^m + b_{m-1} s^{m-1} + b_1 s + b_0} \tag{B-24}$$

then the poles occur at the roots of the denominator (assuming that they are not cancelled by roots of the numerator); for example,

$$F(s) = \frac{(s + 1)(s + 2)^2}{s(s + 3)^3 (s + 5)^2}$$

has a first-order pole at $s = 0$, a third-order pole at $s = -3$, and a second-order pole at $s = -5$. In this example, the roots of the denominator are real; however, they need not be and the poles can occur at all points in the $s$-plane. If the coefficients of the denominator polynomial are real, then the poles will always occur in conjugate pairs. If $n > m$ in Eq. B–24, then $F(s)$ approaches infinity as $s$ approaches infinity. In this case, $F(s)/s^{n-m}$ will approach a bounded, nonzero number as $s$ approaches infinity. Then $F(s)$ has a pole of order $n - m$ at $s = \infty$.

When $s$ is equal to one of the roots of the numerator of Eq. B–24, then $F(s) = 0$. Those values of $s$ for which $F(s) = 0$ are called the *zeros* of the function. In general, if $F(s)$ is analytic at $s_0$ and in a region about it, and if $F(s)/(s - s_0)^n$ is bounded and nonzero at $s = s_0$, then $s_0$ is a *zero of degree $n$*. In the previous example, $s = -1$ is a first-order zero and $s = -2$ is a second-order zero. Also, if $s^k F(s)$ is bounded and does not approach zero as $s$ approaches infinity, then $F(s)$ has a zero of order

$k$ at $s = \infty$. Note that zeros are not, in general, singular points. In the examples cited, the function is analytic at the zeros. Zeros are discussed here since their definition is similar to that of poles.

**Essential Singularity.** In general, if we have a function:

$$F(s) = \frac{a_{-n}}{(s - s_0)^n} + \frac{a_{-(n-1)}}{(s - s_0)^{n-1}} + \cdots + \frac{a_{-1}}{s - s_0} + F_a(s) \qquad (B-25)$$

where $F_a(s)$ is analytic in a region about $s_0$, then $F(s)$ has a pole of multiplicity $n$ at $s = s_0$. If, however, $n$ "becomes infinity," then the singularity is no longer called a pole but an *essential singularity*. For example (see Eq. B–5a),

$$e^{1/s} = 1 + \frac{1}{s} + \frac{1}{2!s^2} + \frac{1}{3!s^3} + \cdots \qquad (B-26)$$

has an essential singularity at $s = 0$. Note that $e^s$ also has an essential singularity at $s = \infty$. It can be shown that, in the neighborhood of an *isolated essential singularity* a function will approach any numerical value arbitrarily closely.

**Branch Points.** A function is, by definition, single valued. Accordingly,

$$F(s) = s^{1/2} \qquad (B-27)$$

is not a function, since it is *multiple valued*. However, we can, by appropriate restrictions, cause $F(s)$ to be single valued. If $\theta$, the angle of $s$, is restricted to the range

$$-\pi \leqq \theta \leqq \pi \qquad (B-28)$$

then in place of Eq. B–27, we can write

$$F_1(s) = \sqrt{|s|}\, e^{j\theta/2} \qquad (B-29a)$$

$$F_2(s) = \sqrt{|s|}\, e^{j((\theta/2) + \pi)} \qquad (B-29b)$$

Note that $F_1(s)$ and $F_2(s)$ are each single valued functions of $s$. Each is called a *branch* of $F(s)$. Thus, "multiple valued functions" can often be treated as several single valued functions or branches.

Let us now consider a procedure whereby "multiple valued functions" can be restricted to single valued branches. Equations B–29 are only single valued if $\theta$ is restricted as in Eq. B–28. Actually, other restrictions can be used as long as $\theta$ is only permitted to vary $2\pi$ radians (e.g., $0 < \theta < 2\pi$, $-\pi/2 < \theta < 3\pi/2$, etc.). To indicate that a restriction is imposed on $s$, a line called a *branch cut* can be drawn on the $s$-plane. If the value of $s$ is *not* allowed to cross this branch cut, then its angle is restricted as desired. If $\theta$ is restricted as in Eq. B–28, the cut consists of the negative $\sigma$ axis. This is shown in Fig. B–3. (Note that if $s$ starts at 0 radian, it can only vary

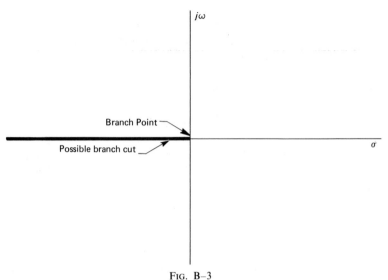

FIG. B–3

Illustration of a branch cut and branch point for $F(s) = s^{1/2}$

as restricted in Eq. B–28.) If the restriction on the angle of $s$ is $0 < \theta < 2\pi$, the branch cut becomes the positive $\sigma$ axis. Actually, any curve which does not cross itself and which extends from $s = 0$ to $s = \infty$ is a suitable branch cut in this case.

If $F(s)$ is only defined as in Eq. B–29a, then, as $\theta$ varies between $-\pi$ and $\pi$, the first branch is obtained.

If $s$ crosses the branch so that $\theta$ lies between $\pi$ and $3\pi$, the second branch is obtained. In this case, the $s$-plane can be thought of as two sheets (one corresponding to each branch of the function). If $s$ crosses a branch cut, it passes from one sheet to the other. These sheets are called *Riemann surfaces*. If $s$ crosses a branch in the same direction twice, $\theta$ will increase to be $4\pi$ and the function will again be the first branch. For other $F(s)$ there may be more than two Riemann surfaces; e.g., $F(s) = s^{1/3}$ will have three.

Let us consider the example of Eq. B–27 again. There is a small neighborhood about $s = 0$ where the function is not single valued. Hence, the function does not exist at $s = 0$. This is then a singular point which is called a *branch point*. In general, the branch cuts run from the branch points.

An example at a function with more than one branch point is

$$F(s) = \sqrt{\frac{s + 1}{s - 1}} \tag{B–30}$$

This will have branch points at $s = +1$ and $s = -1$. If *both* $s + 1$ and $s - 1$ have in increase in angle of $K\pi$ radians, then the function will not have an ambiguity, since $(s + 1)/(s - 1)$ will *not* have an increase in angle of $2k\pi$ radians. Thus, the branch cut need only keep the angle of $(s + 1/(s - 1))$, and not $s$, from varying by more than $2\pi$ radians. A branch cut running between the two branch points will accomplish this. Another possibility is a pair of cuts extending from each branch point to $-\infty$ and $+\infty$ along the $\sigma$ axis.

## B-5. LINE INTEGRALS

The calculation of such things as the inverse Laplace transform requires the evaluation of *line integrals* of functions of a complex variable. In order to evaluate a line integral, we must not only know $F(s)$, which is the integrand, but also the path of integration in the $s$-plane. Such a path is shown in Fig. B-4. Now assume that the function $F(s)$ is continuous along the path of integration. The endpoints of the path are labelled $A$ and $B$. Choose $n + 1$ points on the path, as shown. ($s_0$ is one endpoint, $s_n$, the other.) Choose another set of points $\alpha_1, \alpha_2, ..., \alpha_{n-1}$ which lie on the contour such that $\alpha_k$ lies between $s_{k-1}$ and $s_k$. Then form the sum

$$S_n = \sum_{k=1}^{n} F(\alpha_k)(s_k - s_{k-1}) \qquad (B-31)$$

The line integral is defined as the limit of $S_n$ as the number $n$ of points increases to $\infty$. The number of points must be chosen in such a way that, as $n$ approaches

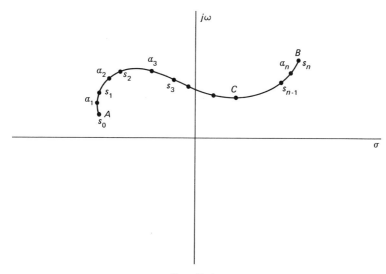

Fig. B-4
Illustration of a path $C$ in the $s$-plane

infinity, the largest segment $|s_k - s_{k-1}|_{max}$ approaches zero. The line integral is written as

$$\int_C \mathbf{F}(s)\, ds = \lim_{\substack{n \to \infty \\ |s_k - s_{k-1}|_{max} \to 0}} \sum_{k=1}^{n} \mathbf{F}(s_k)(s_k - s_{k-1}) \qquad (\text{B--32})$$

The value of the integral *depends* upon both the function $\mathbf{F}(s)$ and the path of integration $C$.

If the contour $C$ of integration is closed (i.e., if the endpoints $A$ and $B$ coincide), then the line integral is called a *closed line integral* and is written as

$$\oint \mathbf{F}(s)\, ds$$

An example of a closed path is shown in Fig. B–5. It is conventional to speak of a *positive direction* when traveling a closed path. As one traverses the path in the positive direction, the area enclosed is to the left. This is illustrated in Fig. B–5.

As an example let us evaluate the integral $\oint [1/(s - s_0)^n]\, ds$ around a closed circular path whose center is $s_0$. This is illustrated in Fig. B–6. Let us assume that the radius of the curve is $\rho$. Then, on the path of integration $s - s_0 = \rho e^{j\phi}$ where the angle $\phi$ is illustrated in Fig. B–6 and $ds = j\rho e^{j\phi}\, d\phi$.

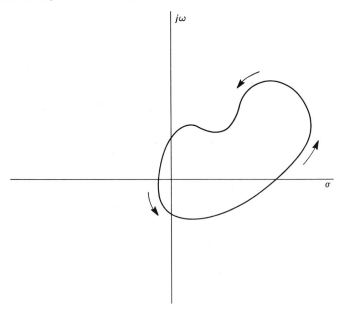

FIG. B–5

Closed path. The positive direction of integration is shown

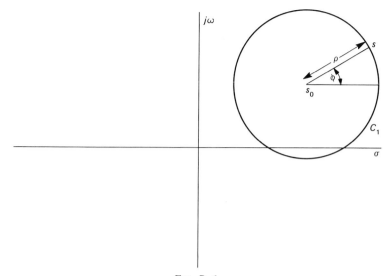

FIG. B-6
Circular path of integration about the point $s = s_0$

Hence,

$$\oint \frac{1}{(s - s_0)^n} \, ds = j\rho^{1-n} \int_0^{2\pi} e^{j(1-n)\phi} \, d\phi$$

If $n = 1$, then $e^{j(1-n)\phi} = 1$ and the value of the integral is $2\pi j$. (This is evaluated as a Riemann integral. Note the similarity of the definitions.) If $n \neq 1$, then

$$\int_0^{2\pi} e^{j(1-n)\phi} \, d\phi = \frac{1}{j(1-n)} \left[ 1 - e^{j(1-n)2\pi} \right] = 0$$

Thus,

$$\oint \frac{1}{(s - s_0)^n} \, ds = \begin{cases} 2\pi j, & n = 1 \\ 0, & n \neq 1 \end{cases} \tag{B-33}$$

Note that this integral is independent of the radius of the path.

## B-6. CAUCHY'S INTEGRAL THEOREM

If a region $R$ is such that any closed curve lying in $R$ can be continuously shrunken to a point, the region is said to be *simply connected*. If a region is not simply connected, it is *multiply connected*. Simply and multiply connected regions are illustrated in Fig. B-7. Note that the simply connected region has no "holes" in it. A multiply connected region (see Fig. B-7b) is defined by $C_1$ and $C_2$. It has a hole. A curve

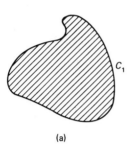

(a)

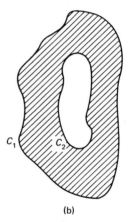

(b)

Fig. B–7

Connected regions; (a) simply connected; (b) multiply
connected

which surrounds such a hole cannot be continuously shrunken to a point, so the
region is multiply connected.

Let us assume that we have a simply connected region within which lies a closed
contour $C$ and that there is a function $F(s)$ which is analytic within that region.
We also assume that $C$ encloses an area $R$. In this discussion we shall make use
of Green's theorem, which states that *If $P(\sigma, \omega)$ and $Q(\sigma, \omega)$ are continuous, single-
valued, real functions of two variables with continuous partial derivatives in a simply
connected region $R$ which is bounded by a closed curve $C$ (where $R$ is included in
$C$; i.e., $P$ and $Q$ are continuous and single valued etc. on $R$), then*

$$\oint_C (P d\sigma + Q d\omega) = \int_R \int \left( \frac{\partial Q}{\partial \sigma} - \frac{\partial P}{\partial \omega} \right) d\sigma \, d\omega \qquad (B\text{–}34)$$

Thus, the line integral of a function on the boundary of a region is related to an
area integral over the enclosed area.

Now let us consider $\oint F(s) \, ds$. Making use of Eqs. B–14 and B–22, we have

$$\oint_C F(s) \, ds = \oint_C [U(\sigma, \omega) + jV(\sigma, \omega)] (d\sigma + jd\omega) \qquad (B\text{–}35)$$

Rearranging, we obtain

$$\oint_C F(s) \, ds = \oint_C [U(\sigma, \omega) \, d\sigma - V(\sigma, \omega) \, d\omega] + j \oint_C [V(\sigma, \omega) \, d\sigma + U(\sigma, \omega) \, d\omega]$$

Applying Green's theorem to the right-hand side of this equation yields

$$\oint_C F(s)\,ds = \int\int_R \left[ -\frac{\partial V(\sigma, \omega)}{\partial \sigma} - \frac{\partial U(\sigma, \omega)}{\partial \omega} \right] d\sigma\,d\omega$$

$$+ j \int\int_R \left[ \frac{\partial U(\sigma, \omega)}{\partial \sigma} - \frac{\partial V(\sigma, \omega)}{\partial \omega} \right] ds \qquad \text{(B–36)}$$

Since the function is analytic, the Cauchy-Riemann equations are satisfied. Substituting Eqs. B–19 into Eq. B–36, we determine that each of the bracketed terms are zero; thus,

$$\oint_C F(s)\,ds = 0 \qquad \text{(B–37)}$$

This is a representation of *Cauchy's integral theorem.* This states that: *if* $F(s)$ *is analytic in a region, then the line integral of* $F(s)$ *over any closed contour within that region is zero.*

Let us now extend this theorem to multiply connected regions. Assume that $F(s)$ is analytic in a multiply connected region $R$ whose outer contour is $C_0$ and that $C$ is a contour within the region such that $F(s)$ is analytic on $C$ and in the entire region between $C$ and $C_0$; i.e., all the holes in $R$ are enclosed by $C$ (see Fig. B–8). Then let $C_1, C_2, ..., C_n$ be contours within $R$ which are enclosed by $C$. Each $C_1, C_2, ..., C_n$ encloses one of the holes in the multiply connected region. (There are $n$ holes.) Now suppose a straight line is drawn from $C$ to each of the internal contours, as shown. Then $C, C_1, C_2, ..., C_n$ and the straight lines now form the boundary of a simply connected region such that $F(s)$ is analytic in the region and on its

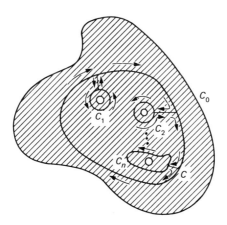

FIG. B–8
Contours in a multiply connected region
(function is analytic in shaded areas)

boundary. (Note that because of the straight lines, this new region has no holes.) Cauchy's integral theorem then yields

$$\oint_C F(s)\,ds - \oint_{C_1} F(s)\,ds - \oint_{C_2} F(s)\,ds - \cdots - \int_{C_n} F(s)\,ds = 0 \qquad (\text{B--38})$$

There is no net contribution from the integrals over the straight line segments. This is because the integral over each segment is evaluated twice, once entering the inner contour $C_j$ and once leaving it. Another way of considering this is that each "pair" of straight lines (e.g., one entering *and* one leaving $C_j$) constitute a closed curve in a simply connected region. Thus, by Eq. B--37 their net contribution is zero. The minus signs are placed before the integrals over $C_1, C_2, ..., C_n$ since their direction of integration is negative (see Section B-5). Note that $\oint F(s)\,ds$ implies that the path is taken in the *positive direction*. Thus,

$$\oint_C F(s)\,ds = \oint_{C_1} F(s)\,ds + \oint_{C_2} F(s)\,ds + \cdots + \oint_{C_n} F(s)\,ds \qquad (\text{B--39})$$

This can be considered a generalization of Cauchy's integral theorem.


## B-7. CAUCHY'S INTEGRAL FORMULA

In this section, another relation which is of fundamental importance in the evaluation of complex integrals shall be discussed. We now consider a simply connected region $R$, within which a function $F(s)$ is analytic. Choose a closed contour $C$ which lies within $R$. Let $s_0$ be any point within $C$. This is illustrated in Fig. B--9. Let us determine the value of the integral

$$\oint_C \frac{F(s)}{s - s_0}\,ds$$

Note that $F(s)/(s - s_0)$ is *not* analytic within $C$. Enclose the point $s_0$ by a circle $C_1$ of radius $d$ which lies entirely within $C$. The curves $C$ and $C_1$ define a multiply connected region within which $F(s)/(s - s_0)$ is analytic. Thus, using Eq. B--39,

$$\oint_C \frac{F(s)}{(s - s_0)}\,ds = \oint_{C_1} \frac{F(s)}{(s - s_0)}\,ds \qquad (\text{B--40})$$

Let us use the notation that on $C_1$

$$F(s) = F(s_0) + \delta F_2(s) \qquad (\text{B--41})$$

where $F(s)$ is equal to its value at the center of the circle plus a correction factor. Since $F(s)$ is analytic in the region

$$\lim_{d \to 0} \delta F(s) = 0$$

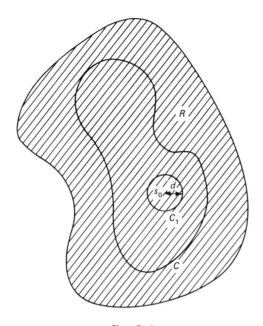

FIG. B–9

Contours used in the development of Cauchy's
integral formula ($F(s)$ is analytic in the shaded area)

That is, as $d$ approaches zero, $F(s)$ approaches $F(s_0)$ at all points on the circle $C_1$.
Then, for very small $d$

$$\oint_C \frac{F(s)}{s - s_0} = F(s_0) \oint_{C_1} \frac{ds}{s - s_0}$$

Using Eq. B–33 to evaluate the right-hand side of this equation, we obtain

$$F(s_0) = \frac{1}{2\pi j} \oint_C \frac{F(s)}{s - s_0}\, ds \tag{B–42}$$

This relation is *Cauchy's integral formula* and it illustrates a remarkable property
of analytic functions. If a function is analytic on and within a closed contour $C$
and its value is only known on $C$, then its value may be *found at all points within
C* using Eq. B–42. This process wherein the value of an analytic function can be
determined in regions where it is unknown is called *analytic continuation*. Actually,
more general analytic continuations procedures have been developed.

Now let us use Eq. B–42 to obtain the derivative of $F(s)$ at $s = s_0$ within $C$.

$$\left. \frac{dF(s)}{ds} \right|_{s = s_0} = \lim_{\Delta s \to 0} \frac{F(s_0 + \Delta s) - F(s_0)}{\Delta s}$$

$$\frac{dF(s)}{ds} = \lim_{\Delta s \to 0} \frac{1}{2\pi j} \frac{1}{\Delta s} \oint_C \left[ \frac{F(s)}{s - (s_0 + \Delta s)} - \frac{F(s)}{s - s_0} \right] ds$$

Assuming that the limit process and the integration can be interchanged, we have

$$\frac{dF(s)}{ds}\bigg|_{s=s_0} = \frac{1}{2\pi j} \int_C \frac{F(s)}{(s - s_0)^2} ds \qquad (B\text{--}43)$$

Proceeding similarly, we obtain

$$\frac{d^n F(s)}{ds^n}\bigg|_{s=s_0} = \frac{n!}{2\pi j} \int_C \frac{F(s)}{(s - s_0)^{n+1}} ds \qquad (B\text{--}44)$$

On the contour, $F(s)/(s - s_0)^{n+1}$ will be bounded. Hence, all of the derivatives will exist.

## B-8. TAYLOR'S SERIES—LAURENT SERIES

We shall now expand an analytic function in a power series. It is assumed that $F(s)$ is analytic in a simply connected region and that $C$ is a circular contour within the region. To avoid confusion, let us rewrite Eqs. B–42 and B–44 in the following way:

$$F(s) = \frac{1}{2\pi j} \oint_C \frac{F(z)}{z - s} dz \qquad (B\text{--}45a)$$

$$F^{(n)}(s) = \frac{n!}{2\pi j} \oint_C \frac{F(z)}{(z - s)^{n+1}} dz \qquad (B\text{--}45b)$$

where $z$ ia a dummy variable of integration and we have replaced $s_0$ by $s$; that is, Eq B–45 can be used to evaluate $F(s)$ at any point $s$ within $C$. Now choose $C$ to be a circle whose center is a point $s_0$. (Note that $s_0$ is not the point where $F(s)$ is evaluated, but the center of the circle.) We can write the following:

$$\frac{1}{z - s} = \frac{1}{z - s_0} \left( \frac{1}{1 - \dfrac{s - s_0}{z - s_0}} \right)$$

The term in parentheses can be written as a finite series:

$$\frac{1}{1 - \dfrac{s - s_0}{z - s_0}} = 1 + \frac{s - s_0}{z - s_0} + \cdots + \left( \frac{s - s_0}{z - s_0} \right)^{n-1} + \frac{(s - s_0)^n}{(z - s)(z - s_0)^{n-1}} \qquad (B\text{--}46)$$

This can be verified for any specific $n$ by simply carrying out the indicated algebraic operation. Substitute into Eq. B–45a and compare the result with Eq. B–45b. This yields

$$F(s) = F(s_0) + (s - s_0) F'(s_0) + (s - s_0)^2 \frac{F''(s_0)}{2!} + \cdots$$

$$+ (s - s_0)^{n-1} \frac{F^{(n-1)}(s_0)}{(n-1)!} + \delta$$

where $\delta$ is a remainder term given by

$$\delta = \frac{(s - s_0)^n}{2\pi j} \oint_C \frac{F(z)\, dz}{(z - s_0)^n (z - s)} \tag{B–47}$$

We shall now show that, as $n$ approaches infinity, $\delta$ approaches zero. The point $s$ lies within $C$ while $z$ lies on $C$. Thus, $|(s - s_0)/(z - s_0)| < 1$. Hence, as long as $s_0$ lies within $C$

$$\lim_{n \to \infty} \left| \frac{s - s_0}{z - s_0} \right|^n = 0$$

Since the length of $C$, $F(z)$ and $1/(z - s)$ are bounded (on $C$) $\lim\limits_{n \to \infty} \delta = 0$ and the series converges. (The latter can be seen from the ratio test.)

Thus, we can see that if $F(s)$ is analytic on a closed circular contour $C$ with center $s_0$, we can express $F(s)$ at any point within $C$ as

$$F(s) = F(s_0) + F'(s)(s - s_0) + \frac{F''(s_0)}{2!} + \cdots + \frac{F^{(k)}(s_0)}{k!}(s - s_0)^k + \cdots \tag{B–48}$$

This is often written in compact form as

$$F(s) = F(s_0) + a_1(s - s_0) + a_2(s - s_0)^2 + \cdots = \sum_{n=0}^{\infty} a_n(s - s_0)^n \tag{B–49a}$$

where

$$a_n = \frac{F^{(n)}(s_0)}{n!} = \frac{1}{2\pi j} \oint_C \frac{F(z)}{(z - s_0)^{n+1}}\, dz \tag{B–49b}$$

Note that $a_0 = F(s_0)$. This is called a *Taylor's series*. Note that the Taylor's series converges for values of $s$ which lie within a circle drawn about $s_0$ if $F(s)$ is analytic within and on that circle.

**Laurent Series.** We shall now assume that $F(s)$ is analytic in an annular region defined by two concentric circles (see Fig. B–10) and on those circles. Now suppose a radial line is drawn from $C_2$ to $C_1$ as in the figure. This line, $C_1$, and $C_2$ define a simply connected region within which and on whose boundary $F(s)$ is analytic. Applying Cauchy's integral formula (Eq. B–45a) to this boundary and noting that the contribution on the straight line portion is zero, we have

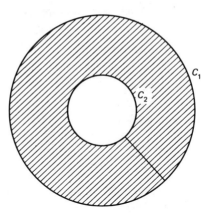

FIG. B-10

Contours used in obtaining a Laurent
series expansion ($F(s)$ is analytic in the
shaded area and on $C_1$ and $C_2$)

$$F(s) = \frac{1}{2\pi j} \oint_{C_1} \frac{F(z)}{z - s} \, dz - \frac{1}{2\pi j} \oint_{C_2} \frac{F(z)}{z - s} \, dz \qquad \text{(B-50)}$$

The first integral can be evaluated in the same manner as Eq. B-49. Note that we
do not require analyticity of $F(s)$ at $s = s_0$ there. Hence, we can write

$$\frac{1}{2\pi j} \oint_{C_1} \frac{F(z)}{z - s} = \sum_{n=0}^{\infty} a_n (s - s_0)^n \qquad \text{(B-51)}$$

where $s_0$ is the center of the circle $C_1$ and the constants $a_n$ are defined by Eq. B-49b.
(The derivative relations cannot be used here since $F(s)$ is not analytic at $s = s_0$.)
This expansion converges for all $s$ *within* $C_1$. For the second integral of Eq. B-50,
we proceed in a slightly different fashion, since we can only obtain convergence
for points *outside* of $C_2$. We write

$$-\frac{1}{z - s} = \frac{1}{s - z} = \frac{1}{s - s_0} \left( \frac{1}{1 - \dfrac{z - s_0}{s - s_0}} \right) \qquad \text{(B-52a)}$$

The term in parentheses can be written as (see Eq. B-46)

$$\frac{1}{1 - \dfrac{z - s_0}{s - s_0}} = 1 + \frac{z - s_0}{s - s_0} + \cdots + \left( \frac{z - s_0}{s - s_0} \right)^{n-1} + \frac{(z - s_0)^n}{(s - s_0)^{n-1} (s - z)} \qquad \text{(B-52b)}$$

Substituting in Eq. B-52a and then substituting the results in the second integral
of Eq. B-50, we have

$$-\frac{1}{2\pi j}\oint_{C_2}\frac{F(z)}{z-s}\,dz = \sum_{k=1}^{n}\frac{1}{2\pi j}\oint_{C_2}F(z)\frac{(z-s_0)^{k-1}}{(s-s_0)^k}\,dz + \delta' \tag{B-53}$$

where

$$\delta' = \frac{1}{2\pi j}\oint_{C_2}\left(\frac{z-s_0}{s-s_0}\right)^n\frac{1}{s-z}\,dz$$

Since $s$ is a point outside of $C_2$, then $\left|(z-s_0)/s-s_0)\right| < 1$. Thus, $\lim_{n\to\infty}\delta' = 0$.

Hence, we can write

$$-\frac{1}{2\pi j}\oint_{C_2}\frac{F(z)}{z-s}\,ds = \sum_{n=1}^{\infty}\frac{b_n}{(s-s_0)^n} \tag{B-54}$$

where

$$b_n = \frac{1}{2\pi j}\oint_{C_2}\frac{F(z)}{(z-s_0)^{-n+1}}\,dz \tag{B-55}$$

Then, using Eqs. B–51 and B–54, we obtain

$$F(s) = \sum_{n=0}^{\infty}a_n(s-s_0)^n + \sum_{n=1}^{\infty}\frac{b_n}{(s-s_0)^n} \tag{B-56}$$

This can be written in more compact form. Compare Eq. B–49b with Eq. B–55. If we write

$$b_n = a_{-n} \tag{B-57}$$

then we can express both $b_n$ and $a_n$ by one integral.

$$a_n = \frac{1}{2\pi j}\oint_{C_1}\frac{F(z)}{(z-s_0)^{n+1}}, \qquad -\infty < n < \infty \tag{B-58}$$

The series can then be expressed as

$$F(s) = \sum_{n=-\infty}^{\infty}a_n(s-s_0)^n \tag{B-59}$$

This is called a *Laurent series*. It converges in the annular region between $C_1$ and $C_2$. (The summation for $n$ between 0 and $\infty$ converges inside of $C_1$, while the summation for $n$ between 0 and $-\infty$ converges outside of $C_2$.

A simple special case of the Laurent series occurs if $F(s)$ is analytic within and on a circle $C_1$ except for a pole of multiplicity $m$ at $s = s_0$; where $s_0$ is the center of the circle. Then, $F(s)(s-s_0)^m$ is analytic and can be expanded in a Taylor's series.

$$F(s)(s-s_0)^m = \sum_{n=0}^{\infty}b_n(s-s_0)^n \tag{B-60}$$

Now, divide both sides of Eq. B–60 by $(s - s_0)^m$; thus,

$$F(s) = \sum_{n=0}^{\infty} \frac{b_n(s - s_0)^n}{(s - s_0)^m}$$

This can be rewritten as

$$F(s) = \frac{a_{-m}}{(s - s_0)^m} + \frac{a_{-m+1}}{(s - s_0)^{m-1}} + \cdots + \frac{a_{-1}}{s - s_0}$$

$$+ a_0 + a_1(s - s_0) + a_2(s - s_0)^2 + \cdots$$

where

$$a_{j-m} = b_j.$$

Thus,

$$F(s) = \sum_{n=-m}^{\infty} a_n(s - s_0)^n \tag{B–61}$$

The $a_{-1}$ coefficient (i.e., the coefficient of the $1/(s - s_0)$) is called a *residue*. It is very important in the evaluation of certain contour integrals (see Section B-9). Then $a_{-1}$ corresponds to $b_{m-1}$ and, from B–58 and B–49b, we have

$$a_{-1} = \lim_{s \to s_0} \frac{1}{(m-1)!} \frac{d^{m-1}(s - s_0)^m F(s)}{ds^{m-1}} \tag{B–62}$$

Note that, when $m = 1$,

$$a_{-1} = \lim_{s \to s_0} (s - s_0) F(s) \tag{B–63a}$$

If

$$F(s) = \frac{N(s)}{D(s)}$$

where a zero of $D(s)$ results in a *first*-order pole at $s = s_0$, then Eq. B–63a can be evaluated using L'Hospital's rule. This yields

$$a_{-1} = \lim_{s \to s_0} \frac{\dfrac{d}{ds}(s - s_0) N(s)}{\dfrac{d}{ds} D(s)}$$

Evaluating, we have

$$a_{-1} = \frac{N(s_0)}{D'(s_0)} \tag{B–63b}$$

where

$$D'(s_0) = \left. \frac{dD(s)}{ds} \right|_{s = s_0}$$

## B-9. EVALUATING CONTOUR INTEGRALS WITH RESIDUES

The series expansions and residues discussed in the last section can greatly simplify the evaluation of certain closed contour integrals. Suppose in a connected region, $F(s)$ is analytic, except for a finite number of poles. Let $C$ be a closed contour in the region such that $F(s)$ is analytic on $C$ and that $n$ poles at $s_1, s_2, \ldots, s_n$ are enclosed in $C$. This is illustrated in Fig. B–11.

Now let us evaluate $\oint_C F(s)\,ds$. Draw a circle around each pole centered at the pole. The radius of each circle should be such that all the circles are contained in $C$. (Let $C_1$ enclose the pole at $s_1$, etc.); then (see Eq. B–39).

$$\oint_C F(s)\,ds = \oint_{C_1} F(s)\,ds + \oint_{C_2} F(s)\,ds + \cdots + \oint_{C_n} F(s)\,ds \qquad \text{(B--64)}$$

We shall evaluate each of the integrals on the right-hand side of Eq. B–64. Consider the pole at $s = s_k$. Expand $F(s)$ in a Laurent series about $s = s_k$; thus,

$$F(s) = \sum_{v=-m_k}^{\infty} a_{k,v}(s - s_k)^v$$

where $m_k$ is the multiplicity of the pole at $s_k$ and $a_{k,1}, a_{k,2}, \ldots$ are the coefficients. This can be broken into the sum of two series

$$F(s) = \sum_{v=-m_k}^{-1} a_{k,v}(s - s_k)^v + \sum_{v=0}^{\infty} a_{k,v}(s - s_k)^v \qquad \text{(B--65)}$$

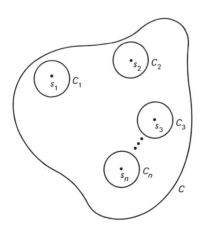

FIG. B–11

Contour enclosing $n$-poles

The second summation is an analytic function; thus, we can write

$$F(s) = \sum_{v=-m_k}^{-1} a_{k,v}(s - s_k)^v + F_a(s) \tag{B-66a}$$

where $F_a(s)$ is analytic within and on $C_k$. Alternately, this can be written as:

$$F(s) = \sum_{v=1}^{m_k} \frac{a_{k,-v}}{(s - s_k)^v} + F_a(s) \tag{B-66b}$$

Then

$$\oint_{C_k} F(s)\, ds = \sum_{v=1}^{m_k} \oint_{C_k} \frac{a_{k,-v}}{(s - s_k)^v}\, ds + \oint_{C_k} F_a(s)\, ds \tag{B-67}$$

Using Cauchy's integral theorem (Eq. B–37) we see that the last integral is zero. Then, applying Eq. B–33 to the summation, all terms except the first become zero; thus, we have

$$\oint_{C_k} F(s)\, ds = 2\pi j a_{k,-1} \tag{B-68}$$

However, $a_{k,-1}$ is the residue of $F(s)$ when it is expanded in a Laurent series about its pole at $s = s_k$. Then, applying this result to each of the integrals on the right-hand side of Eq. B–64, we obtain

$$\oint_C F(s)\, ds = 2\pi j \sum [\text{Residues of poles enclosed in } C] \tag{B-69}$$

where the residue of a pole is the $a_{-1}$ term in the Laurent series expansion about the pole in question. Thus, if $F(s)$ is analytic in a region, except for a finite number of poles, $C$ is a closed contour in the region, and there are *no* poles on $C$, then $\oint_C F(s)\, ds = [\text{sum of the residues enclosed } in\ C]$.

Let us consider an example. Suppose

$$F(s) = \frac{s + 4}{(s + 1)(s + 2)(s + 3)^2}$$

and the contour of integration is illustrated in Fig. B–12. The poles of $F(s)$ are marked by $X$'s and the zeros by $0$'s. This is called a *pole zero diagram*. The path of integration only includes the poles at $s = -2$ and $s = -3$. Thus, only the two residues corresponding to these two poles contribute to the integral. Then, using Eq. B–62,

$$\left[ \text{Res of poles at } s = -2 = \lim_{s \to -2} (s + 2) F(s) = \frac{s + 4}{(s + 1)(s + 3)^2} \right]_{s = -2} = -2$$

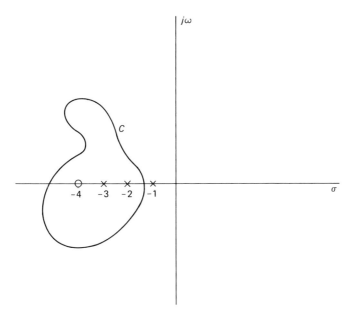

FIG. B–12

Pole-zero diagram showing a path of integration

$$\left[\text{Res of poles at } s = -3 = \lim_{s=-3} \frac{d}{ds}(s + 3)^2 \, F(s)\right.$$

$$\left. = \lim_{s=-3} \frac{d}{ds} \frac{s + 4}{(s + 1)(s + 2)}\right] = \frac{5}{4}$$

Thus,

$$\oint_C \frac{s + 4}{(s + 1)(s + 2)(s + 3)^2} \, ds = 2\pi j(-2 + \tfrac{5}{4}) = -\tfrac{3}{2}\pi j$$

Note that the integral will have this value for *any* closed contour which contains the poles at $s = -2$ and $s = -3$, but which does not contain the pole at $s = -1$. The zero may or may not be enclosed; this will not affect the value of the integral.

The residue method is a very powerful procedure for evaluating closed line integrals. It would have been extremely difficult to evaluate the integral over the irregular contour of Fig. B–12 using standard methods.

Residue methods can only be applied to closed contours. However, there are times when they can be extended to infinite contours. Consider Fig. B–13. Suppose the contour of integration is the infinite straight line parallel to the $j\omega$ axis with a $\sigma$ axis intercept of $\sigma = C$. (Its equation is $s = C + j\omega$.) Then, the line integral is

$$\int_{C-j\infty}^{C+j\infty} F(s) \, ds$$

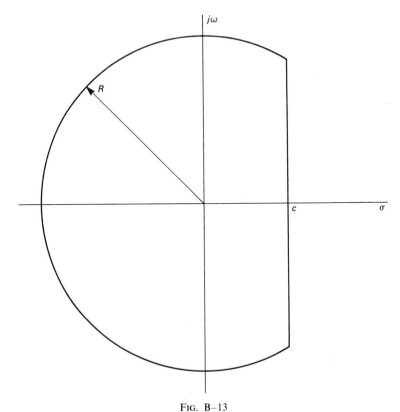

Fig. B–13
Contour of integration which, in the limit, contains an infinite line segment

Fig. B–13
Contour of integration which, in the limit, contains an infinite line segment

Now consider a contour which consists of a finite straight line, (see Fig. B–13), and the segment of a circle of radius $R$ centered at the origin. If $R$ approaches $\infty$, then the straight line portion of the path becomes the desired one. Assume that

$$\int_{C_R} F(s)\, ds = 0 \qquad\qquad (\text{B–70})$$

where $C_R$ is the circular portion of the path; then,

$$\int_{C-j\infty}^{C+j\infty} F(s)\, ds + \int_{C_R} F(s)\, ds = \oint_{C_c} F(s)\, ds \qquad (\text{B–71})$$

where $C_c$ is the closed contour (as $R \to \infty$) shown in the figure. If the only singularities $F(s)$ are poles which are at finite points in the s-plane, and if $F(s)$ is analytic on the straight line contour, then, for sufficiently large $R$, $F(s)$ will be analytic on all of $C_c$. Thus, as $R$ approaches $\infty$,

$$\oint_{C_c} F(s)\,dx = 2\pi j \sum [\text{Res of all poles to left of line } s = C + j\omega] \qquad \text{(B--72)}$$

Substituting Eq. B–70 into Eq. B–71, we obtain

$$\int_{C-j\infty}^{C+j\infty} F(s)\,ds = 2\pi j \sum [\text{Res of all poles to left of } s = C + j\omega] \qquad \text{(B--73)}$$

Thus, this line integral can be easily evaluated if the only singularities of $F(s)$ are poles which do not lie on $s = C + j\omega$ or at infinity and Eq. B–70 is satisfied.

Let us consider a class of $F(s)$ which satisfies Eq. B–70. If as $s$ approaches infinity

$$\lim_{s \to \infty} |F(s)| \leq \left| \frac{K}{s^{n+1}} \right|, \qquad n > 0 \qquad \text{(B--74)}$$

where $K$ is a constant and $n$ is real, then

$$\lim_{R \to \infty} \int_{C_R} F(s)\,ds \leq \lim_{R \to \infty} \int_{C_R} \left| \frac{K}{s^{n+1}} \right| ds \qquad \text{(B--75)}$$

On $C_R$ $s = Re^{j\theta}$ and $ds = jRe^{j\theta}\,d\theta$. Substituting in Eq. B–75, manipulating and noting that $|e^{j\theta}| = 1$, we obtain

$$\lim_{R \to \infty} \int_{C_R} F(s)\,ds \leq \lim_{R \to \infty} \frac{\pi k}{R^n} = 0 \qquad \text{(B--76)}$$

Thus, one class of $F(s)$ for which Eq. B–70 is satisfied is given by Eq. B–74. We shall discuss this further in Section 3-11.

## BIBLIOGRAPHY

Guillemin, E. A. *The Mathematics of Circuit Analysis*. Chap. 6. New York: Wiley, 1949.

Pennisi, L. L. *Elements of Complex Variables*, New York: Holt, 1963.

Peskin, E. *Transient and Steady State Analysis of Electronic Networks*. pp. 115–140. Princeton, N.J.: Van Nostrand, 1961.

Scott, E. J. *Transform Calculus with an Introduction to Complex Variables*. Chap. 1. New York: Harper, 1955.

# Matrices

The manipulation of simultaneous equations or systems having large numbers of variables can often be simplified by using *matrices*, which are arrays of numbers. A *matrix* is usually symbolically denoted by a set of square brackets. For example, a matrix $[A]$ could be

$$[A] = \begin{bmatrix} a_{11} & a_{12} & \cdots & a_{1n} \\ a_{21} & a_{22} & \cdots & a_{2n} \\ \hline a_{n1} & a_{n2} & \cdots & a_{nn} \end{bmatrix} \tag{C-1}$$

The terms $a_{ij}$ are called *elements* of the matrix, where $i$ and $j$ in the subscript are integers. Their location in the array is usually designated by the double subscript $ij$, where the first coefficient specifies the row, and the second, the *column*. If a matrix has only one row, it is called a *row matrix*; if it has only one column, it is called a *column matrix*. If the number of rows and columns are equal, the matrix is *square*. The notation of a "hat" over an element will also be used to indicate a matrix; for example

$$\hat{A} = [A] \tag{C-2}$$

## C-1. MATRIX ALGEBRA

**Equality of Matrices.** If two matrices are equal, every element of one must be equal to the corresponding element of the other. This requires that each matrix have an equal number of rows and also an equal number of columns; for example, if

$$\begin{bmatrix} a_{11} & a_{12} & a_{13} \\ a_{21} & a_{22} & a_{23} \end{bmatrix} = \begin{bmatrix} b_{11} & b_{12} & b_{13} \\ b_{21} & b_{22} & b_{23} \end{bmatrix} \tag{C-3}$$

then

$$a_{ij} = b_{ij}; \quad i = 1, 2, \quad j = 1, 2, 3$$

**Addition and Subtraction of Matrices.** When two matrices are to be added or subtracted, each must have the *same* number of rows and each must have the same number of columns. When matrices are added or subtracted, the corresponding elements are added or subtracted; for example,

$$\begin{bmatrix} a_{11} & a_{12} \\ a_{21} & a_{22} \\ a_{31} & a_{32} \end{bmatrix} + \begin{bmatrix} b_{11} & b_{12} \\ b_{21} & b_{22} \\ b_{31} & b_{32} \end{bmatrix} = \begin{bmatrix} a_{11} + b_{11} & a_{12} + b_{12} \\ a_{21} + b_{21} & a_{22} + b_{22} \\ a_{31} + b_{31} & a_{32} + b_{32} \end{bmatrix} \tag{C-4}$$

**Multiplication of Matrices.** The following rule is used when matrices are multiplied:

$$
\begin{bmatrix}
a_{11} & a_{12} & \cdots & a_{1m} \\
a_{21} & a_{22} & \cdots & a_{2m} \\
\cdots & \cdots & \cdots & \cdots \\
a_{n1} & a_{n2} & \cdots & a_{nm}
\end{bmatrix}
\begin{bmatrix}
b_{11} & b_{12} & \cdots & b_{1j} \\
b_{21} & b_{22} & \cdots & b_{2j} \\
\cdots & \cdots & \cdots & \cdots \\
b_{m1} & b_{m2} & \cdots & b_{mj}
\end{bmatrix}
=
\begin{bmatrix}
c_{11} & c_{12} & \cdots & c_{1j} \\
c_{21} & c_{22} & \cdots & c_{?i} \\
\cdots & \cdots & \cdots & \cdots \\
c_{n1} & c_{n2} & \cdots & c_{nj}
\end{bmatrix}
\quad \text{(C-5)}
$$

where
$$c_{ik} = a_{i1}b_{1k} + a_{i2}b_{2k} + \cdots + a_{im}b_{mk} \tag{C-6}$$

If the matrix multiplication is allowed, the *number of columns of the first matrix must equal the number of rows of the second matrix.* Such matrices are said to be *conformable.* If the two matrices are not conformable, their matrix product does not exist. Also, even if $\hat{A}\hat{B}$ exists, $\hat{B}\hat{A}$ may not; i.e., if the number of columns of $\hat{A}$ equals the number of rows of $\hat{B}$, the converse need not be true. Even if $\hat{A}\hat{B}$ and $\hat{B}\hat{A}$ both exist, we *cannot*, in general, state that $\hat{A}\hat{B} = \hat{B}\hat{A}$. Thus, we must distinguish between *premultiplying* and *postmultiplying* by a matrix.

**Scalar Multiplication.** If each element of the matrix has the same factor $a$, then the following notation can be used

$$
a\begin{bmatrix}
a_{11} & a_{12} \\
a_{21} & a_{22}
\end{bmatrix}
=
\begin{bmatrix}
aa_{11} & aa_{12} \\
aa_{21} & aa_{22}
\end{bmatrix}
\tag{C-7}
$$

**Diagonal Matrices–The Unit Matrix.** In a square matrix, the number of rows or columns is called the *order* of the matrix. If a square matrix is of order $n$ and all

$$a_{ij} = 0, \qquad i \neq j \tag{C-8a}$$

and all

$$a_{ii} \neq 0, \qquad i = 1, 2, \ldots n \tag{C-8b}$$

then the matrix is said to be *diagonal*; for example, $\hat{A}$ is a diagonal matrix if

$$
\hat{A} = \begin{bmatrix}
a_{11} & 0 & \cdots & 0 \\
0 & a_{22} & \cdots & 0 \\
\hline
0 & 0 & \cdots & a_{nn}
\end{bmatrix}
\tag{C-9}
$$

The elements $a_{11}, a_{22} \ldots, a_{nn}$ constitute the *principal diagonal* of the square matrix.

If all the principal diagonal elements of a diagonal matrix are 1s, the matrix is called the *unit matrix* $\hat{U}$ or $[U]$; thus,

$$
\hat{U} = \begin{bmatrix}
1 & 0 & \cdots & 0 \\
0 & 1 & \cdots & 0 \\
0 & 0 & \cdots & 1
\end{bmatrix}
\tag{C-10}
$$

If the matrices are conformable, then

$$\hat{U}\hat{A} = \hat{A} \tag{C-11a}$$

$$\hat{B}\hat{U} = \hat{B} \tag{C-11b}$$

This can be verified by carrying out the rules of matrix multiplication.

**Partitioning of Matrices.** It is often desirable to break a matrix up into sub-matrices. This is called *partitioning* the matrix. For example, we can subdivide the matrix

$$\hat{A} = \begin{bmatrix} a_{11} & a_{12} & a_{13} & | & a_{14} \\ a_{21} & a_{22} & a_{23} & | & a_{24} \\ ---&---&---&|&--- \\ a_{31} & a_{32} & a_{33} & | & a_{34} \\ a_{41} & a_{42} & a_{43} & | & a_{44} \end{bmatrix}$$

(C–12a)

into

$$\hat{A} = \begin{bmatrix} \hat{B} & | & \hat{C} \\ ---&-&--- \\ \hat{D} & | & \hat{E} \end{bmatrix}$$

(12–12b)

where

$$\hat{B} = \begin{bmatrix} a_{11} & a_{12} & a_{13} \\ a_{21} & a_{22} & a_{23} \end{bmatrix}$$

(C–12c)

$$\hat{C} = \begin{bmatrix} a_{14} \\ a_{24} \end{bmatrix}$$

(C–12d)

$$\hat{D} = \begin{bmatrix} a_{31} & a_{32} & a_{33} \\ a_{41} & a_{42} & a_{43} \end{bmatrix}$$

(C–12e)

$$\hat{E} = \begin{bmatrix} a_{34} \\ a_{44} \end{bmatrix}$$

(C–12f)

In general, as long as the partitioning is done in accordance with the rules of matrix algebra, the algebraic operations can be performed on the partitioned form of the matrix; for example,

$$\begin{bmatrix} \hat{B} & | & \hat{C} \\ ---&-&--- \\ \hat{D} & | & \hat{E} \end{bmatrix} \begin{bmatrix} \hat{F} & | & \hat{G} \\ ---&-&--- \\ \hat{H} & | & \hat{I} \end{bmatrix} + \begin{bmatrix} \hat{B}\hat{F} + \hat{C}\hat{H} & | & \hat{B}\hat{G} + \hat{C}\hat{I} \\ ---&&--- \\ \hat{D}\hat{F} + \hat{E}\hat{H} & | & \hat{D}\hat{G} + \hat{E}\hat{I} \end{bmatrix}$$

The reader can verify that, if the original matrices are conformable and if the partitioning is done conformably (i.e., in this example if the number of columns of $\hat{B}$ equals the number of rows of $F$), then all the multiplications are conformable and the results are valid.

## C-2. MATRIX REPRESENTATION OF SIMULTANEOUS EQUATIONS—INVERSE MATRICES

Let us consider a set of simultaneous equations and show how matrices can be used to simplify their manipulation.

$$\begin{aligned} y_1 &= a_{11}x_1 + a_{12}x_2 + \cdots + a_{1n}x_n \\ y_2 &= a_{21}x_1 + a_{22}x_2 + \cdots + a_{2n}x_n \\ &\cdots \cdots \cdots \cdots \cdots \cdots \cdots \cdots \cdots \cdots \\ y_n &= a_{n1}x_1 + a_{n2}x_2 + \cdots + a_{nn}x_n \end{aligned}$$

(C–13a)

In matrix form, these equations become

$$
\begin{bmatrix} y_1 \\ y_2 \\ \cdot \\ \cdot \\ \cdot \\ y_n \end{bmatrix}
=
\begin{bmatrix}
a_{11} & a_{12} & \cdots & a_{1n} \\
a_{21} & a_{22} & \cdots & a_{2n} \\
\multicolumn{4}{c}{\dotfill} \\
a_{n1} & a_{n2} & \cdots & a_{nn}
\end{bmatrix}
\begin{bmatrix} x_1 \\ x_2 \\ \cdot \\ \cdot \\ \cdot \\ x_n \end{bmatrix}
\tag{C–13b}
$$

To represent these equations in compact form, let

$$
[y] = \begin{bmatrix} y_1 \\ y_2 \\ \cdot \\ \cdot \\ y_n \end{bmatrix}
\tag{C 14a}
$$

$$
[A] = \begin{bmatrix}
a_{11} & a_{12} & \cdots & a_{1n} \\
a_{21} & a_{22} & \cdots & a_{2n} \\
\multicolumn{4}{c}{\dotfill} \\
a_{n1} & a_{n2} & \cdots & a_{nn}
\end{bmatrix}
\tag{C–14b}
$$

$$
[x] = \begin{bmatrix} x_1 \\ x_2 \\ \cdot \\ \cdot \\ x_n \end{bmatrix}
\tag{C–14c}
$$

Then, we can write Eqs. C–13 as

$$[y] = [A][x] \tag{C–15a}$$

or, equivalently, as

$$\hat{y} = \hat{A}x \tag{C–15b}$$

**Inverse Matrices.**   Equations C–13a directly express all the $y$'s in terms of the $x$'s. That is, if the $x_1, ..., x_n$ were known, the $y_1, ..., y_n$ could be found directly by substituting the $x_1, ..., x_n$ in Eqs. C–13. Usually, this is not the case. The $\hat{y}$ is known, while the $\hat{x}$ is unknown.

Let us consider how Eqs. C-13 can be solved for $\hat{x}$. Assume that we have a square matrix (see Eq. C–14b) of order $n$. Let us call this matrix $[A]$ and assume that we can find another square matrix $[A]^{-1}$ which is such that

$$[A]^{-1}[A] = [U] \tag{C–16}$$

The matrix $[A]^{-1} = \hat{A}^{-1}$ is called the *inverse* of $A$. Assume that $[A]^{-1}$ exists and is known. Premultiply both sides of Eq. C–15 by $[A]^{-1}$; this yields

$$[A]^{-1}[y] = [A]^{-1}[A][x] = [U][x] = [x] \tag{C–17}$$

Thus, the unknown $[x]$ is now expressed in terms of the known $[y]$ and $[A]^{-1}$.

An inverse matrix can be obtained by using determinant procedures for solving simultaneous equations. Let

$$
\Delta = \begin{vmatrix} a_{11} & a_{12} & \cdots & a_{1n} \\ a_{21} & a_{22} & \cdots & a_{2n} \\ \cdots\cdots\cdots\cdots\cdots\cdots \\ a_{n1} & a_{n2} & \cdots & a_{nn} \end{vmatrix}
\tag{C-18}
$$

where $\Delta$ is the determinant composed of the elements of $[A]$. Also, $\Delta_{ij}$ is the *cofactor* of the *ij*th element of $\Delta$; i.e., $(-1)^{i+j}$ times the determinant formed by striking out the *i*th and the *j*th column of $\Delta$. Then,

$$
[A]^{-1} = \frac{1}{\Delta} \begin{bmatrix} \Delta_{11} & \Delta_{21} & \cdots & \Delta_{n1} \\ \Delta_{12} & \Delta_{22} & \cdots & \Delta_{n2} \\ \cdots\cdots\cdots\cdots\cdots\cdots \\ \Delta_{1n} & \Delta_{2n} & & \Delta_{nn} \end{bmatrix}
\tag{C-19}
$$

(Note the order of the coefficients.) This relation can be verified by considering the determinant procedure for solving simultaneous equations. $\Delta$ is called the determinant of $[A]$. The matrix

$$
\hat{A}_a = [A]_a = \begin{bmatrix} \Delta_{11} & \Delta_{21} & \cdots & \Delta_{n1} \\ \Delta_{12} & \Delta_{22} & \cdots & \Delta_{n2} \\ \cdots\cdots\cdots\cdots\cdots\cdots \\ \Delta_{1n} & \Delta_{2n} & \cdots & \Delta_{nn} \end{bmatrix}
\tag{C-20}
$$

is called the *adjoint* of $[A]$. Hence, the inverse of a matrix is equal to its adjoint divided by its characteristic determinant. An interesting fact about the inverse matrix is that $[A]^{-1}[A] = [A][A]^{-1} = [U]$.

**Rank of a Matrix.**  The inverse of a square matrix does not exist of $\Delta = 0$. In this case, the set of simultaneous equations (see Eq. C-13) will not be linearly independent. The matrix $[A]$ is then said to be *singular*.

The *rank* of a matrix is a number which is often used to characterize its singularity. If a square matrix is nonsingular (i.e., $\Delta \neq 0$) then the rank $r$ of the matrix is equal to the order $n$; i.e., $r = n$. If $\Delta = 0$, but at least one determinant formed by striking out one row and one column of $\Delta$ is nonzero, then the rank is defined as $r = n - 1$. If $r \neq n$ and $r \neq n - 1$, but if any determinant formed by striking out two rows and columns from $\Delta$ is not zero, then $r = n - 2$. Corresponding definitions are given for $r = n - 3$, etc. Note that if $r = 0$, every element of the matrix is zero.

## C-3. EIGENVALUES AND EIGENVECTORS—DIAGONAL FORM

Operations with diagonal matrices are often much simpler than with other matrices; for example, if

$$[A] = \begin{bmatrix} a_{11} & 0 & \cdots & 0 \\ 0 & a_{22} & \cdots & 0 \\ \hdotsfor{4} \\ 0 & 0 & \cdots & a_{nn} \end{bmatrix} \qquad (C-21)$$

Then

$$[A]^{-1} = \begin{bmatrix} 1/a_{11} & 0 & \cdots & 0 \\ 0 & 1/a_{22} & \cdots & 0 \\ \hdotsfor{4} \\ 0 & 0 & \cdots & 1/a_{nn} \end{bmatrix} \qquad (C-22)$$

In this section, we shall consider a procedure where square matrices can be transformed into diagonal form. To do this we shall study some special topics.

**Eigenvalues and Eigenvectors.** Any column value, such as that given C–14a is called a *vector*. If $n = 3$, then $y_1$, $y_2$ and $y_3$ can be thought of as the $x$, $y$, and $z$ coordinates of a vector in space. Thus $\hat{y}$ can be considered to have a magnitude and direction. For $n$ greater than 3, this concept is extended to a multidimensional space.

Let us consider the set of simultaneous equations characterized by Eqs C–13 through C–15. If $\hat{A}$ is nonsingular, then, for eacy $\hat{y}$, an $\hat{x}$ can be found. Now let us determine if there is a set of values $y_1, y_2, ..., y_n$ such that the corresponding $\hat{x}$ is given by a constant times the $\hat{y}$.

$$\hat{x} = \frac{1}{\lambda}\hat{y} \qquad (C-23a)$$

or, equivalently,

$$\hat{y} = \lambda\hat{x} \qquad (C-23b)$$

where $\lambda$ is a constant (i.e., $y_j = \lambda x_j$). That is the $\hat{x}$ and $\hat{y}$ vectors have the same direction. Let us determine if such a $\lambda$ and $\hat{y}$ can exist. Substituting Eq. C–23b into Eq. C–15 yields

$$[\hat{A} - \lambda\hat{U}]\hat{x} = \hat{0} \qquad (C-24)$$

This is the characteristic equation of $\hat{A}$. Here $\hat{0}$ is a column matrix, all of whose elements are zero. Since $[\hat{A} - \lambda\hat{U}]$ is a square matrix, this represents a set of simultaneous equations where all the driving functions (knowns) are zero. Thus, $\hat{x} = \hat{0}$ *unless the matrix* $\hat{A} - \lambda\hat{U}$ *is singular*; that is, the determinant of $[\hat{A} - \lambda\hat{U}]$, called the *characteristic determinant*, must be zero. Hence, if a nonzero $\hat{x}$ exists

$$\begin{vmatrix} a_{11} - \lambda & a_{12} & \cdots & a_{1n} \\ a_{21} & a_{22} - \lambda & \cdots & a_{2n} \\ \hdotsfor{4} \\ a_{n1} & a_{n2} & \cdots & a_{nn} - \lambda \end{vmatrix} = 0 \qquad (C-25)$$

The $a_{ij}$ are given constants. Thus, this represents an algebraic equation of degree $n$ in $\lambda$. Hence, there are $n$ values of $\lambda$ which will result in a singular matrix and so there will be a nonzero $\hat{x}$ in Eq. C–24. The values of $\lambda$ which satisfy Eq. C–25 are called the *eigenvalues* of the matrix $\hat{A}$. Note that all $n$ eigenvalues need not be different. That is, Eq. C–25 may have two, or more, equal roots.

Let us call the eigenvalues $\lambda_1, \lambda_2, ..., \lambda_n$. In general, it can be shown that

$$\lambda_1 + \lambda_2 + \cdots + \lambda_n = a_{11} + a_{22} + \cdots + a_{nn} \qquad \text{(C–26)}$$

and

$$\lambda_1 \lambda_2 \ldots \lambda_n = (-1)^n |A| \qquad \text{(C–27)}$$

Corresponding to each eigenvalue, there is an $\hat{x}$ which satisfies Eq. C–24. This $\hat{x}$ is called an *eigenvector*. In general

$$[\hat{A} - \lambda_j \hat{U}]\hat{x} = 0 \qquad \text{(C–28)}$$

represents a set of $n$ singular simultaneous equations. Then, at least one of the elements of $\hat{x}$ can be chosen at random and one equation eliminated. Usually, the remaining $n - 1$ equations can then be solved for the remaining elements of $\hat{x}$. This $\hat{x}$ is the eigenvector. We shall call this $\hat{x}_j$ and the corresponding eigenvalue is $\lambda_j$. If $\hat{x}_j$ satisfies Eq. C–28, then so will $k\hat{x}_j$. Thus, the eigenvectors are not unique. Let us illustrate this with an example:

$$\hat{A} = \begin{bmatrix} 2 & 2 \\ 1 & 3 \end{bmatrix}$$

Then, to determine the eigenvalues, we use the equation

$$\begin{vmatrix} 2 - \lambda & 2 \\ 1 & 3 - \lambda \end{vmatrix} = (2 - \lambda)(3 - \lambda) - 2 = \lambda^2 - 5\lambda + 4 = 0$$

Thus, the eigenvalues are $\lambda_1 = 1, \lambda_2 = 4$. To determine an eigenvector corresponding to $\lambda_1$, substitute $\lambda_1$ into Eq. C–28.

$$\begin{bmatrix} 2 - 1 & 2 \\ 1 & 3 - 1 \end{bmatrix} \begin{bmatrix} x_{11} \\ x_{21} \end{bmatrix} = \begin{bmatrix} 0 \\ 0 \end{bmatrix}$$

The second subscript of $x$'s is added to indicate that this eigenvector corresponds to $\lambda_1$. Manipulating the equation, we obtain

$$x_{11} + 2x_{21} = 0$$

$$x_{11} + 2x_{21} = 0$$

This is a singular set of simultaneous equations. Choose $x_{11} = 1$. Then $x_{21} = -1/2$. Then, an eigenvector is

$$\hat{x}_1 = \begin{bmatrix} 1 \\ -1/2 \end{bmatrix}$$

Note that if this vector is multiplied by a constant, it will still be an eigenvector; e.g., choose $x_{11} = 2$, then $x_{21} = -1$. Corresponding to the second eigenvalue, we have

$$\begin{bmatrix} -2 & 2 \\ 1 & -1 \end{bmatrix} \begin{bmatrix} x_{12} \\ x_{22} \end{bmatrix} = \begin{bmatrix} 0 \\ 0 \end{bmatrix}$$

Letting $x_{12} = 1$. Thus, a second eigenvector is

$$x_2 = \begin{bmatrix} 1 \\ 1 \end{bmatrix}$$

Now let us form some matrices from the eigenvalues and eigenvectors. We define

$$\hat{\lambda} = \begin{bmatrix} \lambda_1 & 0 & \cdots & 0 \\ 0 & \lambda_2 & \cdots & 0 \\ & & \cdots & \\ 0 & 0 & \cdots & \lambda_n \end{bmatrix} \tag{C-29}$$

That is, $\hat{\lambda}$ is a diagonal matrix whose principal diagonal consists of the eigenvalues. We also define a matrix of eigenvectors:

$$\hat{H} = \begin{bmatrix} x_{11} & x_{12} & \cdots & x_{1n} \\ x_{21} & x_{22} & \cdots & x_{2n} \\ \cdot & \cdot & & \cdot \\ \cdot & \cdot & & \cdot \\ \cdot & \cdot & & \cdot \\ x_{n1} & x_{n2} & \cdots & x_{nn} \end{bmatrix} \tag{C-30}$$

It can be proved that $\hat{H}$ will be nonsingular if all the eigenvalues are distinct. Even if two or more eigenvalues are the same, $\hat{H}$ *may* be nonsingular, although this will not be true in general.

**Diagonalization of Matrices.**   If we substitute Eq. C–23 into Eq. C–15, we have, for each eigenvalue,

$$\hat{A}\hat{x}_j = \lambda_j \hat{x}_j, \qquad j = 1, 2, ..., n \tag{C-31}$$

This represents $n$ matrix equations which can be written in compact form as

$$\hat{A}\hat{H} = \hat{H}\hat{\lambda} \tag{C-32}$$

and this can be verified by applying the rules of matrix algebra. We shall assume that $\hat{H}^{-1}$ exists. Now, premultiplying both sides of Eq. C–32 by $\hat{H}^{-1}$, we obtain

$$\hat{H}^{-1}\hat{A}\hat{H} = \hat{H}^{-1}\hat{H}\hat{\lambda}$$

Thus,

$$\hat{H}^{-1}\hat{A}\hat{H} = \hat{\lambda} \tag{C-33}$$

where $\hat{\lambda}$ is a diagonal matrix. Thus, we can state that $\hat{A}$ has been transformed into a diagonal form. An alternate form of Eq. C–33 can be obtained by premultiplying both sides by $\hat{H}$ and then postmultiplying by $\hat{H}^{-1}$. This yields

$$\hat{A} = \hat{H}\hat{\lambda}\hat{H}^{-1} \tag{C-34}$$

Let us consider some advantages of this diagonalization. Suppose we wish to raise a matrix to the $k$th power ($k$ is a positive integer); that is, the matrix is multiplied by itself $k$ times. (Note that such a matrix must be square.) This involves many tedious multiplications (see Eqs. C–5 and C–6). If $\hat{A}$ is in the form of Eq. C–34, great savings can result; for example

$$\hat{A}^2 = \hat{A}\hat{A} = \hat{H}\hat{\lambda}\hat{H}^{-1}\hat{H}\hat{\lambda}\hat{H}^{-1}$$

but $\hat{H}^{-1}\hat{H} = \hat{U}$; thus,

$$\hat{A}^2 = \hat{H}\hat{\lambda}^2\hat{H}^{-1}$$

Proceeding similarly, we have

$$\hat{A}^k = \hat{H}\hat{\lambda}^k\hat{H}^{-1} \tag{C-35}$$

Thus, only a diagonal matrix need be raised to the $k$th power. This is simple, since it only involves raising each diagonal term to the $k$ power.

For another application of diagonalization, consider the set of simultaneous equations

$$\hat{A}\hat{x} = \hat{y} \tag{C-36}$$

Now define a new set of variables

$$\hat{x}_d = \hat{H}^{-1}\hat{x} \tag{C-37a}$$

and

$$\hat{x}_d = \hat{H}^{-1}\hat{y} \tag{C-37b}$$

Substituting in Eq. C–36 (e.g., $\hat{x} = \hat{H}\hat{x}_d$), premultiplying by $\hat{H}$, and substituting Eq. C–33, we have

$$\hat{\lambda}\hat{x}_d = \hat{y}_d \tag{C-38}$$

Thus, the transformed variables $\hat{x}_d$ and $\hat{y}_d$ are related by a diagonal matrix, which can be very easily inverted.

In practice, the following procedure can be used. First obtain $\hat{y}_d$ from the given $\hat{y}$ using Eq. C–37b. Then obtain $\hat{x}_d$ using Eq. C–38. Finally, obtain $x$ by solving

$$\hat{x} = \hat{H}\hat{x}_d \tag{C-39}$$

At times, the $\hat{H}$ and $\hat{H}^{-1}$ are much simpler than $\hat{A}$, so the procedure saves much work.


## C-4. CAYLEY-HAMILTON THEOREM

In this section we shall derive some results which are very useful when functions of a matrix are encountered. Let us start by defining a polynomial function of a matrix. Consider the ordinary scalar polynomial;

$$P(\lambda) = a_k\lambda^k + a_{k-1}\lambda^{k-1} + \cdots + a_1\lambda + a_0 \tag{C-40}$$

where $\lambda$ is a scalar variable and the $a$'s are constants.

Now consider a square matrix $\hat{A}$. We define the matrix polynomial of $\hat{A}$ as

$$P(\hat{A}) = a_k \hat{A}^k + a_{k-1} \hat{A}^{k-1} + \cdots + a_1 \hat{A} + a_0 \hat{U} \qquad (C-41)$$

Note that since the matrix is square, the powers of the matrix exist. Also, we define

$$\hat{A}^0 = \hat{U} \qquad (C-42)$$

where $\hat{U}$ is the unit matrix whose degree is the same as that of $\hat{A}$.

Let us represent $\hat{A}$ in diagonal form by Eq. C-34. Note that $\hat{\lambda}$ is the matrix of eigenvalues (see Eq. C-29) and $\hat{H}$ is the matrix of eigenvectors (see Eq. C-30). We shall assume in this section that the inverse matrix of the eigenvectors $\hat{H}^{-1}$ exists. Then, using Eq. C-35, we can write Eq. C-41 as

$$P(\hat{A}) = \hat{H}[a_k \hat{\lambda}^k + a_{k-1} \hat{\lambda}^{k-1} + \cdots + a_1 \hat{\lambda} + a_0 U]\hat{H}^{-1} \qquad (C-43)$$

Suppose $\hat{A}$ is a square matrix of order $n$ and its characteristic equation (see Eq. C-25) is given by

$$C(\lambda) = a_n \lambda^n + a_{n-1} \lambda^{n-1} + \cdots + a_1 \lambda + a_0 \qquad (C-44)$$

The roots of the equation are $\lambda_1, \lambda_2, ..., \lambda_n$. Thus, we define the diagonal matrix of eigenvalues as

$$\hat{\lambda} = \begin{bmatrix} \lambda_1 & 0 & \cdots & 0 \\ 0 & \lambda_2 & \cdots & 0 \\ \multicolumn{4}{c}{\cdots\cdots\cdots\cdots\cdots} \\ 0 & 0 & \cdots & \lambda_n \end{bmatrix} \qquad (C-45)$$

We shall now work with the matrix polynomial

$$C(\hat{\lambda}) = a_n \hat{\lambda}^n + a_{n-1} \hat{\lambda}^{n-1} + \cdots + a_1 \hat{\lambda} + a_0 \hat{U} \qquad (C-46)$$

This equation can be written in a compact form. Since $\hat{\lambda}$ is square and diagonal, we have

$$\hat{\lambda}^k = \begin{bmatrix} \lambda_1{}^k & 0 & 0 \\ 0 & \lambda_2{}^k & 0 \\ \multicolumn{3}{c}{\cdots\cdots\cdots\cdots} \\ 0 & 0 & \lambda_n{}^k \end{bmatrix} \qquad (C-47)$$

Thus, the following is equivalent to Eq. C-46.

$$C(\hat{\lambda}) = \begin{bmatrix} C(\lambda_1) & 0 & 0 \\ 0 & C(\lambda_2) & 0 \\ \multicolumn{3}{c}{\cdots\cdots\cdots\cdots\cdots} \\ 0 & 0 & C(\lambda_n) \end{bmatrix} \qquad (C-48)$$

where the $C(\lambda_j)$ are scalar polynomials (see Eq. C-44). However, since $\lambda_j, j = 1, 2, ..., n,$

are the eigenvalues (i.e., the roots of the characteristic equation), then

$$C(\lambda_j) = 0, \quad j = 1, 2, ..., n \tag{C–49}$$

Thus,

$$C(\hat{\lambda}) = \hat{0} \tag{C–50}$$

That is, each element in the $C(\hat{\lambda})$ matrix is zero.

For the moment, let us ignore the fact that $C(\hat{\lambda}) = \hat{0}$ and compute the matrix polynomial $C(\hat{A})$. From Eqs. C–43, C–46, and C–48, we obtain

$$C(\hat{A}) = \hat{H}C(\hat{\lambda})\hat{H}^{-1} \tag{C–51}$$

Substituting Eq. (C–50), we have

$$C(\hat{A}) = \hat{0} \tag{C–52}$$

This will be true for any square matrix $\hat{A}$. Hence, *any square matrix satisfies its own characteristic equation.* This is called the *Cayley-Hamilton theorem.*

Let us consider some practical implications of this theorem. Suppose the characteristic equation of a square matrix $\hat{A}$ is

$$a_n\lambda^n + a_{n-1}\lambda^{n-1} + \cdots + a_1\lambda + a_0 = 0 \tag{C–53}$$

Then, we also have

$$a_n\hat{A}^n + a_{n-1}\hat{A}^{n-1} + \cdots + a_1\hat{A} + a_0\hat{U} = 0 \tag{C–54}$$

Rearranging, we obtain,

$$\hat{A}^n = -\frac{a_{n-1}}{a_n}\hat{A}^{n-1} - \cdots - \frac{a_1}{a_n}\hat{A} - \frac{a_0}{a_n}\hat{U} \tag{C–55}$$

Thus, we have expressed $\hat{A}^n$ in terms of powers of $\hat{A}$ less than $n$. Now multiply by $\hat{A}$:

$$A^{n+1} = -\frac{a_{n-1}}{a_n}\hat{A}^n - \cdots - \frac{a_1}{a_n}\hat{A}^2 - \frac{a_0}{a_n}\hat{A} \tag{C–56}$$

We can substitute Eq. C–55 for $\hat{A}^n$. Thus, we can express $\hat{A}^{n+1}$ in terms of powers of $\hat{A}$ up the $(n-1)$th.

Proceeding in this way, we can express any power of $\hat{A}$ in terms of the first $n-1$ powers of $\hat{A}$; thus, if

$$F(\hat{A}) = \sum_{i=1}^{K} b_i\hat{A}^i \tag{C–57}$$

where $\hat{A}$ is a square matrix, we can write $F(\hat{A})$ as

$$F(\hat{A}) = c_{n-1}\hat{A}^{n-1} + c_{n-2}\hat{A}^{n-2} + \cdots + c_1\hat{A} + c_0\hat{U} \tag{C–58}$$

where the $c$'s are *constants.* Let us determine them.

Equate Eqs. C–57 and C–58. Then use Eq. C–43 to express the matrix polynomials. This yields

$$\hat{H}\left[\sum_{i=1}^{K} b_i \hat{\lambda}^i\right] \hat{H}^{-1} = \hat{H}[c_{n-1}\hat{\lambda}^{n-1} + c_{n-2}\hat{\lambda}^{n-2} + \cdots + c_1\hat{\lambda} + c_0\hat{U}]\hat{H}^{-1} \quad (C-59)$$

This equation will be true if

$$\sum_{i=1}^{k} b_i\hat{\lambda}^i = c_{n-1}\hat{\lambda}^{n-1} + c_{n-2}\hat{\lambda}^{n-2} + \cdots + c_1\hat{\lambda} + c_0 U \quad (C-60)$$

The matrix equation actually represents $n$ scalar equations. Since $\hat{\lambda}$ is a diagonal matrix, these scalar equations are

$$\sum_{i=0}^{K} b_i\lambda_j^i = c_{n-1}\lambda_j^{n-1} + c_{n-2}\lambda_j^{n-2} + \cdots + c_1\lambda_j + c_0, \quad j-1,2,...,n \quad (C-61)$$

where $\sum_{i=0}^{k} b_i\lambda_j^i$ is a scalar. It is obtained from the matrix polynomial $F(\hat{A})$ by replacing $\hat{A}$ with the scalar $\lambda_j$. Thus, Eq. C–61 can be written as

$$F(\lambda_j) = c_{n-1}\lambda_j^{n-1} + c_{n-2}\lambda_j^{n-2} + \cdots + c_1\lambda_j + c_0, \quad j = 1,2,...,n \quad (C-62)$$

where the $\lambda_j$ are the known eigenvalues. Note that $F(\lambda_j)$ is a scalar. Thus, we have $n$ linear simultaneous equations which can be solved for $c_{n-1}, ..., c_1, c_0$. Hence, using Eq. C–58, we have replaced a $K$ term power series by one which has only $n$ terms.

We have represented $F(\hat{\lambda})$ as a matrix polynomial. However, $K$, the number of terms, is unlimited. Thus, this can be an infinite series. Hence, $F(\hat{\lambda})$ can be any matrix function that can be represented by an infinite series. This result is a very general one. It allows us to express many matrix functions as finite series.

As an example, let us represent $\hat{A}^n$ as a finite series, where

$$\hat{A} = \begin{bmatrix} 2 & 2 \\ 1 & 3 \end{bmatrix} \quad (C-63)$$

Then (see Section C-3) the eigenvalues are $\lambda = 1$, $\lambda = 4$. Hence, we solve the simultaneous equations

$$\lambda_j^n = c_1\lambda_j + c_0, \quad j = 1,2$$

This yields

$$1 = c_1 + c_0$$
$$4^n = 4c_1 + c_0$$

Solving, we obtain

$$c_0 = \frac{4 - 4^n}{3}$$

$$c_1 = \frac{4^n - 1}{3}$$

Hence,

$$\hat{A}^n = \frac{4^n - 1}{3} \hat{A} + \frac{4 - 4^n}{3} \hat{U} \qquad \text{(C–64)}$$

where $\hat{A}$ is given in Eq. C–63 and

$$\hat{U} = \begin{bmatrix} 1 & 0 \\ 0 & 1 \end{bmatrix}$$

This expression is only valid for the specific $\hat{A}$ used. However, it may be used to evaluate any power of $\hat{A}$. For large $n$ this can result in great simplification. (This would be especially true if $\hat{A}$ is of larger order than 2.)

We have thus far assumed that all the eigenvalues are distinct; i.e., all are different. This need not be the case. Suppose two or more of the eigenvalues are the same. Equation C–62 will still be valid and will represent $n$ equations with $n$ unknowns. However, two or more of the equations will be identical. Such redundant equations should be eliminated. We will then have $k$ linear simultaneous equations with $n$ unknowns, where $k < n$. In this case, we can arbitrarily specify $n - k$ of the unknowns and use the simultaneous equations to solve for the remaining $k$ unknowns.

Let us illustrate this. Let us again obtain $\hat{A}^n$ where, now

$$\hat{A} = \begin{bmatrix} 3 & 0 \\ 0 & 3 \end{bmatrix} \qquad \text{(C–65)}$$

The eigenvalues are $\lambda = 3, \lambda = 3$. The simultaneous equations that we must solve are

$$\lambda_j^n = C_1 \lambda_j + C_0, \qquad j = 1, 2$$

This yields

$$3^n = 3C_1 + C_0$$
$$3^n = 3C_1 + C_0$$

We can eliminate one of these equations. Thus, the equation which must be satisfied is

$$3^n = 3C_1 + C_0 \qquad \text{(C–66)}$$

We can arbitrarily choose $C_1$ or $C_0$. Since the equations are simple, let us not do this but write $C_0$ in terms of $C_1$. Doing this and substituting in Eq. C–58, we have

$$\hat{A}^n = C_1 \begin{bmatrix} 3 & 0 \\ 0 & 3 \end{bmatrix} + (3^n - 3C_1) \begin{bmatrix} 1 & 1 \\ 0 & 1 \end{bmatrix}$$

Manipulating, we obtain

$$\hat{A}^n = \begin{bmatrix} 3^n & 0 \\ 0 & 3^n \end{bmatrix}$$

This result could have been obtained more easily by assuming that $C_1 = 0$ in Eq. C–66.

In the previous examples the eigenvalues were real numbers, but they may at times be complex numbers. The same procedures are valid, except that complex algebra must now be used.

## BIBLIOGRAPHY

Chirlian, P. M. *Basic Network Theory*. Pp. 159–171. New York: McGraw-Hill, 1969.

Guillemin, E. A. *The Mathematics of Circuit Analysis*. Chaps. 1, 2, and 3. New York: Wiley, 1949.

Tropper, A. M. *Matrix Theory for Electrical Engineers*. Chaps. 1, 2, 3, and 6. Reading, Mass.: Addison-Wesley, 1962.

# Index